WHY BAD THINGS
HAPPEN IN YOUR
GAME
OF LIFE

WHY BAD THINGS HAPPEN IN YOUR GAME OF LIFE

Since You're in the Game, Play to Win!

HARRY E. HUBBARD

XULON ELITE

Xulon Press Elite
555 Winderley Pl, Suite 225
Maitland, FL 32751
407.339.4217
www.xulonpress.com

© 2024 by Harry E. Hubbard

All rights reserved solely by the author. The author guarantees all contents are original and do not infringe upon the legal rights of any other person or work. No part of this book may be reproduced in any form without the permission of the author.

Due to the changing nature of the Internet, if there are any web addresses, links, or URLs included in this manuscript, these may have been altered and may no longer be accessible. The views and opinions shared in this book belong solely to the author and do not necessarily reflect those of the publisher. The publisher therefore disclaims responsibility for the views or opinions expressed within the work.

Unless otherwise indicated, Scripture quotations taken from the King James Version (KJV)–*public domain*.

English Standard Version (ESV). Copyright © 2001 by Crossway, a publishing ministry of Good News Publishers. Used by permission. All rights reserved.

Amplified Bible (AMP). Copyright © 1954, 1958, 1962, 1964, 1965, 1987 by The Lockman Foundation. Used by permission. All rights reserved.

New International Version (NIV). Copyright © 1973, 1978, 1984, 2011 by Biblica, Inc.™. Used by permission. All rights reserved.

Living Bible (TLB). Copyright © 1971 by Tyndale House Foundation. Used by permission of Tyndale House Publishers Inc., Carol Stream, Illinois 60188. All rights reserved.

New King James Version (NKJV). Copyright © 1982 by Thomas Nelson, Inc. Used by permission. All rights reserved.

Holy Bible, New Living Translation (NLT). Copyright ©1996, 2004, 2007 by Tyndale House Foundation. Used by permission of Tyndale House Publishers, Inc.

The Holy Bible: International Standard Version. Release 2.0, Build 2015.02.09. Copyright © 1995-2014 by ISV Foundation. ALL RIGHTS RESERVED INTERNATIONALLY. Used by permission of Davidson Press, LLC.

The Message (MSG). Copyright © 1993, 1994, 1995, 1996, 2000, 2001, 2002. Used by permission of NavPress Publishing Group. Used by permission. All rights reserved.

New American Standard Bible (NASB). Copyright © 1960, 1962, 1963, 1968, 1971, 1972, 1973, 1975, 1977, 1995 by The Lockman Foundation. Used by permission. All rights reserved.

The Voice Bible (VB) Copyright © 2012 Thomas Nelson, Inc. The Voice™ translation © 2012 Ecclesia Bible Society All rights reserved.

The Jubilee Bible 2000 (JUB). Copyright © 2000, 2001, 2010. Used by permission of LIFE SENTENCE Publishing. All rights reserved.

Contemporary English Version (CEV). Copyright © 1995 American Bible Society. Used by permission. All rights reserved.

American Standard Version (ASV))–public domain

Paperback ISBN-13: 978-1-66285-124-7
Ebook ISBN-13: 978-1-66285-125-4

Endorsements

I am very impressed with *Why Bad Things Happen In Your Game of Life: Since You're in the Game, Play to Win!* Harry has a gift for translating deep doctrinal truth into an easy-to-understand-and-apply format. I have sets of theology books in three to eight-thick volumes on my shelves that cover the ground he covered. It is evident that the counsel offered in this book comes not only from much research and reflection but also from the living experience of both him and the members of his family.

I have not been as involved with some of his sources, but he stuck with the Truth. It was a privilege to review this major commentary on the principles of the Christian life, so uniquely expressed in a format that our current generation could grasp. This should result in widespread circulation.

Dr. Gerald Small, retired pastor

Why Bad Things Happen In Your Game of Life is a must-read for all who have a love for truth. It is written with biblical precision that unveils the gross darkness attempting to operate in our personal lives as well as in the world today. However, this book delivers a hope in a greater authority, power, and love that always leads us in victory over evil—Jesus Christ and His kingdom.

Minister Brian Eichelberger
Eagle Eye Perspectives podcast

Harry Hubbard dives into the deep end of the theological ocean with a noteworthy compassion for the reader. Though this work is as thorough as any systematic book you've ever read, you won't want to stop reading. This volume offers a fresh perspective on ancient truths from a man who loves and knows the Game Master.

Pastoral Associate JJ Engelbrecht
Middle School Ministry, Immanuel Bible Church

Harry presents a refreshing look on life. This book reveals his gifted insight and understanding.

Jerry Kelleher
Director of AV Technologies, Immanuel Bible Church

Table of Contents

Endorsements v
Preface xvii
Foreword xix
About This Book xxi
What This Book Will Do for You xxiii
PART 1: The Game of Life 1
   Life's Game Introduction 2
      Life's Rules 3
      Natural Rules 3
      Social Rules 4
      Moral Rules 4
      Legal Rules 4
      Spirit Rules 5
   Obstacles of Life 7
      Spiritual Obstacles 8
         Curses 8
         Spiritual powers 9
      Physical Obstacles 11
      Obstacle Summary 11
   Help from the Game Master 12
   Winning the Game 15
      Bonus Round Rewards 18
   Losing the Game 20
   Part 1 Conclusion 22
PART 2: Perspectives On Our Game of Life 23
   Why Life Happens to Us and What to Do about It 24
   Game Layout 25
   Game of Life Terms 29
Section I: The Game of Life 31
   The Setup 31

  Bad stuff..33
  The fix..33
 Game Synopsis..34
 The Game of Life..36
  The essence – belief...38
Section II: The Game Setup..40
 Clash of Titans..41
  Game Master vs. the Serpent.......................................41
  The Early Rounds...41
   Round 1..42
   Round 2..43
   Round 3..45
   Round 4, etc..50
   The Win..52
   The endgame..53
   Exit thought...53
 Game Master: The Serpent's Fall Guy...........................56
 The Game Master Is Not Powerless...............................61
  Cause and Effect...62
   The twist..64
   Our cost...65
 Job's Story..66
   Kiosk explanation...67
   The lesson of Job..68
   Job was persecuted..69
 Game Setup Conclusion..71
 The Problem of Peace..72
Section III: The Hurt Zone...75
 Why Bad Things Happen to You....................................75
  Bad stuff..76
 10 Big Reasons for Bad Things.......................................78
  1. Free Will..78
  2. Spirit Laws & Power...86
   Occult...90
   Voodoo/hoodoo/WitchTok....................................96
   Folklore...97
   Fate..98

Luck 99
  Miracles 100
  Spirit guides 101
  Dreams of Jesus 102
  Visions 104
  Pseudoscience 105
  Aliens 105
3. Curses 106
  Signs of a curse 108
  Sources of curses 110
  Covenants 112
  Words 112
  Jinxes 117
4. The World 118
  Physical world 118
  Disease & injury 119
  World system 123
  The pre-Apocalypse 136
  The Apocalypse 143
  Armageddon–Judgment Day–The Day of the Lord 148
  Post Apocalypse 149
  Armageddon: round two 149
  Game over 150
  Summary: the World 150
5. The Flesh 150
  Appetite 153
  Charms 154
  Attitudes 155
  Stronghold 156
6. The Devil–Serpent 158
  Serpent hierarchy 160
  Deception and skepticism 161
  Spiritual factor 162
  Fake gods 169
7. Bad Decisions 171
8. Bad People 174
  Psychopaths 176

    Predators 177
    Is it you? 179
  9. Persecution 181
  10. God Only Knows 184
    Game Master's perspective 186
    Game Master's testing 186
    Game Master's discipline 187
    Game Master's glory 188
    Game Master's judgment 190
    Conclusion 199
Hurt Zone Summary 200
Section IV: The Cure Zone 203
  Fixing your Broken Life 203
Obstacle Diagnosis 204
  10 Reasons Diagnosis 205
    Free Will 205
    Spirit Laws and Power 206
    Curses 207
    The World 207
    The Flesh 207
    The Devil 208
    Bad Decisions 208
    Bad People 209
    Persecution 210
    God Only Knows 210
    Diagnosis Conclusion 211
  Barriers to Healing 211
    Unbelief 212
    Un-forgiveness 213
    Evil Spirits 213
    Confession 214
  Soul Healing 215
Personal Healing Journeys 217
  Family Testimonials 219
Cure Zone Introduction 226
  Your Cost 227
  Victory over Guilt 228

- Qualifiers 229
  - Mainstream view acknowledgment 229
  - Mainstream View: To Be Healed—or Not. 230
  - Literal vs. symbolic 231
  - Mainstream View – Trials of Life 233
- Cure Zone Synopsis 234
- Solutions 237
  - Skills Needed 237
    - Read your manual 238
    - Mission ready 241
    - Combat ready – engage. 247
    - Mainstream View – Healing & Miracles Contexts with Spiritual Authority.. 249
    - Mainstream View – Ask vs. Command for Healing.. 250
  - Transformational Power 253
    - Power source. 253
    - Golden ticket application 254
    - The power fizzle 256
  - Faith Power 257
    - Faith defined 259
    - Faith connection. 261
    - Leading questions 262
    - Doubt and unbelief 263
    - Hard-hearted. 264
    - Weak faith vs. strong faith 265
    - Rate your faith 267
    - Mainstream view – If it be Your will 270
  - Spiritual Authority 271
    - Authority examples 272
    - Authority factor 273
    - Spiritual warfare. 274
    - Guest imitations 276
  - Prayer, Praise, & Fasting 276
    - Prayer 276
    - Praise 278
    - Fasting 281
  - Aim & Fire 283

      Effective prayer..284
      Prayer vocabulary 284
      Moving mountains..285
      Blessing your life 286
   Healing..287
      Authoritative healing..288
      Authoritative healing example.......................................288
      Lack of healing evidence..289
      Unequal healing 292
   Life Issues..293
      Circumstances 293
      Conditions...294
      Blessed living 295
   Consistency...298
      Power fade...300
Cure Zone Summary 301
Conclusion 303
PART 3: Section I: Players & Terms 305
Game of Life Terms..307
   Bonus Round..310
   Gameplay – The Way You Play Your Life 311
   The Manual – The Holy Bible 313
      Old Testament 315
      Apocrypha..316
      New Testament..317
      Summarized game rules 318
   Game Master – God, the Father, Creator.......................... 322
   The One – Jesus Christ, Son of God, Messiah, Advocate, Emmanuel (God with us).. 325
   Spirit Master – Holy Spirit, Holy Ghost, Spirit of Truth, Comforter, Intercessor, Guide into All Truth...327
   Guardians – Angels..328
   Serpent – The Devil, Satan 329
   Henchmen – Fallen Angels...332
   Minions – Demons..333
   Players – People 339
   Guest Players – Good People, Innocents, Serfs of the Serpent 342

Guest players – bad people, guilty, serfs of the Serpent	343
Member Players – Righteous People, Adopted Family of the Game Master	344
Fake member players – false prophets	351
Master Players – Advanced Member Players	353
Game Environment	354
Game World Origins	355
New Game Environment	364
Golden Ticket – Eternal Life	365
Golden ticket benefits	369
Ticket acquisition	372
Fire insurance	372
Losing golden tickets	373
Game Violations – Sin, Iniquity, Transgression	373
Noahide laws	375
The Big Ten	377
New Testament commandments	379
Seven abominations	380
Three abominations	382
Seven deadly sins	383
Religious Kiosks – Church, Mosque, Synagogue, Temple	384
Cults and false teaching	385
Meat offered to idols	387
Bonus Round – Eternal Life	388
Bonus round – heaven, the New Jerusalem, the new earth	388
The Day of the Lord – Apocalypse	390
New heaven, new earth	391
Heavenly rewards	391
Headquarters – Heaven, Game Master's Throne	395
Field headquarters	395
Hell – Lake of Fire	396
Obstacles	401
Solutions	402
Section II: Final Points	403
Full Player Membership	404
Membership Details	407
Membership status	407

- Overlooked rules ... 407
- Transfer of rights ... 408
- Citizenship transfer ... 410
- Transfer of ambition ... 410
- Losing Your Golden Ticket ... 413
  - Eternal Security ... 415
    - Texts on assurance of eternal security ... 416
    - Texts on no assurance of eternal security ... 417
- The Almost Christian ... 420
- God's Lemonade Stand ... 424
  - God's lemonade stand – aka all things work together ... 427
  - God is sovereign ... 429
  - Restoration ... 430
- The Sovereignty of God ... 433
- Faith Deconstruction ... 438
- Prosperity Gospel ... 444
  - Blessed living ... 445
- Spiritual Gifts ... 446
  - The One & Spiritual Gifts ... 447
  - Speaking In Tongues ... 448
- Acknowledgments ... 450
- About the Author ... 451
- Bibliography ... 452
- Appendix A: Resources: Counseling & Deliverance ... 484
  - Counseling Centers ... 484
  - Prayer Hotlines ... 486
  - Deliverance Ministries ... 487
  - Sexual Brokenness ... 490
- Appendix B: Resources: Healing & Recovery ... 491
- Appendix C: Resources: Membership Testimonials ... 494
  - Muslim Conversions to Jesus ... 495
  - Shinto and Buddhism Conversions to Jesus ... 496
- Appendix D: Resources: Life Helps ... 497
- Appendix E: Resources: Christianity ... 499
  - Roman Catholicism ... 502
  - Calvinism ... 502
  - Islam ... 503

Appendix F: Resources: YouTube Channels & Websites 504
Appendix G: Resources: Bible, Martyrs & Power for Living. 507
    Martyrs & Survivors. 508
    Power for Living 509
Appendix H: Resources: Demonology & Spiritual Warfare. 510
Appendix I: Resources: Prehistory, Apocalypse, Giants, Aliens, Assorted Topics 517
Appendix J: Resources: Music. 522

Preface

To explain the principles of this book, I have chosen to use the analogy of a video game involving two competing teams. This context of a game easily relates the rules and parameters of life to our collective situation. Because there are rules governing life that are never properly explained, describing those rules in a game setting makes it easier to quickly understand how all the factors come together and affect each other. It is also an easier way to simplify complex spiritual concepts into a sensible format that everyone can use.

This is not a sequential book, where information is confined to a single section, but where it is interwoven, giving an understanding of how multiple factors come together to define a given situation. Throughout the book, there are places where the same information is restated. There are many overlapping topics where those points are repeated by way of explanation.

There is no quick fix when you choose to rise above the circumstances of your life. If you are looking for easy answers to life's problems that will cost you nothing, this is not the book for you. Winners don't just wander over the finish line.

Foreword

PRETTY MUCH EVERYONE in today's world understands board games and video games. Such games have transcended cultures so much that book and movie writers have used them to explain how life works. This conduit allows influencers to plunge into and offer solutions to many of the human dilemmas. In fact, using games to explain life has grown in popularity through the years; movies like *Free Guy*, *Ralph*, and *Tron* have made their mark by successfully contrasting video games to life itself.

This book, *Why Bad Things Happen In Your Game of Life: Since You're in the Game, Play to Win!*, attempts to do the same, with one major difference: it takes a biblical perspective. The hope is that, in doing so, the Bible's message will be better understood, so the reader will be effectually changed into realizing that the biblical worldview is the viable perspective for all of life.

Connecting the Bible to today's culture is a challenge. The Bible is seen as antiquated, if not obsolete. On the contrary, the biblical text, as a timeless "manual," dives deep into the human heart. When we examine our hearts in light of the Bible, we notice our yearnings for eternity and immortality are placed there by God, who is the "Game Master." The Bible makes a clear call to "play the game of life" by following its instructions; it provides real solutions to those human yearnings while dealing with the problems of evil and death.

Mr. Hubbard has hit a vital chord by bringing our big life questions down to a few simple ideas:

We all are in our own game of life. It is in our best interest to know how "to play," considering that the game does not end when this life is over. Since you are already a player, *play to win!*

Pastor Lemuel Lara
Iglesia Bautista Betel, Midland, Texas
Founder of forgod.net *ministries*
Works with Hispanic Southern Baptist Churches in Texas, has pastored several Spanish churches, and engaged in early ministry work with Baptist Student Ministries

About This Book

THE BOOK WAS inspired after the author's youngest son repeatedly received questions about why bad things happened to good people, and he wanted a better answer for them. While he was in an Air Force tech school, he began to reply, "Life is a game, and the name of the game is – *Surprise!*" He quickly found that most people do not want a long answer about this question, and their eyes glaze over when the explanations start. After those detailed reasons are explained here, it should be easier for you to find a shorter answer to the problems you see as they happen to come your way.

This book is intended to give you the tools to figure out why things go wrong in your life and then point you to solutions that can reverse the trends you experience. It's impossible to squeeze huge amounts of help into a few pages, so a resource appendices section will provide additional information with practical details for your complete success.

Life's issues are rooted in spiritual sources connecting the spirit realm to our situations in life. Bible references cite the source material for the points that are explained. If you prefer a nonreligious approach, it will leave out the spiritual dimension that drives the causes of life's problems. If you are convinced there is no spiritual factor in our lives, your answers will never reach deeper than the surface psychological level.

Everybody has an opinion and may assume that they have figured out how life works, or else their church, temple or other philosophical source would have already told them differently. For you who are looking for answers, this book is for you.

What This Book Will Do for You

THIS BOOK IS a practical warfare book to help you fight back and take back both what you lost in life and are destined to lose in your coming years if nothing changes for you. It pulls back the veil and explains the hidden forces driving the events that impact our daily lives.

There is really little mystery as to why bad things happen; the problem is that religious people are really bad at explaining how life's pieces fit together. The question is what combination of forces affects you specifically in any given life event. While there can be patterns to them, not all bad things are from a single cause.

To wage inter-dimensional war with the spirit realm and impact your real-world life in the physical realm, you need Spirit-infused weapons. Make no mistake; what happens before your very eyes isn't the entire picture or the whole story. Your belief system will directly impact your success. We will cover tools and strategies to not only parry the blows of life but to overcome them as well (Jer. 29:11–14).

For those who have suffered great loss, the best place to find comfort is in the Holy Bible—the Manual—in the Author of the Manual (God), and in the Spirit Master Comforter (Holy Spirit) He provides. From compassion for your situation, this book is written to point you to the One (Jesus Christ) who has the power to forgive you and give you hope, restoration, and a future.

If you need comfort, counseling, and healing for your losses, see the Resource appendices section, where links to prayer and crisis hotlines from free and confidential organizations and book lists from various authors provide insight and tools for recovery. It is possible to not only come back from crippling blows to your body and psyche, but you can also finish life strong (Joel 2:23–27).

If you think this book is too good to be true, you may be right because even member players (Christians) who claim to know the score and already have the needed weapons at their disposal rarely choose to pick them up to rise above their circumstances and fight to win. The One promised a seat on His throne to the overcomer, so choose to be a winner (Rev. 3:21).

PART 1
The Game of Life

Life's Game Introduction

HAVE YOU EVER played a game when you only knew part of the rules, and your opponent was beating you with rules you didn't know? How did that work out? That's how we play our Game of Life. We all learn the rules as we go, but there's a rule set that keeps tripping us up no matter how skilled in life we get. Our game has a handbook for that elusive rule set, but most players never pick it up to win the game.

You've been playing the Game of Life for a while now. Perhaps your life has been turned upside down, and things can never be the same again because of what happened to you. Maybe you seem to be in a long run of bad luck, had a period of specific trauma, or you face random calamities in your life. You may experience reverse karma and seem to get punished for the good things you do.

We're all on a quest to find our advantage and make life meaningful to us. Maybe you know what you want from life, or maybe you are still idling and figuring it out. This game you're in needs a simple explanation of how life works so you can overcome those hardships and curveballs that come your way.

Your solution can become more than just a way to cope with your limitations. Your life has great value to God, the Game Master, and He can infuse grace into your situation, which brings you peace and makes you a blessing to others as a result of or despite your traumatic experience. He wrote the handbook to win the game. It's time to get your life in gear and make it count now and for the next round.

We've all played games. You win some; you lose some. Games come in many types. They can be physical, like sports, intellectual, like puzzles, psychological, like cards, and include a range of objectives and elements to keep them simple or make them sophisticated. Computer games are popular and provide a way to infuse human characteristics or personalities into the characters (avatars) that represent the type of person the player wishes to express.

Regardless of the type, all games have rules and objectives. To win, you play by the rules and meet the objective before or better than your opponents. Sometimes we change the rules to make the game easier to play or adapt to the players so it will be a fair game. We can change rules to stop arguments and level the playing field, whether it is an activity game or a board game.

Games are most fun when you know you have an even chance of winning or if the prize is worth your trying to beat the odds. Then there are some of you sadistic players who revel in the sheer pleasure of crushing your opponent no matter how unevenly matched in your favor it may be. Our Game of Life also has that one sadistic personality running its environment, the Serpent also called Satan, who lays a wide swath of destruction as he revels in the sheer pleasure of crushing our spirit, destroying our future, or ending our life. We are his prize when our time in the game is up, or if we joined the Game Master's team, the Serpent can prevent us from getting a prize from the Game Master.

The Game of Life has rules like any game we play, and it has an objective and a final score. We all are rule breakers somewhere as we try to gain an edge in life. We did not make the fundamental rules of our Game of Life, and we cannot change them. Unfortunately for us, the game also has twists added to it that have given us a less-than-even chance of winning the game. The good news is that every player has a chance to win if they choose to go for it.

Life's Rules

Our lives have layers of rules that apply to us to different degrees depending on our economic sophistication and level of participation in society. Poor players don't worry about hedge funds or international travel. Rich players don't worry about going hungry, freezing to death, or getting eviction notices.

When you know the rules, you can use the rules to your advantage. We do this all the time using natural rules to fly in planes and float on boats or surf the waves, by using social rules to get friends and influence, using moral rules to gain prestige or notoriety, and using legal rules to get rich or get acquitted. Being good at navigating all these rules helps us stay alive, get ahead in life, or take advantage of life's situations.

Natural Rules

Natural laws also include the forces of nature and wildlife. We have a sense of gravity. Things consistently fall to the ground. We are familiar with all types of natural rules, and we follow them to stay alive and healthy. Those who are daredevils or adrenaline junkies like to see how closely they can supersede natural rules to set personal or world records. Some of their death-defying feats are amazing, and others are just plain crazy. GoPro cameras make it all the more thrilling and spectacular—or cringe-worthy.

Social Rules

Every country or culture has its own set of social rules. It is usually a good idea to find out what not to do to insult the locals when you travel to foreign countries, especially where they may jail you for your ignorance. Nowadays in America, it's okay to be unrefined and do your own thing. People who call out bad behavior are more likely to get themselves shamed on social media because everyone has a right to self-expression—until the social community police or Ministry of Truth disapprove. Social norms are breaking down because nobody wants to be told what to do or how to act. This is an area where the rules of life can change with the times.

Moral Rules

This could be coupled with social rules because the two are usually linked together through laws and local ordinances. Moral rules transcend social rules in that moral rules or standards are more universally recognized and less likely to change across the world. Religious players more typically classify moral rules as absolute rules, which are always right or always wrong.

For example, cheating, lying, stealing, assault, and murder are consistently considered wrong to do, and religious players should say they are always wrong. Some of these items may get justified or explained away under extenuating circumstances by society at large, but the majority of society frowns on making a practice of them.

Legal Rules

All nations, cultures, and tribes have rules that dictate how their members can operate within the group. These rules can affect all areas of life. Advanced societies developed court systems to handle civil issues, criminal issues, family issues, financial issues, environmental issues, and so on. Wherever rules are made, someone is designated to judge by those rules. Sometimes they are based on moral or social rules, and sometimes rules are made for practical reasons, to generate income for the community, or punish those who use more than their fair share of available resources.

> We have either too many rules or not enough police.

Most of the time, they serve a purpose for the greater good of the community, and sometimes they can be annoying, like the homeowner's association rules that keep you from adding that bigger deck to your house or swimming pool in your own backyard. There are now so many rules that we sometimes see stories about how everyone commits two or three felonies per day without ever realizing it. Depending on your perspective, we have either too many rules or not enough police.

Have you ever wondered how we happen to have a similar code of player behavior across all cultures and religions of the game? These are called the Noahide laws. The Game Master is said to have given six laws to Adam at the start of the game and reissued them again with seven laws to Noah after the great flood. When the players scattered across the globe after the failed Tower of Babel, when their language became confused, they kept these laws largely intact as the universal basis for all player behavior in the game. They are explained in the Terms section.

Spirit Rules

The one set of rules that causes the most trouble for players is the elusive area of spirit rules. All the other rule sets help us navigate through life, and many players become experts in using those rules. The spirit rules are the underlying key to success during life and ultimately to winning our Game of Life, but hardly anyone becomes good at them, much less an expert in this rule set. This rule set has a handbook to finish with a win.

Spirit rules are typically described as what is right or wrong, but what is right and wrong only refers to a set of *moral* rules that are based on the spirit rules. Even during a bygone era when America was considered a Christian nation, many of its Christians did not know how to use the spirit rules that impacted their daily lives. In our post-Christian nation, players follow their own opinions and speculate what the spirit rules could be depending on their own experiences and personal philosophy. Our society is getting less religious (church) and more spiritual (New Age) but less adept with spiritual success (faith).

> **OUR SOCIETY IS GETTING LESS RELIGIOUS (CHURCH) AND MORE SPIRITUAL (NEW AGE) BUT LESS ADEPT WITH SPIRITUAL SUCCESS (FAITH).**

The Game Master used spirit rules to create the cosmos, including players and all life around us, and these rules are used in the way we interact with Him or the Serpent. The Manual does not have a section listing all the spirit rules. Instead, the rules are largely declared or inferred, and we have to identify them by their description. We identify the value system of the spirit realm and the explained process of how to operate within its parameters to get what we want and need from the Game Master. There are also defined limits of what He can do for you when you don't follow the spirit rules.

> **Faith is the currency of heaven.**

The key to the spirit rules is faith. Think of faith as the currency of heaven. To acquire tools, weapons, or skills in a game usually involves a transaction through money or bartering. Our Game of Life also requires something from us to acquire benefits from the Game Master. Following His directions is how we stay connected with Him. Then, whatever transaction you want from the Game Master is activated or energized by your faith. There is a sequence in how we apply faith to our interactions with Him.

As we make transactions with Him through faith, He can change our circumstances and the outcomes of what we face in all the other rules of life. Faith is required to win the Game of Life, but going on from that starting level to becoming an expert in faith transactions will improve your quality of life during the game itself. Even though many of us have obstacles to overcome, the good news is that anyone can open a faith account with the Game Master and begin a winning streak through life.

Obstacles of Life

THINGS GO WRONG for us in so many ways that it sometimes seems like life is just a series of mishaps or periods of tranquility that are punctuated by overwhelming problems. Living life like you are always waiting for the other shoe of bad stuff to drop on you is terribly discouraging.

The areas of life that negatively impact us are in our physical, emotional, mental, psychological, and spiritual realm. We humans are a three-part being composed of physical, psychological (mental/emotional), and spiritual aspects. Many players in modern society operate exclusively in the physical and psychological aspects of their makeup and largely ignore any spiritual connection that they have. They may identify with a religion and perhaps even practice it, but most have an ineffective working knowledge of it, meaning that religion should not only answer the dilemmas of life but also have a spiritual solution that can even change your physical and relational environment.

There are many reasons bad things happen to us, and while we can usually point to a logical explanation or the consequence of a bad decision, we never look beyond the physical reality around us and account for the spiritual layer of consequences that cause our distress and weigh us down with a burden of hopelessness. This is how we end up physically and psychologically scarred and never realize that we possess a spiritual component that can neutralize and reverse the physical and psychological damage that comes against us.

There is usually a combination of physical and spiritual issues at play in things that happen to us. When you are able to recognize the spiritual factor that affects your circumstances or events of life, it becomes easier to diagnose root causes and deal with them. Take note that everything we face may not be necessarily tied to spiritual opposition, so don't get so tightly wired that everything becomes a conspiracy against you.

Sometimes we trip and fall because we weren't paying attention. If we are consistently tripping and bumping things because we seem inherently clumsy, there may be more than just a physical imbalance or situational awareness issue. If we somehow manage to fall at times when it causes a real hardship at those points in our lives, there is probably a spiritual component to that physical issue. Patterns of personal problems or events that strategically disadvantage us in life may well have more than just a logical explanation.

Spiritual Obstacles

Because players are uniquely spirit beings, we can directly interact with the spirit realm and download protection for ourselves, break the spirit powers that come against us, or defend ourselves against evil spirit forces. Animals are not spirit beings and have no power to counteract any evil spirit influence that comes against them.

Players who are tuned in to the spiritual reality that is coupled to our physical existence understand that there are several avenues of evil that contribute to the frequency and types of bad things that happen to us. When you can discover how your physical or psychological problems are connected to a spiritual source, you can use the spirit rules to fix the spiritual cause and then break its power over you in your physical or psychological life.

Before this becomes too mumbo jumbo, let's make some connections with practical examples. Remember, we look at the real-life issue and identify the spirit source and cause of that issue. Although the Serpent is the originating source power of all evil, there are several emanating spirit sources of evil that interact with our physical life issues. There can be different combinations of physical and spiritual forces at work in various scenarios we face.

CURSES

We usually think of black magic when curses are mentioned. These types of rituals tend to be directed toward specific victims, but anecdotal remarks can be found about the rock music industry regarding rituals to place curses on all those who listen to those music albums. Whether this is true or not in your perspective is up for debate, but those who professionally experience and confront spirit forces do make a connection between them and pair evil spirits with rock music and drug use. During the Trump presidency, there were news articles, usually from California or New York City, interviewing witches who very matter-of-factly discussed placing curses on the president or hosting special rituals to invoke curses (Dancyger 2017, ¶ 3-4; DiTrolio 2018, ¶ 4; Kazdin 2017, ¶ 1).

Curses are the one area of negative spiritual influence that impacts the most players across the globe in all strata of society. The chance that you have a curse against you is very high. Most players around the globe are affected by curses that come from a violation of the Game Master's moral code. He explicitly identifies curses associated with violations of specific moral rules. Curses can last for three or four generations, so what your ancestor did one hundred years ago can still affect and disrupt your life today.

Have you had a parent or grandparent who caused great frustration or distress in your life and you vowed that you would never be like them? But now your spouse or friends say that you act just like them? That is likely the effect of a curse. Curses that last for ten generations could have been activated 300 years ago. Most players have no clue what all their ancestors were up to one hundred years ago, much less 300 years or more.

Curses can affect every area of life: your finances, relationships, health, mental state, career, creativity, and so on. Clues that you may have a curse at work against you include circumstances that are recurring, such as illnesses that run in the family, a continual insufficiency of resources, volatile family relationships, a lack of success when things should be going your way, and so on.

If you notice a negative pattern in your life or in your family history, it is probably more than a coincidence and exists for a reason. Your spouse can bring a curse into the family, your sexual promiscuity can open you up to a curse from every partner you have (1 Cor. 6:16), or your involvement in extra-biblical spiritual rituals are other avenues where curses are introduced in our lives.

Curses don't necessarily have an expiration date and can last for millennia. They are a legacy passed on to your children for generations to come. A curse remains in effect over you until you specifically break it. This is done through a prayer to the Game Master to repent or turn from the activity that caused it, whether it was you or your ancestor, and to renounce your association with that activity from that point on. By extension, you can also break the curse from being passed on to your young children.

Spiritual powers

There are two types of spiritual entities that have power. The Game Master and His guardians represent His character of goodness. The Serpent, Satan, with his fallen henchmen and minions (demons), who are lower-level evil spirits, represent evil. These evil spirit beings exert influence over our lives with our permission.

Players will likely say that they do not give minions permission to influence them. Because the Serpent's craft is done through subtlety and deceit, how certain can we be that his kingdom of evil spirits has no influence on us? Every time we ignore what is the right thing to do or we make excuses to do something wrong for the right reasons, we are choosing to let the Serpent's agents reinforce that choice into an activity, a habit, and, eventually, a way of life. Over time, the things that bother the Game Master don't seem to bother us; this is what He calls a seared conscience.

The Serpent's counter philosophy saturates the media through TV, music, situational ethics, and every area of public discourse, whether it is political, philosophical, ethical, educational, or even religious. You grew up on a diet of his philosophy and ethics. That may be why conservative members seem to be totally out of step with general society and its fluid morals and ethics. Additionally, members who are caught up in or influenced by this counter philosophy can hardly agree with each other.

Sometimes we are committed to doing the right thing, but part of our world falls apart at that point. There could be a direct spiritual attack against you that prevents you from doing what you want and believe you ought to do. This would be a good time to assess whether a curse is at work or if it is a specific case of spiritual opposition. Such a scenario tends to look too suspicious to be mere coincidence.

There is a growing discourse on demonic influence. In the nonreligious society, it shows up in creepy, scary, or supernatural movies, shows, and games that depict a realism not seen in previous decades. In religious society, news warnings are going out about the rise of demon possession in Western nations, with headlines that the Roman Catholic Church has an acute shortage of exorcists (Sinnenberg 2023, ¶ 2; The Los Angeles Times 2005, ¶ 1).

Minions connect with players through activities, such as stealing and assault, through emotions like envy, anger, and fear, through choices like lying and gossip, or through self-help classes like yoga. This can happen suddenly or over a period of time. It can happen to a bully or to someone who is victimized. Once their influence takes hold on a person through their choices or experiences, it will continue to affect them until the minion is banished.

Movies may gratuitously portray the most extreme aspects of demonization with eyes rolling back or going black, superhuman strength, levitation, and the like. Typically, minion influence is an extension of someone's personality, where nobody suspects it is happening. Perhaps they have anger issues, a mean streak, a lewd persona, conniving traits, are manipulative toward others, or have illogical fears or phobias that may or may not be guilt-associated. Many traits of minion influence are psychological, but they can also affect a player's physical well-being.

Those who are concerned about a spiritual influence against them should get professional counseling and pair that with a member who has experience in discerning such matters.

Physical Obstacles

This is the catch-all section that intersects the spiritual with the natural or circumstantial areas of life. We are familiar with the dangers of the natural world: driving on wet roads, going down icy stairs, sticking a knife in the toaster, cutting through dark alleys alone at night, or being too trusting on social media. Then, there are other players who should be good and kind toward us, but they cut us off in traffic, steal stuff from our porch or an unlocked car, or randomly sucker punch us on the street.

We learn to be careful in life, but circumstances and other players sometimes conspire to turn our lives upside down. This is usually where we wonder why the Game Master let bad things happen to us. Yes, that accident or assault happened in the real world. Yes, it seems you were targeted for no reason. Yes, the Game Master still loves you and cares about what happens to you. Are you sure there is no underlying spiritual factor in your circumstances?

Most accidents and auto mishaps that my own family has had since the turn of the millennium had a spiritual backstory to them that we could identify. Some of them could have ended in death or permanent disability. Divine protection was the factor in the outcome of all those cases, and intercessory prayer in at least one of them. Where spiritual issues were brought to light, we took action to address them. We still needed new cars and time for physical rehabilitation in some cases, but the Game Master provided resources and expedited healing.

If your problems are nothing more to you than an outcome of circumstances, there is nothing more you can do to prevent them from recurring other than trying to be more careful in what you do. Someday, when you become complacent again, the other shoe may drop, and you'll remember you didn't want to go through that circumstance again. But you did.

Obstacle Summary

Bad things happen around us and to us. They may or may not be our fault. You can still take action to stop them from happening again. Perhaps you are living with brokenness from an accident or mishap. There is healing and restoration available to you physically, emotionally, and circumstantially from the Game Master.

Help from the Game Master

THE GAME MASTER is like the Head Coach in the Game of Life Who put His Son in the game on your behalf. He knows the obstacles and pitfalls of the game, and He knows the strategy of the Serpent and how you can beat his agenda. Do you need answers? He's got the answers. Do you need a game plan? He's got a game plan for you. Are you in crisis? He's the Wonderful Counselor. Do you need help? He's the mighty God. Are you abandoned, cast out, or left to fend for yourself? He's the everlasting Father. Have you lost hope or live in turmoil? He's the Prince of Peace (Isa. 9:6).

When we suffer loss or endure traumatic experiences, there are hotlines and help centers to provide grief counseling, crisis intervention counseling, abuse counseling, and more. These sources range from community services to parachurch organizations. Many of them have trained staff and licensed counselors and can recommend medical services as needed. The Resource Appendix A offers suggestions.

If you find yourself in need of help, locate a professional counseling center to begin your physical and emotional healing. If you have not already done so, contact a religious kiosk or professional religious center that can assist you from the Manual with a spiritual understanding of what the Game Master can do for you and how He can heal you and bring peace to your soul.

A member friend suddenly lost his wife of fifty years. It took him two months to emerge from the fog that enveloped him, which included the bewildering change in the dynamics of his circle of friends. He was no longer part of a couple seeing other couples and interacting with widows. He became a single man with no real place among his circle of married friends, and the relationship with the widows who comfortably and regularly conversed with him as a married man suddenly projected a sense of awkwardness when he saw them. The quiet times of night were now the endless lonely times that dragged on and on until the daylight finally came again.

This happened in a religious setting where the dynamic of member relationships is described as a "family" in a congregation called the "body of believers." If isolation happens this quickly among the religiously connected, those without a religious affiliation are surely equally susceptible to despair.

This friend began attending a grief counseling group in another kiosk where nobody knew him and where he could comfortably express his emotions and loss. This man, who is one of the most patient men I know, experienced outbursts of anger that were uncharacteristic of him and which shocked him. He now had to reign in this ugly emotion and apologize while at a loss to understand its source. He would become suddenly emotional with no warning or apparent reason. The counseling has helped him navigate a path through this loss and unexpected range of emotions.

For people of the faith, the Game Master calls Himself the healer and helper of the brokenhearted. His Spirit Master is called the Comforter. There is divine comfort and help for broken souls who turn to Him through His Manual, the Bible, and through the dynamic of prayer. Those who need a helping hand can find faith-based groups to assist in their recovery.

During the same period, I watched another nonreligious disabled, homeless acquaintance who had lost his wife, then his oldest son several months after I met him, and then, a few months after that, the daughter whom he relied on the most. I was his last phone call before the despair drove him to suicide in an undisclosed place where he said no one would find him. Because he was calling from a remote location in another state, we could only pray after calling 911. A month later, we learned that his youngest son had found him fifteen minutes later and got him to the hospital. His other daughter connected him with her pastors, who helped bring him back from the brink.

> Everyone has a choice to either pursue God or to find their own way.

Throughout all those months that I knew him, he consistently talked about the day he was practically electrocuted on a job site, died three times in the hospital, and lost his arm and the use of both legs. Life was good, and the money was easy until that day. Then for the next twenty years, his luck never turned around, and finally, his family started dying around him. Despite knowing his luck was bad and repeating it often, he steadfastly refused to engage in conversations about the Game Master or what could improve his current circumstances from a spiritual level.

Everyone has a choice to pursue the Game Master or find their own way. With all the negative spiritual influence we are exposed to and accept in our choices of life, He is not likely to be the one to blame or the reason bad things happen to us. He alone can free us from the negative spiritual issues that prevent us from having a life of inner peace, joy, and prosperity.

If physical or emotional healing is your desire, the Cure Zone and Resource appendices provide guidance and sources to help you on that journey. If you want freedom from the circumstances that are against you, using the currency of faith in Him, you can shatter the darkness that binds you, dispel the spiritual oppression that overshadows your world and circumstances, turn your night mourning to morning joy, and make peace your habitation. The One simply repeated the Game Master's original offer when He said, "Come to me, all of you who are weary and loaded down with burdens, and I will give you rest. Place my yoke on you and learn from me, because I am gentle and humble, and you will find rest for your souls" (Matt. 11:28–29 ISV; cf. Jer. 6:16).

Healing starts with renouncing this world system's kingdom of darkness and turning to the Game Master's kingdom of light. His healing is the best solution for your entire being—spirit, soul, and body. For you who need hope, master player Paul repeated the prophet Isaiah's message: "But as it is written, 'No eye has seen, no ear has heard, and no mind has imagined the things that God has prepared for those who love him'" (1 Cor. 2:9 ISV; cf. Isa. 64:4).

Winning the Game

WINNING IS THE point of the Game of Life. Period. If your game has been going badly for you, if you are tired of your Game of Life and want to quit and check out of the game, *do not give in or give up until you win the game*. Whatever it has cost you, whatever you have lost in this game so far, whatever regret you have from life is nothing compared to the regret you'll have if you lose the game. You must win this game at any cost. The One said it is much better for you to be crippled as you win the game than to be whole and gain the world but lose the game (Matt. 5:29–30; 10:39; 16:24–27; John 12:24–26).

> WINNING IS THE POINT OF THE GAME OF LIFE. PERIOD.

If there is something to win, that means it is also possible to lose. Getting cheated by friends, family or the government is not the game. Cheating to get ahead in life is not the game. Your walk through life punching a time clock is not the game. Finishing life with a good retirement is great, but that's not the game. Being happy with family and life is not the game. These are examples of how we traverse the game, not the objective of the game.

Everything we have discussed up to this point refers to our participation in this current Game of Life on planet Earth. This current life we are living is only the qualifying round that determines whether we reach the next level in the Game of Life: the bonus round.

Qualifying for the bonus round, heaven, is the winning objective. Players who choose to become members of the Game Master's kingdom of light must make a deliberate choice to leave their current boss, the Serpent, whose kingdom of darkness we are all born into, and choose the Game Master as their new boss. Only as members of His kingdom can He give us the power to overcome the evil spiritual forces of the Serpent's kingdom that work against us in our daily lives.

This is where the game gets real. You must level up to membership status to win this game. Master player Paul explains to members the Game Master's perspective of our dire situation and how He made it possible for us to become members:

Once you were under God's curse, doomed forever for your sins. You went along with the crowd and were just like all the others, full of sin, obeying Satan, the mighty prince of the power of the air, who is at work right now in the hearts of those who are against the Lord. All of us used to be just as they are, our lives expressing the evil within us, doing every wicked thing that our passions or our evil thoughts might lead us into. We started out bad, being born with evil natures, and were under God's anger just like everyone else.

But God is so rich in mercy; he loved us so much that even though we were spiritually dead and doomed by our sins, he gave us back our lives again when he raised Christ from the dead—only by his undeserved favor have we ever been saved—and lifted us up from the grave into glory along with Christ, where we sit with him in the heavenly realms—all because of what Christ Jesus did. And now God can always point to us as examples of how very, very rich his kindness is, as shown in all he has done for us through Jesus Christ.

Because of his kindness, you have been saved through trusting Christ. And even trusting is not of yourselves; it too is a gift from God. Salvation is not a reward for the good we have done, so none of us can take any credit for it. It is God himself who has made us what we are and given us new lives from Christ Jesus; and long ages ago he planned that we should spend these lives in helping others (Eph. 2:1–10 TLB).

Your ability to win is a simple but eternal choice: 1) choose His lifeline and live to please the Game Master Who made you and Who can give you the best life you could have both here on earth and in the age to come; 2) ignore Him, live to please yourself, and perish in the end with your Serpent boss; or 3) if you decline to choose, option number two has already been applied to you as the default choice since we all were born as subjects and slaves in the Serpent's kingdom (John 8:34).

To become a member, you must RSVP to the Game Master. He sent out the invitation to you, saying, "For God expressed His love for the world in this way: He gave His only Son [Jesus Christ] so that whoever believes in Him will not face everlasting destruction, but will have everlasting life" (John 3:16 VOICE). The Game Master is waiting for your response.

How much does God really love you? "He made Christ who knew no sin to [judicially] be sin on our behalf, so that in Him we would become the righteousness of God [that is, we would be made acceptable to Him and placed in a right relationship with Him by His gracious lovingkindness]" (2 Cor. 5:21 AMP). The Game Master treated the One as though He had committed every sin you have and ever will commit and punished the One by death on a cross for what you did and will do. The One was your substitute in death for your game violations.

When you become one of those "whoever" players that "believes in Him," suddenly the record book item for your life is changed so that when the Game Master looks at you, He doesn't see the guilty you who deserves to die for your corrupt status and game violations; He sees the holy righteousness of His Son who died for you (Rom. 8:16–18; Gal. 2:20).

Why did God have to die? Because somebody must die in a blood sacrifice to blot out your corrupt status as an enemy combatant with your game violations, and it's either you or Him (Lev. 17:11; Rom. 6:23; Col. 1:12–17; Heb. 9:22–28; 10:10–22). But even then, being corrupt in a corrupted game environment, your sin-induced death is already appointed, and it isn't nearly enough to cover your debt to God. So, the One, Jesus Christ, volunteered to come to Earth on a rescue mission to die specifically for you to pay off your corruption and game violations so you could gain an eternal life through His sacrifice and qualify to become a member of the family of God. The moment you repent, turn from living a life of game violations (sin) against God, and believe in Jesus Christ as the only Savior for you because of what He did for you, the Spirit Master comes to live in you, and your golden ticket is secured (Eph. 3:14–19; 4:29–30).

There is no such thing as being a Christian (member) all your life, being born a Christian or because your family is Christian, being baptized to become a Christian or getting religion, and now you are a Christian. No, it isn't by being good or doing penance that we become members on the Game Master's team. It is not a ritual; it is a relationship that comes from a change of heart. It is according to His mercy that we switch teams, by His grace and through our faith in Him (our RSVP) that we receive His gift of eternal life (Titus 3:4–6; Eph. 2:8–9; 1 Pet. 1:3–4; Rom. 5:19–21).

To RSVP to the Game Master, you must release your grip on life with the Serpent as your boss, declare the One (Jesus the Christ as your Lord [your new boss]), and believe in your heart (to the depths of your soul) that the Game Master raised the One from the dead (after He died to cover your game violations [sin]), then you will be saved (from the Game Master's judgment over your game violations) (Rom. 10:9–13; 1 Cor. 3–4; John 3:16–18).

This is the most important faith transaction you will ever make. If you don't personally RSVP to the Game Master's open invitation yourself, it hasn't been done because no one else can do it for you. William Ernest Henley wrote the final verse of his poem, *Invictus*: "It matters not how strait the gate, How charged with punishments the scroll, I am the master of my fate, I am the captain of my soul" (Henley 1875, ¶ 4).

Such self-reliance loses the game. Will you enter that strait (narrow) gate of the Game Master of which Henley speaks, put your fate in His hands by faith, and pursue Him into the bonus round? The One said that many, like Henley, will crash against that gate and still fail to enter (Luke 13:23-25).

This strait gate of the road of salvation and eternal life Henley speaks of is the juncture of life where you must choose to no longer control your fate and call the shots. The Game Master is the only one who can expunge your punishments from the scroll. In exchange, He becomes the captain of your soul. He said that only a few players find that strait gate and make it through. Will you be one of them? This is the cost of your RSVP (Matt. 7:13-14; Luke 13:23-30).

Bonus Round Rewards

So, what's in it for you? What's your prize for winning the game as a member? There are multiple rewards available to you.

You immediately receive eternal life with the Game Master and the One—the relational objective of the game (John 17:3). You get access to the bonus round's new heaven and earth environment—the environmental objective of the game. An abode is being prepared for members by the One, perhaps in the New Jerusalem city (John 14:2-3). Your security is assured with no more death or sorrow or tears, negative outcomes, or harassment against you with all curses expired in the bonus round (Rev. 21:4).

Those are the entry-level prizes. After that, your gameplay on this game level determines the rewards you can earn. You can earn treasure—gold, silver, precious stones—given for character development, overcoming obstacles in the game, recruiting new members, keeping your focus, and staying faithful in your allegiance to the One. You can earn a crown. You can earn a place of authority in the Game Master's kingdom by following the One's commands. There are additional undefined rewards that the One did not explain but simply called them great rewards (Luke 6:23, 35).

Some members who play poorly will reach the bonus round by the skin of their teeth, able to experience the relationships and environments but having no rewards or authority in the bonus round kingdom. All their gameplay on this game level will have been proven worthless to the Game Master—wood, hay, stubble—which will become a smoking ash heap in the fire that determines their quality of rewards. Don't be that player (1 Cor. 3:11–15).

Losing the Game

HAVE YOU EVER thought you could lose this Game of Life? I don't mean losing your health, wealth, or well-being. Those issues have no bearing on whether we win or lose the game. There's still hope for recovery while we play through those setbacks. We can win this game during our gameplay, but our last breath is the end of our gametime. If you haven't won this game before your last breath, you have lost the game.

> **IF YOU HAVEN'T WON THIS GAME BEFORE YOUR LAST BREATH, YOU HAVE LOST THE GAME.**

Maybe you've heard the statement, "Nobody lives forever." That is true for this game level because we all have an appointment with death (Heb. 9:27). But it is doubly true for guests who lose this game level. They will be appointed to a second death on Judgment Day (Rev. 21:8). The lifeline that members reached for during this game level is eternal life (John 3:16). Members will bypass the second death and live forever in the bonus round (Rev.20:6).

Most of us don't even think there's more to lose when we die. We just find our groove and try to enjoy life until it's over. Then things go black, and the afterlife can sort itself out. Because this game level is only a qualifying round, the stakes are so much higher than anyone has ever told you. What's worse is that winning is hard, and losing is easy. And losers go to hell.

While there are various names for hell, the operational term is "Lake of Fire." Players aren't supposed to go there, so if you end up there, it wasn't supposed to end that way for you, except that it will have been your choice. Hell was only prepared and intended for the Serpent and his henchmen. However, since guests are on his team too, the Manual says their fate will be to share in his destruction (Matt. 25:41).

Many religions, perhaps yours, offer an escape hatch from hell, where the subpar, bad, or evil player can reflect on how they messed up during this game level and then meet some requirement or payment plan to finally leave their torment behind and reach a better afterlife. These concepts are taught by Muslims and Hindus who believe hell is a temporary stop on their way to heaven (Silawan 2021, ¶ 2; Hinduism n.d., ¶ 1–18; Tibetan Buddhist Encyclopedia n.d., ¶ 2). Some hope for only a pit stop in Purgatory (Turner 2021, ¶ 9–11).

All these false hopes of postmortem redemption encourage players to be careless in their gameplay, ignore the Game Master's terms, immerse themselves in and love all the pleasures of this Serpent kingdom's game environment, and end their gameplay on their own terms as they captain their soul into hell while fully expecting to recover from any afterlife penalties imposed by cosmic authority.

If you think you can't know before you die whether you will reach heaven, you have bought the Serpent's lie. The Serpent uses kiosks to cloud life's outcome and procrastinate your decision for eternal life until you perish in the grave and can't change your mind. By contrast, the One said that you should do everything you can to avoid ending up in the Lake of Fire (Mark 9:43–49 NLT; cf. Isa. 66:24). The Game Master insists that you can know right now whether you have eternal life, because this life is through His Son (1 John 5:10-13).

Most players lose the game by neglecting the Game Master's great salvation (Heb. 2:1–4). The price for living like the Game Master's Manual means nothing to you, and just running out your game clock pursuing your version of freedom and fun is not some hellish timeout penalty box where you get a divine do-over; it is the end of the road for you and your chances. You don't get multiple tries after this qualifying round you are now living (Heb. 9:27–28).

After death, it's judgment time and the Lake of Fire, where the worm doesn't die, and the fire never goes out. The Lake of Fire is the second death. If you are a guest player, your body will have already died by the end of this game level's time span, but then your soul will be brought up for judgment and sentenced to the Lake of Fire, and that will be your second death. When the Game Master doubles down on your death sentence, what makes you think you're coming back from it? (Mark 9:43–49; Heb. 9:13; Rev. 20:10–15). To perish is to not come back. *Ever*.

Part 1 Conclusion

PART ONE INTRODUCED the way the game operates and its main objective. Part Two covers in great detail the many ways bad things affect our gameplay and how to neutralize them. Being a guest on a gaming app is casual fun because it doesn't cost you anything except advertisement time and perhaps a few purchases.

> God's choice for you is always to *Choose Life.*

Rewards come with a membership signup. We've seen a sampling of the afterlife rewards available to players who level up to membership status. Part Two explains how members can improve their gameplay on this game level as well.

Perhaps this section ended with way too much religion for your taste. You can't afford to lose this game round. The objective of the Game of Life is to qualify for the bonus round and pursue the Game Master for His rewards. We all have a choice to remain a guest and face a second death after we die in this game level or to become a member and go for the gold. If you don't know what to pick, the Game Master's choice for you is always to *choose life. Don't neglect to RSVP to the Game Master!* (Deut. 29:9; 30:19–20; Rev 20:11–15).

PART 2

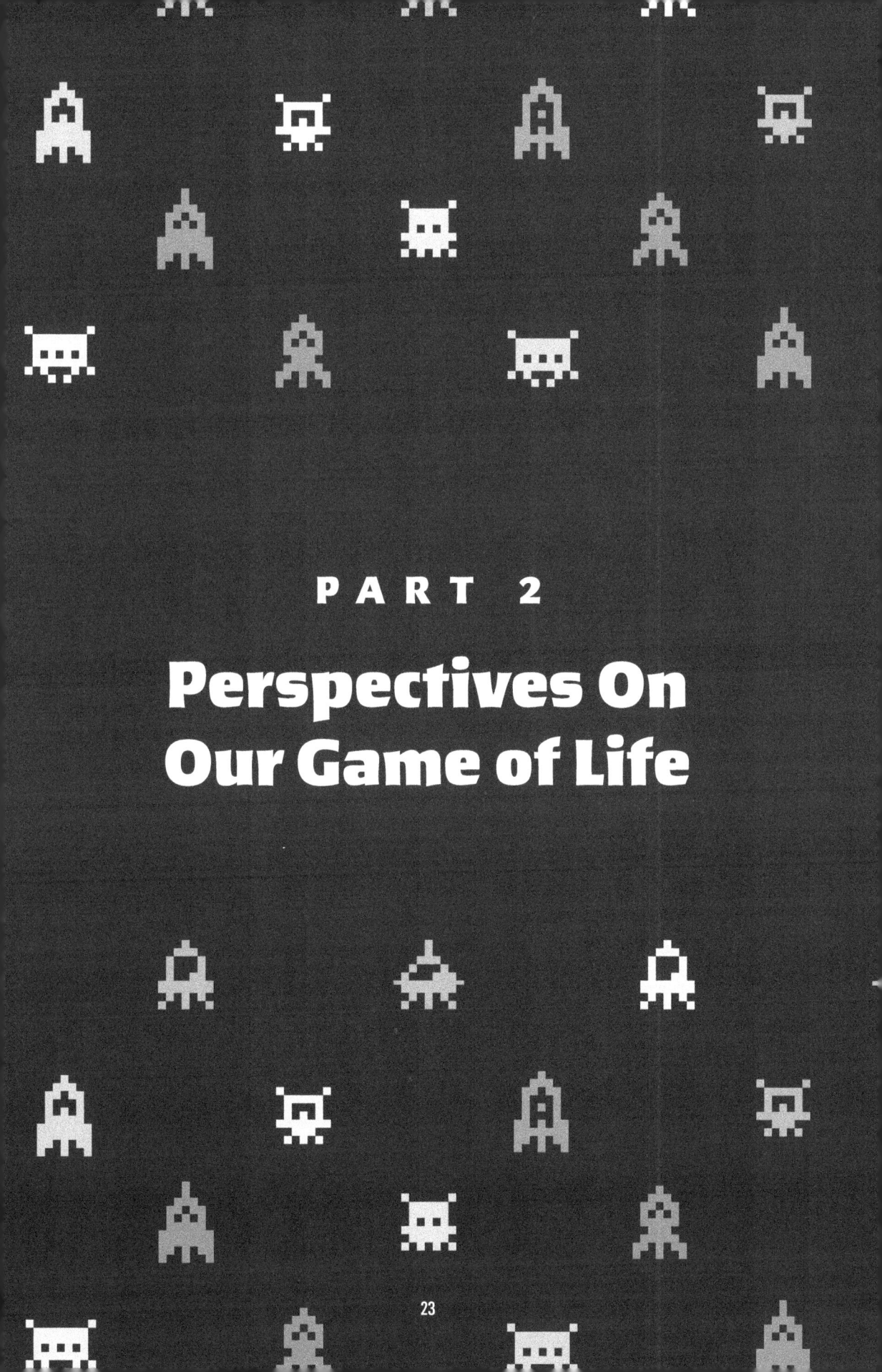

Perspectives On Our Game of Life

Why Life Happens to Us and What to Do about It

WHY DO BAD things happen to good people? Nobody fully answers the question or shows us how to make it stop. This part will first explain how it all started. Then, it will give you factors and formulas to apply to the bad things that happen to you so you can discover and diagnose what is going on in your life. Finally, you will see how you can stop bad things from happening to you and how to turn your life from a cursed existence into a blessing.

Bad things that happen to us are a collective common experience. An easy conversation starter is asking, "Don't you just hate it when . . . ?" As you share your recent experience, even strangers chime in and have something to add about how their lives take a predictably bad turn in some similar way.

Living on a cursed earth has predictable harms we face through disease and nature. Although we insulate ourselves through better medicines and safe shelter, other types of harm turn up, like bad circumstances and bad people. Throw in a diabolical element like evil spirits or what some describe as bad juju or bad karma, and you have the inevitable recipe for disaster scenarios. Fortunately, most of us don't deal with it every day, but bad things are bad enough and last too long when they do come around and hit us. If you live in a perpetually bad situation, life itself can become unbearable. Let's see how this happens and work out an escape plan.

Game Layout

THIS WHOLE GAME globe environment we live in, planet Earth in its galaxy and universe, has only one valuable commodity: *you*. The human race of players on earth are the only beings constructed in the image of their Creator, God, the Game Master. You were made to be spirit-synced with Him like no other creature He made on Earth. But He keeps the universe expanding and the galaxies spinning as light finger work while He struggles to get your attention (Ps. 8:3; Quayle 2013, 10–11).

Players are the most valuable aspect of the Game of Life. The Game Master puts a premium on your value as a player, and nothing in the game environment compares to you individually or collectively. Governments may calculate your worth based on the productivity of your work, as collateral against the national debt or by your carbon footprint, but the Game Master calculates your worth as His created being. Your personhood is worth more to Him than the mere wealth of the entire world, which your government will never fully possess.

Heaven and earth will pass away (Matt. 24:35; 2 Pet. 3:10; 1 John 2:17; Rev. 21:1). The spirit of the player, or what is usually called the soul, is the only eternal feature of this game. We hold the choice to pursue eternal life or settle for the destruction of our souls. Because our eternal soul is encapsulated inside a decaying body in a sustained but declining game world environment, we have a hard time distinguishing our temporary game life from our eternal potential, so our perspective is naturally drawn toward the game's daily temporary things, which become the defining elements of our existence.

Players generally don't seriously consider the value of their soul but choose to pursue their own game objectives of fame, fortune, or family at this game level instead of investing in their eternal future bonus round potential by pursuing the Game Master's priorities for their life, which may include fortune, fame, and family—or not. The One describes it like this:

> Then he called his disciples and the crowds to come over and listen. "If any of you wants to be my follower," he told them, "you must put

aside your own pleasures and shoulder your cross, and follow me closely. If you insist on saving your life, you will lose it. Only those who throw away their lives for my sake and for the sake of the Good News will ever know what it means to really live.

"And how does a man benefit if he gains the whole world and loses his soul in the process? For is anything worth more than his soul? And anyone who is ashamed of me and my message in these days of unbelief and sin, I, the Messiah, will be ashamed of him when I return in the glory of my Father, with the holy angels" (Mark 8:34–38 TLB).

If you acquired all the world's wealth, it would still not compare to the value of your soul. Nothing you could attain or offer can equal your value to the Game Master. It doesn't matter what you think of yourself. You know how much you are worth by the price the Game Master was willing to pay for your soul's redemption. To Him, you are worth dying for, and so He died and rose again to offer you a new life in Him (Prince 2022a, min. 1).

> **YOU KNOW HOW MUCH YOU ARE WORTH BY THE PRICE THE GAME MASTER WAS WILLING TO PAY FOR YOUR SOUL'S REDEMPTION.**

The game's players were spirit beings adapted and limited to a physical game world. Their soul was the bridge between the spirit realm and the physical realm, and this soul was where they were given their free will. Unlike all other animal life forms and perhaps other spirit beings, these players had a choice to side with the Game Master or to reject His ways.

Note that some kiosks teach that we are a two-part being (dichotomy: body and spirit) and not a three-part being (trichotomy: body, soul, and spirit). This book refers to players as three-part beings ("Trichotomy vs. Dichotomy of Man—Which View Is Correct?" n.d. ¶ 1)

The term "soul" is often interchanged with the word "spirit," such as when we say animals have no soul. There is a self-awareness or psyche associated with living creatures. When religious discussions refer to the soul, they usually indicate the indestructible spirit that lives on after the body has died. Because that usage is so common, it will be applied in this book as well, with the word "soul" also generally referring to the eternal spirit of an individual ("Trichotomy vs. Dichotomy of Man—Which View Is Correct?" n.d., ¶ 2).

Creatures made in His image require freedom of choice, so the Game Master can't make you choose Him. Instead, He can show you the path to Him and perhaps even compel you toward Him, but you can go off in your own direction. And that's where the Serpent, His archenemy, discovered a way to keep the Game Master from what He wants.

There is a conspiracy to keep you from syncing up with the Game Master (God the Creator) and living a life of inner and outer peace. The bad things that happen to you are part of the collateral damage from the epic struggle the Serpent (Deceiver or Satan) instigated. To him, it's just part of the game to deprive the Game Master of His prized players, but to you, it is personal, and sometimes it hurts more than anyone can imagine.

The Game Master has a way for you to avoid tremendous losses, recover from those losses that take you down, and see you come back for a win. So, let's get started. This book is a look at what you are up against in this life and is explained like a video game. Here are the book's main sections that remain starting in this **Part 2** section:

Section One: *The Game of Life* explains the scenario that put us in life's bad situations and gives a synopsis of the game.

Section Two: *The Game Setup* section shows how the combat between the Arch Rivals affects the moves of the players. When you understand this section, there is very little mystery about how the bad things of life reach us.

Section Three: *The Hurt Zone* spells out areas of all players' lives' troubles as you play the game and helps you identify the causes for those bad things that affect you.

Section Four: *The Cure Zone* tells how you can get immunity and power to combat your troubles and neutralize them. Here you collect and assemble the armor and weapons needed to change the course of your life.

Part 3

Section One: *Players and Terms Defined* glossary section identifies the environment for the Game of Life and introduces the players and tools. This is an extensive section for those who would like explanations about life's spiritual elements.

Section Two: *Final Points* include topics that elaborate on points made earlier or that cover some controversial issues related to this book's topics.

Appendix: *Resource* appendices include suggested lists of experts, print and media materials who have the answers you need and can explain them in an even more practical, logical, and thorough way.

Game of Life Terms

Game of Life – Refers to the qualifying level for the bonus round; your personal life that you live on earth; collective lives of all people and how they live; game ends for each player upon their death; collective game will end at the apocalypse

Game Master – God, Jehovah, Yahweh, Creator, God the Father

the One – Jesus Christ, Messiah, God the Son, Son of God

Spirit Master – Holy Spirit, Holy Ghost, Comforter, God the Holy Spirit, Spirit of Truth

guardians – God's angels—all classes, spirit beings

Serpent – Satan, devil, prince of this world, dragon, fallen angel, a spirit being, previously called Lucifer, the boss of this game level

henchmen – Serpent's angels, fallen angels, spirit beings

minions – Demon spirits: disembodied spirits, haunting spirits, spirit guides, evil spirits

players – People, sometimes refers to all game participants, also called gamers

guest players – Default player status; non-believers in Jesus, member of the Serpent's kingdom, not found listed in the Book of Life

member players – Believers in Jesus (Christians), member of God's kingdom, listed in the *Book of Life*, bonus round players

master players – Expert level member players

game environment – Earth, solar system, Milky Way, universe, physical non-spirit dimension

game world – Planet Earth

spirit realm – Non-physical dimension of game

headquarters – God's throne in heaven, great white throne of judgment

bonus round – Heaven, God's next kingdom, the new Earth, the Holy City, bonus level

hell – Hell, Hades, Lake of Fire, the second death

kiosk (religious) – Church, temple, mosque, shrine, seminary, religious publication or blog, TV, radio, or other source of religious information, including pagan or non-Christian spiritual sources; may be identified by type: Protestant, Catholic, Pentecostal, Baptist, Wiccan, New Age, Communist, philosophy, and so on

Manual – Holy Bible, Word of God, Scriptures; a compilation of sixty-six smaller books, Game Master's Handbook

book of life – Official list of bonus round players

golden ticket – Eternal life, qualifies player for bonus round, qualifies player for miracle-working power, access to God, the fix

game violations – Sin, violation of God's code

Big Ten – the Ten Commandments, summary of rules for interacting with the Game Master and fellow players

New Testament commands – Rules for interacting with the Game Master and fellow players

gameplay – The way you live your life

obstacles – Bad things that happen, just bad stuff

solutions – Description of obstacle fixes

synced – Spirit connection to the Game Master; abiding in the One; led by the Spirit Master; learning the Manual so it abides in the player improving their behavior; acquiring the thought process and attitude of the One; required for miracles and answered prayer

---

NOTE: Many of these **Game of Life terms** are defined in **Part 3** for players who want an in-depth explanation of their meanings. Member players may find some alternative views from the generally accepted teachings of their kiosk. Also, a number of these terms are never explained in detail even in the best of kiosks or even in kiosk-related seminaries, colleges and universities. Most players will never get a complete picture of the spirit forces that affect them or receive tools to help them even if they faithfully attend a kiosk or study group for decades. This knowledge comes from a purposeful quest to learn the truth.

Your Game of Life
Rate your Gameplay

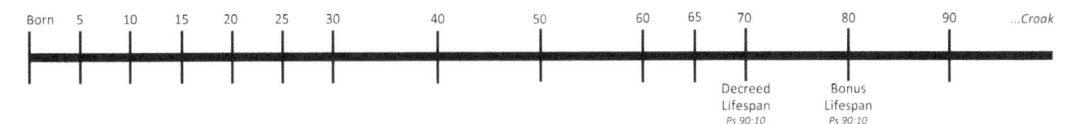

Born 5 10 15 20 25 30 40 50 60 65 70 80 90 ...Croak

Decreed Lifespan
Ps 90:10

Bonus Lifespan
Ps 90:10

Quality of Life at Each Stage — *Accomplishments? Obstacles? Blessings? Miracles?*

Age 5 - Walk & Talk & Choices + _____   **Goals** - *Current Game or Bonus Round*
Age 10 - _____   _____
Age 15 - _____   _____
Age 20 - _____   _____
Age 25 - _____   _____
Age 30 - _____   _____
Age 35 - _____   _____
Age 40 - _____   _____
Age 50 - _____   _____
Age 60 - _____   _____
Age 70 - _____   _____
Age 80 - _____   _____
Age 90 - _____   _____
...Croak - __ *Bonus Round* or __ *Lake of Fire?*   **Golden Ticket** Acquired at Age: _____

Section I: The Game of Life

WHY DO BAD things happen to good people?
    Easy Answer: Because life is tough, and nobody gets a free pass. If you want things to be different, you must change them yourself.

Long Answer: The Game of Life didn't start like this. Originally, the Game Master created a perfect game environment for two perfectly created players, Adam and Eve, who were made in His image. He put them in charge of the game world with one rule: don't eat the fruit from the forbidden Tree of Knowledge of Good and Evil. So they didn't—until the Serpent got an idea.

The Setup

The Serpent saw that the new players had control of the game world and were synced up to the Game Master daily. He wanted to be in charge of everything and realized he could spite the Game Master by taking away His prized creatures, so he persuaded the players that they would become godlike if they tried the fruit from the forbidden tree. When they chose to listen to him and eat the fruit, it was their moment of death, where their spirit connection to the Game Master was broken (Gen. 3).

They had *one job* and broke that rule; the rest is history, and here we are. This was the Pandora's box moment for the Game of Life, where everything in the game environment was cursed or contaminated. Today, all the bad things that happen to us are the result of this fateful day when the players chose to follow the Serpent instead of the Game Master.

They understood good and evil but didn't become godlike. They simply exchanged one boss for another. Plus, they ceded their authority over the game environment to the Serpent by disobeying the Game Master, and the Game Master now calls the Serpent the "prince of this world." Now, by default, you were born as a subject and slave in the kingdom of the prince of this world.

The Game Master installed a governor on the game to thwart the Serpent's ambition for total domination of the game. This governor has kept things restrained, so we haven't been totally overwhelmed by evil. The Game Master will have the governor step aside heading into the Apocalypse after self-professing members abandon the Game Master, which is now starting to happen. You may notice it as popular members deconstruct their faith and publicly walk off His team. Then the Serpent's plan to fully control the game will soon come together (2 Thess. 2:1–12).

The Serpent was the Trojan horse who infected the entire game with malware. He now acts as though he owns the game, and we all run his plays and dance to his tunes. He has taken control of the game's systems of philosophy, religion, entertainment, media, politics, judiciary, education, sports, industry, and so on. Players may say the Game Master is in charge, but most don't even notice that the plays they run and tunes they dance to belong to the Serpent.

THE SERPENT WAS THE TROJAN HORSE WHO INFECTED THE ENTIRE GAME WITH MALWARE.

This runs our whole life long until we individually choose to be disinfected by the Game Master and play the game with His plays and sing a new tune (Ps. 40:6; 94:1; 96:1). In the end, this game level will be fumigated into oblivion along with the Serpent and his infected guest players while the Game Master starts up the clean bonus round with His disinfected member players.

Bad stuff

Bad things that happen to us come from four main sources: 1) a violation of spirit laws—the Game Master's moral code, 2) influence by the Serpent and his spirit-being henchmen and minions, either directly or indirectly, 3) the result of the curse on the game environment plus all the curses triggered by the players upon themselves, all of which collectively include disease, hostile living conditions like from the plants, animals or the forces of nature, and the pressures of life, and 4) players: other players who do bad things, whether physically or psychologically, or the bad choices we make that result in harm.

Bad things that hit us can be multiple combinations of any of these four sources: spirit laws, the Serpent, the game environment, or player choices. Most players never notice the influence of the spirit realm; that reason is the least understood and the most disregarded.

It's sad when players make dumb choices and then ask why bad things happen to good people as those consequences come back to bite them. Assuming there isn't a self-defeating curse at work, some bad things are preventable, and it helps to pay attention.

The fix

The Game Master has not forfeited the game but is playing it out from a huge disadvantage since none of the players start on His team anymore. Notice that none of the bad stuff comes from the Game Master. Instead, He is the source of power through Whom you overcome the onslaughts of the Serpent's henchmen, break and defeat the curses of the game environment, and mitigate the losses from other player activity.

Additionally, the Game Master can bring restorative power to your life and empower you to succeed against obstacles that come against you. The fix is only available to players who leave the Serpent's team and join the Game Master's team. When the Serpent flips a coin with you on his team, his condition is, "Heads, I win; tails, you lose." You cannot expect to overcome problems instigated by the Serpent while you're still playing on his team. You will always lose.

> The Serpent's Coin Toss:
>
> "Heads, I win; tails, you lose."

If you want solutions to change the turmoil of life, you must choose them on purpose and pursue the success that is waiting for you. Joining the Game Master's team is only the first step to getting you in the door that offers you an array of successful options; the rest depends on how well you can sync up with Him.

Game Synopsis

Game Objectives: *Qualify for the bonus round and sync up with the Game Master.*

Why bad things happen is a near-universal question. Life is the game we play for keeps. When you get hurt, that's not your avatar bleeding; it's you. Everything we do or say in this life counts for us or against us because this Game of Life is not the main round; it is only a setup for the real game after this one—the bonus round. This life is simply the qualifying round where every player has a chance to keep all the bad things that happen to them limited to this level. All the bad things that happen to players in this game world are the result of a corrupted game environment.

The first goal of this game level is to qualify for the bonus round. After you qualify for the bonus round and continue to play out your time on this game level, you can make yourself eligible for power-ups that can mitigate or even eliminate the bad things that come your way. Players who choose not to go for the bonus round never have access to the Game Master's power plays that prevent bad things from happening to them. They live an exposed, unblessed, and unprotected life.

> **Goal 1**
>
> Qualify for the Bonus Level

This is how the One describes the value of the bonus round: it is like a businessman who finds a highly valued pearl in a field, swaps everything he has, and leverages all he can to buy the field just to get this pearl-of-great-price (Matt. 13:45–46). When you find eternal life—*knowing the true God and Jesus Christ whom He sent*—you're a winner because you are in the Game Master's kingdom and will reach the bonus round even if you get totally wiped out and lose all your points in this qualifying game level based on your society's measures of success. Along the way, you have a chance to beat the odds in this life too (John 17:3).

All players play this Game of Life as either guests or members, with guests playing on the Serpent's team and members on the Game Master's team. If you are not sure which team you are on, you are a guest player. At the end of the game, all the players report to the Game Master. He pulls up their records to confirm who qualifies for the bonus round (Rev. 20:11–15).

Members are listed in the Book of Life and go on to the bonus round of perpetual life minus all the bad things. Gone are their tears with all life's miseries (Rev. 21:4; 22:1–3). For this bonus round, members will now have an upgraded trans-dimensional body with superhero capabilities (Luke 24:36–37; John 6:19–21; 20:19, 26; Acts 8:39–40).

Guests are all the remaining players who stayed on the Serpent's team and either refused or didn't bother to join the Game Master's team as members. Since all players are born as default guests of the Serpent's team, each player must make an individual and deliberate decision to switch teams during their gameplay lifetime. If no decision is made, that player stays on the Serpent's team.

Although there are no reliable statistics reaching back to the start of the game, based on current player assessment, on what happened in the days of Noah and after the great flood, and observing the following civilizations through the millennia, this number of guests could include well upwards of ninety-five percent of all players since even many professing members will not pan out. Statistically, across the game timeline, your chance of becoming an actual member player is slim to none. The good news is that, despite the weight of history stacked against you, you personally can still beat the odds.

Guests are not listed in this Game Master's Book of Life and don't make the bonus round. Instead, they will have a charge sheet of all their game violations from start to finish. Because they didn't allow the Game Master to expunge their violation record during their gametime, they are now held liable to pay for all the damages. This is where "shock and awe" will take on a sickening new meaning as guests learn too late that being a good person was not good enough (Rev. 20:11–15).

As a guest, if you can't think of anything bad that you are responsible for seeing as you're a good person, the Game Master said that even the work you did to feed your family, your community service, your faithful religious participation, and those miracles you did will all count against you because you were working in the service of the Serpent the whole time (Prov. 21:4; Matt. 7:21–23).

If you are one of those players who say, "I may have done a little bad stuff perhaps, but not enough to go to hell," you don't really understand the chasm between your corrupted soul and the Game Master's perfect holiness. The chasm is so great that His Son had to die to even give you a chance at eternal life. In the Game Master's perspective of perfection, it isn't just the bad stuff we do that He despises, but the best and most noble and even heroic deeds we do still look like menstrual rags to Him (Isa. 64:6–7).

Until you get yourself off the Serpent's team, no good deed goes unpunished (Prov. 15:26; 21:4, 27; Isa. 64:6). Guests who try to curry favor with the Game Master without actually joining Him are called workers of evil, the lawless ones (Matt. 7:21–23). Since we can't make the rules, we also can't choose which ones apply to us. Remember, we're just playing this game with the hand we are dealt; we don't own it.

Most all the players throughout the history of the game world will be faced with the reality that all their good efforts counted for nothing. All the guests who are not listed in the Book of Life will be found guilty of game violations, sentenced to a degree of punishment based on their violations, and scheduled for destruction along with their leader and boss, the Serpent (Martin and Zaspel n.d., ¶ 1–33). Whoever runs out their clock without the golden ticket is a loser, gates of hell and all. *Game Over* (Matt. 13:44–50; Luke 12:42–48; John 17:3; Rev. 20:11–15; 21:6–8; 22:14–15, 19).

The second objective is to become like the One. After a guest becomes a member, the Manual explains how to develop Jesus' characteristics. The benefits to the players include personal growth in character and wisdom, effective prayers, miracle power, and authority to effect change in the physical environment and spirit realm. For the bonus round, the character development completed in this first round of life improves the player's value to the Game Master (Mark 10:45; Luke 9:23–25; Phil. 2:5–8).

This power explained by the One is real and amazingly impressive, but hardly any players use it. Most of them don't understand the Manual well enough to activate that kind of power. Members have access to it and will more likely tell you it's not even available anymore, but the Game Master still gives it to those who go for it.

Goal 2
Become Like the One

The Game of Life

This Game of Life was already running and had rules in place before we showed up in the garden of Eden. The game started before mankind came on the scene, but now that we are here, our presence generates a lot of attention, both good and bad. The game world has been referred to as the "psychic center of the universe" by entities on the Serpent's team (Branton 1999, 91). The current game environment was made to be suitably excellent, and the players created for it were perfect.

The Game of Life was intended to be played by members only—players who were synced up and spirit-connected to the Game Master. When the first two members, who were on the Game Master's team and ideal in every way, threw a wrench in the works and teamed up with the Serpent, they were downgraded to guest player status—by breaking their syncing spirit-connection to the Game Master—and they corrupted the game environment in the process.

Since then, all players now start the game as guests without the Game Master's advantages, and the objective is to get back on the Game Master's team (2 Cor.

5:14–15; 2 Pet. 3:9). Unfortunately, current membership status is not equal to the original game status because all players must still compete in this corrupted game environment. That won't be fixed until the bonus round.

The tree of the knowledge of good and evil is continually referenced in this book. So, what was the point of planting a tree whose fruit would open your awareness of good and evil, kill your spiritual awareness and connections, and physically condemn you to death? That is the starting point for all the trouble we face in this game (Gen. 3).

The Game Master is all about choices. He didn't create this game world as the ultimate experience for His perfectly created players. It was simply excellent for us but not the ultimate we could have. We are not playing in a one-round game scenario. This game world is simply the starting point for us, and the question is whether we will lose this round in a double-death experience or make it to the next round, where we will have the ultimate life experience with Him (Rev. 21:8).

We are all taking the Game Master's test in this life. You are taking His test. Just like Adam and Eve's single choice about the fruit in the garden of Eden, your single choice today is exactly the same: whom will you choose to listen to, whom will you choose to obey, the Game Master or the Serpent? (Gen. 3).

WE ARE ALL TAKING THE GAME MASTER'S TEST IN THIS LIFE.

Adam's choice looked easy: leave the tree alone and gain eternal life, but the Serpent framed his choice to look like he was a loser if he didn't choose the tree of knowledge. The Serpent may also make you look like a loser if you choose to walk away from him today. The question is, how much longer will you believe him?

The world is full of religions. Most players choose the Serpent's team by joining his kiosks, any kiosk in the world except the Game Master's kiosk. Others may choose a kiosk that masquerades as a Game Master kiosk, deceiving those who thought they found eternal life. Many players nowadays reject both the Game Master's and the Serpent's religious kiosks, saying religion isn't for them, and instead choose the Serpent's kiosks of philosophy and vainglory.

Still others, like the atheists, choose the Serpent's kiosk of pride and purposely reject a chance for the bonus round. Some who affiliate with the Game Master's kiosk will enjoy the experience or respectability it may bring but aren't interested in giving up their own agenda on life by crossing the Serpent's fence and actually choosing to serve the Game Master. If nothing changes their minds, all these players will lose this round of the game and slip away to their eternal second death. Will this include you?

Because we, today, already started on the wrong side of the fence in this game round, there are only choosers and losers. Only a few will jump the fence, choose the Game Master, and join His kiosk but are willing to walk out of their kiosk with

Him as "Ichabod" (where is the glory?) is stamped over its doors when that kiosk gets infected by the Serpent's agents, as is happening more often these days (1 Sam. 4:21–22; Matt. 24:10–14).

The Game Master wants players who are committed to Him, and having a choice is the only way He confirms that we want to be with Him on purpose. Those who pass the test qualify for the upgraded level He offers, the bonus round.

"For the eyes of the Lord search back and forth across the whole earth, looking for people whose hearts are perfect toward him, so that he can show his great power in helping them" (2 Chron. 16:9a TLB).

Each player on Earth is a unique player, and everybody has a chance to win. The Game Master left enough clues for everyone to win if the players don't get distracted (Rom. 1:16–21). Distractions are the hallmark of the game environment, and players are exceptionally easy to distract. Most will lose out because they never get their focus or learn to play to their advantage. Even though the odds don't favor the players, the game is winnable for all, and each player is responsible for his own win or loss.

There are only winners and losers. Don't be fooled; life is not an easy game. One of the hardest parts of playing the game as an expert is getting the details of the rules correct, but those who do so learn that they can call in supernatural powers straight from the Game Master Himself. Those powers will last as long as they can keep their focus—that's the hardest part (1 Cor. 9:24–27).

THE ESSENCE – *BELIEF*

The Game of Life is all about belief. After the first two players in paradise chose not to believe the Game Master and threw the game into chaos by eating the forbidden fruit, it has *always* been about whom the player will believe, the Game Master or the Serpent.

What the player believes and whom the player believes in determine his outcome at the end of the game: going to the bonus round or perishing in the Lake of Fire. These are stark choices. The Game Master is looking for members who will choose to totally believe Him and play the game His way. They will be the ones who qualify for the bonus round (2 Chr. 16:9a).

During this current Game of Life level, the arsenal they get will also source its energy level from the strength of their own belief in the Game Master's Manual. This is usually called faith, but its strength comes directly from whether the player believes the instructions of the Manual with all his heart—without doubt— even in the face of impossible odds. This is where players usually fail because doubt

> Doubt is a Faith-killer.

can be instantly injected into any situation. Few players—including members—recognize doubt as a problem or cause for failure (James 1:5–8).

Doubt is a faith-killer. The Manual explains that doubt is the one ingredient that interferes with or even cancels all the power that is generated through belief and will sink any chance for a miracle. Making miracles happens on the depth of a player's belief for it and on the total absence of doubt.

Warning: this Game of Life is saturated with deceit. Deceit infuses doubt about the rules. Enough doubt will make players disqualify themselves from reaching the bonus round. The hardest part is finding the truth and then keeping it free from getting mixed with deceitful doubt, whether from your own deceit or from an outside source or kiosk source. Those who get the truth have a chance to expose the deceit and beat it or outmaneuver it, but the need for vigilance never ends.

Section II:
The Game Setup

WHY DO BAD *things happen to good people?* Maybe you've heard it something like this:

God loves you (true), *and He wants to make you a better person even through the bad things* (also true), *so He allows these bad things to happen to you for your own good* (not so true), *and there's nothing you can do to change it* (really not true).

Most of the reasoning sounds like it's based on a simple 1+2=3. But this sentence doesn't add up based on the Manual's own text and the character of the Game Master.

That's why it can sound illogical to guests. Why would the Game Master make life hard for you and then offer to fix it? When members try to explain it, they can sound incoherent because the backstory is missing, and what they do know about it is too sketchy. It isn't a hard answer; it's just not a short answer. But once you know the context and parameters of the game, you'll also know more of the Game Master's perspective and how to find solutions. So here is the backstory.

Clash of Titans

Game Master vs. the Serpent

ACCORDING TO THE Manual, the Game Master is clearly superior in power to the Serpent, but the Serpent does not concede. Even in his rebellious condition, the Serpent does not have the power to neutralize or overcome the Game Master. This does not keep him from trying. Members who confront occultist players can demonstrate power over them in the name of the One, but vigilance is still required because the Serpent is a formidable and sly adversary who can devour them (1 Pet. 5:8).

The Game Master and Serpent are fighting over you. They both want your worship and complete devotion to them. If you think you'll worship neither one and just be your own independent player going your own way with nobody bossing you around, your game status is that you already have a boss. You are actually enslaved to the Serpent because you started life on his team; he already wins you by default (Rom. 5:12; 1 Cor. 15:21–22; Eph. 2:1–2). This is why the Serpent's Emergent teachings, Wicca, New Age, and Eastern religions and philosophy are so appealing: players think they are creating their own path to the divine, feeling empowered without being controlled by an outside entity.

> You are the Cosmic Prize in this Game.

The game's players are the object of this rivalry. When the Serpent saw how much the Game Master loved His newly created players, he saw an opening to use them against the Game Master. Here's a quick rundown condensed into four rounds.

The Early Rounds

From the Garden of Eden (circa 4,000+ BC)
to the resurrection of the One (circa AD 35)

Round 1

There were two important trees in paradise, the garden of Eden, when the current game world was created. The first one was the Tree of Life, where those who ate its fruit would live forever. The second tree, the forbidden tree, was the Tree of Knowledge of Good and Evil. The newly created players, Adam and Eve, could eat fruit from any of the trees in the garden they wished except from the forbidden Tree of Knowledge of Good and Evil. The Game Master told Adam that the day he ate from the forbidden tree, he would die.

So, they began life in paradise and in charge of the new game environment, hanging out with the Game Master in the evenings and ignoring both of the special trees. Adam tended the garden, so there was proximity to both trees where he probably tended them. Where did Adam get his tools?

But the Serpent was watching and realized that the choice given to the players, eating or not eating the forbidden fruit, could be used against them as a wedge issue. He told the woman, Eve, that the Game Master was just trying to keep them from being like Him because He knew that they would become gods if they ate the fruit (yes, he [the Deceiver] transformed into an actual serpent animal and talked to Eve, who was not alarmed about having a conversation with an animal). So he convinced her to try the forbidden fruit, the only single thing they were not allowed to eat. Upon closer inspection, she decided it looked desirable for food and wisdom, took a bite, and gave it to her husband. Adam recognized it as a ploy but chose to join Eve in eating the fruit (Gen. 3:1–7; 1 Tim. 2:13–14).

At that moment, they realized, OMG, they were naked! They suddenly grew a conscience, got terribly embarrassed, covered up with fig leaves, and ran off to hide. You know they were in total panic because they chose fig leaves. Fig leaves have serrated edges, a sandpaper-like top, and stiff hairs on the bottom ("Fig Leaves" n.d., ¶ 1). If they had their wits about them, they would have chosen any of the more than a dozen large-leaf plants that didn't chafe so much. Adam ran the garden, after all; he should have known.

Of course, that evening, the Game Master "found out" when He had to go looking for them. Adam scolded the Game Master for giving him that weak woman and blamed Eve; Eve promptly pointed at the Serpent and said, "He tricked me!"

> The Garden of Eden had a "magic" sword.
> Gn 3:22–24

The Game Master then cursed the ground so Adam would now have to pull weeds and work for crops with hard sweat equity, Eve was cursed with pain in childbirth, and even though she would want to control her husband, he would be her boss (Gen. 3:16 NLT). The Serpent was cursed to crawl on the ground and eat dust (the serpent animal was cursed because that was the guise used by the Serpent Deceiver).

Because the Serpent tricked Eve, the Game Master predicted that Eve's descendant (the One) would bruise his head even though the One's heel would get bruised (Gen. 3:14–15). Then the Game Master made some proper leather clothes for Adam and Eve, drove them out of the garden, and set cherubim angel guardians and a flaming sword, which turned every direction to protect the Tree of Life from anyone trying to eat it (Gen. 3:22–24). This is probably the first example of what one might call a magic sword, a spiritually animated object. This arrangement lasted for over 1,600 years until the great flood, which destroyed the game environment (Gen. 6–7).

Adam and Eve were made in the image of the Game Master (a spirit), having a spirit connected to a body and soul. Their spirit died on that fateful day in that it was disconnected from the Game Master (Gen. 2:16–17; Rom. 5:12; 1 Cor. 15:21–22; Eph. 2:1–2). That event also triggered the biological countdown of their physical body's decline toward death. The Tree of Life's fruit would have stopped the clock, but it wasn't a big deal until now. The game environment was cursed with weeds, thorns, and deadly plants. This is also where some say that the animal kingdom turned carnivorous, arguing that death was not listed at all as a factor in the game environment before now (Ham n.d., ¶ 8–18; Stambaugh n.d., ¶ 30–61).

The worst result for the players was that now all players who are born since then belong to the Serpent's team because the first two players purposely chose his team. Adam and Eve did not gain independence from the Game Master or become equal to Him; they simply swapped masters from the Game Master to the Serpent when they chose to disobey the Game Master.

Round one went to the Serpent, an easy, early victory. Now the Serpent had taken control of the game environment from Adam as the ultimate boss, the new prince of this world. This event marks the origin of spiritual slavery in the game. All players are now the Serpent's slaves to their death and must purposely break their bondage to the Serpent. He is their ultimate boss who calls the shots.

Round 2

The Game Master's prediction in the first round of a coming Messiah who would fix the Serpent's game interference gave the Serpent his next idea: corrupt the players' bloodline so there could be no Messiah.

He already had the players being born on his team, but that wasn't enough to guarantee a win. The icing on the cake was that if the entire player bloodline was contaminated, no one could qualify for the bonus round, and no Messiah could be born to free his slaves.

Back in the early days of our current earth, the Game Master's watcher guardians (angels) were mesmerized by the earth's exceptionally gorgeous women (i.e., perfect specimen Adam plus perfect specimen Eve, both with perfect DNA; you do the math). Twelve watcher leaders convinced about 200 of the watcher guardians in a plot to transform themselves into men and take up harems of these beautiful women. Their children were hybrids, part human and part supernatural beings of gigantic heights. They are the source beings for the legends of the Greek and Roman gods. Those may be widely considered as fables, but there is a bedrock of truth down there (Quayle 2013, 61–80).

Rob Skiba has a YouTube video entitled, "Moses Tells Us Exactly How the Nephilim Returned after the Flood," that goes into more detail about this event, citing the books of Enoch, Jasher, and Jubilees as cross-reference material (Skiba 2016, 158–195).

Being trans-human, these children were disqualified from the bonus round when they died. It is thought by some that they became the demons, or minions, that were consigned to roam the earth until the end of the game as disembodied spirits looking for new players to inhabit. Having previously been alive, they still have personalities, feelings, and appetites, and they crave the chance to possess a body once again.

By the time Noah arrived in the game in its tenth generation about 1,600 years later, the entire player bloodline was corrupted except for Noah, his wife, and his three sons—the Serpent was close to winning this round. The Game Master was left with no choice but to rid the game world of the corrupted players. He directed Noah to build an ark, a large barge-like boat, to save his family and specimens of all the game environment's animals from a game-world flood (Gen. 6).

The ark's dimensions were about 475 feet long (144.6 m), 79 feet wide (24.1 m), and 47 feet high (14.4 m). Skeptics say that wooden ships this big could not be built to withstand ocean forces, thereby disproving this story. However, the Ming dynasty appointed admiral Zheng He in the early fifteenth century to launch a fleet of 317 ships, including 60 galleons that were more than 400 feet long (122 m) and 150 feet wide (45.7 m). An excavated rudder was figured to fit a ship approaching 500 feet long (152 m). These mammoth-sized, sea-going treasure junks sailed throughout Indonesia to India to Africa (Greenberg 2021, ¶ 1). Since the Chinese could accomplish seven ocean voyages with wooden vessels that were

NOAH ONLY NEEDED ONE BOAT TO SAVE THE WORLD.

twice the size of European sea-going ships, Noah's ark was also very feasible, and Noah only needed one boat to save the world (Hadingham 2001, ¶ 4).

The ensuing forty-day torrential rains depleted the protective canopy that gave the game environment its extra solar radiation shield and higher levels of oxygen for a greenhouse atmosphere, and the fountains of the deep were torn open to flood the earth to at least twenty feet (6 m) above the highest mountains. All land life outside the ark was destroyed in floodwaters that took a year to subside (Gen. 7:17–24). It is estimated that there is still an ocean of water in today's atmosphere. With the recent discovery of ringwoodite stone deep in the earth, there is reported to be a water reservoir containing three times the volume of all the current oceans (Coghlan 2014, ¶ 1; Woo 2018). Scientists have also discovered that the earth is eating its oceans, cycling in more water than the crust emits (Pappas 2018, ¶ 1). Those who claim that Noah's flood was only a local event have not accounted for the tremendous volume of water that was released from beneath the earth.

This was the first game-world climate change event that triggered ice ages as the planet adjusted to its new climate conditions in the current game world. The earth's tectonic plates are now again becoming more active in recent years, indicating that recurring and coming climate change issues are both atmospheric and topographic, as the Game Master predicted (Matt. 24:3–8, 21–22; Mark 13:23–25; Luke 21:7–11, 25–28).

While Noah's bloodline itself was clean, at least one or more of his son's wives were still carriers of the corrupt bloodline (Skiba 2012, 177–184). So, the game environment retained its potential for bloodline corruption, and giants could once again roam free after the flood. The Serpent *barely* lost round two, but the stage is set for the next attempt.

Round 3

These series of clashes are important because many players believe the Game Master is the instigator of brutality toward them for no reason. They are wrong on both counts. This round is where many of those accusations originate.

Round three was a two-prong attack against the Game Master. Instead of going for a total corruption of the player bloodline again, the Serpent went for players' spiritual connection to the Game Master by first introducing alternate and eventually competing religious systems that would disqualify all players from the bonus round. Now you can pick from a wide variety of religions to suit your own interest in the divine.

Belief systems are much easier to spread than corrupted bloodlines, and it only takes minor deviations from the truth to cause a major bonus round disqualification. Besides, all the 200 watchers with their dozen conspirators were shackled in oppressive darkness as a lesson to any other guardians or henchmen who would think about trying their tactic again (2 Pet. 2:4).

Part one. First, the players didn't want to fan out across the game environment as the Game Master instructed them after the great flood. Round two retained strong spiritual interaction between players and spirit beings. The players, with their descendants, wanted this to continue after the flood, so they built what was called the Tower of Babel (Gen. 11:1–11). These players were still highly intelligent like their ancestors. It could have been a literal skyscraper tower intended to breach the atmosphere. It may have been a high place like a ziggurat with a temple on top, where they were perhaps building a stargate to reestablish their connection to the spirit realm.

Along with this, they were formulating false history and religions originating with Nimrod and based on the Serpent's influence with alternate source stories of how the game began, and became the era when the pantheons of gods were established. The Book of Jasher mentions a possible origin of the Hindu gods, Ganesha and Hanuman, from this time. The Game Master noticed their distractions from His directive and confused their language into the major language groups we have today (Gen. 11:6–9) (Skiba, 2015, min. 1:26:53).

Tower of Babel: the Original Stargate?

> And the Lord smote the three divisions that were there, and he punished them according to their works and designs; those who said, We will ascend to heaven and serve our gods, became like apes and elephants; and those who said, We will smite the heaven with arrows, the Lord killed them, one man through the hand of his neighbor; and the third division of those who said, We will ascend to heaven and fight against him, the Lord scattered them throughout the earth. And those who were left amongst them, when they knew and understood the evil which was coming upon them, they forsook the building, and they also became scattered upon the face of the whole earth (Book of Jasher 9:35–36; cf. Josh. 10:13 and 2 Sam. 1:18–27).

As the players scurried across the game environment, they took their new religious views with them as they continued attempts to locate portals and construct pyramids around the globe. All these religions that sprang up were the perfect way to distract the players throughout the entire game from learning the Game Master's truth. Part one of the Serpent's plan was now firmly in place as a failsafe against part two.

Part two. After these events, as giants were again proliferating, the Game Master called a player originally named Abram to head to the land He would promise to give him: today's land of Israel. Technically, wherever this Abraham walked was to be his inheritance from the Game Master, which is said to run from the Euphrates River down to the River of Egypt, but that's another topic (Gen. 15:18–21).

The second part of this round was set up when, after Abraham reached this promised land, the Game Master informed him that his promised descendants would head to Egypt and eventually be enslaved during a 430-year period before returning to their promised land (Gen. 15:12–16). This gave the eavesdropping Serpent his next chance with 400 years to specifically target a player group, the Hebrews or Jews as we call them today, for the corrupt bloodline.

While the Hebrews were slaving away in Egypt, the Serpent was filling up the promised land with more giants who came from the corrupted bloodline that was recessive in Noah's daughters-in-law. The Hebrews called themselves grasshoppers by comparison; they meant it literally (Num. 13:33). Notably, the Game Master Himself did not contradict them but actually agreed and acknowledged that He destroyed the Amorites, "whose height was like the height of the cedars" (Amos 2:9–10).

The smallest mature cedar tree is about 35 feet tall (10.67 m). Stephen Quayle"s book, *Genesis 6 Giants,* collates reports and documented giant heights of up to 25 feet (7.62 m) across Asia, Europe, and the Americas, and he also includes information about the more extreme heights of those up to 36 feet tall (11 m) (Quayle 2013, 213, 448, front cover face page). Rob Skiba's book, *Archon Invasion*, details the bloodline and giant aspect of the story (Skiba 2012, 208–212).

This point about the Amorites is where most kiosk teachers do not take the Manual text literally because no one can imagine anyone being close to that tall, even though the Game Master mentions it. The Hebrews, now called Israelites, having just escaped from Egypt after their leader Moses unleashed the ten plagues (Exod. 7–13), refused to fight these giants out of heart-melting fear. They were consigned to wander in the Sinai wilderness for forty years until the older, unbelieving, fearful, and faithless generation had died (Num. 13–14).

If you as a member are thinking, "It serves them right but I'm not unbelieving, fearful or faithless like those weak folk," give yourself an honest inventory of your faith walk, because those are the very characteristics that can keep you out of the bonus round (Rev. 21:8). The Game Master is deadly serious about expectations that we too often so casually brush off thinking He's not that serious or He is just being dramatic because it makes good poetry or prose (Matt. 7:24–27). Consider what your personal responses are to His Word, commands, and promptings.

During Israel's time in the Sinai wilderness, the Game Master drove out the biggest of the giants for them (Amos 2:9–10), leaving them to fight giants that were fifteen to twenty-five feet tall (4.5–7.6 m) (Deut. 3:1–13). These were partly dispatched by Israel, led by Joshua and Caleb. Some were said to retreat from Canaan and migrate to Europe and North Africa (Quayle 2013, 217–219). By the time David, the famous shepherd boy, came along, Goliath was a comparative pipsqueak at about 12 feet (3.66 m).

Modern texts, both religious and secular, leave out any records or mention of giants across the globe, so all players have the impressions that giants were maybe eight feet tall at most and were limited to a few scattered, aberrant individuals when in fact they composed entire tribes and people groups who were two or three times that height.

The Roman author, Pliney the Elder, who lived in the First Century and died at the Mount Vesuvius eruption in AD 79, relayed an account of a human more than 40 feet tall (12.19 m). He wrote,

> Ambassadors from Olisipo, sent on a mission with this purpose in view, reported to the Emperor Tiberius that a Triton, whose appearance is well known, had been seen and heard playing on a shell in a certain cave. I have illustrious knights as authority for the assertion that a Triton has been seen by them in the Gulf of Gades, perfectly resembling a man in his physical appearance. They say that he climbs aboard ships during the night, and that the side of the ship on which he sits is weighed right down, and, if he should happen to stay there an unduly long time, the ship is submerged. The bones of this monster . . . were bought by Marcus Scaurus from Joppa in Judea . . . The monster was over 40 feet long [12 m], and the height of his ribs was greater than that of Indian Elephants, while his spine was 1½ feet thick [0.45 m] (Quayle 2013, 213).

Typically, it took relatively few giants to be in charge of greater numbers of normal size players because of their imposing stature, so their actual numbers probably never exceeded the population of normal players in most locations. They were still estimated to run in the hundreds of thousands in Europe and the Middle East as late as two thousand years ago. The Roman Army was the first to successfully develop tactics to defeat them, and Julius Caesar is credited with dispatching a majority of them in Gaul (Quayle 2013, 226–230).

There are still giants on the earth today. If you search the Internet for Guadalcanal giants, you will find articles and stories through the twentieth century of 15-foot giants (4.5 m) and other cryptids found on the Solomon Islands and in the caves of Guadalcanal by the Japanese and American militaries during the Second World War. They are still there to this day and may also populate other areas of the globe (Not from Earth n.d., ¶ 7–20).

In March 2004, one of these 12-foot (3.66 m), 1,100-pound (499 kg) giants, likely referred to online as the Giant of Kandahar, was killed in the caves of Afghanistan by US Marines, so they are still not quite extinct (Quayle and Long 2008, 274–279).

To enter the promised land, the Game Master said that the Israelites, with their leader Joshua, had to purge the land of six specific nations: "namely, the Hittites, and the Amorites, the Canaanites, and the Perizzites, the Hivites, and the Jebusites" (Quayle 2013, 69–72), meaning none of them could be left alive including their livestock. Then, all their religious artifacts were to be completely destroyed (Deut. 20:16–18; 2 Sam. 23:20). The Game Master didn't want the Israelites' religion corrupted or their bloodline from where the One would originate to be contaminated by the giants. Later, Israel's first king, Saul, was ordered to destroy the Amalekites in this fashion (1 Sam. 15:2–3) (Eredin 2024, min. 17:30)

No other people groups in Canaan were treated like this. The standard operational tactic for all the other nations that Israel fought had their women, children, and livestock preserved as the spoils of war. The first order was to make peace with a city and have them pay tribute. If they refused tribute, the next order was to besiege them and kill only the men, never annihilating the population (Deut. 20:10–15).

This genocide order on the six nations is where many players accuse the Game Master of heartless cruelty. However, if players have contaminated bloodlines and become trans-human, it appears they lose their freedom of choice to reach the bonus round because the One did not sacrifice Himself for non-human or trans-human players. This was instead a heartless and cruel tactic by the Serpent to use these player nations as cannon fodder simply to ensure all future players like you would stay on his team (Quayle 2013, 139–140, 142).

Also, we do not know where the tipping point is in the trans-human process, where a player would lose the quality that defines his having been created in the image of God. Scientists are now commonly exploring trans-human cures for diseases from the animal kingdom and turning us into cyborgs with chip implants or DNA splicing using nano-technology (McNamee and Edwards S D 2006, 513–518; Malik 2023, 1-13; Mirkes 2019, 115–126). This sparks concern among some about players losing their spirit-being status.

So, extermination orders to Joshua and King Saul were issued for a total of seven nations in the promised land, where the Israelites would reside. Except for this one issue, any call for genocide was not condoned by the Game Master, and subsequent history shows that genocide was not a normal practice for Israel, unlike other invading nations, such as the Assyrians or even what the series of today's major current player nations repeatedly did to the New World's native peoples in their recent history with the mantra credited to General Philip Sheridan in 1869 that, "The only good Indian is a dead Indian" (Fixico 2018, ¶ 1-26; Lewy 2004, ¶ 1–67; Ostler 2015, ¶ 35). In these modern cases, religion or trans-human contamination was not a driving factor; it was simply a brutal, inhumane conquest exhibited by both sides.

The Serpent's chances to specifically contaminate the bloodline of the One were again thwarted. But his alternate religious exploits have now thoroughly permeated the entire game world up to the current day, ensuring that most players, perhaps even you, will never see the bonus round.

Round 4, etc.

These rounds just didn't stop in the race to prevent a Messiah for the players. The Serpent used false religions as a wedge to get the Game Master to punish His chosen people by causing them to commit game violations (sin) and turn their back on Him. Balaam, with his talking donkey, was only the first of many enticers who advised the local tribes to have their women persuade the men of Israel to marry them and accept their pagan religions (Num. 22-24, 31; 2 Pet. 2:15–16; Rev. 2:14).

After the Game Master announced to King David that he would forever have an heir for his throne, the Serpent focused efforts to exterminate David's specific bloodline. He occasionally tried total extermination of Israel again as well (2 Kings 11:1–3; Esther 3:5; Matt. 2:13–18).

When it finally came time for the One to be born, conceived of the Spirit Master to the virgin Mary, the Serpent had King Herod wipe out all the toddlers and infants around His birth town of

> The execution of the One was the greatest miscarriage of justice in the history of the Game.

Bethlehem (Jer. 31:15; Matt. 2:16–18). During His lifetime, the Serpent tried to distract the One from His mission, and a few more attempts were made to kill the One prematurely, but the Serpent thought he finally got Him where He was crucified on a cross at Calvary: Golgotha, the place of the skull. The execution of the One was the greatest miscarriage of justice in the history of the game.

Ironically, the accusation that brought down the One was His claim to be equal to the Game Master, which is actually the truth (Matt. 26:63–66; 27:27–44; Mark 14:61–64; Luke 22:67–71; John 5:18). That claim merited capital punishment. The problem was that the Jewish religious leaders could not legally kill him after a night of beatings and false charges, so they went to Pontius Pilate, the Roman governor, to request his execution. After examining him, Pilate found no legal reason to detain the One, much less kill him.

After more pressure from the Jewish leaders, Pilate gave them a choice to choose Barabbas or the One for release. The Jews chose Barabbas, a thief, for release instead. Pilate still resisted killing the One and asked why they wanted him to kill their king. Here the political card was played, and the Jews insisted they had no king except Caesar.

When Pilate saw he couldn't win, he got a bowl of water and dramatically washed his hands of the whole fiasco while the Jews insisted the One's blood would be on them and their children. Pilate gave the One a horrendous flogging, jammed a crown of thorns on His head, and turned the One over for execution. By the time the One was compelled to carry His own cross to the execution spot outside the city, the Manual says his appearance was so messed up from the beatings that He hardly looked human (Isa. 52:14; 53). He collapsed on the way, and Simon of Cyrene was compelled to carry it for him (Matt. 27).

This was the one chance the Serpent had to beat out his millennia-long frustrations on the Game Master's Anointed One. Those beatings and ripping out His beard were most certainly done with a derisive and savage vengeance. He was more dead than alive by the time He was crucified. Lee Strobel details the torture the One endured in chapter 11 of his book, *The Case for Christ* (Strobel 1998, 191–204).

What do you think a messiah does? A messiah is an anointed one, a chosen one who is supposed to be a savior or liberator to free players from bondage. He isn't supposed to die before liberating those players. There have been numerous messiahs identified in history across many cultures in the game. When the Game Master announced a coming messiah at the garden of Eden, the context was to free players from their spiritual bondage and slavery to sin and the Serpent so they could qualify for the kingdom of heaven, the bonus round (Gen. 3:14–15). Unlike our view of a messiah, this required a blood sacrifice, which was represented by the blood of lambs, bulls, and goats.

The One's crucifixion and death was the final blood sacrifice for all time with Him, the Game Master's Messiah, completing that blood requirement to break players' bondage to sin (game violations) and the Serpent. This caused the Game Master to turn His back on the One when He was shouldered with your game violations on the cross, leaving Him to suffer alone while He called out, "My God, my God, why have you forsaken me" (Matt. 27:46–47)? As the One died, He declared, "It is finished!" (John 19:30). Your game violation pardon was finally paid in full, so the Game Master ripped apart the temple's heavy curtain to the most holy place from top to bottom, granting you access directly to Him because of the One's sacrifice for you (Matt. 27:51; Heb. 9:27–28; 10:1–14).

No other messiah in history was qualified to free your soul and grant you eternal life, and no other messiah has come to give up his life for you. Master player Paul declared the One's purpose:

> How true it is, and how I long that everyone should know it, that Christ Jesus came into the world to save sinners—and I was the greatest of them all. But God had mercy on me so that Christ Jesus could use me as an example to show everyone how patient he is with even the worst sinners, so that others will realize that they, too, can have everlasting life (1 Tim. 1:15–16 TLB).

The Win

Everybody then thought the One was finished and that was the end of Him. The death of the One should have ended this epic struggle with the Serpent gaining the upper hand, except the Spirit Master resurrected the One three days later, throwing the win to the Game Master (Matt. 28:5–8; Mark 16:6; Luke 24:5–6; Phil. 2:8–11). The One's sacrificial death that poured out His sinless and pure blood atoned for all the game violations (sins) of all players, past, present, and future. Now the path to the bonus round is assured and available to all players who have a passion for qualifying. There is nothing the Serpent can do to rescind the offer except deceive and lure you away or help you die before you choose to level up on eternal life.

> If the One was not resurrected, then the Manual itself would be pointless and there would be no cosmic power that could help you.
>
> (1 Cor 15:12-22)

The One's death was necessary to cover game violations and sin's curse, but His resurrection from the dead is the key component that completed the golden ticket transaction and infused life-giving power to His sacrifice on your behalf. The extreme importance of this detail is epic from the Manual: *if the One was not resurrected, then the Manual itself would be pointless, and there would be no cosmic power that could help you* (1 Cor. 15:12–22). That is why Easter, resurrection day, is the major celebrated event in Christendom.

It is puzzling that the Serpent didn't see this loss coming since it was predicted in detail, but being the ultimate narcissist, perhaps he didn't believe it would hinder him. The One resurrected players from the dead during His lifetime, one of them after half a week in the grave. This also happened in earlier history with the Game Master's prophets, so pulling a resurrection move should have been totally expected and easily within His capability (1 Kings 17:17–22; 2 Kings 4:32–36; 13:21).

THE ENDGAME

Now that the Serpent lost the match through the entire bloodline fight from the garden of Eden, his only consolation now is to keep as many players from joining the Game Master's team as possible. Having all players born on his team, he has the home-court advantage. Killing them off in ever greater numbers runs up the Game Master's losses in his favor, so endless wars, global pandemics, and famines are used to great advantage by the Serpent, are growing more widespread these days and coming to neighborhoods near you.

The Game Master is not willing that any player should perish, but He can't force players to want eternal life in the bonus round, force them to change their minds, or drag them across the finish line (2 Pet. 3:9). Instead, He sent his members out to call all players to turn their allegiance to Him (Matt. 28:19–20). He extends His offer of grace to all players until the end of the game at its apocalyptic finale between Him and the Serpent, where all remaining players will be the stakes in the game and the prize to be won in a final showdown. Some of you reading this book could be around to watch it happen. It will be a climate change event to end all worlds. Guest player, it will end very badly, and ringside seats are not recommended (Rev. 20:6–10).

EXIT THOUGHT

What religion or philosophy do you follow? What god or deity do you believe in? What prophet do you cling to? What saint do you pray to? What spirit guide do you pursue? Who is your divine aspiration?

What have they specifically done for you? How do they guarantee your eternal future? Do you have to die before they'll tell you that you achieved heaven? Is your god or guide willing to die for you like the One died for you? Has it crossed their mind? Instead, they make you do all the heavy lifting to reach your place in the afterlife, don't they? All religions are give-and-take. You must do something to earn acceptance by their deity. It's your blood that they require. It's all on you.

Neither the Serpent nor any god he established has ever offered to die for anyone or give himself up on your behalf. His goal was to enslave you. Mission: Accomplished. Every god or divine path that is not from the Game Master and the One has been created by the Serpent. The New Age universalism theology that we are all god's children is true in the sense that we are all children of the god of this age, the Serpent, who is the source for and the shadow god of every other religion. None of them will pay the ultimate price to rescue or help you escape the clutches of your Serpent boss (Dougherty 2021, min. 10:49).

We have seen the Game Master fight for your redemption through the Manual's Old Testament, and He will give you every chance to choose life to the end of the New Testament. The entire Manual is about His plan to convert us unworthy players into adopted and accepted heirs of His grace. He was willing to pay the ultimate price to have His Son humble Himself and die for us who despised Him so we could have a chance to become more than we could ever make of ourselves. Eternal life, His gift of grace, is believing His account of His Son's sacrifice for you. He loves you despite your sorry condition. There are no prerequisites; come to Him with your messy life, and He will make you whole (Isa. 1:18; John 3:16–18; Rom. 5:6–11; Eph. 2:8–9; Phil. 2:5–11).

Master player Paul explains this to members:

> When we were utterly helpless, with no way of escape, Christ came at just the right time and died for us sinners who had no use for him. Even if we were good, we really wouldn't expect anyone to die for us, though, of course, that might be barely possible.
>
> But God showed his great love for us by sending Christ to die for us while we were still sinners. And since by his blood he did all this for us as sinners, how much more will he do for us now that he has declared us not guilty? Now he will save us from all of God's wrath to come.

> And since, when we were his enemies, we were brought back to God by the death of his Son, what blessings he must have for us now that we are his friends and he is living within us! Now we rejoice in our wonderful new relationship with God—all because of what our Lord Jesus Christ has done in dying for our sins—making us friends of God (Rom. 5:6–11 TLB).

Did you know that God can be your friend? Our status before membership is the enemy of God. The first two commands of the Big Ten are to worship the Game Master exclusively. You cannot add Him to your set of gods. He is extremely jealous of your worship and loyalty (Exod. 20:3–6).

What if you don't have any gods you worship? Master player James wrote to members:

> You adulteresses [disloyal sinners—flirting with the world and breaking your vow to God]! Do you not know that being the world's friend [that is, loving the things of the world] is being God's enemy? So whoever chooses to be a friend of the world makes himself an enemy of God (James 4:4 AMP).

Even members who love the things of this world can make themselves the Game Master's enemies when their loyalty and desire are to be accepted by the world system and what it offers. Your treasure and what you treasure are where your heart lies. It is a very big deal to be called a friend of God (Matt. 6:19–21; Luke 12:32–34; James 2:23).

IT IS A VERY BIG DEAL TO BE CALLED A FRIEND OF GOD.

Game Master: The Serpent's Fall Guy

IT STARTED WITH an innocent question in the garden of Eden (Gen. 3). The first lies came from the cunning Serpent, who is also called the Father of Lies (John 8:44). The first lie was, "Has God really said you shall not eat of every tree of the garden (Gen 3:1)?" implying that **the Manual is unclear**, that His instruction about not eating the fruit from the tree of knowledge of good and evil was an inconclusive or perhaps mistaken directive (Asscherick 2019, min. 9:28).

The second lie is that **the Game Master is a withholder** who wants to keep something from you. Then the Serpent explains that the Game Master is keeping Adam and Eve from a "higher, better, and nobler experience," the god-like knowledge of good and evil (Asscherick 2019, min. 11:22).

Even today, he gets tremendous mileage out of that same lie to current gamers that "fundamentally, God is trying to keep something from you that would be in your best interests to have" (Asscherick 2019, min. 9:28; Gen 3:1–5).

As the prince of this world, the Serpent controls whatever narrative he wants all players to believe. The Game Master is the Serpent's fall guy, his scapegoat, whom the Serpent gets all players (including members) to blame for their tragedies of life. This is a very well-crafted deception and is still a top hit today.

If you search "blaming God" and "blaming Satan," the top Google articles in 2015—about whether the Game Master deserves blame for our hard times and trouble in life—do not factor in the influence of the Serpent or the "fallen condition" of man as possible reasons, even from Christian sites. Interestingly, in 2016, the first Google search return about blaming Satan was from a 2013 *Charisma Magazine* article entitled, "Stop Blaming the Devil!" (Savard 2000, ¶ 1–36). The following returns mostly tracked along the same line, telling us to take responsibility for what we do. In 2022, the top result was from Fairview Bible Church entitled, "Stop Blaming Satan for Your Sin" (Preston 2021, ¶ 8). So even in a casual perusal of the topic, the Serpent somehow gets off the hook every time. How can the Serpent be blamed when most of the players already think as he does and have taken ownership of his way of thinking?

Here is another explanation from Christian Media Research, showing how today's deceptive kiosk philosophy was first used by the Serpent in the garden of Eden.

> In its simplest form, the **Diaprax** system is a process whereby the entire world will eventually dialog until they reach a consensus. The 3 part formula consists of 3 essential components: **Thesis**, **Antithesis**, and **Synthesis**. Simply put, a "thesis" is combined with the opposing view, the "anti-thesis," and the result is called the "synthesis."
>
> In the Bible we see **Satan** cause the fall of man through the use of **Diaprax** (the practice of the dialectic). **Eve** tells the **Serpent** that **God** has commanded that of the tree in the midst of the garden, that they "shall not eat of" it. That is the thesis. Then **Satan** offers an opposing opinion (the antithesis) that flies in the face of the Word of God, telling Eve about the benefits of eating the forbidden fruit. Eve joins the two views and comes up with the synthesis–the fruit is "good food," "pleasant to the eye" and will "make one wise." Through Adam and Eve's reasoning, God's eternal truth was reasoned away, and the curse of death replaced the gift of eternal life (Hudson and Lloyd n.d., ¶ 4–5).

It is understandable that the average player would identify the Game Master as a source of trouble. Many of His members make a clear point that nothing happens to us without the Game Master's oversight. This perspective leads to the faulty conclusion that He is in charge of dispensing both good and evil in the game world.

This is how we got to this place: the Serpent makes the Game Master out to be the bad guy, then members take an example like the story of the prophet Job, who lost all his possessions and children in one day and was then struck with boils all over his body, and interpret the dialogue between the Game Master and Serpent to mean that the reason bad things happen to us is that the Game Master lets them happen to us, that He allows it or with the logic ending that He gives it to us. Kiosk leaders then say that the Serpent can't harm you without the Game Master's permission. Sorry, player, but that's not in the Manual nor grants you immunity. Besides, you give him plenty of permission all on your own in ways you may not notice.

Dr. Brian Mattson wrote an enlightening review, entitled, "Sympathy for the Devil." He explains in detail how our culture has come to accept the Jewish gnostic philosophy of Kaballah, how it is quickly spreading through our collective experiences through the Hollywood film industry, and the fact that practically no religious kiosk leaders of any persuasion even recognize it. According to Dr. Mattson, the1994 *Noah* film's director and an atheist, Darren Aronofsky, used Kaballah philosophy in the *Noah* film and in his first feature film in 1998 called *Pi* (Mattson 2014a, ¶ 13-19; 2014b, ¶ 39-53; 2014c, ¶ 13-14).

The cultural philosophy of our secular society, along with the religious kiosk culture, both leave us with the impression that the Serpent was right: *the Game Master does not fundamentally want the best for us because of all the bad things that He allows (or makes) to happen to us* (Asscherick 2019, mins. 9:28).

Although guests may agree with that statement, I expect that member leaders will strongly disagree. They will rightly say that the Game Master wants what's best for us, and they will have Manual texts to prove it. But when they go on to say that the Game Master will allow or even put trouble in our lives to make us better, they really are saying that the Game Master is, in fact, responsible for both the good *and* the bad stuff in our lives. Did the Game Master really have to burn down your house on Christmas Eve to help you become a better player? And yes, I know two Christian families who experienced this.

I have observed this concept across three kiosk denominations. If this is not what kiosk leaders mean, the problem is that the average member understands it that way and expresses it that way when normal conversations turn to matters of life's troubles. Kiosk leaders who disagree with this interpretation should consider setting the record straight by teaching their members properly, vetting their staff, and providing better clarity in their doctrine.

The apostle member Paul said we are to glory or give praise to the Game Master in tribulations, and apostle member James says to count it a joy when we fall into troubles of all kinds because the testing of our faith is a practice toward patience or endurance (Rom. 5:3-5; James 1:2-3). Both apostles spell out the character development that can come through testing and trouble.

Members would point out that trouble is to be expected, and we typically consider it a bad thing until we can see the hand of the Game Master making us a better person because of it. But many members who experience this also go on to assume it was the Game Master's intent to put us through the trouble because He helped us through it, and we benefitted from it.

Philosopher Friedrich Nietzsche said, "That which does not kill me, makes me stronger." (Nietzsche 1911, 2). Research indicates that traumatic experiences can make us more resilient (Association for Psychological Science 2011, ¶ 1). Challenges in life give us experience in what some like to call the school of hard knocks. It is unfortunate when you require more remedial education than those around you. With the Manual as their guide, players can graduate early from that school: "Great peace have those who love your law; nothing can make them stumble" (Ps. 119:165 ESV).

Testing and troubles are part of the contaminated game world situation and happen to all of us and are good for us, and we should thank the Game Master for His hand in the process of bringing us through them. That being said, none of the Manual texts point to the issue that the Game Master is the instigator of those troubles. He said that He can make all things work together for the best, but it does not follow that He is the source of life's trials (Rom. 8:28).

The Manual is clear that the Game Master corrects and redirects His members (Prov. 3:12; Heb. 12:6–7), but it does not mean that correction must equal personal disasters from the hand of the Game Master. Throughout the Manual, it is very clear that the player group of Israel always connected bad days and personal or national disasters with their own rejection of the Game Master, never calling it a blessing from Him because He never blessed them with evil when they obeyed Him.

The One made a strong point to relate the goodness of the Game Master with His very character, saying, "If you then [member players], being evil, know how to give good gifts to your children, how much more will your Father who is in heaven give good things to those who ask Him!" (Matt. 7:11 NKJV). He portrayed the Game Master as a benevolent Father Who will treat us much better than our own imperfect fathers do. According to the One Incarnate, it does not follow that we would get hit with evil by the hand of the Game Master.

Bad things that happen to you are not the Game Master's fault. This is usually the first reason we think of when we start pointing fingers, but this shouldn't even be on the list. There are many reasons why bad things happen, and none of them require the Game Master's participation. While they don't have His approval, whether or not He can stop them depends on you.

The typical member takes the phrase commonly used by their kiosk leaders, "God will allow trouble," and translates it to mean "God will bring us trouble" when they explain it to fellow players. Kiosk leaders sometimes even use this altered explanation too, perhaps to get players to not fight with the Game Master about their problems or not lose faith and hope because of them since "He has a purpose and a plan." Neither phrase accurately describes why we get into trouble, as will be explained in the next section.

This perspective of the Game Master's contribution to our suffering has a very tenuous Manual foundation, with the prophet Job cited as a main example. Blaming the Game Master by default is a beautiful example of how the Serpent can bring misery to everyone, including members, and get them to unwittingly pin the blame on the Game Master and even be encouraged to thank Him for giving them their misery because He's going to make them a better person from it. It's diabolical. So, let's see what's really happening.

The Game Master Is Not Powerless

Why doesn't God do something about all the suffering in the world? Why does God let people do bad things to me and those I care about? If God is sovereign, in charge, and all-powerful, why can't He do something?

These questions are very sincere and real to those who experience loss and trauma. The good news is that you can check out of this cycle of trouble, and the Game Master can specifically shield you from life's troubles and even protect you from their consequences.

Don't confuse limited influence with powerlessness. The Game Master set the parameters of how He interacts in players' lives, and that is where He is limited—by how much players choose to connect their lives to Him. Changing that balance is entirely up to you, the player (2 Chron. 16:9; 1 Pet. 3:12).

He is constantly scanning the game for players who will connect with Him and is listening for their prayers so He can demonstrate His strength on their behalf (2 Chron. 16:9). The Game Master made the opportunity for you to connect to Him through the One, but you must initiate the relationship with Him, and you must pursue Him so He can then show His power to your benefit.

Here's a sample list from the Game Master of specific things a member can expect from Him:

> He is listening for their call when He can come deliver them out of all their troubles,
> He is close to the brokenhearted and those with a crushed spirit,
> He looks out for them so no bones are broken, and
> No matter how many things go wrong for them, He will fix them all
> (Ps. 34:15–20).

Members have His attention, and He is waiting for their call to Him. He calls Himself a deliverer, comforter, and protector, and He takes action to get them out of trouble and keep them from trouble.

There is another list of protective promises in Psalm 91 for those who abide in the One. He calls Himself "the Almighty." Tremendous favor, protection, and healing power from the Game Master are available to members who are synced up with Him.

All this stuff we are talking about here can be summarized as a transfer of spirit realm power injected into our physical situation to improve or fix us and our circumstances at the speed of thought. The Game Master cannot help you if you don't get yourself prepped to receive His transformational power into your life situation. He made the required mechanisms so simple that a child can do it. This will be specifically addressed in Section Four.

Cause and Effect

Things don't just happen without reason. Investigations into disasters are sometimes called an act of God. A lightning strike could be called an act of God for insurance purposes. But is the Game Master out to get you, or were you simply in the wrong place at the wrong time, or was it from a curse, or was it a minion attack?

There are dynamics in how the Game Master operates toward us. When we are synced up to Him, there is a free-flowing interaction that can occur between us and Him, where promptings and insights come to us in our daily routines. Conversely, most players are synced with the Serpent's agenda, where their thoughts track according to the world views and attitudes that appeal to the player's self-centered side. Those who think that because they are not influenced by—or that they refuse to be influenced by—the Game Master, there is no influence on them are actually being influenced by the Serpent's point of view. There is no neutral ground, and whatever neutral ground you think exists also belongs to the Serpent (Eph. 2:2).

> **THERE IS NO NEUTRAL GROUND, AND WHATEVER NEUTRAL GROUND YOU THINK EXISTS ALSO BELONGS TO THE SERPENT.**

Beyond being synced to the Game Master, He does not necessarily micromanage our lives where everything that happens to us is Him moving the pieces on the board of life. Yes, technically, He could do that, and such circumstances can occur as part of His protective care, but such attention to your life is still subject to your free will and character deficiencies. It could generally be considered under the category of blessings or curses, which are cause-and-effect scenarios.

> Living a blessed life means that whatever you do will most often turn up for the best.

An extreme example of micromanagement is when a player specifically chooses to have the Spirit Master direct all aspects of their lives down to the mundane daily choices.

In the 1800s, a fellow named George Müller opened orphanages in Bristol, England, that were built and operated only through donations with prayer lists provided. The catch was that he never asked anyone for donations; he prayed to the Game Master for what they needed. Over the years, he fed and cared for 10,000 orphans this way and started 117 schools for 120,000 children. He traveled 200,000 miles during his life before airplanes were around and always planned to pay his way (Muller n.d., ¶ 2, 7, 12–13).

George said, "The orphan houses exist to display that God can be trusted and to encourage believers to take him at his word." He had a passion "to display with open proofs that God could be trusted with the practical affairs of life" (Piper 2004, ¶ 20).

For those who prefer sequenced instructions, the Proverbs say, "With all your heart you must trust the Lord and not your own judgment. Always let him lead you, and he will clear the road for you to follow. Don't ever think that you are wise enough, but respect the Lord and stay away from evil" (Prov. 3:5–7 CEV). How many times do we read this passage, and the impact of those instructions just floats past our conscience? We too often believe it is good to know but fail to practice it for our daily benefit.

When the Game Master says He can supply all our needs, that isn't empty talk. George Müller's preferred experience is unique, and the Game Master doesn't micromanage our life like this without our asking for it (Phil. 4:19).

The Manual says that the steps of a member are established or made secure by the Game Master, and some Manual text interpretations indicate that their steps are ordered or set in place by Him (Ps. 37:23). This is descriptive of a blessed life. Living a blessed life means that whatever you do most often turns up for the best and that your path in life doesn't have potholes that most other players get.

This attention from the Game Master is not necessarily micromanaging. As we are synced to Him, it should be expected that He would have a deeper influence on our circumstances. Technically, members understand that the Game Master is not in charge of the world system as it is under the control of sin and the Serpent (Rom. 8:19–22), but when they say that "God is in control," it leaves a strong impression that the Game Master is the cause of the game world's good aspects and the game world's downward spiral, even though they may not mean it that way. The day is coming when the game will end, and all player accounts will have to be settled with Him, and His sovereignty will be undisputed. Until then, we must navigate this game world with its evil, but we get to choose Him to make things better for us.

Having a positive attitude or trusting the Game Master are good things that ought to be done because they can reduce suicidal tendencies by keeping us from losing hope, but without a strategy to put an end to the cycle of bad things that come against us, trust and positive attitudes only get us through the current problems or, at best, prepare us for the next round of obstacles. The good news is that we can stop the next round of disaster, but it takes much more than passive trust, desperate prayers, and grim smiles.

Members like to call the Manual their handbook for living, but too often, they ignore its actual instructions or get lost and confused in the details and end up playing through their game life broken and unfixed. Instead of living from blessing to blessing, they live from miracle to miracle, where the Game Master is regularly bailing them out of trouble and picking up their pieces of brokenness. Understand, He responds to their call, but if there are spiritual hindrances to their ability to live a blessed life, He can only assist them after the damage is done.

Unfortunately, a typical religious kiosk connection will not likely give you specific instructions to change your lot in life because some of the tools available for your ability to overcome obstacles are rarely mentioned and practically never taught. Most teaching about successful gameplay is described in the ethereal, spiritual realm and never quite makes it to the real game world where we feel it happen to us every day. Sermons don't explain how the spiritual translates explicitly into the physical realm where we live.

THE TWIST

The Game Master has put physical laws, moral laws, and spirit laws in place. Much of what happens to us is the result of how we interact with those laws, complete with reward and retribution but with a twist. You have to factor in the effects of our interaction with other players, including what they might do toward you, and if you invited the Serpent to your party through indulgent behaviors, his mischief has to be considered as well. Or you could be hit out of the blue with seemingly no reason behind it. Random mayhem can include being in the wrong place at the wrong time.

We prefer to think that the Game Master looks out for us, guiding our every move. This could be true in a broad sense, but divine protection that plays out in specific ways, as described in the Manual, requires that we meet the conditions found there, which describes a blessed life (Ps. 91). If you want Him to guide your every move in a micromanaged way, you must pursue His response at every move you make. Few players have done it as effectively as George Müller.

OUR COST

Too often, we assume that the Game Master's enhanced benevolence toward us requires no contribution on our part, but that is simply not the case. How much you receive from the Game Master is correlated to how committed you are to Him and how closely you pay attention to what He specifically says (2 Tim. 2:15).

This concept runs throughout the Manual. Receiving from Him is not a one-way street, and simply being a "born-again" member neither makes you automatically eligible for all the protections and power-ups He offers, shields you from consequences of your own making, nor suspends all the bad spiritual baggage you already have.

We have been conditioned to think that everything that happens to us, including the bad things, is the direct hand of the Game Master, that He has done it to us on purpose or just let it happen because, after all, "God is in control" of everything, and "nothing happens to us unless He allows it" implying that He does it to us.

Job's Story

A Classic Player Beatdown – Or Is It?

THE OLD PROPHET, Job, who lived about 4,100 years ago, is the universal gold standard classic example of someone suffering (seemingly) at the hands of the Game Master. Since his torment was done with the Game Master's permission, we assume that when bad things happen to us, it is also done with the Game Master's permission or by His hand, as the Serpent apparently accused Him in the text. Here's Job's story (Job 1; 2; 42).

The Serpent showed up at headquarters when the guardians came to give their reports to the Game Master. He saw the Serpent among them and asked what he'd been doing. The Serpent said he'd been around, you know, here and there, so the Game Master asked him if he'd checked out His player Job, who was the most perfect gamer at that time and a multi-millionaire. His personal wealth was greater than anyone who lived in the East (the land of Uz, an unclear location but associated with the ancient land of Edom, which includes perhaps the areas of northern Arabia, western Jordan, southern Israel, and the eastern Sinai Peninsula) ("Land of Uz" n.d., ¶ 3; Paterson 2016, ¶ 3–6).

The Serpent said that Job was so good and prosperous because he was the Game Master's pet player, and if He took away everything he had, then Job would curse Him to His face. So the Game Master said, "Game on; do what you want, but don't touch him."

Suddenly, in one day, all Job's livestock was carried away by Sabean raiders (southern Arabia), Chaldean raiders (southern Mesopotamia), or consumed by fire from heaven with most of his servants killed (7,000 sheep, 3,000 camels, 500 yoke of oxen [1,000], and 500 donkeys), and then his ten children died when a tornado collapsed the house on them at their banquet. But Job only said, "The Game Master gives, and He takes away; His Name is blessed." This was a "death by Serpent" series of events, and only five of Job's servants survived to report his losses.

When the Serpent reported back later, the Game Master said, "I told you so," whereupon the Serpent replied, "Yeah, yeah, easy come, easy go, but he still has his health; take that away, and he'll curse you for sure." So the Game Master said the Serpent could strike Job down, but he couldn't kill him.

Then Job was struck with painful boils all over his body, so he sat in a heap of ashes and scraped at his boils. His wife finally said, "Why don't you just curse the Game Master and die?" Job replied, "Should I only get good things from the Game Master and not bad things too?" and refused to curse Him (Job 2:9–10, paraphrased). The rest of the book talks about his three friends who only offered cold comfort and spent most of their time accusing him of game violations while Job wished he were dead. They might as well have been his enemies too.

This whole account is estimated to have lasted about a year. After that, the Game Master stepped in and made Job's friends beg Job to forgive them for being so nasty to him.

After Job prayed for them, the Game Master doubly restored all the possessions Job had lost (14,000 sheep, 6,000 camels, 1,000 yoke of oxen [2,000], and 1,000 donkeys), along with ten more children, including three daughters who were the most beautiful women in the land. (He didn't get twenty more children because the first ten who died reached the bonus round, so they were not permanently lost to him.) We don't know if the servants' families were compensated.

Then all his brothers and sisters and everybody who knew him before belatedly showed up and gave him a piece of money and a gold earring and offered comfort. In addition, Job lived another 140 years and saw his fourth generation of grandchildren. Based on tradition, Job was 70 when everything collapsed around him, so a double restoration of everything, including his life span, would have made him 210 years old.

Job's wealth upon his restoration was perhaps about $56 million dollars in liquid assets with his herds. Adding his lands of at least 8,300 acres and estates to his value, he held a probable worth of $60 million dollars (Heartstrings 2014, ¶ 6, 16–17).

Kiosk explanation

A theme of this Manual's story is: *why do the righteous suffer?* Job's friend observed that "man is born to trouble as surely as sparks fly upward" (Job 5:7 NIV). That sounds like a precursor of our modern version of Murphy's Law: *Anything that can go wrong will go wrong.* But all the clichés in the world that explain how it will happen to us as life gives us one beatdown after another never go on to tell us how to make it stop.

Religious kiosks interpret the dialogue between the Game Master and Serpent to mean that the reason bad things happen to us is that the Game Master lets them happen to us, He "allows" it, or He "gives" it to us. Other texts in the Manual can be construed to support this (Rom. 8:28), but because the Game Master goes out of His way throughout the Manual to insist that members are given special care, this conclusion contradicts Him, is therefore illogical, and does not square with His character. A theme about learning patience is also taught.

Kiosks also say that the Serpent can't touch members without the Game Master's approval, but that doesn't account for the relatively equal amount of trouble members and guests alike receive today. The part they leave out, especially since it is bad form to tell this to players who are grieving over catastrophic losses, is that players have things come against them for reasons that could have been of their own making—this will be explained in the next section.

Also, the Serpent was not allowed to kill Job, but that didn't mean Job's wife couldn't encourage him to kill himself. Her statement to "curse God and die" (Job 2:9) can be argued as a Serpent-inspired statement in the same vein as when the One told Peter to "get behind me, Satan" (Mark 8:31–33). Job's wife could have merely been a mouthpiece for the Serpent, who hoped to kill Job during his depression. It seems to be out of character for the spouse of a devout member, but she was also grieving and deeply suffering from the sudden loss of all her children, and the Serpent found his angle of attack.

For those who say that the Serpent can never harm members without the Game Master's permission, this exchange shows that the Serpent has ways to easily bypass that stipulation. The loss of hope is a path to suicide, but Job's faith in the Game Master sustained his hope in the face of total loss.

Besides that, it doesn't answer the question of *why the righteous suffer*. Saying the Game Master allows it could also imply He does it on purpose. Following this line of thinking that He allows or inserts trouble in our lives, a logical conclusion would be that if you have a good life and even try to be a Mother Teresa toward other players as Job was, the Game Master can still put you in your place, stink up your life, and turn the Serpent loose on you so you can learn some patience. Ergo, keep your head down, stay wretched, broke, and sick so maybe the Game Master won't notice you, and then you can get on with your miserable existence without Him blessing you with the Serpent. It seems everybody's out to get you! What a set of choices!

The lesson of Job

Notice what happened here. Job was prosperous and pious. The Serpent was given a chance to hurt Job to prove his sincerity toward the Game Master. The point is that the Serpent was trying to force Job to curse the Game Master, Who said Job wouldn't do it. Whatever happened to Job was actually instigated and orchestrated by the Serpent.

It was the Serpent who drove the perspective that if the Game Master would hurt Job, he would then turn his back on Him. To prove His point, the Game Master cleared the path against Job, but He did not cause him harm. It seems like a nitpicky thing, but that's how lies are born, in the details. The Manual does not make a practice that the Game Master will hurt His members or give the Serpent permission to hurt members who are synced up to Him like Job was. This issue about Job's suffering is not a typical or model circumstance. It is not a guide for how the Game Master interacts with members.

Those who know a little about the Manual may bring up the point about master player Paul, who had a henchman from the Serpent attacking him. This instance is a direct attack on Paul strictly because of his extreme gaming skills and was not a situation where the Serpent was allowed to make his life a living hell as a matter of principle. Paul was told specifically what was going on and told to deal with it as persecution, unlike most players who run into problems and then make unverified and unsubstantiated assumptions that the Game Master is letting the Serpent slip in some punches on them (2 Cor. 12:6–10).

> Job was *persecuted* for his faith and passed the test.

JOB WAS PERSECUTED

A good explanation for what happened to Job is that he was *persecuted* for his connection to the Game Master.

Persecution is an attack against a member for his association with the Game Master. Since the start of the twenty-first century, members are increasingly being penalized and violently assaulted daily across wider expanses of the game world. Historically, the choices they are given are to renounce the Game Master or else:

- pay a fine or get their livelihood destroyed,
- be brutalized, tortured, or the family hurt, or
- they will be killed.

These are still the same choices for members that are announced on the news today. Renounce or die. Nothing has changed.

Job's experience easily fits the description of a member who was persecuted. The unique part about his situation is that Job didn't know where it was coming from or why it happened because the Serpent didn't threaten him directly like is typically done to members. The dispute with the Game Master was happening at headquarters, and Job was left in the dark but feeling all the effects of it. That first strike against Job came with no warning out of a clear, blue sky. His wife became a mouthpiece of the Serpent's objective when she told Job to curse the Game Master and die.

Job is not an example of the Game Master bringing suffering to him, his family, and his servants, nor does He allow or insert trouble in our lives to teach us patience. This test on his character proved that he already had patience, and the Game Master was counting on it (2 Pet. 1:5–8). The building blocks of spiritual and character development start with faith. From that foundation, a member adds in sequence: 1) *virtue* – resolve for moral excellence, 2) *knowledge* of the Manual, 3) *self-control*, 4) *patience* or endurance, 5) *godliness*, 6) *brotherly affection*, and 7) *sacrificial love* (2 Pet. 1:2–10).

Patience is halfway up the sequence of things that need to be added to faith. If Job was only halfway up the list of qualities on his faith journey, his ability to pass a test of patience of this magnitude would have been questionable at best. The Game Master would not have showcased an unseasoned and still-developing player. This could not have been his first real test of patience. Job's descriptions of how he cared for the weak and needy show that he was at the top of the list and at the top of his game.

Instead, this was a case where the Game Master allowed the *persecution* of His master player, and the Serpent threw in a lot of collateral damage in the loss of life for his children and servants. Pay close attention that this is also an example of how much collateral damage the Serpent is willing to spread to those you care about and throughout your sphere of influence to specifically target just you or influence your choices.

For many persecuted members since the first century, the choice they usually get is to renounce the One or die, and the Serpent was trying to force Job to curse the Game Master, in essence, renounce his membership with Him. *The Manual does not give members an exemption from persecution.* That's the one category of obstacles where immunity is not assured (John 15:19–21).

For the master player Job, the Serpent was eager to bring the pain to him, but the Game Master would not allow him to be martyred. The result was that Job suffered severe persecution with the loss of family, livelihood, and health, but he did not lose his golden ticket "nor charged God foolishly" (Job 1:22 KJV).

Game Setup Conclusion

IF YOU STILL decide that the Game Master is, in fact, the cause of your troubles, how do you propose to get Him off your case? Spite Him? You'll only hurt yourself. Appease Him? How? The One ended all sacrifices and penance.

> **The Declaration of Bethlehem**
> *Glory to God, Peace on Earth for All Those Pleasing Him*
> (Lk 2:14 TLB)

When He killed His own Son, the One, on a cross at the place of the skull (John 19:16–18), your game violations toward Him were included and covered, just waiting for you to come to Him to have your full pardon authorized by getting your golden ticket, so *there is no reason for the Game Master to be a scourge in your life* and make you miserable. He even gave a preemptory Declaration of Bethlehem when His host of the guardians announced, "'Glory to God in the highest heaven,' they sang, 'and peace on earth for all those pleasing him'" (Luke 2:14 TLB).

Guest player, do you realize that the Game Master declared peace toward all players who switch to His side? The long war to recover the chance for you to win eternal life is over, all player game violations were covered, and the ransom for your soul was made with His Son's own blood when the Serpent thought he had Him crushed.

Now you just have to decide whose team you're going to be on. So, if the Game Master doesn't want you to lose, why does trouble stick to you like a shadow? Where does it come from, and what is behind it?

The Problem of Peace

JUST WHEN WE reached the conclusion, here's a dilemma: the One is called the Prince of Peace (Isa. 9:6), and we have just declared that the Game Master had a message of peace for players at the time of the One's birth. However, when the One grew up, He instead announced:

> **Do not think that I have come to bring peace to the earth. I have not come to bring peace, but a sword.** For I have come to set a man against his father, and a daughter against her mother, and a daughter-in-law against her mother-in-law. And a person's enemies will be those of his own household (Matt. 10:34–36 ESV, emphasis added; cf. Micah 7:6).

Not only did He *not* come to bring peace but to cause division. He even came to set the earth on fire: "**I've come to set the earth on fire**, and how I wish it were already ablaze! I have a baptism to be baptized with, and what stress I am under until it's completed!" (Luke 12:49–50 ISV, emphasis added).

This certainly appears to fit the stereotypes of the Game Master as a wrath-filled vengeful Creator, which seem to be well-documented in His own Manual. How can the Game Master call Himself a peacemaker while His Son goes off script and wants to burn the place down? Somebody needs to get with the program, right?

It's too bad for us that the Game Master's objective is not to generate peace between gamers. If you want peace with your fellow player, that is something you have to work out between you. Good luck with that.

Instead, these remarks emphasize the heavy price for Him to offer peace to players and the ensuing conflict that happens when players agree to His terms to find their own inner peace with the Game Master.

Here are the passages again in the Amplified Bible version, with the explanation in bold print:

> Do not think that I have come to bring peace on the earth; I have not come to bring peace, but a sword [**of division between belief and unbelief**]. For I have come to set a man against his father, and a daughter against her mother, and a daughter-in-law against her mother-in-law; and a man's enemies will be the members of his [own] household [**when one believes and another does not**] (Matt. 10:34–36 AMP; cf. Micah 7:6).

Regarding the One's mission of His personal sacrifice by death:

> I have come to cast **fire** (**judgment**) on the earth; and how I wish that it were already kindled! I have a **baptism** [**of great suffering**] with which to be baptized, and how [greatly] I am distressed until it is accomplished! (Luke 12:49–50 AMP).

The coming of the One changed the dynamic of how players could once again have direct access to the Game Master. As we have documented, the Serpent had struggled through the ages to cut off our path back to the Game Master.

The One was under great distress to reach the finish line and make our spirit connection to the Game Master complete. He finally did this by His death on the cross (His "baptism") and sealed that victory with His resurrection from the dead three days later. Now, the Spirit Master convinces the game world of judgment because the prince of this world, the Serpent, is judged (John 16:7–11).

Players who turn to the Game Master will now find peace for their souls with Him, but in many cases, the player's family will become their enemy because they vehemently oppose this change of religion. Many players from Eastern religions who walk away from their family's religion to receive the One already know they are choosing a death sentence by their family, but peace with God and the peace of God are more compelling than the threat of death (Rev. 3:20). Those in modern Western societies may not see this occur as often because the secularized Western world simply does not care about one's spiritual bent. But even in these societies, as ideologies become more intolerant of those who think differently, it may well become very real for players who choose the Game Master. Master player Paul describes the process:

> Therefore, since we have been justified [that is, acquitted of sin, declared blameless before God] by faith, [let us grasp the fact that] we

have peace with God [and the joy of reconciliation with Him] through our Lord Jesus Christ (the Messiah, the Anointed) (Rom. 5:1 AMP).

Our peace, which transcends the typical player's understanding or doesn't make sense, is the peace from the Game Master that offers hope through our worst and darkest hour.

> Do not be anxious or worried about anything, but in everything [every circumstance and situation] by prayer and petition with thanksgiving, continue to make your [specific] requests known to God. And the peace of God [that peace which reassures the heart, that peace] which transcends all understanding, [that peace which] stands guard over your hearts and your minds in Christ Jesus [is yours] (Phil. 4:6–7 AMP).

This is how you can personally and finally have "peace on earth."

Section III: The Hurt Zone

Why Bad Things Happen to You

WHY DO BAD *things happen to good people?* More pointedly, when asking that question, we usually have a specific scenario in mind like, "*Why do* [insert-bad-things-here] *happen to me?*" Those who do not claim to be very religious express the same frustrations as religious players do, and while they may draw different conclusions, many times neither has been offered clear reasons or solutions.

You have a personal perspective on what the bad things are for you. In the bigger picture, we see suffering all around us, and we wish somebody would make it stop. Accidents are tragic, disasters are frustrating, diseases are troubling, prolonged suffering is heartbreaking, meanness is aggravating, violence is horrifying, and brutality is appalling. Stories with these themes come to us in the daily news from around the game world, and it's just depressing when we feel helpless to fix it. Sometimes it affects our region, city, and neighborhood, where we pause and vow to live with caution. When it happens in our workplace, school, or home, our very world can be turned upside down.

And then there are the personal problems that plague us or seem to have just grown up with us and never go away. Physical issues, emotional traumas, relational conflicts, destructive vices and habits, financial shortfalls, constant unexpected bills or repairs, worrying situations and pressures, unfulfilled aspirations, and the list goes on. The good things or opportunities that do come along for us are somehow changed or twisted into something different from what we wanted, and life just doesn't look like what we hoped it would be.

The religious kiosks technically have all the answers, but it seems they keep them bottled up under lock and key in the seminaries, so even their members can't explain it to you.

Do you find yourself saying, "Could this day get any worse?" or "Why me, God?" Do you feel helpless because things go wrong at the worst times? Does bad luck or fate seem to follow you around? Do you get kicked by karma? Do you worry about jinxing the good times? It is shocking how much the word "jinx" comes up, and the phrase "knock on wood" is mentioned or practiced by members. There's no effort to control their circumstances or outlook by using their religious belief system. It seems fate steps in when God is off the clock.

This simple question of why bad things happen has a complicated answer, but the reasons are not unknowable. In fact, when you see them, you'll realize they make sense. But going one step further, there are immunities you can get to stop those bad things. Few members talk about this, and that is what this book is about: not just why bad things happen but how to understand and stop them.

> IT SEEMS FATE STEPS IN WHEN GOD IS OFF THE CLOCK.

BAD STUFF

Bad things that happen to us come from four main sources:

1) violating spirit realm moral code: spirit laws
2) influence by the Serpent and his spirit-being henchmen and minions, either directly or indirectly
3) the result of the curse on the game environment, plus all the curses triggered by the players upon themselves, all of which collectively include disease, and hostile living conditions like from plants and animals or the forces of nature, and the pressures of life (work, government, home life, etc.)
4) players: other players who do bad things, whether physically or psychologically, or our own bad choices we make that result in harm

Bad things that hit us can be multiple combinations of any of these sources: spirit laws, the Serpent, the game environment, or players. This section of bad stuff will be explained in ten major categories: 1) Free Will, 2) Spirit Laws and Power, 3) Curses, 4) The World, 5) The Flesh, 6) The Devil, 7) Bad Decisions, 8) Bad People, 9) Persecution, and 10) God Only Knows.

Four Sources of Trouble
Mix & Match
1. Spirit Laws
2. Serpent & Henchmen
3. Game Environment
4. Players: You & Others

As you go through the categories of bad stuff, notice these combinations of sources that interact with each other, and that can be applied to them: Spirit Laws, the Serpent, the game environment, or player choices.

DISCLAIMER: THE GAME MASTER DID NOT CAUSE NOR CAN HE BE HELD RESPONSIBLE FOR THE BAD STUFF THAT HAPPENS TO YOU; NOR DID HE BREAK YOUR LIFE IN THE MAKING OF THIS GAME WORLD. HE CANNOT BE HELD ACCOUNTABLE FOR THE BONE-HEADED DECISIONS YOU MAKE NOR BE HELD LIABLE FOR WHAT OTHER PLAYERS CHOOSE TO DO TO YOU. IF YOU ARE NOT A MEMBER OF HIS TEAM, HE HAS LIMITED THE RESOURCES TO ENHANCE YOUR GAMEPLAY OR TO ALLOCATE FOR YOUR SECURITY.

10 Big Reasons for Bad Things

> **Author's Note:** There are a number of compiled lists in these following Sections that are sourced from other authors, bloggers or groups. These are compiled and provided for information purposes only and may not be complete views held by this author. Where you have points of disagreement, refer to the provided source.

THIS SECTION SPELLS out obstacles that impact us, with some that contribute to the limitation of the Game Master's assistance in our gameplay. These are categories of possible reasons for the trouble that finds us. Here they are described and explained. Some may apply to you and others may not. Suggestions and strategies for removing these obstacles of life will be offered in Section Four.

1. Free Will

A major gift to you and a huge limitation that the Game Master put on Himself is that He gave us the free will to either choose Him or ignore Him. This does not mean that there are no consequences or repercussions to your choices.

For example, if you sincerely say in your heart or out loud that you are done with God, and you want Him to leave you alone, your wish can be granted. If you don't feel a cold chill come over you, you may still get a sense that something has changed. There are cases, such as the experience of Pastor Billy Crone, who said this as a sixth grader, but later grew up, changed his mind in a minion-fueled panic at the age of twenty-five, and turned to God (Jesus4Evers 2015, min. 3:22). However, saying something like this could have possible permanent results because the Game Master may also remove any desire for you to ever look for Him again. That was your choice. When you get mad, make sure your anger is pointing in the right direction (Phil. 3:18–19; Heb. 6:4–6).

When the Game Master gives you a choice, He may give you strong hints or a heaviness of heart (also called "conviction" in religious jargon) about what is in your best interest (Deut. 30:19), but He is limited to interfere and compellingly force or pressure you to do what He sees to be in your best interest. He can bring you to the moment of decision, but He cannot make that choice for you. You still have the capacity to resist His promptings toward your spirit. He has been described as the "Hound of Heaven," Who pursues players to turn from their self-destructive path.

He will stay out of your business if you don't want Him to interfere with your life. If you feel yourself under strong conviction to make a decision about switching to the Game Master's team, the outcome will still be your choice alone. Can you honestly blame the Game Master for life's troubles if you don't want Him in charge of you? He would rather help you, so the trouble you face in life isn't coming from Him. Understand, though, that He may take advantage of those troubles to get your attention and prompt you to change your life's trajectory.

Some members have spoken of numerous experiences or an extended time period where, while they were guests, it seemed the Game Master was keeping them from the consequences of their choices as they lived for their own pleasure and tried to avoid Him. Usually, there was a member, perhaps a mother or grandparent or friend, whose prayers gave them protective cover until the guest became a true member. This is called intercessory prayer, or prayer on behalf of another player. Intercessory prayer is a powerful tool in the spirit realm.

Your free will to live your life like you please and being accountable to nobody does not mean that you are not enslaved to anybody. The One said that whichever master you choose by your free will, whether the Game Master or the Serpent, you will pursue the passions of your master. That is the natural outcome of your choice (Matt. 6:24; Luke 16:13; John 8:30–59).

> **YOUR FREE WILL TO LIVE YOUR LIFE LIKE YOU PLEASE AND BEING ACCOUNTABLE TO NOBODY DOES NOT MEAN THAT YOU ARE NOT ENSLAVED TO ANYBODY.**

If you are not a member, the fact that you refuse to recognize the Serpent as your boss has no bearing on that reality. This includes Hindus, Buddhists, Shintoists, Muslims, Roman Catholics, Jews, Wiccans, atheists, and all others who do not accept the One and exclusively worship the Game Master (1 John 5:1–12). Many of these players are religious and kind, and they worship gods whom they definitely don't refer to as the Serpent. However, those gods originated from the Serpent because the Game Master shares His glory with no one (Isa. 42:8). As your gameplay evolves, your daily free-will choices follow the trajectory of your master's character until your time in the game is up. Then you get to spend the next game level with your chosen master.

When another player's free will gets into your business, or you see bad things happening around you, and you want the Game Master to fix it, you're asking Him to interfere with the free will He gave to those players who choose to do bad things.

So, when is it okay for the Game Master to tell the *bad people* what to do but not right for Him to tell *you* what to do? We don't want Him telling us what to do, but we're glad to send Him after someone else.

The Manual has a string of stories that symbolize the excitement of the Game Master when a player chooses His team (Luke 15:1–10, 11–32). The third story in one series is commonly titled The Prodigal Son. Briefly, the younger son of a wealthy man told his father, in effect, that he wished his father were dead and demanded his share of the inheritance. The father granted his wish and watched him ride off to a distant land where he lived a raucous, party-driven life until his money ran out and drought and famine destroyed the economy.

One day, while feeding the hogs and snatching some of their scraps, he came to his senses and remembered how good things used to be back home, so he set out to see if his father would give him a job like a servant. Always hoping for his return, the father saw him coming in the distance and made an embarrassing spectacle of himself for that culture by running down the road to hug his dusty, wayward son. Before the son could finish his speech, his father called for the best robe for him; he put a ring on his finger, shoes on his feet, and prepared a huge homecoming party, saying, "My son was dead and is alive again; he was lost and is found!"

This story illustrates how much it means to the Game Master when a single player comes to Him. Headquarters lights up with a celebration in the presence of the guardians (Luke 15:10). There's a party in heaven when you turn to the Game Master for a new life (John 3:16).

You have the free will to choose the One and get your golden ticket. The Game Master does not oblige Himself to respond to those who don't choose Him (Prov. 15:29; 28:9), but if you sincerely look for Him, He says that He will be found by you (Jer. 29:13–14). If you go to Him and want to be on His team, the One said that there is no chance He'll turn you down or kick you out (John 6:36–37). Therefore, you do have hope for the best He can give you.

There is a growing boldness across blogs, social networks, and news comment threads, where player commenters feel comfortable disparaging the Game Master and expressing contempt for the One when topics or other comments in the news take a religious turn. This may be coupled with the rising disbelief in a heaven or hell. Since the Game Master does not accept players who reject the One, it is logical for such players to also reject the bonus round.

After all, players who despise the One shouldn't want to reach the bonus round and all it represents because that would put them in direct proximity to both the Game Master and the One. Being in the bonus round with those sentiments would be miserable for sure, in addition to constantly being around all the odious goody-goodies who got there. Free will doesn't mean we can pick and choose the outcomes or consequences of our choices. So it's just as well that the Game Master's despisers can't turn up in the bonus round and spoil everyone's health and happiness after so many members suffered their own hell on earth during this game world level because of their devotion to the Game Master (Rev. 6:9–11).

A new wrinkle is developing on this issue of free will. It seems the government is weighing in with its version of free will management. History professor Yuval Harari, a World Economic Forum (WEF) advisor, said in an interview with journalist Romi Noimark,

> Ideally, you have people forming up opinions and desires and then voting for a government that represents them. But we know it works both ways. The government has enormous power to shape the opinions and desires of the population, and this power only increases today with the new technologies of surveillance, of mass surveillance, of social media and so forth. So, the government is not just responsive to the will of the people, it can shape the will of the people. And this really destabilizes the democratic system. Also, the media has an enormous role to play in this, that if the government has too much control over the media, then it's not like people are forming their own independent views about what's happening (The Hebrew University 2021, min. 23:39).

> We now have the power—not we, but some governments and corporations, for the first time in history, have the power to basically hack human beings. There was a lot of talk about hacking computers, hacking smart phones, hacking bank accounts, but the big story of our era is the ability to hack human beings, and by this I mean, if you have enough data, and you have enough computing power, you can understand people better than they understand themselves, and then you can manipulate them in ways which were previously impossible. And, in such a situation, the old democratic system stopped functioning. We need to reinvent democracy for this new era in which humans are now hackable animals. You know, the whole idea that humans have, you know, this soul or spirit and they have free will, and nobody knows what's happening inside me, so whatever I choose, whether in

the election or whether in the supermarket, this is my free will, that's over (The Hebrew University 2021, min. 24:35).

No matter what you think ultimately what is the truth of the universe, you have to realize that practically, today, we have the means to hack human beings on a massive scale, and this means we need to reinvent democracy, we need to reinvent the market. Again, the whole idea of the customer is always right, we just do whatever the customers want. Yes, but you can now hack the customers, you can manipulate the customers to want what you tell them to want. So this whole idea that corporations just serve the needs of the customers, this is over (The Hebrew University 2021, min. 25:55).

Ah, those days when restaurants would manipulate your appetite with their corporate color schemes or waft aromas through their air systems seem like a bygone era. Have you noticed that your free will is being hacked? Do you consider yourself un-hackable? Harari says that you are now being hacked by the messaging of the government, tech companies, and the complicit media, and all you know is that nobody is interfering with your free will. The fact that you agree with so much of their agenda and perspectives doesn't prove anything. This also brings up a question of where indoctrination ends and hacking begins.

Mass hypnosis is already being practiced regularly in our kiosks, concerts, and media programs. Dick Sutphen's 1995 article called "Born Again Brainwashing" explains the step-by-step techniques an audience is hypnotized in kiosks. He then shows how it can be used in other venues, including crowd control. He summarizes the article with an example of television usage.

> The techniques and staging will vary from church to church. Many use "**speaking in tongues**" to generate catharsis in some while the spectacle creates intense excitement in the observers.
>
> The use of hypnotic techniques by religions is sophisticated, and professionals are assuring that they become even more effective. A man in Los Angeles is designing, building, and reworking a lot of churches around the country. He tells ministers what they need and how to use it. This man's track record indicates that the congregation and the monetary income will double if the minister follows his instructions.

He admits that about 80 percent of his efforts are in the **sound system** and **lighting**.

Powerful sound and the proper use of lighting are of primary importance in inducing an altered state of consciousnes [*sic*]—I've been using them for years in my own seminars. However, my participants are fully aware of the process and what they can expect as a result of their participation (Sutphen 1995, point 12, ¶ 1–3).

The more we find out about how human beings work through today's highly advanced technological research, the more we learn to control human beings. And what probably scares me the most is that the medium for takeover is already in place. The television set in your livingroom and bedroom is doing a lot more than just entertaining you.

Before I continue, let me point out something else about an altered state of consciousness. When you go into an altered state, you transfer into right brain, which results in the internal release of the body's own opiates: enkephalins and Beta-endorphins, chemically almost identical to opium. In other words, it feels good . . . and you want to come back for more.

Recent tests by researcher Herbert Krugman showed that, while viewers were watching TV, right-brain activity outnumbered left-brain activity by a ratio of two to one. Put more simply, the viewers were in an altered state . . . in trance more often than not. They were getting their Beta-endorphin "fix."

To measure attention spans, psychophysiologist Thomas Mulholland of the Veterans Hospital in Bedford, Massachusetts, attached young viewers to an EEG machine that was wired to shut the TV set off whenever the children's brains produced a majority of alpha waves. Although the children were told to concentrate, only a few could keep the set on for more than 30 seconds!

Most viewers are already hypnotized. To deepen the trance is easy. One simple way is to place a blank, black frame every 32 frames in the film that is being projected. This creates a 45-beat-per-minute pulsation perceived only by the subconscious mind—the ideal pace to generate deep hypnosis.

The commercials or suggestions presented following this alpha-inducing broadcast are much more likely to be accepted by the viewer. The high percentage of the viewing audience that has somnambulistic-depth ability could very well accept the suggestions as commands—as long as those commands did not ask the viewer to do something contrary to his morals, religion, or self-preservation.

The medium for takeover is here. By the age of 16, children have spent 10,000 to 15,000 hours watching television—that is more time than they spend n [sic] school! In the average home, the TV set is on for six hours and 44 minutes per day—an increase of nine minutes from last year and three times the average rate of increase during the 1970s.

It obviously isn't getting better . . . we are rapidly moving into an alpha-level world—very possibly the Orwellian world of "1984"—placid, glassy-eyed, and responding obediently to instructions.

A research project by Jacob Jacoby, a Purdue University psychologist, found that of 2,700 people tested, 90 percent misunderstood even such simple viewing fare as commercials and "Barnaby Jones." Only minutes after watching, the typical viewer missed 23 to 36 percent of the questions about what he or she had seen. Of course they did—they were going in and out of trance! If you go into a deep trance, you must be instructed to remember—otherwise you automatically forget (Sutphen 1995, point 46, ¶ 1–9).

I have just touched the tip of the iceberg. When you start to combine subliminal messages behind the music, subliminal visuals projected on the screen, hypnotically produced visual effects, sustained musical beats at a trance-inducing pace . . . you have extremely effective brainwashing. Every hour that you spend watching the TV set you become more conditioned. And, in case you thought there was a law against any of these things, guess again. There isn't! There are a lot of powerful people who obviously prefer things exactly the way they are. Maybe they have plans for . . . (Sutphen 1995, point 47, ¶ 1)?

These mass hypnotic techniques were in use and spreading thirty years ago. We are now daily immersed in a sea of subliminal messaging to keep us in a hypnotic state. You will take ownership of those thoughts and accept them as your own. The minions already do this daily to billions of players across the globe in their daily thoughts and conversations. Since you are likely being hacked, what are the odds that you will change your mind and choose to join the Game Master's team?

If you are a member and you have taken on the mind of Christ (the One), you should be more likely to recognize thought patterns and perspectives that run contrary to the Manual, whether they come to you through the media or a technological or subliminal channel. A big reason that members are increasingly persecuted across the game is that the Manual is contrary to the Serpent's game world philosophy. Getting rid of members who think differently will finally bring unity to his guests across the globe (Rom. 13:14; 1 Cor. 2:15–16; Gal. 3:27; Eph. 4:17–24; Phil. 2:5–8; Col. 3:9–14).

It turns out that your religious faith can be downgraded through transcranial magnetic stimulation (TMS).

> *Religion is an ephemeral connection between humans and God*, a private and direct bond that is, paradoxically, mediated by ancient traditions and group practices in houses of worship. People believed in supernatural beings for about as long as they were human:
>
> We can ask a question: **can the invisible link between the faithful and God be severed by a third party** armed with the tools provided by the latest scientific advances?
>
> Disturbingly, the answer may be yes. Scientists led by Dr. Colin Holbrook at UCLA undertook a multi-year endeavor to discover ways to stop "religious beliefs and right-wing prejudice." They attempted to apply direct *electromagnetic stimulation* to the brain to alter human beliefs, specifically *turning off belief in God*.
>
> That study was extremely unethical! When recruiting study subjects, **Dr. Holbrook lied about the purpose of the study** (using

electromagnetic waves to reduce belief in God) and offered participants $25 while promising "ostensibly unrelated" activities:

Now, as we know, to religious people, **abandoning belief in God is blasphemy** and puts them at risk of going to Hell, shunning, and so on.

The outcome was, indeed, a *dramatic reduction of religious beliefs*:

Also consistent with predictions, **participants who received cTBS reported an average of 32.8% less positive religious conviction** . . . relative to the sham participants.

Colin Holbrook was supported by the U.S. Air Force Office of Scientific Research (Chudov 2024, ¶ 2–3, 6–7, 14–15, image 7).

When the Game Master gave players free will, it set the stage for a competition between Him and the Serpent for your loyalty. The One explained the situation by saying, "If you are not on my side, you are against me" (Matt. 12:30 CEV). The point He made is that if you don't choose the Game Master's team on purpose, you have already chosen to keep the Serpent as your boss. Because Adam committed the first game violation (disobedience) by eating the forbidden fruit, all players since that baneful day are born as children of disobedience, having inherited the consequence of his game violation, with the Serpent as their boss (Eph. 2:1–3; 5:5–7; Col. 3:5–7). If you want to change that, you must decide for yourself to choose the Game Master on purpose. Free will to the end. Choose wisely, if you can.

> **WHEN THE GAME MASTER GAVE PLAYERS FREE WILL, IT SET THE STAGE FOR A COMPETITION BETWEEN HIM AND THE SERPENT FOR YOUR LOYALTY.**

2. Spirit Laws & Power

There are only two sources of spirit power in the universe. If it does not come directly from the Game Master and matches His Manual, then it is from the Serpent. There is no power besides these two. There is no neutral power or benign power from a third party.

Laws govern the spirit realm. Many of these are discovered through directives in the Manual and can be loosely summarized: do things right and keep it orderly. The Game Master is not the author of confusion (1 Cor. 14:32–33, 40). You can see this concept in action as you look at the game world and the whole game environment's creation.

We are familiar with some of the laws that control our physical world, like those dealing with gravity and hydrology and physics and chemistry, and we are accustomed to working within the parameters of those laws to keep ourselves healthy and alive. But sometimes players can get fuzzy on the details, like mixing the wrong cleaning products with potentially deadly results. The point is to make things sparkle and shine, but how we do it can matter too.

Whenever you see a statement in the Manual about what you should do or how you should do it when discussing how to receive something from the Game Master or to accomplish an objective like an answered prayer or healing or favorable status or success in a situation, those instructions are spirit laws. Mark them down. Getting what you want or losing out is not based on the capricious whims of the Game Master. It is based on the spirit laws He wrote down for you. Follow the law to get what you want. If it doesn't work, find the missing ingredient for success.

This doesn't only apply to instructions. When you read statements about how things work, such as the power of the tongue as described in the book of James or the creation explained in Hebrews 11, these are insights to spirit laws. Understanding how this realm works and interacts with our physical realm will improve your gameplay.

The Manual contains instructions on how to conduct business with the spirit world, specifically with the Game Master Himself. When players engage with Him, it is called faith. When players engage with the spirit world but not with the Game Master, these transactions are controlled by or are under the dominion of the Serpent, and it is called witchcraft. The spirit world of witchcraft here includes all other religions, such as Eastern religions, Wicca, New Age, Native religions, Islam, Roman Catholicism, Mormonism, and so on, and even the peripheral and mainstream Christian religions and perhaps your own kiosk now need to be vetted as well since the Serpent has infiltrated practically all the Game Master kiosks.

The Manual gives many warnings to stay away from witchcraft. Don't assume your preferred group is exempt from scrutiny because the Serpent's use of witchcraft across the religious spectrum comes in a myriad of flavors and styles so that there is something appealing to each player's perspective. Members are instructed to keep their own kiosks under scrutiny (Acts 17:10–11; Gal. 1:6–9; 1 John 4:1–3).

The Manual is a completed book and binding or unchanging, so the Game of Life must run its course as written. Real confusion happens because players don't know the Manual, but they think their own philosophy of justice lines up with the Game Master (which may only be partly true on points). Then, they wrongly conclude that there are no rules in place setting parameters that the Game Master is required to follow. He can just do what He wants because He's the Game Master, after all.

Not so. For one example, the Game Master explained that Israel's lack of cooperation with Him as a nation limited what He could do for them when they left Egypt for the promised land (Ps. 78:40–42). For another example, consider this:

"Husbands, in the same way be considerate as you live with your wives, and treat them with respect as the weaker partner and as heirs with you of the gracious gift of life, so that nothing will hinder your prayers" (1 Pet. 3:7 NIV).

Husband, if you think you can treat your wife poorly, without consideration and deference and respect, and still get your prayers answered, you are dead wrong and have a bad theology. Then again, if you're mistreating your wife, what are the odds that you're actually praying?

Even members who take communion can become weak, sickly, or even die because of their unworthy participation.

> So then whoever eats the bread or drinks the cup of the Lord in a way that is unworthy [of Him] will be guilty of [profaning and sinning against] the body and blood of the Lord. But a person must [prayerfully] examine himself [and his relationship to Christ], and only when he has done so should he eat of the bread and drink of the cup. For anyone who eats and drinks [without solemn reverence and heartfelt gratitude for the sacrifice of Christ], eats and drinks a judgment on himself if he does not recognize the body [of Christ]. That [careless and unworthy participation] is the reason why many among you are weak and sick, and a number sleep [in death]. But if we evaluated and judged ourselves honestly [recognizing our shortcomings and correcting our behavior], we would not be judged. But when we [fall short and] are judged by the Lord, we are disciplined [by undergoing His correction] so that we will not be condemned [to eternal punishment] along with the world (1 Cor. 11:27–32 AMP).

Do you think a doctor would ever diagnose anemic conditions, illness, or a cause of death as a result of a bad communion experience? How much damage can crackers and wine do, after all? Yet, carelessness with spirit laws can lead to a judgment of illness or death from the spirit realm into the physical realm.

Logically, the spirit world runs by laws because that realm existed before our physical world (Heb. 11:3). However, we like to think that how we deal with spiritual things doesn't matter as much as how sincere or needy we are. We get some things right and others wrong, but we still expect good results every time. Carelessness with the Manual's details is a big hindrance to getting the results we want. Learn and play by the rules to find your edge for success.

If you don't want anything from the Game Master, then don't pay close attention to what He says because that's all you'll ever get. Don't think that you can invoke His spirit realm, including prayer, and get results to your advantage by ignoring His rules, including those about prayer.

It is true that He knows our hearts and that His Spirit Master makes intercession for our deficiencies (Rom. 8:26–27). It is sadly unfortunate that members are not taught how to get it right to improve their results, and so they attribute their inadequacies of life to Him through their unanswered prayer when they have only themselves to thank for that.

> *What percentage of your prayers get answered?*

If you call yourself a spiritual player, take a quick assessment of your spiritual connection. What percentage of your prayers get answered? What kinds of prayers are you confident of answers? Big ones? Small ones? How confident are you of your prayers being answered without using talismans, or prayer chains—just you and the Game Master with perhaps a few members? When I say answered prayers, exclude those that are typically 100 percent guaranteed, like getting better on a recognized timed schedule for the flu (five to seven days) or a cold (three to fourteen days) unless you can pray and get healed in a significantly shorter amount of time.

My son called us on a couple of instances to pray about situations that would likely upend his world and impact his future career opportunities. These were bad spots of his own making where he knew he had messed up. He prohibited us from calling on prayer chains and anyone outside the immediate family.

When your son's future depends on the strength of your faith to get the job done, how confident are you that the Game Master will hear you and pull out a total miracle? This was when the NATO air base commandant was cracking down on behaviors related to his situation. In these cases with him, his supervisors and colleagues who knew the score and his circumstances were amazed at the unprecedented favor and good fortune he got. The consequences were far lighter than anyone had expected. His immediate supervisor, who was on his way up the stairs but missed the opportunity to plead his case, met my son on the way out of his meeting with the commandant and was astounded at the outcome. It was to the point of him and others repeatedly saying that nobody gets treated that good.

We didn't grovel and beg or chant or hold marathon prayers. The One said the Game Master doesn't like those prayers where we just run our mouths incessantly and repetitively or wail away as though He were deaf (Matt. 6:7–8). We prayed together fervently as a family as the Manual says (John 15:16), and then as his situation crossed our minds later, we'd add a sentence or two on our own. Confidence with the Game Master is a game changer.

The Manual also includes specific instructions to get prayers answered and how to have the Game Master respond to us. A reason that members can see little progress or have uneven success is that they get most of the instructions right but fail to follow through, or they void the process by adding to or removing from what the Manual says.

There is no question from the rules that the Game Master wants to answer our prayers because the One said that "anything you ask the Game Master invoking the One's name will be done for you because that shows the Game Master's power" (John 14:13). Answering our prayers in the One's name demonstrates the majesty of the Game Master, but asking in the One's name is not the only ingredient. When we follow the process to the letter as written in the rules, then His power in the spirit realm reaches across the dimensions into the real game world on our behalf.

OCCULT

The Serpent has power too. Occult things relate to the supernatural, mystical, or magical realm that derives its power from the Serpent. We typically think of voodoo and witch doctors and casting spells, but the occult encompasses the entire spectrum of Satan's dominion, whether we recognize it or not, believe it or not. Some activities like drug use and rock music can open avenues of compliance to the occult as well.

In transactions with the Serpent's spirit realm, there can be specific preparations to make, specific things to say, and specific things to do. Using objects and saying certain things and including blood are usually recognized as part of the Serpent's realm. Examples of how magic generally works or types of mechanisms that enable it can be found in popular books, movies, or TV series, and in occult literature, commercial games, and even performing arts, things that many players are regularly exposed to.

However, the Serpent does not need chants and rituals to gain influence with a player. Any form of participation in his occult realm is an invitation for him to begin influencing their thoughts, words, motivations, and activities. Motives don't matter. Players can participate out of ignorance, unwittingly, as an adventure, as a joke, or simply through an emotional response. *Participation is consent*, and that consent is for his influence upon the player, any player. Understand that your participation in any occultic activity or accepting talismans and the like is your defiance of the Game Master's spirit laws.

Simply dabbling in any occult practice, whether it's a Ouija board, a séance, or even something as simple or seemingly harmless as a palm reading, yoga, or popular games that come around like Charlie Charlie can open your spirit or grant your permission to be affected by the Serpent and his power realm. John Ramirez explained that the popular Ice Bucket Challenge of 2014 was a Haitian Sansi voodoo initiation ceremony ritual. Did you participate? It does not matter if you go looking for answers or if you do it as a joke, your act of participation equals your permission for the spirit world to have power in your life. The influence can stay with you indefinitely until you deliberately rid yourself of it (Ramirez n.d., min. 16:00).

Unlike the Game Master, your lack of sincerity or faith is not a limiting factor for the Serpent. Furthermore, if you take a child with you who is too young to understand, because they are in your care, your participation also grants permission for the spirits to affect that child into adulthood even if they were not directly included in the activity, were too young to understand, or have no knowledge of the event. Following horoscopes, reading tea leaves, palmistry, Eastern religious good fortune activities, yoga, living by Zodiac principles, and the like are invitations to the spirit realm to influence your life.

Fortune-telling is easily ridiculed. As with all fantastical opportunities, there are sure to be scam artists, but there is occult power that validates those predictions. When master player Paul reached the major city of ancient Philippi with his assistants, they encountered the local fortune teller:

> One day, on our way to the place of prayer, a slave girl ran into us. She was a psychic and, with her fortunetelling, made a lot of money for the people who owned her. She started following Paul around, calling everyone's attention to us by yelling out, "These men are working for the Most High God. They're laying out the road of salvation for you!" She did this for a number of days until Paul, finally fed up with her, turned and commanded the spirit that possessed her, "Out! In the name of Jesus Christ, get out of her!" And it was gone, just like that.
>
> When her owners saw that their lucrative little business was suddenly bankrupt, they went after Paul and Silas, roughed them up and dragged them into the market square. Then the police arrested them and pulled them into a court with the accusation, "These men

are disturbing the peace—dangerous Jewish agitators subverting our Roman law and order." By this time the crowd had turned into a restless mob out for blood (Acts 16:16–21 MSG).

This was the first recorded exorcism that happened simply because the member player was annoyed and then finally exasperated. The psychic was telling the truth about Paul. This is an example of the Serpent's agent presenting itself as an angel of light (2 Cor. 11:13–15). When Paul evicted the minion from her, the slave girl's owners realized they had just lost a good income because her predictions were not fake. Without the psychic spirit, she couldn't accurately make predictions.

Occult participation can start innocently. If you crack the door open just to peek in, even if for nothing more than simple curiosity, minions may force it wide open and take liberties with your life that you never saw coming. It only takes a single encounter to have a perpetual minion influence over you.

What if you are just watching TV or a movie? You're not participating in the activity. Maybe. But from the occult spirit realm perspective, your emotional response to what you see attributes consent, and your consent determines how you are affected.

The story of the first martyr mentioned in the Manual identifies the instigator of the coming persecution against members. It says he was just holding the coats of the guys who stoned Stephen to death. But it includes the comment that he was consenting to Stephen's death (Acts 7:58; 22:20). His attitude from this event inspired him to start a deadly inquisition. Your attitude toward what you surround yourself with does matter, and you are influenced by it whether you want to believe it or not.

My son met a priest of Wicca through his work. This wasn't just someone interested in Wicca. This was a man who was steeped in Native American spiritual practices, including a journey through the desert with no food or water to have his own vision with the spirit realm. One night, when a group of colleagues was sitting around respectfully talking about it, one person asked the witch about communication with minions. The witch responded, "Don't do it. When you summon them, you have no control over what happens." He said, "Even as a witch, I don't summon demons. If they show up, then I'll talk with them. But I refuse to summon them."

How interesting that a player who chooses the power of the Serpent still does not trust him because of the negative effects on himself. Yet many players, even among members, think that it's okay to expose oneself to all the demonic things that are out there, like occultist horror movies or magic, which increasingly have strong, overt minion influence.

Many players shrug off points like this, saying, "I like getting scared," "It's just a movie," or "Yeah, but I don't believe in that stuff." Postings on viewer forums for these types of films show strong mockery toward those who express fear of the spiritual reality they portray. Before and increasingly since the beginning of this twenty-first century, TV shows and feature films with occult or spirit elements are being portrayed with much more realism and accuracy than before.

Jenny Weaver, a former Wiccan, was drawn into the occult through *The Craft* film. Weaver points out that the movie that introduced her to the dark side was remade in 2020.

> "They recreated the movie, and they invited real witches on the set, and they had the witches before they would do a scene to cast spells and to invite the actresses to come into this circle with them while they were releasing spell words over the viewers and over the scene," said Weaver. "People are playing it in their homes and it's entertainment. The first part of entertainment is 'enter.' So be careful what's entering your home."

> "She went on to say, 'I went to this store, it's a very popular store, and I even hate to say their name, but it was Marshalls. And I was just blown away that Marshalls had actual witchcraft books. Like you can come in here, and you can do this spell. And you can get this sage, and you can get these; it was like a whole kit. And they're selling it like it's a holiday kit that you would buy someone.

> "And so, it's really starting to be very mainstream, and I just feel like the church needs to be aware. The Bible says to stay away from those things of darkness but rather expose them, not to partake in them,'" said Weaver (Aaron 2021, ¶ 15).

PLAYERS WHO NEVER GO TO ANY TYPE OF RELIGIOUS KIOSK CAN WALK OUT OF THE THEATER, NEVER REALIZING THEY GRANTED PERMISSION FOR A SPIRITUAL INFLUENCE UPON THEM COURTESY OF HOLLYWOOD.

If your hackles rise when watching these shows or you feel a sudden chill or emotional bonding, there's a good chance you aren't as alone as you think. Spirits can become attached to a person through their expression of emotions, and fear is a very convenient avenue. Also, what better place to provide an opportunity for a minion influence en masse than in crowded theaters? Players who never go to any type of religious kiosk can walk out of the theater, never realizing they granted permission for a spiritual influence upon them courtesy of Hollywood.

Occult transactions don't usually happen in dark graveyards. These normal seeming encounters in public places or through the pursuit of personal interests toward enlightenment usually do not have immediately noticeable effects. A gradual influence over thoughts and actions can occur over an extended period of time. Players affected by this assume their thoughts and actions are always without outside influence, and they appear normal in every way.

There are well over two hundred avenues of activities where the occult interacts with players. The Deliverance Ministries section in Resources Appendix A has an occult worksheet link from Cornerstone Assembly of God kiosk. This worksheet lists hundreds of categorized occult activities so you can do a self-examination on your exposure to the occult. The worksheet provides steps to freedom and a prayer of deliverance.

What is it like to have witchcraft affect you? Here are some symptoms suggested by the Four Corners Free organization:

> Traveling pain throughout the body, confusion, inability to think clearly, losing track of your thoughts, sleeplessness, fitful sleep, waking up after only a short time of sleep, fatigue, inability to dream or remember dreams, inability to control food cravings, lack of appetite, disinterest in Bible reading, distraction during prayer, inability to follow a train of thought, bursts of anger, feelings of hatred and resentment, strange noises, sudden sense of cold, headaches, burning eyes, suicidal thoughts, violent thoughts, thoughts of a particular person out of nowhere (especially from a past toxic relationship), perverse thoughts, sexual urges, lack of sexual desire, imbalance in body systems, forgetfulness, losing or misplacing items, machinery breaking down, lack of ability to connect to God in worship, wanting to run and hide, fear of public places, fear of people, gossip, false accusations, misunderstandings, chaos, feelings of low self image, feelings of self loathing, worthlessness, wanting to disappear, addictions, depression, overwhelming sorrow, sudden sickness, bloating, indigestion, heart burn, clumsiness, self injury, lack of personal boundaries, inability to speak up for yourself, hearing random song lyrics run through your head, hearing voices, hearing thoughts of self harm, self criticism,

constant complaining, inability to see beauty in life, hopelessness, scatter brained, arguments erupting out of nowhere, bickering, wanting to crawl out of your skin (Four Corners Free n.d.b, ¶ 2).

These look like typical ailments or phobias we all may experience. However, put them in context with your life history. When did the symptoms start? Was it too much Italian or Mexican food the other day? Did you just mess up a big event in your life? Is it part of another diagnosed ailment like having brain fog from a fatty liver?

If logical factors don't address the cause, perhaps there is a spiritual element involved. Check your routines, your exposure to something different recently or a new activity. Are there any occult factors associated with recent events in your life?

Since we've already turned onto Weird Street here, let's talk about astral projection. "Astral travel allows human souls to leave their body and they are invisible invaders into any space. Charles Manson said he didn't mind being locked in a jail cell, he could go anywhere he wanted. He was speaking of astral travel" (Four Corners Free n.d.a, ¶ 2). Those who practice astral travel can invade your private space without your permission. You may not know anyone who can astral travel, but perhaps there is someone who has taken an interest in you or who has asked an astral traveler to check on you. They can really mess up your day. The Four Corners Free organization says,

> The Lord has revealed covens coming in groups to do an astral ritual in people's homes, in churches, in places that are supposed to be our safe havens. We have to WAKE UP!
>
> What are the signs? Sudden inexplicable sickness, discomfort, uneasiness, chaotic behavior, outbursts of anger, intensified symptoms of a "normal" malady, feeling restless, waking suddenly for no apparent reason, feeling weak and dizzy, extreme fatigue, feeling like you are dragging yourself along, everything going wrong, frustration, helplessness, deep sudden depression or sorrow. (Insert your bad day here.) (Four Corners Free n.d.a, ¶ 4–5).

Julie Lopez, a former 5th generation witch had a dream where she saw her former witch teacher doing rituals to try to find her but she couldn't see Julie. When Julie woke up, the Spirit Master told her that she was covered with the blood of the

One, a cloth of invisibility, and they would never find her again (CBN News 2023, min. 25:35).

It is not true that the power of faith is real, but the power of witchcraft is fake. The Manual isn't the only source for curses. There is the realm of witchcraft, where curses or spells can be invoked upon others. Faith and witchcraft are very real and potent, and they are the only two choices of spiritual power. Without question, the power of the Game Master is greater, and a member who knows how to work with it can break the power of the Serpent.

However, many members live as though they have no power over curses, which is awkwardly true. Although they are on the side of the Game Master, they are not taught how to work and live in the authority He gave to them to keep trouble out of their lives, in general. More specifically, they don't know how to recognize the manifestation of curses or become trained to break the power of curses.

In fact, many members are likely to say that they have little belief that the Serpent is responsible for anything specific. Many certainly mistakenly believe that his curses are ineffective, especially toward members. So if you expect a member to identify or fix a curse for you, good luck finding one who can do either of those things. They do exist more often in Pentecostal-type kiosks as master players, but even there you will search much, much harder than you should need to search because they are very few and far between. Check the Resource appendices section for help.

Voodoo/hoodoo/WitchTok

Voodoo or Vodu refers to a wide range of Afro-American religions or spiritual traditions originating in West Africa that were influenced by Christianity in the New World, more specifically Roman Catholicism, and Islam. It spread and developed across the Caribbean, Latin America and the Southern United States ("African Diaspora Religions" n.d., ¶ 1).

Some historians frame Voodoo as simply another religion unfairly associated with "black magic, devil worship, and witchcraft" (Edwards 2022, ¶ 19–21). The Manual is clear that the practices and rituals associated with Voodoo in the veneration of spirit minions is idolatry and witchcraft (Exod. 20:3–5). Voodoo curses can be powerful enough to kill you.

Curses that are brought on directly through witchcraft may not be commonly reported in your area. The police and local government are not going to announce that occult activity is happening in your neighborhood. There may be unusual break-ins, property destruction, missing cats, and such, but whatever they know will likely be framed out of context as individual crimes so the local community does not panic. The chances of you being personally targeted may be less likely, but just remember that freedom from curses is available.

Hoodoo is practiced in the American Deep South and involves charms, potions, and spells that originated in African traditional folk magic. It is associated with jinxes, bad luck, and so on ("Hoodoo (Spirituality)" n.d., ¶ 9).

The avenues of occult exposure are vast and varied, and there is growing interest in understanding it from guests and members. WitchTok videos on the TikTok social media platform reached 30 billion views by 2022 and continue to rapidly grow, mainstreaming access to occult knowledge. Jenny Weaver is raising the alarm on its accessibility and tailoring to children (Wise 2022, entire article).

Folklore

The occult realm operates with four elements: fire, earth, air, and water. This includes all fairy types or fae folk, merfolk, and cryptids. The *Minions* movies have popularized Gru's henchmen as funny little guys, mischievous but always causing trouble, and we tend to fall in love with them. We are familiar with stories of all types of fairies, such as the Scandinavian trolls, Irish leprechauns, and Iberian or Spanish *duendes* (pixie, goblin, gnome-like). These cryptids or spirits can be described as *espiritus chocarreros*, pesky spirits.

This entry includes some stories from my Mexican family located in the central eastern part of Mexico in the 1930s. Most interactions were attributed to duendes, small humanoid creatures about three or four feet tall.

My grandfather traveled the range on horseback. The ranch hands warned him not to go to a particular area at night because of duendes, but he didn't listen. As he returned to the ranch from this area one night, his horse suddenly seemed to get bogged down in mud. He dismounted, found it was dry ground, and pulled the horse along. When he arrived at the ranch, he noticed that the leg hairs on the horse were very twisted with rope pieces around the legs.

As a young boy, my uncle went close to the well on the ranch one day, then returned and told his mother that he saw little kids coming in and out of the well. She kept him away from the well after that.

One morning, my grandfather met the cowboy crew at the corral and reprimanded them, demanding to know who had ridden the horses that night. They insisted that nobody rode them. He took them to the stable, and the horses were sweaty, and their manes were tangled like they had been twisted and held. The crew said they never heard anyone around the stable that night.

When my mother was a month old, she would cry all the time. One day, my grandmother told my grandfather that a *zopilote* (small, black vulture—or a *chupilote*, a sucking vulture) was coming in and pecking and sucking blood from my mother's big toe. Grandpa hid in the wardrobe the next day. When the bird came inside, he shut the window and started beating it, almost killing it before it escaped. The following day, he learned that a witch in town had received a very bad beating the day before.

In February 2023, Mexico's president, Andrés Manuel López Obrador (AMLO), made headlines when he posted a photo of what he described as an alux, a Mayan woodland type of elf, in a tree (Reed 2023, ¶ 1–9).

Such stories are repeated around the globe and across many cultures. Other story types about merfolk, werewolves, and vampires are featured prominently in our culture. Many such movies and shows are popular because of our fascination with the magic of their storylines. Accounts and explanations from both Christian and spiritist sources attest to their reality on a paranormal level. Member organizations that deal with the occult find themselves discovering new aspects of the Serpent's bondage over these players who try to escape his binding clutches.

This topic of folklore is easy for rational players to dismiss as pretend fun. I was like most everyone else until I wrote this book. I thought all those folklore stories and fairy tales I read since childhood were make-believe. My cousin asked me to research vampires because his sons are very interested in such TV and movie topics. I was surprised to learn that it isn't simply some medieval scare that sells tickets and tourism.

The overwhelming majority of players, guests and members alike, are unaware of the vast depth and breadth of the Serpent's kingdom of darkness. What little we see around us suggests that there is not much to his kingdom, so we go our merry way as though the devil still lives in Africa and doesn't bother us here. Players who live in a region of prevalent witchcraft or those who participate in occult venues like my family has, see stories like these become more than folklore.

FATE

Belief in luck, destiny, and superstitious codes run deeply through popular cultural sayings and can include the use of talismans or good luck charms. There is a paradox of our observation of omens and our belief in their validity. They can be good or bad, from butterflies to black cats. Rituals done to bring good luck or ward off bad luck are widely accepted, even though some observing players are bemused as they watch them played out, wondering if the other player really believes in luck but is not willing to interfere with their psyche in the matter—like lucky underwear, a lucky ritual, or a lucky ring, and so on.

A lot of this begins in early childhood with a parent, grandparent, babysitter, or friend who tells the child what to do to make something happen for them. It can be as simple as doing a snow dance, wearing a snow cap or pajamas, or throwing ice cubes in the toilet to make the snowfall happen. That's not too far removed from the Native American rain dance ritual. Such activities are considered harmless fun, but they acclimate young players to accepting the greater world of good and bad luck and then participating in it.

There is a broader issue of blessings versus curses, but that topic has its own category. This entire concept of luck, fate or destiny, omens, reading tea leaves, fortune-telling, and so on is part of the occult realm where most of it seems totally harmless, making you think that whatever helps you gain an edge is okay. A deception of the Serpent is to make players think that anything said to be associated with him appears so patently ludicrous that any sensible player can plainly see that he has nothing to do with it.

So, "your fate is in your hands." This is literally an occult Chinese palmistry discipline, but it is also the mindset of many successful people. However, "fate" in the sense of making your destiny through your effort is not what we are discussing here.

The fate we are talking about is an interference with your life that you did not choose, and it works in a way that hinders your success. Nobody confuses self-help or successful living concepts like the power of positive thinking with belief in luck, but the two are not as far apart as one would think. The Manual says that the way a player truly thinks of himself, is what he is (or becomes) (Prov. 23:6–7).

Luck

Wishing someone good luck is widely used as the equivalent of cheering them on in a generic sense, like telling them to do well, giving them best wishes, or hoping they will succeed. It can also be a sarcastic or generic way of telling a player they set their expectations too high. It is a catch-all, throw-away line.

> **Luck:**
> **Real or Fake?**
> *Can be Real* – when anything becomes connected to a spirit source, it has real power potential.

Although there are spiritual connections to luck, it is not true that good luck comes from the Game Master and bad luck comes from the Serpent. As mentioned in the beginning of Spirit Laws, since luck and fate do not come from the Game Master, the only source of both is from the Serpent. Therefore, the Serpent can grant good luck and bad luck.

It is a mantra among members and some kiosk teachers to adamantly say that there is no such thing as luck. They make a strong point that members are blessed by the Game Master and not by random good fortune (which should be the case). This statement identifies both sources of power: the Game Master (blessing) and the Serpent (luck). However, their statement that there is no luck is simply not true. If your run of good fortune is statistically beating the law of averages, it is possible, and perhaps likely there is a spiritual dynamic that is driving that prosperity.

This issue of luck brings up the point that you can generate the power to succeed or fail through what you believe in. There is power in beliefs, even in the little things. Even if you don't put much stock in luck yourself, but you seem beset by or pushed around by what could be described as bad luck, that's not your imagination, and it is probably not random. If you frame your situation that "the stars are aligned against you," their power has a source. And where a source can be identified, it can be stopped and reversed. In this case, check the category of Curses.

Miracles

The Serpent performs miracles, too. As Rumpelstiltskin reminded and cautioned his many eager clients in the *Once Upon a Time* TV series, "All magic comes with a price" (TV Show Clips 2016, min. 1:35).

If you run to the Serpent to get your miracles, they will cost you much more than you thought you agreed upon. Seriously, how binding is a promise from the Father of Lies? How can you ever be sure of a bargain with him? Even if you read the fine print, did he mean it the way you read it?

Because miracles originate from the spirit realm, they can be enacted by agents of good or evil. However, the realm of evil is limited compared to the range of power held by the Game Master. That is why the Serpent uses deception as a major tool to give the illusion that the Game Master is weaker in power and disinterested in helping you.

> **BECAUSE MIRACLES ORIGINATE FROM THE SPIRIT REALM, THEY CAN BE ENACTED BY AGENTS OF GOOD OR EVIL.**

When the One cataloged His ministry to give proof to his cousin, John the Baptist, that He was the Messiah, 87 percent of the reasons he listed for John were miracles of healing that improved the lives of all the ordinary players who went to Him for help (Isa. 35:3–6; Luke 7:18–23). In one instance, He specifically cautioned an individual who was healed to stop his game violations unless something worse happened to him (John 5:14). He gave examples of how a good deliverance from minions (exorcism) can end badly (Matt. 12:43–45; Luke 11:24–26).

This supports the understanding that it is possible for the benefits of healing to be reversed by the choices we make. We may not intend to lose the miracle we got, but if we don't take steps to ensure its permanence, the Serpent's minions can snatch it away and make our condition much worse than before.

During a college-level class on world missions, weekly instructors came in from working around the game world. One of them remarked that the Pentecostal missionaries were finding more success with converts because they backed up their message of the gospel of peace with miracles. A common question they got was, "Is your God stronger than the witch doctor?" This was a very real problem because if players left the village religion and the Game Master wasn't stronger, there was nothing to save them from retaliation. Many believed in the One because they became convinced by miracles that He is sovereign.

The Gospel for Asia organization catalogs similar stories of its native missionaries who bring healing to those who found no help from the regional witch doctors and spent their livelihood savings without results. Miracles for ordinary players were important to the One, and they still matter to Him for you today.

Spirit guides

The average player does not experience the phenomenon of spirit visitations. They are likely to begin through participation in spirit-related environments, all of which can also open the door to alien encounters. These environments include Wicca; Masonry; New Age practices, including yoga; African or Native American or Eastern culture religions; occult practices, such as séances or Ouija boards or fortune-telling; or through drug use and occultist rock music.

Some players experience angel visitations or spirit guides who are kind, loving, comforting, and full of light. Many people find peace and assurance in these visitations. A meditative state with a mix of spirit guides and the One that has been recounted in a Reiki experience is an antichrist appearance rather than Jesus Himself, even if he brings healing (Feather n.d., ¶ 1–8). Here is a 2,000-year-old test from the Manual to find the source of a spirit:

> Don't believe every spirit, but quiz them whether they are from the Game Master: because many false prophets overspread the [game] world. Here is how you know the Spirit of the Game Master: Every spirit that confesses that Jesus Christ is come in person is of God: And every spirit that confesses not that Jesus Christ is come in person is not of God: and this is that spirit of antichrist. You've heard that

it should come; and even now it is already in the [game] world (1 John 4:1–3).

The Game Master says that He shares His glory with nobody: "I am the Lord: that is my name: and my glory will I not give to another, neither my praise to graven images" (Isa. 42:8). Master player Paul says that if we are told anything different from what the Manual says, by him or anyone else or even from an angel from heaven, he is to be cursed. This is so important that he said it twice in a row (Gal. 1:8–9).

> Despite the claims of New Age practitioners, spirit guides are anything but benevolent. They are not the spirits of dear, departed loved ones, nor are they ascended masters who have crossed over some mystical plane. They are what the Bible calls "familiar spirits" (Lev. 20:27 NKJV). They don't announce their evil nature but portray themselves as beneficial. 2 Corinthians 11:14–15 says, "Even Satan disguises himself as an angel of light. So it is no surprise if his servants, also, disguise themselves as servants of righteousness." Satan's lies are most effective when they look and sound like the truth, when they seem helpful. Spirit guides are actually demonic spirits [minions] who masquerade as helpers in order to trap and destroy people with false teachings and occult practices ("What Are Spirit Guides?" 2022, ¶ 3).

DREAMS OF JESUS

What if the One comes to me in a dream? Dreams from the One neither bypass the gospel or good news of the Manual nor instruct a player to do or believe anything contrary to the Manual.

Someone commented in an Internet question forum that he began seeing the One in dreams as he pulled away from Christianity, and his continued visitations confirmed to this player that he was on the right path. Such a scenario meets the description of a spirit guide and a minion visitation. It does not pass any Manual test, and the fact that the player was not directed back to the Manual makes this Jesus identity suspect.

By contrast, there are multiple reports and personal stories on the Internet from member sources about guest players in Iraq, Iran, Afghanistan, and across the Middle East and Asia in recent years where they had a dream of Jesus coming to them and telling them where to find out about Him or where to go where they will meet someone who will tell them about Him. In these countries, there is virtually no access to a Manual where players can find the Game Master without assistance.

Author and filmmaker Dinesh D'Souza has a short video entitled "Millions of Muslims Are converting to Christianity after Having Dreams and Visions of Jesus Christ." D'Souza says that, although numbers are hard to confirm, it is estimated that about six million Muslims are converting to the One each year. They clearly indicate that it is not the prophet Isa that appears to them but the Christian Christ. This is unprecedented in history for large numbers to convert from Islam. Many of the reports claim that it is the direct result of dreams about the appearance of Jesus Christ (D'Souza 2021, min. 3:30).

Notice some key points to these remarks about dreams. First of all, contrary to a member teenager I heard who exclaimed with relief to her friend in the school hallway one morning, "Thank God dreams don't mean anything!" there is evidence in the Manual showing the Game Master's connection with us through dreams. Eliphaz, a friend of the prophet master player Job, explains how a vision came to him and describes it like this, "In disquieting thoughts from the visions of the night, when deep sleep falls on men" (Job 4:12–17 NKJV).

The prophet master player Joel prophesied it (Joel 2:28), and the apostle master player Peter confirmed its fulfillment that, in the last days [our current time], the Game Master would pour out his spirit on all players to include visions and dreams and to prophesy (Acts 2:16–18). There are Christian books assisting with dream interpretation, including examples and symbolism, but many Protestant kiosks dismiss them. Although the last days began during the era of the apostle players with the pouring out of the Game Master's spirit with visions, dreams, and prophesying as confirmation, that aspect is treated as a bygone era since kiosks don't discuss or affirm such phenomenon today. You have to learn about it on YouTube instead of in kiosks.

Second, apparently, the Game Master is still using dreams as he has for the past 4,000 years. Next, in all the cases of reported dreams where Jesus came to them, the dreamers are given instructions on how, who, or where they will find the answers about Him. How many people who saw the One didn't believe in dreams and chose not to go? Would the Game Master give them another dream? In some rare instances, it took more than one dream before they responded.

Most players in the reports did not mention a second dream invitation or a hesitation to respond because the encounter was too real to ignore. The dream was profound enough that they took it as being genuine. They either had to go meet someone, go to the place where they would find their answers, or locate someone who would come to them. In one story, Afshin, a devout Muslim held in an Iraqi prison, said that he encountered Jesus and prayed, "God, send me a Bible." The next day, a prisoner from another section of the jail unexpectedly passed by and handed him a Manual, saying, "This is what you asked for" (Planet Zion 2014, min. 14:00).

Because the Game Master told members to tell the good news about Him (Mark 16:15), He does not step in and explain it Himself or "save" the dreamer in their sleep. It appears that he points them in the right direction to find their answers, which are expected to be revealed and confirmed through His Manual.

VISIONS

Visions are not dreams. They happen when a player is awake or thinks they're hallucinating. Three visions are mentioned in the story of guest player Saul's conversion into becoming the apostle member player Paul. On a trip to the town of Damascus around noon, the One knocked Saul to the ground and struck him with blindness in a vision of bright light where everyone with him saw the light and heard a voice but didn't see anyone. The One instructed Saul to continue into the city as he had planned, where he would be told what to do. Then, through another vision, the Game Master instructed a member, Ananias, to go to a specific street address to meet Saul and pray for Saul to receive his sight. He also explained to Ananias that Saul was already waiting for him because Saul had also seen a vision of a man named Ananias coming to him and praying for him to receive his sight.

The Game Master did not do these jobs Himself but sent Saul into town and then sent His member, Ananias, to go meet Saul. Ananias wasn't so sure about doing it because Saul had come to town to round up all the members he could find and drag them back to Jerusalem for trial and probable execution. It took some convincing, but in the end, Ananias went to Saul, who got his eyesight back. If Ananias had refused to go to Saul, the Game Master would have had to find someone else. He would not have restored Saul's sight Himself (Acts 9:1–20).

In a clip from the documentary *Father of Lights*, Ravi had a film team drive five hours to a particular temple in India one morning. The Game Master had told Ravi to find a man with a white beard, an orange robe, and a turban on his head. They walked around and searched for a while before they found him. He was a maharishi, a guru of gurus, like a bishop, whose life had been given to the Botswana god. In his dreams, someone told him to meet a man on a particular day and showed him a picture of Ravi. He recognized Ravi when they met, and he learned that it was Jesus who had talked to him in his dreams. Ravi had his undivided attention, and he soon became a member (Hall 2014, entire video).

A lesson about the Game Master sending members to deliver His message is that He will not do a job for members that He assigned to them. The Great Commission from the One telling members to announce to all players the good news about the golden ticket is an example of this (Mark 16:15). He will help and guide those who need it, even through their dreams, and even to both parties involved. If the job doesn't get done, the members are responsible for its failure.

Pseudoscience

The realm of pseudoscience is very, very broad, and the categories are extensive, covering physical sciences, life sciences, applied sciences, social sciences, religion, the paranormal, and so on. This includes the Bermuda Triangle, hypnosis, chiropractic, crystal healing, pyramid power, and so on.

Those fields that include the supernatural or have claims that engage the spirit world or realm of the interdimensional should be thought of as something related to the occult. This simple reason is that all displayed power in the game environment is likely from the Serpent because he is in control of the game environment. Thank you, Adam. Until a clear connection can be made of a phenomenon directly linked to a scientifically understood principle, prudence and caution are advised with the recommendation to stay away.

Aliens

A June 2019 Gallop UFO Poll tells us that forty-nine percent of Americans believe that people like us exist on other planets. This number rose to seventy-five percent of those who say life of some form exists elsewhere. Forty-one percent claim to have seen an alien spacecraft (Saad n.d., ¶ 1–3). Two to three percent claim to have been abducted (Alien Resistance n.d., ¶ 3–5).

While many religious players may express disbelief in alien life, three-quarters of Americans polled are willing to say it is possible. This topic is quietly gaining wide acceptance. Now that the CIA has made documents available with the Freedom of Information Act, and European countries have put their UFO data online, a comment here for those interested in the alien phenomenon is appropriate (Elliott 2021, ¶ 3; The National Archives n.d., entire article).

Member teachers, including Chuck Missler, former UFO enthusiast and former Druid priest Dr. William Schnoebelen, and member researchers into alien matters consistently conclude that the alien phenomenon is either wholly demonic or largely influenced by the minion spirit realm. A Christian symposium on aliens' presence online offers specific topics from a Manual perspective for those interested. Also, these researchers have found that dealing directly with aliens should be done the same way members would deal with minion spirits as described in the Manual's gospels and its book of Acts of the Apostles.

They found that those who reported abduction events showed an interest in or had exposure to the supernatural and the occult. They say that abductions can be stopped, and resistance to them is successful in the name of Jesus, but those who are not Spirit-filled members remain susceptible to repeated and increasingly hostile visitations. Their reported benevolence and kindness only last as long as the abductee is compliant or agreeable with them; otherwise, they can quickly become hostile. Aliens are not a third power player in the spirit realm but are part of the occult and aligned with the dominion of the Serpent.

3. Curses

Curses can be broken or their effects neutralized, depending on your perspective. However, any player—guest or member—can activate a curse against themselves or their family. There is no automatic or blanket immunity from a curse; they must be repelled. There are cautions about curses throughout the Manual. Many are not verbal curses but are based on actions. They are activated following a violation of the Manual's laws, and they are identified from specific directives of what to do or what not to do. The primary cause of curses is rebellion, an unwillingness to obey the Game Master.

> "Like a flitting sparrow, like a flying swallow, so a curse without cause shall not alight" (Prov. 26:2 NKJV).

Curses affect guests and members, and both groups can activate a curse. There is always a reason for a curse. Curses are consequences of our breaking divine law, and they position us against the Game Master. The trouble that comes upon us through a curse is not the Game Master's fault. Life does not line up in our favor until we deal with a curse that hinders us by turning to the Game Master to have it removed.

Curses waste away the blessings and resources of the present and rob the prosperity and potential of the future.

Curses are corrosive in their effects. They not only affect the player who caused the curse; they can also affect the family associated with the player, the home, the workplace, and the player's entire sphere of influence. Curses waste away the blessings and resources of the present and rob the prosperity and potential of the future.

A thorough description of blessings and curses with their effects is located in the Manual text of Deuteronomy 28. In contrast, Derek Prince summarizes by category the blessings that the Game Master prefers to bestow:

- exaltation
- health
- reproductivity (in every area of your life)
- prosperity
- victory
- God's favor (Deut. 28:1–14) (Prince 2006, 48)

This comparatively short list of blessings covers all the bases of life. The rest of the long chapter describes wave after wave of curses and their devastation.

There are specific actions that cause a curse to be activated in our lives. Unfortunately, many of them can be put upon us by our ancestors: parents, grandparents, great-grandparents, and so on. Some curses can last three or four generations, going back to a source pool of about 30 people, and some last for ten generations with at least 2,046 ancestors, where any one of them could have started a curse on the family line. Can you guarantee that none of your 30 ancestors in four generations ever activated a curse? What do you know about your previous 2,046 ancestors from ten generations? Any saints or scoundrels you don't know about?

> There is always a reason for a curse. *Find the source and break the curse.*

I was shocked to recently learn from a cousin that part of my Mexican family had many witches and warlocks. My mother neglected to mention it while living. I knew a story about my grandmother and idol worship but had no idea that it was a major factor in the extended family. These things mentioned in a passing moment can quickly change the landscape of your gameplay.

Curses can also last centuries or millennia. These may be identified by characteristic issues that affect various people groups such as nations: American, Somali, Russian, and so on, or in regions: European, African, Asian, and so on, or cultures: Native American, Hispanic, Korean, and so on, or blood lines: Irish, Scandinavian, Armenian, and so on. Curses can affect individual players on multiple levels of sources from the present day to the ancient past.

Dr. William Shnoebelen has a video clip on his YouTube channel discussing the curse of the Irish, and he frames it as a generational curse. If you have Celtic lineage, he says that this curse may impact you (Schnoebelen 2023, min. 11:00).

A number of curses are conditional upon the behavior of the players. In many cases in the Manual, they appear to be explicitly directed toward the Israelite nation. However, all players are subject to the moral standards of the Game Master, which includes each player's relationship to the Game Master. Therefore, every curse in those parameters affects all players across the Game of Life.

SIGNS OF A CURSE

Prince suggests a summary of the curses or the opposite of the blessings:

- humiliation
- barrenness (inability to reproduce in any area of your life)
- mental and physical sickness
- family breakdowns
- poverty
- defeat
- oppression
- failure
- God's disfavor (Deut. 28:16–68) (Prince, 2006, 49)

Check your life to see if you or your family are being affected or influenced by a curse. Explained another way in his book, *Blessing or Curse*, Prince (2006) identifies seven indicators of curses from Deuteronomy 28. Jonas Clark also lists a similar set of indicators. Lists from both authors are integrated here:

1. mental or emotional instability or breakdown (Deut. 28:28–29)
   a. insanity, craziness, foolishness, irrational behavior, flakiness
   b. blindness: confusion, indecision, wonderment, inner struggles
   c. fearful, unsettled, frustrated
2. repeated or chronic sicknesses (especially if hereditary) (Deut. 28:21–22, 27, 35)
   a. consumption: COPD (chronic obstructive pulmonary disease), lung cancer, emphysema
   b. arthritis, Alzheimer's
   c. leukemia, diabetes, cancer, and so on
   d. botch (open sores), wounds that won't heal
   e. all other hereditary diseases
3. barrenness, a tendency to miscarry or related female problems (Deut. 28:18)

a. menstrual problems ("the curse"), PMS (premenstrual syndrome)
   b. hormone problems, infections, cramps, fibroids, cysts, tumors
   c. painful sex, bladder problems, kidney stones
   d. male impotence, ED (erectile dysfunction)
   e. miscarriage, stillborn child
4. breakdown of marriage and family alienation (Deut. 28:30–32, 41)
   a. divorce, family divisions, intra-clan feuds
   b. dispersed family, jailed children, estranged relationships, no fellowship
5. continuing financial insufficiency (Deut. 28:17, 29, 47–48)
   a. financial lack, inability to save money, squander and waste finances
   b. poverty, indebtedness
   c. financial drought, failed job ventures
6. being "accident-prone"
   a. clumsy
   b. random cuts, scrapes, bumps, bruises, broken bones
7. no ambition (Deut. 28:29)
   a. No goals or visions, dreams or aspirations
   b. Negative, apathetic
8. bondage and slavery (Deut. 28:43–44)
   a. literal bondage and slavery
   b. easily controlled and manipulated
   c. loss of personal freedoms and identity
9. a history of suicides and unnatural or untimely deaths (Deut. 28:20–21)
   a. lost hope, acute depression
   b. dying younger than normal (Clark n.d., ch. 2; Prince 2006, 53)

Do you get sick repeatedly? Do certain illnesses "run in the family?" Are you "accident-prone" or "clumsy?" Are you typically hit financially when things seem to be just about to go right? Are you under continued emotional or mental pressure? Are your close relationships full of turmoil? Do you watch others succeed but see it always slip past you, *even when it's your turn for success?* When you plan ways to succeed, do you get a sense of paralysis or helplessness? Do you manage to sabotage your own success and somehow always snatch defeat from the jaws of victory? Would you describe yourself as a loser in any area? (Prince 2006, 53).

If these categories or situations describe you, there is a very real possibility that you are being buffeted and limited by one or more curses. Because curses are woven into the fabric of our daily lives, we don't recognize the source of what seems to be just a run of bad luck or nothing more than what other players do to us.

You could very well have activated a curse. For many members and guests living under a curse, it isn't necessarily their fault, even though the outcome plays out in their lives. Perhaps you had nothing to do with getting them yourself, but somewhere in your bloodline, somebody else could have activated a curse that now affects you. If you are married, your partner may have brought the effects of their cursed life into your family.

Whether or not you are the source of a curse, if you are burdened by a curse in your life, then you are still responsible for breaking it off for yourself. Curses don't just wear out and disappear. They must be identified before they can be revoked. Reversing a curse requires identifying and renouncing it along with any other Manual guidelines.

CURSES DON'T JUST WEAR OUT AND DISAPPEAR.

Sources of curses

There are several sources that cause a curse to be activated. Curses are easy to acquire and hard to remove. Most players are affected by one or more curses. Derek Prince has identified sixteen sources of curses:

- **God Himself** – (Exod. 20:3–5) Commandments 1 and 2 of the Big Ten include worshiping any god instead of the Game Master or in addition to the Game Master and worshiping idols. This includes any form of occult practice.
- **disobedience** – (Deut. 27:15–16) This includes disrespect for parents (Eph. 6:1–3).
- **treachery** – (Prov. 17:13) "If anyone returns evil for good, evil will not depart from his house" (ESV).
- **injustice to the weak or helpless** – (Prov. 28:27) "He who gives to the poor will not lack, But he who hides his eyes will have many curses" (NKJV)
- **illicit sex** – (Lev. 20:10–16) unnatural sex, especially incest
- **anti-Semitism** – (Gen. 12:3; 27:29) This curse can come against an individual or a nation.
- **trust in man** – (Jer. 17:5–6) "Cursed is the man who trusts in man and makes flesh his strength, whose heart turns away from the LORD" (ESV).
- **perjury & theft** – (Zech. 5:1–4)
- **stinginess toward God** – (Mal. 3:8–10)
- **preaching a false gospel** – (Gal. 1:8–9)

- **God's "mouthpieces"** – (Josh. 6:26) a curse pronounced by member players
- **relational authority**. Authority originates with the Game Master; players did not create it. Negative words by an authority figure to those under their authority have supernatural power. This includes a husband-and-wife relationship (Gen. 31:30), parent to child, teacher to student, boss to employee, and so on. There is usually a minion element to this (James 3:14–15).
- **self-Imposed curse** – (Gen. 27:11, 46; Matt. 27:24–25) Revoke it with a positive. antidote: Psalm 118:17, "I shall not die, but live, and declare [or proclaim] the works of the Lord (NKJV).
- **unscriptural covenants** – (Exod. 23:32) such as freemasonry
- **servants of Satan** – (Num. 22:4–6; 1 Sam. 17:43) Includes witchcraft
- **abominations in the home** – (Deut. 7:26) Objects associated with idols or the occult, charms, horseshoes, pagan souvenirs, and so on; they are an avenue for the Serpent's intrusion. If children are frightened at night, search the home and clean it out (Prince 2021a; 2021b; 2021c).

Here is an example from Derek Prince of a curse from the Native American Indians for injustice to the weak or helpless:

> In other messages I deal with the fact that American Indians in the United States placed a curse on the White House because the American government regularly broke its treaties with American Indians. And believe me, Indians know how to curse! That's why from 1860 to 1980 every President elected in the 20th year died in office. You can trace that back to two things: the American government's unfaithfulness to the American Indians and the fact that Abraham Lincoln, who was the President elected in 1860, permitted a spiritist seance to be conducted in the White House by his wife, who later ended up in a mental institution. So you see that curses not only affect individuals, but whole nations (Prince 1994,17).

> I believe that the same would have happened to President Reagan, who was elected in 1980. It seemed that the curse was being fulfilled when an attempt was made on his life early in his presidency. But just before he took the oath as President, a group of us in a large meeting had combined in prayer and faith and released him from the curse—not just him, but the presidency. The bullet lodged within one inch of

his heart, but his life was spared. I believe this was God's vindication of the prayer that released the curse. Once again, we see that this is no abstract theory. It is something that affects the lives of people and nations everywhere (Prince 1994, 17).

Covenants

I want to add a point here about secret societies, covenants, and blood oaths. Freemasonry is typically identified in this category but can also include Druidism, Kabbalah, water spirits, and all types of tribal and secret organizations where you swear allegiance and many times involves blood. We occasionally hear about politicians and upper-level officials in all branches and departments of the government being allegedly involved in secret societies and rituals such as the Skull and Bones or the Bohemian Grove. They publicly laugh it off or ignore questions when faced with a camera. The deeper you become involved in occult things, the more that blood becomes a required element in rituals.

There are also line-crossing ceremonies for inductees who cross the equator for the first time. It includes a baptism to Neptune (Buys n.d., 8). Many navies of Europe and the Americas, along with merchant ship lines, have conducted this ritual over hundreds of years, with it being mandatory up to recent years (Buys n.d., 2). How many of those sailors or passengers took it seriously? No matter how much humor or goodwill you infuse into such ceremonies, the occult bondage is real.

Detailed prayers of renunciation are available at kanaanministries.org (Buys n.d., 11–18). If you are breaking curses and need to break a spirit covenant, a simple exorcism or deliverance prayer may not be enough to complete the process. These are not contracts where you can simply walk away. The Resource appendix A lists ministries that include help with such deliverance.

Words

Your words also speak curses. Typically, a curse is a simple or quick personal expression of opinion said in the heat of the moment, usually negative, negative and sarcastic (meant to be "funny"), or a pointed remark that we just feel compelled to say to put someone in their place or set the record straight. We all say them, sometimes on purpose, sometimes reflexively (James 3:8–10).

The Manual says that "Death and life are in the power of the tongue" (Prov. 18:21). It also describes the spoken blessings and curses that even members too frequently engage in (James 3:8–12). Our words have power to the point of literal life and death.

The fact that we may choose not to believe this does not make it untrue, nor does our skepticism cancel the power of our words.

An example of a literal death sentence happened when King Ahaziah sent a captain to fetch the prophet master player Elijah, and here is the dialogue:

> Then the king sent to him a captain of fifty with his fifty men. And he went up to him [Elijah], and behold, he was sitting on the top of the hill. And he said to him, "You man of God, the king says, 'Come down.'" But Elijah replied to the captain of fifty, "If I am a man of God, may fire come down from heaven and consume you and your fifty." Then fire came down from heaven and consumed him and his fifty men (2 Kings 1:7–15 NASB).

This happened twice, and the third captain got wise and humbly begged Elijah to come with him, whereupon a guardian told Elijah that he could safely go with him.

The first thing we will notice is that none of us is the prophet Elijah, so obviously, nothing we could say would kill anyone, especially so dramatically as that. That makes this story pointless. True, maybe, except for the fact that when the Manual says that death and life are in the power of the tongue, that really does include literal death, and that text does include you.

In another example, the One's disciples, James and John, asked if they should call down fire on a Samaritan village that refused to shelter them. The One was shocked at them:

> He (the One) sent messengers on ahead of Him, and they went into a Samaritan village to make arrangements for Him; but the people would not welcome Him, because He was traveling toward Jerusalem. When His disciples James and John saw this, they said, "Lord, do You want us to command fire to come down from heaven and destroy them?" But He turned and rebuked them [and He said, "You do not know what kind of spirit you are; for the Son of Man did not come to destroy men's lives, but to save them."] And they journeyed on to another village (Luke 9:52–56 AMP).

The One stopped them because James and John had the wrong attitude and response; He did not dispute their ability to destroy the village.

For a modern example of this, a preacher on national television, Andrew Wommack, told the story of when he was invited to a religious kiosk where they had just suffered the tragic, sudden loss of a boy in a car accident. Andrew happened to be staying in the home of the family who lost their son. They and the whole kiosk were completely flummoxed as to why the Game Master would take the boy from them.

While at the home, Andrew sat in the kitchen and watched the mother severely berate the teenage daughter for not making her bed one morning, giving her a really hard time. He told the mother that he hadn't made his bed either and asked her why she didn't scold him. She answered that he was a guest and not expected to make his bed. He then explained that the mother treated strangers better than her own family.

At this point, the mother began to cry and said that the day their son died, she had a big argument with him at breakfast about some small thing and angrily told him she didn't want to see him again as he walked out the door. She never saw him alive again (Wommack 2008, min 35:50–37:10).

Andrew concluded his story with a text from the Manual, "For where envying and strife is, there is confusion and every evil work" (James 3:16 KJV). The Game Master did not "take" this boy in the way the kiosk thought; his own mother sent him away, and the powers of darkness were empowered and happy to grant her wish. Their family fights apparently drew a crowd from the spirit realm. We have no idea the amount of destruction we can unleash on our lives and on those around us when we let our passions run loose and give the Serpent an avenue to empower them.

Do you know someone living with guilt because they said something to a player or about another player, and then it happened? Maybe they said directly to someone, "I don't ever want to see you again!" or to someone else, "I wish he/she were dead!" and suddenly, it came true. Perhaps a freak accident or unexpected situation occurred, and the player who said those feelings is left wondering if it is their fault. The hard truth is that, yes, it could very well be their fault. Players facing their guilt may be unable to forgive themselves, but forgiveness is available when they turn to the Game Master for it.

Anything that does not speak well about you can be empowered against you. Sometimes we say negative things about ourselves, cursing ourselves and paying for the privilege. Here are some typical types of curses we hear: You'll never amount to anything, you're stupid, you're a clumsy oaf, you never hold on to anything you make, you're going to have an accident, you're going to fall down from there and break your neck, you're going to get sick, you'll catch your death of cold, your dreams are stupid, you'll always be fat, and there's nothing you can do about it—that's just your lot in life.

These words rarely come from strangers unless, perhaps, you are on social media. In essence, the people who know you the best and claim to love you the most can be your worst fortune tellers. If they got paid for the entire bad verbal juju they spread around, they would be filthy rich.

But you can always refuse to accept a curse; reject it out loud even if you have to say it in a whisper under your breath and behind their back. Don't let negative comments toward you hang in the air where they can work their way into your psyche and soul or empower any spirit listeners to bother you because you didn't reject those words—that's tacit consent.

The power of words is innately sensed by normal players who will never stop to think about this phenomenon. Have you ever watched when a sick player says they will never get better, perhaps because they just feel so bad? However, their loved one immediately scolds them, saying, "Don't say that! Of course you'll get better, and you'll be up and around in no time," or when a frustrated child says, "I'll never get this right." Their companion or caregiver contradicts them with what we usually interpret as encouragement.

Something inside us wants to repel the thought of negative consequences in the hope that they don't happen. Those in the medical profession do, at times, assess someone's chances of survival based on their "will to live," where they may say, "He's a fighter." Even nonreligious professionals recognize that what we think and choose to say can make the difference between death and life (Prov. 18:21).

While the Serpent is always looking for an opening to harm you and doesn't have to be asked twice, the Game Master is willing to give you a chance to reconsider. Andrew Wommack was in the Vietnam War and at a point in life where he felt his connection with the Game Master was so close that he just wanted to die and move on to the bonus round, so he prayed for the Game Master to kill him. That day he almost died twice and suddenly realized he wasn't ready to end the game, so he rescinded his request. However, if you pray and ask Him to let you die, be prepared for Him to grant your request and remove His protective care from you—but don't say He did it to you (Wommack 2105, min. 18:37–21:09).

We like to pick and choose which words or sayings will have any real meaning or influence and which ones won't, but the spirit powers that give words their potency don't play by our rules. You have to remember their perspective: evil spirit powers don't see this as a tragedy; to them, it's an opportunity.

Our modern, scientifically enlightened minds consider it superstitious, therefore untrue to believe that we could say something and that our mere words would be a death sentence upon us or someone else. But the power of the spirit realm does not change or get nullified based on our skepticism or personal opinions. Instead, our thinking needs to be adjusted to the spirit reality.

The Manual is clear that we will be called into account for every idle word we speak, "By your words you will be justified, and by your words you will be condemned" (Matt. 12:36–37 NKJV). Whether we think we meant it or not or insist that *we were just joking* does not reduce the potential power or effects of accountability for what we say. Don't hang around players who enjoy hurling verbal firebombs of negativity and then say they are joking.

The mouth simply says what comes out of the sincerity and fullness of our heart (Matt. 12:34), including what is known as a Freudian slip. Derisive jokes have a measure of truth. Even players who recognize that it is more than a simple joke publicly tend to shrug it off. The old saying, "Sticks and stones may break my bones, but words will never hurt me," to cover hurt feelings has faded out of popularity. The mindset behind it and hurt feelings, however, remain. Alternative phrases said toward those who do get offended are, "Don't get butt-hurt," "Man up," or "People are too easily offended nowadays."

Does every negative observation, every angry or bitter word result in a curse? Not necessarily. In the best scenario, you can just brush it off and be done with it, but if they are regularly being stacked against you, the chances that they mean nothing will greatly diminish over time.

For example, you make a practice of using harsh language, sarcasm, and angry outbursts; you are showing your willingness to let emotions overwhelm you. This practice is how you align yourself with the spirit realm of darkness, and at some point, a minion watching you could choose to agree with you and begin helping to make sure such characteristics become part of your pathological personality traits. It can happen gradually or suddenly.

In extreme cases, you eventually may not be able to control your outbursts or temper because that fit of rage may be supernaturally enhanced. Alcohol, rock music, or drugs can inflame the situation and speed up the process. Have you seen players like comedians talk about how mean their fathers were? They sometimes describe it as though they escaped the clutches of pure evil and could be more right than they know.

Notice what happens from a spirit-view when you lose control. To yourself and everybody else, it looks like you just have attitude problems, maybe to the point that someone thinks you need help. Usually, you just get ostracized, fired from your job, or kicked out of your club. Nobody lets you stick around long enough to realize that the impulses that get out of control are more than just you acting out—try telling anyone the rage isn't you, and they'll call you crazy and refer you to a psychiatrist.

Maybe you feel stuff just comes over you, but since those are your thoughts and your words, you yourself also conclude that it must be only you with no outside influence. When deviant minion spirits have an opportunity to interact with us, they suggest thoughts to us in our mind that sound like something we might say or think, so we take ownership of those thoughts or attitudes and claim them as a part of us. The transition is quite seamless and may likely be completely undetectable without insight from the Spirit Master.

Not every thought that pops into your head is necessarily yours (John 12:40; 2 Cor. 4:3–4). This is why members are told to reign in their thoughts as part of their obedience to the One (2 Cor. 10:4–5). Letting thoughts run loose in your head that will negatively affect others or your outlook on life is not a good practice.

> **NOT EVERY THOUGHT THAT POPS INTO YOUR HEAD IS NECESSARILY YOURS.**

As we gradually get immersed in negative attitudes over weeks, months, and years, we cede our control to those passions. The Manual tells us not to give a beachhead to the Serpent (Eph. 4:27). The spirit realm is engaged all the time, 24/7/365[25], never resting, always watching for an opening, and words spoken in anger, fear, and frustration can be spiritually activated and supernaturally enhanced. The fact that you may refuse to believe in the power of your words and don't believe the Manual to be literally true about them does not prevent their effectiveness in the spirit realm. From there, the curses we speak become manifested in the real world.

Jinxes

Jinxes are superstitions of bad luck that everyone just knows are true. Even if they say they don't believe them, many players fear them because their evidence appears real. Actually, this reality is very likely the case, and even many sincere members, both children and adults, are heavily influenced by the threat of a jinx upon their good fortune. It is dismaying how often it is referenced among religious members because they are the ones with the spiritual authority to quickly break a jinx. They don't recognize or operate in the spiritual authority that has been granted to them.

Speaking a jinx or trying to reverse a jinx are the most common ways normal players express or relate to the power of their words. So, the real "curses" that we say all the time against others are fake, but jinxes are like, you know, "play curses" and more "real" but not "serious." Got that? Are you listening, powers of the cosmos? Yeah, well, we didn't mean it, so that one didn't count!

4. The World

The world is both the game world that embodies the physical aspects we live in and the system of governance that controls it in both the physical and spiritual senses. What we do in this world and how we interact with it affect how long we can stay here. The Game Master's intent for you is to stick around as long as possible and be healthy and happy until the very end, when we buy the farm, kick the bucket, sprout daisies, cross the river, go to glory (Exod. 15:26; Deut. 30:19–20; Ps. 91:14–16; 1 Cor. 15:53–58; Eph. 5:18–20).

The Manual has a grouping regarding the world, the flesh, and the devil from Ephesians 2:2–3. The context for the world means this world system, which is communicated to us through philosophy, entertainment, the media, and so on. It encompasses the values of the world's institutions. We discuss this elsewhere and are instead focused here on the natural world around us and the government systems that control us (which also convey the values of the world system). Derek Prince described it like this,

> What do we mean by the world? I'll give you my definition. The world is a social order or a system of life which refuses the righteous government of Jesus Christ. Because Jesus is God's appointed governor, He's qualified, He met the conditions, He's the only one God will appoint as ruler of the human race. But the world is a system, an attitude that refuses the righteous government of Jesus. Worldly people can be religious, they can be nice, they can be respectable, but when you challenge them with unreserved submission to the Lordship of Jesus, that attitude comes out. That's the world (Prince n.d.a, min. 44:14) (John 15:18–19; 1 John 2:15–17).

Physical world

Accidents happen. They could be caused by mechanical failures from tools and equipment we use, natural disasters or mishaps, a miscalculation by us or someone else resulting in an accident, or by our own physical limitations. We use the term "Mother Nature" to describe things happening in our natural world that appear beyond our control.

Our interaction with the natural world requires care and good sense. Heat in the summer, cold in the winter, and murky depths of water we enter are just some things that prepare us to ensure our safety. As advanced as our automotive technology has gotten, we still must use caution and preparation when crossing deserts and traveling lonely, snow-covered roads. Having a vehicle breakdown in the desert or getting snowbound on an empty road can reduce our chances of survival to that of pioneers of the 1800s.

With its easy comforts, our modern world can make us forget to be alert as we become more removed from nature. We occasionally hear about hikers who must be rescued from their own absentmindedness because they were caught on a mountainside unprepared for the weather or conditions.

Disease & injury

It is routinely and truly said that sickness is part of the curse from Adam's epic game violation. The implication, though, can be that players get sick and die, and we can do nothing about it. But the issue of disease is true of every other aspect of life that is affected by a curse: healing can happen, and curses can be broken.

The animal kingdom poses threats that usually seem remote in our urban existence. Bacteria and viruses appear to be a closer threat as new diseases or previously eradicated ones periodically come on the scene and can now travel around the globe in a matter of days. Seeing a 2015 headline of bubonic plague in the fleas of rats in New York City seemed so medieval (Guion 2015). There are still about seven cases of the plague reported in the United States each year (Sullivan 2020, ¶ 6). The COVID-19 pandemic turned the world's routines upside down, shutting down the global economy for two years with lingering effects.

Our diet affects our general well-being, health, and longevity. Every day we can choose to eat right or take a break and indulge ourselves. What we eat directly impacts health risk factors affecting our body systems. Some diseases seem obviously preventable with proper diet, and others may take decades to reveal themselves.

Injuries like those related to sports appear self-explanatory, as are accident-related traumas. Occasionally, the medical world may be mystified at first about a unique medical condition, but most of the time, diagnoses are made and treatments prepared. Many diseases are now treatable and curable, but there are still many that elude a cure. Some of them can be managed and controlled, while the successful treatments of others involve too many factors to predict the outcome.

COVID-19. When the COVID-19 virus sped across the globe in late 2019, there was great fear of its deadliness. Since then, there has been growing fear and mounting evidence that the vaccines and boosters themselves are now contributing factors in many deaths worldwide.

Here are sample headlines as more continue to surface month after month:

- "1 Million COVID Deaths: Here's the Real Reason Why More People Died from COVID In The United States Than Every Other Country" (Powe 2022)
- "'Everyone is at Risk for Blood Clots!' – CDC and Pfizer Issue Urgent Warnings on Blood Clots Even in 'The Healthiest Athletes'" (Mek 2022a)
- "Germany Admits Covid 'Vaccine' 40 Times Deadlier Than Previously Known" (Mek 2022a)
- "Study Warns of Possible Reproductive Crisis as Sperm Counts Drop Worldwide" (Carter 2022)
- "Australia Sees 63% Drop in Births After Introduction of Covid 'Vaccines' – What Will the Government's Excuse Be?" (Huff 2022)
- "'Died Suddenly' Film Connects the Dots on the Depopulation Agenda Behind COVID Vaccines" (Mangiaracin 2022)
- "Deborah Birx Openly Admits to Lying About the COVID Vaccines to Manipulate the American People, (Bonchie 2022)"
- "Vaccine Injury Treatment–Fasting for 48-72 Hours Creates Autophagy–The Body's Detox Process that Kills COVID-19 Vaccine Spike Protein Damaged Cells and Reboots the Immune System" (Vigilant News 2023)
- "Swiss Study: Heart Injuries from COVID Vaccine 3000x Higher Than Thought," (Strom 2023)
- U.S. Has Recorded Over 1 Million Excess Deaths Among People Aged 65 And Older Since The Rollout of Covid-19 Vaccines (Johnson 2024)
- Top Virologist Warns 'Massive Tsunami' of 'Death' among Vaccinated Is 'Imminent' (Bergman 2024)

This seems to be a case where the cure is worse than the disease. Perhaps the COVID disease or vaccine has affected you or someone you know. The impacts addressed in these articles can include increased cancer risk, hepatitis risk, heart disease risk, suppressed immune system, reduced sperm counts, and suppressed reproductive rates with highly increased miscarriage rates, and increased mortality rates at all ages.

Dr. Anthony Fauci, Bill Gates, and the World Health Organization (WHO) continue to assure us that more and deadlier pandemics are on the way. There is conjecture that this is government-approved biological warfare against you and your loved ones, and it will soon become much harder to navigate ways to stay healthy and alive. A global depopulation plan will be addressed under the World System heading. The use of disease is only one facet of that program, and huge swaths of the population will continue to be impacted by it.

Man-made disaster. We occasionally hear of dams that fail and bridges that collapse due to faulty engineering or infrequent structural inspections. Learning from previous disasters can lead to safer conditions, such as earthquake-resistant buildings (Rethinking the Future n.d., entire article; Scoggins 2019, entire article).

Everybody knows that we don't control the weather, right? According to a 2009 History Channel series entitled, *That's Impossible!*, episode three discussed Weather Warfare. In it, they showed the mechanics of artificially creating a weather event and then applied their findings to Hurricane Katrina.

Their conclusion was that this hurricane fit the elements of a manmade event and could have been an attack on the United States since several countries have that technology. They also pointed out that in the next hurricane season, a high-pressure zone unusually showed up in the Caribbean and prevented all hurricanes from making landfall the next year (Nico Christodoulou 2012, min. 38:38). Was that also a natural happenstance?

> **Natural Disaster?**
>
> If Man can replicate or weaponize a natural disaster, when is it an act of God, a political objective, or an act of war?

Researching similar areas like scalar technology, weaponry, and electromagnetic research takes one to topics that border on the unbelievable. Some discussions include the deliberate triggering of tsunamis and earthquakes as well. Planet Earth has so many pressure points it is conceivable that scientists would want to poke and prod to explore the possibility of creating events to study their effects and harness their use. We have studied the microscopic world for more than a century, and it should be no surprise to turn our attention to the game world's mechanical systems.

On February 13, 2022, popular Romanian Senator Diana Sosoaca declared,

> "We have lived to witness production of earthquakes on demand. NATO disliked being set up by President Erdogan," a furious Sosoaca stated.

> "Moreover, his position of neutrality and mediator in the Ukrainian-Russian war deeply disturbed them. His position to block Sweden's accession to NATO and his speech in Davos as well as the gesture of leaving in the middle of a press conference defying Schwab did not remain without an echo in the cold world leaders of the world.

"But no one thought that people would have to die so many in such a terrible way.

"But ten seconds before the occurrence of the so-called earthquakes the Turks closed these (oil and gas) pipelines.

"In addition, 24 hours before the earthquakes 10 countries withdrew their ambassadors from Turkey.

"Five days before its occurrence the Romanian Ministry of Foreign Affairs issued a travel warning for Romanian citizens in Turkey."

These damning accusations are prima facie evidence of a deliberate attack on Turkey by Deep State using HAARP technology (Lee 2023, ¶ 2–8).

At the time of this report, thirty-three thousand people had died from a series of earthquakes starting February 6 (Lee 2023, heading 1).

This topic of man-made events on a massive scale that can encompass whole nations is where most players hop off the crazy train. However, the History Channel introduced it as a serious possibility among other things like energy weapons in its six-part series, and the subject is now on the table.

> "Others [terrorists] are engaging even in an eco-type of terrorism whereby they can **alter the climate, set off earthquakes, volcanoes remotely through the use of electromagnetic waves** . . . So there are plenty of ingenious minds out there that are at work finding ways in which they can wreak terror upon other nations . . . **It's real**, and that's the reason why we have to intensify our (*sic*) [counter terrorism] efforts." - Defense Secretary William Cohen, 1997 (Morgan 2007, §3, #1, box 2).

The coming Apocalypse in the Manual's text of Revelation will include judgments executed through the hand of players, nature, and an invasion from the spirit realm into our dimension of the game world. Based on alleged technology, mankind himself has the potential to cause great harm using the forces of nature.

The year 2023 saw an array of natural disasters ramping up across the globe, encapsulated in a headline, "Wake Up! Highly Destructive Natural Disasters Are Suddenly Striking Areas All over the Earth" (Snyder 2023b, entire article). Concerning hurricanes in a story by Ian Livingston, Jason Samenow remarked, "For the first time on record, storms have reached top-tier Category 5 strength in every tropical ocean basin in the same year" (Livingston and Samenow n.d., ¶ 1).

The 2023 fires in Maui, Hawaii, are being called a Directed Energy Weapon (DEW) event by skeptics of the government narrative (Freeman 2019, ¶ 1). If science can make a weather event or natural disaster appear to be part of a completely normal terrestrial cycle to players who don't know what telltale signs to look for, then aside from arson or negligence, at what point are we actually aware that it is something else than an act of God?

Extensive droughts, prolonged rain and flooding, wildfires, temperature extremes, and so on are all classified under a Climate Change heading, along with storms, tornados, earthquakes, tsunamis, and volcanoes. This Climate Change reference implies that gamers are not causing specific events but that mankind collectively is making the world a worse place to live. This raises the questions of why create disasters and whether any of these climate change events are deliberate.

World system

The American Declaration of Independence, signed in 1776, contains a phrase that "governments are instituted among men." The rest of the phrase that they are "deriving their just powers from the consent of the governed" is a matter of debate depending on the type of nation you come from (Jefferson 1776, ¶ 2).

Governments came into existence after Noah's flood about 4,375 or 5,375 years ago, which is the traditional biblical date or its corrected date, when the Game Master announced to Noah, "Whoever sheds man's blood, by man shall his blood be shed" (Gen. 9:5–6 NKJV), thereby authorizing corporate oversight of what players do to each other (Meehan 1999, ¶ 1, 7). Since players had done such a bad job policing themselves in the early game, they would now get policing done to them from a hierarchy of other players through tribes, people groups, and nations.

Fast forward to century twenty-one. Here we are, watching the fabric of society unravel on multiple levels and in numerous nations and regions. The game world in modern nations is hardly recognizable from fifty or even twenty-five years ago, and there seem to be even more significant changes happening lately within five-year increments and now even annually. The long-held notions that your government is looking out for your best interests and will protect you are falling on seriously hard times these days.

Your life can be turned upside down in a flash. The Silicon Valley Bank failed in mid-March 2023, leaving hundreds of small businesses, including the online marketplace Etsy, unable to access their funds (Moynihan and Gasparino 2023, ¶ 18). This event is seen as a catalyst to transition America to digital currency that was the first in a continued series of bank failures. Government policy affects the size of your paycheck, your mortgage interest rates, the cost of food and its availability, your health care options and medicine prices, the cost of energy, the prices of cars and gas, the rise in crime, and your safety and security. Your life can be easily spun around by executive order and government mandate.

Corruption in government and industry are more common than we want to believe because if the truth were told, we would probably lose hope for justice and getting a fair shake in most every area of life, especially when it seems like they are doing bad things to good people on purpose.

Nation-building is a term used for one country to set up a government in another country and is the result of or an alternative to outright war. Foreign industrial investment is a way to expand markets and influence. Many times, this is helped along with government negotiations. Economic forces can be artificially manipulated to destroy another nation's industry or its entire economy. Sometimes it's obvious when embargoes or sanctions against another country are announced. Even foreign aid is susceptible to corruption.

The rise of the Nanny State is a response to our desire for protection from harmful things, accidents, and trouble. Governments, both local and national, are exploring ways to protect us from ourselves using Big Tech. We are hearing more often about the social credit system.

> "China's social credit system is a combination of government and business surveillance that gives citizens a 'score' that can restrict the ability of individuals to take actions—such as purchasing plane tickets, acquiring property or taking out loans—because of behaviors. Given the position of several major American companies, a similar system may be coming here sooner than you think" (Tate 2021, ¶ 2).

> A Rair Foundation USA article about The Great Reset states, "The WEF's digital identity scheme is laying the foundation for a global social credit system that will give them the power to control citizens and punish those they deem 'untrustworthy'" (Flanagan and Warren 2022, 20–27; Mek 2022b, ¶ 7).

"In February 2022, Klaus Schwab's World Economic Forum (WEF) released a new report, 'Advancing Digital Agency: The Power of Data Intermediaries,' which lays out their plans for the creation of the Fourth Industrial Revolution, a fusion of the "physical, digital and biological world" (Flanagan and Warren 2022, 20–27; Mek 2022b, ¶ 1).

"The unelected WEF globalists have capitalized on Covid and are using the 'vaccine passports' to lay the foundation for widespread digital identity adoption. This is just one more part of the great reset in action" (Flanagan and Warren 2022, 20–27; Mek 2022b, ¶ 2).

With a Fourth Industrial Revolution upon us, you can count on the fact that your government keepers don't want bad things to happen to good people and may someday soon feel obligated to lock you up or quarantine you for your own safety. Wasting away in a government penalty box is a tough way to play out the game.

Disinformation. You can't have a depopulation plan without a comprehensive disinformation campaign. Like basic things such as good governance, information has now been weaponized against us.

Hoax journalism has been around as long as there have been newspapers, but perhaps it reached its zenith of popularity in the 19th century. Many of these stories were not just exaggerations of fact, or sloppy reporting. Some of the most well-known were complete fabrications from beginning to end. Amazingly in this era, newspapers from the smallest weekly publications to the biggest daily city press printed hoaxes. Also, some of the most famous names in American literature were behind the stories. Famous hoaxers include Mark Twain, Alexander Hamilton, Edgar Allen Poe, and perhaps Benjamin Franklin. "As the 19th century was left behind and the 20th century dawned, the public began to demand more accuracy from their newspapers. Most dropped their hoax stories and many required independent fact checking on important articles" ("Hoax Journalism" 2008, ¶ 3–9, 15–18, 21).

It's hard for us to imagine, in our day and age of radio and television, how much a part of 19th century entertainment centered on the tall tale and the hoax. Journalistic hoaxes, even in the largest newspapers, were standard fare. Readers were expected to guess about which stories were true and which were fictional. Almost every small town had a "lair club" where tall tales were swapped ("The Mystery Airship of 1896" 1996, ¶ 15).

Rising from hoax journalism, the government found ways in the mid-twentieth century to make disinformation part of the official government narrative and policy position. Disinformation campaigns by the government use the media to tell the public what to believe and think. In 2022, Edward Snowden tweeted a 1983 video interview of a former CIA operative explaining how the 1960s and 1970s disinformation campaigns used disinformation in up to 70 to 80 percent of their data exclusives to targeted journalists. Some of this was intended to shape legislative policy and public perspective on the Vietnam War, and it succeeded (NTB Staff 2022, entire article).

In the 1980s, then CIA director, William Casey, said, "We'll know our disinformation program is complete when everything the US public believes is false" (Broadbery 202, ¶ 1). Do you realize your government has been practicing lying to you through legislation and the media for more than fifty years? How successful do you think that government disinformation program is by now? How many legislative initiatives include hidden poison pills? Have you noticed any government and media disinformation campaigns over the past forty years since Bill Casey said that? How many more are still unnoticed today?

The Intelligence Community is sometimes described as a fourth branch of government that has great influence on the other government branches. In January 2017, Senator Chuck Schumer responded to MSNBC host Rachel Maddow's remark that President-elect Donald Trump was taunting the Intelligence Community, saying, "Let me tell you: you take on the intelligence community—they have six ways from Sunday at getting back at you. So, even for a practical, supposedly hard-nosed businessman, he's being very dumb to do this" (Terje 2021, min. 1). Ever since then, we have watched the Intelligence Community oppose President Trump using intelligence and narratives that were confirmed to be disinformation both during and after his time in office.

Twitter (now X) user Greg Price has a thread about the Deep State saying, "Pretty much everything you learned about American history in the 20th century is a lie. The CIA killed JFK. The FBI killed MLK. The intel community launched the downfall of Nixon. The Deep State has changed our country's history in ways we still don't fully understand" (Price 2023, ¶ 1).

Fox News host Tucker Carlson detailed how President Richard Nixon was removed from office by "the FBI's COINTELPRO program, which was designed to secretly discredit political actors the federal agencies wanted to destroy, people like Richard Nixon" (News Clips 2023, min. 2:50).

When we assumed that everything we saw on the evening news was factual, we had no way of knowing if that was true or if there was more to any story. We were apparently wrong. Do you read both sides of the issues? Whose narrative do you follow? Are you sure you're told the truth and could spot a falsehood? Dennis Prager has an article that explains how to know which side is telling the truth. He concludes that the liar is "the one that censors and suppresses dissent. The Left" (Prager 2022, ¶ 22–23).

The short-lived Disinformation Governance Board was created in April 2022 as part of the Department of Homeland Security. "The board was intended to coordinate department activities related to disinformation aimed at the US population and infrastructure" (Sands 2022, ¶ 3). How ironic that a government practiced in providing disinformation and lying to the public would need a board with a disinformation czar to track alternative propaganda. Perhaps the counter-disinformation competition was getting too good–or you weren't getting the government memo.

The complicit media are assisting governments at all levels and Big Tech social media companies who report the acceptable narrative, enforce politically correct dialogue in their apps, and provide governments with personal information on non-compliant players. Technology companies are now heavily involved.

Elon Musk bought Twitter (now X) on October 27, 2022. By Christmas Eve, 2022, Musk announced, "To be totally frank, almost every conspiracy theory that people had about Twitter turned out to be true. Is there a conspiracy theory about Twitter that didn't turn out to be true? So far, they've all turned out to be true. If not more true than people thought" (ProTrump News Staff 2022, ¶ 2).

Matt Taibbi released The Twitter Files, Part Six, TWITTER, THE FBI SUBSIDIARY thread December 16, 2022, saying, "2. The #TwitterFiles are revealing more every day about how the government collects, analyzes, and flags your social media content. 3. Twitter's contact with the FBI was constant and pervasive, as if it were a subsidiary. 4. Between January 2020 and November 2022, there were over

150 emails between the FBI and former Twitter Trust and Safety chief Yoel Roth" (Taibbi 2022a, ¶ 1).

The thread continues up to 32 posts. Taibbi also posted "Twitter Files Thread: The Spies Who Loved Twitter, From FBI to DNI the DNI to 'OGA,' the full thread on Twitter and its intelligence partners" (Taibbi 2022b, full article).

This is just Twitter. Imagine what Google, Facebook, YouTube, Reddit, TikTok, and your other favorite apps are doing to drive narratives and suppress valid information by working hand in glove with the government.

So, how many of the government pandemic or recent crisis narratives were true? All of them? Any of them? Have you noticed that accusatory narratives before elections change after the elections or the bad news is withheld until after the elections? When a story breaks that impacts the administration or its party, how much of the response are spins and lies? Or is the story fake?

On March 9, 2023, feminist author Dr. Naomi Wolf posted a lengthy apology to American conservatives for believing all the lies that the government and legacy media made against them from the Russian collusion hoax to the COVID narrations and the January 6 narrative exposed by Twitter and Tucker Carlson (Wolf 2023, ¶ 1–86). It is extremely rare for a public figure to offer a genuine apology and acknowledge the politically incorrect view, especially when they detail so many divisive topics.

Nobody likes to believe they've been told wrong, but not everybody is right. Historically, dissenters who did not cooperate with the government and national media narrative in other countries were portrayed to us as authentic resisters speaking truth to power. When such dissenters speak up in our own country, such as at school board meetings, they are suddenly viewed as divisive and on par with terrorists. Don't tune out the dissenters if you are sifting for the truth.

> **NOBODY LIKES TO BELIEVE THEY'VE BEEN TOLD WRONG, BUT NOT EVERYBODY IS RIGHT.**

A quote attributed to both Elena Gorokhova and Aleksandr Solzhenitsyn is a good perspective to have toward our government and media: "The rules are simple: they lie to us, we know they're lying, they know we know they're lying, but they keep lying to us, and we keep pretending to believe them" (Gorokhova 2009, 172).

The game world you knew may soon become a world you only saw in the movies. Let the gaslighting begin.

Violence. Have you been affected by violence? The rise of violence is worrying as a statistical factor, and it is especially alarming when it comes through our neighborhoods. In the times leading up to the Apocalypse, the One explained that we would hear about wars and rumors of wars, but members shouldn't freak out because those things aren't the end of the world, they're just the first part of the countdown. Examples will be that nations will war against nations and kingdoms against other kingdoms (Matt. 24:6–7; Mark 13:7–8; Luke 21:9–11).

The phrases nation vs. nation and kingdom vs. kingdom refer to countries at war with each other, as well as tribes or people groups or ethnic groups at war with each other, like what typically happens in civil wars. According to the Wars in the World website, as of April 2015, 65 conflicts around the game world involved 632 groups of separatists, guerillas, and militia. By March 2024, there were 70 countries in conflict around the game world involving 893 groups of separatists, guerillas, and militia (Wars in the World 2024, full article). The numbers continue to grow. Add to this mix the threats made by ISIS and Iran to flood the Western nations with Middle Eastern refugees with the announced intent of subverting those nations who opposed them. Israel's war with Hamas is now making headlines.

We usually think that things have been relatively quiet much of the time, but most of those conflicts that don't affect us never make it into the daily news. Now, with instant access to events worldwide, we are becoming more aware that things are happening, but the actual number is probably much higher than we would have thought.

Crime. This is the category of violence that the average player experiences or perceives on a personal basis. While crime can be organized and regional, players usually feel it as random and local, ranging from property crime to physical crime against an individual. How many malls or neighborhood stores have you quit patronizing because of rising crime? Local crime statistics can usually be found for those who are concerned about their safety. The personal aspect of violence against a person or property will more often raise the question of, "Why me?"

Democide. A term called "democide" describes the murder of civilians by their own government, whether by genocide, politicide, or mass murder (Rummel n.d.b, ¶ 1). In the twentieth century alone, the number of deaths by democide reached 262 million players. Every so often, we become aware of an oppressed player group like the plight of the Armenians or the Chinese Uyghurs. Democide accounts for six times more than those who died in any type of combat in that century (Rummel n.d.a, ¶ 4).

According to the One, violence and war will become more common as we are seeing today. This phenomenon of seventy countries in conflict around the globe affecting 36 percent of the world's nations paints a grim picture of endless suffering.

The game world is dangerous enough in its natural condition, and the multiplication of violence perpetrated by players or governments against civilian innocents is just appalling.

Genocide. The Merriam-Webster Dictionary defines genocide as "the deliberate and systematic destruction of a racial, political, or cultural group" (Merriam-Webster 2022, ¶ 1). The United Nations also defines and describes genocide. The concept of genocide can now be applied to politics, religion, and health as observable patterns.

There is an actual Global Depopulation Plan. A Rair Foundation USA article states,

> "Crisis is the rallying cry of the tyrant"
> – James Madison
> (Moore 1997, ¶ 34)

> At a March 9th, 2015 International Conference titled "The New World Order – A Recipe of War or Peace!" Former Malaysian Prime Minister Mahathir Mohamad warned that the 'Elites want to reduce the world population to 1 Billion' and will go to any length necessary to achieve their goal (Kennington 2021a, ¶ 1).

> PM Mohamad stated that the Trans-Pacific Partnership Agreement (or TPPA) is a strategy lead [sic] by the United States to dominate the world economy. Several guest speakers focused on borderless trade and globalization being used to usher in a one-world government (Kennington 2021a, ¶ 2).

> "Basically, it is about having a world government. We should abolish all states, nations, and bodies but instead have only a one-world government. And that world government is to be by certain people, elites. People who are rich, intelligent, and powerful in many ways. They are the ones who will govern the world. There was not much talk about democracy or the choice of leaders, instead, there was to be a government by these elites who will impose their rules on everyone in this world. And for those who are unwilling to submit to them, there will be punishment,' Dr. Mahathir explained (Kennington 2021a, ¶ 3).

> "And the peace that we will get from this is the peace of the graveyard because the intention also is to reduce the number of people in this world. At the time when the New World Order has [sic] annunciated,

the population of this world was only 3 billion. The intention was to reduce it to 1 billion. Now the population of the world is 7 billion. There would be a need to kill many billions of people or to starve them to death, or to prevent them from giving birth to reduce the world's population" (Kennington 2021a, ¶ 4).

The article goes on to identify several avenues to achieve these goals. **Agenda 21** and **Agenda 2030 for sustainable development** are blueprints for world control and depopulation.

Mass, forced migration to the West promoted by multilateral organizations, left-wing governments, and organizations has been another vehicle for erasing borders. But as citizens push back against unvetted and potentially dangerous people flooding their countries, the globalist left has seized upon a new weapon to impose their agenda: the coronavirus pandemic (Kennington 2021b, ¶ 8).

The border crisis, COVID-19 lockdowns and vaccine mandates prepare the way for depopulation. Agenda 2030 has "17 Sustainable Development Goals with 169 associated targets that are integrated and indivisible" (United Nations 2015, ¶ 26). This went into effect on January 1, 2016, and is the road map for the following fifteen years, according to points 18 & 21 (United Nations 2015, ¶ 26, 29).

In September 2022, Bill Gates announced that they were halfway toward the goals of the Great Reset. In his remarks, he said, "As it stands now, we'd need to speed up the pace of our progress five times faster to meet most of our goals—and even that might be an underestimate because some of the projections don't yet account for the impact of the pandemic, let alone the war in Ukraine or the food crisis it kicked off in Africa" (Dowling 2022, ¶ 4).

The pace of things changing around us is disturbing enough. What would it look like to accelerate five times heading toward 2030? Are you ready? Let's hope we stay behind schedule for a long time.

When you see talk about depopulation, do you ever wonder how it will affect you? How hungry do you get before you depopulate from the game (Kottusch, Tillmann, and Püsche 2009, abstract)? It sounds like a third-world issue. The America First Report has an article titled "How the Jabs Will Be Used to Control Those Who Haven't Already Been Depopulated Into the Grave." The subheading goes on, "They want us under their control, or they want us dead. It really doesn't matter to them as long as we're not causing trouble. Are the jabs the easiest way for them to gain compliance and depopulation?" (Rucker 2022, Title).

Notice that all these economic and political issues are usually blamed on unresponsive leadership: open borders and migrant crises, supply chain crises, food shortage crises, energy crises (with high gas prices), housing crisis, inflation, pandemic mandates, violence, social credit discussions, digital currency transition, climate change agenda, and so on.

These aren't simply from bad government; they are all part of The Great Reset as agenda-driven objectives in cooperation with the United Nations' goals. They are doing it on purpose. The globalization of America has been incrementally planned and systematically implemented for decades down to your local government. For example, the new unused bike lanes that reduce your city traffic lanes are only ridiculed as stupid government, but the goal is to eliminate automobile access. It has only recently become evident to the average player that something is wrong when so many painful changes suddenly impact them. Are you surprised at the recent turn of events these last few years?

> "Who controls the food supply controls the people.
>
> Who controls the energy can control whole continents.
>
> Who controls the money can control the world."
>
> - Henry Kissinger
> (The Thinking Conservative 2021, ¶ 1)

Although these Reset issues can be framed in political terms, politics is the short-term view. We are not living through simple government inaction or incompetence. Yes, the previous president managed things better, but he wasn't supposed to win in 2016. Every so often, a president gets in the way and partially rights the ship of State. Now that he is out of office, the trend toward Apocalypse continues apace. The America you've known will soon be only a historical memory. Bad things are coming to you on a pre-planned schedule with a goal of implementation by 2030.

How will they begin depopulating us? Let's count some ways: 1) food production facilities are being destroyed (mysteriously) with more than one hundred gone in the United States alone in the past three years, 2) the avian flu continually requiring millions of poultry preemptively destroyed and is now infecting cattle and humans, 3) drought across the United States leading to cattle culled and seventeen states canceling harvests in 2022 and 2023, 4) global rice production collapsing in 2022 and 2023, 5) vaccination-related deaths (allegedly) rising among those under sixty-five (suddenly dead with causes unknown), 6) vaccinations put in the food supply, 7) vaccination-related infertility and stillborn deaths rising, 8) euthanasia being implemented in lieu of elderly or disability care (à la Canada), 9) hazardous chemical railway and truck spills or fires including chemical plants and refineries burned in Ohio, South Carolina, Arizona, Nebraska, Illinois, Michigan, North Dakota, Texas, and Florida beginning early 2023 and continuing, 10) wildfires across the globe, 11) rising murder rates in cities and spreading to suburbs and exurbs, 12) climate change initiatives restricting farming and cattle production, 13) endless pandemics with DNA-altering vaccines, 14) abortion up to birth and beyond, 15) rising suicide rates among the young, 16) fentanyl deaths rising, and 17) incremental starvation and growing food and pharmacy deserts in our cities (Compson 2022, Check it Out section).

These ways do not include the impact of government policies on energy, both oil, gas and electric; water usage; digital currency; labor markets and property rights and the rise of artificial intelligence (AI), which will ensure the trend toward massive poverty. Add to this the constricting government control forming over all areas of our lives, and we get a deep sense of something inevitable, and it isn't good (Whitehead and Whitehead 2023, entire article; MacIntosh 2023, entire article).

We may not have to wait until 2030 to get depopulated from the game. America's population was predicted to decline 68.5 percent by 2025, with many Western nations seeing a decline of 25–70 percent (Hohmann 2023, ¶ 6). Journalist Leo Hohmann writes,

> All the globalist policies over the last three years are driving toward one thing, mass depopulation. Yes, they want to kill us. Until you understand that, you will never understand what's going on. You will never make sense of it.
>
> I know it's a hard pill to swallow, but reject it at your own risk. Those who live in denial will get duped, again. Many of those duped the first time lost their lives, or ended up with life-long health issues.
>
> I like to revert back to the analysis done by Deagel Corp. in 2014, forecasting massive global population declines out to the year 2025, especially in Western countries.
>
> Deagel's founder was a military contractor who had sources well positioned in the deep state. The Deagel Corporation is an offshoot of US military intelligence which collects data for high-level

decision-makers and prepares confidential briefing documents for agencies like the National Security Agency, the United Nations and the World Bank.

According to the Deagel forecast, America's population would plummet from just over 310 million in 2017 down to just 99 million by the end of 2025. Western European nations, especially the U.K. and Germany, were forecast to see similarly drastic decreases in population, as were Canada and Australia.

This population forecast was so controversial, showing population reductions of 68.5 percent in the United States (from 2017 levels) and between 25 and 70 percent for almost every Western European country, that the study mysteriously disappeared from Deagel's website in March 2021.

The COVID Blog suggests "5 reasons to believe the global population is already 1 billion people less than it was in January 2020" (COVID Blog 2023, ¶ 9–53).

1. Numerous countries reported record excess deaths, record-low births in 2021 or 2022.
2. There's no way of knowing exactly what's happening in China and India.
3. The kids die anonymously.
4. How many Dominique de Silvas are out there?
5. Polio and famine in Africa

We are now running a gauntlet from birth to the grave while getting handicapped by our government to stay alive as they pretend you are so silly to think such thoughts. Evidence? Conspiracy? It's simply coincidence, you see. Not our fault. Meanwhile, you will be dominated and made to comply. This is the way your global-invested government loves you. Who would have thought like that before the pandemic lockdowns?

Abortion. Planned Parenthood, an organization that has aligned itself with governments, has a historical mission to cull the earth of its "feeble-minded," "idiots" and "morons" through sterilization as advocated by its founder, Margaret Sanger, who helped inspire laws in thirty American states that led to the sterilization of over 60,000 such people. "In a letter to Clarence Gable in 1939, Sanger wrote:

"We do not want word to go out that we want to exterminate the Negro population, and the minister is the man who can straighten out that idea if it ever occurs to any of their more rebellious members" (Margaret Sanger commenting on the "Negro Project" in a letter to Gamble, Dec. 10, 1939; Grossu 2014, ¶ 4).

In 2022, abortion was the leading cause of death worldwide for the fourth year in a row (Foley 2023, ¶ 1). Walter Hoye, founder and president of the Issues4Life Foundation, referring to the 2008 Guttmacher Institute's fact sheet on abortions, issued statistics in a press conference in 2013, saying,

> Right now to give some of us just a perspective of the impact of abortion on demand in the black community, according to the archives of the Tuskegee Institute, from 1882 to 1968—86 years—the Ku Klux Klan lynched 3,446 Negroes. While it took the Klan 86 years to accomplish this, abortion on demand in America accomplishes that in less than 4 days [4,734 aborted black babies] (MSR News Online 2013, ¶ 8).

Abortions by Planned Parenthood since 1970 are more than 9.4 million. All abortions in the United States since 1973 are more than 64.5 million (Pavone 2023, ¶ 1), with more than 19 million of them being black babies (Number of Abortions n.d., Abortion Clock). In China, the induced abortion rate among married women ages 20–49 was 29 percent up to 2010. (Jiang et al. 2017, 2; Wang & Jiang 2022, ¶ 5).

The worldwide abortion number since 1980 is about 1.728 billion babies or roughly 21 percent of the current world population of 8 billion people (Number of Abortions n.d., Abortion Clock WorldOMeter n.d., Current Population). WHO estimates that the worldwide abortion rate is about 73 million per year or 200,000 per day (World Health Organization 2021, ¶ 1; Novielli 2022, ¶ 10).

> "Those who can make you believe absurdities, can make you commit atrocities"
>
> - Voltaire, 1765 essay (Olson W. 2020, ¶ 1)

The Radiance Foundation says that "In 2021, Planned Parenthood killed an estimated 360 black lives every single day" (Bomberger 2022, ¶ 3). "Abortion is the number one killer in the black community. It outnumbers the top twenty causes of death, combined" (Bomberger

2022, ¶ 5)! "For every 1,000 born alive, there were 1,226 killed by abortion in 2018. The black community is the *only* demographic where there are more induced deaths than births" (Bomberger 2022, ¶ 6). Margaret Sanger's Planned Parenthood's genocidal objectives are succeeding as planned as a healthcare service to the black community while enjoying political approval and protection (The Radiance Foundation 2022, ¶ 3).

The death of innocents becomes our legacy. What cannot be done effectively through sterilization and birth control can be done permanently through abortion. Were all these 1.73 billion aborted babies destined to be bad players, and if so, is an organization like Planned Parenthood actually a Pre-Crime Division that requires public funds?

THE PRE-APOCALYPSE

We are living in pre-Apocalypse times. The current game isn't nearly over even though we will soon reach the Apocalypse and the Battle of Armageddon. Although our gameplay may soon end with these events, the game itself will continue with remnants of players after that for another thousand years before it finally ends at the Game Master's great white throne judgment for all players. We will all be dead for about a thousand years before the lights finally go out on this game level.

There is a lot of attention given to the coming Apocalypse. A long buildup to it is taking place around us. The One described it like this:

> "When you hear of wars and disturbances [civil unrest, revolts, uprisings], do not panic; for these things must take place first, but the end will not come immediately."
>
> Then Jesus told them, "Nation will rise against nation and kingdom against kingdom. There will be violent earthquakes, and in various places famines and [deadly and devastating] pestilences (plagues, epidemics); and there will be terrible sights and great signs from heaven" (Luke 21:9–11 AMP).

He is describing wars like we have discussed, uprisings, famines, plagues, epidemics, and signs in the sky as a prelude to the real Apocalypse. With a casual glance at the game world around us since 2020, we saw the Hong Kong uprising that filled the news, earthquake clusters and increasing earthquake events, increasing volcanic activity, the giant locust plagues devastating Africa and central Asia with coming famines, the coronavirus that impacted local and national economies, talk of super-moons, blood moons, wolf moon, worm moon, and asteroid near misses and the all-encompassing climate change stories describing how the earth is getting stressed.

Preparation for the Great Reset and the Apocalypse includes the construction of SMART cities and is much further along than we realized. Former twenty-five-year Silicon Valley engineer Aman Jabbi said that "SMART Cities" worldwide are being turned into concentration camps.

> [T]he globalists already have the laws and technological infrastructure in place to convert our Republic into a technocratic slave state.
>
> Some of the most advanced elements of this infrastructure, as Jabbi points out, are in states like Florida and Georgia and other red states.
>
> We must recognize that these are the very same tools and products that make our busy 21st century lives so convenient, so efficient and entertaining. And so we buy them on cue, we upgrade them on cue, we hand over our biometric data on cue, until one day we will wake up and realize we have convenienced ourselves and entertained ourselves right into a digital gulag from which there is no escape.
>
> This is how the globalists intend on breaking the backs of free Americans. They will do it through our finances, through the healthcare system and through the entertainment systems. Digital ID cards disguised as "health passports" or "SMART Health Cards," will be required to work a job, to access the Internet and the coming digital bank accounts or digital wallets. The convergence of all these systems will make sure, in the words of U.N. Agenda 2030, "no person gets left behind."
>
> By the time most people wake up and see that they have walked into a trap, it will be too late. They will have all your data, they will know everything about you, your strengths, your weaknesses, your vulnerabilities.

As Jabbi says, "You can deny reality but you can't deny the consequences." Jabbi gives what I believe is the most comprehensive description of the Beast System that I have seen anywhere.

If you pay attention, you will see hundreds of these LED light poles lining streets and highways, and in many cases, they are retrofitted with surveillance cameras and speakers for listening. Jabbi also talks about drones [sic] charging stations being set up and how drones might be weaponized against citizens.

Many of these LED Smart lights are outfitted with what's called **PUKE Ray technology**, which can be weaponized and used to incapacitate humans. This is a military technology being applied in our cities for potential use against civilians, courtesy of the U.S. Department of Homeland Security.

Jabbi describes on video "an extremely invasive technology being set up in SMART Cities—from license-plate readers to SMART Lights and SMART Poles to SMART cars and SMART neighborhoods, SMART homes and SMART appliances—all connected to 5G and wirelessly communicating with each other" (Hohmann 2022, ¶ 8–9, 14–17, 20, 25–26, 30).

Everything is spying on us: our streets, cars, cellphones, watches, banks, appliances, digital thermostats, and every SMART device we use, with artificial intelligence connecting all the dots (Crone 2023b, entire video; Snyder 2024, ¶ 1). Mind reading technology is already available and is being configured for your personal devices (S. Miller 2024, ¶ 6–11). The time when you were your own person doing anything you wanted with no oversight or accountability is practically over.

Another term associated with SMART cities is a fifteen-minute city. These are cities where all you need for work or play is a fifteen-minute walk from home. Journalist Lara Logan describes them like this: "A '15-minute city' is a self-sustaining concentration camp. And the guards are Artificial Intelligence. 'And you'll never be happier.' Wake up" (Rucker 2023, ¶ 3).

For six months in 2020, powerful police spy planes circled Baltimore for 12 hours a day, capturing nearly every movement of the city's residents.

A group of grassroots community activists sued the Baltimore Police Department over the program. They argued, in part, that the powerful technology violated their Fourth Amendment rights. In other words, if police wanted to collect that kind of information, they needed a warrant (Winkley 2023, ¶ 1–2).

San Diego installed more than 3,000 smart street lights by 2020. "Initially sold to the public in 2016 as cost- and energy-saving lights, the smart streetlights also included high-tech sensors equipped with cameras, microphones and other technology. The fact that the lights had cameras didn't really enter the public consciousness until last year" (Figueroa 2020, ¶ 9–10, 28).

Before you know it, the infrastructure to monitor you is in place and ready for activation or already in use. Such intrusion for the purpose of tracking and controlling you will only grow more pervasive.

The artificial intelligence (AI) guards include all your devices, home appliances, vehicles, streetlights, digital ID card, and more. Don't think you'll be going anywhere any time you wish. The objective is to keep you safely on your own fifteen-minute turf.

These events are all a warmup to the major events of the Apocalypse, which will have its own three series of even greater disasters before the earth-destroying final showdown between the Serpent and the Game Master.

Apocalypse time sequence. The Manual book of Revelation is also called the Apocalypse of John, which refers to the time frame of the latter stages of the Game of Life rather than a single event. The timing of the Apocalypse has drawn interest and speculation for the last 2,000 years, starting when the One's disciples asked Him when all the bad stuff would happen and what would be the sign of His return (Matt. 24:3; Mark 13:3–4; Luke 21:7).

The Apocalypse is usually described as a two-part, seven-year scenario where the tribulation period begins. Three-and-a-half years later, the great tribulation kicks in with intensified global catastrophes, ending in the seventh year of tribulation. Although members have been waiting for the imminent return of the One for two millennia, many believe we are now living in the pre-tribulation time, where global unrest is ramping up into an era of general lawlessness (LT Radio n.d., entire source) (Matt. 24:3–14).

The sign that kicked off the countdown to the Apocalypse was what the One called the lesson of the fig tree when it begins to bud. It is generally agreed in the evangelical community that He meant the forming of the state of Israel in 1948. The next marker year, 1967, marked the time when the Jews gathered from across the nations. He said the generation at that event would not pass away until everything was fulfilled (Matt. 24:32–35; Mark 13:28–31; Luke 21:29–33).

A generation in the Manual may be considered 40 years, 70 years, 100, or 120 years. The 70-year mark was 2018 (from 1948) or 2037 from the 1967 marker, and the tribulation has not started. The 120-year mark is the year 2068 or 2087, when everything will have been fulfilled, so many players living today will very likely witness the events of the Apocalypse. Either way, it doesn't seem to add up that we will make it to the year 2100 (Hanley 2018, entire article). The tricky thing, though, is trying to stay alive until it is over. Global depopulation is part of the scenario and is coming to a continent near you. With a global population of about 8 billion in 2022, at least 4 billion players will not survive from only two of the apocalyptic events.

Accounting for prophesied blood moons and other signs of the end times, various scholars of end times prophecy place the Apocalypse era starting anywhere from 2025 to 2050. The speed at which our world system has become unrecognizable since the year 2000 seems to make this plausible.

The rapture. The doctrine of the Rapture, a sudden catching away of members to heaven as portrayed in the *Left Behind* book and movie series, and the following seven years of the Apocalypse period, is the scenario around which the following Apocalypse events are framed in this book. Those who do not hold to this sequential set of events point to John Darby as the source of this recent kiosk doctrine that began around 1830. The Interactive Bible website, hosted by those affiliated with the Church of Christ kiosk, make the following introductory statements on this topic:

> Rapture doctrine is one of the most recent "new doctrines" in the history of the Church. The only doctrine more recent is the invention of the sinner's prayer for salvation by Billy Sunday in 1930, which was made popular by Billy Graham in 1935.

> The fact that John Nelson Darby invented the pre-tribulation rapture doctrine around 1830 AD is unquestionably true. All attempts to find evidence of this wild doctrine before 1830 have failed, with a single exception: Morgan Edwards wrote a short essay as a college paper for Bristol Baptist College in Bristol England in 1744 where he confused

the second coming with the first resurrection of Revelation 20 and described a 'pre-tribulation' rapture. However Edwards' ideas, which he admitted were brand new and never before taught, had no influence in the modern population of the false doctrine. That prize to [sic] goes to Darby.

Prior to 1830, no church taught it in their creed, catechism or statement of faith.

Darby has had a profound impact on religion today, since Darby's 'secret rapture' false doctrine has infected most conservative, evangelical churches. While the official creeds and statements of faith of many churches either reject or are silent about Rapture [sic], neither do they openly condemn this doctrine of a demon from the pulpit.

While not all dispensationalists believe in the Rapture. [sic] All those who teach the Rapture also believe in premillennialism. Both groups use Israel's modern statehood status of 1948 to be a beginning of a countdown to the end.

All premillennialists, rapturists and dispensationalists alive today believe the Bible reveals the general era of when Christ will return. The date setters of the 1800's (Seventh-day Adventists who are date setting premillennialists who reject the rapture, Jehovah's Witnesses who have set many dates) based their predictions upon speculative arrangements of numbers and chronologies in the Bible. Today's date setters without exception wrongly believe that Israel gaining state hood [sic] in 1948 fulfilled Bible prophecy and that Christ would return within one generation.

There are two kinds of premillennialists: Those "Date setters" and "Date Teasers." "Date setters," set specific dates which are in fact a countdown clock to the extinction of their own ministries. (William Miller, Charles Russell, Ronald Weinland, Harold Camping, etc.) "Date teasers," share the same rhetoric of urgency that the "end is very soon," but refuse to lock into a specific date (Jack Van Impe,

Hal Lindsay, Tim LaHaye, Pentecostals, Baptists, Grant Jefferies, Christadelphians.) (Rapture n.d., ¶ 1–7).

Pastor Billy Crone explains that the rapture event will be blamed on aliens who took away the first wave of subjects.

> Channeler Thelma Terrel, who goes by her spiritual name "Tuella," wrote a book called *Project World Evacuation*, and here's what she shares. "The Great Evacuation will come upon the world very suddenly. The flash of emergency events will be as a lightning that flashes in the sky. Do not be concerned nor unduly upset if you do not participate in this first temporary lift-up of souls who serve with us. This merely means that your action in the plan is elsewhere, and you will be taken for your instructions or will receive them in some other manner. Do not take any personal affront if you are not alerted or are not a participant in this first phase of our plan. Your time will come later, and these instructions are not necessary for you at this time" (Crone 2023a, min. 55:14) (1 Thess. 4:16–17).

You should know that there will not be a second evacuation plan in a rapture scenario. That is a deception. Instead, it will be judgment time. There are four major views of eschatology (Logos 2022, ¶ 17). Whether you agree with a premillennial rapture or not, the general public is more aware of eschatology portraying a rapture event followed by a seven-year Apocalypse countdown scenario than any other explanation of end times events. I use this context simply because it is the most widely known explanation by the general public.

One final remark on the countdown of the ages is that the Manual says that 1,000 years is like a day for the Game Master.

> And by the same word, the present heavens and earth have been stored up for fire. They are being kept for the day of judgment, when ungodly people will be destroyed.

> But you must not forget this one thing, dear friends: A day is like a thousand years to the Lord, and a thousand years is like a day. The Lord isn't really being slow about his promise, as some people think.

> No, he is being patient for your sake. He does not want anyone to be destroyed, but wants everyone to repent (2 Pet. 3:7–9 NLT).

The current game cycle started with a seven-day week.

> So the creation of the heavens and the earth and everything in them was completed. On the seventh day God had finished his work of creation, so he rested from all his work. And God blessed the seventh day and declared it holy, because it was the day when he rested from all his work of creation (Gen. 2:1–3 NLT).

For those who follow a six-thousand-year timeline from the creation of the current game to the present day, the time of man (whose number is six) is coming to an end, and the Sabbath rest will soon begin with the 1,000-year reign of the One. This would make the current game cycle a one-week event for the Game Master (Bible Study n.d., ¶ 1).

We are very quickly reaching the final climax of this game level's six-day run of the time of man with the Serpent at the helm. Most guests will not survive this first climactic round of conflict between the Serpent and the One, which ends at the Battle of Armageddon. The seventh day of 1,000 years of peace follows that before it is punctuated with a Battle of Armageddon 2.0, which ends in Lights Out for this game level at the Game Master's great white throne judgment on the game. Buckle up because your game experience will soon become much worse than you have imagined.

The Apocalypse

Since the trend toward violence and increasing natural disasters is escalating, it is appropriate to briefly describe how the game will finally end. Even though a divine judgment may be executed using a person, nation, or natural event, all these scenarios are still credited to the hand of the Game Master by His decree.

When the Game Master brought judgment in various instances through the Manual, like Noah's flood, Sodom and Gomorrah, Jericho, the fall of empires like those successively prophesied about Babylon, Assyria, Egypt, Greece, Rome, and so on, common elements in many of these situations are that "nature" was "harnessed" to complete the decree, or it was carried out by other players, where, in one case, the Game Master called the pagan King Nebuchadnezzar His servant and sent word to all the surrounding nations and especially to the stubborn king of Judah to surrender to His servant Nebuchadnezzar to avoid destruction. Of course, he didn't listen (Jer. 27:5–18).

According to the One, increasing violence and natural disasters across the globe are only precursors to the actual Apocalypse. What we see around us and whatever economic or personal hardship we experience from it is not the big stuff that's coming.

The raging debate about climate change is the nonreligious explanation for the countdown to the end of the game before ushering in a time of peace. Both sides, religious and secular, are probably correct that there is at least one generation currently living today that will be around when the game reaches Armageddon. Both sides also have a somewhat similar version of how the Game of Life will finally end—badly.

But for all their hysteria, the climate change proponents greatly underestimate just how badly the game will really end. The Game Master explicitly describes a vastly worse scenario, and He concludes that without His direct intervention, no players will survive. That, my friends, is truly apocalyptic (Matt. 24:22–24).

Various lists of apocalyptic scenarios on the Internet explain how different types of disasters could individually and theoretically cause life on earth to end. There's usually an action film available to depict them. According to the Manual, the timeframe of the Apocalypse will include a combination of such events from a possible asteroid strike to volcanoes to earthquakes and tsunamis, and so on, in addition to all the man-made and Serpent-infused horrors. For brevity, this account leaves out major players, plot twists and some significant events.

Let's start with some non-Manual descriptions. The New Age book, *Book II: The Earth Changes*, chapter 4, refers to "Earth Changes" for the cleansing of Mother Earth that involve a tilt of its axis resulting in natural global catastrophes. This is quite a sterile, gentle phrase for such a horrific time (Sartorius and Sartorius 2022, chapter 4).

The Georgia Guidestones, also known as the American Stonehenge, is a monument anonymously built east of Atlanta, Georgia, in 1980 (and bombed in 2022) that outlines ten guiding principles in eight languages:

1. Maintain humanity under 500,000,000 in perpetual balance with nature.
2. Guide reproduction wisely—improving fitness and diversity.
3. Unite humanity with a living new language.
4. Rule passion—faith—tradition—and all things with tempered reason.
5. Protect people and nations with fair laws and just courts.
6. Let all nations rule internally, resolving external disputes in a world court.
7. Avoid petty laws and useless officials.

8. Balance personal rights with social duties.
9. Prize truth—beauty—love—seeking harmony with the infinite.
10. Be not a cancer on the earth—Leave room for nature—Leave room for nature ("Georgia Guidestones" n.d., ¶ 18).

Haven't we heard talk lately about social duties trumping personal rights? Something about being selfish. There is no one to directly associate with these guidelines, so why make a statement at all? This gives rise to speculation that it is the 10 Commandments of the Illuminati, assuming they exist. Perhaps. If you are aware that the Serpent is the prince of this world system who spreads evil influence over the nations of the earth, then the possibility of a diabolical source is understandable and logical. Notice item number ten on the Guidestones is a call to protect nature, sounding like the call for you to do your part about climate change, except that in this context, it appears that you are the "cancer" on the earth.

Two points about item number one are: 1) how do "they" propose to reduce the population of the game world to below half a billion players? That requires the death of 7.5 billion players. As mentioned earlier, Agenda 21 and Agenda 2030 are current roadmaps for that. And 2) if you read the apocalyptic book of Revelation, by the time it gets to the seventh guardian sounding his trumpet, the game world's population will have been decreased by at least 50 percent from only two disaster series: the fourth seal with its Pale Rider who kills 25 percent of all players with war, famine, plagues and wild animals; and the sixth trumpet that releases the Four Angels who assemble a monstrous army of 200 million players to kill 33 percent of all players with fire, smoke, and sulfur (nuclear?) (Rev. 6:8; 9:14–21).

Journalist Leo Hohmann reminds us that, "There is no more efficient way to depopulate than through war, famine, and plagues. Isn't it interesting that all three of these time-tested methods of murder are in play right now" (Fielding 2024, ¶ 24)? Some news sites say that the COVID-19 pandemic and its mandates are a practice run for global depopulation and total government control of your choices and life—out of an abundance of caution for your health and well-being, of course (Toledo 2022, ¶ 1–5). The pandemic has also tilted the balance toward global food supply shortages, increasing the odds of widespread famine for all nations. The weekly destruction of America's food production facilities since 2021 reached one hundred by mid-2022 (Hoft 2022, ¶ 2). It has since continued worldwide and will soon bring that famine home to all of us. It seems our benevolent governments are facilitating things for the Pale Rider of the Apocalypse (Rev. 6:7–8).

> Let's pause to reflect on the Agenda 21 and 2030 efforts toward depopulation and the disparaging remarks by world leaders who describe you as a cancer on the earth in light of climate change that we have discussed. Your worth to the Serpent's team is nothing; you and your fellow guest players' very existence is a problem for the Serpent. To him and his world leaders, you are ultimately better off dead.
> Contrast this with the Game Master Who said that He loves all His players so much that sent the One to rescue you from perishing, Jn 3:16 and that He is not willing that any player should perish, but instead come to Him for everlasting life before it's too late. 2 Pt 3:7-9; Ps 95:8; Heb 3:7-9, 14-16; 4:6-8

Our discussion has not even included the rest of Revelation's "seven seals" (which include the four horsemen of the Apocalypse) and "seven trumpets" judgments on mankind: aggression, world war, famine, 33 percent of all land plant life destroyed, 33 percent of sea life destroyed, 33 percent of fresh water contaminated, 33 percent of light from the sun and stars removed, a minion locust-like swarm tormenting players for five months, an earthquake, and hailstorm (Rev. 6–11).

During this time, there will be incredible conflict among the nations and civil unrest that are currently in the formative stages around us. The Game Master will finally send out a personal call by His guardians for all players to switch sides to the Game Master before it's too late, with another guardian following behind them to explain the torment of those who stay on the Serpent's team, including those who take the mark of the Beast on their forehead or hand—they cannot buy or sell without it (Rev. 14:6–13).

Mark of the Beast. The Beast will be a popular leader who drives the global agenda during the Apocalypse. The mark of the Beast is the name of the Beast or the number of his name (666) on a player's right hand or forehead. It is widely thought to be a chip implant that could be an ID connected to the coming new global currency. All your government and financial and social information would be stored on that chip, which would be used for transactions and societal interaction. This is similar to the social score phone apps that China currently uses to control various populations. What you see happening around you with the use of this technology is simply a precursor to that mark. Getting UPC tattoos or chip implants right now are voluntary and isolated to compatible transactions with individual companies. All governments will make the mark of the Beast compulsory and universally mandated.

Dalton Thomas, the president and founder of Frontier Alliance International (FAI), says that rather than technology as is traditionally thought, the mark of the Beast could very well be Islamic and Jihadist in nature that simply identifies those who have the right to buy or sell. He details how and when this particular mark will be deployed. It will be rolled out at the final forty-two months before Armageddon when Jerusalem is besieged and occupied by foreign armies. The Beast will declare war on all members and will crush them in an era of full martyrdom. Being a member in this game level event will have the likelihood of death. There will be military domination and a refugee crisis. Global worship of the Beast will be mandated. This is the main issue; it is about worship and control, not technology. These events are the backdrop to the implementation of the mark (D. Thomas 2020, min. 48:24–1:01:08) (Zech. 14:1–4; Rev. 12:11; Rev. 13).

Game Over Tripwire: *If you worship the Beast and his image and accept his Mark, you are doomed to the Lake of Fire. In that moment, your choice and chance to become a member is gone. The pressure to take the Mark will be so great because you will need it to stay alive in your SMART city concentration camp. The Game Master says that staying alive will be the least of your worries as you are cast into the Lake of Fire. If you've been a good citizen, following community expectations all your life, and going along with society's trends and mandates, what are the odds that you'll finally rise up to buck the system, listen to the Game Master, and refuse the mark? You're better off taking your chances siding with the Game Master Who restores life.*

This is why the fear among members is so great lest they somehow accidentally take the Mark and lose the bonus round, but this will be a purposeful choice. Without the Mark, you will be homeless and starving, so your game time outlook is dim either way. Your chance of finding a black market is slim. Your phone and every Smart device you own are already tracking you and telling your secrets. Noncompliant players who refuse the Mark will be ostracized or killed. Just look at the rage we've seen against those who refused the COVID-19 vaccines. That was with generally voluntary compliance. The Game Master declares that members who die from this point on are blessed.

> "This calls for patient endurance on the part of the people of God who keep his commands and remain faithful to Jesus" (Rev. 14:12 NIV).

Along with all these fourteen devastating calamities come the Big Ones from the "seven bowls": boils and sores, 100 percent of sea life destroyed, 100 percent of fresh water destroyed, the sun burns through the atmosphere, scorching everything, the game world goes dark, then the mother of all earthquakes the game world had ever seen since players were on the earth occurs with all the islands overwhelmed and with a horrific hailstorm, having every hailstone weighing 130 pounds (1 talent, 58.9 kg) (Rev. 16:17–21).

ARMAGEDDON–JUDGMENT DAY–THE DAY OF THE LORD

Then it's time for the big showdown between Serpent and the Game Master. Now it's "High Noon" for Planet Earth as Ground Zero in the war between good and evil. The One remarked that unless those days should get shortened, no players will be left, but they'll be shortened for the sake of the members (Matt. 24:22). Speaking to fellow Israelites about this day, master prophet Amos said,

> Woe (judgment is coming) to you who desire the day of the LORD [expecting rescue from the Gentiles]! Why would you want the day of the LORD? It is darkness (judgment) and not light [and rescue and prosperity]; It is as if a man runs from a lion [escaping one danger] And a bear meets him [so he dies anyway], Or goes home, and leans with his hand against the wall And a snake bites him. Will not the day of the LORD be darkness, instead of light, Even very dark with no brightness in it? (Amos 5:18–20 AMP).

Some say the sixth trumpet and sixth bowl poured out in Revelation chapters 9 and 16 both refer to the same event. However, the trumpets and bowls should be viewed as simultaneous events. One is the spiritual perspective, and the other is the real-life perspective (Bowman 2022, 91–92).

The battle of Armageddon at the Plain of Megiddo in Israel is the climax location of the Apocalypse. The Serpent will collect a massive army of 200 million from the kings of the East to finally wrest control of the game. The One, the Lamb of God, Who is the Lion of the tribe of Judah, will descend from the clouds with His guardians and the members from the game's timeline plus those who were raptured away during the Apocalypse phase. They will confront the army of the Serpent.

The Serpent's army will be crushed with what appears to be neutron weaponry.

> "And the LORD will send a plague on all the nations that fought against Jerusalem. Their people will become like walking corpses, their flesh rotting away. Their eyes will rot in their sockets, and their tongues will rot in their mouths" (Zech. 4:12 NLT).

The Serpent's leaders who deceived the players (the Beast and the False Prophet) will be captured and tossed alive into the Lake of Fire, the army remnant will be killed, and the Serpent boss chained in the bottomless pit for 1,000 years and sealed to not deceive the nations during that time (Rev. 19–20) (Ames 2020, entire article;

Figgs 2018, image; "What Is the Battle of Armageddon?" n.d., entire article; Nito 2014, entire article; Prophecy News Update 2011, entire article).

Exit question: How many of these apocalyptic events do you think you can survive? It seems we'd stand a much better chance of living through climate change. Golden tickets are still available, and one has your name on it. *Make sure you RSVP to the Game Master.*

Post Apocalypse

This is the source for where world leaders get the idea of creating a 1,000-year empire. Following Armageddon, the One will set up His kingdom in the game world and rule with an iron rod for 1,000 years. All the members will rule with Him. There will be enforced peace across the game world. This millennium will be a recovery period for remaining players who survived the apocalyptic events. The game environment will also have a chance for nature to stabilize once again (Rev. 2:27; 20). The best way to ensure you can make it to the post-Apocalypse phase is to become a member player. Have you ever wondered why our governments want to kill us now since we still have a thousand more years remaining of this game?

Armageddon: round two

You didn't really think this was over, did you? After 1,000 years and many generations from now, the old Boss returns. The Serpent is released from the bottomless pit for a season so he can deceive the nations once again and persuade them to throw out the government of the One. Those who were born during the thousand-year era will have never experienced the wiles of the Serpent. Many will be deceived, and this time, he gathers an army that blows past the size of his previous 200 million-player army and will number like the sand of the sea (Rev. 20:7–8).

This army will be summarily destroyed by the Game Master Himself with fire from heaven (Sodom and Gomorrah style?) (Gen. 19:24–29). The Serpent will be hurled into the Lake of Fire with the Beast and the False Prophet to be tormented forever and ever (Rev. 20:9–10). The Game Master will set up His great white throne of judgment field headquarters to judge all the guest players, living and dead. Master player John explains:

> And I saw a great white throne and the one sitting on it. The earth and sky fled from his presence, but they found no place to hide. I saw the dead, both great and small, standing before God's throne. And the books were opened, including the Book of Life. And the dead were

judged according to what they had done, as recorded in the books. The sea gave up its dead, and death and the grave gave up their dead. And all were judged according to their deeds. Then death and the grave were thrown into the lake of fire. This lake of fire is the second death. And anyone whose name was not found recorded in the Book of Life was thrown into the lake of fire (Rev. 20:11–15 NLT).

Game over

This game level ends roughly a thousand years from now with the great white throne judgment. Because every prophecy in the Manual regarding the current Game of Life will have been fulfilled to that point, this current game with its earth and heaven (surface and atmosphere) will then be destroyed with fire (2 Pet. 3:7–14). The game world gets reset, and the bonus round now begins with a new heaven and a new earth for member players only. The new Jerusalem city descends from heaven (Larken 1920, 434–446) (Rev. 21:1–2).

> **THIS GAME LEVEL ENDS ROUGHLY A THOUSAND YEARS FROM NOW WITH THE GREAT WHITE THRONE JUDGMENT.**

Summary: the World

This is a very long section, where most of it focuses on the world system, those governments and influential organizations that we see and know, and those clandestine international ones that prefer to remain anonymous but who wield great influence over our lives and futures. Not all the topics that will cause harm to us could be covered.

Lord Acton summarized this current world situation in these two ways: "Power tends to corrupt and absolute power corrupts absolutely." "And remember, where you have a concentration of power in a few hands, all too frequently, men with the mentality of gangsters get control. History has proven that" (Dalberg-Acton n.d., ¶ 1–2).

5. The Flesh

Most players would say they lead responsible lives, earn an honest living, and raise their children to be good citizens. Being comfortable enough in life to lack an interest in choosing the Game Master's team is perhaps the lowest threshold the Serpent needs to persuade guests to give up the bonus round. The consequence is death with hell to pay at the end of the game, ultimately a bad thing, but such a distant and vague concept when satisfaction with life and family is here and now.

The "flesh" can refer to the "lusts of the flesh" as mentioned in the Manual. This flesh goes beyond our physical body and is part of the passions of the world system, along with the "lust of the eyes" and the "pride of life" (1 John 2:15–17).

In times past, those whom we consider less responsible in their habits were described as "given to excess." Nowadays, we say they have a disorder. This is because the things we excessively indulge in can cause bad things to befall us. This should be self-explanatory, but let's continue.

Guest players are more likely to reign in their fleshly inclinations based on what may be good social behavior or by what will keep them from getting arrested. Members engage in a much more fierce inner struggle with the flesh because those inclinations are at war with the Game Master. Derek Prince explains how the rebellion of our fleshly nature can prevent professing members from reaching the bonus round.

> Galatians 5:24. Those who are Christ's have crucified the flesh, with its passions and desires. What's the deliverance from there? Crucified the what? The flesh. What are you delivered from there? The flesh, that's right.
>
> We have to define what the flesh is. The flesh is not your physical body. It's the nature that you received when you were born in your physical body. It's essentially the nature of a rebel, it has all sorts of desires and feelings that are not in line with God's will and are not subject to God.
>
> God's remedy is crucifixion. You see, as far as God's concerned, the crucifixion . . . Well, let me say a little bit more about the nature of the flesh. Notice that phrase there, first of all. Galatians 5:24: Those who are Christ's have crucified the flesh, with its passions and desires. That's not a denomination but those are the people who belong to God. It's not Baptists or Pentecostals or Presbyterians. It's those who are Christ's. What's the mark, what separates them out from the others . . . They have crucified the flesh.
>
> If you turn for a moment to 1 Corinthians 15:23, you'll find the people that Jesus is coming back for. Do you want to know who they are? It's not the Presbyterians, nor the Baptists, nor the Pentecostals, nor the Catholics. It says in verse 23 about the resurrection:

Each one in his own order: Christ the first-fruits [He's already risen], afterward those who are Christ's at His coming. Who is He coming for? Those who are Christ's. What's the mark of those who are Christ's? Galatians 5:24, they have crucified the flesh. So who is Jesus coming back for? Christians who have crucified the flesh with its passions and desires.

So now you know how you have to qualify. We had a lady in our church in London years ago, whenever she prayed she said, "Lord, help us to remember it'll be too late to be getting ready." I have never forgotten that. You can't leave it to the last moment; you've left it too late. You have to have already dealt with the flesh. You see, this nature that we're talking about is in direct opposition to the will and the way of God.

Romans 8:7–8, Paul says the carnal mind. Now the word carnal is the same as fleshly, it's just a different word derived from a Latin root. The fleshly mind is enmity against God; for it is not subject to the law of God, nor indeed can be; so then those who are in the flesh cannot please God.

Those who are controlled by their fleshly nature cannot please God. There is no way you can do it. You can try as hard as you will, you can be as religious as you please but you cannot do it.

And then in Galatians again, 5:17, Paul brings out the same thought. Galatians 5:17: For the flesh lusts against the Spirit [the Spirit of God], and the Spirit against the flesh; and these are contrary one to another. Your natural fleshly desires are contrary to the way, and the will of the Spirit of God. So that you do not do the things that you wish. Maybe that's a revelation to some of you.

You set out with all sorts of good intentions, you consecrate yourself, you go forward at the altar of the church, pray a nice prayer and say, "That's it." And about a month later you say how could I have ever got so far away from what I intended to be and do? The answer is the flesh lusts against the Spirit. You have in you an enemy of God and that enemy has to be dealt with. You cannot lead the Christian life successfully until the flesh has been dealt with in you.

Paul had that problem. Perhaps that will encourage you. It's not a problem just a few people have, it's universal. You need to read Romans 7 right through sometime and see Paul's personal struggles against the flesh.

My observation is the most dedicated Christians and the ones whom God intends to use the most are the ones who have the main struggles. Pentecostals used to have the attitude, I think it's changed. I've been a Pentecostal for 48 years. The attitude used to be you get saved, baptized in water, baptized in the Spirit, speak in tongues, and you have no more problems.

How many of you know it doesn't work that way? Wish it did. I know it doesn't. Why? Because it didn't work with me. And furthermore, I pastored Pentecostals long enough to find out it isn't like that. The reason is the flesh. It's an enemy, an enemy of God (Prince 2024, min 27:24).

Appetite

Appetites can include a desire for, a liking for, or a craving for food or pleasures of life. A healthy appetite would be characterized by moderate consumption of foods or pleasures that, in measured doses, are helpful to our health and well-being or not harmful to us. An unhealthy appetite includes too many of those things that are either helpful or unhelpful to us, transitioning to an obsession where our ability to control them has been lost and where they are no longer conducive to good health, good reason or logic, common sense, moral codes, or lawful practices.

Addictions such as excessively consuming things like alcohol and drugs, whether legal or illegal or prescribed, can harm oneself or others. Addictions to activities can cause discomfort or harm to oneself or other players or cross the threshold of societal acceptance. For example, several gamers have died from playing video games for up to three weeks straight or who resorted to stealing and killing over games (Nguyen 2017, full article).

Curse of poverty. While this title would be more appropriate in the section on curses, the effects of a curse of poverty may reveal themselves in the appetites of the flesh. A curse of poverty or a continual sense of inadequate resources can attach to a person on the spiritual level. It could be triggered by a short, intense period of great need or a prolonged period of poverty and hardship.

The result is that a player affected by this difficult time of life develops a persistent need to indulge himself or collect resources greatly beyond what is needed for sustenance or survival. Examples could be the consistent tendency to eat more than being comfortably filled, like being in the "clean plate" club, stocking the pantry or freezer so full that there is no reasonable way to clear things out in four to six months or keeping them so full that food and goods cannot get properly cycled out before they expire.

Another clue could be hoarding goods and supplies, not for natural disasters like government agencies encourage players to do, but because of a fear or feeling of running out of them or not having enough. Many of our great-grandparents who went through the American Great Depression and the Dust Bowl of the 1930s never recovered from the need to scrimp and save, and we heard stories of houses full of junk or mattresses stuffed with hundreds of thousands of dollars while they lived modest and even meager lives.

Some of their tendencies have been passed on to current generations, and these tendencies could have a spiritual root as a spirit of poverty. A spirit of poverty can affect every economic level, from the poorest to the richest players. Personal hardship is very difficult to overcome and develop into a balanced life even when our situation improves.

Charms

The pleasures of life charm or mesmerize us to stay in the Serpent's kingdom where self-indulgence is our reward. In the context of the Manual, riotous living (extravagant or dissolute—indifference to moral restraints) leads to pain and deprivation where others who are worse than you can take you to the cleaners, leaving you enslaved to them and utterly miserable. You may have heard stories where young players go on an overseas holiday of freedom and fun, then get arrested and potentially imprisoned for life in another country because they were allegedly returning home as a drug mule. Most insist they were framed.

This seems like an odd entry, but the long view is that, according to the Manual, the "pleasures of sin" are very real and desirable, but they are not fulfilling and only last for a season, as described about Master player Moses' choice to "suffer affliction with the people of God, considering the reproach of Christ greater riches than the treasures of Egypt" (Heb. 11:24–26 KJV). Our perspective on what is the purpose of our gameplay drives the choices we make.

The Manual is clear that life in the Serpent's kingdom has great advantages for our comfort and indulgence. After all, who, in their right mind, would want to turn down the actual riches of Egypt? That had to be huge since Moses lived like a son in the Pharaoh's palace. In the Manual, Egypt is always symbolically equated with the Serpent's realm and his ways of the world system, so symbolism is also going on here. The text is not saying that the riches themselves or using them were a game violation.

We may hear religious players talk about sin as though it were always dirty and undesirable. If that were the whole story, fewer players would choose obvious game violations. But the point of sin, before it becomes vile, is alluring with real pleasure and fun, holding and even delivering on the promise of indulgence or comforts and security through its early stages. Some players live to regret their years of wild living, while others never seem to tire of it.

Attitudes

Attitudes lead to actions. How we think about others affects the way we treat them. Discrimination toward those who are different from us or our culture can be mild, where players are ignored, common courtesies are not extended, or they can escalate to the degree where those who are not wanted in the neighborhood are verbally harassed, threatened, or suffer property damage or personal injury.

Civil rights laws were enacted to discourage discrimination between people groups and cultures when they mix in the larger community settings. When one group is pitted against another or one people group is perceived to have a favored status to the exclusion of what may be considered fair, hard feelings can develop. These issues can be artificially driven by failed government policy meant to generate a desired outcome for a particular group to the exclusion of others or by cultural norms where differing homogenous groups have not previously had to mingle together in close proximity.

Examples can include immigrants suddenly taking over neighborhoods or relocated refugees displacing town folk. Whether these are bad things is debatable, but the point is that learning to get along with different cultures can be an uncomfortable experience for those who never envisioned it happening to them. This "melting pot" process may include tension and misunderstandings.

Whatever the reason, when players feel threatened in how they wish to conduct themselves comfortably, cultures clash and conditions form where isolated incidents can escalate to greater perceived or even very real violence. On a regional level, this seems to be a persistent issue across the Middle East, with a specific example of how the function of the Iraqi government finally failed because of distrust among the various religious and ethnic groups. Afghanistan is a country that can be described as being forever in turmoil among all the cultural factions within its borders. It can also happen locally now in our own cities.

Stronghold

A stronghold is a negative spiritual addiction or vice that has a rock-solid grip on your mind and displays itself as an addiction or compulsion in your life through your habits by the things you say and do and in the attitudes you have.

The Manual only refers to it briefly by name (2 Cor. 10:4) but describes its grip on us quite extensively. The concept is typically overlooked in the religious world as an issue that merits specific attention and treatment.

The intersection of a spiritual stronghold and its manifestation in our life begins in our mind through unbelief and fear. It originates and operates spiritually as a curse but can be fortified through minion activity as an addiction having physical attributes, which leave us virtually powerless to break it. As a curse, it can cross generational boundaries, where the children follow the path of their parents even if they don't want to go that way.

It does not matter if you are a member or guest player. It does not matter if you have ever heard of strongholds or not. It does not matter if you don't believe in them. Any time you hit a spiritual tripwire by what you do or what is done to you, you can activate a baser element of life or a curse against you that eventually becomes a defining characteristic of you or your personality. Therapy and prescription drugs may be part of an addictive treatment plan since a spiritual stronghold affects any combination of mental, emotional, or physical health issues. However, once it has a settled foundation in your life, it is usually treated as a compulsion or an illness with no cure.

For example, a recovering alcoholic is rarely described as a former alcoholic or a healed alcoholic because even though they overcome the stronghold of alcohol addiction, they never have an assurance that they actually broke the power of that stronghold of addiction in their life. It is a physical realm example of a spirit realm condition exhibited in a player's life. Although it is physically apparent, the source of the stronghold is in the spirit realm; few players go there to finally and forever crush its power over them. Instead, they languish forever in recovery, never resting, never at peace or finally free.

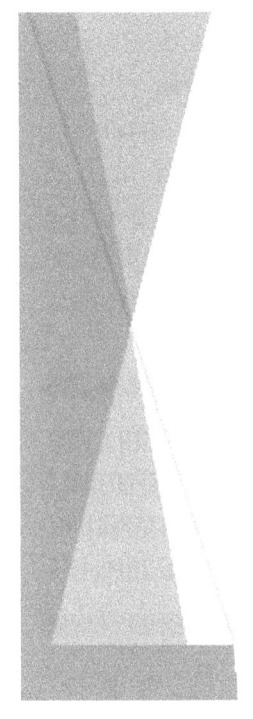

The Anatomy of a Stronghold

Jesus said, "You shall know the truth and the truth shall make you free"

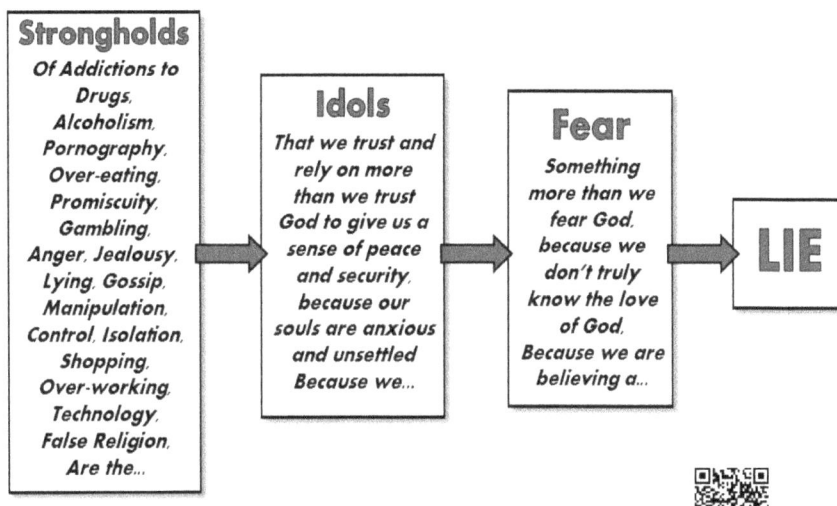

Strongholds Of Addictions to Drugs, Alcoholism, Pornography, Over-eating, Promiscuity, Gambling, Anger, Jealousy, Lying, Gossip, Manipulation, Control, Isolation, Shopping, Over-working, Technology, False Religion, Are the... → **Idols** That we trust and rely on more than we trust God to give us a sense of peace and security, because our souls are anxious and unsettled Because we... → **Fear** Something more than we fear God, because we don't truly know the love of God, Because we are believing a... → **LIE**

(One Lord One Body Ministries 2013)

What is the difference between being recovered and healed? It is more than just playing with words. The steps of recovery used by Alcoholics Anonymous originated in the principles of the Manual, so the paths to recovery or healing may run parallel to each other in many respects. The difference in the outcome can range from the conventional, typical result to the transformational, which goes beyond recovery to permanent healing.

Those who achieve conventional results keep their focus on the recovery process, which keeps them perpetually associated with their condition. The fear of a relapse is never far away.

A transformational result taps into a spiritual dimension beyond the steps of recovery. This happens through a faith transaction or series of transactions to break the grip of the addictive stronghold as part of a process to change the focus of the individual to emulate the character of the Game Master. The Manual describes this as a renewal of the mind over areas that control life practices (Rom. 2:12; Col. 3:10). It is not merely "mind over matter" or a sheer will exercise.

This path offers the possibility of a completed and healed recovery. The memory of the addiction or condition may remain, but it is a former part of the individual that they have discarded (1 Cor. 6:9–11). The process can be very short, but that is very unusual. The Resource appendices section includes online testimonials of guests who became members and were instantly released from the power of their addictions to alcohol and cocaine. Typically, change requires time, perhaps a lot of time.

Both paths can have a high rate of failure because neither one is easy. Both require lifestyle and habit changes, and not everyone has the interest or inner strength to persist. Moreover, the scars of addiction and its effects may be permanent because negative spiritual issues always leave a swath of mental, emotional, or physical destruction, especially as they persist and deepen in our lives. Still, for some, healing for this, too, may be possible.

To summarize, a stronghold, a self-destructive habit of life, affecting an individual is a real-life example of a spiritual breach in our character that is empowered not only by our own habitual practice but also by a disconnection from the Game Master's healing power applied to that area, and perhaps, also enhanced by the Serpent's power to enlarge the breach through minion influence. Any player with a vice likely has a spiritual stronghold affecting that area of their life.

> ANY PLAYER WITH A VICE LIKELY HAS A SPIRITUAL STRONGHOLD AFFECTING THAT AREA OF THEIR LIFE.

6. The Devil–Serpent

Anyone who thinks the devil is real probably spends too much time in religious kiosks. Pick a subject like violence or just a personal issue like your computer crashed when your term paper was due, and then tell someone that the devil is causing it— this was an actual online post.

Before you can cough up your explanation, unsympathetic players will ridicule you, then they'll tell their friends and get them to laugh at you too, savoring your delusion. Finally, your credibility will be finished. Just watching what TV preachers say about the devil's work and seeing how the public responds or reacts can tell you which way the wind blows here.

The devil, if he really exists, is well insulated from blame and could hardly be the cause of much harm in the game world since it's so obvious that players are causing most of it, and here you are blaming him for your computer like the dog ate your homework.

Yeah, it's not a good idea to bring him up in any serious conversation, and it doesn't work too comfortably in religious kiosks, either. It is distressingly amusing to watch religious folk who should have answers dance and squirm around the subject as they try not to sound crazy by not giving the devil too much credit for things that he is well capable of doing.

Those who are tuned in to spiritual warfare are more likely to recognize that circumstantial issues and equipment failures, as described above, can be associated with diabolical sources as evidence mounts, but discussing it with other members who are unfamiliar with spirit-induced activity is both unenlightening and nonproductive. The reason is that no one is systematically informed about the Serpent's tactics, shown how to recognize them, or are offered ways to resist him. The Manual says to "resist the devil," but how can you resist him when you don't even notice he's around? (James 4:7).

There is no goodwill from the Serpent toward gamers. The only time he is on our side is to put us at a disadvantage in his favor. He played the gamers at the garden of Eden with a successful ploy to get Adam to 1) eat the forbidden fruit, 2) choose to join the Serpent's side, and 3) cede his authority of dominion over the game world to the Serpent (Gen. 3).

The Manual explains that Adam knew what he was doing; he wasn't tricked, and he made a deliberate choice, which makes you wonder if he expected more godlike symptoms than he got or if he just ate the fruit to stay with gorgeous Eve, who brought it to him after she had tried it. Apparently, he was willing to risk death to find out (1 Tim. 2:14). How long do you think it took for him to realize he just got a new Boss and that he wasn't in charge of the game world anymore?

That situation could be why, when the Serpent offered to give the One all the kingdoms of the game world as they viewed them together in a moment of time—including the country you currently live in—in exchange for worshiping the Serpent, the One did not correct him because those kingdoms were the Serpent's to give. The issue was whom to worship or whom to call Master (Luke 4:5–8).

> **The Serpent has plans for you - *to Steal and to Kill and to Destroy:***
>
> You & Your Loved Ones
> Your Possessions
> Your Relationships
> Your Health
> Your Opportunities
> Your Dreams
> Your Future Jn 10:10

The One describes characteristics of the Serpent as a murderer from the beginning, without an ounce of truth in him, a liar, and the Father of Lies (John 8:44). Furthermore, He tells us what the Serpent wants to do to you: his agents are thieves who come "to steal, and to kill, and to destroy" (John 10:10).

There is always stuff for you to lose. The things in life that the Serpent will choose to steal from you (opportunity, possessions, relationships, and so on), to kill (you, loved ones, dreams, and so on), or to destroy (health, future, your purpose in life, and so on) will get your attention. This is when he suggests you point the finger at the Game Master and blame Him for your ruined life while he comforts you with commiserating friends or drugs or alcohol and prepares the next round against you.

For citizens of the kingdom of the Serpent, life can be pretty quiet, with a few hiccups like illness or the death of an older relative, but nothing unusual or unpredictable. As long as they mind their own business and don't get too radical about religion and begin loving the Game Master, things just seem to flow along, and life goes according to plan.

If you make the mistake of deciding to leave his kingdom and choose the Game Master and get your golden ticket, things may somehow start breaking, and life just goes very wrong. This could be the Serpent's doing to get you to settle down, or it could be related to a curse that's been dormant, and now where you are seeing hope of deliverance, it rises up against you.

Some players decide to join the Serpent's party because the money is great, the booze flows, or the good times never end. This path includes plenty of landmine curses that can be activated while the party rolls on. Some who finally left that lifestyle report a feeling like their life force being drained from their soul and emptiness just pouring in.

A good example of this scenario is the story of a Baptist pastor, Billy Crone, who gives a testimonial available on YouTube that narrates his hatred for God as a sixth grader, his decision to give himself to the Serpent, and immerse himself in the pleasures of life with his rock band and alcohol, trying everything to fill the void in his life. He recounts how the money poured in until everything went south, ending badly with minion visitations (Crone 2016, min. 11:00).

Those who join gangs may be required to steal, kill, and destroy like the One describes of the Serpent Thief. They've got protection with their group, and it's just like family. It's worth the risk while they stay above ground, but upon death, the good times end forever, and there is no eternal advantage to being a player in his kingdom.

SERPENT HIERARCHY

The Manual's text about the prophet master player Daniel reveals a hierarchy ranking of spirit beings that control the kingdoms of the game world (Dan. 10:12–14). In this case, the henchman overseer of the kingdom of Persia prevented a messenger of the Game Master from reaching Daniel for twenty-one days until the messenger called in Michael, one of the Game Master's chief warrior guardians, to help him get the message to Daniel. Here's the story.

At the time of Daniel's encounters with the messenger, he was living in Babylon, the capital city of Persia, as a high-ranking government official, where Cyrus the Great was ruler. Persia was the world's superpower at that time, and the Serpent had his henchman ruler, called the prince of Persia, watching over the kingdom.

It seems that since there was no opposition to Daniel's prayers the first time the messenger Gabriel visited him (Dan. 8:15–16), the prince of Persia may not have realized there was very much importance about Daniel until Gabriel zoomed in at high speed. The second time around, the Game Master again responded to Daniel and sent Gabriel off with an answer just as soon as Daniel began praying, but the prince of Persia was watching and ready this time to repel His messengers. The ensuing struggle took three weeks until the reinforcement of Michael arrived (Dan. 10).

Do you think there are any countries in the game world today that would have henchmen hosts overseeing them? What about their capital cities, the world's financial, entertainment, or religious capitals? As part of his résumé for being a notable leader before his presidential election, Ronald Reagan liked to boast that as the governor of California, he managed the equivalent of the world's sixth-largest economy. Would California attract any henchman attention?

Based on the account in the book of Daniel, there is a spiritual layer of influence over the nations of the game world that would have probably included all the major civilizations around the globe through the ages up to today's nations. There could very well be henchmen rulers for every country, capital, and major city right now. The Game Master's guardians still come and go, but special deliveries may require additional postage like prayer and fasting since the game world is considered hostile territory to His team.

If the Serpent felt compelled to stir the pot and mess up paradise when there were only two players on earth, why would he keep his hands off our affairs with eight billion to herd? But to the skeptical mind, it's all cool 'cause the devil only lives in our imagination.

Deception and skepticism

A primary tool of the Serpent is deception. Guests may think they are earning points toward the bonus round, but their efforts never actually qualify them to arrive there, and they remain perpetual guests. For members, his deception is designed to make them miss rewards or bring a curse upon themselves by reverting to practicing the law of Moses or accepting New Age mysticisms in their worship or health routines (Deut. 27:26; Gal. 3:10–11). Another side of his deception targets the nonreligious gamers who are just looking for a good time and a good, uncomplicated life without getting tied up with religious rules.

Skepticism is an effective tool used for more technologically advanced societies where science is worshiped in the public square, and intellectual reason reigns supreme. The Serpent's original ploy in the garden of Eden was to introduce skepticism about the Game Master's interest in the well-being of His players and cast doubt about His motives for making that single rule about the forbidden fruit. While these two factors still flood players' commentary in online discussions of moral issues, that original skepticism has progressed to the point where guests today confidently deny the very existence of the Game Master.

Skepticism is viewed as a healthy trait to keep us from becoming gullible to swindlers and frauds. A healthy dose of skepticism is extremely valuable as a matter of general practice. It is good in a religious context to confirm the truth of the Manual against what religious leaders may say, including yours.

In religious matters, guests tend to employ skepticism as a reason why they don't need to locate the truth. They are products of a philosophy of relativity: religion is all opinion, and there is no single truth or actual real spirit power. What little they know of the Game Master makes no logical sense, so their mind is made up, and they firmly choose disbelief in the possibility of a good God who would do anything for them.

SPIRITUAL FACTOR

There is a cosmic war happening right now for the loyalty of your soul. Every player the Serpent can keep from turning to the Game Master is a win for him. Every player he can bring to the grave without a golden ticket is a win for him. When he fails, and someone gets their ticket, every member he can keep distracted and interested in the pleasures of his kingdom—this game world's distractions—is a consolation to him. But when he can get a member to walk away from the Game Master on purpose, to deconstruct their faith, he wins again (Matt. 13:1–9, 18–23).

Religion. As explained in Section One, the Serpent established and owns all the religious franchises of the game world—except the few that are still loyal to the Game Master's Manual. Excluding these few Game Master kiosks, all the competing religions you see around you are not merely choices of what fits your style. They are designed to satisfy your need for a spiritual connection while keeping you away from the Game Master's truth. Many are full of love and light and quests for inner peace, but they all lack the power to transform your life into a supernatural expression of the Game Master's own love and peace (Phil. 4:6–7).

False prophets. This may seem off-topic, but the Serpent's objective is to keep players from the bonus round, and this is such an effective means that the One felt compelled to make major points about it. At the time of the One's life on earth, He said,

"Difficult is the way and small is the entrance that leads to eternal life with few finding it, but wide is the path and broad is the entrance that leads to destruction and most players will end up there" (Matt. 7:13–14, paraphrased).

Statistically, your chance of missing the bonus round with eternal life is nearly 100 percent. The Serpent's track record for keeping players out of the bonus round is excellent, even superb. It continues to be extremely successful and only improves by the decade.

For those who are thinking about turning to the Game Master, the Serpent has his false prophets in place, including in allegedly every major Christian denominational kiosk headquarters, ready and looking to help players make decisions and join the kiosk so they will feel close to the Game Master—but not actually be on His team.

The Protestant religious groups are generally factions of members who take strong exceptions to what are technically the minor points of difference among them. Most agree on the major points of doctrine. However, over the past several decades, there is a growing danger as they increasingly incorporate the Serpent's religious philosophies into their practices affecting worship music and mixing syncretism of New Age and Emergent theologies in greater numbers of kiosks across a broad spectrum of denominations from conservative to liberal kiosks.

Many members willingly accept whatever is put before them, perhaps not realizing the subtle significance of the new and innovative ideas their kiosk has discovered. These networked kiosks have developed techniques to gradually incorporate change and deal with the few dissenters who are "unduly" alarmed.

False teachings. Go to any religious kiosk in the country and ask them, pastor, priest, or lay person, if they have false teachers in their kiosk, and not one of them will say yes. They may point to the kiosk down the road and tell you it's full of false teaching, but that kiosk will totally disagree. So, you must get to the truth for yourself.

Even false prophets can also be sincerely duped. If your false teacher is sincere and says he's right, and you're sincere too and accept his words, how will you know if he's right or how much of it is right—since you don't know he's a false teacher? Sometimes there are small phrases or just a twist of perspective on a small aspect of a spiritual point that does not match the Manual. It can go by so quickly in a sermon or kiosk lesson that it's not convenient to sidetrack the discussion or belabor the point.

False teaching originates with the Serpent and has continued since the start of the game. How wrong does a remark, explanation, or teaching need to be before it rises to the level of serious error and is tagged as a false teaching? Some problems of false teachings are that some teachings themselves may be widely accepted, plausible interpretations of the Manual or are glossed over as part of a bigger point, making them less detectable or susceptible to scrutiny.

Compound the problem with players who logically decide that the kiosk is right because who am I, an unlearned player, to challenge a religious expert? So, there is an inherent perception that the listening player probably just doesn't understand the Manual well enough to read it right. But there's always the Spirit Master who can provide insight and clarity and "guide you into all truth" (John 16:13).

A logical line would be that if they don't alter major doctrinal teaching, then there is no need to worry. However, if tweaking words and phrasings mean the difference between getting your prayers answered, having a miracle happen, leaving you languishing in your sorry situation, or missing the bonus round, perhaps the details would matter a little more than usual.

Although there is not a category listing all false teachings, the Manual gives some specifics and descriptions of what constitutes false teaching.

> See to it that no one takes you captive by **philosophy** and **empty deceit**, according to **human tradition**, according to the **elemental spirits** (spiritual principles) **of the world** (perhaps a reference to ancient philosophies based on the belief that only the material world is real), and not according to Christ (Col. 2:8 ESV, AMP, emphasis added).

Players have an increasing tendency to frame the Manual's teachings around their own life experience, which includes the world's philosophy toward life instead of adjusting life perspectives to scriptural truth. This mixture becomes their spiritual perspective, superseding what is written in the Manual. The outcome is a Christian perspective riddled with and supported by non-Manual philosophy. Those who then share these hybrid spiritual insights with family, friends, and study groups are spreading false teaching, which is spiritual but not scriptural.

This scenario easily happens in conservative kiosks. Member players in conservative kiosks will say, "God won't give you more than you can handle," "You have an angel in heaven looking out for you now that your mother has died," "I only do yoga for the exercises; the spiritual part doesn't affect me," "I have to love them, but I don't have to like them," and speaking of someone who may not have been a

SINCERITY ALONE DOES NOT AFFIRM SPIRITUAL TRUTH NOR QUALIFY YOU FOR THE BONUS ROUND.

member, "Now he's in a better place." Sincerity alone does not affirm spiritual truth nor qualify you for the bonus round. And don't forget to "knock on wood."

The Cultural Research Center conducted An America's Values Study in July 2022 regarding America's foundation for determining right and wrong.

> A new study reveals that less than one-third of Americans believe the Bible should serve as the foundation for determining right and wrong, even as most people express support for traditional moral values (Foley 2022, ¶ 1).

> Overall, when asked to identify what they viewed as the primary determinant of right and wrong in the U.S., a plurality of participants (42 percent) said: "what you feel in your heart." An additional 29 percent cited majority rule as their desired method for determining right and wrong. In comparison, just 29 percent expressed a belief that the principles laid out in the Bible should determine the understanding of right and wrong in the U.S. That figure rose to 66 percent among Spiritually Active, Governance Engaged Conservative Christians. Only 66 percent (Foley 2022, ¶ 3).

> "Three-quarters of Americans maintain that people are basically good, and less than half of all Americans believe in God or that the Bible is God's true, relevant, and reliable words to humanity," said George Barna, the director of research at the Cultural Research Center, in response to the survey's findings (Foley 2022, ¶ 11).

> "Consequently, Americans have become comfortable with the idea of being the arbiters of morality. In the same way that most Americans contend there is no absolute moral truth, they now believe that there is no divine guidance required or even available to define right and wrong," Barna said, lamenting that most Americans "are now more likely to take their moral cues from government laws and policies than from church teachings about biblical principles (Foley 2022, ¶ 12).

> One could reasonably argue that the nation's ideas about right and wrong are now more likely to come from the White House and the halls of Congress than from our houses of worship" (Foley 2022, ¶ 13).

The Cultural Research Center at Arizona Christian University also has a poll of 1,000 Christian pastors published on May 17, 2022, regarding a biblical worldview.

> People have many expectations of pastors of Christian churches. One of those expectations is that pastors possess a philosophy of life that largely reflects biblical principles, a perspective commonly called a biblical worldview (Unruh 2022, ¶ 4).

> But a new nationwide survey among a representative sample of America's Christian pastors shows that a large majority of those pastors do not possess a biblical worldview. In fact, just slightly more than a third (37 percent) have a biblical worldview and the majority—62 percent—possess a hybrid worldview known as Syncretism (Unruh 2022, ¶ 5).

Here is the biblical worldview breakdown among the pastoral staff: senior pastors—41 percent, associate pastors—28 percent, teaching pastors—13 percent, children's and youth pastors—12 percent (one out of eight), executive pastors—4 percent. Only 2 percent of preteen parents in the general population have a biblical worldview (Unruh 2022, ¶ 11).

Overall, you have a two-thirds statistical chance of hearing the wrong Manual perspective in a given Christian kiosk, and it rises to 88 percent in the youth ministries. If you think your kiosk fully teaches the Manual, perhaps you should give it a second thought. If your child is a teenager or younger, they are less likely to be hearing the Manual teaching you think they are getting. Their lessons may include the well-known Manual stories, but whose philosophy are they being framed around?

A good kiosk may have false teachers sprinkled among the staff and grade-level leaders, and it may be impossible to differentiate the good from the bad since the pastor overseeing all the small groups and classes cannot vet every one of them every week. Yes, the lesson outline may be approved, but the lesson itself can be delivered with non-Manual interpretations based on the lesson giver's different worldview. Your child may give spiritual answers about the lesson but not know the Manual's perspective.

If you are counting on your kiosk to help give your children a Christian worldview, think again. My children went to conservative kiosks and schools. I was appalled to realize their spiritual training didn't begin to cover all the bases. I had to ramp up a systematic doctrinal study program at home as they were going through middle school. There was no effective kiosk partnership with the family to raise them with a biblical worldview. It looked good in the early years but didn't pan out.

My son told me that everything he learned about the Game Master in church and school he had learned by third grade. The rest was just rehashing those same things for years. Josh McDowell said in a radio clip that this is why most young members walk off the team by their second year in college. Their parents' religion never became theirs; the Game Master didn't do anything for them and wasn't their God.

For a family, enforcing rules without cultivating a relationship with the child is a breeding ground for rebellion. On a spiritual level, the transference of faith is done through relationships in daily opportunities (Deut. 6:6–8), but it's easier and quicker to transfer faith by listing for children the rules of God because, how do you transfer a relationship, anyway? So, the kids grow up hearing all the God rules, then find new friends who don't go by any God rules and are living just fine. Many young adult players see this and walk away from their unimpactful family faith.

Parents generally don't practice the God relationship with their children. The Game Master told Joshua to collect twelve stones from the Jordan River and build a monument.

> Then Joshua said to the Israelites, "In the future your children will ask, 'What do these stones mean?' Then you can tell them, 'This is where the Israelites crossed the Jordan on dry ground.' For the LORD your God dried up the river right before your eyes, and he kept it dry until you were all across, just as he did at the Red Sea when he dried it up until we had all crossed over. He did this so all the nations of the earth might know that the LORD's hand is powerful, and so you might fear the LORD your God forever" (Josh. 4:21–24 NLT).

The demoniac of Gadara wanted to follow the One after he was freed from his minion oppression, but the One said,

> "Go home to your friends," he told him, "and tell them what wonderful things God has done for you; and how merciful he has been." So the man started off to visit the Ten Towns of that region and began to tell everyone about the great things Jesus had done for him; and they were awestruck by his story (Mark 5:19–20 TLB).

That one moment of incredible deliverance had a deep and lasting impact. Other examples are the woman-at-the-well story (John 4:5–30) and a blind man who was healed (John 9:1–38).

Does your family have any God moments or God stories where the children learned or saw the blessings of the Game Master on the family or the children? Helping the children experience the relationship of the Game Master and teaching them to get their own blessings from Him will encourage their faith in Him. The Game Master is the God of relationships. Eternal life is actually knowing Him (John 17:3).

The first apostle master players who knew the One face-to-face had to deal with false teachers inside their own religious kiosks. Now that those original eyewitnesses are dead and long gone, you can be sure that the problem of false teaching is only more widespread than it was 2,000 years ago. Here is how the One explains this mess:

> Enter by the narrow gate; for wide is the gate and broad is the way that leads to destruction, and there are many who go in by it. Because narrow is the gate and difficult is the way which leads to life, and there are few who find it.
>
> Beware of false prophets, who come to you in sheep's clothing, but inwardly they are ravenous wolves. You will know them by their fruits. Do men gather grapes from thornbushes or figs from thistles? Even so, every good tree bears good fruit, but a bad tree bears bad fruit. A good tree cannot bear bad fruit, nor can a bad tree bear good fruit. Every tree that does not bear good fruit is cut down and thrown into the fire. Therefore by their fruits you will know them.
>
> Not everyone who says to Me, "Lord, Lord," shall enter the kingdom of heaven, but he who does the will of My Father in heaven. Many will say to Me in that day, "Lord, Lord, have we not prophesied in Your name, cast out demons in Your name, and done many wonders in Your name?" And then I will declare to them, "I never knew you; depart from Me, you who practice lawlessness!" (Matt. 7:13–23 NKJV).

The odds are so stacked against the players that the One's own followers were dismayed and asked Him how it was even possible for *anyone to be saved* (Matt. 7:13–14; 19:23–26; Luke 13:23–24; 18:22–27).

Nobody ever tripped into heaven. You won't reach the bonus round by accident, good fortune, family or kiosk credentials, or even a sincere heart. Many sincere players are put on the wrong gospel train by those helpful false prophets the One mentioned because they didn't check the Manual at the station to ensure they got only His exact, unfiltered details straight from the Game Master Himself.

The One said plainly in this above-quoted text that many apparently good players (who worked in His name and genuinely believed that they were servants of the Game Master) will find out only too late that they missed eternal life in the bonus round because they "work iniquity," are "evildoers," "practice lawlessness," "break the Game Master's law," or "disregarded My commands."

> **NOBODY EVER TRIPPED INTO HEAVEN.**

It takes no effort to serve the Serpent because we were born into his kingdom of death, and living to please ourselves is all he needs to keep us from drifting away. If you think you want eternal life, you must escape from this game world pleasure kingdom and find the Game Master. He is sending out His members, and many are trying to spread His gospel news, but they're not getting the job done. If you don't find them, and they don't reach out to you, don't wait for them. Find His Manual, read it, and don't get fooled.

This game world we live in is under the dominion of the Serpent, the Great Puppet Master behind all its turmoil and trouble. If you still doubt this, there are plenty of online conspiracy videos that document it. If you won't believe the Game Master and His Manual, then He said that nothing would convince you even if players start coming back from the dead (Luke 16:20–31).

Fake gods

The Serpent is the shadow god behind every non-Manual religious teaching. Every founder or leader of a non-Manual religion or religious practice is a false prophet or false god. You may call your leader or god by a different name, but they have "Serpent" written all over them. This includes leaders who use the Manual but also have alternately inspired teachings. This also includes leaders who use the Manual but include non-Manual philosophy in their teaching. Plus, it includes all leaders who do not use the Manual at all. They all provide the Serpent's great cloudy haze of light and goodness, which give you that aura and feeling of spiritual fullness and belonging but leave your soul unchanged and unsatisfied.

Then there are the agnostics and atheists. Many players in the Western game world these days don't put much stock in the spirit world. It means nothing to an increasing number of players. Movies that portray aspects of that realm are fake just like Asgard and the Marvel universe; it's all make-believe.

When the evil lord of the spirit realm and god of this age can successfully make the Creator Game Master into a fantasy of the masses on par with unbelievable and mythical lore, there is little worry that anyone will go looking for Him. Peer pressure alone is enough to keep most players from asking serious questions or finding the meaning of life (Prov. 29:25).

As the Serpent deceives players into believing there is no spiritual reality, the more easily he can encourage them to focus on themselves, entertain themselves, find fulfillment in their busyness of life and thereby distract them from his scheme to steal their soul from the Game Master, and find forgiveness for their game violations that was already paid in full and is waiting for them to claim.

In the Manual text of 2 Kings 18–19, Sennacherib, the king of Assyria who was immortalized in the poem by Lord Byron, repeatedly told King Hezekiah of Judah that they would become the slaves of Assyria. He told them that the Game Master wouldn't deliver them because no god ever before could save a nation from Assyria. To him, the Game Master was just Judah's entertainment (i.e., just a movie). He didn't believe in that stuff about the Game Master's invincibility.

In one night, the Game Master's guardian singlehandedly killed 185,000 troops from the army of Assyria. To put that into perspective, it was the equivalent of killing in one single night almost every American soldier (186,300) deployed during the height of the war in the Iraq and Afghanistan theaters in the fiscal year 2009 (Belasco 200, 39).

Refusing to acknowledge power does not make it disappear or render it ineffective (just ask Saddam Hussein how that worked out in Kuwait). The purported lack of corroborative texts about this incident from the ancient world assumes that those texts without this account are complete and accurate. However, adding accounts of Sennacherib's defeat to official records would have proven to his enemies that he wasn't invincible after all.

In recent decades, it was said that some nations of Africa stopped reporting accurate numbers of devastating HIV casualty rates because they didn't want neighboring countries to try a military takeover. And recently, there were accusations of COVID-19 deaths being misreported to cover mishandling of various States' state of emergency practices or hospital systems to collect extra federal funds by reporting higher death rates. That gunshot victim was actually a COVID death, you see. Truth is skewed or suppressed to fit the narrative.

King Sennacherib's lack of belief in the Game Master's power did not stop Him from using it. The Game Master had reminded Israel that all the gods of the other nations could not help them or stand against Him because they were not powerful like Him. Sennacherib noticed this lack of power in the gods of the other kingdoms and took advantage of it during his conquests. His mistake was applying that previously accurate observation to the Game Master God of Israel, Who swore to defend them when Hezekiah turned to Him for help. Incidentally, Sennacherib's sons later killed him in his own god's temple—as predicted by the Game Master (2 Kings 19:7, 35–37).

Guests who choose to disbelieve in the spirit realm have little to work with in explaining how this game world has devolved into the mess we see around us today. If players are basically good, as is widely claimed, and there's no outside interference from a nonexistent Serpent, why isn't the game world becoming a better place to live? Where are those elusive good players? Or do they just need to learn good manners? But why should they need to learn good manners if they are already good to begin with?

7. Bad Decisions

Players have the freedom of choice, or if you are cynical or know something different, at least the illusion of freedom of choice. Whatever the case may be, whether choices are made freely or under pressure, calculated or unplanned, or simply mistakes that end badly, the human factor accounts for a lot of discomfort, trauma, and tragedy in our lives. This is also an area where players are told to stop blaming the devil and take responsibility for their failures and game violations.

Choices can impact our ability to make a living, build up good retirement savings, keep good friends, simplify life, or find inner peace. Sometimes the choices we make result in a deferred disaster, such as a decision to buy a home in a disaster-prone area and then expecting no problems. Who hasn't heard of the Ring of Fire, Tornado Alley, the San Andreas Fault, or the New Madrid Fault or hurricane-prone coastlines?

Sometimes these decisions are not obvious, like for those living in the American Midwest whose communities were flooded for the first time in nearly a century back in 1993. They lived in a floodplain that so rarely flooded that it's possible many players did not even know the probability of a flood or the distant history of the countryside. During a six-month period, this flood disaster covered nine states, with an area larger than West Virginia being underwater and included more than a thousand levees breached and ninety-two water gauges that reached all-time record levels. The Great Flood of 1993 was considered one of the biggest natural disasters in America, cost an estimated $15 billion in damages, and about fifty players lost their lives (Lada 2018, ¶ 1–4, image 4).

Within this saga, James Scott of West Quincy, Missouri, decided to remove several sandbags from the levee guarding the town, telling several friends that he wanted to break the levee so that his wife would be stranded on the other side of the river. Scott's wife at the time worked in Taylor, Missouri, at a restaurant/truck stop. Scott allegedly told his friends that if his wife was stranded, he could party, have an affair, and create ideal fishing conditions.

> On the day of the infamous flood, July 16, 1993, the Mississippi River had stopped rising and was one-and-a-half feet below the levee. However, around 8 p.m., the Mississippi River began cascading through the main stem of the levee and traveled five miles inland, destroying acres and acres of farmland. Between 12 and 15 feet of water flooded West Quincy, a mile-long strip of gas stations, a beauty salon, a restaurant, and other businesses. The flood also destroyed several truck stops and closed the Bayview Bridge, a main link between Missouri and Illinois. The bridge was closed for 71 days. Without it, thousands of people who lived in Missouri and had businesses in Quincy had to fly, take a ferry, or drive 80 miles to get to work. And some of the flood water remained in Quincy for months after the break in the levee ("Missouri v. James Scott: 'The Midwest Flood Trial'" 2007, ¶ 5).

This story belongs in the "Bad People" section describing a psychopath who certainly made a bad decision by showing disregard for others and willfully causing them extensive and long-lasting harm. Insurance is purchased not because we plan to have disasters but to help us after a loss while we hope we never have to call it in.

After a major earthquake with a tsunami that hit Japan in 2011, stories turned up that those living along the coastlines of Japan up to 600 years previously had set up stone markers warning future generations of the tsunami danger of building below that high water mark. The memory of danger fades with time, and the convenience of proximity to the shoreline is too economically inviting ("Ancient Stone Markers Warned of Tsunamis" 2011, ¶ 4–5).

David Mc Dermott has a blog that discusses decision-making. He describes the bad effects of bad decisions and why we continue making them. Bad decisions leave us with circumstantial consequences where we are shortchanged in what we expected, with consequences in relationships, with emotional and physical consequences where we feel very bad about what happened and can even become ill because of it, with resource consequences where we lose time or money, and eventually, lifetime consequences where too much of our gameplay was spent living with consequences of bad decisions (Mc Dermott n.d., ¶ 11).

Bad decisions can also become habitual when our focus is on other players. We want them to think well of us, so to please them, we do things we would rather not do. We may feel pressured to do things because we feel forced or obligated to help or be part of the team. These habits often begin when we are young and are required to follow the directions of those in charge of us. This may be part of a proper upbringing, but as we grow, we do not transition to a place of personal responsibility where we make decisions based on our set of life responsibilities and what we should accomplish through them. This dynamic could also be the effect of a generational curse upon us where we don't develop our own identity and are too easily manipulated by more assertive players (Deut. 28:43–44).

Sometimes our choices have immediate consequences. For example, drinking and driving are a lethal combination that is well-known in advance. Sometimes a job needs to get done, and precautions are not taken because we don't have the time or the tools. I did this as a teenager when I moved a big telephone pole by myself so I could stack bus seats behind it. That mistake triggered my eventual fibromyalgia.

We also just make dumb choices, like the time as a teenager when I took a bike without brakes down a steep hill, fully expecting to make the hairpin turn. Fortunately, while getting scraped by a tree or two and banged up by the rest of the hill, I landed on the only patch of grass between a brick wall and a brick house. Then, I had to limp a few miles home, dragging my cousin's borrowed bike. Youth seems indestructible.

As the One told the Serpent, who wanted Him to jump off a pinnacle because the Game Master promised to save Him, "It is written, you shall not tempt [test] the Lord your God" (Deut. 6:16; Matt. 4:5–7; Luke 4:9–13). The Manual indicates that the Game Master is not keen on the notion that purposely exposing oneself to imminent danger compels Him to protect you.

He does not validate those who choose to live their lives on their own terms. Precautions you take are, therefore, advisable and can affect the degree to which you improve your margin of safety. From that point, you and the Game Master can have a dialogue.

8. Bad People

The Manual says, "The heart is the most deceitful thing there is and desperately wicked. No one can really know how bad it is!" (Jer. 17:9 TLB). So, how well do you really know yourself? Every one of us can commit the most heinous acts against other players while we call ourselves good people. Our choices can take us so far down a path where we don't recognize ourselves anymore and didn't imagine we would do the things we did.

We live in the game's last days as the Apocalypse overtakes us. Master player Paul warned his student, Timothy, about what players will be like. There seem to be news stories increasingly describing players with these qualities. Does this list remind you of players you know at work, family, community, or school?

> But understand this, that in the last days dangerous times [of great stress and trouble] will come [difficult days that will be hard to bear]. For people will be lovers of self [narcissistic, self-focused], lovers of money [impelled by greed], boastful, arrogant, revilers, disobedient to parents, ungrateful, unholy and profane, [and they will be] unloving [devoid of natural human affection, calloused and inhumane], irreconcilable, malicious gossips, devoid of self-control [intemperate, immoral], brutal, haters of good, traitors, reckless, conceited, lovers of [sensual] pleasure rather than lovers of God, holding to a form of [outward] godliness (religion), although they have denied its power [for their conduct nullifies their claim of faith]. Avoid such people and keep far away from them (2 Tim. 3:1–5 AMP).

For those who read the Manual, do you notice how often the traits of gossip or being a meddler or busybody show up in the lists of what to avoid or as characteristic of those who hate the Game Master? (Prov. 16:28; 26:17; Rom. 1:28–32; 2 Cor. 12:20–21; 1 Pet. 4:14–15). We pay lip service to acknowledging that it should not be done, but the practice seems to be common in the kiosk culture as we share the "news" about what's happening in our kiosk world or in our concern about a "matter of prayer" for a fellow member. Perhaps gossip too often crosses into abomination territory as a lying false witness or one that stirs up hard feelings in the kiosk community. But we're good people—we're members, after all (Prov. 6:17–19).

Michael Snyder remarks in his article titled "America Is Being Transformed Into a Really Bad Version of 'Grand Theft Auto,"

Have you noticed that more people than ever in our society seem to be going completely crazy? And when I say crazy, I don't mean it in a fun, non-threatening way. All over the country, we are literally seeing people "go psycho" and commit some of the most heinous acts of violence imaginable. It is almost as if we have all been transported into a "Grand Theft Auto" game where people feel free to indulge their basest instincts. In recent months I have repeatedly written about the fact that crime rates have been soaring, but it isn't just the number of crimes that is alarming. We are starting to see things happening in our streets that are so bizarre that it is difficult to believe they are real. In fact, many of them seem like they have been pulled right out of an extremely violent Hollywood movie (Snyder 2022, ¶ 1).

Civil unrest is on the rise all over the globe, and we are now warned that "the worst is undoubtedly yet to come" as food supplies get tighter and economic conditions continue to deteriorate. And if the streets of major U.S. cities are filled with violence while economic conditions are still relatively stable, what will they look like when the economy really deteriorates (Snyder 2023a, ¶ 34)?

The truth is that the whole world is simply not prepared to handle the exceedingly difficult challenges that are ahead of us. As a result, the thin veneer of civilization that we all take for granted on a daily basis is getting thinner and thinner, and eventually, it will be gone completely (Snyder 2022, ¶ 42).

Let's discuss the base element of evil, "For the love of money is the root of all evil: which while some coveted after, they have erred from the faith, and pierced themselves through with many sorrows" (1 Tim. 6:10). Here we see that covetousness is the driving force at the root of evil, a Big Ten violation (Exod. 20:17; Deut. 5:21; Ps. 119:36; Prov. 28:16; Rom. 7:7; 13:8–10). Now we are back to square one where it's all about us. Do you know some good people around you who just love getting new things or expanding their influence or power for how it lines their bank account? They are constantly looking for their big break or finding an edge to make it big. Are you one of them? Surely, we haven't tapped into the root of evil—we're good people!

> **COVETOUSNESS IS THE DRIVING FORCE AT THE ROOT OF EVIL, A BIG TEN VIOLATION.**

The most basic characteristic we have is self-centeredness or selfishness. It plays itself out in our love of money and the pursuit of what we can gain from it, which is the catalyst that spreads to the capacity for all kinds of evil. It can be so alluring that even professing members are willing to give up the bonus round for it (Mark 4:7, 18–19; Luke 8:14; 21:34–35).

Have you been tempted to do the wrong thing so life will be easier for you—and then do it again? Pablo Escobar, the Columbian Medellin Cartel drug lord, said, "Everyone has a price, the important thing is to find out what it is" (Escobar 2023, ¶ 1). We occasionally see government officials compromised by illegal payouts. Businesses may cut corners on quality and safety to increase profit margins. Those with drug or gambling addictions become more apt to steal and commit violence to feed their habits. Good people eventually get hurt by those who pursue such selfish ambitions.

The Baltimore Police Department created a special Gun Trace Task Force unit in 2007. Instead of cleaning up the crime in the city, the task force stole and resold guns and drugs. Crime skyrocketed in Baltimore until 2017, when eight officers were indicted. The ten-year story was documented in an HBO miniseries, *We Own This City*. Trust in the Baltimore police may never recover from their corruption and betrayal in the pursuit of money (Bates 2022, ¶ 15).

Psychopaths

Have you ever rubbed shoulders or crossed paths with a psychopath? We don't usually think we'll ever meet one in real life. Traits of a psychopath include antisocial behavior, narcissism, superficial charm, impulsivity, callousness, unemotional traits, lack of guilt, and lack of empathy (Morin 2007, ¶ 6). Do these traits ring any bells? About 29 percent of the American population (96 million) has one or more of these traits, but only about 0.6 percent (2 million) fit the definition of a psychopath (Morin 2007, ¶ 7). "Clinical observations at ASH [Atascadero State Hospital] have suggested 4 possible subtypes of psychopathy: narcissistic, borderline, sadistic, and antisocial" (Murphy and Vess 2003, 11).

Kevin Dutton, author of *The Wisdom of Psychopaths: What Saints, Spies and Serial Killers can Teach Us about Success*, conducted the Great British Psychopath Survey:

> To assess the prevalence of psychopathic traits within an entire national workforce. Participants were directed onto my website, where they completed the Levenson Self-Report Psychopathy Scale and were then given their score. But that wasn't all. They also entered

their employment details. What would turn out to be the U.K.'s most psychopathic profession? (Dutton 2012, 161–162).

Professions with the most psychopaths in order were CEO, lawyer, media (TV/radio), salesperson, surgeon, journalist, police officer, clergy person, chef, and civil servant. Professions with the least psychopaths in order were care aide, nurse, therapist, craftsperson, beautician/stylist, charity worker, teacher, creative artist, doctor, and accountant (Dutton 2012, 161–162).

Those with the most psychopathic traits tend to oversee the company, the narrative, surgery, law, spiritual perspective, and the function of government. For example, of the fourteen lead pastors of kiosks I attended over the last sixty years, three of them exhibited psychopathic traits and were eventually forced out of the kiosk for bad behavior. Do you have such a story?

Does this study remind you of any trips to the department of motor vehicles or the post office? A bad boss? How about a blue-light "roadside service" anomaly? Suddenly, we all may know a psychopath!

It hurts when you are in a situation where you can't just walk away. At some point, we have a one-third chance of having someone with psychopathic traits bossing us around or making choices for us in life. Let's all hope we don't meet the 0.6 percent—except, it seems, they're running the country!

The Serpent is the ultimate psychopath. He exhibits all the traits of the psychopath plus those of its possible subtype categories (Isa. 14:12–16). Players who display a psychopathic trait or two simply reflect the character quality of their Serpent boss (John 8:44). A member with a psychopathic trait demonstrates a stronghold of opposition to the One in their life. This is a character trait that must be discarded as part of their obedience to the One and replaced with the character of the One through the Spirit Master (2 Cor. 10:3–5; Rom. 13:8–14).

Do you know any bad people? Have you been victimized or traumatized by someone you know? Are you still a hostage to someone else's agenda for you or their control over you?

Predators

Human predators are among the worst reasons that we are harmed in life. At one of my first school jobs, a maintenance chief would periodically tell me, "Locks don't stop the bad people; they only keep the good people honest." We can only take precautions; we cannot guarantee safety. Those who know their Manual may find an exception to that statement in Psalm 127, but prudence is still in order.

An acquaintance asked my son why God let their boyfriend kill their child. He responded that the boyfriend chose to commit murder and was responsible for what he did. The Game Master was not liable or the perpetrator; He is keeping score but does not necessarily interfere with the choices of bad players because of the game rules.

Players who are controlled by vices, addictions, passions, and ideological causes can commit aggravating campaigns of mayhem and the most heinous atrocities. In addition, prestige and power issues can escalate to impact greater populations from neighborhoods to cities to regions via gangs, militias, and resistance groups.

> Evil is the exercise of power…to commit crimes against humanity.
> (Zimbardo 2008, min. 2:29)

In what he calls the Lucifer Effect, where "Lucifer descends into Hell, becomes Satan, becomes the Devil and the Force of Evil in the Universe" (Zimbardo 2008, min, 1:57), Philip Zimbardo, Professor Emeritus of Psychology at Stanford University, described the arc of the cosmic transformation where humans "are transformed from good, ordinary people into perpetrators of evil" (min. 2:19). In this Ted Talks forum on the psychology of evil, Zimbardo gives his psychological definition of evil:

> Evil is the exercise of power, and that is the key—it's about power, to intentionally harm people, psychologically; to hurt people, physically; to destroy people, mortally or ideas; and to commit crimes against humanity" (Zimbardo 2008, min 2:38).

The source of evil is the Serpent boss, whose team members then follow his example. Zimbardo simply explained evil in the One's description of what the Serpent wants to do to you through his agents as thieves who come "to steal, and to kill, and to destroy," using bad players to accomplish these ends (John 10:10).

In November 2022, Tom Knighton of Bearing Arms said,

> The average number of friends a person has on Facebook is 338. Obviously, some have more, and some have less. That's . . . kind of how averages work.
>
> Why would I bring this up on a site about guns? Because we also talk about crime, and according to a recent study, if the murder rate trends continue as they have been, either the Facebook user themselves or

at least one of their friends will become a murder victim (Knighton 2022, ¶ 1–3).

A study by Just Facts, a nonprofit research institute, examined the number of murders in 2021 based on death certificate data and found that if the current 2021 crime rate continues, one out of 179 Americans will eventually be murdered over the course of their lifetimes (Knighton 2022, ¶ 4).

Jim Agresti, president and co-founder of Just Facts, who authored the study, told Fox News Digital, "That means if you're in the United States, you live here, you're born, and you spend your life here, your odds of your life ending by murder are one in 179 over your life. Not over a year or any other timeframe (Knighton 2022, ¶ 5).

"It's just somebody's gonna murder you before you die of natural causes, an accident, suicide, whatever it may be," he continued (Knighton 2022, ¶ 6).

Our chances of staying alive and well seem to fade by the decade. Those who live in crime-ridden cities likely have a much lower chance of survival for now until the crime reaches our outlying neighborhoods. Recovering from personal harm caused by other players is difficult because it can include a loss of livelihood, physical mobility, a good future, a legacy of accomplishment, and so on.

The rise of advocacy voices in society points to the increased sense of personal loss that creates the desire to raise awareness about dangers related to a particular trauma. Personal crusades are marked by making some perpetrator pay reparations or ensuring the problem doesn't happen to someone else. Healing the scars of loss is affected by how we view the cause, where we place the blame, and how we choose to move forward from it.

Is it you?

What if it's you? What if *you're* the bad person? Have you messed up your life, your chances, your future? Do you have a sense of entitlement that has run off with your better judgment? Maybe you've been caught; maybe you are still running free and playing the odds. Do you have a certain reputation?

Perhaps you broke the law or the Game Master's moral code. Other players who look at you don't see a good person because you've crossed the line, and now the label "bad person" or "psycho" or "predator" or "creep" goes with your name. Game violations against fellow players can reach the point of being unforgivable for them, their families, or the community. Even if you do your time or pay your dues, you can't erase your past or reputation.

What is your response? Are you sorry you did wrong or just sorry you're caught, but it's no use changing or crying about it because it won't make any difference for you? Do you justify your actions because you are better than other lowlifes? Do you do evil for the greater good? Have you reached a point of no return where you just don't care about anyone except yourself and convinced yourself that it doesn't matter what anyone thinks of you so long as you're okay with how you are?

The Game Master has some thoughts about that. He knows how low you can go and how utterly evil you can be. If you made your bed in hell, He would be there watching you in the blackest darkness, probing the deepest, secret recesses of your darkened heart. When you've finally had enough of yourself and are looking for a way out, He's still there with you, waiting to straighten your crooked path and give you peace (Jer. 17:9–10; Ps. 139:8–12; Heb. 4:12; Isa. 59:1–8).

When you are ready to dialogue with the Game Master, He will reason with you. He says that though your evil ways are like the stain of deep, red blood, when you turn to Him from doing wrong (repent), His Son's blood will wash your crimson stains and make your status with Him as white as snow (Isa. 1:16–18). If you are paying for your crimes, you were judged by His agents of justice and may not see a reprieve on this game level or until your debt to society is paid. When you take His lifeline and become a member, you become the Game Master's ambassador of His grace no matter where you live or languish (Rom. 13:1–5; 2 Cor. 5:17–21).

> The Ten Commandments were given so that all could see the extent of their failure to obey God's laws. But the more we see our sinfulness, the more we see God's abounding grace forgiving us. Before, sin ruled over all men and brought them to death, but now God's kindness rules instead, giving us right standing with God and resulting in eternal life through Jesus Christ our Lord (Rom. 5:20–21 TLB).

> Blessed and happy and favored are those whose lawless acts have been forgiven, And whose sins have been covered up and completely buried. Blessed and happy and favored is the man whose sin the Lord

will not take into account nor charge against him (Rom. 4:7–8 AMP; Ps. 32:1–2).

Even if your victims or society will never forgive you, the Game Master can forgive you. When you turn to Him for His lifeline, you are no longer condemned by the Judge of all the earth (John 3:16–21; Gen. 18:25; Ps. 96:12–13; 98:8–9; John 8:10–11).

9. Persecution

This is one case where there is no question why bad things happen to good people or whether they will occur. This point is noteworthy because persecution is the only situation where the Game Master offers no promise to deliver His own members from hard times of persecution or death. The One said that if the Master is persecuted, His servants should expect nothing better (John 15:19–21). This does not mean members cannot receive help from Him when they are persecuted.

In this section, I am speaking specifically of persecution against members, believers in the One, Jesus Christ, the citizens of the kingdom of the Game Master according to the Manual. This section does not include martyrs of any other religion or ideology; they are still victims of atrocities and bad people nonetheless.

This point is a contrast to all the other points that have been listed. Since the Game Master is not the cause or reason for trouble in our lives, His ability to prevent or protect us from trouble in all the other points we have listed can be requested by us and granted by Him on His terms.

However, about persecution, He said that what was done to Him and the prophets He sent will also be done to members. The *Book of Martyrs* by John Foxe (1709, full book) catalogs the untimely deaths of those who, through the ages, chose to keep their ticket, their faith in the One, and accept death instead. The book, *Persecuted: The Global Assault on Christians*, discusses the current persecution of members across the game world (Marshall, Gilbert, & Shea 2013, full book). Those who endure to the end are promised a Crown of Life. Master player Paul said, "Yes, and all who desire to live godly in Christ Jesus will suffer persecution" (2 Tim. 3:12 NKJV). Those who track religious intolerance observe that Christianity is the most persecuted religion in the game (Bandow 2013, ¶ 17).

The One reminded his members that He had already told them the servant isn't greater than his lord; since He was persecuted, they would be persecuted too (John 15:20). The years 2013 and 2014 and following saw the greatest persecution of Christians around the globe in modern days and increasing each year. Going into 2024, persecution is intensifying in India's Manipur state, where the United

Nations experts have appealed the government, and Nigeria, where more than 18,000 churches have been set ablaze since 2009 and five million Christians internally displaced. Pakistan and many Middle East nations and Africa are seeing violence increase against Christians (Snyder 2023a, ¶ 5–9).

It is reported to be especially acute in Middle East countries where the number of professing members has dropped from 20 percent to four percent in the region (Šerić, 2023, ¶ 4). Their livelihoods, safety, and very lives are imperiled with no apparent hope for a reprieve from the game world community's United Nations. Persecution concerns can be tracked around the world. Organizations like Voice of the Martyrs and Open Doors offer ways to assist those persecuted for their faith.

Instead of promising blanket protection, the One said that believers in Him will be mistreated, tortured, killed, and hated by "all nations" on earth (Matt. 24:8–9). It was hard to imagine persecution happening in the "Christian" nations before the turn of the millennium. However, attitudes among the game world populations toward members are quickly changing as they are now viewed more like troublemakers and contrary to everyone else. A new term, Christofascist, was coined in early May 2022 to describe conservatives who push their "religious morals on the rest of the nation—whether they like it or not" (Charles 2022, ¶ 4).

One way to gauge and observe this shift is to read the comments players make about religious players in web articles that include religious or moral themes or where commenters may insert a religious context. Many guests are comfortable with making disapproving statements about members, going so far as saying the game world will be a better place when they are finally gone with their fairy tale god.

Andrew Brunson and his wife were missionaries to Turkey for twenty-five years. One day, they were invited to the police station, where he was subsequently held for more than two years. He relates that:

> They wanted to make an example of someone in order to intimidate other Christians, and they chose me. They threatened to give me three life sentences in solitary confinement.
>
> I thought of myself as a relatively tough missionary—we had faced threats before; I had even been shot at once. But I was not prepared for what I experienced in prison. It was much more difficult than I imagined it would be, and I almost didn't make it through. Persecution almost knocked me out.

Many Christians do not think this can happen in the United States, but it can. Followers of Jesus throughout history and in countries around the world have experienced persecution. In fact, our experience of very little persecution up to now is the exception (Brunson 2022, ¶ 1, 3–5).

Many members in Western nations still hold the mistaken belief that their own country is still a generally God-fearing nation. Unfortunately, those actual numbers of professing members do not reflect the sincerity of their belief and so are not likely nearly as high or firm as the polls suggest.

In the member community, there is reportedly little difference in many moral indicators compared to the general player population. Thinking that their worldview is still in the majority, there is a tendency for religious players to scold the nation about its ungodly ways. But they are no longer speaking to like-minded fellow citizens. Instead, their lectures are annoying more and more players who have walked away from the Game Master and chose to play the game by their own code because the Serpent doesn't bother them.

Choosing the Game Master's team includes the very real possibility of personal danger. How imminent that is depends on the country or family you live in, but as Moses chose to give up even Egypt's riches and instead suffer with the other members on the side of the One, we have the same choice today with the same expected outcome (Heb. 11:24–26).

> Dear friends, do not be surprised at the fiery ordeal that has come on you to test you, as though something strange were happening to you. But rejoice inasmuch as you participate in the sufferings of Christ, so that you may be overjoyed when his glory is revealed. If you are insulted because of the name of Christ, you are blessed, for the Spirit of glory and of God rests on you. If you suffer, it should not be as a murderer or thief or any other kind of criminal, or even as a meddler.
>
> However, if you suffer as a Christian, do not be ashamed, but praise God that you bear that name. For it is time for judgment to begin with God's household; and if it begins with us, what will the outcome be for those who do not obey the gospel of God? And,

"If it is hard for the righteous to be saved, what will become of the ungodly and the sinner?" So then, those who suffer according to God's will should commit themselves to their faithful Creator and continue to do good (1 Pet. 4:12–19 NIV; Prov. 11:31).

Precious in the sight of the LORD is the death of his saints (Ps. 116:15).

10. God Only Knows

The final point here is a catch-all statement that is used when we are totally perplexed by life's misfortunes: God works in mysterious ways. Apparently, the Game Master keeps secrets too, saying that He doesn't think the way we do because our perspectives are worlds apart and so much more limited than His (Isa. 55:8–9).

Master prophet Job said in his suffering that even if the Game Master killed him, he would still trust Him (Job 13:15). Job knew his eternal outcome in the bonus round was assured. Even today, when we have pursued every avenue for healing or help and still come up short, what fear is there of death when you can know the Game Master keeps you in His care and is your hope beyond the grave? (Rom. 8:35–39; 1 Cor. 15:51–58; Phil. 4:6–7; Jude 1:20–25; Rev. 12:11).

Many kiosk scholars teach or imply that the Game Master allows suffering and injects suffering into our life experience to make us better players. They use the Manual to prove that their teaching and perspective is Manual-based. However, as you read these texts, which are used to prove the point, notice that 1) the source or instigator of suffering is not clearly identified, and 2) regardless of the source, the Spirit Master can provide the player with comfort and support for us as we push through times of suffering toward a beneficial development of character with personal and spiritual maturity. Speaking to members, the authors Paul, James, and Peter tell us,

> Therefore, since we have been justified by faith, we have peace with God through our Lord Jesus Christ. Through him we have also obtained access by faith into this grace in which we stand, and we rejoice in hope of the glory of God. Not only that, but **we rejoice in our sufferings**, knowing that **suffering produces endurance**, and **endurance produces character**, and **character produces hope**, and **hope does not put us to shame**, because **God's love has been poured into our hearts** through the Holy Spirit who has been given to us (Rom. 5:1–5 ESV, emphasis added).

So be truly glad. There is wonderful joy ahead, even though **you must endure many trials for a little while. These trials will show that your faith is genuine. It is being tested** as fire tests and purifies gold—though your faith is far more precious than mere gold. So **when your faith remains strong through many trials, it will bring you much praise and glory and honor** on the day when Jesus Christ is revealed to the whole world (1 Pet. 1:6–7 NLT, emphasis added).

Consider it pure joy, my brothers and sisters, **whenever you face trials of many kinds**, because you know that **the testing of your faith produces perseverance**. Let perseverance finish its work so that you may be **mature and complete**, not lacking anything (James 1:2–4 NIV, emphasis added).

Players may experience wavering faith in trials, but the Game Master provides reasons to hold on to that faith even through an unknown cause. Notice that the troubles we feel in this physical realm can be catalysts to strengthen our psychological and spiritual resolve. This is something we must choose to do on purpose.

As you search for comfort in your losses, you will rarely find kiosk leaders assisting you in finding your trouble's source or root cause. Finding a source or cause for suffering is not on the agenda. Their typical focus in the aftermath of loss is comfort, healing, and moving on. But if you are walking through a field of tripwires from an unresolved spiritual cause, you may simply be moving on to the next tripwire of trouble instead of removing them.

It is said that knowledge is power. Knowing why you experience what happens to you can be helpful in knowing what to do next. This book aims to help you find those causes and apply the Game Master's fixes to help you recover and prosper and prevent recurrences. Even though we have now come to the end of finding reasons, we are not without solutions and benefits from what happens to us.

> We may run out of reasons for our trouble, but we still have solutions and choices.

Whatever touches your experience, the Game Master can apply a purpose to it so you can become a better player from having gone through what you did, whether it was something good, bad, or indifferent that happened to you. If all other reasons are exhausted, you can still create value through personal growth from an unknown source of trouble when the Game Master's love has been poured into your heart through the Spirit Master (Rom. 5:1–5).

Game Master's perspective

The Game Master has another perspective of suffering, which is typically left unsaid. What you suffer can help you become a helper to others in their suffering.

> Praise be to the God and Father of our Lord Jesus Christ, **the Father of compassion and the God of all comfort, who comforts us in all our troubles, so that we can comfort those in any trouble with the comfort we ourselves receive from God.** For just as we share abundantly in the sufferings of Christ, so also our comfort abounds through Christ. If we are distressed, it is for your comfort and salvation; if we are comforted, it is for your comfort, which produces in you patient endurance of the same sufferings we suffer (2 Cor. 1:3–6 NIV, emphasis added).

I printed a poster with these verses and displayed it in the main lobby of a Baptist school during the aftermath of the 9-11 attacks in 2001. Many of the children in the school knew somebody who was affected by the attack on the Pentagon in Washington, DC.

When we experience the compassion of the God of all comfort, we should take the comfort He gave us and pass it on to those who suffer. The Game Master wants you to become a comforter to others as a result of what you experienced. This is how we show the love of the Game Master when they don't feel Him near to them.

Game Master's testing

Another aspect of the Game Master's perspective is that He would test the resolve of those who say they are committed to Him. Those who overcome the temptation would continue having His blessing, and those who succumb to the test would face the consequence or get the curse associated with that failure.

He gives an example of a prophet or visionary who, using a miraculous sign or wonder, counsels others to participate in the religion of their neighbors, a direct Big Ten violation of His explicit Rules 1 and 2 about the worship of other gods:

"For the Lord your God is testing you to know whether you love the Lord your God with all your heart and mind and all your soul [your entire being]" (Deut. 13:3b AMP).

Every week, the Game Master tests many members in this way by the syncretism and the Emergent and New Age philosophies and practices that come floating through their kiosks. Do you recognize them? Do you accept them? Which of your pastors or leaders likes to be on the cutting edge of different new teachings?

In another example, the Game Master instructed His prophet Jeremiah to bring the family group of the Rechabites into a temple room, set wine before them, and have them drink it. They refused because their ancestor Jonadab, the son of Rechab, charged his sons and their descendants forever to never drink wine, among other things. Because his family refused the wine and refused to disobey Jonadab, the Game Master immediately pronounced that there would always be a male descendant of Jonadab (Jer. 35).

The Game Master doesn't post your test dates on the bulletin board. Always evaluate your choices from the Game Master's perspective and according to His commands. Many circumstances of life provide a means or opportunity to develop character or correct deficiencies, to navigate a solution with Spirit Master guidance, or to recalibrate our connection or commitment to the Game Master. Some situations, like Job's, may require great patience or personal growth, but success is possible with the Game Master's resources (1 Cor. 10:13).

> THE GAME MASTER DOESN'T POST YOUR TEST DATES ON THE BULLETIN BOARD.

Members who know the Manual and have a habit of responding to the promptings of the Spirit Master are more likely to naturally pass these types of testing. Guests would not be tested in this manner since they are not on His team.

GAME MASTER'S DISCIPLINE

There is also the matter of being disciplined by the Game Master for not following His directives. Master player Paul ordered the discipline of some members of the Corinthian kiosk by excluding them from the group for immoral behavior (1 Cor. 5). After they corrected their behavior and changed their ways, he urged the kiosk to restore those members to the group to prevent their discouragement as members (2 Cor. 2:6–11).

This scenario is also called church discipline. It is sometimes used in this described manner. However, if a minor is involved in a case of abuse by an adult, the minor is more likely to be punished and the adult only has to say they are sorry and perhaps move on to another kiosk.

Kiosks also insert church discipline into the home when a couple is separated due to infidelity or abuse, usually by the husband. If the husband says he's sorry, the kiosk pressures or disciplines the wife for not returning home or allowing him back home. Rather than resolving issues, the kiosk picks a side based on whether the offended party forgives and lets bygones be bygones. This empowers the offending party to insist things return to normal rather than holding them accountable to demonstrate a change of heart which takes time. Many times, even when trauma is involved, the kiosk is more interested in the impact on the public image of the situation and the kiosk, saying it reflects poorly on the cause of Christ.

The purpose of discipline is a corrective measure because the Game Master loves His members (Prov. 3:12; Heb. 12:5–7). This means that disciplinary action is done with a purpose and is not random or undeserved. It also means that His discipline does not deliver knockout blows that devastate a member. If a member experiences an overwhelming disaster, then there is likely a different issue at work.

Game Master's glory

This seems to be the very favorite reason from most kiosk leaders and teachers, which may generously account for 90 percent or more of the reasons cited for our sufferings. Not only do they not have to diagnose any spiritual baggage you may have, but they also don't have to figure out why bad things happen to you because it's obviously for the Game Master's glory, whatever that means. A Manual passage supporting this says,

> As he was walking along, he saw a man blind from birth. "Master," his disciples asked him, "why was this man born blind? Was it a result of his own sins or those of his parents?" "Neither," Jesus answered. "But to demonstrate the power of God. All of us must quickly carry out the tasks assigned us by the one who sent me, for there is little time left before the night falls and all work comes to an end. But while I am still here in the world, I give it my light."
>
> Then he spat on the ground and made mud from the spittle and smoothed the mud over the blind man's eyes, and told him, "Go and wash in the Pool of Siloam" (the word Siloam means "Sent"). So the man went where he was sent and washed and came back seeing!
>
> His neighbors and others who knew him as a blind beggar asked each other, "Is this the same fellow—that beggar?" Some said yes, and some said no. "It can't be the same man," they thought, "but he surely looks like him!" And the beggar said, "I am the same man!" Then they asked him how in the world he could see. What had happened? And

he told them, "A man they call Jesus made mud and smoothed it over my eyes and told me to go to the Pool of Siloam and wash off the mud. I did, and I can see!" "Where is he now?" they asked. "I don't know," he replied (John 9:1–10 TLB).

There you have it. The beggar was born blind only to bring the Game Master glory, not for any underlying sinful cause or spiritual baggage. The difference is that the Game Master healed the blind man—for His glory, but your kiosk leader may likely tell you to live with it—for His glory (2 Cor. 12:8–10). The Game Master's glory was in the healing, not in blinding him, which He did not claim to do. However, our kiosk leaders don't follow His example and heal the hurt, which questions the Game Master's glory.

Let's address the cause of his blindness. The One said that game violations by him or his parents were not the cause. This leaves other game world environmental causes on the table. "Vitamin A deficiency is a major cause of preventable blindness in the world" and is prevalent in developing countries (Oregon State University n.d., ¶ 3, 26, 28–29).

> The National Library of Medicine gives the leading causes of infant blindness. "The causes of SVI [severe visual impairment] and blindness may be prenatal, perinatal, and postnatal. Congenital anomalies such as anophthalmos, microphthalmos, coloboma, congenital cataract, infantile glaucoma, and neuro-ophthalmic lesions are causes of impairment present at birth" (Gogate, Gilbert, and Zin 2011, ¶ 1).

The passage does not say that the Game Master blinded him to leave him blind, but He used the blindness to demonstrate His power. But did the Game Master really blind him? God only knows, but the disciples didn't imply that. The One did not say He did that or elaborate on the cause but focused on the solution.

Given the many thousands of players that He healed, why did He need an object lesson? The story goes on that after the One healed the beggar, He ghosted him. The healed beggar only heard the One's name but didn't know where He went or what He looked like. Was this healing a lesson for the priests? The beggar was left defending the One by himself, concluding He was a prophet and ended up getting kicked out of the local kiosk.

The One later connected with him and asked if he believed in the Messiah. The beggar believed, and he worshipped Him when the One revealed His identity. Then the One said, "I have come into the world to give sight to those who are spiritually blind and to show those who think they see that they are blind" (John 9:39 TLB).

This is the other purpose of this story. The One came to give sight to the spiritually blind and used a physically blind beggar who suffered through his life as a lesson on the impact of His healing grace both now and for eternity. The beggar's life was transformed so he could live on par with those in the community, and although he was excommunicated by the kiosk, his eternal gameplay was assured.

This lesson also points out that even though you may not come up with a cause for your life's problems, you can still find help from the Game Master. He came to give you spiritual sight, but you can ask Him for physical help too, which gives Him glory.

Game Master's judgment

There are appointed judgment times for nations that the Game Master sets. The wickedness of the Amorite people hadn't reached the point of no return when the Game Master was talking to Abraham, so he let another 400 years transpire before He brought judgment against them (Gen. 15:16). The image shown to King Nebuchadnezzar in his dream was interpreted by Daniel as successive world powers that would rise and fall over thousands of years until the Game Master's kingdom would clear the playing field and reign over the game world (Dan. 2:31–45).

Jonah. One story that illustrates the Game Master's patience with players is the account of Jonah and the whale as told in the Manual book of Jonah (Jonah 1:1–4:11). Jonah, the prophet, was minding his own business when the Game Master told him to go the city of Nineveh (in northern Iraq) with the message that Nineveh would be overthrown in forty days. Jonah knew the Game Master was allowing them to clean up their act and refused to go in case the Ninevites repented. So he hopped on a ship to Spain and took off in the opposite direction.

> But as the ship was sailing along, suddenly the Lord flung a terrific wind over the sea, causing a great storm that threatened to send them to the bottom. Fearing for their lives, the desperate sailors shouted to their gods for help and threw the cargo overboard to lighten the ship. And all this time Jonah was sound asleep down in the hold.

So the captain went down after him. "What do you mean," he roared, "sleeping at a time like this? Get up and cry to your god, and see if he will have mercy on us and save us!"

Then the crew decided to draw straws to see which of them had offended the gods and caused this terrible storm; and Jonah drew the short one. "What have you done," they asked, "to bring this awful storm upon us? Who are you? What is your work? What country are you from? What is your nationality?"

And he said, "I am a Jew; I worship Jehovah, the God of heaven, who made the earth and sea." Then he told them he was running away from the Lord. The men were terribly frightened when they heard this. "Oh, why did you do it?" they shouted. "What should we do to you to stop the storm?" For it was getting worse and worse.

"Throw me out into the sea," he said, "and it will become calm again. For I know this terrible storm has come because of me" (Jon. 1:3–12 TLB).

The crew didn't want to throw Jonah overboard and tried more to ballast the ship but finally gave up and heaved him over the side. Suddenly, a big fish gulped Jonah down, and a great calm came over the sea.

Jonah spent three days and nights inside the fish pondering his choices, repented, and decided to obey the Game Master. After he was vomited out on a beach, he made his way to Nineveh and began giving his message that the city would be destroyed in forty days. It's said that Nineveh was so big that it took three days to cross town. It is estimated that Nineveh had about 600,000 inhabitants (Geisler and Howe 2014, ¶ 2).

Word got to the king, and he decreed that the entire citizenry stop their evil deeds and—including animals—eat or drink nothing, put on sackcloth, and strenuously pray for mercy from God in the hope that He would spare them.

The Game Master relented and spared the city. Jonah got steaming mad and seethed, "I told you this would happen! You're too gracious, merciful, patient, excessively loving, and eager to relent! That's why I headed for Spain! I wish I were dead!" Jonah then set up a booth east of town to watch for the coming disaster. The Game Master made a vine grow and gave him some relief from the heat. Jonah was extremely happy for the shade.

Then the Game Master sent a worm to chew through the vine and kill it. As he fainted from the heat and wished for death over his anger about the dead vine, the Game Master responded,

> "You pity the plant, for which you did not labor, nor did you make it grow, which came into being in a night and perished in a night. And should not I pity Nineveh, that great city, in which there are more than 120,000 persons who do not know their right hand from their left, and also much cattle?" (Jon. 4:10–11 ESV).

It is said that Nineveh lasted another 150 years after this event. The repentance of the city gave life to the following several generations.

Disasters. Sometimes you will hear from a broadcast preacher that a particular natural disaster is the hand of "God's judgment" on a city or country for certain sins. It could be an earthquake, hurricane, tornado, crippling storm, or devastating disease. If it's true that He's the instigator, then those events could certainly be called an act of God.

Comments like these make players nationwide rise up in anger against these "preachers of hate." Historically, however, this connection from the pulpit—associating the Game Master's judgment with national or natural crises—has been going on for millennia. However, a major difference is that only now are we in a country that is secularized to the point that it is no longer well-received by hardly any faction.

That question, whether disaster equals the Game Master's judgment, seems to persist. This same point was brought up to the One after the Roman governor, Pontius Pilate, killed some Galileans and mixed their blood with the holy sacrifices. The assumption was that this was God's judgment on those Galileans for their worse game violations and perhaps they wanted the One to confirm it.

But the One asked them, "Do you suppose that these Galileans were worse sinners than all other Galileans, because they suffered such things? I tell you, no; but unless you repent you will all likewise perish" (Luke 13:2–3 NKJV).

This was probably a shock to their theology and the opposite of what they expected to hear. Then He went on to press the point, saying, "Or those eighteen on whom the tower in Siloam fell and killed them, do you think that they were worse sinners than all other men who dwelt in Jerusalem? I tell you, no; but unless you repent you will all likewise perish" (Luke 13:4–5 NKJV).

So, was it the Game Master's judgment? The One clearly said no. He did not go on to give other possible reasons for those tragedies, but He made it clear that the sinful condition of those players was not the reason for their deaths. Instead, He reminded them that they were all under the same condemnation of the Game Master unless they repented. This is a perspective of the Manual text where the One said, "He who believes in Him [Jesus] is not condemned; but he who does not believe is condemned already, because he has not believed in the name of the only begotten Son of God" (John 3:18 NKJV).

Yes, it remains possible for the Game Master to wipe out a city for its game violations, but anyone who has not believed in the One is already living under the condemnation of the Game Master. That point could be raised about any disaster area. All the other reasons we've discussed could have been associated with those incidents the One discussed, but He didn't elaborate for those who asked.

Anti-Semitism. This point belongs in the section on Curses but will be addressed here as a national issue. First, let's look at the Game Master's blessing to Abraham:

> And I will make of you a great nation, and I will bless you and make your name great, so that you will be a blessing. **I will bless those who bless you, and him who dishonors you I will curse**, and in you all the families of the earth shall be blessed [or, by you all the families of the earth shall bless themselves] (Gen. 12:2–3 ESV, emphasis added).

In the next generation, Isaac blesses his son Jacob:

> "Let peoples serve you, and nations bow down to you. Be lord over your brothers, and may your mother's sons bow down to you. **Cursed be everyone who curses you, and blessed be everyone who blesses you!**" (Gen. 27:29 ESV, emphasis added).

The Game Master extended to Abraham and all his descendants conditional blessings or curses upon all players and nations that interacted with him or his descendants. This means that, even today, the treatment of Israel by individual players or nations will result in either a blessing or a curse. Israel is the only nation in the game world to have such a conditional promise associated with it.

John McTernan wrote a book called, *As America Has Done to Israel*. McTernan goes through America's history and correlates its rise as a powerful nation with its treatment of the Jewish people. In recent decades, he identifies when the American government publicly declined to support Israel's interests and instead pressured her to exchange land for peace with her enemies. He found that, within twenty-four hours of its decisions, America suffered dramatic catastrophes with the losses of hundreds of lives and up to hundreds of billions of dollars in damages (McTernan 2012, back cover).

These events include hurricanes suddenly turning toward and reaching landfall, earthquakes, floods, wildfires, major tornadoes, financial market crises, and so on. In all events, major damage was done to the American regional or national economy.

Another author, Geoffrey Grider, has an article that identifies eleven disasters since the Perfect Storm of 1991 to Hurricane Katrina in 2005 that each struck within twenty-four hours of the American government's pressure against Israel (Grider 2014, entire article). Who were America's presidents during those years?

Most television preachers fail to draw a connection to this specific curse regarding Israel. Instead, they usually identify the sins of the affected city, region, or nation as the cause of these disasters. The answer to this issue of God's judgments on America appears to be, yes, there can be a spiritual cause, and Israel may be a determining factor.

The interesting aspect of this blessing and curse dynamic with Israel is that it may also happen on a case-by-case basis. If so, it suggests that supporting Israel should conversely result in an outcome of blessing for America on a case-by-case basis.

An example of this blessing could be the exceptional prosperity America saw during the time when President Trump was supporting Israel throughout his presidency by moving the US Embassy to Jerusalem, brokering the Abraham Accords peace agreements between Israel and the Arab nations, and canceling the nuclear agreement with Iran, Israel's archenemy. He also provided support in Palestinian matters and in security and economic growth.

During that time, America saw phenomenal prosperity with record and historic employment across the board, real wage increases for the working class, achieving energy independence for the first time, low gas prices and low inflation, record stock market prices, greater border control, and maintaining peace with other nations (Archives 2021, ¶ 1–2, 4, 11, 15, 38–46).

Although the COVID-19 pandemic stalled the nation, a solid recovery was in progress when a new administration stepped in. We have since learned that all this prosperity happened despite the continued efforts of deep state operatives across the government bureaucracy and intelligence community to handicap and thwart President Trump's initiatives and remove him from office.

When the following administration took over, President Biden reversed course and shut down support for the Israeli gas pipeline to Europe, looked to reverse the US Embassy move, drove wedges into the peace agreements, began affirming

Palestinian grievances, and resumed nuclear negotiations with Iran. During his first year and beyond, America's energy independence evaporated, and the economy went up in smoke with historically high gas prices and rising inflation that devoured the wage increases from the Trump years and imperiled the nation's food supply.

It's easy to say that President Trump was a good manager and President Biden was not. However, given the subversive opposition President Trump faced throughout his presidency from his Cabinet, agencies, Congress, and the courts, plus his own bellicose ways, his political missteps, and the poor advice he received in choosing advisors and Cabinet appointments, there was arguably a success in America that transcended his management skills. It seems plausible to argue for a spiritual factor regarding Israel that drove his success than for his winning against all odds through his own ability alone.

We have some current examples of the curse dynamic impacting President Biden's treatment of Israel in 2024.

> Is the destruction of the temporary pier President Joe Biden ordered erected on the coastline of the Gaza Strip just the latest example of God judging this administration for its push to have Israel divide its land?
>
> Less than two weeks after its completion, the pier broke into pieces and much of it submerged "[d]ue to high sea states and a North African weather system," Pentagon spokeswoman Sabrina Singh said Tuesday, according to Stars and Stripes.
>
> The weather-induced destruction of the structure, coupled with a deadly string of tornadoes in the American heartland, not seen in years, appears to fit a pattern: Whenever the U.S. has pressured Israel to divide its land, bad and often catastrophic things have happened.
>
> Bible scholars have pointed to the Bible's book of Genesis, Chapter 12 as an explanation for this phenomenon in which God says to Abraham: "I will bless those who bless you, and I will curse him who curses you."
>
> A Gallup poll published in December showed 65 percent of Israelis opposed the two-state plan, while 25 percent supported it. In January, Politico reported, "The two-state solution is dead," citing that polling.

The clear concern is that if more territory is ceded to the Palestinians, it would just offer more opportunities to strike Israel.

Yet on May 19, Biden reiterated during his commencement address at Morehouse College in Atlanta, "I'm working to make sure we finally get a two-state solution, the only solution for two people."

That same day, Biden National Security Advisor Jake Sullivan was meeting with Israeli Prime Minister Benjamin Netanyahu, having just come from talks with Crown Prince and Prime Minster of Saudi Arabia Mohamed bin Salman "focused on a comprehensive vision for an integrated Middle East region," the U.S. Embassy in Israel said in a news release.

That "comprehensive vision" includes "a two-state solution that meets the aspirations and legitimate rights of the Palestinian people," the administration said, according to Politico.

So rough seas destroying the pier came the same week that the Biden administration was negotiating with Saudi Arabia and no doubt trying to pressure Israel to give up more of its land.

The timing of the destruction of the Francis Scott Key Bridge in Baltimore Harbor last month came in even closer proximity to an adverse action taken by the U.S. toward Israel.

On March 25, the United Nations Security Council passed a resolution calling for an immediate cease-fire in Israel's war with Hamas.

Rather than exercise its veto power, as the U.S. has done consistently in the past to protect the Jewish state from the U.N.'s pronounced, long-standing anti-Israel bias, the Biden administration abstained from voting.

"The U.S. declining to protect Israel from a resolution it passionately objects to by not providing a veto is an extraordinary thing," Hussein

Ibish, a senior resident scholar at the Arab Gulf States Institute in Washington, told CNBC.

The following morning at 1:30 a.m., a cargo ship ran into the Francis Scott Key Bridge, causing it to collapse and killing six workers, as well as shutting down the Port of Baltimore, one of the busiest in the country, for the foreseeable future.

As the Biden administration continues to push a two-state solution, the U.S. has gone through one of its worst tornado seasons in years, USA Today reported Wednesday.

"Since April 26, the U.S. has experienced 18 killer tornadoes in which 36 people have died," the news outlet said.

"We've had a lot of tornadoes and several 'big' days," Harold Brooks, a senior scientist at the National Severe Storms Laboratory in Norman, Oklahoma, told USA Today.

"Preliminarily, the U.S. has seen four days with at least 30 tornadoes rated EF1 or stronger," Brooks told the news outlet. "The average is two a year. That likely puts 2024 in the top 10% of years."

Between April 25 and May 27, tornadoes touched down on all but two days, The Washington Post noted.

Further, during that time period, 17 of those days "had PDS [particularly dangerous situation] tornado warnings, the most on record for that stretch" of time.

Divine judgment, or just coincidence?

Only God knows for sure, but there has been a pattern going back decades that makes one believe He's seeking to communicate to America's leadership: "Stop trying to force Israel to divide its land" (DeSoto 2024, ¶ 1–2, 5–6, 12–22, 47–54).

Other spiritual dynamics are impacting America's trend lines, but focusing on Israel's blessing and curse dynamic shows an astounding contrast over eight years. One of the dynamics driving the economic downturn is the Biden administration's pursuit of the Agenda 21 and Agenda 2030 initiatives that cause economic hardships. This could be argued on a spiritual level as well. So, the next question is, is the downturn part of a divine judgment on America?

The Game Master detailed judgment on guest nations of the ancient world ranking from small regional countries to consecutive superpowers. He gave reasons for judgment against them and sometimes explained how they would fall into the ashbin of history. During those times, many of the pagan nations also associated punishing judgment or their weak gods with the loss of their national power. So, there is precedence for spiritual factors with those associated statements about regional and national disasters.

The Game Master declared His sovereignty in that, He sets up the nations and brings them down (Ps. 75:6–7; Dan. 2:21). What will happen at the end of the game was explained by the One, and as players increasingly travel a path away from the Game Master, hard times of their own making will follow as the game now heads toward the Apocalypse.

The Game Master called out the Serpent for his hand in the trend toward Apocalypse when He said, "How you are fallen from heaven, O Lucifer, son of the morning! How you are cut down to the ground, You who weakened the nations!" (Isa. 14:12 NKJV).

Has anything changed? Yes, the playing field has changed since the Old Testament. The Game Master's host of guardians proclaimed, "Peace on Earth, good will toward men." Master player Peter said the Game Master is not a promise breaker but is holding out until the end of the Game, hoping for all guests to join His team (2 Pet. 3:9; 2 Cor. 6:2; Heb. 3:7–19).

We still have natural disasters, epidemics, and conflicts that increasingly circle the globe, but these are not necessarily the Game Master's judgment for game violations. He could be applying pressure to turn players' attention toward Him as the Apocalypse approaches, or they could be consequences of players' game violations through curses, or they could be Serpent instigations through players, or all the above.

He does not deal with us like He did in the previous millennia B.C. Game violations have been paid for and covered by the blood of the One. He was the Game-Changer whose death and resurrection ushered in an age of grace, making it possible for you to see the bonus round.

Conclusion

For now, we don't operate with the complete body of knowledge that the Game Master has, and we don't have the perspective from His vantage point of time so that some things will remain hidden for now. The time is coming when the members will see the whole game and understand (1 Cor. 13:12). As master player Moses put it, "The secret things belong to the Lord our God: but those things which are revealed belong to us and to our children forever, that we may do all the words of this law" (Deut. 29:29 KJV).

Undoubtedly, we don't have all the answers, but most of what happens to us in life is not mysterious. There is a reason, and only when we have pursued every avenue and returned empty, then this is the conclusion of last resort: God only knows.

> **WE DON'T HAVE ALL THE ANSWERS, BUT MOST OF WHAT HAPPENS TO US IN LIFE IS NOT MYSTERIOUS.**

Hurt Zone Summary

HAVE YOU ALREADY experienced overwhelming loss? Do you see catastrophic losses headed your way? Are your storm clouds black and your future days even darker?

The prophet Habakkuk called out to the Game Master because half of the nation was in exile, and it didn't seem like He was listening. The Game Master replied and told Habakkuk that he had a plan, and worse days were coming with the Chaldeans, who would displace the Babylonians. How do you respond when your only source and hope of good news turns out to be even worse bad news? (Pastor Landon 2019, entire video).

> I heard and my whole inner self trembled; My lips quivered at the sound. Decay and rottenness enter my bones, And I tremble in my place. Because I must wait quietly for the day of distress, For the people to arise who will invade and attack us.
>
> Though the fig tree does not blossom And there is no fruit on the vines, Though the yield of the olive fails And the fields produce no food, Though the flock is cut off from the fold And there are no cattle in the stalls, Yet I will [choose to] rejoice in the LORD; I will [choose to] shout in exultation in the [victorious] God of my salvation!
>
> The Lord GOD is my strength [my source of courage, my invincible army]; He has made my feet [steady and sure] like hinds' feet And makes me walk [forward with spiritual confidence] on my high places [of challenge and responsibility] (Hab. 3:16–19 AMP).

The Amplified Bible footnote for this passage says that, "The troubled times of life may actually be the "high places" of spiritual growth for the believer who remains stable when tested by God" (*Amplified Bible* 2015, 1419, Hab. 3:19 footnote).

Is this your situation? What is your response when bad things happen to you? Will the Game Master be your source of courage, strength, and stability in your dark days?

We have described major devastations through war, violence, genocide, disease, and natural disasters that have impacted many millions of players, with up to billions of us unnaturally ending our gameplay in the coming years. These seem like nameless and faceless issues, but they hurt and distress millions of individuals, families, and perhaps players you know or love.

Whatever way we view the reasons described in this section and whether we choose to accept these as valid points, it has been explained that the Game Master has revealed the many causes of human suffering beyond what we see around us.

There may be more nuanced reasons than are mentioned here, but these main reasons listed should give you some tools to identify different ones you may experience. Once we know the source of the trouble, we can then check for solutions. Ultimately, what you choose to do with your knowledge will identify whom you blame.

10 Reasons for Bad Things

What is your source of trouble?

Free Will - 1 4

Spirit Laws & Power - 1 2 3

Curses - 1 2 3 4

The World + Gov't - 2 3 4

The Flesh - 2 3 4

The Devil - 1 2

Bad Decisions - 1 3 4

Bad People - 2 4

Persecution - 2 4

God Only Knows - 1 2 3 4

Four Sources of Trouble
Mix & Match

1. Spirit Laws
2. Serpent & Henchmen
3. Game Environ. + Curses
4. Players: You & Others

Section IV: The Cure Zone

Fixing your Broken Life

> *"If your life isn't supernatural, then it's superficial"* —Andrew Wommack (Wommack 2022b, entire; cf. 2022c, ¶ 3)

IT'S TIME TO put on your game face. This is the members section, where faith is applied to life. This section aims to translate spiritual truths and concepts into a practical way for you to improve your life situation, daily circumstances, and future prospects. Having a faith that doesn't significantly help your life on earth is a faith that's hard to keep alive and hold close to you or pass on to your children. Miracles in the Manual were demonstrated as signs reinforcing the authority of the One by those who followed and represented Him. Members are both the recipients and the dispensers of His miraculous grace.

Obstacle Diagnosis

ALL SUCCESSFUL CURES start with a correct diagnosis. Before we work on the cure, we need to learn how to diagnose the causes related to your situation. In the previous two sections, we outlined how bad things that happen to us come from four main sources:

1) Violations of Spirit laws, God's moral code: curses, strongholds, sin
2) Influence by the Serpent and his spirit-being henchmen and minions, either directly or indirectly
3) The result of the curse on the game environment plus all the curses triggered by the players upon themselves, which collectively include disease, hostile living conditions, the pressures of life, and so on
4) Players: other players who do bad things, whether physically or psychologically, or the bad choices we make that result in harm or a violation of spirit laws

Bad things that hit us can be multiple combinations of any of those four sources: Spirit laws, the Serpent, the cursed game environment, or player choices. The previous section of bad stuff explained how these sources present themselves across ten major categories: 1) Free Will, 2) Spirit Laws and Power, 3) Curses, 4) The World, 5) The Flesh, 6) The Devil, 7) Bad Decisions, 8) Bad People, 9) Persecution, and 10) God Only Knows.

A section with barriers to healing will also be included here. Healing is of great interest to most players, and understanding how to improve your prospects for healing is part of the diagnosis process.

Perhaps you are looking for a miracle to undo the damage or loss you have experienced, a solution to stop continuous cycles of bad things that come against you, or a way to change your life experience to one with consistent and expected goodness and peace. All these things require an injection of supernatural power. This is where the Game Master operates best.

Many stories in the Manual's historical books describe how His members started with a disadvantage so large that it took a miracle to pull them through their tight spot. His point repeatedly was that if He is going to pull you through and make you prosper, you must do it His way, and He gets all the credit.

We are not talking about matters where simple persistence will help you overcome, like immigrating to a new country with a dollar in your pocket and working your way up to be the CEO of a company. If all your solutions are found within you, the credit is all yours. Simple talent and positive thinking don't cover all aspects of your gameplay.

10 Reasons Diagnosis

> **Disclaimer**: As you read these diagnoses and prescriptions, understand that this author is not a medical professional, mental health advisor, nor an ordained minister. Your condition or circumstances are best diagnosed and treated through trained professionals. In all respects, physical, mental or spiritual treatment should be applied in ways that improve your condition or circumstances of life. It is expected that this book will identify avenues where you can further pursue successful solutions for you and your loved ones. For additional spiritual insights, the Resources Section will include experienced ministerial professionals whose detailed instruction can provide clarity and guidance.

The following areas include a diagnosis from Section Three plus a suggested prescription to apply solutions. The diagnosis assumes a negative starting point where you are at a disadvantage; it can affect either guests or members. *The prescription only works for member players—or for guest players in some cases at the request of members.* Additional how-to instructions for preparing the prescriptions cover the remainder of this section.

Free Will

Every player has free will to choose their daily activities, their path through the game, and their final destiny. Some cultures limit the array of choices on the first two points, but the final destination choice of eternal life belongs to every player.

Prescription. Because all players start their gameplay with guest player status, the most important choice is whether to switch teams or not. From there, those who become members have the free will to continue toward the Game Master's spirit power that improves their gameplay. For players in some cultures, simply becoming a member is their death sentence. The Game Master reserves special rewards in the bonus round for all players who "did not love their life and renounce their faith even when faced with death" (Rev. 12:11 AMP).

Spirit Laws and Power

Worship in another religion or mixing non-Manual philosophy into your life is prohibited by the Game Master. The influence of the occult is mainstream, permeates our society, and has a global reach. This is where philosophies of physical, mental, or spiritual well-being are commonly sourced in New Age and Eastern religious concepts and applied to our daily lives.

For example, yoga is one of the more widely recognized and respected activities that promote whole-being wellness. It is well established in social groups, churches, and retirement homes. While yoga is not a religion, it is a spiritual discipline from a Hindu doctrinal foundation. Most players will never learn Hindu doctrine; they just breathe in and out while they flex into different poses. Perhaps they don't even bother to empty their minds and calm their thoughts in the process, and religious players may instead think about Jesus and listen to Christian music in their sessions. In the Serpent's realm, participation is consent for him to gain access to influence players. Any religion or religious philosophy that replaces or displaces the Game Master belongs to the Serpent's realm and is Numero Uno as a Big Ten violation with an accompanying curse.

> **ANY RELIGION OR RELIGIOUS PHILOSOPHY THAT REPLACES OR DISPLACES THE GAME MASTER BELONGS TO THE SERPENT'S REALM.**

Players may be involved in more obvious or recognized occult practices like Wicca. There is a bondage from the Serpent's realm that prevents players from experiencing miracles, healings, and prosperity from the Game Master.

Prescription. Those who have hindrances from receiving life blessings from the Game Master must separate themselves from all participation of an occult nature, past or present. First, identify the possible spirit source, then renounce your participation with it in the name of Jesus, repent and turn toward the Game Master as your source of blessing, and pray for his provision on your behalf in the name of the One. Deliverance through exorcism may possibly be needed for those who have been exposed to idol worship and occult practices.

Curses

The categories of curses include the several major types of generational curses, curses we invoke, activate, or that are made against us, and curses resulting from activity in the previous point on Spirit Laws and Power regarding the occult. Guest or member status does not affect the acquisition or continuation of a curse through the generational lines. If it was running in your family before you became a member, it will continue to run in the family until you break the curse. If you begin participation in a cursed activity as a member, the curse and its effects will still apply to you.

Curses are spiritual attacks that affect our physical, mental, or emotional health, physical environment, life circumstances, or any combination of these areas. Curses are set in motion by a word or an action of a player, then their power is applied from the spirit realm, and they are finally brought against the player or object in the physical realm. The effects of a curse can begin manifesting within hours.

Prescription. Recognize the effects of a curse upon you or your family. Identify the source of the curse, if possible. If a source cannot be determined, go through the list of sources that may apply to your situation and renounce them one by one. Repent and turn from any activity that could be a source for a curse. Pray a blessing upon you and your situation for the present and the future. If you have children in your care, renounce any curse against them as their authority figure and pray a blessing in its place.

The World

The world may be spinning out of control, but you can hop off that spin cycle—mostly. This includes the physical world of disease and injury, the world system's philosophy worked out in government and society, and the threat of violence.

Prescription. Care must be taken in the way we live: dress for the weather, drive defensively, eat vegetables, and so on. Prudence in life is an individual responsibility. If your environment is unsafe, relocate. If you can't relocate and are stuck by your circumstances in an ill-advised situation, pray for a solution and act when it arrives. In all things, you can pray a blessing and protection upon you and your sphere of influence.

For matters of illness and injury, healing is available from the Game Master. Locate kiosk leaders or master players who can pray with you for healing.

The Flesh

These are the appetites of life where we over-develop our passions, interests, and attitudes. They can also be described as strongholds. These appetites of life can affect us financially, physically, or emotionally when they are misused and become vices. Wherever there is a habit or an addiction of some type, there is the potential for a minion spiritual connection or attachment as well.

Strongholds. Strongholds may be associated with a curse, minion influence or control, and addictions or compulsive, habitual behavior.

Prescription. Reigning in appetites may be more than a process of sheer will. This could be a strong bond where we associate the vice or addiction with our very identity. A negative spiritual attachment associated with it is also possible. Check any spiritual factor from an occult association or curse and deal with that aspect accordingly.

Renew a spirit connection with the One through the Manual and use His power to break the addictive bond of the flesh in your situation. Being filled with the Spirit Master, as He instructs, assists in displacing the power of addictions (Eph. 5:18). Create a plan to guard yourself in that area and remove the temptation to relapse. If professional help is desired, arrange to pursue it. Expect to make permanent life changes in your routines and perspectives to achieve permanent results.

THE DEVIL

Deception about the truth of the Game Master and skepticism of whether there is a true path toward recovery and prosperity in life through religion are legitimate issues spawned by the Serpent since the start of the game. However, players willing to go on a path of discovery can come to a knowledge of the truth and meet the Game Master through a spirit connection from His Manual, the book He imbued with Spirit power.

Prescription. You may choose to set aside a final decision about the Game Master and His claims, but begin reading the Psalms, Proverbs, and New Testament section of the Manual. The Game Master said that "He will be found by you when you search for Him with all your heart" (Jer. 29:11–14). Skeptical authors and video testimonials of players who went on their own path of discovery like this and who found the Game Master are listed in the Christianity segment of the Resource appendices section.

BAD DECISIONS

Effective choices are the result of good decisions. Consequences are the result of bad decisions. If your life can be described as a series of consequences, something needs serious fixing.

Prescription. First, identify any patterns or cycles of decisions that leave you with regrets. If there is a distinctive element of inevitability where you know what's coming next and it isn't good, treat it as a curse and take steps to break it. This may also require a proactive response change from you when you are faced with that scenario again, so prepare to treat it differently the next time it arises.

Second, the Manual says to get wisdom and pursue understanding (Prov. 4:4–7). The Manual is the source of wisdom for life from the Game Master's perspective. Sync up with Him through the Manual. Third, if you need wisdom, ask the Game Master for it directly through faith, and He will provide you with wisdom for life and for your specific situation (James 1:5–8).

Wisdom can be downloaded to you from the Game Master in your moment of need. When I was a high school dean of students, sometimes I was at an impasse in finding a disciplinary solution with an uncooperative student. In those times, I would pause and silently pray for an answer. When I started the dialogue again in a few moments, it took a different direction than I had thought of before, and the solution resulted in the student's cooperation.

Bad People

Living in a community of bad people is dangerous but unavoidable for many players, especially those in urban areas. Even those in quiet communities can find themselves victims of criminal behavior. Outbreaks of violence can be sudden, unexpected, and random. As a result, fear becomes a perpetual emotion of life for many players.

Prescription. Protection from evil starts on a spiritual plane and translates from there into your physical world. The Game Master Himself must be your protector, and obviously where living in the presence of evil is part of your routine existence. Psalm 140 is a prayer for protection from evil and violent players. The night that the One was betrayed to be crucified, He prayed for you as a member that the Game Master, through His Manual, would keep you from the evil that would come against you (John 17:14–16).

Psalm 23 is an assurance for members that, *though they walk through the valley of the shadow of death, they are able to proceed and to fear no evil toward them.* Psalm 91 describes the protected life of a synced-up member who has divine protective intervention over every aspect and situation of life. Qualify yourself for His protection and claim His blessing upon you.

Using His Manual as your guarantee, pray to the Game Master for daily protection. As you take precautions and reject fear with an assurance of His care, be sensitive to sudden inspirations or insights in your spirit to follow a different direction or go to a different place than you had planned. As you walk in His care, His guidance can be a simple thought that pops into your mind, taking you to safety. It may seem insignificant, but sometimes you later learn that the outcome made a dramatic difference. This is a literal way we sometimes walk with His Spirit.

Even players who don't face the daily stress of violence should remember that *unless the Lord keeps the city safe, the sentries stay awake in vain* (Ps. 127:1b paraphrased). This applies to your home and community.

PERSECUTION

Persecution of members is again ramping up across the game world and becoming more public and condoned as the United Nations steadfastly declines to condemn it. The One predicted this, and members should not assume they will be continually immune from its reach. Eventually, and perhaps soon, there will be no nation in the game where members are guaranteed safety (Matt. 24:9).

Prescription. As with the prescription offered regarding Bad People, divine protection and guidance is required. The One's prayer of protection in John 17:14–16 applies to those facing circumstances or environments of persecution against them. Those who are detained, arrested, or subjected to persecution are encouraged to remain true to their faith and not fear those who can only destroy the body but cannot harm their spirit (Matt. 10:28; Luke 12:4–5). This is a point where the members' perspective may move past current suffering and imminent death and turn to the final outcome of guaranteed rest and peace when they cross over from death to eternal life with the Game Master in the bonus round (Rev. 2:10–11).

GOD ONLY KNOWS

When we pursue all the avenues of causes for the bad things we face and come up empty, we may never know the reason until we reach the bonus round. After all the scenarios we have described, this final reason that only God knows should be a rare occurrence.

The point of diagnosing the sources of our psychological and physical maladies is to expose and remove any underlying spiritual causes that are barriers to our healing. If you conclude there is no other explanation than the general trials of life, then pursue divine help and healing (John 9:2–3).

Prescription. If your situation is truly puzzling, go through the combinations of causes (Spirit Laws, the Serpent, the game environment, and other players) as systematically as possible. You may need a different perspective from a kiosk group or master player.

A strong clue that seems to indicate another diagnosis is needed is when those who advise you, especially kiosk leaders, tend to quickly dismiss the factor of a spiritual source that could be at work against you. Usually, they will redirect that concept and turn directly to physical solutions, such as seeing your doctor, getting psychological help, saying the problem is you, and so on.

I have experienced and heard of this redirect from professional spiritual leaders who speak as though there is no spiritual perspective on the matter. While you may need to do these other things, those issues are not necessarily the root cause. Remember, very little happens to us in this physical realm that does not have a factor in the spirit realm.

> Take comfort in the promise from the Game Master that no temptation or trial overtakes us beyond what is the common experience of players, and that He is faithful to prevent us from succumbing to more than we can handle, and He will provide relief for us so we can prevail (1 Cor. 10:13, paraphrased).

Finally, when all avenues are exhausted, understand that *the hidden things belong to the Lord* (Deut. 29:29). Trust Him to strengthen and sustain you.

Diagnosis Conclusion

Notice that every prescription offered here includes a spiritual factor associated with it. Successfully navigating the game requires a connection to the spiritual source, which can prevent or undo the negative things we experience so that we may experience and become a source of blessing and prosperity in our gameplay. The rest of this section explains how to connect to that Spirit power.

Barriers to Healing

The pursuit of physical or emotional healing affects every player's family. Most often, it is provided by the medical community through pills, shots, or surgery. Players rarely pursue healing through the spiritual realm until they are dealing with a life-changing crisis or a serious or terminal illness. In these cases, most members ask their kiosk for prayer while they navigate the issues with their doctors or surgeons.

The Game Master can enhance their healing or recovery process within the natural process or through a dramatic, miraculous recovery. Very few members look for healing primarily from the spiritual realm for the purpose of no longer needing medical help or depending on medical solutions. They often only ask for enough healing to get by or get better for the immediate future.

The medical community offers clinical reasons that they call barriers to healing. These are quantifiable and observable issues that, in most cases, have a cure or strategy that can be applied to resume the healing process. Because the spirit realm impacts the physical realm, there can also be resistance toward healing within the body system from spirit-derived sources. Even when using prescribed medications and treatments that are supposed to work, they can be hindered by a spiritual element that slows down or stalls recovery.

The question of why not everyone gets healed is rarely answered with specific reasons. There is no systematic kiosk training to give players tools to diagnose their own situations. Usually, the entire question is left in the category that God Only Knows, which seems very vague and unhelpful. However, that points out a key clue as found in the text we cited for that particular reason for bad things.

> "The secret things belong to the Lord Our God, but those things which are revealed belong to us and to our children forever, that we may do all the words of this law" (Deut. 29:29 NKJV).

There are two things referenced: 1) *secret things* that belong to the Game Master, and 2) *revealed things* that belong to us. We cannot know what the Game Master keeps from us, but those He has revealed, we can act upon them.

Derek Prince, who has provided insight on barriers to healing, said he has found that barriers are not from the Game Master. Rather, barriers are contained in the hearts and lives of members. So, when you begin a quest for healing, save yourself some time by first removing as many barriers as possible. Prince's source material also includes suggested prayers for each of these areas: 1) Ignorance, 2) Unbelief, 3) Unconfessed sin, 4) Un-forgiveness, 5) Occult Involvement, 6) Freemasonry, 7) Effects of a Curse, 8) Evil Spirits (Prince n.d.b, entire article). We'll cover three areas here.

Unbelief

Doubt is unbelief. Unbelief is a game violation. The Manual calls an unbelieving heart evil. This is unbelief in the Manual, unbelief in the promises of the Game Master, and includes anything contrary to what He says (Prince n.d.b, ¶ 18).

> "Take care, brothers, lest there be in any of you an evil, unbelieving heart, leading you to fall away from the living God. But exhort one

another every day, as long as it is called 'today,' that none of you may be hardened by the deceitfulness of sin" (Heb. 3:12–13 ESV).

"My people are destroyed for lack of knowledge. Because you have rejected knowledge, I also will reject you from being priest for Me; because you have forgotten the law of your God, I also will forget your children" (Hosea 4:6 NKJV).

The antidote to unbelief is faith. Faith can be acquired and received through the Manual: *Faith comes from hearing, and hearing through the Manual* (Rom. 10:17, paraphrased). Repent of this game violation and build up your faith, your belief in what the Game Master says (Leggatt n.d., ¶ 19–20).

"Therefore I say to you, whatever things you ask when you pray, believe that you receive them, and you will have them" (Mark 11:24 NKJV).

Un-forgiveness

Un-forgiveness is a choice, not an emotion. We consider this an emotional issue, but a heart of unforgiveness is a decision to not forgive. When you pray, any time you pray, make sure un-forgiveness does not hinder your prayers (Prince n.d.b, ¶ 34).

> **UN-FORGIVENESS IS A CHOICE, NOT AN EMOTION.**

Get a clue: If you want the Game Master to forgive you, it's in your best interests to drop all grudges and forgive anyone and everyone who has ever wronged you.

If your relative or that evil player down the street is already dead and gone, you still tell the Game Master that you forgive them—and mean it. In these cases, clearing your accounts with Him is still not too late.

"And when you stand praying, if you hold anything against anyone, forgive them, so that your Father in heaven may forgive you your sins" (Mark 11:25 NIV).

Evil Spirits

We have already covered specific barriers to healing from exposure to the **occult** or through **curses**. These are very widespread, common sources. Minion spirits can grip a player through illness. There are two main types of illness-inducing minions: those that cause **actual illness** (e.g., asthma, arthritis, unnatural pain, a crippling spirit like scoliosis or curvature of the spine) and those that cause **emotional distress** (rejection, grief, depression, tension) (Prince n.d.b, ¶ 77–82).

> Now when the sun was setting, all those who had any who were sick with various diseases brought them to him, and he laid his hands on every one of them and healed them. And demons also came out of many, crying, "You are the Son of God!" But he rebuked them and would not allow them to speak, because they knew that he was the Christ (Luke 4:40–41 ESV).

> And behold, there was a woman who had had a disabling spirit for eighteen years. She was bent over and could not fully straighten herself. When Jesus saw her, he called her over and said to her, "Woman, you are freed from your disability." And he laid his hands on her, and immediately she was made straight, and she glorified God. But the ruler of the synagogue, indignant because Jesus had healed on the Sabbath, said to the people, "There are six days in which work ought to be done. Come on those days and be healed, and not on the Sabbath day." Then the Lord answered him, "You hypocrites! Does not each of you on the Sabbath untie his ox or his donkey from the manger and lead it away to water it? And ought not this woman, a daughter of Abraham whom Satan bound for eighteen years, be loosed from this bond on the Sabbath day?" (Luke 13:11–16 ESV).

Confession

In the Manual, confession is speaking the truth. In this case, you declare what the Game Master says about you. Find Manual texts that speak of your status as a member. If you have spoken negative words about yourself or your physical or emotional condition, replace those negative confessions with a positive one (Prince n.d.b, ¶ 83–93).

> "For by your words you will be justified, and by your words you will be condemned" (Matt. 12:37 ESV).

> "Therefore, holy brothers and sisters, you who share in a heavenly calling, consider Jesus, the apostle and high priest of our confession" (Heb. 3:1 ESV).

"The LORD is my strength and my song; he has become my salvation. I shall not die, but I shall live, and recount the deeds of the LORD" (Ps. 118:14,17 ESV).

Soul Healing

It is hard to address the components of our soul or the psyche of our being, namely the mind, will, and emotions. Issues of the soul involve many universal factors that can be diagnosed and addressed. However, unlike the physical body, each player's personal experience contributes differently to the hurts in our soul that can shape and drive the trajectory and outcome of our lives.

> "Mental pain is less dramatic than physical pain, but it is more common and also more hard to bear. The frequent attempt to conceal mental pain increases the burden: it is easier to say 'My tooth is aching' than to say 'My heart is broken'" (Lewis 1996)

Who is willing to tell the world they have mental or emotional problems? Those problems show up in the way we act and speak. They could be prejudices, mental turmoil, emotional hang-ups driven by psychological pressures, abuse and traumas, post-traumatic stress (PTSD), and the like. The COVID-19 pandemic, with its broad lockdown on society and life routines, created many mental health issues in children and adults. These problems created during a two-year period will impact players for decades.

The Manual says that trusting the Game Master keeps us in perfect peace (Isa. 26:3; 57:19; Phil. 4:6–7). The One was sent to heal our souls and declared,

> "The Spirit of the Lord GOD is upon me, because the LORD has anointed me to bring good news to the poor (afflicted); he has sent me to bind up the brokenhearted, to proclaim liberty to the captives, and the opening of the prison to who are bound" (Isa. 61:1 ESV; cf. Luke 4:17–21) (see also Guzik 2021, A.2.).

Are you afflicted or distressed or depressed? Are you brokenhearted? Are you being held captive mentally or emotionally? Are you imprisoned and powerless to escape your situation or circumstances? There is healing and freedom through the One.

Discussing physical health is easier than addressing mental and emotional hurts. The Manual has a purpose to give us "the mind of Christ" (1 Cor. 2:15–16). As we apply it to our lives, we gain knowledge of the Manual (2 Pet. 1:1–8), and we develop the character of the One through the work of the Spirit Master (Gal. 5:16–25; Eph.

5:8–10; Phil. 2:5–13). The crazed demoniac of Gadara was healed in his spirit, mind, and body (Mark 5:1–20; Luke 8:26–39).

We have briefly discussed that the battle for control of your soul is waged in the mind, and the journey through the game is a transformation of our mind through the influence of the Manual, which then permeates our being. Applying the Manual to yourself changes your way of thinking and can also be applied to your emotions so that you prosper in your spirit, soul, and body (3 John 1:2).

Mental and emotional health may also need counseling and mentoring, just as some use doctors and life coaches. As with every source of help, make sure it meets the standard of the Manual in its spiritual path.

Personal Healing Journeys

The Lord is gracious and righteous; our God is full of compassion. The Lord protects the unwary; when I was brought low, he saved me. Return to your rest, my soul, for the Lord has been good to you.

For you, Lord, have delivered me from death, my eyes from tears, my feet from stumbling, that I may walk before the Lord in the land of the living (Ps. 116:5–9 NIV).

BEFORE WE COMPLETE the gameplay process, here are some stories from my family showing some outcomes of putting these principles into practice. We have had our successes and failures, but through them all, God is faithful.

Ordinary players can have their extraordinary blessing and miracles. A book like this should have a resurrection story.

My sister-in-law had a heart attack and died in the early morning hours of September 7, 2022. My nephew performed CPR for ten minutes until the paramedics arrived. She was dead for about forty-five minutes before paramedics were finally able to revive her after shocking her four times. Upon arrival at the hospital, the medical team advised my brother to have them stop treatment. He refused and told them to give her a chance. They sedated her while they worked to stabilize her vital signs over the next several days.

On September 13, they ran an MRI scan. My brother said, "The MRI results are back, and they are very bad. She had a massive heart attack, and it can't be fixed; she had a global brain loss of oxygen that is unrepairable. The movements that she has are just reflex movements from her brain stem. The doctor said there is no hope for her. I just can't pull the plug on her. It is when you are at your lowest, that is when God will shine the brightest. Please pray that we will be strong and trust in God in the valley of death. They don't think she will recover from this, but I think God will heal her! We are not going to give up on her. Keep praying for a full recovery!"

My nephew later said it was so hard to be strong in the face of ten doctors who showed them the report and said it was time to pull the plug because, with half her heart dead and no brain function, there was no coming back from this, and she was going to stay comatose. The family insisted on maintaining life support based on my niece's word that the Game Master told her that her mother would fully recover.

On September 14, I talked to my brother about his situation after the MRI scan and encouraged him to remain steadfast in his hope. I gave him some prayer phone hotlines, and I contacted a cousin who could also come alongside to join with his faith for healing. My brother dialed the Andrew Wommack ministry prayer hotline, and they encouraged him and prayed with him over his wife's status report.

Heading into September 21, she was coming off the sedation, her eyes came alive again and she responded to comments with a look and a smile, indicated that she had no pain, and could slightly squeeze the doctor's hand and wiggle her toes, surprising the doctor. The ventilator was turned off for a few hours and then for several hours the next day. She was mouthing words and seemed to understand what she was told. This two-and-a-half-week mark is where the doctor would have expected at least six months of progress to reach this stage.

Over the next week, she began moving more, sat up, and by October 4, finally stood up and wanted chocolate. Her appetite returned, and by October 19, she was moved to a rehabilitation center. She had therapy three hours a day with physical, speech, and occupational therapy. She learned to walk, do things for herself, get in and out of a car, and be mobile. Finally, she was sent home November 10 with continued home therapy, nine weeks after her heart attack.

Setting aside the fact that the doctors wanted to pull the plug right away and that the heart and brain damage were total and irreparable, what would have taken up to a year or more for someone with better chances was accomplished in two months through faith when no hope was offered.

This was a very difficult and grinding challenge for my brother, his son, and daughter. They had never stretched and challenged their faith to take on any miracle prayers, and the first try was to raise the dead. During this time, well-meaning member players cautioned my brother to not get his hopes up and be prepared for slow, long-term progress like the doctor described. My brother rejected those concerns and insisted on praying for a full and quick recovery.

On November 19, we celebrated my sister-in-law's Lazarus moment of returning from the dead. Her mental acuity and speech were excellent at the party and when we met again the next day. She was relearning her arithmetic and reading an analog clock. Her body was still recovering, and she moved with a walker like she was in recovery, not like she was feeble.

Family Testimonials

On a personal note, I grew up in a mainstream independent Baptist church from the 1960s to the 1980s, where answered prayer was not assured as a matter of teaching. Prayers had to agree with what the Game Master wanted for us, and we had to keep a clean slate with Him so our spirit connection to Him was solid, two accurate points from the Manual. Instead of encouraging us that keeping our spirit connection enabled could result in answered prayer, we were admonished not to expect anything from the Game Master if it was disabled. That did not encourage teenagers to get it right—toward the faith that was required for assured answered prayer.

The Wednesday evening services and youth praise sessions included adequate time for individuals to give testimonials of answered prayer or personal blessings. This helped encourage others who were waiting for answered prayers.

A missing element of prayer that former classmates have related is the personal confidence of faith that the Game Master wants to answer our own prayer. We saw others receive blessings, which gave us hope, but it did not dispel the nagging question of whether it could happen for us. I always viewed healing and blessing as a crapshoot; you meet all the requirements but still have no guarantees. What's the difference between getting surgery and getting healed, of getting therapy or getting healed, of popping pills or getting healed? I'll use our family as an example in the following stories.

If you are looking for healing, as my wife and I both needed, you will not find evidence of consistent healings or repeated significant healings in kiosks or their denominations, which teach about healing like it's a roll of the dice, and you can never really know if it is meant for you, you know, God's will and all. We found it to be a lonely journey over more than a decade with no local support or encouragement from our own or other kiosk denominations we checked, but the Game Master brought us to those who could help, and He healed me of fibromyalgia and my wife of Crohn's disease.

2003 car accident. In 2003, a single mother came to work at our school. She was key to our finding more information on healing as written in the Manual. Over several months, it became clear that she was struggling financially. My wife and I believed the Game Master wanted us to help her, so we met with her at the end of November and discussed what we would do for her.

The next Wednesday at the intersection of the school, she witnessed the high impact accident as my van's passenger side was T-boned by a work van that ran the red light. I had just finished our daily prayer with two of my sons before we would turn in to the school access drive. Such accidents were always one of my fears, but I watched it happen with great calm.

After I came to my senses from the impact, I helped one of my sons out the passenger window while seated in the driver's seat. He had a fractured leg, lacerated liver, and "angel kisses" on his face from the shattered glass. My youngest son in the center bench seat got a checkmark cut on his forehead to catalog the event. We all had scrapes and bruises, and both boys needed stitches. The van looked like it would forever go in circles, never to make a left turn again.

In the early hours that morning, the Game Master woke up the mother of my youngest son's friend and urged her to pray for our family. She didn't know why she needed to pray for us, but her intercession kept us from permanent harm. All our injuries healed without complications. I believe this was a minion attack executed through a vehicle accident.

The aftermath of this accident triggered my wife's Crohn's disease, forcing us to now look for healing from two major medical issues.

Fibromyalgia. This condition may not require surgery but is incurable. The onset began in my late teens in high school when I moved a large telephone pole by myself at work. I had a job to do and didn't think to ask for help. One of the staff members who heard me later say that my back hurt took it seriously and told me to get it checked out. Back in the 1970s, there weren't as many specialists around, and most of the doctors pronounced me fit as a horse. Finally, one chiropractor diagnosed muscles pulled from the rib cage and ordered a two-week bed rest.

Ever since that incident, the ensuing pain from manual labor grew more consistent, and I began a long trend of weekly chiropractic care and pain pills. In the early 1980s, for the first time, I quit my job specifically because I had to see the chiropractor too often just to be able to keep working. By the time I was thirty-five, the pain dictated what family activities we could do, and I couldn't sit in most chairs for more than an hour. I woke up one day and thought that I would rather die than grow old with this increasing pain. As a band director, constantly moving band equipment and holding up my arms became so painful that one day in the 1990s, I walked into the school administrator's office and quit. He said, "Oh, no, you don't. You're going to the doctor, and I'll find a band director."

This was the point where I eventually found a pain management specialist and began injections along the spine. I improved from doctor visits twice a week until

I was seeing him every three or four months, so I thought I could teach band again. Big mistake. I relapsed and thereafter hit a plateau where I could never go more than two weeks without shots. His physician assistant, certified (PA-C) then managed my case; she saw 300 patients, and I was the only male. The issue I dealt with was that the ligaments were too weak to hold the muscles along the spine, especially on my right side. It's like having tight muscles from working all day, but then they relax overnight in normal people. Mine would continue to tighten up; the inflammation was hot enough to melt large ice cubes in a minute or two, and the PA-C could see those back muscles spasm from across the room.

Every two years, she would do a full workup, including an MRI and X-rays, to see if there was something that could be found or if a new treatment was in the works. The last time she did that, she showed my results to seventeen specialists from Annapolis to Johns Hopkins Hospital. They all said that it was classic fibromyalgia and told her there was nothing they could do.

During this time, a coworker introduced us to kiosk leaders who used familiar texts in the Manual to show how the Game Master will heal us. Eventually, I was introduced to a local master player who, along with his friend, prayed for my healing. I had been trying to get an introduction to this guy for over a year, and here we were, and nothing was happening. After a minute or two of praying, he asked me what I was thinking. I told him that I was thinking this was stupid and was not going to work. He suggested that I fast (from eating) for three days and come try again. (This exchange is an example of minion interference with a healing that I desperately wanted.)

After three days of fasting, my wife and I went back. We had a two-hour session with the last thirty minutes being prayer. As he prayed, I could feel the pain begin evaporating. Wherever there was still pain, his friend would place his hand on it, and it would melt away as he prayed. I left that night pain-free for the first time in about twenty-five years. This new acquaintance told me how to pray and end the pain if it came back, but I didn't understand enough to believe I could do it.

I went back to my pain specialist a few times afterward while I started learning about healing. Eventually, I began to try praying before medicating. The first time, it took about an hour for the pain to disappear because I said the wrong thing: I told it to "begin to dissipate," and so it did—gradually after an hour. As I realized what I had said, the next time I prayed, paying better attention to what I said, and the pain left within five minutes. After that, whenever I recognized the kind of pain I used to have, I would pray right away, and it finally stopped recurring. I saw the pain specialist for follow-up visits, but they didn't require shots, and now I haven't returned for more than a decade.

After I was healed, I decided to teach band again since healing should also mean no relapse. I was back in the classroom for another ten years and four years directing the church orchestra with only a few rare instances of pain, which were quickly dispatched through prayer.

Crohn's disease. My wife was diagnosed with Crohn's disease in the months following my major car accident in 2003, where two of our boys and I providentially survived with relatively minor injuries. This happened the week when my wife and I had just decided to begin financially assisting a single mother who was our only contact with resources about healing.

In the following years, I was able to pray for healing with specific bouts of pain my wife endured but could not see her healed completely. Eventually, she went to a women's conference where someone prayed with her, and she was finally completely healed. Subsequent colonoscopies came back with healthy reports.

Her doctor refused to release her from Remicade treatments because once they are stopped, she can never start them again as the risk factor is too high. As long as the treatments were covered for her by insurance, she continued with them. As she passed through the office over the years, she was the only patient she knew of who had no pain, symptoms, or residual issues from the disease. The Remicade treatments were eventually discontinued due to insurance changes, and she has had no symptoms of Crohn's.

Stressed ligaments. I had two separate instances of injured shoulder ligaments, one on the right and the other on the left. I was diagnosed with the injury on my left shoulder and prescribed exercise therapy, and the shoulder healed. When the right shoulder was injured later, I was again prescribed therapy. At this time, we had pulled up an Internet broadcast of a religious kiosk conference and recognized a friend we had met on a visit to the conference center. The program had already started, and she was in the middle of prayer for healing to the audience and viewers. Then she said the next prayer was for those with right arm injuries and told them to hold up their arm, and so I did. During that prayer, my shoulder was healed and pain-free.

Karen's 2016 accident. My wife was hit on the driver's side in a T-bone car accident Friday, March 11, 2016, while paused in the median for a left turn on a country highway. An officer stopped by the house to let me know that "she had her bell rung pretty good" and was flown to the shock trauma center in Baltimore, where she stayed a week until March 18. She had surgeries for a ruptured bladder and broken left pelvis and treatment for a collapsed lung with a fractured rib and dislocated elbow, along with bruising and minor cuts on her foot. There were no head or spinal injuries, and her general healing progressed on a natural schedule.

She was then moved to a rehabilitation center for two weeks for physical therapy to get her mobility improved enough for her to get up, sit down, and move around unassisted. She came home on April 6 and for the next two phases of rehabilitation, but there was no in-home therapy treatment available. Instead, she was scheduled to go to a treatment center for seventeen weeks. She was finally discharged after seven and a half weeks. The treatment center could not justify charging the insurance company because she had improved so quickly.

She was able to work at CVS again on June 11, three months after the accident and at least four months ahead of the estimated schedule. She has had no residual effects from the accident. The blessings of her divine protection were no head injuries, swift treatment, and expedited healing. A nurse remarked to her that a ruptured bladder is a significant cause of death from car accidents, and it was discovered and treated the first day.

Pinched nerves, headaches, injuries. Have you ever sneezed and suddenly you couldn't stand up, or you got a splitting headache? As I began practicing healing prayers for myself and my family, the time frame for healing got shorter. At first, it would take half an hour, then ten or fifteen minutes, then five or less, and eventually, I was healed mid-sentence.

For healing pinched nerves like from sneezing or twisting the wrong way, a quick prayer with a step or two or flexing the spine if I were driving would put everything back in place without pain. Once I got a stabbing, back muscle pain right after I had just gotten in bed, and I didn't want to get up for a pain pill, so I started praying, and after a few words the pain disappeared before I could finish the sentence. I thanked the Game Master and went to sleep.

Another time, I got a bad headache and took some pain pills, which, from my long experience, take up to half an hour to take effect. Right after that, I remembered that I should have prayed about it, so I prayed anyway, and the headache was gone in a couple of minutes. Allergy issues work the same way.

One morning while walking through the dark band room before class, I whacked my shin really hard on the music stand cart. That one hurt! Almost immediately, a large lump swelled up at that point, and the pain was distracting. This class started before the school day. I only had a few minutes to prepare, and the nurse wasn't there yet. I didn't want to take the time to make an ice pack, and I was going to be standing up for the next hour. Then I remembered to pray. I said a quick healing prayer, thanked the Game Master, and started prepping for class. A few minutes later, while walking back to the band room from my office, I noticed the pain was gone. I felt my shin, and the swelling was gone too! I had no residual pain or discomfort after that.

My son had finished an Emergency Medical Technician (EMT) course and was training for entry to the Air Force Pararescue program, which required tremendous amounts of running, swimming, and exercise. Once he sprained an ankle on a run, walked off the sprain in several steps as he prayed over it, and then finished the run pain-free. Another time, he suffered a stress fracture where he could feel the bone displaced, so he prayed over it, and it healed immediately as it had been before.

Diabetes. A few years after being healed of fibromyalgia, I was diagnosed with a severe case of diabetes. It was so bad with inflamed hands and feet that my primary doctor couldn't diagnose it from my health history. Six months before, he had remarked that the blood A1C went above six points. When I was finally diagnosed by my pain specialist PAC, my blood A1C was at 10.8. My primary doctor said it was unexpected because the symptoms were more typical of someone who had been a diabetic for ten years. My PAC swore (literally cussing mad) that my bloodwork had been swapped because it was so unrecognizable and had ordered a complete workup to prove it.

Diabetes is a generational disease on both sides of my family as well as a broader culturally prone disease of Hispanics. It has been a discouraging journey. I visited a kiosk in Canon City, Colorado, with a son, where they preached the information explained in this book that the Game Master wants to heal us. I went forward during worship time, and the prayer team prayed over me about my diabetes. I was off my insulin from that day, and my condition was stable that week.

The next kiosk I went to, the pastor friend had seen a parishioner die over the issue where faith healing did not happen for her, and she had refused medical care. He was strongly opposed to these perspectives that the Game Master wants us well and that healing is available simply through prayer. That day, my sugar spiked again, and I was back on the insulin. This situation is the reason the One took the blind man out of Bethsaida for

STRONG UNBELIEF HAS A SPIRITUAL EFFECT AND IS A FAITH AND MIRACLE KILLER.

his healing and told him to go straight home, stay out of town, and not tell anyone in town about his healing. Strong unbelief has a spiritual effect and is a faith and miracle killer (Mark 8:22–26; Luke 10:8–14).

As of this writing, I continue to experience the symptoms and effects of diabetes. I do not expect to end my gameplay from diabetes. I have had prayer for it at an Andrew Wommack meeting and in various kiosk settings. My doctor has remarked that, given the length of time I've had with diabetes, my body systems are remarkably resilient and quickly respond to treatment adjustments. This has still not yet translated into weight loss or stable sugar readings. I believe my healing will come and look forward to the time when it is complete, where the eroding health effects from diabetes, such as neuropathy, dental, vision, physical stamina, and so on, are reversed too.

Cure Zone Introduction

AS ADOPTED BENEFICIARIES of the Game Master's grace, the intent here is to show you how to develop a strong faith that can work miracles to benefit you and others in this game world with the Game Master's blessing and tips. Instead of wondering whether good things will come your way, make supernatural blessing a common way of life for you and your family.

Ephesians 3:14–21 encapsulates for members how completely we can connect with the Game Master and the capacity of power available to members—tremendously more than we could ask or think as a conduit of the Game Master Himself. This alone should encourage your pursuit of Him and improve your outlook on life and hope for a future.

> Now to Him Who, by (in consequence of) the [action of His] power that is at work within us, is able to [carry out His purpose and] do superabundantly, far over and above all that we [dare] ask or think [infinitely beyond our highest prayers, desires, thoughts, hopes, or dreams]—To Him be glory in the church and in Christ Jesus throughout all generations forever and ever. Amen (so be it) (Eph. 3:20–21 AMP).

The Game Master has made available to members *everything they need that pertains to life and godliness* (2 Pet. 1:3, paraphrased). That blanket statement covers every issue of life in every aspect of your being, spirit, soul, or body. Anything you can think of that pertains to your life, spiritual life, emotional life, physical life, family life, financial life, vocational life, and quality of life can be applied to your benefit from Him.

Clarke's Commentary describes it like this:

> By *life* and *godliness* we may understand, 1. a *godly life*; or, 2. eternal life as the end, and godliness the way to it; or, 3. what was essentially

necessary for the *present life*, food, raiment, etc., and what was requisite for the life to come. As they were in a suffering state, and most probably many of them *strangers* in those places, one can scarcely say that they had *all things that* pertained *to life* and yet so had God worked in their behalf, that none of them perished, either through lack of food or raiment. And as to what was *necessary for godliness*, they had that from the *Gospel ministry*, which it appears was continued among them, and the *gifts of the Holy Spirit* which were not withdrawn; and what was farther necessary in the way of personal caution, comfort, and instruction, was supplied using these *two epistles* (Clarke 1832, ¶ 2).

The Manual has guidelines for qualifying, but for those who do qualify, the Game Master has promised that He will not hold back anything that's good for His members. All His gifts are good and perfect, consistent, and straightforward (Ps. 84:11; 1 Cor. 7:7; James 1:17).

Now that we have reached an overview of the Game of Life and skipped our way through the Manual, this section explains how to play the "away game" with a home team advantage. The causes of life's bad things seem to be uncontrollable, but that is only an illusion perpetrated by the Serpent and believed by many guests and members. The less you know, the better he can hurt you.

Your Cost

There is usually no quick fix when you choose to change the trajectory of your life. If you are looking for easy answers to life's problems that will cost you nothing, this book is not for you. The solutions won't work for skeptical or casual readers because of their unbelief. You have to make a commitment of active faith if you want to find results.

The Game Master had to turn His back on His own Son while the One died to give you hope for eternal life by absorbing all the game violations for you and every other player throughout the entire time span of the game. Therefore, his pure blood qualified to make you as pure as the righteousness of the Game Master when you choose to have it applied to your game violation account (Matt. 27:27–44; Mark 15:12–39; 1 Pet. 2:21–25).

In exchange, your cost is that your life then belongs to Him, who ransomed you from the Serpent for the Game Master to live so that His power can make you become a better player, improve your personal circumstances, and make you a helper and a blessing to other players (Rom. 6:5–7; 2 Cor. 5:14–15; Gal. 2:19–21; Col. 3:1–11).

The difference between your life on the Serpent's team and life on the Game Master's team is that your full cost as a guest comes due at the end of your gameplay, where nothing was expected from you until it is over after you ran out your clock and it is too late to change your mind. Becoming a member, improving your life, and changing your outcome requires an up-front, deliberate commitment to play the game by the Game Master's rules—His rules for His abundant life and miracles (John 10:10; Eph. 3:20–21).

If you are a member and still living like a guest who answers to nobody, now would be a good time to check your membership status. The One said that nobody can serve two masters and that you know whom your master is by identifying which one you are actually obeying (Matt. 6:24, paraphrased). Being a guest or a member, whatever choice you make will cost you something either way (Luke 16:13; Rom. 6:15–16; James 4:4).

> **PLAY THE GAME BY THE GAME MASTER'S RULES—HIS RULES FOR HIS ABUNDANT LIFE AND MIRACLES.**

Victory over Guilt

The thought that we deserve what comes to us and that we are undeserving of something better is a powerful weapon of the Serpent that keeps us from hope and a change in our circumstances. Those who join the Game Master's team can legally reject the Serpent's powerful weapon against them: guilt.

The war to defeat the Serpent in the cosmic realm has already ended in victory for the Game Master by the death and resurrection of the One. The Serpent (who accuses all players) is the Accuser of the members, using guilt with its shame to keep us from fighting back so we will stay defeated and burdened under our circumstances. Master player John wrote:

> Then I heard a loud voice in heaven say: "Now have come the salvation and the power and the kingdom of our God, and the authority of his Christ. **For the accuser of our brothers**, who accuses them before our God day and night, **has been hurled down**" (Rev. 12:10 NIV, emphasis added).

Members should not accept his accusations because they have been forgiven. Master player Paul explains:

> When you were dead in your sins ... **God made you alive with Christ. He forgave all our sins**, having cancelled the written code, with its regulations, that was against us and that stood opposed to us; **he took it away, nailing it to the cross.** And having **disarmed the powers and authorities** [Serpent and his henchmen], he [the Game Master] **made a public spectacle of them, triumphing over them by the cross** (Col. 2:13–15 NIV, emphasis added).

The Game Master forgave all our sins. How can you remain guilty if you have been forgiven? Spiritual warfare begins in the battle for your mind. The Helmet of Salvation is the assurance that you are forgiven, never to be accused or condemned by the Game Master, and able to resist the accusations of the Serpent (Rom. 4:7–8).

The Serpent has not accepted his defeat and will continue the fight to the bitter end at the Apocalypse, where he will be shackled and ultimately destroyed (Rev. 20:10). He still remains a very dangerous and lethal enemy, but you have the high ground and access to the weapons of victory. It is time to start living guilt-free and actively overcoming the bad circumstances of life.

> "Blessed is the one whose transgressions are forgiven, whose sins are covered. Blessed is the one whose sin the Lord does not count against them and in whose spirit is no deceit" (Ps. 32:1–2 NIV; Rom. 4:7–8).

Qualifiers

Mainstream view acknowledgment

This section will have "Mainstream View" parts that identify mainstream views on doctrinal issues, where points of disagreement between some denominations will be stated. Retired minister, Dr. Gerald Small, has graciously provided conservative mainstream views on these points (Dr. Gerald Small, pers. comm.). Although some denominations agree with all the doctrinal tenets of this section, some Protestant denominations may view some of these teachings as containing doctrinal error. But whether they are widely taught or not, even though there may be interpretive differences with the Manual, some denominations doctrinally agree with the points that will be presented.

Mainstream denominations usually interpret our interaction with the spirit realm from a perspective where we ourselves cannot proactively and fundamentally change the outcome of our circumstances or the impact they have on us. Because of this, there will be points presented in this section that appear to overstate our power in the spirit realm and understate or dispute the need to develop patience in suffering and accept suffering as an intent of the Game Master as part of His greater purpose for us. You can choose to act with power or patience in this dynamic. Both can be employed as a matter of persistence.

Having spent most of my time in Baptist-type kiosks, I agree with Dr. Small on most mainstream viewpoints. I see them as a different facet of the issue being discussed rather than a conflicting issue. They are included in the text because those views are usually the types expressed to refute or caution the points I make when, in fact, they likely address another aspect of the matter at hand. This is an example of juxtaposing differing denominational perspectives, and I don't see it as a truth vs. heresy argument because I believe both to be true.

Mainstream View: To Be Healed—or Not.

> There are cases in the Manual where even master players were not always granted physical relief from the pains of life: Paul's thorn in the flesh, Job's physical pains and torments, as well as unwanted experiences. Ultimately, they were relieved, but not until other matters were dealt with. Sufferings that no one in his right mind would want to go through have often been allowed to continue for the benefit of others. Many are encouraged by the brave attitudes of those who suffer or lose their physical capacities; the Game Master is involved for their good (Dr. Gerald Small, pers. comm.) (Rom. 8:28).

Paul's thorn in the flesh is a disputed point where many say it was a disease put on him, perhaps an eye problem. Whatever it was, a messenger or emissary of the Serpent afflicted him to limit his gameplay. Three times, Paul asked the Game Master to remove the hindrance, but the Game Master finally said, "My grace is sufficient for you: for my strength is made perfect in weakness" (2 Cor. 12:7–10 NKJV). This was the point where Paul accepted it as part of his gameplay hindrances. The issue of Job was described in the last section.

You are welcome to associate your circumstances of suffering by comparing your trials with these men as a validation of the Game Master's purpose for you in your own suffering. These universally used examples appear to have been the direct result of their successful gameplay and not some random affliction that had no underlying cause. The benefit to us in seeing the physical and spiritual dimensions to these examples is that the Game Master did not abandon them in their trials of life. Their steadfastness is a point of encouragement to us that the Game Master will also be faithful to us through our suffering (Rom. 5:3–5).

Literal vs. symbolic

The word "literally" may seem much overused. A problem in the religious kiosk world is that faith is supposed to be practical, but it is being elevated or relegated to a spiritual ideal that no longer touches our life's circumstances in the way it was intended to do. Kiosk leaders need to explain why life goes wrong, so they minimize the Manual's texts of personal help by cautioning players not to interpret its promises as specific to them or directed toward their exact situation.

Players then don't get their hopes up in case nothing happens. This keeps kiosk leaders from becoming liable for players' failures to receive actual relief from their bad situations, and it takes away a reason for players to blame them or the Game Master for any failure. If help isn't literal but only spiritual or emotional, then players' expectations were misplaced if they thought the Game Master could actually do something for them.

So the word "literal" reminds you to expect literal, real-life results from your faith, not some future, ethereal potential reserved for the blissful afterlife. When things go wrong in the here and now, active faith can set them right when you know how to use it to your advantage. Literally.

This is also the most controversial section. Having participated in conservative religious kiosks for more than five decades, the answers here may appear to wander off the narrow path. They will include topics or areas where members may strongly disagree. The first point is to urge them to check the Manual on its own merits and not rely solely on the long-held interpretations of their religious kiosks. The second point is that, after finding the answers and seeing results, it became clear to the author that those who most strongly disagree with recommended points also tend to demonstrate inconsistent success in reversing their own fortune or the fortunes of others.

Guest players: You will get limited value from this section because the power to defeat the Serpent's environment does not come from his team. His power is used to incapacitate and kill you. You must switch to the Game Master's team to use the solutions found here.

Until then, you remain the Game Master's opponent. Even though He has the best intentions for you and your success with real world power to back them up, you don't have the capacity to receive them or use them when you're not synced up with Him. They simply will not compute without a golden ticket (1 Cor. 2:14).

If you don't believe in faith stuff and religious "mumbo jumbo," the rest of this section will be a tough read. But it may be interesting for you to have a look at the psyche of the masters who take hold of their life situations and have learned to keep the bad stuff from even starting. If you think this is just a positive mental attitude pep talk, you haven't even reached the playing field; you're still sitting in the parking lot.

If you are thinking spiritual talk is stupid, ignorant, and delusional, you're right—from your vantage point. The Game Master Himself said that His wisdom is totally upside down and plain foolish to guests and hopelessly incomprehensible for players without reconnected spirits (1 Cor. 2:13–14). So you can walk away from this book knowing that the Game Master completely understands your perspective. He doesn't agree with you, but He understands where you are coming from.

Member players: It takes time and an intentional refocus of your spiritual understanding to get accustomed to living a consistently supernatural life. We all know the same Manual texts and can spar with each other on their meanings or applications. The difference in your success is in how you apply the Manual. The ensuing power to make miracles is awesome.

For some with less religious baggage, results can come quickly, but for us who have had to unlearn common faith-destroying habits of doubt and unbelief ingrained over many years in sincere religious kiosks, it requires a serious spiritual exercise regimen and continual maintenance. The saying, "Don't get your hopes up," is a typical example of steeling yourself against the possibility that things won't happen as you want them to. When we put out the effort to believe in a favorable outcome for ourselves and then temper it with this philosophy of unbelief, we effectively choke off the faith-induced power that our belief could have had.

While there are singular exceptions, dealing effectively with your life situations doesn't happen with no preparation. For me, it took about four years to finally and clearly understand what you are about to read and another three years to implement it successfully. It took about a year or two for my sons, who didn't have as much religious baggage to unload and unlearn.

Don't wait until things go wrong for you before you decide to get your spirit synced up with the One and learn His skills. It's no benefit to anyone in your life for you to be caught flat-footed in the execution when you knew what needed to be set in place beforehand. If the life or future of your loved one is in the balance, it's better to confidently get results with joy than to fearfully see them slip away with regrets. Don't get caught unprepared.

MAINSTREAM VIEW – TRIALS OF LIFE.

Dr. Gerald Small writes:

> The bondservant of the One will not always have it easy in the physical or spiritual realm. 1 Cor. 10:13 – . . . (as to trials) God is faithful who will not let you be tried beyond what you are able (to bear), but with the trial will also make a way of escape that you may be able to ENDURE it. Phil 3:8 – suffered the loss of all things in order that . . . 2 Cor. 12:7ff – Lest I should be exalted above measure by the abundance of revelations, a thorn in the flesh was given to me, a messenger of Satan to buffet me, lest I be exalted beyond measure . . . I pleaded with the Lord three times that it might depart from me . . . infirmities, reproaches, needs, persecutions, distresses—for when I am weak then I am strong.
>
> 1 Pet. 3:15 – Sanctify the Lord God in your hearts, and always be ready to give a defense (answer) to everyone who asks you a reason of the hope that is in you . . . . (The context implies that there is not any logical reason for a person to have hope in this circumstance, whatever it might be.) It may have been threatened persecution against Christian servants, such as exists in many parts of the world today, and is knocking at the doors of this country. Yes, there is healing, but not as an end in itself, but in the context of serving and glorifying our Lord. All of this is for the glory of God, but it also allows for enduring the undesirable by God's glorious grace. However, I wouldn't for the life of me hinder anyone seeking healing of any sort (Dr. Gerald Small, pers. comm.).

Master player Paul says plainly that, "all who will live godly in Christ Jesus shall suffer persecution" (2 Tim. 3:11–12). Within the context of living to please the Game Master, afflictions and suffering of all types are an expected potential factor. **This book does not intend to assert that members will have a problem-free life**, but just as Paul kept pursuing relief or healing (from the Serpent's revenge for his expert gameplay) until the Game Master explicitly told him to live with it by His grace, the Manual does not prohibit us from pursuing solutions to life's problems. Whatever blessing or healing you can receive, go for it: the prayer of faith will heal the sick (James 5:14–15, paraphrased).

Cure Zone Synopsis

THE SOLUTION TO minimizing the hits you take from the Game of Life will be covered here first, then the explanation will follow. If you are inclined to skip the rest of the book, the details are there when you're ready to check them out. If you have a standard or mainstream religious doctrine, don't assume you know what will be said; your kiosk doesn't explain things very thoroughly.

Those with competing or conflicting doctrinal positions within Protestant denominations find it easier to stay inside the fenced-in denominational yard. They do not seriously consider other teachings—which they may even describe as sinful—practiced by other members of mainline Protestant denominations and which originate in the Manual.

Don't rely on your denominational kiosk's interpretation of the Manual, but use the Manual itself as your authority with the Spirit Master guiding you to discern error. Kiosk leaders interpret the Manual based on their denominational affiliation, and they rarely accept a Manual interpretation that goes outside the lines of denominational teaching. Unfortunately, to do so means they may have to leave the denomination if they even appear to accept a different interpretation of a topic.

I attend denominational kiosks that are different from my denominational perspective. While growing up, my kiosk occasionally dropped a missionary from their support because of a change in a single doctrinal perspective. As part of the application process for an advanced degree in a Bible college in 2022, My wife's friend's husband was required to disavow that the manifestation gifts of the Spirit Master are still in effect today. Aside from social issue exceptions, denominational boundaries are firmly held.

If you become convinced of a differing perspective on a Manual topic, don't try to convince your denomination leaders to change their views or accept what you have discovered. Finding answers that finally work for you can be a very lonely road when you are surrounded by members who believe the same fundamental doctrines as you do but can't relate to your understanding of the Manual. The Game Master can make the results worthwhile even when you have no one to share your journey or joy.

Changing your thinking is sometimes easier when you finally realize, as I did, that your very life depends on it. But still, for all of us, facing change is hard.

Membership. This section is about fixing life's problems. You can't fix your gameplay as a guest. You *must* join the Game Master's team. Membership connects you to the resources that give you the power to change your circumstances.

Solutions start in the spirit realm and transfer into the physical realm through faith. Without membership, there is no spiritual connection to transfer power or healing. Can you be blessed or healed without membership? Anecdotally, yes. But then, why stay a guest when it only benefits you at this game level?

Character. Becoming like the Game Master in your character will put you in sync with His objectives for successful play. You must develop the capacity to handle the power available to you; this power is ineffective when you continue playing with the same kind of character you had on the Serpent's team. The goal of character development is to have the work of the Spirit Master flow through you, energizing your gameplay.

> SOLUTIONS START IN THE SPIRIT REALM AND TRANSFER INTO THE PHYSICAL REALM THROUGH FAITH.

We are commanded to live our lives controlled by the Spirit Master. The character of the Game Master expressed in us is referred to as the **Fruit of the Spirit**: **love**, **joy** (gladness), **peace**, **longsuffering** (patience), **gentleness** (kindness), **goodness** (benevolence), **faith**, **meekness** (humility), and **temperance** (self-control) (Gal. 5:16–23).

These qualities are the natural result of your tuning in to the Manual and practicing it. They describe the way you think, the way you act, your emotional state, your inner strength, your will, and your perspective.

Arsenal. Weapons and defensive armor originate in the spirit realm. They are integrated from our spirit into our soul as part of our "renewal of the mind" transformation (Rom. 12:1–2). As our character becomes more like the Game Master, the armor is strengthened, and the weapons increase their potency.

The armor of the Game Master includes: 1) Belt of Truth, 2) Breastplate of Righteousness (integrity, synced to the One), 3) Faith and Love, 4) Boots of the Gospel of Peace (feet stabilized with this good news), 5) Shield of Faith, 6) Helmet of (the hope of) Salvation – Golden Ticket, 7) Sword of the Spirit – the Manual, and 8) Effective Continual Prayer (staying alert and assisting other members) (Eph. 6:10–18; 1 Thess. 5:8).

Faith is the energizing factor that can change your game world. It is not just what you believe but how you believe it that causes faith to power up your weapons or shut them down. The lack of power we typically observe causes many players to wrongly conclude that faith is only meant for spiritual enlightenment. Faith was intended to move mountains figuratively and literally, just like the One literally killed a fig tree. Most players need mountains of circumstances moved; faith reaches into the spirit realm and gets the job done in the real world in real time to our real circumstances (Matt. 21:17–22; Mark 11:12–14, 19–24).

Engage. As your character develops, as your armor is put on, and your weapons become energized with faith, practice is the key to skill and greater power. The Manual has a set of strong encouragements for the current age we live in that includes three points: "Rejoice always, pray continually, give thanks in all circumstances; for this is God's will for you in Christ Jesus" (1 Thess. 5:16–18 NIV). Rejoicing all the time and being thankful in all circumstances are not normally possible. When a member uses the spirit connection to pray continually, circumstances have less influence on their outlook on life. Spiritual warfare is a big part of the membership experience and will be detailed in this section.

Let's add up some of the initial instructions. The One put it like this, "If you:

1) abide in me, and
2) my words abide in you,
3) you will ask what you want and
4) it shall be done for you
5) that the Father may be glorified in the son" (John 14:12–14; 15:6–8, paraphrased)

Do it. Practice it.

Solutions

Skills Needed

SUPPOSE YOU WERE in a video war game. What would a team leader think of a soldier who bumbles around in combat drawing enemy fire, exposing his team's position, and misfiring his weapons while he then stumbles into the kill zone, all because he somehow skipped training (learning the controls and strategy) but still got assigned? The first question might be, "Who took the controls?" Ever had anyone like that on your team? Do you want them watching your back?

Here is where members are likely to say it was "God's will" for him to die and "his time was up" or "God took him so young." *Ya think?* Everyone else is thinking, "With gameplay like that, it's a wonder he lasted so long. Blaze of glory, man, blaze of glory."

That's not how the Game Master wants it to end for you; He expects you to still be standing when the dust settles and the battle is over (Eph. 6:13; Deut. 30:19–20). A major point of the armor of God is to prevent you from becoming a casualty in life's conflicts. Getting incapacitated or dying before your time is not His will. We assume that whenever we die, that is our appointed time. The Manual gives tips on how to live a long life (Eph. 6:1–3). This means that you have the capacity to extend your life by implementing the Manual's commands and principles. You can defy your rendezvous with death as expressed by Alan Seeger's poem (Seeger 1917, entire poem). We may not know when our end will come, but the inevitable can be stayed through our cooperation with the Game Master and our use of the armor He provides.

> "Turn the other cheek" does not apply to spiritual combat.

The scenario of a stumbling, bumbling player is what it probably looks like to the Game Master who watches His members choose to ignore their training. They're still at war with a Serpent who can take them out of action and even kill them, but He can't make them train because—free will (1 Pet. 5:8–9). That's the worst scenario of a volunteer army that doesn't think the orders apply to them. With an army like that, this is where the term "Banana Republic" comes to mind for a religious kiosk, with nothing professional or serious about it, just run by personalities and platitudes. Perhaps you know of some.

Many members have learned very few skills and expect the Game Master to break the rules and fight their battles for them while they don't lift a finger themselves. Where's the old Hebrew spirit that said, "With my God, I'll run through a battalion!" (2 Sam. 22:30; Ps. 18:29, paraphrased).

Skill acquisition isn't just a point-and-shoot setup, and no one can pick up another player's weapons and make them work because they are individually programmed. The weapons are integrated into the player himself, and they require players to be tuned in to the things that make their weapons lethal.

"Turn the other cheek" does not apply to spiritual combat. Master players should exhibit the gentle character of the Game Master toward all other players. There is no appeasement toward evil forces at the spirit level; attack and resist with zero tolerance are the only commands ordered by the Game Master (2 Cor. 10:3–6; James 4:6–8). What activities and philosophy do you accept which compromise your spiritual effectiveness?

As we review the needed skills, they will include not just strength of character but a lion-hearted attitude. The Manual says to not let the sun set on your anger (Eph. 4:26–27). Most members say that means don't go to bed angry, and that's not a bad idea. But the context is to never let your anger set against the realm of the Serpent, and never let your guard down where he can slip a dagger into you or knock you off your feet. In addition to keeping a focused anger smoldering, the text continues and says to not give ground to the Serpent. It is possible to let your anger toward him cool down multiple times a day in distracted moments. When your anger cools, complacency sets in, and you will begin to cede the territory of your life to his influence.

We are now in the section of power, and you can turn your ordinary life into a supernatural one with the weapons and approval of the Game Master. If you're doing okay under the circumstances, that's your choice, but nobody needs to live burdened down by circumstances. To change your situation, you need a skill set that is tremendously better than what you've been working with, and this is where it starts.

Read your manual

The Manual is the source of power with the strategy to win the game. If you want to win this Game of Life, you need to read the Manual continually. Reading it keeps the rules of the game in front of you and gives you insights when you run into a problem.

This is the single most helpful task for skill development. The process is: read the Manual and practice the Manual. Most players are never helped to understand how the practical value of learning the Manual can change their real-world circumstances (Luke 6:46–49). Master player James cautions against only reading the Manual but not practicing it; that causes self-deception (James 1:22–26).

You know the old song: "Read your Bible, pray every day, and you'll grow, grow, grow." Kiosk leaders strongly promote reading the Manual and praying as the two basics for spiritual growth. This is true, but they leave the desired outcome of "spiritual growth" as a vague concept that doesn't mean much when prayers don't get reliably answered. There is little concrete correlation taught in kiosks about how reading the Manual can directly lead to answered prayer, nor is anyone told how these habits can translate into successful living where you can expect the good stuff in your life and proactively keep the bad stuff away.

Derek Prince explains,

> So, this is a staggering thought that I want to impress it upon you. When you are reading your Bible and absorbing it and letting it do its work in you, all the creative power of Almighty God is at work in you. Because, God used nothing but His word and His spirit to create the universe. And the same word, the same spirit are available to us when we read the Bible. So never set limits to what the Bible can do in your life. Go out, look at the stars, look at the sun, look at the oceans, look at the mountains, the tremendous creative power of God demonstrated, and then say to yourself: "the same agents that created all those things are working in me when I read my Bible" (Prince 2021e, min. 1:08; see also Prince 2021d) (Ps. 33:6).

Memorization of the Manual is an effective way to develop divine characteristics because it is internalized for immediate application in your daily circumstances. Reflecting on the text has a more profound effect than just reading it. Also, when situations come up at home, work, school, or play, The Spirit Master can use the texts you have memorized to encourage you in what is the right thing to do—or to remind you after the fact of what should have been done differently (Ps. 119:11; 2 Tim. 3:16–17).

Master players are mature players characterized as skillful in the Manual and who, through practice, can discern good and evil (knowing the difference is not always as obvious as one would assume, hence the need for discernment). They consistently demonstrate supernatural power in their daily lives. Unskilled members who don't really know the Manual like this are contrasted as comparative babies, and that is where a majority of us seem to be living based on our gameplay (Heb. 5:12–14).

Spiritual skill development involves a transformation of the mind toward the thought patterns of the Game Master, which is achieved by reading the Manual. The battle for your spiritual success takes place in your mind through your way of thinking. As this battle is won and your thoughts and perspectives become transformed toward those of the Game Master, you can then change your circumstances of daily life.

The instructions from the Manual are simple and straightforward, but their application requires members to unplug themselves from the fun distractions and worrying cares of the game environment to the degree of the amount of power they want to have. The more spiritually connected we are to the One, the better our overcoming powers can grow (2 Tim. 2:15–16).

Joining a monastery is not required or advised, but regularly turning off or ignoring the TV, Internet, games, and phones for extended periods of time is a lot to ask. Even twenty or thirty minutes to one hour a day of replacing these activities to study the Manual with the purpose to take its advice can bring measurable change within a month. Read it as literal truth, not as a good concept. To get literal results, you must take the Game Master at His literal word and believe He meant what He said while you keep it in context. Then hold Him accountable for what He said. The Game Master is not afraid of accountability (Isa. 55:10–11; Jer. 23:28–29; Mal. 3:10–11; 2 Cor. 1:20).

I was amazed at the insight of my teenage son, who did this. While he still had his teenage inexperience, his Manual-perspective of universal truths that he could discern and apply to his daily situations was astounding. His prayers began to get consistently answered, and his confidence in getting results encouraged him to continue reading and praying.

Master players know the Manual. The Spirit Master who energizes their weapons must have something to work with because the power resides in the Manual. Those who don't know the Manual can't be enlightened by the Spirit Master. It doesn't help to flip the switch when the light bulb is missing. That catastrophically eliminates your light bulb moments of life.

Weapons in the hands of clueless, ignorant members who don't carefully read the rules are useless. That's where they get the notion that the Game Master chooses to let bad things happen to them—because they don't have focus and their weapons are always misfiring. It never connects that most of their wounds are avoidable or self-inflicted.

Quick objectives here are to 1) love the Game Master above all and 2) love other players like the One loves you, 3) strengthen your faith through the Manual, 4) obey the One, and 5) learn to understand and play the game from His perspective (Matt. 7:34–35; 22:37; Mark 12:30; John 13:34; Rom. 10:17; Phil. 2:3–8; 2 Pet. 1:5–11; 3:17–18; 1 John 5:3–4).

Mission ready

The more you are like the One, the better your gameplay will be. He wants members to be mission ready, become like Him, and take on His way of thinking (Phil. 2:5–8).

There is a sequence of self-development toward the master player skills starting from the least to the greatest. Now that you have *faith* as a member, add: 1) *virtue*—resolve for moral excellence, 2) *knowledge* of the Manual, 3) *self-control*, 4) *patience* or endurance, 5) *godliness*, 6) *brotherly affection*, and 7) *sacrificial love* (2 Pet. 1:2–10).

Godliness is a turning point in the list toward the upper level, where members begin thinking more like the One and start to habitually filter their thoughts through the Manual's perspective. But godliness is only part way up the list. That is typically viewed as the highest level, but when we can love others who seem unworthy more than we love ourselves, that is where we have become most like the Game Master Whose defining characteristic is love (1 John 4:7–8, 16).

You can rarely comment on patience, the fourth item, without some member saying, "Don't pray for patience because God will give you tribulation (trouble)!" Many members never reach the top three levels because they never learn patience. Patience means to endure, and there is no way to learn patience except to endure and hold out until the tough time is over. Endurance requires self-discipline, which is the next step up from developing self-control.

Self-control is a harnessing of emotions and impulses. Patience is the practice of self-control extended over a period of time or through an intense period of trouble. Dropping the emotion that your time is being wasted is the progression from self-control toward patience. A simple way you can develop your patience on a daily basis is to practice it with family members, friends, or coworkers in your daily routines. When you are out of the home, practice patience in traffic and in the check-out line at the store.

There are many opportunities for self-control that we can use for short-term practice that will develop an attitude of patience. Your motivation for doing this is to practice the Game Master's attitude toward you: we forgive others because He forgave us; we love others because He first loved us (Eph. 4:32; 1 John 4:7–8, 19).

Watching your young adult children learn endurance without a family safety net is fascinating. This indicates how well they were raised to be independent, responsible adults and reminds you as a parent of everything you forgot to tell them. One son miscalculated his funds a couple of times, which put him in a tight spot for a few months (technically, he had other money but wouldn't touch it). He would tell me his situation but insisted I stop offering to help him. He had a plan and wanted to work out his plan even if it meant reduced food and fun. Learning patience doesn't require a hammer-drop from headquarters. Many members reflexively pull back from an opportunity to develop their inner strength.

Meditation. The New Age movement draws heavily from Native and Eastern religions, and meditation is a major part of this practice, with yoga as a well-known example. New Age meditation is about finding your center and emptying your mind and bringing you closer to a state of inner peace. This is how the Serpent can 1) more easily influence meditators and also 2) equate meditation with the illusion of a "lack of influence" upon them as they feel more spiritual, with an added bonus that 3) they think that emptying their thoughts is the same meaning for meditating as in the Manual.

The *last thing* the Game Master wants a member to do is to empty his mind. Instead, members need to do the *opposite* and fill their minds with the perspective of the Game Master as they memorize the Manual (Ps. 1:1–2; 119:10–18). The original Hebrew language for meditation in the Manual refers to a muttering or mumbling to yourself the teachings and thoughts of the Game Master as found in His Manual. An example of how this process is done is to reflect on the words about the goodness of the Game Master and promises of the Manual's text (like a psalm) and personalize them for yourself as you meet the qualifications. This is the way the Spirit Master can help you understand the One's perspective, energize those spirit rules that you internalize, and turn them into major weaponry.

Geared-up – spiritual warfare. The Game Master does not want members running around the game world without full and proper armor, not even half-dressed. So, getting suited up is important as a daily check since the Serpent prefers sneak attacks. You don't always know when your overwhelming evil day is coming (Eph. 6:10–18; 1 Thess. 5:8).

Much of the war is engaged in your mind. It's a battle of perspectives and ways of thinking. The way you think proceeds to what you will become (2 Cor. 10:4–5). However, it can spill over into your daily circumstances. If you can successfully think like the Game Master and use His armor to protect you, then you can start to change your game world through miracles, change how your life plays out on Friday the 13th, and inspire other players to get active in the war. This requires the Serpent to waste resources to attack you, hence the need for armor.

Examples in the Manual of our struggle with the spirit realm describe close combat, whether it is a wrestling match or hand-to-hand combat (Eph. 6:12–18). It is up close and personal, and the wounds can cut clear to the bone because the Serpent's minions have no hesitation about invading your personal space and turning your life upside down. The Manual emphasizes three times in a row that the purpose for your armor is so you will still be standing against the Serpent's treachery when it's over on your day that's overwhelmed with evil. All this armor comes from the Manual, and learning it well gives you full coverage.

The whole armor of the Game Master includes: 1) Belt of Truth, 2) Breastplate of Righteousness (integrity, synced to the One), 3) Faith and Love, 4) Boots of the Gospel of Peace (feet stabilized with this good news), 5) Shield of Faith, 6) Helmet of (the hope of) Salvation—Golden Ticket, 7) Sword of the Spirit—the Manual, 8) Effective Continual Prayer (staying alert and assisting other members) (Eph. 6:10–18; 1 Thess. 5:8).

Dr. William Schnoebelen identifies a dozen more pieces of armor: 9) Garment of Vengeance (Isa. 59:17), 10) Cloak of Zeal (Isa. 59:17), 11) Armor of Light (Rom. 13:12), 12) Shield of Salvation (Ps. 18:35), 13), Girdle of Righteousness around our loins, (Isa. 11:5), 14), Girdle of Faithfulness around our reins (viscera—vital organs, "the seat of the feelings or passions" (Merriam Webster n.d., ¶ 2) (Isa. 11:5), 15) Robe of Righteousness, (Isa. 61:10), 16), Large Shield of Favor "like a spiritual tank" (Ps. 5:12), 17) Glittering Spear of Yahweh (LORD) (Heb. 3:11), 18) Rod of Strength (Ps. 110:2), 19) Battle Ax of Yahweh (Jer. 51:20), and 20) Buckler of Truth (larger shield protecting the whole body (Ps. 35:2; 91:4) (Bible Study Tools n.d., ¶ 2–3) (Schnoebelen 2015, min. 5:56).

Defensive armor. The One spoke that famous line, "You will know the truth, and the truth will set you free" (John 8:32 ISV). Unless you know your Manual, you will never know the truth and, therefore, can never be set free. Having it spoon-fed to you at your religious kiosk is a starvation diet. All the defensive armor and weaponry are sourced in the Manual. The better you know it and apply its principles to change your life, the faster you will be able to recognize thoughts, ideas, perspectives, and situations that are out of place. The Game Master describes Himself as our rear guard. He is watching your back while *you* face the enemy (Isa. 52:12; 58:8).

"Guard your heart above all else, for it determines the course of your life" (Prov. 4:23 NLT). The breastplate of righteousness protects your heart from Serpent attacks and wandering into game violation territory. Something you see or hear during your day may spark a thought or memory. You face a choice to indulge yourself in an old habit or enjoy something you discarded from your guest player days.

Do you keep that breastplate of righteousness and girdle of righteousness and faithfulness on, or do you set them down for a few moments of pleasure or indulgence? Can your heart handle an unguarded session of fun? Is the Spirit Master cautioning you to turn away, reminding you whose team you're on? These may be fleeting thoughts, but your armor can help you choose to stand in a moment of weakness. It is mighty, through God, to help you pull down that stronghold that once had a grip on you.

Offensive weapons. We'll highlight two offensive weapons: prayer and the Manual. Prayer seems like it doesn't belong on the list, but Derek Prince pointed out that it is the equivalent of a spiritual ICBM (intercontinental ballistic missile) that any member from anywhere can launch and hit a specific, even individual target anywhere in the game environment (Prince 2022c, min. 3:25). While we may think of prayer as a personal, intimate issue, when it is coupled with an understanding of the player's spiritual authority from the Game Master, it is effective for defensive and offensive use. The Manual as a weapon deserves its own category.

The Sword of the Spirit. The Manual is the Sword of the Spirit. Derek Prince explains that the Sword of the Spirit is the spoken word of the Game Master, not the Bible on our shelf. We use the Bible from the shelf to speak what is written. "When you take the Scripture in your mouth and quote it direct, then it becomes the sword of the Spirit" (Prince 2022b, min. 6.33).

It can be used in similar ways as prayer, but the main difference is that it is itself authoritative and its own source of power as opposed to prayer, which derives its power from the strength of the faith of the one who is praying. The Manual is the authority upon which prayer is based and is the *source of the faith* that gives prayer its power (Rom. 10:17).

> The Manual is the authority upon which prayer is based and is the *source of the faith* that gives prayer its power.
> (Rom 10:17)

The Manual is our singular multifunction weapon that has an array of capabilities depending on the type of combat we face. Master player Paul describes our weapons as "mighty through God," explaining one way the Manual is used to overcome spiritual opposition of resistance to its truth.

> For though we live in the world, we do not wage war as the world does. The weapons we fight with are not the weapons of the world. On the contrary, they have divine power to 1) demolish strongholds. We 2) demolish arguments and 3) every pretension that sets itself up against the knowledge of God, and 4) we take captive every thought to make it obedient to Christ. And we will be ready to punish every act of disobedience, once your obedience is complete (2 Cor. 10:4–6 NIV).

Here is an example of the effectiveness of the Sword of the Spirit with two translations to describe it:

> For the word of God is living, and active, and sharper than any two-edged sword, and piercing even to the dividing of soul and spirit, of both joints and marrow, and quick to discern the thoughts and intents of the heart (Heb. 4:12 ASV).

> For the Word that God speaks is alive and full of power [making it active, operative, energizing, and effective]; it is sharper than any two-edged sword, penetrating to the dividing line of the breath of life (soul) and [the immortal] spirit, and of joints and marrow [of the deepest parts of our nature], exposing and sifting and analyzing and judging the very thoughts and purposes of the heart (Heb. 4:12 AMP).

It has several characteristics: 1) alive in spirit, 2) full of power, and 3) sharper than any two-edged sword.

It also has several capabilities: 1) penetrates the dividing line of the soul and spirit, 2) penetrates the physical joints and bone marrow, and 3) discerns and analyzes the thoughts and motivations of the heart.

Like any spiritual text with a spirit source or blessing, the Manual is derived from and empowered by the Spirit Master Himself. That makes both its blessings and curses binding, very real, and capable of affecting even the physical game environment, including your surroundings and your physical body. It is a precision instrument and an extremely sharp weapon of unequaled power beyond anything the

Serpent could assemble. The Manual specifically mentioned its capabilities that the Serpent cannot match.

The concept of something sharper than a two-edged sword reminds me of a day in Mexico as a youngster. We stopped by an uncle's ranch, where the ranch hands were hand-sharpening their new machetes. By late morning, they had a pile of filing dust almost a half-inch high running the length of the blade, and they still weren't finished sharpening them. Almost every kitchen knife I have used seemed dull compared to those razor-sharp machetes. Yet the sharpness of those machete blades is no match for the Manual.

Soul and spirit. The Manual can find the place where the players' souls and spirits are joined and separate them. The Game Master is the only One who can destroy a player's spirit, and He tells players not to fear those who can only destroy their body because any threats against their spirit are empty threats (Matt. 10:28). He is the only judge of both the living and the dead (Acts 10:42).

Joints and marrow. The Manual says that the life of the body is in the blood (Lev. 17:11). It's interesting to read that people who have an organ transplant may suddenly develop lifestyle habits of the donor, like going from a vegetarian to a burgers and beer diet or from a couch potato to a fitness freak. In any case, the joints are where cutting most easily takes place, and the marrow gets to the source of the blood. This is why the Manual is effective in literally healing any disease because it can impact the player's physical life all the way to its source in the marrow.

Discerner of the heart. The Manual goes beyond anguished or conniving thoughts and reaches to the very recessed motivations of the individual. It calls the player's heart more deceitful than anything and desperately wicked (Jer. 17:9). Keeping thoughts bottled up inside usually leaves telltale signs of a player's disposition. If they are suicidal, it is sometimes only realized too late to help. But we have a tendency for deepest, darkest secrets known only to ourselves that the Manual can still perceive.

While players have an enormous capacity for good, we are also capable of the worst evils and can do them while we still say that we are a good person. It's easy to find someone worse than ourselves (2 Cor. 10:12). This is a cause of some Manual warnings because players can deceive even themselves. That is sometimes the most difficult deception to recognize (2 Tim. 3:13; James 1:22), but the Manual can shine a light on the most hidden secrets to bring solutions and healing where we are most deeply hurt.

The armor of light. The armor of light may be considered a behavioral rendering of the armor of the Game Master. Master player Paul explains:

And now consider this. You know well the times you are living in. It is time for you to wake up and see what is right before your eyes: for salvation is nearer to us now than when we first believed. The darkness of night is dissolving as dawn's light draws near, so walk out on your old dark life and put on the armor of light. May we all act as good and respectable people, living today the same way as we will in the day of His coming. Do not fall into patterns of dark living: wild partying, drunkenness, sexual depravity, decadent gratification, quarreling, and jealousy. Instead, wrap yourselves in the Lord Jesus, God's Anointed, and do not fuel your sinful imagination by indulging your self-seeking desire for the pleasures of the flesh (Rom. 13:11–14 VOICE).

Kingdom character begins in this game level. As members, with the end of the age upon us, we need to wake up, discard unholy living, and clothe ourselves in the nature of the One and with His mindset, living with our actions guided by the One's truth, righteousness, and godliness, the elements of His armor. The contrast is that, as guests, we were in darkness under the power of the Serpent, but as members, we are light in the Lord and are called the children of light (G. Thomas 2009; "What Does It Mean to Put on Christ in Romans 13:14?" 2023, ¶ 3; Henry 1706, ¶ 1–7) (Isa. 2:5; Eph. 2:1–2; 5:8; Col. 3:10; Acts 26:18).

Dr. Schnoebelen asserts that this armor "empowers all the rest of the parts of the armor" (Schnoebelen 2015, min. 6:20) He continues,

> The armor of light flows through you. It's like you have a spiritual nuclear reactor inside of you that gives you the power to live a victorious life, to have victory over sin, to have victory over bondage, and to walk in a way that the Almighty wants you to walk . . . it turns your regular old suit of armor, like you might see in a museum, into like the Iron Man's suit of armor, like the comic book character, because that armor is not only defensive. It gave him the power to be strong, it gave him like jets that he could fly with . . . it's going to give you the power to live a mighty and victorious life in Moshiach [Messiah]" (Schnoebelen 2015, min. 6:12) (Rom. 13:12).

Combat ready — engage

Developing the character of the Game Master and suiting up with His armor are prerequisites to being combat ready. This next set of items that channel the supernatural power are not in a single listed location. They are scattered about the Manual and require players to recognize and pick them up. It's like assembling your own weapon; the parts you leave out greatly affect its lethal capacity.

This is a reason most players don't work miracles. Recognizing the components as weapons-grade materials is the first problem. The next is sequencing them together to make them work; the third is actual practice so they can start taking down even small targets as they work toward bigger and bigger objectives. Only a few kiosks are very effective at assisting with this concept, and they are also very hard to find.

To make miracles, to put a protective shield around you and your family, and turn circumstances to your favor, these are some areas you need to master: 1) faith, 2) spiritual authority, and 3) prayer and praise.

Faith. The Manual says that our faith is the victory that overcomes the game world (1 John 5:4). It seems like faith is a passive thing, and for most players, it's always passive. But faith becomes active when it is applied to a situation where we expect a certain outcome—not just wish for it or know it could theoretically happen, but fully and literally expect it.

Then it changes from a passive faith, where we believe the Game Master *can* make that thing happen as a matter of principle to an active faith, where we believe He *will* make that thing happen for us. This is how faith becomes weaponized, where it can be used as the main component to get the results we need. Our belief system controls the active ingredient for faith.

Spiritual authority. The authority of the One is available and transferred to members who play under His authority. Authority figures who don't use their authority are ineffective. Those who don't have authority themselves but are doing a job with their boss's authority can operate with whatever level of authority their boss has delegated.

The One said that all authority in the spirit realm and the game environment is His (Matt. 28:18), so members who operate with His authority anywhere in the game world can overcome their obstacles and circumstances in life (Mark 16:15–20), just like He demonstrated for them and expects of them (John 14:12). The Manual is the source players invoke when exercising their authority in the name of the One by citing its specific promises or declarations.

Prayer and praise. The Manual says that effective and intense prayer gives players their advantage (James 5:16), and the player's praise toward the Game Master is a sacrifice in His view (Jer. 33:11; Heb. 13:15). Prayer and praise can seem inconsequential as weapons. Praise is like the weapon scope that aligns and focuses the player's confidence in the Game Master and also the battery pack that fully charges faith so the player's faith can most quickly increase and become active, ready to fire. Prayer is the trigger for that activated faith that moves mountains.

If you are in an overwhelmingly bad situation, praise the Game Master for His goodness according to Psalm 100, remind Him of His promises of care and solutions for members, and bless His care on you and your problem as you work to fix it. You simply *must know* (memorize) the Manual; when you're crying too hard to read or look it up, what you already memorized gets told back to Him a lot faster.

The way players talk about their circumstances shows their level of faith and the effectiveness of their prayers. An outcome can be predicted based on the way they talk. How they praise and pray can tell if they have an active faith, passive faith, faith mixed with unbelief (or fear), or no faith. Victory and defeat are predictable outcomes.

There may certainly be more key elements for combat available from more experienced players and facets of gameplay that are not covered here. With attentive application, what is explained here is good enough to raise the dead.

While all this can seem ponderous, overwhelming, and digging way too deep into each area listed, it only scratches the surface. There are recommended books that more thoroughly explain them. Becoming a member starts a journey toward becoming a master player. If all members understood the Manual like they say they do and played with the master skills like the Manual says they should have, this section wouldn't have to explain so much.

MAINSTREAM VIEW – HEALING & MIRACLES CONTEXTS WITH SPIRITUAL AUTHORITY.
This is a preemptive point to acknowledge what is certain to be a major issue of difference with the mainstream kiosk view. What will be covered through this section does not disparage the methodology of miracles taught by mainstream kiosks.

There are two approaches to receiving from the Game Master. Both ways are correct and have corresponding texts describing them. These two approaches are the dynamics of asking from the Game Master versus using His authority to change your situation. Both approaches have a prescribed formula; both require the same faith, but the task at hand may call for one instead of the other.

This section explains how to assert your spiritual authority in a situation. This is not the approach taught in the majority of kiosks and not the only approach, but it is the lesser-known approach and not used even when appropriate to do so.

Asking from the Game Master. The universally taught and practiced approach for receiving from the Game Master is to ask for the blessing: "Do not be anxious about anything, but in everything by prayer and supplication with thanksgiving let your requests be made known to God" (Phil. 4:6 ESV). The formula here includes: 1) without fearfulness (use confidence—faith), 2) pray and ask, and 3) be thankful. The next text verse assures that the peace of the Game Master will guard our hearts and minds in the One. As with all spiritual transactions, fear must be dispelled because it cancels faith. The Game Master's love dispels fear (1 John 4:18–19).

The Manual describes the care of the Game Master toward his members, where the One says, "And I tell you, ask, and it will be given to you; seek, and you will find; knock, and it will be opened to you. For everyone who asks receives, and the one who seeks finds, and to the one who knocks it will be opened" (Luke 11:9–10 ESV; Matt. 7:7–8).

Players fall short of receiving what they seek because they are not confident that they will receive (doubt vs. faith). When you focus on your unworthiness instead of confidence in His benevolence, you will continually wonder whether you will receive what you ask for. Uncertainty results in disappointment (James 1:5–7).

Ask versus command. This area is a major dividing line of Protestant denominations where the manner of healing is practiced differently, and the context in which we make or expect miracles is different.

This assertive command prayer is not us commanding God. Walking by faith in His delegated authority, we practice what the One demonstrated, and His followers copied. Peter's command to the lame man to rise up and walk was not Peter commanding God to raise the lame. He followed the prescription given by the One and told the lame man to rise and walk (Acts 3:1–13). He spoke directly to the man's issue by telling him how to respond. Just like asking prayers, command prayers require the same faith, and both are accomplished in the name of the One (John 14:12–14).

Mainstream View – Ask vs. Command for Healing.

> "Most kiosk members have never been in a setting where a disease was commanded to be healed. They are familiar with the procedure of placing a hand on the subject by the elders, and praying with confidence in the Game Master's willingness to heal" (Dr. Gerald Small, pers. comm.).

While only some denominations include an assertion of spiritual authority to command healing as practiced in the Manual, all denominations practice the laying on of hands by elders as described in the Manual.

Nineteenth-century theologian F. L. Godet, Th. D. (1957, 196–197), says in his 1886 commentary that "Faith is the root of the Christian life, not one of its fruits.". He then describes it as "the possession of salvation taking the character of assurance in God, of heroic daring, resolutely attacking and surmounting all the obstacles which are opposed to the work of God in a given situation" (197). In applying this understanding of the power of faith, he explains,

There follow the gifts of healings, which are closely connected with faith thus understood, for they have as their basis confidence in the power of God applied to disease. Here there is not only a confident prayer; there is a command given in the consciousness of complete harmony with the will of God such as the "Rise, and walk," of St. Peter (Acts iii. 6). The substantive gifts and healings are put in the plural as relating to the different classes of sicknesses to be healed (Godet 195–197).

There is a general belief that: "The Game Master could give a person in some special case the power to command healing within the framework of allowing the subject to continue in some kiosk ministry or divinely appointed task" (Dr. Gerald Small, pers. comm.).

The Matthew Henry Bible commentary describes it as Dr. Small related it in the 1 Corinthians 12:9 passage (Henry 1991, 458–460). However, few members ever witness healing by command through faith or the traditional laying on of hands. It is simply not an area where results are commonly reported in a majority of denominations, but perspectives remain very strong about how it should be properly done and whether it is something the Game Master desires for you. Anecdotes about healing may be found within select kiosk organizational newsletters or reports.

The perspectives of Dr. Godet and Mr. Henry highlight different conclusions on the aspect of how healing can be achieved. It should be noted that both men frame miracles in the context of it being God's will to heal—that is also a point of dispute where some argue that one should not ask for healing unless they know it is already the will of God, while others say that multiple scriptures indicate that His will to heal is part of the atonement for man's soul and that faith should be applied accordingly. Whichever view you choose to follow, the type of faith you employ will affect your results and how diligently you pursue healing when it doesn't happen on your first, second, third, or fourth try.

Healing for divinely appointed tasks. This general view that healing may be authoritatively accomplished for continuation in kiosk ministry or in a divinely appointed task is a qualifier meant to acknowledge that healing is possibly available within narrow parameters but not generally available simply because God wants to heal you (Matt. 8:1–3; Mark 1:39–41; Luke 5:12–13). However, there are no scriptural limitations where the One decided not to heal an individual based on their lack of kiosk ministry or divinely appointed tasks. Instead, all types of players poured out of the cities and towns to be healed, and it is more often stated that He healed all who came to Him. The disciples later followed His example (Matt. 4:24; 8:16; 12:15; 14:14; 15:30; 19:2; 21:14; Mark 1:34; 3:10; Luke 4:40; 5:15; 6:17–19; 9:10–11; Acts 5:16; 19:11–12).

Whether it was by command, a touch, the shadow passing over them, or a handkerchief or apron, healing was granted indiscriminately with no strings attached. The sensationalism of modern healing ministries on TV have soured the public on God's power to heal and on the love of God to care about you who hurt in your hopeless situation. Don't let money-grubbers or charlatans discourage your quest for divine help (Smith 2011, 99–109).

There is virtually no teaching on the active pursuit of healing within the mainline Protestant kiosks today despite it being a sign of the One's divine authority and a practice among His first-century followers. We are discussing concepts that a minority of Protestant kiosks practice.

Mainstream View. There is also the matter of the believer's authority expounded in this section, another major untaught concept in mainline Protestant kiosks. It will be partly addressed in the command to "move mountains," as the One explained it.

> "The majority understanding is that the faith to move mountains applies to those members who are accomplishing the will of the Game Master in their divinely appointed task" (Dr. Gerald Small, pers. comm.).

Reported miracle results on these topics in daily life for the average player from mainline kiosks is sparse. Understand that you may find more major points of disagreement here, but there are growing numbers of mainline kiosk believers who, after searching for help, are finding their miracles through the application of the Manual's teaching as described throughout this section.

Changing your perspective is more important than conceding a point here and there. The following sections outline ways to develop your faith so you can receive the Game Master's full array of blessings that already await those who pursue Him. If your different way of doing it gets the results you need, praise God and carry on.

Transformational Power

This is how divine power flows: When members have a clear and literal understanding of the Manual, when they get synced up to the One and energized by the Spirit Master, the power of the Game Master is theirs when they invoke the name of One on their behalf. *That's how miracles are made by you* (John 15:1–14).

After the One rose from the dead—as He predicted that He had the power to give up His life by choice and that He had the power to get it back (John 10:17–18)—He announced to his first members that all authority in the spirit realm and the game environment was now His. He then instructed the members to play the game using His authority to run up the score and recruit guests to become master players on His team (Matt. 28:18–20).

Most members today let His authority lie dormant in their gameplay. That's why they don't look like winners to the guests. Use this section to change that.

Power source

The Manual says that the same Spirit Master power that raised the One from the dead now lives in the members. It's like having the Game Master's cosmic power generator—in pocket-size! (Rom. 8:11; Phil. 2:13).

This power potential only comes with the golden ticket. But wait—*there's more!* Every aspect of the player's life has His restorative power available to them.

Several things happen when a guest becomes a member. Most members are only shown the first one where their game violations were covered. Their religious kiosks insist that the Manual doesn't literally mean the rest are covered because the evidence is not there as they see it, but that's because the fixes are misapplied. Here are the members' personal benefits:

1. *spirit life restored*—game violations erased, bonus round achieved, golden ticket acquired—eternal life
2. *soul given peace*—mental health, emotional health, hope in circumstances and future
3. *physical healing*—healing for all body systems, injury restoration, resurrection power both now and later

These three areas encompassing the players' spirit, soul, and body are each specifically mentioned in the prophecy of what the One would complete in His sacrifice at the place of the skull:

> "But he was pierced for our transgressions, he was crushed for our iniquities; the punishment that brought us peace was on him, and by his wounds we are healed" (Isa. 53:5 NIV).

The Resource appendices section includes testimonial video links of players who dramatically experienced the overwhelming love and peace of the Game Master flooding their soul upon receiving their golden ticket. Others also experienced physical healing as well at that time.

The Game Master does not provide for the restoration of our spirit, soul, and body to no purpose. Players who get membership become His ambassadors who serve as representatives of His grace in their lives (2 Cor. 5:19–21).

A great example of this complete healing of spirit, soul and body is the account of the demoniac of Gadara. The minions and the pigs grab attention in this story, but the Manual says that the healed demoniac was found by townsfolk to be sitting at the One's feet, clothed and in his right mind. He was a new believer whose mind and body were also healed (Mark 5:1–20; Luke 8:26–39).

Golden ticket application

The golden ticket does not automatically change every aspect of a player's life situation. Some parts of your life may turn up rainbows and roses, but the rest of it may still look like a war zone. Here's the reason: during gameplay, parts of your personal game environment can get destroyed or left in shambles after an accident, serious illness, injury, years of debauchery, generational curses, lifestyle choices, being victimized or abused, a spiritual invasion, or other life-changing events.

The golden ticket doesn't fix the damage automatically. It is your insurance policy to cover the repairs and includes acquiring all the materials you need to fix your broken life. But you must still get the repairs done yourself or find a master player who can help you speed up the process. Otherwise, you keep limping along in those broken areas until your game time expires.

The sacrifice and resurrection of the One provided for the breaking of all their curses and the healing and restoration of every aspect of the players' life, but each aspect of their life must have the cure applied to it, and those cures are not done the same way across the board.

This is not a universal health bonus where you find the medic kit and just inject it for a full health power-up—that will happen at the bonus round. For now, you must apply stitches and bandages to every cut and scrape, then make sure you don't let infection set in so the cure can be permanent. Sometimes it can be done in one fell swoop with a master player in the lead, but it's usually a process.

Notice I did not say that the One's sacrifice broke all curses. Only the curse of game violations against the player is broken when the ticket is acquired. Personal curses that players trigger and accumulate during their gameplay or because of their ancestors' gameplay remain to be broken specifically and individually. The game violation is forgiven at membership, but the consequences and effects of the curses can live on.

This issue of curses I mention here refers to the Curses category back in the Hurt Zone of Section Three, which enumerates the kinds of curses against you that can be activated by you, your parents, grandparents, ancestor, or by someone else who has a vendetta against you. Because they are not curses against your spirit but are instead curses against your soul or body, they are dealt with differently and specifically through the power of the One because of your golden ticket possession.

All curses will finally expire at the bonus round, but you don't have to wait until then to deal with curses that are personally active against you (Rev. 22:3).

1. Spirit Life Restored. When a player comes to the Game Master and accepts His solution for eternal life, that act of faith breaks the original game violation curse with all game violations to that point in life, restores the spirit connection to the Game Master and is a task that only He can complete for you. In their spirit-being aspect, all members have the same fix applied, so the spirit connection to headquarters is reestablished with the Game Master's industry standard link through the Spirit Master. Game violations committed after membership must be addressed and confessed during gameplay (1 John 1:9).

The curse against your spirit is broken. Now the rest of your being, soul and body, needs to have the cure applied. This is where misunderstandings happen toward those who believe and understand it this way.

2. Soul and Body Healing. The curse and the effects of the curse against the players' soul and body still remain, but the cure was also made available with the golden ticket. Categories listed in the Hurt Zone cataloged many of the curses and oppressions that are brought against the players through a myriad of pressure points.

Identification of the source of trouble is the hard part of finding healing and restoration for the soul and body. Players are not affected by every curse or minion. They don't all have the same diseases or injuries or emotional scars. They don't all have the same pressures of life or suffer the same degree of bad stuff. Minion attacks against them do follow patterns but are individually tailored and different.

So, while every player had the same disconnected situation in their spirit being, they all have varying soul and body situations where each situation needs specific solutions applied. The provision for healing in soul and body is universally available because of the golden ticket, but the specific application is unique to each player.

In the bonus round, we find that the Tree of Life, which was planted back in the garden of Eden at the start of the game, shows up again giving twelve kinds of fruit, one for each month, and its leaves are provided for the healing of the nations (Rev. 22:2). We would think that the Game Master could have decreed healing for everyone and be done with it. Instead, each member can eat the fruit to live forever and use the leaves to apply them for healing in whatever way they were specifically affected.

Go through the Hurt Zone, identify sources of life's trouble as you review your life and circumstances and research your family history, and then use this Cure Zone section to apply healing to those areas of your life.

THE POWER FIZZLE

Many members are passive in their gameplay. They line up all the texts about how great and powerful the Game Master is and how He can do everything for them and how He has the power to beat every challenge, and there are even great songs written to that effect. All this is true, except for the missing ingredient: the actual application and infusion of His power into their life situations. Too many members don't have much experience in wielding power themselves.

Psalm 18 is a good text for this issue. The first twenty-eight verses graphically describe what the Game Master will do on behalf of His members who call on Him. The rest of the psalm describes how the member's gameplay was enhanced by the Game Master's assistance. He didn't just sit back and watch; he got into action because the Game Master was running flank operations and interference for him. He took matters into his own hand and beat his enemies as small as dust and threw them out like dirt.

That's not passive; that's aggressive. Yet the focus of the kiosk worship and the attitude of members is limited to the first part of the psalm where we just watch like it's on TV. If the Game Master didn't come through for us, oh well, we didn't get our hopes up anyway.

I should mention here that while members in this age of grace are not called to physically pummel other players as described in Psalm 18, this kind of action should be executed in the spirit realm against the game world events and disasters that come upon us. We are not called to harm other players, but we have the spiritual authority to stop them in their tracks.

Faith Power

All spiritual transactions that reach the physical game world are done through faith. Faith is the currency of the spirit realm that transfers power into our dimension of the game environment. Running gameplays without faith is a game violation (Heb. 11:6). The Game Master doesn't approve gamers playing life without the power-filled faith factor because that is the *only thing* that energizes their arsenal to overcome our hostile game environment (Eph. 6:16; 1 John 5:4).

> **FAITH IS THE CURRENCY OF THE SPIRIT REALM THAT TRANSFERS POWER INTO OUR DIMENSION OF THE GAME ENVIRONMENT.**

Playing without faith means that members are playing without power. They are relying on their own game world skills to win a game that is interdimensional. That's a guest player move, but too many members don't transition out of guest mode when they switch teams. This is also an area of ridicule where guests criticize members for being inept—because they are inept.

The Manual says that your faith is your spirit shield (Eph. 6:16). If you give up your faith, your shield is down, and you are personally exposed to the Serpent's flaming arrows. The Manual says that it's impossible to please the Game Master if you don't have faith. It doesn't say it's hard to please Him; it doesn't say it will take longer to please Him. It is *impossible*, without any remote possibility of pleasing Him (Heb. 11:6).

> Running gameplays *without faith* is a game violation.
> (Heb 11:6)

There are two minimum conditions you need to qualify for as someone who has faith: 1) believe the Game Master exists, and 2) believe that He rewards those who unrelentingly pursue him (Heb. 11:6). This is where most members say they totally agree, as they should since it's straight from the text. But most trip up on condition number two: believing that He rewards those who pursue Him.

Check your stance: As you watch bad things happen to you, who do you blame (or praise) for your troubled times? If you are a member who calls the bad things in life a blessing from the Game Master—to help you be a better person—your perspective of Him has gotten twisted by deductive reasoning, not from the actual text of the Manual. Bad things for relentlessly pursuing Him are no reward.

When He speaks of a "good man" or a "righteous person," the Game Master does not associate their life situation with bad things from Him. He admires strong faith and doesn't limit the categories of blessings and miracles that apply to you. Becoming an expert in your faith power-up gives Him a chance to shoot some awesome miracles into the game environment for your personal benefit while He gets the credit (John 14:13).

Trials and Temptations. There is always the need to thread the needle on this issue of bad things happening to synced-up members. Of course, bad things will come against us during gameplay. This book is not an argument for a problem-free life. Problems can build character and should be used to keep us focused and strong, but the Game Master does not need to be a source of trouble for you to get character. Master player Paul said,

> We can rejoice, too, when we run into problems and trials, for we know that they are good for us—they help us learn to be patient. And patience develops strength of character in us and helps us trust God more each time we use it until finally our hope and faith are strong and steady. Then, when that happens, we are able to hold our heads high no matter what happens and know that all is well, for we know how dearly God loves us, and we feel this warm love everywhere within us because God has given us the Holy Spirit to fill our hearts with his love (Rom. 5:3–5 TLB).

> Master player James said, "Dear brothers, is your life full of difficulties and temptations? Then be happy, for when the way is rough, your patience has a chance to grow. So let it grow, and don't try to squirm out of your problems. For when your patience is finally in full bloom, then you will be ready for anything, strong in character, full and complete" (James 1:2–4 TLB).

As a member, you can go through life with trial after trial and not learn character or patience, just slogging through until the next one comes along. Paul and James don't say your problems come from the Game Master. They said to be constructive with the problems that come your way. Use your faith power to minimize the number of problems you get and the amount of damage they cause, and also become a better player from the ones that reach you.

Paul advised Timothy,

Endure suffering along with me, as a good soldier of Christ Jesus. Soldiers don't get tied up in the affairs of civilian life, for then they cannot please the officer who enlisted them. And athletes cannot win the prize unless they follow the rules. And hardworking farmers should be the first to enjoy the fruit of their labor. Think about what I am saying. The Lord will help you understand all these things (2 Tim. 2:3–7 NLT).

FAITH DEFINED

The Manual says that *faith is the manifestation of what you hope for and the evidence of what you can't see* (Heb. 11:1, paraphrased). What you believe or don't believe is your faith or lack of faith. It says that, *with this faith, we know the game environment was framed by the word of the Game Master so that what we see of our game world wasn't made by something that was already here* (Heb. 11:3, paraphrased). So while the game environment was framed in the physical realm having scientific and mathematical laws, it was manufactured from the spirit realm as the Game Master spoke it into existence.

That's the cosmic explanation for how our game environment arrived here. We still use this same faith factor to control our game environment and control the things that happen to us or don't happen to us.

Faith source. Here's the sequence: *Faith comes by listening, and listening comes from the Manual* (Rom. 10:17, paraphrased). The Manual says that faith *comes* to us, so if you need faith, you can get it, but how? Start reading the Manual. If you don't know where to start, try the book of St. Mark and then Acts, and also the Psalms and Proverbs. The book of St. John goes more specifically into points of belief and your connection to the One.

The whole dynamic of faith is that it starts in the spirit realm and is activated by our belief system, just like in the Christmas movies—the wind chimes start—the magic happens because the character's belief is finally genuine. With faith, what you believe in and how you believe it determine what benefit you get from it.

Generally, assume that you should read the Manual literally, but it should also be read in context. But besides the real world versus symbolism, there is also the physical reality versus the spiritual aspect of a topic. For example, here is a controversial rendering in the book of 1 Peter:

> Wives, in the same way submit yourselves to your own husbands so that, if any of them do not believe the word, they may be won over

without words by the behavior of their wives, when they see the purity and reverence of your lives. Your beauty should not come from outward adornment, such as elaborate hairstyles and the wearing of gold jewelry or fine clothes. Rather, it should be that of your inner self, the unfading beauty of a gentle and quiet spirit, which is of great worth in God's sight. For this is the way the holy women of the past who put their hope in God used to adorn themselves. They submitted themselves to their own husbands, like Sarah, who obeyed Abraham and called him her lord. You are her daughters if you do what is right and do not give way to fear.

Husbands, in the same way be considerate as you live with your wives, and treat them with respect as the weaker partner and as heirs with you of the gracious gift of life, so that nothing will hinder your prayers (1 Pet. 3:1–7 NIV).

Based on your cultural background, there are some potentially charged words here like "submit," "obeyed," and "weaker partner." These tend to be fighting words in sophisticated Western cultures. Some may render them as a literal directive while others interpret them as a point to be wise in your relationships, among other possibilities. Note that the passage does not prohibit having a good fashion sense, but that is the interpretation of some members. The first part of this passage is speaking about a wife's goal to win her partner over to the Game Master's team.

While this contains an apparent set of dos and don'ts, the end of the passage identifies the rest of the point: *be nice, treat your wife with respect, and work on your home relationships so you don't get your spirit powerline disconnected.*

Husbands, how you treat your partner directly affects what the Game Master can do for you. If you are mean to your wife, your prayers will get deflected. Your character matters and can affect your faith power. Take the Manual literally but read with understanding.

A problem with religious kiosks, even conservative ones, is that they tend to transfer too much of the text into a symbolic or spiritual plane where something that could have been applied literally is instead symbolized. The most common reason they do this is because they look around the game world and don't see evidence of

> Losing hope that you can have your needs met is where miracles go to die.

actual blessings happening, so they assume it does not apply anymore to our real-life situation.

For example, I observed a kiosk teacher explain this section's opening text that the Game Master has the power to grant us all things that pertain to life and godliness, to say that it does not literally mean our physical life but instead our spiritual life. That takes physical healing and help for any real-life situation off the table in one easy sentence, and the Game Master is off the hook (2 Pet. 1:3). While "life" can refer to either physical or spiritual life, the passage does not exclude the physical aspect of life for the spiritual. So, if you need a blessing on your life in a physical sense, expect it; if you need a blessing for your spiritual life, ask for it.

A kiosk leader at a different denomination told the congregation one day during the opening worship and prayer session, "You people here who keep looking for healing need to stop because it's not going to happen for you." Losing hope that you can have your needs met is where miracles go to die.

If you need a miracle, you must start believing the Game Master meant what he said in a literal sense because *if medical science can match your needs in both time and space, you haven't yet reached the miracle threshold*. Believing the Game Master for the impossible means believing what He said in His Manual that seems impossible. *He prefers to run a supernatural game with you, and He gets no credit when your pain pill works faster than He does*. While not all healing is instantaneous and some healings can develop over a period of time, it is generally reasonable to expect immediate results or an early manifestation toward the desired outcome.

The Manual indicates that healings and miracles were often referred to as a sign showing the divine authority of the One or the divinely delegated authority of His apostle members (John 4:46–54; 6:24–36; Acts 5:12; 14:3; Rom. 15:18–19; Heb. 2:3–4; 2 Cor. 12:12). The Game Master's chosen nation, Israel, is a group of players that takes things literally, so when He made promises to them, they expected literal results, and sometimes the One's symbolic talk totally confused them (John 6:47–60). That process of literal promises hasn't changed going into the last half of the Manual.

FAITH CONNECTION

Many members confuse a lack of response from headquarters with negative feedback from headquarters. There's no response, so ergo, headquarters must not want to process that request. They don't realize that their frequency dial got moved. If there's static on the line, it doesn't mean headquarters isn't broadcasting. They need to get their tuner fixed or get technical support from their Spiritual Service Provider—the Spirit Master.

Most members are told by religious kiosks that the Game Master answers prayers with three or four codes: Yes, No, Wait, or (always) Grow. The "yes" answer is easy and obvious because when things go your way, you assume you know the answer was yes. The rest of those answers are usually deciphered by their observation of circumstances where nothing happens, so they assume their request was denied or figure the timing was off (2 Cor. 1:20).

The problem is also likely that members are using the wrong codes and misinterpret the signals they aren't getting. Furthermore, they assume that nothing is wrong on their end of the line when that's usually where everything went wrong. The Spirit Master is with them, waiting to light up the connection, but the member is not giving Him anything to work with, so the transmission is lost.

All faith is not equal. Most members assume their quality of faith is enough to get the job done. If that were true, cross-country prayer chains would be superfluous since the One said it only takes two or three members agreeing with each other in prayer, and He is right there ready to respond (Matt. 18:19–20). It should be hard to imagine members not being able to find one or two members to agree with them for a specific miracle, but I have found that it is, in fact, quite difficult to find those who can help you achieve that miracle.

A reason that miracles happen when boatloads of members pray together is because at least one of them in that huge number has a solid faith connection to headquarters. But you should also be able to get the job done by yourself without a boatload of help. Doubt and unbelief are where the signal goes dead, and that is caused by weak faith.

Leading questions

When you ask the Game Master for an answer to prayer, don't ask leading questions that paint Him into a corner. Let's say you're selecting a new job and want Him to choose for you; players usually ask if they should work at this job or that job. The Game Master's answer may be one of them or it may be neither, or He may have a preferred third choice that wasn't listed as part of the prayer question. You may get an answer based on your question but which isn't what He preferred for you, so you still can end up in a place that's different from what He wanted for you. When you pray about decisions or choices, try not to limit yourself to what you've already thought about.

What if you go to a kiosk leader for advice about what you should do? Is their answer the voice of the Game Master? It may be good advice, but then it may not be what you should do. There may be a personal perspective or agenda included in that spiritual advice.

Master player King David asked the prophet Nathan if he should build a proper temple for the Game Master. Knowing this was the king's long-held desire, Nathan told him to go ahead, and the Game Master would prosper him in it. That night, the Game Master told Nathan in a vision to go back to King David and tell him he was *not* to build a temple because as a warrior, he was a man of blood; the temple would instead be built by his son. Nathan had to go back and correct himself for speaking out of turn (2 Sam. 7:1–17).

I once heard Barry Black speak at a conference. He has been the chaplain for the US Senate since 2003. When he was searching for a job, he was contacted for a leadership position at a college in the South. He said that after visiting and praying about it, this would have been a very good move for him, but he was still unsure. He asked friends and those he respected what they thought. All said it was a great opportunity for him, and he should take the job. He still had no peace about it, so he turned down the job. At the airport heading home, Senator Trent Lott called Barry and asked him to consider becoming the chaplain for the US Senate. When he took the job, there were challenges regarding housing, but he felt peace that this was where the Game Master wanted him to land.

Not every kiosk or mentor answer is what the Game Master intends. Seek counsel, but check in with the Spirit Master to shed light on your question.

Doubt and unbelief

A fast way to get a member angry at you is to tell them they don't have enough faith. The Manual says you only need faith the size of a mustard seed to get mountain-moving miracles done. A more accurate but probably equally enraging comment is to say they have weak faith. Members assume they have a standard quality of faith that does not fluctuate or need cultivation. Nobody tells them otherwise.

When the One scolded His member team saying they had little faith as their boat was sinking, and Peter, who was walking on the water, suddenly began to drown, it was in the context of weak faith because he ended the sentence asking them why they doubted they would be okay (Matt. 14:29–31). That moment certainly got their blood pumping with panic, but their faith was totally overwhelmed. The Manual explains in detail what the difference is between weak faith and strong faith (Rom. 4:16–22).

Doubt and unbelief are the mindsets that weaken or destroy faith. It's like water in the gas tank or potatoes in the tail pipe. Why are you even praying if you have doubt, the one thing that will guarantee a misfire?

Andrew Wommack tells of a time when a young boy with seriously crossed eyes came to a meeting for healing. Before he even began to pray, while Andrew explained to him that sometimes healing doesn't happen right away, the boy's eyes straightened out, and he could see straight. Andrew was shocked, and the first thing out of his mouth was, "I don't believe it!" As soon as he said that, the boy's eyes crossed back, and no amount of praying could change it again. There is no follow-up report whether his condition was later reversed (Wommack, 2012c, min 10:35–11:50).

> **DOUBT AND UNBELIEF ARE THE MINDSETS THAT WEAKEN OR DESTROY FAITH.**

A total engine flush is required to remove doubt and its lingering effects. Saturate your mind and heart with the promises of the Manual and totally believe they are true for you. Even before you see results of your belief, set your remarks to a preemptive praise and a thank you (2 Cor. 1:20).

Hard-hearted

The One performed a big miracle of feeding 5,000 men plus women and children (15 to 20 thousand players) with only five loaves of bread and two fish, the contents of one meal, like a large anchovy pizza. That night, when the One sent his disciples across the Sea of Galilee, a fierce storm whipped up, and they were only halfway across this 8- by 15-mile sea after about five or six hours of rowing. The One, who was walking across the sea on the water, got into the boat and the storm suddenly calmed down. The disciples were stunned. The Manual said that their response showed that their hearts were hardened because they didn't consider or understand the miracle of the supper that day (Mark 6:51–52).

Members can have a hardened heart where they are close-minded or have a lack of understanding of the Manual. This comes from a perspective of doubt or disbelief in what the Manual says.

Limits of miracles. Through the last few centuries, it is consistently reported by master players that nations and cities with enlightened intellectual philosophies and advanced technologies are more likely to have a resistance to miracles. Members in these areas tend toward skepticism of the supernatural and a very large measure of unbelief in their success. There is a tendency to dismiss those in backward societies for their beliefs in the supernatural and their fear of dark powers.

The One experienced limited miracle potential in cities where unbelief was strong among the players, specifically condemning the cities of Chorazin, Bethsaida, and Capernaum. In one case He had to take a blind player outside of the city limits of Bethsaida to remove him from the city's atmosphere of unbelief. We imagine the One never had to struggle to make a miracle, but this is an instance where the player was not immediately healed on the first try.

When the healing was finally complete, the One insisted the healed player stay out of town, not tell anyone in town about his miracle, but instead go straight home. The unbelief of others can influence, reverse, and even undo the miracle that has been received, and it doesn't happen much faster than a bucket of cold water of negativity dousing your excitement over your miracle (Matt. 11:20–24; 13:53–58; Mark 8:22–26).

Weak faith vs. strong faith

A most offensive thing to say to a member is that they "didn't have enough faith," especially when a loved one dies. That is also the worst of times to bring it up. This is a point a fellow kiosk member has raised several times whenever the matter of faith for healing comes up as proof that healing is not meant for everyone since all members obviously have enough faith.

The One did say that all we need is faith the size of a mustard seed (Matt. 17:20; Luke 17:6). That's not all He said about making miracles happen, but everything else He said after that is consistently ignored. He was only making the point that the issue is not the size of our faith.

He made it very clear that *unbelief* is a factor that affects the strength of our faith (Matt. 17:19–21). Unbelief will undo the positive outcome of our faith, and this is where we most often see miracles slip through our fingers. The One's solution to combat unbelief was prayer and fasting—topics we will address later.

When the Game Master gives a promise to members that challenges our faith, it is somehow connected to the completion of a divine purpose. There are both the promises written in the Manual that members can choose to receive by faith as they meet the qualifications, and perhaps a promise for a specific personal matter where a member may feel a confident assurance of the outcome by the Game Master.

The most thorough Manual explanation and the best description of how the dynamics of faith works is the example of master player Abraham. He was given a staggering promise that required faith to believe and receive it as a true outcome. Here is the text in the Amplified Bible version:

> Therefore, [inheriting] the promise is the outcome of faith and depends [entirely] on faith, in order that it might be given as an act of grace (unmerited favor), to make it stable and valid and guaranteed to all his descendants—not only to the devotees and adherents of the Law, but also to those who share the faith of Abraham, who is [thus] the father of us all. As it is written, I have made you the father of many nations. [He was appointed our father] in the sight of God in Whom he believed, Who gives life to the dead and speaks of the nonexistent things that [He has foretold and promised] as if they [already] existed.
>
> [For Abraham, human reason for] hope being gone, hoped in faith that he should become the father of many nations, as he had been promised, So [numberless] shall your descendants be. He did not weaken in faith when he considered the [utter] impotence of his own body, which was as good as dead because he was about a hundred years old, or [when he considered] the barrenness of Sarah's [deadened] womb. No unbelief or distrust made him waver (doubtingly question) concerning the promise of God, but he grew strong and was empowered by faith as he gave praise and glory to God, Fully satisfied and assured that God was able and mighty to keep His word and to do what He had promised. That is why his faith was credited to him as righteousness (right standing with God) (Rom. 4:16–22 AMP).

Let's translate this: the Game Master told Abraham when he was ninety years old that his wife—who was too old to have children—would have a son. This is the kind of remark where unbelief is easy and faith is hard. In addition to this, the Game Master waited another ten years before making the miracle; that's a long time to hold on to faith when the circumstances were already beyond the possible when he first heard the promise (Gen. 15–18, 21).

So, He laid down some outlandish promises to Abraham and then explained to us what weak faith looked like contrasted with the strong faith that Abraham showed.

*If Abraham's faith was **weak***, he would have 1) decided his body was too old to have a son and that 2) Sarah was too old to have children and 3) concluded it couldn't happen, thereby staggering at the promise because of unbelief (vv. 19–20).

*Instead, Abraham's faith was **strong*** because he 1) had hope in the face of "no hope" based *only* on what the Game Master said, 2) he agreed and he declared it to be so, 3) he gave praise to God for His promise, and 4) was fully persuaded that it would happen because 5) he *believed in his heart* that what the Game Master had promised He also was able to follow through and perform the miracle (vv. 19–22).

This is the Game Master's best explanation describing to you specifically what He is looking for from you when He tells you to have faith in God, walk by faith, ask in faith without wavering, and not doubt in your heart (Mark 11:21–24; 2 Cor. 5:6–7; James 1:6).

Do you have the faith of Abraham? What did he do? Abraham ignored the two obvious obstacles to the Game Master's promise of a son that stared him in the face, namely, his and Sarah's ages. He totally expelled disbelief and unbelief that the promise might not happen for him. He didn't even get rocked back on his heels because of doubt or stagger at the promise by playing "what if" scenarios that it might be "too good to be true" or our other modern-day equivalent of "don't get your hopes up."

Abraham's perspective was different. He embraced faith toward the Game Master by praising Him and giving Him glory. (Try practicing the directions of Psalm 100 or 150 to encourage and strengthen your faith.) He was fully persuaded without an ounce of doubt that the Game Master would deliver on His promise. (Have you ever assured someone that you would do something, but as the words came out of your mouth, you knew deep in your heart that it would not really happen, or you heard a promise toward you and silently dismissed it because you just knew it wouldn't happen? This was not Abraham.) He was fully and totally persuaded in the apparently impossible promise of the Game Master to the very depths of his soul.

Sarah laughed at the promise. Perhaps her faith was not as strong as Abraham's faith. It seems she had her doubts by having Abraham father a son with her maid Haggar, birthing Ishmael, who is the father of today's Arab nations. But whatever unbelief Sarah may have held, in the end, she showed her faith by concluding the Game Master was faithful to His word (Heb. 11:11).

Sometimes as we exercise our faith and it seems inadequate, it can help to have a fellow member who is strong in faith to come alongside and believe with us the promise and blessing we want from the Game Master.

Rate your faith

Do you stagger at the promises of the Game Master?

When you see a Manual text that describes a blessing you would like to have from the Game Master, such as healing, prosperity, or a future, do you think He would really give it to you? Literally, in real life?

As you read passages in the Manual, notice also the requirements to receive the promise, and notice the instructions given to receive the provision. Some are simple declarations that you must believe apply to you. Can you accept for yourself, being fully persuaded like Abraham in the promises of the Manual?

> "And *this is the confidence that we have in him*, that, *if we ask anything according to his will*, **he hears us**: And *if we know that he hears us, whatever we ask*, **we know that we have the petitions that we have asked of him**" (1 John 5:14–15 NKJV, emphasis added).

The point is about our confidence that the Game Master hears us and will grant us our petition. The Manual does not tell us to ask Him whether it is indeed His will as so many members do. This is not a matter of pride vs. humility. It is an encouragement toward confidence. Using the phrase "if it be Your will" is not a statement of faith and belief; it is typically *used to hedge our unbelief* just in case the Game Master does not come through for us and answer our prayer *because we are not confident He will hear us*. Hedging against disappointment is a blessing killer (Mark 11:23).

There are various perspectives to frame our thoughts without calling it unbelief. Perhaps we feel it is respectful to not run ahead of the Game Master by acknowledging that we only want what is His will; perhaps we are hoping our request is the avenue He will choose for us; perhaps we don't want to place demands on Him and instead ask that His will is done in that situation.

The Manual author of Hebrews said that because the One is our high priest who knows the struggles we face, we should *come boldly to the throne of Grace to get mercy and find grace to help in time of need* (Heb. 4:16, paraphrased). Do not use a phrase that would minimize your statement of confidence in the Manual's encouragement toward unwavering belief. Drop it from your vocabulary and drop the doubt. Instead, thank Him by faith for His provision on your behalf.

Do you find yourself staggering at the literal provision of all these promises? Does your religious kiosk or its leaders teach that healing and prosperity are not for today? Do any guidelines exempt areas of your life or anything that pertains to your life, namely your spirit, soul, or body, from the Game Master's blessing? If you need encouragement, hop on YouTube and check out all the scores of new members in other countries who don't know any better describe how they got their miracles and healings by simply asking the Game Master for them.

Some teachers in religious kiosk schools explain that healing and prosperity are only spiritual, not usually physical. The Manual's text of anointing with oil and healing in James chapter 5 has been explained by a kiosk leader as a spiritual event, not necessarily a physical healing or for emotional or psychological issues.

Many kiosks view this same text as a primary sanctioned avenue for physical healing and list it like that in a doctrinal statement. Laying on of hands and anointing with oil are rarely done in the majority of Protestant denominations. They are reserved for special and specific requests for such prayer.

Kiosks regularly collect and pass around a list of members who need healing and will praise the Game Master when it happens, but nobody goes to the hospital to anoint them with oil or lay hands on them. If an explanation is given about the Game Master's desire to heal all players, kiosk leaders are likely to frame it in the context that He uses the skills of the medical professionals as part of the healing process. Much prayer is directed toward the attending doctors and staff. The Game Master answered prayer and healed through the doctor's skill, you see.

When the skill of medical professionals is considered a key factor in the recovery of the sick, it becomes easier to predict who will more likely be healed. Occasionally, someone will beat the odds, and praise for their miracle healing will be lifted to the Game Master, but when their story is recounted in the following months and years, a list of the treatments applied will also be offered as a significant element in their recovery.

Just remember that if you are in dire straits in a lonely place, the Game Master can heal you without a doctor's intervention. There are also stories online of His guardians who stepped in to bring such needy players to safety or medical services when their lives were on the line, including guest players.

Before my wife's father died when she was four years old, their kiosk leaders prayed over him, anointing him with oil for the purpose of his physical healing from Hodgkin's disease. I have participated in a session like this as a Baptist deacon. When I was healed of fibromyalgia and my wife later from Crohn's disease, we were not anointed with oil but were prayed for by kiosk elders or master players who laid hands on us.

Does the Manual encourage you with a confident assurance that the Game Master means exactly what He says? I see a Savior who is happy to answer our prayers in His name (Jesus) that the Game Master Father may be given glory in His Son (John 14:12–14).

In fact, the One insists that He will answer us by saying exactly that—twice in a row. He doubled down and says it applies to *anything*. This question needs to be settled completely in your mind and heart so you can receive from the Game Master without doubts. As you read your Manual, passages of promises and blessings will appear (Matt. 21; Mark 11).

Mainstream view – If it be Your will

> This is not necessarily unbelief—servants of Christ sometimes need guidance—[In making hospital calls in D.C., when I had more than one location, timing was important. So I asked for His will, or to guide my choices as to which is first. Arriving at the right time could be critical. This was before we had cell phones, so I prayed for Him to guide me according to His will. This is not a case of unbelief or doubt (Dr. Gerald Small, pers. comm.).

The above description is an acceptable use in prayer of the clause, "If it be your will." Here is the original context from the Manual:

> Come now, you who say, "Today or tomorrow we will go into such and such a town and spend a year there and trade and make a profit"— yet you do not know what tomorrow will bring. What is your life? For you are a mist that appears for a little time and then vanishes. Instead you ought to say, "If the Lord wills, we will live and do this or that." As it is, you boast in your arrogance. All such boasting is evil (James 4:13–16 ESV).

From passages just before His execution, the One prayed not for His will but rather for the Game Master's will to be done, when He was casting about for another solution to His redemptive sacrifice for you before He followed through with it (Matt. 26:39; Mark 14:36; Luke 22:42).

Most kiosks will provide the proper teaching when covering the text, but in the context of the prayers where it is constantly and exclusively spoken, that is not the context in which the phrase is meant. The issue I described in this section does not refer to divine guidance but pertains to its wide use in prayers where divine help or healing is desired.

The One answered this question of His will to heal when a leper asked Him if He wanted to heal him. Just because the leper knew stories of His miracles and perhaps even witnessed them, he still wasn't sure the One would help him personally.

Large crowds followed Jesus as he came down the hillside. Look! A leper is approaching. He kneels before him, worshiping. "Sir," the leper pleads, "if you want to, you can heal me."

Jesus touches the man. "I want to," he says. "Be healed." And instantly the leprosy disappears.

Then Jesus says to him, "Don't stop to talk to anyone; go right over to the priest to be examined; and take with you the offering required by Moses' law for lepers who are healed—a public testimony of your cure" (Matt. 8:1–4 TLB).

Not only did the One want to heal him on His busy day, but He also took extra time to remind the healed leper to follow the process required to be accepted again by his community.

Many Manual texts describe the Game Master's desire to heal and to help His players. Invoking this phrase of whether it truly is His will in such a prayer actually questions His desire to do what He said. Of course we want His will played out for healing and help, but He already said many times that He will respond to our call. Unless and until He specifically tells us otherwise, we already know His will is to heal and help; the next step is to find the way to get that healing and help.

Spiritual Authority

The authority you have affects your perspective on a situation. If you're not in charge and don't have any authority to change things, there's less incentive to get involved. You may stay back and watch things happen, or if you want to do something, you'll go ask someone in charge to handle things.

Where you see yourself in the ranking of authority has a lot to do with your perceived ability to effect change. It's never a good moment to find out after things went badly that you actually had the authority to prevent or stop problems. This was the case for the Uvalde, Texas, school district police chief, who said he didn't believe he was in charge at the scene during the mass shooting at Robb Elementary School in May 2022 ("Uvalde Schools Police Chief: I Didn't Know I Was in Charge at the Shooting Scene" 2022, ¶ 1).

Members generally don't believe they have the authority to change their circumstances or the issues of life that push against them. Kiosks don't train members to live with a sense of delegated authority. When they pray for things that weigh heavily on them, it's with a heart of uncertainty in the outcome or with a fearful hope because they are at a loss and can't even see the Game Master Who is the only one Who can set things right.

Instead of focusing on their favored position of "abiding in Me [the One]," they focus on His final phrase that "without Me you can do nothing" and actually translate it to mean "I am nothing" (John 15:5). It is discouraging to hear kiosk elders refer to us as worthless and worms in their prayers. It should be noted that the Game Master never devalues the worth of a player. When He calls out their ineffective actions or their own sense of righteousness, He never disparages their personhood. Even when the wicked are described in their final punishment at the end of the game, it is based on their actions from their choices, not their personal value (Ps. 103:13–14; Isa. 42:1–4; Matt. 12:15–21; Rev. 20:11–15).

> The Game Master never devalues the worth of a player.

Sometimes members have great confidence in the Game Master and pray and ask Him to do the job on their behalf while they decide to wait until He comes through for them (Ps. 27:14; Prov. 20:22). There are texts that seem to support these action plans, but limiting action to these options leaves out the authority factor. If you want to get things done, understand the authority structure of the spirit realm and play with confidence within it.

> **IF YOU WANT TO GET THINGS DONE, UNDERSTAND THE AUTHORITY STRUCTURE OF THE SPIRIT REALM AND PLAY WITH CONFIDENCE WITHIN IT.**

AUTHORITY EXAMPLES

David/Goliath (1 Sam. 17:1–11, 42–51), David/Saul (1 Sam. 18:18), and Moses/God (Exod. 3:11)

We'll focus on two examples from Israel's King David. The classic story of David the shepherd boy killing Goliath, the twelve-foot giant (3.66 m) is a good example of two authority issues. David brought food from home to his brothers in the army who were in a standoff with the Philistine army. While there, David heard their champion, Goliath, challenge any man to a duel, and the loser's army would be subjects of the winner's army.

This had gone on for forty days. David got angry because Goliath dared to challenge the army of the living God. He got so worked up about it that the king found out and let him go challenge Goliath. In their verbal sparring, David declared the issue to be a spiritual one and told Goliath he had the authority from God to kill him.

And so he did. One stone into the forehead with his slingshot, and a lopped-off giant's head using Goliath's sword (1 Sam. 17:1–11, 42–51).

Panicking, the shocked Philistines turned and fled while the amazed Israelites pursued and killed them to the gates of their cities. However, the Philistines did not keep their bargain to become servants of the Israelites. Instead, they continued to war against each other. David got his big victory and rescued his nation that day, but this was only day one of the ensuing battles he would face for decades thereafter (1 Sam. 18:2, 5, 30).

David framed his fight with Goliath as God vs. evil. A lesson from that perspective is that when you take on the devil's challenge and beat him against all odds, he won't concede and let you have your victor's reward. It doesn't matter what you've earned, it may still be nothing gained beyond the immediate crisis. The Serpent, the Father of Lies, isn't in the business of paying tribute just because his champion fell. It simply becomes a war of attrition until he finds the next advantage against you. Eternal vigilance is expected of members until the end of their game (Rom. 7:18–25; Eph. 6:10–13; 1 Pet. 5:8–9).

After his stunning victory, the king kept his word that David could have his daughter in marriage. Suddenly, David became very uncertain about this because he was the least, youngest of his father's house in the tribe of Judah, which was only a small tribe of Israel. David felt he was at the bottom of the list in the lowest family of the lowest tribe of the nation. He had no authority to become part of the king's family (1 Sam. 18:14–18).

In these two stories, we have the same character who viewed his authority in two different ways. In his family's perspective, he had no authority at all with the king. In his faith perspective, he had the authority of the Game Master ensuring his success against Goliath.

You may be the least successful, least worthy, or least in the pecking order in your family or job, but even you can play the game with cosmic power because you have the authority of the Game Master Himself to change your situation and help others too.

Authority factor

The greatest understanding of authority resulted in the greatest display of faith. A Roman centurion with a sick servant asked the One to heal His servant. But as the One moved to go to his house, the centurion stopped Him and said that he understood authority and that his men did what he said. He told the One to just say the word, and he knew his servant would be okay. The One was shocked and exclaimed that He hadn't seen faith that strong in the entire nation of Israel. So He gave the word, and the centurion's messenger confirmed that the servant's fever broke the hour it was declared (Matt. 8:5–13; Luke 7:1–10).

Those who understand how authority works are quicker to realize how to use it effectively. The degree of authority you think you have in the spirit realm will determine the focus of your faith and how effective it will be. When the One declared that all authority in the spirit realm and game environment was His and sent His members to declare the good news of the golden ticket, He sent them out in His authority (Matt. 28:18–20).

What did His authority allow them to do? Cast out minions, speak in new tongues, heal the sick, cleanse lepers, raise the dead, handle serpents with impunity, drink poison without effect, and have power over the enemy Serpent. Freely they had received His authority and power, and freely they were to give the benefit to others (Matt. 10:7–8; Mark 16:15–18; Luke 10:19, paraphrased). How much of His authority are you using today?

The handling of serpents and drinking poison were not recreational devices or proofs of faith, which fall under the category of foolishly testing the Game Master, but rather, in the course of getting the job done and these things come upon you, the authority from the One is yours to neutralize the danger (Acts 28:1–10).

In the early 2000s, a newsletter from Gospel for Asia told the story of a group of native missionaries who traveled to a distant village to tell the good news of the Game Master. The village men welcomed the travelers and gave them something to drink. When noticing the villagers had expectant expressions, the missionaries realized they'd been poisoned. They quickly prayed together that the poison would have no effect, and no one got sick. Exercising spiritual authority with faith is very effective.

Spiritual warfare

One of the least discussed areas of spiritual authority is spiritual warfare. It's not that it doesn't affect us; it's that we don't recognize it when it happens, don't believe it for what it is, and have not picked up any tools to deal with it anyway. Besides, if you told anyone that you suspect something, they might sign you up for some electro-therapy. Try finding a religious kiosk that believes in exorcism and is willing to teach you how to effectively deal with minions and malevolent spirits. Some methods are more effective than others, but finding a place to learn how is quite rare.

Casting out minions is one of the stated uses of the authority we have from the One (Matt. 10:7–8; Mark 16:15–18). This can include oppressed players or even locations like those that creep you out when you go in or what could be termed haunted houses. If you suspect a minion-enhanced environment, whether at school, work, public place, hotel room, and so on, speak a blessing over that space and command any minions to get out and not come back. My son did that in a dorm room that was creeping him out where he felt like he was being watched. After blessing his room like this, the creepiness was gone.

Sometimes you deal with players who are real grouches, but occasionally you may get one who suddenly has a vendetta against you for no reason. This happened to my son at the community college. One of his classmates started coming in and telling him off and criticizing him for no reason about schoolwork that was none of his business. They weren't friends or lab partners and didn't need to even talk to each other about anything.

After a couple of days, he was talking to me about how crazy it was that this guy was suddenly getting mad at him when they never talked before. I told him to bless the room when he went to class the next time and, under his breath, command any minion there or connected to that guy to leave. From that point on, the confrontations stopped. Later, the guy met my son in the parking lot and apologized, saying he didn't know what came over him. My son accepted his apology and thought, "Yeah, I know exactly what came over you."

A similar situation happened again with my son about a year later in another tech school, and he blessed the room and commanded any minions attached to the other guy to leave. He had the same immediate results with no further problems.

When my wife cleaned houses, she would pray for the owners while she worked. One day, a client came home while she was there and said that the house always had a calming atmosphere on the days she came to clean. You can control your personal space and the atmosphere of where you are.

Tactics of witchcraft include infiltrating religious kiosks to negatively charge the atmosphere of their worship services. Most members never notice, and those who do recognize a restless atmosphere are not likely to correctly identify its source. Some witches join the custodial staff for access to the building, others become teachers or helpers in the children's services, join the worship team or even join the pastoral staff.

Spiritual armor listed in the Manual is given for frontal attacks (Eph. 6:13–18). The Game Master is our rear guard as we fight (Isa. 52:12; 58:8). Spiritual warfare isn't always obvious, and you can engage under your breath because the minions can hear you just fine.

We have not gotten into exorcisms, but that is a topic where advice from experienced players will be most helpful. Most members may not directly experience this but might recognize the situational encounters described here. The Resource appendices section includes literature and video teachings on deliverance, demonology and exorcism.

Guest imitations

Guests sometimes get in on the action of spiritual warfare, but because they are sabotaging their own team, the results can backfire. As we have mentioned before, the One will declare many players to be lawless ones who did miracles in His name (Matt. 7:21–23). This seems to support the fact that the Serpent does allow some miracle working done for players if it will deceive well enough to distract players from actually joining the Game Master's team.

One example of exorcisms gone wrong happened with traveling Jewish exorcists who didn't believe in the One and refused to join the Game Master's team but saw that Master player Paul was getting results. Sceva, a chief priest, had seven sons who started copying Paul. They would exorcise minions "in the name of Jesus whom Paul preaches about." They did a particular exorcism like this, but the minion controlling the man shot back, saying, "I know Jesus, and I know Paul, but who are you?" The man then jumped them all, beat them up, and they ran out of the house stripped naked and bleeding (Acts 19:13–18).

When you deal with minions and your authority gets challenged, that's the time to pack it up and head for the exit while you still have a chance. Even though they respond to the name of the One, invoking His authority won't help when you get challenged if you are not on His team and don't actually possess His authority to back up your bluster.

Prayer, Praise, & Fasting

Prayers, praise, and fasting are just as much a part of the package for successful living as the other components of faith. Prayer can be a request, a blessing, or expression of thanks for ourselves or on behalf of other players. Praise and fasting eliminate unbelief and infuse a filtered or purified doubt-free faith into our prayers.

Prayer

Our communication with the Game Master through prayer can be as personal and casual as talking to your best friend when the moments pop into your head, sharing your observations of what is happening in your life, thanking Him for keeping things together for you, praising Him for His goodness, asking for directions when you have a decision to make, or just asking for His favor on something happening in your life. The Game Master is not your buddy, but while he is your chosen Master, He is also your spirit Father (Rom. 8:15), the One is your spirit Brother (Matt. 12:50; Mark 3:35), and the Spirit Master is your Comforter (John 14:16, 26). These are family associations that help us understand and relate to the type of close bond we have with the triune Godhead (Acts 17:29).

Prayer is also serious business when trouble is headed our way. The Game Master said to call on him, and He will answer us (Jer. 33:3; 1 John 5:14–15). He also reminds us that we can boldly approach headquarters, what He refers to as "the throne of grace," where we can receive mercy (benevolence and compassion) from Him and find grace (free and undeserved favor) and kindness to help us in our time of need (Heb. 4:16). Having the Game Master in your corner, Who embodies these qualities of mercy and grace, is the best advantage a player could have.

Prayer is communication with headquarters, and there are no restrictions on your keeping the line open for chit-chat. A habit of routine discussion with the Game Master makes it easier for you to remember to call Him up on the fly. The less we talk to Him, the longer it takes to realize that prayer is as much a measure of prevention against the troubles of the game as it is a rescue call amid our losses.

Intercessory prayer. Our prayer benefits other players when we intercede for them. Prayer using weekly kiosk lists or the missionary bulletin or requests from friends and family is intercessory prayer. Most prayer that is not for personal needs is intercessory on behalf of others.

If someone you know has a needy situation that pops into your head, send off a quick prayer to headquarters while it's fresh on your mind. As you pass an accident on the road where help is at the scene, pray for those affected by it. We are also told by the One to pray for players who treat us badly. This is possible to do as we reflect on the Game Master's love for them despite their hurtful ways (Matt. 5:44; Luke 6:28).

Soulish prayer. Not all prayer is helpful. There is a class of prayer that can be called soulish prayer, where prayers are made from a selfish or game world perspective.

First, the player's focus is on this game level. Then, it descends toward an egocentric perspective where the focus is all about self. This increasingly allows the minions to exploit the players' self-centered focus and turn their spiritual power into a game world novelty. It's like having the firing pin of your weapon removed: it still looks powerful and feels powerful, and you may carry it like it's lethal, but nothing happens when you pull the trigger. And the minions are sitting back, holding your firing pin while savoring the look on your face when you can't figure out what's going wrong.

An example of soulish prayer is the type described by master player James, who said that prayers don't get answered because of wrong motives and selfish objectives

(James 4:1–4). Players use prayer for personal gain, or they pray for others based on their personal agenda for the other player. If you sense such prayer being made on your behalf, limit your spiritual contact with that player when possible and make a point to reject a line of concern that could hamper your gameplay.

This can apply to players who pray regularly for others, such as a parent with a growing or grown child who prays that the Game Master will set the child straight according to their expectations, which could be either noble or manipulative. These prayers can also be driven by fear that something bad will happen because the other player is not listening to them enough or to the Game Master. There is a difference between praying fervently or with passion, and praying with panic or anger.

Praise

The Psalms has several short poems of praise. Praise is an expression of appreciation and acclaim for the majesty and benevolence of the Game Master and a sincere giving of thanks for the Game Master's listed promises of help toward members. Praise is the mechanism we use to align our attitude with the Manual's description of the Game Master's character. It is a powerful way to quickly boost your faith as you recount His blessings and promises toward you.

> **PRAISE IS THE MECHANISM WE USE TO ALIGN OUR ATTITUDE WITH THE MANUAL'S DESCRIPTION OF THE GAME MASTER'S CHARACTER.**

Kiosk services are usually designed with a worship time of praise before the leader's message. The reason is to prepare the members to be spiritually receptive to the teaching of the Manual. This is the same format to use when you need to claim a promise from the Game Master to have your request granted or your miracle empowered.

Praise and worship music in the Manual is described as psalms, hymns, and spiritual songs (Eph. 5:19). Generally, psalms can be lifted wholesale from the book of Psalms, hymns can be thought of as doctrinal-centric songs, and spiritual songs are typically inspired by Manual verses or concepts, like most modern worship music. Although there are hymns that need doctrinal correction, the spiritual songs categorically are more likely to need vetting since they are composed from the artists' perspective, which may or may not faithfully align with the Manual's teachings.

> **Ingratitude**, including an attitude of grumbling and complaining, is a game violation.
> (Rom 1:21; 1 Cor 10:9-11; Phil 2:13-15)

Psalm 100 has different facets of praise and describes the attitude with which we should give it. If you cannot praise Him, you will not thank Him. Ingratitude, including an attitude of grumbling and complaining, is a game violation (Rom. 1:21; 1 Cor. 10:9–11; Phil. 2:13–15).

Praise is called a sacrifice and is explained as a vocal expression of thanks (Jer. 33:11; Heb. 13:15). Notice that praise is a voiced opinion where you actually say it out loud. The psalmist says in the Manual that he will sing of the Game Master's mercies, and with his mouth, he'll make known His faithfulness (Ps. 89:1). When you speak it, your entire being gets the message, and your perspective is more quickly synced with the Game Master.

Master player David was on the run from King Saul, his own countryman, so he went to his Philistine enemies for refuge and was given a city called Ziklag. He destroyed an Amalekite city to prove his loyalty to the Philistines, but when it came time to fight against Saul, the other Philistine lords refused to have him join them in case he turned against them. When David returned with his 600 men to Ziklag, they found that the city had been burned down and all their families had been taken captive by the Amalekites.

Everyone sat down and cried until they had no more strength, and then they got angry and were preparing to stone David to death for letting it happen. David himself was already "greatly distressed" by the loss of his family, and his impending execution was not a welcome thought. His response is different from most players because David "encouraged himself in the Lord his God." He then roused himself, got a signal from the Game Master, and recovered all the kidnapped families and an abundance of spoils (1 Sam. 30:1–31).

How can you be thankful or encouraged when your game world just collapsed? Do you focus on the problem or on the One who can help you solve the problem? Being thankful is a choice, and in moments of despair, it can be a very hard choice. In times like this, you must sacrifice and put an end to your bitterness and despair and change your attitude to thankfulness and encouragement from the Game Master. Thankfulness that He gave you the problem or let it happen to you? No! Thankfulness that He will give you grace to overcome your problem and help you thrive despite it (2 Cor. 9:8).

If you can't bring yourself to praise the Game Master despite all your bad gaming circumstances, your faith can blow out like a candle, and lack of faith is a lack of power. Bitterness will leave you powerless and can put you in a frame of mind to walk away from the Game Master's team, which comes all the more easily when you have already been subsisting with no supernatural power available to turn things around in your life.

Your decision to praise during the hard times will brighten your faith and encourage your confidence in the One Who can meet your need and empower you to overcome your circumstances.

Psalms of Praise: Psalm 8, 19, 29, 33, 65, 66, 100, 104, 105, 111, 113, 114, 117, 135, 136, 145, 146, 148, 149, 150.

Psalms with Blessings and Promises: Psalm 1, 4, 18, 23, 24, 25, 27, 31, 34, 37, 40, 41, 46, 61, 81, 84, 89, 91, 103, 112, 121, 128, 146.

Count your blessings. There is a hymn that encourages us to count our blessings when we are discouraged. The first verse says, "When upon life's billows you are tempest tossed, When you are discouraged, thinking all is lost, Count your many blessings, name them one by one, And it will surprise you what the Lord has done" (Oatman 1956, 318 verse 1).

Remembering past blessings can be hard in a moment of discouragement. If you need a list to help you get started, read Psalm 103 (AMP):

Bless *and* affectionately praise the Lord, O my soul, And do not forget any of His benefits;

- Who forgives all your sins,
- Who heals all your diseases;
- Who redeems your life from the pit,
- Who crowns you [lavishly] with lovingkindness and tender mercy;
- Who satisfies your years with good things, So that your youth is renewed like the [soaring] eagle.
- The Lord executes righteousness And justice for all the oppressed.
- The Lord is merciful and gracious, Slow to anger and abounding in compassion *and* lovingkindness.
- For as the heavens are high above the earth, So great is His lovingkindness toward those who fear *and* worship Him [with awe-filled respect and deepest reverence].
- As far as the east is from the west, So far has He removed our transgressions from us.
- Just as a father loves his children, So the Lord loves those who fear *and* worship Him [with awe-filled respect and deepest reverence].
- But the lovingkindness of the Lord is from everlasting to everlasting on those who [reverently] fear Him, And His righteousness to children's children, To

those who honor *and* keep His covenant, And remember to do His commandments [imprinting His word on their hearts].

Bless *and* affectionately praise the Lord, O my soul!

Thank the Game Master for His care for all aspects of your life. Apply these blessings specifically to you and your situation. If you need these blessings in your life, qualify to receive them as directed and pray for Him to apply them to you in your moment of need.

If you don't have a past blessing that relates to the crisis you face, find a promise in the Manual that covers that type of situation, confirm that you qualify to receive that blessing, and pray it to cover you in the name of the One.

Every hard situation you face in life should end with an infusion of encouragement from the Game Master Who overwhelmingly loves you and stands ready to apply His blessing to your need. As you read through the Psalms, it starts with a grateful heart, even in our deepest despair (Rom. 5:3–5).

Fasting

Fasting is an all but forgotten faith-building spirit power enhancer. Today, an alternate form of it is coming back in vogue as religious kiosks mimic the game world concept of fasting by substituting "digital detox" and "relationship reconnection" to unplug from the fast pace of the game world and rejuvenate their lives. There is also intermittent fasting promoted as a good way to lose weight. Those are good and wholesome things, but they are not what the Manual refers to by fasting.

Fasting is the denial of self in one of our most basic functions of life: eating. There is a point where denying food for a prescribed period of time, whether it's a meal on a prescribed day of the week, an entire single day or a series of days, is practiced to accomplish a spiritual purpose. When you need to make a major life decision or perplexing choice, a time of fasting and prayer toward that issue is appropriate. If you need a breakthrough in an area of life and seem to be at an impasse, fasting can be the key for success. The worst thought about fasting is that you will starve because fasting is a battle where the spirit exerts authority over the soul by denying the body of a basic need, something we always try to avoid.

> IF YOU NEED A BREAKTHROUGH IN AN AREA OF LIFE AND SEEM TO BE AT AN IMPASSE, FASTING CAN BE THE KEY FOR SUCCESS.

The objective of fasting is to enforce the authority structure within your being by making your soul's will and emotions obey your spirit. Fasting is an intense spiritual skirmish to eliminate unbelief, but it plays out in the physical game world with your body deprived of food. When your spirit is in authority over your body and soul, your faith will become stronger and more effective as the unbelief is vanquished (Matt. 17:20-21; Mark 9:28-29). Your soul, through your mind and emotions, will howl and wail that you're trying to kill your body. Do you give in, or do you enforce your choice to push through despite your feelings?

There are differing types of fasting. Skipping entire meals is the most common form of fasting. Occasionally, a player may exclude both food and water with their fast. Master player Daniel recorded one fast that was accompanied with prayer while he sat wearing rough sackcloth in an ash heap, interceding in prayer for the sins of his fellow tribe players (Dan. 9:3-6ff). Another time, he excluded meat, desserts, and wine and wore no cologne during a three-week fast while he was in mourning (Dan. 10:1-3). It's curious how he could sit in an ash heap since he was one of the highest-ranking officials in an ancient superpower, but he wasn't too proud to humble himself.

Derek Prince has some helpful booklets on fasting that we used when the children were in middle school and we first learned how to fast as a family. We took a day to substitute pure fruit juice for food at mealtimes. This gave the boys an understanding and confidence that they could successfully complete a fast. We did this a few times for teaching purposes, but after that did not impose a family-wide fast. The boys did not fast on their own again until they were college age when they decided there was a direct purpose for them to get divine answers to their direction in life. Since then, they have fasted more often, ranging from one day to one week at a time.

Two of my sons had a failed fast on separate occasions where each decided to fast for a week. One of them realized he had no clear purpose for a week-long fast and couldn't keep his motivation going, so he ended it early. The other son said he had the right idea but the wrong motive, where he was using it to curry favor with the Game Master, and it didn't work out so well, so he ended it and chose to try another time when his motives were right.

Someone remarked once that they used a fast to lose weight. That may be a byproduct of fasting, but if it becomes the motivation for it, then it's really a diet and not a spiritually beneficial fast. Motives matter when you engage the spirit realm, and what you do in the game world realm can have spiritual benefits, bonus round benefits, or no benefit at all beyond the moment of action.

What if you have a medical condition and can't fast? Perhaps you can work out a scenario where you can modify a fast without jeopardizing yourself. As a diabetic, my fasts consist of a liquid-only diet with perhaps protein shakes supplemented with a sugary drink or a piece of candy as needed. Protein is needed to accompany the recovery from a drop in blood sugars.

You can also ask a fellow member to fast on your behalf while you focus more time on the Manual and prayer. Or you can fast and pray for another player without their participation. Daniel and Nehemiah fasted on behalf of their nation, so intercessory fasting is documented (Neh. 1:3–4ff; Dan. 9:3–6ff).

The One said that when you fast, keep it personal and private. Don't spread the word that you are fasting or look or act like you're sacrificing yourself for a cause, but keep yourself well-groomed and go about your business like nothing's different. (If someone else prepares your meals, don't surprise them with your week-long fast after they have already set the table!) Just like with all spiritual game points, your motive for doing it determines whether it benefits you. The Game Master is paying attention to what you do. The breakthrough and success you need to get are between you and Him, so keep it between you (Matt. 6:16–18).

Aim & Fire

Those of us who are not used to making miracles don't know what to say that would make any difference. What you say and how you say it determine your success or failure as much as your strength of faith to believe for it. This is where misfires can happen. Sure, the Game Master knows what we mean, but we also need to say it the way we mean it. Your habits of speech can offset your intentions as they are blurted out the wrong way, so *think before you talk*.

In the second half of the Manual, the One and his apostle team recorded prayers to heal or change things up. All these prayers directly address the issue itself. They don't pray to the Game Master to fix what they're pointing at; they point at it and command it to be fixed or make a statement of what they want that disease or situation to do.

It feels weird to talk to an illness or injury like it's another person and expect it to do what we say. When you engage the spirit realm, it responds to words energized by faith or total belief. The game environment was assembled with words. As you read the first chapter of the Manual, the game environment was told what to do and instructed how to exist, and it has done so since then (Gen. 1). Giving instruction and expectations to the issue you face is no different than the One and his apostle team demonstrated. Start practicing, and you'll soon get comfortable with seeing results.

They used the authority they had been given instead of asking the Game Master to do it for them as is universally done today. Follow their example and instructions to effect the change you want to see.

EFFECTIVE PRAYER

You can't have a casual relationship with the Spirit trio—Game Master, the One, and the Spirit Master—and expect to get what you pray for. Master player James says that a reason members don't get their prayers answered is because they are asking with the wrong motive: to indulge their own passions and pleasures (James 4:3). This comes back to the point that they are not synced up to the One. Members who have only a passing acquaintance with the Manual are more likely to fail on this point.

Let's review the instructions. Here is how the One put it, "If you 1) abide in me and 2) my words abide in you, 3) you will ask want you want and 4) it shall be done for you that 5) the Father may be glorified in the son" (John 14:12–14; 15:6–8).

In asking for wisdom the Manual says,

> "If any of you lack wisdom let him 1) *ask of God* who gives to all men liberally without berating them. *But* let him 2) *ask in faith* 3) *without wavering*, because he who wavers is like a wave of the sea, driven with the wind and tossed about. *Don't let that man think he'll receive anything from the Lord.* A double-minded man is unstable in all his ways" (James 1:5–8, paraphrased). In the spirit realm, wavering faith or having doubt equals double-mindedness (unbelief)).

The One also gave explicit instructions on how to make things happen saying, "Truly, I say to you, 1) if you have faith and 2) do not doubt, 3) you will not only do what has been done to the fig tree, but even if you say to this mountain, 'Be taken up and thrown into the sea,' 4) it will happen. And 5) whatever you ask in prayer, you will receive, 6) if you have faith" (Matt. 21:21–22).

First, you need the right relationship with the Game Master: 1) abide in the One, 2) His word abides in you.

PRAYER VOCABULARY

Whatever you ask in the name of the One will be received. When you meet all the above requirements, ask in confidence because you know He hears you, and since you know He hears you, it will happen for you. Confidence is key to faith because you are sure of what you know: the Game Master wants to help you (1 John 5:14–15).

Drop the phrase, "if it is Your will" from your prayer routine and instead tell Him, "Thank You for Your provision." It is not spiritual or humble to use that phrase when asking the Game Master for what you need when He already said multiple times that He will supply your needs as you meet His conditions—this phrase too easily transposes His guarantee into a question, which is the essence of doubt and unbelief. If you are asking for what you want and are actually *not sure* you should have it, then asking according to His will would be appropriate.

However, if it is being used indiscriminately as a standard rote phrase, it needs to be scaled back and spoken only as needed. That phrase is properly used when talking to *other players* or to the Game Master about your *plans* (James 4:13–16), not when talking to the Game Master about your *needs*. When He declares that He *will supply all your needs according to His riches in Christ Jesus*, there is no question what His will is for you (Phil. 4:19). "Ask what you will" in the name of the One and thank the Game Master for His provision on your behalf. Amen (John 15:7).

Moving mountains

We call this prayer too, but it is more of an assertive, authoritative command and not a request. This language is instructed by the One for us to take His authority and work miracles and healings and exorcisms and change the trajectory of our circumstances.

In this case, you do not pray to the Game Master *about* your mountain, you don't pray *for* your mountain to go away, and you don't pray *for strength to endure* having your mountain. You just move it and tell it where to go.

The One's exact instructions are to "Say to your mountain 'be removed and cast into the sea'" (Matt. 21:21; Mark 11:23). There is no appeal to a higher authority, and there is no negotiating on the matter. If you want to reason with it, then tell it the reason the Manual says it must obey you; find texts that support your authority in the matter.

Say to that lump from a bump on your head, "Swelling, you go down now in the name of Jesus; pain, you stop hurting right now; blood, you don't pool in my head but get absorbed back into my body! God, thank you for your healing in the name of Jesus because You said that by His stripes I was healed. Amen." Say it and believe it (Isa. 53:5; 1 Pet. 2:24).

If you don't care for a strong authoritative approach, you could pray, "Father, thank you for your healing as Jesus took on our sorrows and infirmities (Isa. 53:4; Matt. 8:17) so we could be made whole. I bless this broken arm in Jesus' name and say, 'Heal, be restored as you were before with all strength. Mend now in Jesus' name.' You sent your Word to heal us (Ps. 107:19–21), and I believe Your Word and receive my healing now. Thank you, God, in Jesus' name, amen."

Say to that problem you have at work, "In the name of Jesus, I bless that situation and command it to straighten out with no more delays or disruptions. I bless the attitudes of everyone involved. God, you said that the steps of a good man are ordered of the Lord (Ps. 37:23), and I call upon you now to make order out of this mess in the name of Jesus. Thank you for your provision on my behalf. Amen."

Notice in these examples that they are assertive statements, expecting an outcome. Healing was a completed act as part of the atonement for sin and a reverse of the curse on the game world. It is something to receive, to take hold of based on the finished punishment of the One at the place of the skull. If you feel the need to ask, do so but don't stop there but also walk in His authority to declare it as He promised. Now we take His Word as our authority to heal as He did, and speak it as though it were the reality in the game world, just like it already is the reality in the spirit realm. "The prayer of faith will heal the sick" (James 5:15a NKJV).

BLESSING YOUR LIFE

We have examples of how to bless a location or situation in the spiritual warfare context. Bless your life as different situations come to mind. Bless your finances, classes, car, your job, travels, home, relationships, and so on. Say blessings, "I bless my finances in the name of Jesus. Thank you for Your provision." "I bless my class in the name of Jesus; I bless my understanding, my skill development, and my ability to meet deadlines. Thank you, God, for Your provision in Jesus' name."

Read the Manual and put your faith in its promises, then apply them to your life. You know the Game Master wants you to live long (Ps. 91:14–16) and be in good health and prosper (Deut. 29:9; Ps. 1:3; 3 John 1:2) because He said so (Jer. 29:11). Since He told *you* to heal the sick, add yourself to the list and do it. His intention is not for you to have a short, miserable life. If that's what you're having, He didn't give it to you or sign you up for it.

> **READ THE MANUAL AND PUT YOUR FAITH IN ITS PROMISES, THEN APPLY THEM TO YOUR LIFE.**

One of the ways to ensure long life is to honor your parents (Eph. 6:2–3). Make sure you qualify and then claim the promise. Another way to ensure a long life is to love the Game Master with all your heart (Ps. 91:14–16). Qualify and claim the promise.

If you want to prosper in whatever you do, get synced with the One through the Manual (Ps. 1:1–3). Qualify and claim the promise. This is not a mystical formula; these are declarations from the One who does not lie (Ps. 89:34–35). Get Him to punch your ticket on everything you meet the requirements for. Don't be shy; *of course you don't deserve it* when you *focus on your own righteousness*, but as a righteous player from His perspective, He wants to "show Himself strong on behalf of those whose hearts are pure toward Him." He is looking for you to qualify. Become one of those blessed players (2 Chron. 16:9).

Healing

There is no disease the Game Master is unable to heal even to the point of raising the dead. Among those who have healing ministries, there are accounts of limbs regrown and eyes restored or regenerated. Many members believe that if you are healed, then it was the Game Master's will; if you are not healed, then it was not His will to heal you. There are many reasons why He does not heal, but his lack of willingness is hardly one of them, especially since the One used healing as 87 percent of the prophetic proofs that He was the divine Messiah (Isa. 35:4–6; Luke 7:22). Today, Protestant kiosks, overall, in Western nations, practice healing at about a nearly zero percent rate as proof the Messiah has come. They will typically not encourage the pursuit of divine healing as a standard practice.

The Manual asserts that members should characteristically walk by faith and not by sight (2 Cor. 5:6–7). Couple this with Hebrews 11:1, which says that "faith is the confidence in what we hope for and assurance about what we do not see" (NIV). The point of seeing through the eyes of faith is that the physical evidence, which is staring you in the face, is not the whole story from a spiritual perspective. Looking at evidence of physical illness does not mean that is what you are destined to keep.

Faith takes the perspective of your healed condition in the spirit realm and applies it to your physical illness even before the illness and its lasting effects are physically removed (1 Pet. 2:24). Religious and secular skeptics may call this foolishness, not faith. You still must deal with the physical issues, but the spiritual perspective is assured of a coming different outcome—*through faith*. There can be barriers to healing, and if one or more of those barriers affects you, that must be dealt with before the results of healing will manifest in your body.

On this issue of illness, it seems that many members tend to walk by sight and not by faith, the opposite of what they are supposed to do, because their evidence of what is the Game Master's will for their recovery is based primarily on their current condition. But just as a misdiagnosis doesn't help recovery, so a misapplication of the Manual's diagnosis and prescription can hinder the healing work of faith.

Many members from the pulpit to the pew are so convinced that the Game Master deliberately chooses not to heal someone, that showing textual evidence from the Manual contradicting this perspective or this way of thinking is ineffective in changing their minds. So, the conclusion for most becomes: "God didn't [won't] heal me."

Authoritative healing

Does the Game Master want you to be well? This issue is where most arguments are made that players cannot expect with any confidence that the Game Master wants them to get better every time they get sick. There is no solid Manual text to back up that answer or argument for their condition; it is anecdotal evidence that does not authoritatively create a guiding principle, except that it will probably be argued authoritatively.

Those with this view are likely to concede that some illnesses are obviously the Game Master's will to heal, such as headaches, colds, flu, broken bones, infections, and so on, while others suddenly don't reach that standard of assured healing such as major or chronic illnesses, paralysis, dementia, and so on. How do you know when you crossed from an automatically healed illness to one where it may no longer be His will to heal? Did the Game Master tell you specifically that your condition doesn't qualify for His intervention?

If your answer approaches "yes" that the Game Master wants you well, your faith and confidence in His Manual need to be encouraged. After all the passages in this section, it should be clear that He wants to help you.

Do you believe He will heal you? If you say "no," that's what you'll get. If you say you hope so, that is probably faith mixed with doubt. Doubt is a game violation (Rom. 14:23; James 1:6–7). If you say "yes," you have a fighting chance. It is exciting to see online kiosk testimonials of brand-new member believers across the game world who received instant healings from broken bones, multiple sclerosis, and drug addiction through pure faith and simple prayer.

Authoritative healing example

Praying for healing is usually made as a request to the Game Master for healing, and there are places where the Manual instructs us to pray for the sick. Most examples of healing events in the Manual are declarative statements.

Praying for healing is not the kind of prayer where you need to ask the Game Master to do the job for you. It is the kind where you directly address the issue yourself using His authority that was given to you. We call it prayer because that's the most recognizable jargon to associate with a spiritual connection. It is specifically a statement of faith and a spoken command to the issue. It is a prayer of:

1) praising the Game Master for his power, concern, and (specific) promises to provide healing,
2) speaking by faith with His authority to the illness at hand that

a) it has been defeated at the Cross by the One (sickness is an oppression of the Serpent) (Acts 10:37–38) and has no authority in the body,
  b) by His authority, it is to heal now,
  c) addressing the specific issue: muscles, tendons, joints, bones, inflammation, and so on, and
3) closing the prayer by thanking the Game Master for His healing
4) in the name of the One [Jesus] (John 15:16).

1. Praise is an encouragement of your faith to strengthen your belief in the Game Master's authority and to drive out unbelief from your heart. Memorize appropriate texts.

2. The authoritative speaking to the issue is your exercising the authority you have been granted from the One in the matter. Be specific. Memorize appropriate texts. Expect results.

3. Thanksgiving is expected from the Game Master. He does not accept ingratitude (Rom. 1:21; Phil. 4:6; 1 Thess. 5:18).

4. In the Name of the One [Jesus] is the condition for the request to be granted (John 15:16; 16:23–24). He holds the delegated authority to make it happen, and it is through Him that the Game Master receives the glory.

As you read the Manual, you will notice that the examples of prayers for healing or any other situation are never requests; they are commands or declarative statements. The players do not ask the Game Master to heal; they command healing in the name of the One. The One made miracles using His own authority (Luke 4:39), not asking for results from the Game Master as we habitually do today. Follow their examples.

Lack of healing evidence

Lack of evidence does not mean a lack of willingness on the part of the Game Master. Some healing is instantaneous; some is gradual. Don't pray for gradual healing, but it can arrive that way. If it seems like nothing's happening, shoot it again; just keep firing faith into it. The One told stories for the specific purpose that players should keep praying and not give up (Luke 18:1).

Derek Prince told of the time when he was bedridden for a year in a North African military hospital, praying for healing. He called on everyone he knew who would pray for him, and anyone who came to town with healing experience would be called on to pray for him, all to no avail. Having plenty of time to read, he read through the Manual and underlined with a blue pencil every time it talked about healing. He said that when he reached the end of the Manual, all he had was a blue Manual—no healing. With his perseverance, he eventually was healed with a full recovery using the principles identified in his book, *God's Medicine Bottle* (Prince, n.d., min. 25;30–26:08) (Ps. 107:19–20).

Andrew Wommack told of his breakthrough in healing that happened when he was very sick with a bad cold or the flu. He decided that the Manual said the Game Master would heal him, and he would take His word for it. He spent a very miserable night crawling around on the floor pushing the Manual around with his nose, reading its promises, and refusing to take medicine while he insisted in prayer that he believed the Manual meant exactly what it said. After that long night, the illness left him, and he went on to experience a life of health from that miserable start (Wommack, 2012b, min. 11:46–14:49).

Derek and Andrew went on to have game world ministries that have seen many thousands healed and delivered from minion oppression. Their start on their healing journey was difficult, and perseverance was required. It's hard to choose to believe when you don't see evidence for a year, but that is a measure of the strength of your faith.

Those who insist the Game Master does not want to heal everyone usually say that because they believe their (lying) eyes instead of His Manual. Since they're sincere members, they'll also have texts to presumably back up that opinion. They look around and notice that not everyone who prays to get better actually improves. So, they wrongly conclude that it is the Game Master's will to also keep players sick and let them die or "take them home" as they euphemistically say. This is an example of living by sight and not by faith, where what you see dictates the perspective and strength of faith you will have.

If a disease is brought on by negligence, does that mean you are disqualified from healing? No. Some may argue otherwise, and it seems like that ought to be the case, but the Manual doesn't concur. If you have a pickled liver from drinking or bad lungs from smoking or cancer from an environmental exposure, is your healing beyond the compassion of the Game Master? If you are injured because you somehow decided not to wear protective gear, meaning you deserve what you got, does the Game Master make you live with it?

Running out your game clock before you get healed can be a very real concern. There are many reasons healing does not manifest itself in our body as described in Section Three. Most players rarely look deeper than the outward results, so we usually are not aware of all the negative spiritual baggage we've been carrying around that prevents healing from happening.

What if you pray and believe for healing, and it doesn't happen? 1) First, check to see if there are obstacles that hinder it. 2) Try fasting a few days and pray again. 3) Call a master player who has experience with healing and ask them to pray with you. The encouragement of someone who has strong faith can be enough to finish the job. If you don't know anyone who successfully prays for healing, call a prayer hotline of those who can pray effectively.

Blind faith. Occasionally, a member becomes convinced that the Game Master wants them well or they decide that He will heal them, and to prove their faith, they refuse any medical assistance and pray for healing instead. The general public is aware of this perspective, usually from adherents of the Christian Science church, who have died, or their children died when they refused medical treatment and chose to pray for healing instead. Occasionally, members from mainline religious kiosks will do this too.

Medical professionals are less spiritually sensitive in matters of healing since their focus is always factoring worst-case scenarios, and their first prescription is to use pills and shots. Most of their professors, being good scientists, were likely confirmed agnostics. So they as a whole do not encourage a player's faith nor have they been trained in how to do so.

If you have no prior experience with healing and have not previously exercised your faith to see results and have no spiritual lifeline to call on, to start a healing journey from scratch with an incapacitating illness, your level of faith may not be up to the task of healing yourself in time to outrun the disease. This is just a reality of where we are as players of faith, but regardless, you should pray with fervency and assurance in the hope and belief of the Game Master's promises.

Certainly pray, but observe your condition and how it changes. Continue with your medical treatment as needed. If your prayer is effective, your situation should at least stabilize or improve. Sometimes results are instant, and in other cases, it takes time. Improvement may not happen in a minion-induced illness, but this should not be the focus unless it is confirmed by experienced members who recognize that you are dealing with a direct spiritual opposition of that type.

Some kiosk leaders have given testimonials where they began teaching a series on how the Game Master wants players to be well, and they themselves suddenly became sick throughout the lesson series. In one case, the leader lost his voice. They realized this was an attempt to prove them liars, and they were able to finally overcome the illness through prayer as they continued their teaching series.

A benefit of divine healing is the lack of need for affordable health care. If you are in a serious condition with no access to medical assistance or other help, by all means, pray like your life depends on it. The condition of the Game Master is that you pray in faith without faltering, doubting, or fear because otherwise, you'll certainly come up empty. Your assured confidence is required (James 1:5–8).

Unequal healing

Master players Peter and Paul performed many miracles of healing, including raising the dead, but Paul remarks about two fellow team members, Epaphroditus and Trophimus, who were laid up by sickness. Paul was very concerned about Epaphroditus, who almost died (Phil. 2:25–27). Trophimus had to be left behind because of illness (2 Tim. 4:19–21). I have wondered why he didn't simply heal them and be done with it, but he didn't elaborate on the circumstances. Even the apostle player faced situations of concern regarding healing. This could fall in the category that God only knows.

As you begin your healing journey and start to see results, you may notice healing comes more quickly for some types of problems than for others. Because most of us do not receive the spiritual gift of healing and miracles, our ability to perform them requires a more focused exercise of faith. Our success can be developed over a broad range of illnesses, but we may experience faster progress with some illnesses more than others while we mature in this area.

The man who prayed for my fibromyalgia healing seems to have some difficulty with results for tendons, joints, and flu issues. His friend who assisted with my healing died of cancer. These things can be puzzling but are not necessarily evidence of the Game Master's choice to not heal players. I don't know their specific circumstances.

Some master players have mentioned that there are some diseases that seem to respond better as they pray for them. That does not mean healing will not come for other ailments or that there are limitations to what the Game Master will do. Andrew Wommack's website has stories of members giving examples of raising the dead. These are firsthand stories of healing—normal member players finding their extraordinary miracles. Links are in the Resources Appendix.

A relapse is not evidence of a failed healing. Sometimes it takes additional perseverance to complete a healing or stop its recurrence as it did with my fibromyalgia. The One told a story about a widow who needed justice, so she pestered an indifferent and uncaring judge until he relented and granted her request. This point that the One made about persistence in praying does matter until our objective is finished (Luke 18:1–8).

> **A RELAPSE IS NOT EVIDENCE OF A FAILED HEALING.**

When you are dealing with issues that encompass the spirit realm and the game environment, not every factor is in your control. Understanding that sickness is an oppression of the Serpent, sometimes you must be prepared for an extended process before the issue will respond as it should (Acts 10:37–38). If you have never used your authority from the One before now, the minions may not believe that you mean what you say. In fact, your own body may not believe what you say with your words of unfamiliar spirit authority.

First responses can take time. If you are in a habit of telling lies, even little ones like always being late when you tell others you'll be on time, your entire being responds to the way you make excuses for yourself. Then you tell your body to obey you and heal, but what you say is inconsistent with what you do; sometimes you lie, and sometimes you tell the truth, and who is it to believe? This is a simple example of how our own lack of character can interfere with the transfer of power from the spirit realm to the body.

This is like dealing with a rebellious child; do you stay consistent and firm until they finally respond the right way, or do you just give up and maybe save the struggle for another day? One of the hardest parts of this matter is to have the patience to keep at it until you see the results that you want to happen for you. To repeat the One again, *players should always keep praying and not lose hope* (Luke 18:1).

Life Issues

Healing is a category covering illness and injury. Now we are addressing other life issues that may or may not result in injury but can seem like somebody is out to get you. Being in the crosshairs of bad luck is no way to live.

Life issues can include things that impact your life circumstances and affect your ability to stay alive. This section builds on the principles already discussed, and they apply here too. When you get your life tuned in to the Game Master's spirit frequency, it's just a matter of directing the results of that sync-up to other areas of life. You are not starting from scratch with every area where you need a blessing.

Circumstances

Your life situation includes personal relationships like family, work, and social activities; civic responsibilities like licensing and contractual obligations; life responsibilities like your job or school performance; productivity, including voluntary things like hobbies and community service; and financial responsibilities, like budgeting, savings, and investments.

There may be more that you can think of, but the details don't matter as much as the life principles you apply to them. As you have been reading the first parts of this section, the point has been to apply the Manual to your life and take its principles to heart to become more like the Game Master. The Manual includes principles of living as guidelines for applying the characteristics of the Game Master, so if there is something not specifically mentioned, you can find an approach from the Manual in how you should think about it.

A brief list of optimal characteristics from the Manual is to be content, dependable, diligent, discerning, faithful, forgiving, generous, gentle, grateful, helpful, hospitable, humble, kind, orderly, resourceful, self-controlled, sincere, truthful, wise, and so on. Assuming we are living responsibly and trying to get along with other players, the goal is to work the game with the least number of misunderstandings and turmoil with the players we deal with and in the tasks we must do. How these things intersect can impact our daily gameplay and our future choices (1 Cor. 13:4–8; Gal. 5:22–26; Eph. 4:20–32; 5:15–17; Phil. 4:4–9; Col. 3:8–17; 4:5).

Conditions

The conditions of life can be framed by our faith. Things that seem out of bounds for prayer are within the scope of our ability to change them. For example, weather events can be modified by faith. Traffic signals, machinery, or whatever issue comes your way are subject to faith.

Oops, we just made a left turn onto Weird Circle. This area sounds like something from a metaphysical promotion for pyramid power or mood rings. Most of us don't use our faith like this, but the same prayers of faith for healing or urgent needs can be applied to all areas of life, not just emergencies.

The same authority we use to pray for health can be directed toward conditions of life. All the same principles of character and spiritual growth and faith are required for these things of life. The difference is in the understanding that you can direct a blessing or curse on inanimate objects and game world conditions.

> One day Jesus said to his disciples, "Let's cross to the other side of the lake." So they got into a boat and started out. As they sailed across, Jesus settled down for a nap. But soon a fierce storm came down on the lake. The boat was filling with water, and they were in real danger.
>
> The disciples went and woke him up, shouting, "Master, Master, we're going to drown!"

When Jesus woke up, he rebuked the wind and the raging waves. Suddenly the storm stopped and all was calm. Then he asked them, "Where is your faith?"

The disciples were terrified and amazed. "Who is this man?" they asked each other. "When he gives a command, even the wind and waves obey him!" (Luke 8:22–25 NLT).

What terrified them the most, drowning in the raging sea or the fact that the One could talk to the storm? His response was to question their faith. Not only did they wake Him up, but they were also making Him do all the heavy lifting. The worlds were framed by the word of the Game Master (Heb 11:3). Your faith can also control the elements and inanimate objects. Give it some practice.

Blessed living

Here are several examples of environmental conditions affected by faith. We will start with the One because this kind of talk seems out of place in a discussion of faith, but He gave examples for us to follow. Not every instance was an urgent situation; some of them were only quality-of-life events.

Early age examples. The One used His faith to alter his environment several times. His first miracle was turning water into wine. The only compelling reason to do this was because the wedding host ran out of wine, and His mother put Him on the spot and told the servants to do what He said. It saved time and money. The host was complimented because it was the good stuff, not the cheap wine they served after everyone was well-hydrated (John 2:1–11).

Twice, He multiplied a single meal of bread and fish (maybe the size of a large pizza) to feed several thousand players just so they wouldn't go hungry and faint on the road home (Matt. 14:14–20; 15:32–39). Both times, they had several baskets' worth of food left over, so these miracles included an abundance of food and not just enough to get by.

When He passed a fig tree and saw there was nothing to eat, he cursed the tree, saying that no one would ever eat from it again (Matt. 21:18–21). The next day, when His disciple team passed by it again, they saw it was dead, and He made a point to explain that they could do that too, giving them specific instructions on how to do it. Another point to bring up is that the tree didn't immediately die but died from the roots, so it took a day for it to show up on the leaves and branches. How hungry do you have to be to curse a fruit tree just because it had nothing? This miracle was an object lesson and example for us to keep in mind.

And then there were the times when He calmed storms on the Sea of Galilee and scolded his disciple team for their lack of faith. Storms happen. At least one of those times, He expected them to use their faith instead of waiting for Him (Matt. 14:22–33; Mark 4:35–41; Luke 8:22–25).

There are other types of miracles than these that are just as available to members today as they were 2,000 years ago. The age of miracle-making hasn't ended.

Current examples. I'll start with examples from my family and go from there. When my son was training for the Air Force Pararescue program, he didn't want rainy weather. This was during the winter in Maryland. He wasn't keen on splashing through puddles on his runs, and his body fat was so low that the other guys working out with him had to watch him for hypothermia. He prayed away the snow or rain forecast several times. I finally told him that we needed the rain to prevent another drought, so he relented and said it could only start when he was done with his run. This happened like that a couple of times. Interestingly, our kiosk leader said that several of his public-school elementary children from a certain kiosk denomination were also praying away the snowy weather that winter so their weekly kiosk meetings would not get canceled.

One of those times, there was a strong storm front moving east that stretched from Pennsylvania to the northern neck of Virginia. It was moving into my son's area around the time I got home from work, so I pulled up the radar to see if he was being affected. It was astounding to see a straight line of heavy rain bands across the state on the radar, but the place where he was located had a loop where the rain just circled around his location. He later told me that the rain held off during the workout, started when he got to his car, and was pouring down as he left the area.

There was another time in the summer when we had a derecho storm come through the area. This one had a double front where there was a line of rain that came through, and half an hour later, the main part of the storm was on the way. This was a serious storm with strong winds and hail in the forecast. Our work allowed us to shut down in the early afternoon and head home before it arrived.

As I drove home, I prayed for a blessing of protection on all our property. This turned out to be a lethal storm and struck east and west of our neighborhood. At my house, there was no wind at all and not even a drop of rain. I kept going outside to see if anything was happening, but the storm passed by without affecting us. I checked the radar, and our house was in dark green and yellow rain zones, but outside, it was only cloudy and calm.

When my youngest son was in fifth grade, we read about the fig tree story in the Manual, as mentioned above. He thought that was cool, so he went to school and cursed one of the trees. This was at the start of spring, and that was the only tree that didn't wake up from winter. He finally told me about it when he returned to that school campus seven years later and noticed that the tree he cursed was the only one missing from the landscaping.

A couple of times, we had car trouble where, if that car stopped, we couldn't get it started again for a while. I prayed for green lights the whole way home, and that's what we got (through at least ten traffic lights per incident). Other times, we had situations that would have severely disrupted our family life or finances and prayed for blessings in those situations, which worked out in our favor. In contrast, before this, we would have expected bad results and gotten them because that was typically our history of life issues.

When my son worked at Taco Bell, one of the registers would stop responding and was troublesome to fix. Under his breath, he would pray over it, apply the sequence again to get it working, and the register would respond. When his coworker had trouble with it, he would call him over to see if he could help get it going. Eventually, the coworker caught on and asked, "You just prayed over it, didn't you?" My son affirmed that he had (pers. comm.).

My son told a story where a military coworker who disliked Andrew Wommack with his teaching of faith-filled words went on a trip to England. The coworker told his wife repeatedly that the weather wouldn't be good, but she countered and insisted that they would have great weather. While they were there, the weather was sunny and beautiful to the point that their hosts kept commenting on how unusually nice the weather was. His wife's faith overcame his unbelief, and my son doesn't think the coworker realized what happened in the spirit realm (pers. comm.).

Andrew tells of the summer as a young adult when he cut his mother's lawn, which had a lot of pecan trees. When his father was alive, they would harvest about 500 pounds (226 kg) of pecans each year. After he died, things went fallow, and caterpillars took over, so they got maybe 50 pounds in a season. As he cut the grass that summer, he would put a hand on the trees as he passed by and curse the caterpillars and bless the trees. That was it; no fertilizer, no pruning, or anything else. That season, they harvested 500 pounds of pecans (Wommack, 2012a; min. 2:32–5:00).

An example of tuning in to the Spirit Master happened to me when I was driving to a pain management appointment for shots in my back to deal with fibromyalgia. I approached the bend where an exit before the one I needed made a cutoff, which included another entrance ramp back to the highway. Suddenly, a thought popped in my head: "Take the exit." It didn't say why. Instead of taking the exit, I argued with that voice in my head and said, "Why?" I didn't need that exit, so I didn't take it.

I rounded the bend, and traffic was backed up for the final mile up to my needed exit. If I had taken the first exit, I could have either taken the entrance ramp to get back on the highway or easily gone around the traffic jam through side streets. I sat there for an hour and a half and had to reschedule that appointment with its forty-five-minute commute for another day, enduring the back pain until I reached the next appointment. Sitting in traffic gave me plenty of time to realize the Spirit Master had dialed in.

Life situations are included in the Game Master's blessings, and He responds with as much consistency as your faith to believe Him. Turn your life into a perpetual blessing.

Consistency

Playing in a hostile game environment is hard. The Manual includes repeated calls of perseverance and faithfulness with a reward for those who hold out to the end and overcome their obstacles. This book may leave the impression that it's easy to hold back the tide of evil against you, but that is not the case. The good news is that we don't have to deal with it all at once or all by ourselves, but persistence is required.

Master player Paul was an expert, capable of special miracles that occasionally went beyond the normal miracles that other members could do (Acts 19:11–12). He expressed frustration with how hard it was to do the things he wanted to do, hard to do the things he knew he should do, and stop doing the things that made him ineffective (Rom. 7:14–24). He offers encouragement to all members that our effort has eternal value:

> "So, my dear brothers, since future victory is sure, be strong and steady, always abounding in the Lord's work, for you know that nothing you do for the Lord is ever wasted as it would be if there were no resurrection" (1 Cor. 15:58 TLB).

Paul compares our gameplay with a race where we should all try to win the prize. For his part, he played with a purpose, kept his focus, and worked to consistently practice self-control so that after he told us how to play, no one could call him a hypocrite or see him get disqualified (1 Cor. 9:24–27).

Don't let game violations accrue but deal with them right away by confessing and forsaking them. Delayed correction can lead to insensitivity to the promptings of your conscience and the Spirit Master (Prov. 28:13; James 5:16; 1 John 1:9).

Perhaps you need an intensive jumpstart to get your consistency going. My cousin was ordained as a minister at age twenty-one but finally became a pastor eight years later. He said that he couldn't get focused and be consistent because it was super easy to be distracted by worldly things of his past life in Mexico City as a gang member. He surmises that master player Paul probably didn't go to Arabia only to be taught by the One but also to get all the junk out of him from his former life (Gal. 1:15–18).

You likely know what areas you struggle with and what activities or indulgences take you back to the old days and your former self. The breastplate of righteousness will enable you to guard your heart with all diligence and turn away from things that cause you to lose your focus on the bonus round (Eph. 6:13–16; Prov. 4:23; Col. 3:1–3). Continue to develop the character of the One through the Spirit Master (Gal. 5:22). Good character is a demonstration of consistency.

Master player Paul reminds members, "Don't drink wine excessively. The drunken path is a reckless path. It leads nowhere. Instead, let God fill you with the Holy Spirit" (Eph. 5:18 VOICE). To the degree the Spirit Master fills your life, your focus and interest in doing things that cause you to stumble is also reduced. The One reminds us that following His sayings and taking them to heart will give you a solid foundation against temptation and trials (Matt. 7:24–27).

> If you need a routine, in-your-face approach, follow the example spelled out by master player Moses who said, "You must commit yourselves wholeheartedly to these commands that I am giving you today. Repeat them again and again to your children. Talk about them when you are at home and when you are on the road, when you are going to bed and when you are getting up. Tie them to your hands and wear them on your forehead as reminders. Write them on the doorposts of your house and on your gates" (Deut. 6:6–8 NLT). It doesn't matter if you don't have children; read the Manual and apply this routine to yourself.

Along with these commitments, stay connected to the Manual and memorize it, and pray over your daily life. Find ways to encourage your faith and fellowship with other members through church attendance, a life group, church social activities, church ministry participation, an accountability group, and such things that work for you. Read books on topics of faith and listen to music that aligns with the Manual. Don't overcommit and get so involved that you burn yourself out. Walk through your Christian walk.

Power fade

The key to power is abiding in the One. This means having a consistent connection to Him through the Spirit Master by getting a mastery of the Manual. It is a daily, weekly, monthly, yearly, and lifelong process. As your faith strengthens and your gameplay grows into consistent blessing in all areas of life, you will naturally want to keep the good things coming and make your favored gameplay continue.

> **THE KEY TO POWER IS ABIDING IN THE ONE.**

There is an ebb and flow of life where we get busy or distracted from our power source. We can maintain our situation for a while, but the longer we are disconnected from the One through His Manual, our faith will weaken, and we may notice a lack of response when we pray. We are the ones who change the circumstances by allowing our connection with the Game Master to cool down.

You know what you need to do to strengthen your faith, dispel unbelief, get your prayers answered, and move your mountain: abide in the One and get His Manual abiding in you (John 15:4–8; Ps. 91).

Cure Zone Summary

THE CURE ZONE shows us how to apply faith to our daily life situations and remove obstacles to their outcomes. There are sets of instructions for addressing obstacles such as curses and strongholds that place us at odds with the Game Master's blessing or prevent us from receiving a healing or miracle.

Begin by laying the groundwork for success. First, run an obstacle diagnosis on your situation to identify areas that impact you and hopefully reveal specific sources of your troubles. Then, check for barriers to healing so you don't have any blind spots hindering your healing or recovery. This area also includes soul-healing tips for your mind and emotions. The final areas of preparation in the Cure Zone Synopsis include checks on your membership, character, arsenal, and engagement with the Game Master.

The Solutions section identifies the needed skills: read your Manual, develop your character sequentially, and put on the armor of God. Develop your faith, understand your delegated spiritual authority, and practice prayer, praise, and fasting.

Apply these skills to your situation and pray for your healing and success. It doesn't need to take a long time to get help from the Game Master. You can read it and practice it as you go.

We must discard habits of doubt and unbelief that limit the Game Master's ability to bless our lives, then cultivate a heart of faith. Using the instructions He gave us, we apply our faith to life issues that pummel us spiritually, mentally, emotionally, physically, and circumstantially. Practice in the application of faith improves results.

To summarize, this section is about character development through the renewal of our mind and obedience to the commands of the One (Rom. 12:1–2; 2 Cor. 6:4–6). Our objective is to become like the One in our way of thinking and in our gameplay. When aligned with His agenda for our lives, we can apply His Manual to heal our hurts and bless other players.

As you watch bad things happen to good people, you may not know all the obstacles they face, but you can know why bad things happen to you and work through the Game Master's solutions. When you walk with the One, "you shall know the truth, and the truth shall set you free" (John 8:31–32; 4:16). Walk in His truth to the bonus round.

Conclusion

HERE IS A final blessing by the Game Master and a message from the One:

"May the Lord bless and protect you; may the Lord's face radiate with joy because of you; may he be gracious to you, show you his favor, and give you his peace" (Num. 6:24–26 TLB).

"To him who overcomes I will grant to sit with Me on My throne, as I also overcame and sat down with My Father on His throne" (Rev. 3:21 NKJV).

"Now unto him that is able to keep you from falling, and to present you faultless before the presence of his glory with exceeding joy, to the only wise God our Savior, be glory and majesty, dominion and power, both now and ever. Amen" (Jude 1:24–25).

Since you're already in this game, play to win!

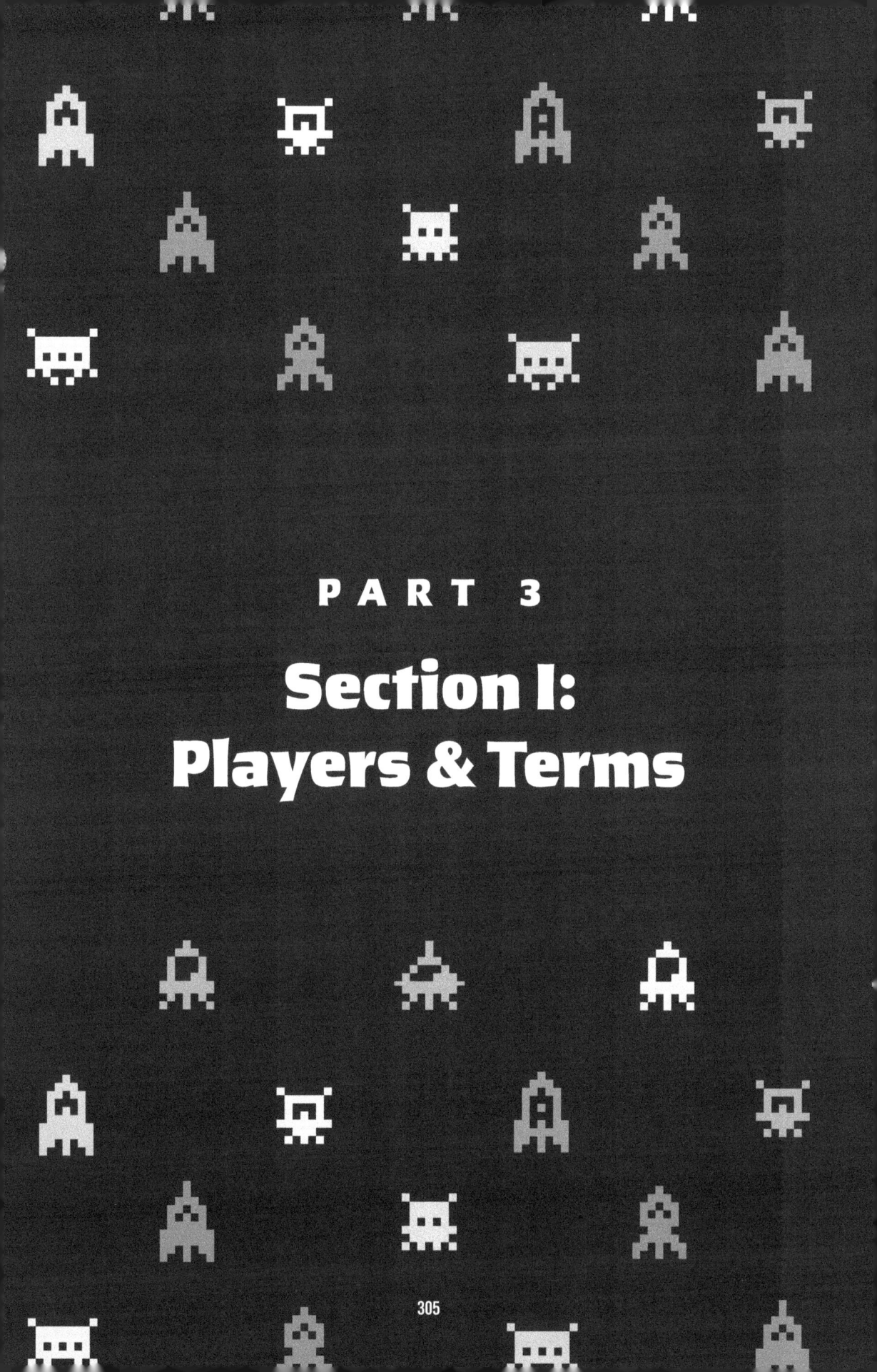

PART 3

Section I: Players & Terms

SINCE OUR UNIVERSE involves an interaction of interdimensional forces, it is important to understand that what happens here on planet Earth can be influenced by what happens in the realm of God or the spirit realm. The occult world and New Age teachings describe these transactions differently. The Manual (the Bible) is our primary reference, and it explains that what came to be called our physical universe started from the spirit realm. There is influence running both ways (Heb. 13:2; Eph. 6:11–18).

Our reaching into the spirit realm of God is a transaction called faith. Member players (Christians) have the benefit of spiritually protective armor. The opponents of our lives are not mainly other players around us but are coming into our dimension from the spirit realm too, so we wrestle *"against principalities, against powers, against the rulers of the darkness of this world, against spiritual wickedness in high places"* (Eph. 6:11–18). Here is a lineup of the players and game environment we face.

Game of Life Terms

Game of Life – Refers to the qualifying level for the bonus round; your personal life that you live on earth; collective lives of all people and how they live; this game level ends for each player upon their death; collective game level will end at the final apocalypse.

Game Master – God, Jehovah, Yahweh, Creator, God the Father

the One – Jesus Christ, Messiah, God the Son, Son of God

Spirit Master – Holy Spirit, Holy Ghost, Comforter, God the Holy Spirit, Spirit of Truth

guardians – God's angels—all classes, spirit beings

Serpent – Satan, devil, prince of this world, dragon, fallen angel, a spirit being, previously called Lucifer, the boss of this game level

henchmen – Serpent's angels, fallen angels, spirit beings

minions – Demon spirits: disembodied spirits, haunting spirits, spirit guides, evil spirits

players – People, sometimes refers to all game participants, also called gamers

guest players – Default player status; non-believers in Jesus, member of the Serpent's kingdom, names not found listed in the Book of Life

member players – Believers in Jesus Christ (Christians), member of God's kingdom, names listed in the *Book of Life*, bonus round players

master players – Expert level member players

game environment – Earth, solar system, Milky Way, universe, physical non-spirit dimension

game world – Planet Earth

spirit realm – Non-physical dimension of the game

headquarters – God's throne in heaven, great white throne of judgment

bonus round – Heaven, God's next kingdom, the new Earth, the Holy City, bonus level

hell – Hell, Hades, Lake of Fire, the second death

kiosk (religious) – Church, temple, mosque, shrine, seminary, religious publication or blog, TV, radio, or other source of religious information, including pagan or non-Christian spiritual sources; may be identified by type: Protestant, Catholic, Pentecostal, Baptist, Wiccan, New Age, Communist, philosophy, and so on

Manual – Bible, Word of God, Scriptures; a compilation of sixty-six smaller books, Game Master's Handbook

book of life – Official list of bonus round players

golden ticket – Eternal life, qualifies player for bonus round, qualifies player for miracle-working power, access to God, the fix

game violations – Sin, transgression, violation of God's code

Big Ten – the Ten Commandments, summary of rules for interacting with the Game Master and fellow players

New Testament commands – Rules for interacting with the Game Master and fellow players

gameplay – The way you live your life

obstacles – Bad things that happen, just bad stuff

solutions – Description of obstacle fixes

synced – Spirit connection to the Game Master; abiding in the One; led by the Spirit Master; learning the Manual so it abides in the player improving their behavior; acquiring the thought process and attitude of the One; required for miracles and answered prayer

Game of Life – Your Life Choice

The tree of the knowledge of good and evil is continually referenced in this book. So, what was the point of planting a tree whose fruit would open your awareness of good and evil, kill your spiritual awareness and connections, and physically condemn you to death? That is the starting point for all the trouble we face in this game (Gen. 3).

The Game Master is all about choices. He didn't create this game world as the ultimate experience for His perfectly created players. It was simply excellent for us but not the ultimate we could have. We are not in a one-round game scenario. This game world is simply the starting point for us, and the question is whether we will lose this round in a double-death experience or make it to the next round, where we will have the ultimate experience with Him (Rev. 21:8).

WE ARE ALL TAKING THE GAME MASTER'S TEST IN THIS LIFE.

We are all taking the Game Master's test in this life. Just like Adam and Eve's single choice about the fruit in the garden of Eden, your choice today is the same: whom will you choose to listen to, whom will you choose to obey, the Game Master or the Serpent? (Gen. 3; Josh 24:14–16; 1 Kings 18:21).

Adam's choice looked easy: leave the knowledge tree alone and get eternal life, but the Serpent framed his choice to look like he was a loser if he didn't choose the tree of knowledge. The Serpent may also make you look like a loser if you choose to walk away from him today. The question is, how long will you believe him?

Most players choose the Serpent's team by joining his kiosks, any kiosk in the world except the Game Master's kiosk. Others may choose a kiosk that masquerades as a Game Master kiosk, deceiving those who thought they found eternal life. Many players reject the Serpent's religious kiosks, saying religion isn't for them, and instead choose his kiosks of philosophy and vainglory.

Still others, like the atheists, choose the Serpent's kiosk of pride and purposely reject a chance for the bonus round. Some who affiliate with the Game Master's kiosk will enjoy the experience or respectability it may bring but aren't interested in giving up their own agenda on life by crossing the Serpent's fence and choosing the Game Master. If nothing changes their minds, all these players, the vast majority of players on Earth, will lose this round of the game and choose their eternal second death. Will this include you?

Because today we already started on the wrong side of the fence in this game round, there are only choosers and losers. Only a few will jump the fence, choose the Game Master, and join His kiosk but be willing to walk out with Him when that kiosk gets infected by the Serpent's agents, as is happening more these days (Matt. 24:10–14).

The Game Master wants players who are committed to Him, and having a choice is the only way He confirms that we want to be with Him on purpose. Those who pass the test qualify for the better level He offers, the bonus round.

The Game of Life is not about the money you earn, the things you collect, the friends and family around you, the experiences you discover. The game experience is framed around all those things as our life completes its journey on Earth. In the midst of those things, our purpose in the game is to choose the Game Master as our God and to show our love for Him in the way we live our lives. Only then will we win the game.

> "For the eyes of the Lord search back and forth across the whole earth, looking for people whose hearts are perfect toward him, so that he can show his great power in helping them" (2 Chron. 16:9a TLB).

Bonus Round

Those who choose life with the Game Master will enjoy a major upgrade from this game round and discover the ultimate game experience. The bonus round environment will be better, the quality of life will be vastly improved, and having an exceptional life with the Game Master will never end.

Then I saw a new earth (with no oceans!) and a new sky, for the present earth and sky had disappeared. And I, John, saw the Holy City, the new Jerusalem, coming down from God out of heaven. It was a glorious sight, beautiful as a bride at her wedding (Rev. 21:1–2 TLB). The Amplified Bible notes about this verse that "Whereas heaven is the abode of God, the sea often represents the abode of evil (see Dan. 7:3; Mark 5:13; Rev. 13:1)" (*Amplified Bible* 2015, 1956 Rev 21:1 footnote).

> I heard a loud shout from the throne saying, "Look, the home of God is now among men, and he will live with them and they will be his people; yes, God himself will be among them. He will wipe away all tears from their eyes, and there shall be no more death, nor sorrow, nor crying, nor pain. All of that has gone forever."
>
> And the one sitting on the throne said, "See, I am making all things new!" And then he said to me, "Write this down, for what I tell you is trustworthy and true: It is finished! I am the A and the Z—the Beginning and the End. I will give to the thirsty the springs of the Water of Life—as a gift! Everyone who conquers will inherit all these

blessings, and I will be his God and he will be my son. But cowards who turn back from following me, and those who are unfaithful to me, and the corrupt, and murderers, and the immoral, and those conversing with demons, and idol worshipers and all liars—their doom is in the Lake that burns with fire and sulphur. This is the Second Death."

Then one of the seven angels who had emptied the flasks containing the seven last plagues came and said to me, "Come with me and I will show you the bride, the wife."

And he pointed out to me a river of pure Water of Life, clear as crystal, flowing from the throne of God and the Lamb, coursing down the center of the main street. On each side of the river grew Trees of Life, bearing twelve crops of fruit, with a fresh crop each month; the leaves were used for medicine to heal the nations.

There shall be nothing in the city that is evil; for the throne of God and of the Lamb will be there, and his servants will worship him. And they shall see his face; and his name shall be written on their foreheads. And there will be no night there—no need for lamps or sun—for the Lord God will be their light; and they shall reign forever and ever.

Then the angel said to me, "These words are trustworthy and true: 'I am coming soon!' God, who tells his prophets what the future holds, has sent his angel to tell you this will happen soon. Blessed are those who believe it and all else written in the scroll" (Rev. 21:1–9; 22:1–7 TLB).

Gameplay – The Way You Play Your Life

All players start the Game of Life in guest mode with a perpetual points deficit. They play through life collecting pats on the back, attaboy awards, and fame or fortune for all their accomplishments but still end the game with a deficit. That guest mode is only good for this level. We are playing this game level to determine our place in the next game round.

Players like to think that all their good deeds and success in this round should qualify them for a place in the bonus round or at least a path to the bonus round in the next life. Unfortunately, it doesn't matter how many points a player accrues; a guest will forever be a guest, never gaining the approval of the Game Master. Even if they can see those pearly gates, heaven will stay beyond reach for even the best guest.

Since most players don't read the Manual, the Game Master's handbook, they never learn that they must first change their status from guest to member. As members, their progress through life can finally amount to positive points and even bigger awards going into the next round.

With member status, it doesn't matter if a member becomes a success, a rich or famous player, or experiences obstacle after obstacle, loses all their accrued points on this level, or gets totally wiped out by another player. All their playing experience in suffering hardships can still be transposed into bonus round rewards as they play for the Game Master's objectives in this round.

Paradise in the garden of Eden kicked off this game level with Adam and Eve. These first two players joined the Serpent, condemning all their descendants to the Serpent's team and their influence. In that moment of decision where they took action to eat the forbidden fruit, the spirit part of their being was deactivated and disconnected from the Game Master and instantly downgraded to guest player status, unqualified for the bonus round.

Since then, the Game Master has chosen to let each player decide whether to stay a guest or become a member. He will probably not intervene to fix their broken gameplay just because they get hurt. It's their choices and their consequences. If players decide they want help, they must ask for it and choose to play the game by His rules. *Then* He will make Himself available to help them fix all their broken aspects of gameplay as they apply His solutions.

To reconnect a player's spirit with the Game Master, each player must find Him and get a golden ticket as proof they are members on His team. At this point, the Spirit Master punches their ticket, joins the player's spirit, and connects them to the Game Master (John 1:11–13; Rom. 8:13–15; Eph. 4:30). Even their thoughts can get a response directly from headquarters. The player's soul still controls, limits, or hinders how much the Spirit Master can help or influence them because the player's free will remains intact.

Peer pressure or the concern about what others will think of them is a common and effective way the Serpent uses to keep players from deciding to join the Game Master's team (Prov. 29:25). As the Game Master and His members become greater objects of public ridicule, there is less incentive to join His team. These days, another widely used technique is to keep players so distracted with the cares of their lives, with social media or with the pursuit of fame or fortune, that the Game Master's advantages seem so inadequate by comparison (Matt. 13:18–23; Mark 4:3–20).

The Manual – The Holy Bible

If someone gave you their career notes full of tips on how to successfully navigate a career path you chose, would you bother reading it? If you decided to go on a cross-country trip, would you read any of the books detailing places to see and places to avoid in your itinerary?

The Game Master wrote the Manual to help you succeed in life and win this game. Even with all the mayhem caused by the Serpent and dealt out by those around you, the Game Master's strategy for life is a strategy for success. Have you ever read it from start to finish?

> **THE GAME MASTER WROTE THE MANUAL TO HELP YOU SUCCEED IN LIFE AND WIN THIS GAME.**

What would you do if you got a book that was supposed to give you a career edge you really need, but it was hard to understand, and then someone stole it from you? Would you care? This can happen to players who hear teaching from the Manual but don't see how it pertains to them, and the Serpent comes along and snatches away the good news they heard using distractions of work or leisure time, social life, or obstacles. Just getting on with life is a strategy to keep you from becoming more than you would otherwise be (Matt. 13:3–4, 19).

Many gamers familiarize themselves with Sun Tzu's Art of War, internalizing his strategies and tactics for success (Tzu 2022, full book). Harvard Business Review lists the top 40 essential business books for corporate success (Harvard Business Review n.d., full article). Many players have figured out keys to success for numerous careers in this game level of the Game of Life. But all those keys to success are only good for this game level.

The Manual is the Game Master's handbook. The Game of Life is based on the Manual and will run its course as written until the final play for all remaining players. The Manual identifies all the players, all the obstacles they face, the complete arsenal for combat, how to use the weapons, how to identify stealth opponents, where to watch for deception, rules of engagement, and how to become like the One. Everything is included. There are no missing instructions for success (James 1:2–5; 2 Pet. 1:2–4). It is the only book that can get you into the bonus round.

In our morally relative society, the Bible is not considered an authoritative work these days. The Game Master declared that the single violation which disqualifies a gamer from the bonus round is unbelief in His account of the One as written in the Manual (John 3:16–18, 35–36). Being bad only makes it worse. Players can choose what they wish to believe, but their choices become permanent and anchored to the stated outcomes at the end of their game life. We only get one shot at this game; there is no retake or reincarnation (Heb. 9:27).

Most players get their advice from religious kiosks of all types scattered throughout the game. Some have been set up by the Game Master, and most by the Serpent. They all have different perceptions and interpretations of the Manual. Most don't use it at all and may actively oppose it. Make sure of this: always believe the Manual when there is a discrepancy between the Manual and others' explanations. Ensure you read it right and get a second or third opinion if you still struggle to understand something.

The Manual is not a living document as the United States constitution is sometimes called, meaning it should change with the times. But it is a living document in the sense that it has a spirit connection and supernatural power within its makeup that probes the soul of the player who reads it.

"For the word of God is living and active, sharper than any two-edged sword, piercing to the division of soul and of spirit, of joints and of marrow, and discerning the thoughts and intentions of the heart" (Heb. 4:12 ESV).

Advantage: Once you get your membership on the Game Master's team, the Spirit Master will join your spirit and help you understand the Manual because He inspired its writings. His clarity will never contradict the Manual or the character of the Game Master. Aim to read it through at least once every two years.

Manual Layout. There is widespread misunderstanding of the Manual's rules and teachings. It's easy to find Internet sites listing rules in the Manual that are considered archaic or outrageous. Many of these lists are dug up in the book of Leviticus. These may range from actual game violations (sins) like theft or murder to ordinances like not mixing fabric types in a garment or pairing milk with meat in food, to penalties like execution for what may today be considered a minor crime, misdemeanor, or perhaps no crime at all.

Leviticus is a Manual rule book of conduct that explains in detail how the specific nation of Israel would operate in every aspect of personal and community life. This code of conduct, called the Law of Moses, became distinctive of the customs and traditions for Israel 3,300 years ago. The player group of Israel is the only group specified to live by the Law of Moses. Today, other nations around the game have their own personalities, distinctive characteristics, and quirks, such as the law in America making it illegal to whistle underwater (Stupid Laws 2022).

The Manual is a counterculture book whose teachings contradict modern enlightened societal tendencies. It contains an absolute set of morals and conditions for relating to the Game Master. Just as He is immutable (unchanging), His Word is also immutable. The resurrection of the One from the dead in the New Testament marks the end of the Law of Moses in its "schoolmaster" role of bringing us to the

One for a golden ticket. It is no longer in force as an acceptable path to the bonus round (Gal. 2:16; 3:10, 23–27).

A guide for today's game players is that prohibitions of practice in the Manual that were part of the Old Testament (i.e., moral codes, et al.) mainly apply today as they were restated in the New Testament—and issues of morality are thoroughly revisited. Simply because a directive was announced in the Old Testament does not follow that it is still practiced today. Civil authority sets the retribution regarding moral codes in each modern nation's society, so statements on moral practices do not bind the modern player to the punishment meted out in the Old Testament. Nevertheless, member players should observe standards that align with holy living because the Game Master is the final arbiter on Judgment Day.

OLD TESTAMENT

This refers to the first thirty-nine books of the Manual from Genesis to Malachi. The timeline for these books covers the start of the Game of Life and runs to about 400 BC. The Game Master initiated the ritual sacrifice for sin after the garden of Eden, and it continued through the rest of the timeline of the Old Testament and into the New Testament. The Old Testament includes historical books, poetic books, and prophetic books. Modern archaeology seems to be reluctant to corroborate recorded history from the Manual in various popular TV shows about history and geography.

To many players, it appears that the way business was done with the nation of Israel by the Game Master paints Him as a vindictive, vengeful, and merciless authoritarian. To be sure, the Game Master calls Himself the final authority on right and wrong, and His decisions are irrevocable (Jer. 4:27–29; Rev. 20:10–15). He also declares that He is full of mercy and willing to take back or withhold vengeance for wrongdoing when players change their minds and ask for mercy (Gen. 18:25–26; Exod. 33:19; Deut. 5:9–10; Ps. 136; Rom. 9:15–21). Many of the Manual's books include entreaties by the Game Master through His prophets for Israel to listen to Him, follow His ways, and avoid calamity.

The Old Testament is a behind-the-scenes look at how the Game Master, a perfect, holy, and righteous spirit being Who cannot tolerate game violations in any form, tries to relate to players who have a natural bent toward game violations and self-destruction with their Serpent boss to help them along.

Finding things to criticize about the Game Master is quite easy for guests with a high tolerance for game violations, for doing their own thing, and who resent divine criticism. Today's tolerant players accept selective murder (abortion) or mercy killing (euthanasia) and alternate lifestyles with no problem. However, they climb on a sanctimonious high horse when their sense of justice is offended by an egregious restriction or even a simple condemnation of their free-thinking choices.

For Israel, this interaction of the immortal Game Master with the mortal player translated into a cycle starting with,

1) favorable status for these players with the Game Master (prosperity),
2) rebellion of these players who do things their way (idol worship, lawlessness),
3) warning and then punishment from the Game Master for sin and rebellion and doing things their own way (enemy oppression, invasion, drought, locusts, disease, etc.),
4) repentance of these players for their sin and rebellion to again do things the Game Master's way (worship Him and keep His Law), and
5) return to favorable status for these players with the Game Master (prosperity).

Then the cycle repeats – usually about every generation or two (Ps. 78).

This cycle occurs throughout the Old Testament but happened intensively in the book of the Judges when Israel had no king, and every player did what was right from their own perspective (Judg. 17:6; 21:25). The result is that it appears that the Game Master is in constant punishment mode. What gets overlooked is the tremendous favor and prosperity Israel enjoyed when they were in a favorable status with Him (Ps. 78).

Israel was supposed to be the example nation to the game's players of how prosperous they could be by following the Game Master's instructions. Instead, Israel often wanted to be like all the other nations around them and thought they wouldn't get disciplined for it. But they were.

Psalm 100:5 can be cited as a conclusive statement of the Game Master that He is good, His mercy lasts forever, and His truth endures to all generations of players. Therefore, finding a way to get on His good side leads to His goodness, mercy, and truth.

Apocrypha

This is a collection of books that fills in the timeline between the Old and New Testaments. Some books also reference early prophets and events back to Adam at the start of the game. Select books were included in the Roman Catholic church canon as well as in the original book list of the King James Version of the Manual. References may be occasionally made to them, such as with the prophet Enoch and the book of Jasher (Josh. 10:13; 1 Sam. 1:18; Jude 1:14). The book of Jasher fleshes out the storyline through the book of Genesis and provides some context to what is left unsaid in the scripture. Generally, they are not widely accepted as authoritative and divinely inspired.

New Testament

Traditional Jews accept some Apocryphal books but do not recognize the New Testament as a divinely inspired book set because they still wait for the Messiah as an unfulfilled prophecy. Christian kiosks are convinced the One came as the Messiah, Who fulfilled hundreds of prophecies and declared that He would return as the ruling King over the game. Both groups now wait for the Messiah for completely different reasons.

The New Testament is the final twenty-seven books of the Manual from Matthew to the Apocalypse (Revelation), for a total of sixty-six books. Technically, the Old Testament sacrifices end at the conclusion of each of the first four books depicting their gospel accounts of the death and resurrection of the One. This event ushered in what is called the age of grace. The timeline for these twenty-seven books runs from about 0 BC to the current day to the (soon) coming Apocalypse. This Testament explains how to get on the Game Master's good side.

There is a tendency to think that the Game Master is mean-spirited in the Old Testament but gracious and kind in the New Testament. He remains the same in His character across both Testament sections of the Manual. However, the dynamics of the way He relates to players changed because of the sacrifice of the One.

All the rules of Moses' law that were laid out in the Old Testament, plus all the new ones added later based on Moses' law by the priestly class, expired at the execution of the One on the cross. The Law no longer qualifies players to reach the bonus round because the focus is now on His finished sacrifice. After His atoning work was done, keeping the law of the Old Testament to experience the favor of the Game Master nullifies the faith required of players to be accepted by Him. Now players need to simply believe that the grace of the Game Master by the death of His Son is enough to qualify them for the bonus round—plus nothing (Acts 15:1–31; Rom. 10:9–10; Eph. 2:8–9).

The One is now our great High Priest. Members can come directly into His presence through prayer and worship without a kiosk priest or traditional sacrifice. As in both Testaments, praise to Him and a humble heart are acceptable sacrifices (Heb. 4:14–16; Ps. 51:17; Jer. 33:11; Heb. 13:5; James 4:6; 1 Pet. 5:5–6).

The New Testament explains the new approach players have with the Game Master and includes extensive teachings on how to develop the lifestyle characteristics of the

Game Master. This emphasis on a positive approach to life, living with a connection to what is holy, and the spirit realm all make for a seemingly stark contrast to the Old Testament. His expectation of holiness from players stays the same across the game from start to finish, but now He is more accessible and relatable to every player.

Various kiosk organizations promote healthy living and healthy lifestyles by reverting to the dietary and customary practices of the Old Testament. The Manual says each-to-his-own for personal preferences and self-discipline, but it draws the line when kiosks or members try to push those practices on players as a condition of their favorable status with the Game Master (Acts 15:1–31; Rom. 14:1–9; Col. 2:16–23).

Finally, for those who say the Manual is hard to understand, nineteenth-century Danish philosopher and theologian Søren Kierkegaard has this remark:

> The matter is quite simple. The Bible is very easy to understand. But we Christians are a bunch of scheming swindlers. We pretend to be unable to understand it because we know very well that the minute we understand, we are obliged to act accordingly. Take any words in the New Testament and forget everything except pledging yourself to act accordingly. My God, you will say, if I do that my whole life will be ruined. How would I ever get on in the world?
>
> Herein lies the real place of Christian scholarship. Christian scholarship is the Church's prodigious invention to defend itself against the Bible, to ensure that we can continue to be good Christians without the Bible coming too close. Oh, priceless scholarship, what would we do without you? Dreadful it is to fall into the hands of the living God. Yes it is even dreadful to be alone with the New Testament (Kierkegaard 2007, 56).

SUMMARIZED GAME RULES

Hardly anyone reads the rules. Many players who feel like they're tuned in to the Game Master go around giving misleading advice or taking the wrong advice. Some of it sounds like the rules or is based on the rules but is inaccurate just enough, so it doesn't help others get the advantages they need or point them to the bonus round.

These are only a summarized set of rules that pertain to the topics of this book. However, learning the rules can mean the difference between being a master player or being a pawn that gets pushed around, unable to do much about what hits them.

- Everybody must play until they die. There is no opting out. The clock starts ticking when players are conceived before birth (Ps. 139:13–17; Jer. 1:5). Living in a bubble by pretending there is no Game Master is a guaranteed loser move and doesn't exempt the player (Ps. 14:1; 53:1). Killing yourself early just ends your chance to earn the bonus round unless you got the golden ticket first. Suicide is not advisable but is not an unpardonable sin, except that, after death, it's judgment time. Golden tickets are not issued postmortem (Heb. 9:27).

- There is no neutral ground. By default, you are on the Serpent's team from birth until you defect to the Game Master. You cannot declare yourself off the two teams and form your own team. Since the Serpent rules the game environment, any group you want to start will automatically include him as a charter member. Self-identifying on the Game Master's team doesn't change your status either. He must confirm your status on His team through the Spirit Master (Eph. 1:12–14).

- You cannot play for someone else. Running their life or manipulating their choices may help them dodge a lot of debris from life's hits but does not get them across the finish line into the bonus round. You can't vouch for someone else with the Game Master. Baptizing, confirmations, church membership, being devoutly religious, and so on are good things but are all non-starters for His team membership (Matt. 7:21–23).

- You cannot cheat and win. There is no fooling the Game Master (Gal. 6:7–8). His records are official and final. The Manual has only one way to win, with no exceptions (John 14:6). The Serpent offers many cheat choices based on what you want to hear and what tickles your ears or stirs your soul, but in the end, they won't work; they are designed to keep you out of the bonus round.

- You are the target. Your starting family situation in the game environment—economically, philosophically, culturally, and geographically—sets your starting circumstances and trajectory of life. Most of your contact in the game involves other players on a visual plane who can be helpful, neutral, or hurtful. You may have an easy life or one of deep struggle, but on both extremes, forces are brought to bear to influence you to keep your attention off the golden ticket and out of the bonus round. The Serpent's objective is for you to lose at all costs. His big advantage is that you already started life on the losing team, and keeping most players there is so easy because almost nobody dares to be different. Are you going to defy your parents, family, religion, town, or government to pick the Game Master as your God? What will that courage (i.e., foolishness) cost you? (1 Cor. 1:18–19; Rev. 12:10–12).

- The Serpent controls the game environment. Unfortunately, the first two players fouled up the paradise environment and ceded their control of it to the Serpent, leaving you stuck with what he dishes out. The good, bad, or hard life all have different pressure points that he applies to encourage you to stay on his team. The downside is that he does not provide lasting protection from the circumstances that come against you, and if you end the game before getting the ticket, he wins, and you lose.

    o The Game Master calls the Serpent the "prince of this world" and the "world ruler of darkness" (obscurity). He has set some parameters in place for now to keep the Serpent from causing a collapse of all the players through murder and mayhem (2 Thess. 2:6–8).

    o As you look around, you'll notice that the Serpent has plenty of leeway to infuse misery at every turn. Joining that maiden voyage to Mars won't change things because the rules apply throughout the universe. They stay with you wherever you go, like Murphy's Law.

- You are fair game. All the mishaps and misfortunes that happen to you during the game are not prohibited. The Serpent takes advantage of this because he has no bleeding heart for the players, only calculating moves. He encourages you to blame the Game Master, and most players do, even those on His own team may unwittingly tag Him for their bad stuff. Most players are easily manipulated and deceived, so the Serpent doesn't have to do much to keep them in line.

    o The Game Master does not force players to join Him; He intervenes when you look for Him or when His members come to find you, and you agree to meet Him. Some members sensed they had a guardian while they were still in guest mode. This may be the case, but the Game Master knows for sure. Most other contact comes from the Serpent.

- Game obstacles impact everyone. There is always a reason for the obstacles. Occasionally, they are simply part of the routines of life, but many times, they have underlying causes. Finding the root cause can be helpful in limiting the types of obstacles that hit a player. Obstacles take on many forms:

    o Some are physical like the weather, accidents, and health issues.

    o Some are pressures like finances and stressful environments or choices we make.

    o Others are ethereal-like circumstances, like clockwork, that always go wrong at the worst time for no apparent reason.

- Nobody gets a free pass. This is related to the universal impact of obstacles. This point is specifically for members who want to claim the promises that "with God all things are possible" (Mark 9:23) and "I can do all things through Christ who strengthens me" [through the hardships he described in the previous sentence]" (Phil. 4:13). Member player, do not associate those promises with a concept that nothing is expected of you or that you automatically have unrestricted enhanced favor. Yes, you can turn your life into a perpetual blessing, which should be typical of all members but is conditional on how you play the game. The Game Master does not play the game for you or call the shots without your cooperation. As you meet the requirements, He infuses blessing and favor where you claim the promises for which you qualify. Those who "abide in Him" find this process more effortless and consistent, even in the face of hardship.

> **THE GAME MASTER DOES NOT PLAY THE GAME FOR YOU OR CALL THE SHOTS WITHOUT YOUR COOPERATION.**

- Game Master weapons are readily available to members. They are "mighty through God" (2 Cor. 10:4–5). Weapons are immediately available even to the brand-new members and are most effective when players are synced with the Game Master and following His instructions. They have unlimited use and can increase their power and potency the more the player uses them and the better the player stays synced to the Game Master. Conversely, their effectiveness decreases the longer players disconnect themselves from the Game Master, and they can even shut down from disuse.

- o Guests occasionally discover Game Master weapon caches and try them out. They do have power over the Serpent's realm, even in guests' hands. The Serpent may allow it for a time or may move to shut down the guest who's causing him trouble (Acts 19:13–17).

- o The Game Master weapons are almost always used to benefit its user or other players. Although the Game Master gets routinely blamed for deliberately hurting players, His arsenal is primarily available to fight the Serpent's agenda and help all players of the game, especially members.

- Serpent weapons are rented. Nothing comes free from the Serpent. Most of the time, there is a deferred payment plan. Players always use his obscure weapons, like curses, without realizing how effective they are. Those who go looking for higher-grade weapons through witchcraft and blood oaths risk getting themselves and their families eventually crippled or destroyed more quickly by the Serpent who lent them out. One of his names is Destroyer—and that means to destroy you.

- o The Serpent's weapons can indeed imitate the Game Master's weapons so that his agent players look like they are member players. The Game Master said to check the results of what they do to discover who is who (1 John 4:1–3).

- o Most players do not realize that while the Serpent's weapons can inflict heavy damage on other players by the user, the user himself also gets damaged by them regardless of their level of potency (Rom. 6:16).

Game Master – God, the Father, Creator

He created the game, its rules, its environment, and all the characters except the One and the Spirit Master, Who are each also equal personalities of the singular Godhead. Having the ability to transcend time, the Game Master has already gone through the entire game and knows what will happen at any point. That's why His prophecies coded in the Manual are always 100 percent accurate (Eccles. 3:11; Isa. 46:9–10; Rev. 1:8; 21:6; 22:13).

He created two original players to be on His team and put them in paradise and in charge of the game. The Serpent saw that the players oversaw their new environment and schemed to get them to give him their authority in the game environment by breaking the Game Master's one rule: eating the forbidden fruit (Gen. 3:1–5).

Since that fateful day, all players are born into the Serpent's team with a death sentence hanging over them, and they are condemned to the Serpent's fate upon their death: no bonus round of eternal life and certain destruction with hell to pay. The game environment was cursed, and players became susceptible to all the obstacles that beset them.

To undo their fate, each player must now have his own death sentence reversed. The Game Master arranged to insert the One into the game over 2,000 years ago to successfully play it as an example for the players, then to die in their place to cover their game violations and death penalty, and finally, to rise again from the dead to empower players to overcome the obstacles they face. This is symbolized in the ceremony of baptism. Players can apply His substitutionary death to their account by faith and switch teams back to the Game Master (John 3:16). Before the coming of the One, the Game Master predicted this moment of redemption, and it has always been a transaction of faith since the game began (Gen. 3:14–15; Isa. 52:13–53:12; Heb. 11).

Any player who wants his death sentence revoked must get his golden ticket from the Game Master. This ticket also entitles him to all the advantages of power held by the Game Master, and it's backed by His promise to honor the requests of players who follow the rules to the letter (John 14:12–14).

There have been times when the Game Master inserted Himself into the game at the national level or at the personal level to give players a chance to join His team. Today, there is an open call with a standing invitation for all players to join His team. His observation is that players who decide to wait and see what will happen never make a move to change sides (John 3:18–20; Acts 17:29–31; Heb. 4:6–8).

Game Master's character – love. There are many attributes for the Game Master: among them, He is *omniscient* (all-knowing) (Rom. 11:33–34), *omnipotent* (all-powerful) (Jer. 32:17; Eph. 3:20), *omnipresent* (everywhere) (Ps. 139:7–10), *immutable* (unchanging) (Isa. 40:8; James 1:17; Heb. 13:8), *holy* (morally excellent and ethically pure) (Prov. 9:10; 1 Pet. 1:15), *righteous* (Ps. 11:7), *just* (incorruptible) (Deut. 32:4; Ps. 11:7), *merciful* (Dan. 9:9; Matt. 5:45; James 5:11), and *love* (Ps. 100:5; Rom. 8:39; 1 Cor. 13; 1 John 4:8, 10). He has hundreds of names in the Manual that describe his characteristics.

His defining characteristic is *love*. The Manual's description of love in a positive light is that it is: long enduring, patient, kind, happy when right and truth prevail, bears up under anything and everything that comes, ready to believe the best, disregards being wronged, unfading, endures everything, and never fails or ends.

From a negative perspective, the Game Master's love is not envious or jealous, boastful, vainglorious, disdainfully proud or arrogant, rude or unmannerly or acting unbecomingly, insisting on its own rights or own way, self-seeking, touchy, fretful, or resentful (1 Cor. 13:4–8).

When you read these Manual characteristics of love, apply them as the Game Master's love toward you: His love is long enduring toward you, His love is patient toward you, His love is kind toward you, and so on. While the impression is spread that He is vengeful and hateful, He declares that He gets no pleasure in the death of any players (Ezek. 33:11; 2 Pet. 3:9). This is why He didn't give up on your soul without a fight until He won the war.

The Manual describes the Game Master's unbreakable love for His members:

> Who shall separate us from the love of Christ? Shall tribulation, or distress, or persecution, or famine, or nakedness, or peril, or sword? For I am persuaded, that neither death, nor life, nor angels, nor principalities, nor powers, nor things present, nor things to come, nor height, nor depth, nor any other creature, shall be able to separate us from the love of God, which is in Christ Jesus our Lord (Rom. 8:35, 38–39 KJV).

Game Master's operation – grace. The perspective of the Game Master toward all players is to operate from a position of grace: bestowing favor and kindness, blessings, and divine assistance toward undeserving players. Kiosks that have divided game history into dispensations of time or ages call these current millenniums AD the age of grace, where salvation for the soul and divine blessings are freely available and easily accessible to all players through the golden ticket.

The sacrificial death of the One for all players was a gift of grace by the Game Master: "And what a difference between man's sin and God's forgiveness! For this one man, Adam, brought death to many through his sin. But this one man, Jesus Christ, brought forgiveness to many through God's mercy" (Rom. 5:15 TLB).

The grace of the Game Master enables members to become better than they would have been on their own (1 Cor. 15:10; Eph. 3:7; 1 Pet. 4:10). The grace of the Game Master who brought the opportunity for salvation to all also provides the impetus for players to become like the Game Master in their character (Titus 2:11–14). He created the game environment to operate with impartiality toward players, as the One notes that, "He makes His sun rise on the evil and on the good, and sends rain on the just and on the unjust" (Matt. 5:44–46 NKJV).

His grace was available to players in all the game's periods of historical time. When the player group of Israel was formed, His character of grace was embodied in the special blessings they received as a nation. This favorable status was intended to be an example to all nations that the Game Master reigned supreme and was the source of goodness for all who called upon Him. Israel's lack of cooperation with the Game Master is chronicled through the Manual, but their uneven record of blessings and chastening is not a fault of the Game Master. On the contrary, even amid their troubles, He is repeatedly described as gracious and full of mercy (Exod. 33:19; 34:6–7, Num. 6:22–27; 2 Kings 13:22–24; 2 Chron. 30:9; Neh. 9:17, 31; Isa. 30:18–19; Joel 2:12–13; Amos 5:14–15; Jonah 4:2; Ps. 77:7–11; 86:15; 103:8; 111:4; 112:4; 116:5; 145:8; Luke 4:21–22; 1 Pet. 2:2–3).

When you hear John Newton's song, "Amazing Grace," sung in a movie you are watching, this overwhelming grace of the Game Master which transformed John's soul and bestowed eternal life to the former slave trader is the amazing grace John was referring to. "The Game Master is not slow in keeping his promise, as some understand slowness. Instead, he is patient with you, not wanting anyone to perish, but everyone to come to repentance" (2 Pet. 3:9 NIV).

The age of grace will continue until the day of judgment when all players will have made their choice to join the Game Master for the win or turn Him down to perish with their Serpent boss.

A Gallup poll released on July 20, 2023, indicates that belief in God has reached a new low in America at 74 percent overall (Brenan 2023, ¶ 1). Coming to the Game Master requires believing that He exists (Heb. 11:6). This is now becoming an obstacle in discussions on the spirit realm.

However, among those 18–34, it is 59 percent (Brenan 2023, chart 3). A Gallup poll reported on June 17, 2022, indicates that almost 30 percent of Americans currently have no religious affiliation (Jaeger 2022, ¶ 11).

The One – Jesus Christ, Son of God, Messiah, Advocate, Emmanuel (God with us)

He is the One, the Messiah who was promised to come and offer all players the life upgrade that would give them a chance to restore their member status and original powers. This upgrade is the golden ticket, which gives players access to the bonus round, supernatural power to change their game environment, and the conditions in which they play. He was the ultimate master player in the Game of Life Who came to set us captives free (Isa. 61:1; Luke 4:18).

It is generally conceded that He played the game with absolute success, but many guests prefer to rank him as only one among many (guest) master players who were great philosophers, humanitarians, prophets, and founders of new religions, so let's include a little perspective here. These alleged master players were great humans and indisputably affected the landscape of the game, but they were not members with any significant power greater than the force of their personalities except to the degree that they were energized by the deficient power of the Serpent. A list of such religious founders would include Nimrod, Zoroaster, Krishna, Buddha, Confucius, Mohammed, Joseph Smith, and others, plus any leaders that are offshoots of the Manual.

Look at His twelve apostle master players who were left behind when He went back to headquarters. These twelve players had supernatural powers recorded in the Manual that are unequaled by any of the religious founders that guests will cite as examples being equal to the One. In fact, few if any of the religious founders could perform miracles of any kind, and their philosophical enlightening prowess still leaves players on the Serpent's team. Yet, the One was even greater than those miracle-working apostle master players because He is the Game Master Incarnate and rose from the dead.

What most players don't realize is that Jesus said that the members can also do all those cool things He did. He isn't just the example of what we should become; *He is the example of how we can play and should play the game.* Then He raised the bar and said that the members would do even greater things than He did because He was leaving to go back to the Game Master (John 14:12).

Players who understand how He did His miracles also realize that He left winning instructions for all the members who joined His team and followed Him. Most players, including members, when asked how He did miraculous things, simply shrug and say that He was God. Their impression is that no one can do what He did. However, by putting His instructions to work, many members have been able to duplicate what He did and even surpass His work, just as He predicted.

Here are some examples of special skills Jesus displayed through spiritual gifts. He did some amazing things like:

- Knowing what players were thinking (gift of discernment) (Matt. 12:24–26; 22:15–22; Mark 2:5–12; 3:1–6; Luke 6:7–11)

- Knowing what others didn't know (word of knowledge) (Mark 5:38–40; John 6:64)
- Knowing where to find things (gift of knowledge) (Matt. 17:24–27; 21:1–5; Mark 11:1–8; Luke 5:3–9; 19:29–36; John 21:3–6)
- Seeing players where no one was watching (gift of knowledge) (John 1:43–50)
- Passing through a mob unharmed (gift of miracles) (Luke 4:28–30; John 8:59)
- Telling a player's future (gift of prophecy) (John 21:18–24)
- Healing numerous multitudes with healings of all kinds, limb regenerations, raising the dead, and so on (gift of healings) (Matt. 4:24; 8:16; 12:15; 14:4; 15:30; 19:2)
- Teleportation (miracle gift—teleportation itself is not a spiritual gift) (Luke 24:36–37; John 6:19–21; 20:19, 26)
- There are more like walking on water, calming storms, and multiplying a bag lunch to feed thousands.

You can get in that circle of power too. Get connected to Him through the Manual; He calls it "abiding" in Him.

When the game ends, we will see the One revealed as the King of kings and the Lord of lords: the supreme ruler of the universe (1 Tim 6:12–16; Rev. 1:9–18; 17:13–14; 19:11–16).

Spirit Master – Holy Spirit, Holy Ghost, Spirit of Truth, Comforter, Intercessor, Guide into All Truth

When a guest receives the golden ticket, that is when the Game Master gives them the Spirit Master to join the player's spirit to help them navigate the game as a member. The Spirit Master generates life into the spirit of the player. This allows the player to connect with the Game Master through prayer and understanding the Manual's spiritual context. He provides a perception of spiritual discernment in the events and circumstances of the player's life (John 1:12; Rom. 8:14).

The Spirit Master has the personality of a peace-loving dove Who can be driven away by a lion-like personality in a player. The One was successful in the game because He operated with a gentle lamb-like personality that kept the Spirit Master connected to Him and could do His work of energizing the Game Master's weapons and gifts in the hands of the One. All three of these divine characters can work in tandem through the member to make them unstoppable.

To get this synergy going, the member must also develop a lamb-like personality so the Spirit Master can energize his weapons and make them formidable to the point of obliterating obstacles. These traits are called the fruit of the Spirit (Gal. 5:16, 22–25). Players develop a different perspective on the game from the Spirit Master as they learn the Manual. Other players will notice this transformative change.

Spirit Master's character – comforter. The night before He was crucified, the One announced to His group of disciples that He was going away but would not leave them without comfort. He explained that His time on earth was ending but that He needed to leave so the Spirit Master could come to them from the Game Master (John 14:16–18, 26).

The One described the Spirit Master as the Comforter who would be sent from the Game Master in the name of the One. Because He has the capacity to be omnipresent (everywhere at once), He is the ideal Guide for members and makes it possible for every member to be simultaneously in touch with headquarters. His influence in the life of a member through what is called the fruit of the Spirit provides members with inner peace regardless of the turmoil of their life experience when mental and emotional stability are most needed (Phil. 4:6–7).

Guardians – Angels

The Game Master created a few types of servants to operate in the cosmic realm of the universe. The Serpent somehow rebelled and persuaded or coerced one-third of them to join him as his henchmen. There are messenger angels, a warrior class, cherubim, seraphim, and perhaps other types as well. The Game Master indicated that he uses them to watch out for players, especially the young ones (Matt. 18:10). It is said that guardians don't have free will like the players do; they are programmed to obey the Game Master. How the Serpent chose to rebel is a speculative discussion topic (Isa. 14:12–17).

The Game Master said that players should be nice to everyone because, on occasion, they may be talking to the guardians without even realizing it (Heb. 13:2). There are many accounts on the Internet, and we even hear them told sometimes by people we know, about how they were in an accident or a serious situation of trauma or danger, and a nice man or a nice woman stopped to help them, and when the players were all set again and turned around to thank them, the nice helper had disappeared, sometimes where it was impossible for someone to simply vanish.

My wife experienced this scenario during some car trouble where a truck driver couple blocked traffic while they helped her and encouraged her, and then the rig was suddenly gone when she was settled back on the road. A colleague described her car trouble story, saying a lady with a piercing gaze showed up and helped her, encouraging her, and disappeared when she turned to thank her for her help.

Guardians can insert themselves into the game and do it on a limited basis. Their purpose is to help players according to the Game Master's agenda.

Serpent – The Devil, Satan

Satan is the archenemy of the Game Master and aspires to be like Him or replace Him. Some guests admire him as an underdog instead of the conniver that he is. All the names he is called in the Manual describe him as sly, most cunning, a liar, deceiver, slanderer, accuser, destroyer, and murderer, with many variations. With characteristics like that, it follows that he does not play by our moral rules. In fact, the one thing a player can be certain about the Serpent is that he cannot be trusted.

The Serpent was originally named Lucifer. He was an angel of light with great power in the administration of the Game Master. He instigated a coup but was expelled from heaven, taking one-third of the angels to join him as his henchmen. Together, they control the minions.

There are growing numbers of players who doubt his existence. If his existence is uncertain to a player, then there is less belief in what the Game Master says or in the credibility of His Manual (Shapero 2023, ¶ 2).

He is highly intelligent and resourceful, but he has no creative power. For example, he cannot create player souls, nor can he destroy them. He and his henchmen team can create life forms only because they originate from existing life. He may not directly kill players but can get them to kill themselves (suicide), influence others to do the job (murder, homicide, manslaughter), have players infect themselves with terminal illnesses through the physical or spirit realms, or encourage players to give up their will to live and stop resisting their inevitable demise. His persuasive powers are quite formidable but can still be stopped by the power of the Game Master.

The Serpent is the leader of the henchmen and minions. Together, they embody and operate all the evil aspects of the game environment. Some guests embrace the thought of evil and gladly choose his rebellious tendencies as an expression of their freedom from the oppressiveness of the (hateful) Game Master and His (odious) Manual.

Those members who have had dealings with players from the occult say that obscurity or deceit is one of its major traits. Players are drawn in by the promise of enlightenment, but the path only leads to more mysteries with more promises of insight. There is no revelation to be found and no freedom of enlightenment until there is no way to escape.

One of his primary weapons against players is guilt. Every player is born with a conscience, a sense of right and wrong. While it begins with an innate sense of what is good or bad, this conscience can be manipulated, molded, or desensitized when players ignore the promptings of their conscience. This commonly happens in our modern society through the philosophy of relativism, where what is good or right for you is fine for you, but it may not be good or right for someone else. This cultural erosion is bringing society back to the days of Noah, where everyone does what is right from his own perspective.

The Game Master placed the conscience of a player as a universal standard for conduct. When a wrong deed violates the conscience, guilt follows. The player should then correct the wrong behavior to prevent more guilt. The Serpent likes to entice players to break the rules and then use their guilt against them, so they feel helpless or unworthy to ever become guilt-free again. A common thought he plants in a player's mind is that God would never forgive them for what they did. The hopelessness the player feels keeps them perpetually on the Serpent's team. Even members can be overwhelmed by this attack of guilt. Kiosks may create a layer of guilt upon members by emphasizing their unworthiness to receive good things from the Game Master instead of focusing on their changed status as justified in the Game Master's view (1 Cor. 6:9–11).

The Serpent's plan is to keep all the guests on his team and deprive the Game Master of their allegiance. He and his henchmen can transform themselves at will back into angels of light and easily persuade players that they are connected to the Game Master (2 Cor. 11:14–15). He toys with them like a lion would play with a wildebeest calf, never concerned about the obstacles that disrupt their lives, helping them along to their own willing destruction with a cold, deadly calculation.

> **THE SERPENT'S PLAN IS TO KEEP ALL THE GUESTS ON HIS TEAM AND DEPRIVE THE GAME MASTER OF THEIR ALLEGIANCE.**

He may not directly injure players unless they allow him to do so by participating in his magic or violating the Manual. He can also convince other players to be the ones who injure and kill others, so he gets results on all fronts with an exceptionally high rate of success.

The Game Master instilled a sense of physical pain for players to protect and remove themselves from harmful elements like thorns and hot stoves. He instilled a sense of moral guilt for players to protect and remove themselves from harmful situations where a moral failure will lead to destroyed relationships, potential retribution, and, ultimately, a rejection of His truth. These are proper purposes for pain and guilt. But the Serpent inflicts destructive physical and emotional pain as an outcome of his enticements to urge players to mistreat themselves and others. He also inflicts false guilt on players to ensure their moral destruction.

The Spirit Master convicts the world of sin, righteousness, and judgment with the purpose of improving the player's condition. The One explained it like this:

> And when he [the Spirit Master] has come he will convince the world of its sin, and of the availability of God's goodness, and of deliverance from judgment. The world's sin is unbelief in me; there is righteousness available because I go to the Father and you shall see me no more; there is deliverance from judgment because the prince of this world has already been judged (John 16:9–11 TLB).

Serpent's operation – guilt, false guilt. The Serpent operates by injecting guilt into the player's soul. The purpose, as the One describes it, *is to steal and to kill and to destroy* (John 10:9–11). The outcome of guilt is a bondage that robs a player of freedom and keeps them on a path to their own destruction, whether it is through lifestyle failings and vices in the short term or by dying without a golden ticket in the long term.

False guilt does not bring a player to the point of repentance or restoration with the Game Master and others and comes from three primary sources: 1) ourselves, 2) others, and 3) the Serpent. Our condition of sin, where our spirit is separated from the Game Master, accounts for the potential of self-guilt and guilt being put on us by others. The Serpent focuses our failings against us and uses them to accuse us of ourselves and to the Game Master (Rev. 12:10).

For ourselves, false guilt can happen through a weak conscience that doesn't know the truth. Players may feel guilty for committing a sin that was not actually called a sin in the Manual. Their sense

> The Serpent is pro-choice until the abortion is over, then he turns pro-life to accuse and blame when there's no chance to undo the wrong.
> (The Ethics and Religious Liberty Commission 2014, ¶ 5)

of right and wrong is based on ignorance (1 Cor. 8:7–13). Players also place guilt on themselves for things that are not their fault, like blaming themselves for their parents' divorce, asking someone to do them a favor and an accident results, or feeling guilt and shame from an abusive home life, whether as a child or as an adult.

There are many avenues where guilt reaches us in our circumstances of life. Other players can use these same avenues to heap guilt upon us as a means for control or simply as a megaphone for the Serpent's mode of operation as an accuser to keep us paralyzed through shame. It's been said that the Serpent is pro-choice until the abortion is over, then he turns pro-life to accuse and blame when there's no chance to undo the wrong (The Ethics and Religious Liberty Commission 2014, ¶ 5).

Suppose we have been properly convicted of having wronged others or the Game Master. In that case, the Serpent can suppress our urge to fix the situation and inject reasons into our thoughts of why making things right will not work out, why trying to do the right thing will get us deeper in trouble, that our past record will make us look like a phony who is just covering his tracks, that we are not worthy of forgiveness, and so on.

> "A sad Christian is a phony Christian, and a guilty Christian is no Christian at all"
> (Manning 2005, 119)

Instead, the Manual says, "Blessed is the one whose transgression is forgiven, whose sin is covered. Blessed is the man against whom the LORD counts no iniquity, and in whose spirit there is no deceit" (Ps. 32:1–2; Rom. 4:7–8 ESV).

The antidote to guilt is the grace of the Game Master, Who offers freedom from guilt to all through the forgiveness of sin (Rom. 5:15; Titus 2:11–14). There is more mercy waiting for us from the Game Master than from any other source. Other players may or may not forgive us, but the Game Master will forgive us of our worst failings and actions and can reach us in our deepest despair to bring rest to our soul. There is no condemnation from Him when players face their guilt and turn to Him for forgiveness and membership (Matt. 11:28–29; Luke 7:46–48; John 6:37; Rom. 8:1).

> Christianity happens when men and women accept with unwavering trust that their sins have been not only forgiven, but forgotten, washed away in the blood of the Lamb. Thus, my friend archbishop Joe Reia says, "A sad Christian is a phony Christian, and a guilty Christian is no Christian at all'" (Manning 2005, 119).

Henchmen – Fallen Angels

These are the Serpent's rebel angels. He didn't create them but enticed or coerced them from the Game Master when he rebelled. It appears their main work is to manage the game world system, oversee the world's nations, and connect with players who want more authoritative influence through the dark realm. The Serpent only has half the number of henchmen angels as the Game Master's guardians, so his forces are probably used more strategically in his quest for world domination.

The henchmen can transform themselves into what the Manual calls "ministers of light," who lure players away from the Manual by posing as accurate guides through the game. They are likely stationed at the headquarters of the major religious kiosks across the game. Many players who claim to have heard from the guardians or even from the Game Master Himself have actually been in contact with disguised henchmen (2 Cor. 11:12–15).

Because deception is their best cloaking device, they are exceptionally effective at persuading players to focus on any goal they choose to highlight.

Minions – Demons

These are the spirits that directly trouble all players and cause tremendous damage to their personal lives. Their fingerprints on the players' circumstances are rarely noticed because players choose to disbelieve that the minions exist, and most don't recognize their mode of operation. Minions do not die and have been operating for thousands of years through hundreds of generations of players, studying them, and perfecting their craft against them. When players say the devil is causing them trouble, it is not the Serpent personally but minions who act on his behalf.

There is disagreement as to the origin of demons. A widely held view is that they were originally hybrid children of henchmen and beautiful player women unions in the early stage of the Game of Life (Gen. 6:4). Because they were trans-human, upon death, they were ineligible for the bonus round and were consigned to languish in the game world where the Serpent conscripted them into his services. They have retained their appetites for life and crave possessing another body. They can coexist together by the hundreds to demonize or possess a single player.

Minions have personalities and oppress players according to the demon's proclivity. The Manual describes various points of attack by minions: physical disease, mental disease, moral impurity, false religious doctrine, spiritual warfare, and oppression. There is a tendency for them to operate in gangs. If a minion influences a player, there are likely more of them at work than just one.

Here's an example of how the average player perceives minion activity. The village of Badi in India, plagued with high suicide rates, had that cause attributed to a demonic presence by the local sarpanch or village leader. A psychiatrist ruled out a spiritual cause and attributed it to depression and schizophrenia, likely driven by financial stress and pesticide exposure. He remarked that the villagers were unable to understand or relate to depression and instead linked the cause to demon activity (Kotwal 2016, ¶ 3–9).

It is possible that the sarpanch and the psychiatrist were both correct. In cases of demonic oppression where physical and emotional pressures exist, a corresponding psychiatric or medical condition or cause can usually be identified. The ability to diagnose an observable condition does not rule out a spiritual element driving it that medical or psychiatric personnel are untrained and unqualified to diagnose or authoritatively dismiss as they are prone to do, like in this case.

The influence of a minion upon a person can be unrecognized by that person and everyone else who knows them. Thoughts can be suggested to an individual who assumes it was their own thought or sudden inspiration. They can immediately take ownership of them and act on or speak out those thoughts. A well-known example in the Manual is a dialogue between the One and his disciples.

> When Jesus came to Caesarea Philippi, he asked his disciples, "Who are the people saying I am?" "Well," they replied, "some say John the Baptist; some, Elijah; some, Jeremiah or one of the other prophets." Then he asked them, "Who do you think I am?" Simon Peter answered, "The Christ, the Messiah, the Son of the living God."
>
> "God has blessed you, Simon, son of Jonah," Jesus said, "for my Father in heaven has personally revealed this to you—this is not from any human source. You are Peter, a stone; and upon this rock I will build my church; and all the powers of hell shall not prevail against it. And I will give you the keys of the Kingdom of Heaven; whatever doors you lock on earth shall be locked in heaven; and whatever doors you open on earth shall be open in heaven!"
>
> Then he warned the disciples against telling others that he was the Messiah. From then on Jesus began to speak plainly to his disciples about going to Jerusalem, and what would happen to him there—that he would suffer at the hands of the Jewish leaders, that he would be killed, and that three days later he would be raised to life again.
>
> But Peter took him aside to remonstrate with him. "Heaven forbid, sir," he said. "This is not going to happen to you!" Jesus turned on Peter and said, "Get away from me, you Satan! You are a dangerous

trap to me. You are thinking merely from a human point of view, and not from God's" (Matt. 16:21–23 TLB; Mark 8:27–33).

The One declared that Peter had been given a divine revelation by identifying Him as the Son of God. Then the topic changed, and the One began explaining how He would soon die. Peter took offense and rebuked Him for it, but the One looked at Peter and said, "Get behind me, Satan!" He did not call Peter Satan but addressed Satan, who spoke through Peter.

Peter acted as the leader and spokesperson for the One's disciple group. In a short time, Peter was a conduit for expressing the thoughts of both the Game Master and the Serpent, and he did not hesitate to respond to the promptings from either of them. It is possible that he himself did not discern the source of those declarations he made, which came from opposing spiritual sources.

Peter was not possessed by the Serpent or necessarily oppressed either as an ongoing experience. This was an instance where the Serpent saw an opportunity, and Peter was an easy target to quickly express the Serpent's views. The One rebuked Satan, and Peter got the message too. In this scenario, the Serpent was likely influencing Peter since he directly opposed the One. We are likely to be influenced by a minion of the Serpent who operates the same way.

Players who allow themselves to be conduits of Serpent or minion perspectives may eventually become their spokespersons. This creates what the Manual describes as a "stronghold." A stronghold is a position of powerful influence that a minion can have on a player. It can control specific areas of life like their thought patterns, infuse motives to trigger the minion's desired speech or actions, exert control over the player's appetites and lifestyles, or take over the player's self-control. A stronghold can even exhibit what is a recognizable case of demon possession. Any of these stages of minion control can be experienced by a guest or member.

Let's continue this example of thought influence. Have you ever paused and wondered where a random thought came from? Have you felt the urge to say something that you don't normally say, perhaps opposing someone else's plans or aspirations? Have you noticed any of your thoughts or remarks that differ from how you approach things or express yourself? Do you simply accept them and add them to your persona?

Since most players are on the Serpent's team as guests in the Game of Life, conveying his perspectives comes naturally through family or cultural tradition, the news, and social media. The question is, how do you know the source of your thoughts? The Manual instructs members to think differently and identifies what the thought patterns from the Game Master look like. As members become accustomed to the

Manual's perspective, it becomes easier to identify the sources of other players' perspectives with whom they associate daily.

This exchange also illustrates how easy it is for players to quickly accept spiritually driven impromptu suggestions and respond to them in the moment as part of a normal conversation. It also suggests that the less a player knows and understands the Manual, the more easily it can be misquoted or even contradicted. The Manual says that those who think they are immune from getting suckered into being manipulated should not be overconfident (Prov. 16:18; 1 Cor. 10:11–12; 2 John 7–8).

Minion activity. There is a long-standing debate running through kiosks as to whether a minion can or cannot actually possess the body of a member. The dominant answer from kiosks is no, but they can possess the body of a guest. The original Manual text uses the term "demonized," which doesn't really answer the question.

> Author and Messianic Rabbi K. A. Schneider wrote, "Demons do not possess believers, but they can become squatters" (2015, 20). Describing this perspective, he explains,
>
> Be assured, though, that even if demons do set up camp in believers' hearts and minds, they cannot possess us. The word *possession*, which is often used when demons are spoken of, implies ownership. Satan can never own us. We have been bought by the blood of the Lamb. After Jesus was crucified, ascended into heaven, and was seated at the right hand of God, the Holy Spirit came. Through the Holy Spirit, Jesus is now living in the hearts of all who receive Him as Lord and Savior. Jesus owns us. We are the Church and the Bride of Jesus.
>
> But demons can occupy our space *illegally*, just as the moneychangers did at the Temple, and when they do they will try to keep us from ejecting them (Schneider 2015, 18) (John 2:14–16; 1 Cor. 3:16).

Whatever the answer, the result is that a player is influenced in mind or body, which may be unnoticeable to them and others or becomes noticeable to others as an actual control over a player by affecting their physical activity or personality in ways that the player does not typically or normally act or respond.

If a player is levitating or bending metal bars barehanded and destroying things around him, a debate about calling them oppressed versus possessed is largely irrelevant. The Manual uses the term "cast out demons" to describe an exorcism. Those who perform exorcisms do not typically hold the popular kiosk belief that members cannot be demonized. They observe minion control or influence in both guests and members alike.

Dr. Gerald Small relates this story from his kiosk ministry days:

> I and another pastor on my staff worked with a young, sweet woman who was having what she thought was Satanic or demonic problems. We brought in our secretary to join with us in trying to understand and remove this influence. We decided to sing a hymn of praise to God, and this woman's voice radically changed, becoming harsh and angry. Later she came back entirely changed. We found out that her unsaved grandmother, with whom she had been staying was a medium. The young woman moved out of her grandmother's home and was immediately freed from all demonic influence. Interestingly the woman claimed to be a born-again believer. After leaving her grandmother's home, she lived a convincingly, untroubled Christian life—interesting! (Dr. Gerald Small, pers. comm.).

Any player can invite minions to oppress them when they break the rules of the Manual or ignore its warnings. Once the oppression starts, their influence on the player becomes greater as time passes and lasts until the player dies, and they move on to find new players to oppress. Players who say God told them to kill their children or loved ones were obeying minion voices; murder is a Big Ten violation and never comes from the Game Master.

When a guest gains membership status, minions are not automatically banished but must still be specifically expelled. Several accounts of exorcisms occurred in the Manual Acts of the Apostles, where players both believed in the One and minions were actively dispatched (Acts 5:14–16; 8:6–8; 18:11–12). Most members are not aware of the parameters or dynamics of this issue.

Exorcism. The primary way to be rid of minions is through exorcism. Members should only practice exorcism because this is a power clash between the Game Master and the Serpent about whether the Serpent's minion will have permission to continue its oppression of the player. Deliverance from minion oppression is more likely to be permanently effective for members (Matt. 12:43–45). Exorcism can involve a stubborn clash over who has the superior spiritual authority over the victim. It need not involve bodily harm or death as is tragically reported on occasion.

However, self-injury or aggression is possible while the minion can still torment or attack the victim and others.

Members are the best contacts for performing an exorcism. While all members have the spiritual authority and potential power to do so available to them, hardly any of them know how. However, it is possible to locate members who can help. The Resource appendices section provides information on how to do this.

Derek Prince has messages others have posted on YouTube about teachings on demonic oppression where those in the audience "cry out," as happened when the One exorcised minions. There are teachings on how to perform an exorcism upon yourself. Rabbi K. A. Schneider (2015) has a book entitled, *Self-Deliverance*. Guests can perform exorcism only at their own peril because they are interfering with their own Serpent master's tactics of oppression (Acts 19:13–18).

Folklore. The occult realm operates with four elements: fire, earth, air, and water. This includes all fairy types, merfolk, and cryptids. The *Minion* movies have popularized Gru's henchmen as funny little guys, mischievous but always causing trouble, and we tend to fall in love with them. We are familiar with stories of all types of fairies, such as the Scandinavian trolls, Irish leprechauns, and Iberian or Spanish *duendes* (pixie, goblin, gnome-like). These cryptids or spirits can be described as *espiritus chocarreros*, pesky spirits.

In February 2023, Mexico's president, Andrés Manuel López Obrador (AMLO), made headlines when he posted a photo of what he described as an *alux*, a Mayan woodland type of elf, in a tree. "According to traditional Maya belief, *aluxes* are small, mischievous creatures that inhabit forests and fields and are prone to playing tricks on people, such as hiding things. Some people leave small offerings to appease them" (Reed 2023, ¶ 1–3, 6).

Stories of fae folk are repeated around the globe and across many cultures. Other story types about merfolk, werewolves, and vampires are featured prominently in our culture. Many such movies and shows are popular because of our fascination with the magic of their storylines. Accounts and explanations from both Christian and spiritist sources attest to their reality on a paranormal level. Member organizations that deal with the occult find themselves discovering new aspects of the Serpent's bondage over these players who are caught up in his binding clutches.

> **THE OVERWHELMING MAJORITY OF PLAYERS, BOTH GUEST AND MEMBER ALIKE, ARE UNAWARE OF THE VAST DEPTH AND BREADTH OF THE SERPENT'S KINGDOM OF DARKNESS.**

This topic of folklore is easy for rational players to dismiss as pretend fun. The overwhelming majority of players, both guest and member alike, are unaware of the vast depth and breadth of the Serpent's kingdom of darkness. What little we see around us suggests that there is not much to his kingdom. Players who live in a region of prevalent witchcraft or those who participate in occult venues, see incidents like these become more than folklore.

Players – People

The original players, Adam and Eve, were created as perfect beings by the Game Master and started the game on His team. They were made in the Game Master's image, not so much in their physical aspects as the Game Master is a Spirit, but in the composition of their being (Gen. 1:26–31; John 4:24).

Adam was created from the dust of the ground and not from an evolutionary biological microorganism (Gen. 2:7). He had a physical body made for the game world earth environment, a soul for self-awareness or psyche, emotions and decisions and intelligence, and a spirit to connect directly to the Game Master.

Players are the most valuable aspect of the Game of Life. The Game Master puts a premium on your value as a player, and nothing in the game environment compares to you individually or collectively. The government may calculate your worth based on the productivity of your work, as collateral against the national debt or by your carbon footprint, but the Game Master calculates your worth as His created being. Your personhood is worth more to Him than the mere wealth of the entire world, which your government will never fully possess.

Heaven and earth will pass away (Matt. 24:35; 2 Pet. 3:10; 1 John 2:17; Rev. 21:1). The spirit of the player, or what is usually called the soul, is the only eternal feature of this game. We hold the choice to pursue eternal life or settle for the destruction of our souls. Because our eternal soul is encapsulated in a decaying body in a sustained but declining game world environment, we have a hard time distinguishing our temporary game life from our eternal potential, so our perspective is naturally drawn toward the game's daily temporary things, which become the defining elements of our existence.

Players generally don't seriously consider the value of their soul and their need to safeguard its survival beyond this game level. Rather, they choose to pursue their own game objectives of fortune, fame, or family at this game level instead of investing in their eternal future bonus round potential by pursuing the Game Master's priorities for their life. The One describes it like this:

> Then he called his disciples and the crowds to come over and listen. "If any of you wants to be my follower," he told them, "you must put

aside your own pleasures and shoulder your cross, and follow me closely. If you insist on saving your life, you will lose it. Only those who throw away their lives for my sake and for the sake of the Good News will ever know what it means to really live.

"And how does a man benefit if he gains the whole world and loses his soul in the process? For is anything worth more than his soul? And anyone who is ashamed of me and my message in these days of unbelief and sin, I, the Messiah, will be ashamed of him when I return in the glory of my Father, with the holy angels" (Mark 8:34–38 TLB).

If you acquired all the world's wealth, it would still not compare to the value of your soul. Nothing you could attain or offer can equal your value to the Game Master. It doesn't matter what you think of yourself. To Him, you are worth dying for, and so He did to offer you a new life in Him.

So, the game's players were spirit beings that were adapted and limited to a physical game world. Their soul was the bridge between the spirit realm and the physical realm, and this soul was where they were given their free will. Unlike all other animal life forms and perhaps other spirit beings, these players had a choice to side with the Game Master or reject His ways.

The original players were not perfect in the sense of having independent godlike powers. They were sinless as they were not tainted by sin or its effects on their spirit or physical being. It is conceivable that they could have had the capacity to effect miracles through the empowerment of the Spirit Master as synced-up master players can do today. The Game Master declared his creative work to be "very good" indicating there were no corrections to be made (Gen. 1:31).

Players' character – self-centeredness (selfishness). While there are many examples of selflessness toward fellow players, the default player character is self-centeredness. This was not always the case. When paradise was created and the first players, Adam and Eve, came on the scene, they were created in the image of the Game Master. They had the same character attributes encompassed by His sacrificial love, which is the opposite of selfishness.

Since they chose to disobey the only rule in Eden's paradise, they lost their condition of perfection with its character quality of love. Instead, they took on the characteristic selfishness of their new boss, the Serpent. This is now our default attribute. Sharing and giving must be taught and purposely practiced rather than having those qualities as part of our intuitive nature. Our sparks of selflessness toward our fellow players are only vestiges of what was once one of our main attributes.

Joining the Game Master's team begins a journey toward recovery. We are called to set aside our self-centeredness and become loving and giving toward others in our life habits as a reflection of the Game Master's unconditional love toward us and as an example of our love for Him (Rom. 12:9–18; Eph. 4:31–32).

Good people (innocent). Good people are considered regular players who are responsible, don't get into trouble, and don't go looking for trouble. Good people look out for their neighbors, help those having a hard time, and assist others in a crisis. They mind their own business but are polite and respectful toward others. Add your own description here because the list can go on.

We can also call these people the innocents, victims of misfortune. Most players would call themselves good as in, "I'm a good person" or "I'm not a bad person." It is unclear what each one's definition of a "good person" or "bad person" would be since we tend to compare ourselves to each other or to a personal code instead of a universally defined standard like the Manual. We can justify our bad decision or behavior and still call ourselves good because we are good-hearted, like when we do the wrong thing for the right reason or are not bad compared to someone else.

Whatever the standard, we consider good people as those who have bad things happen to them for no good reason. Section Three in Part Two explained the sources of those bad things, but to stop the bad things, as explained in Section Four, being a good person isn't good enough. You must meet the qualifications to be a "righteous person" as a member. Unfortunately, almost all good people are actually guests.

Who is a good person? For this book, bad things that happen to good people include players who do not consider themselves bad. You can include yourself in that category because bad stuff happens to practically everyone. We cataloged bad stuff that all players universally feel. However, to apply solutions to fix the bad stuff, you must become more than a generically good person.

The Manual has a completely different standard for being a good person. According to the Manual, a good person has two distinctive characteristics: 1) they first belong to the Game Master's team as members, and then 2) they do good deeds. It is not only an outward action of doing good things, but it starts from an inward heart condition that produces good deeds (Matt. 12:34–35; Luke 6:44–46).

So, what about all the players around the globe who do good things every day? We all ought to be good people as players in general. Doing good things makes you a good person in the eyes of your family, friends, and neighbors, but your good deeds cannot classify you as a good person according to the standards of the Game Master.

Therefore, you must also change your player status for Him to recognize and reward your good deeds and certify you as a good person.

John 3:16 is perhaps the most famous Bible verse saying that "God so loved the world, that He gave His only Son, that whoever believes in Him should not perish but have eternal life" (ESV).

Most players don't know the opposite verse to this in John 3:18 where Jesus goes on to say that "he that does not believe is condemned already, because he has not believed in the name of the only begotten Son of God" (JUB)".

In the space of three verses, the One spelled out the consequences of your free will: believe in Him, and you won't perish; don't believe, and God already condemns you. Until you choose the Game Master's kingdom for yourself, you are living under the Serpent's dominion, including the evil that comes with it. The One said that "everyone who commits sin is a slave of sin" (John 8:34 NASB). From the Game Master's perspective, there is no question of who His people are and who are not His people.

The Manual describes only two kinds of people, the righteous and the wicked. The righteous chose the Game Master as their King and live according to His commandments, and the wicked have not chosen the Game Master and still please themselves, defaulting to the Serpent as their king. Other ways to describe this are saved vs. unsaved, believers vs. non-believers, true Christians vs. fakes plus everyone else, actual good people vs. those who think they are good.

The Game Master says there is no one who is good or does good apart from Him (Ps. 14:1–3; 53:1–3; Prov. 11:17; Eccles. 7:20; Rom. 3:12; 3 John 1:11). Perhaps you would never describe yourself as wicked. You may be popularly defined as a good person who is honorable, kind to others, and helps people, but if you don't belong to the kingdom of the "good God" (Ps. 100:5), then your legal classification is that of a wicked person who is part of the kingdom of the Evil One.

If you consider yourself a good person, if you want to become truly good and want yourself legally classified as a good person by the Game Master, take the next step by renouncing your own goodness and join the Game Master's team by accepting His goodness on your behalf (2 Cor. 5:20–21).

Guest Players – Good People, Innocents, Serfs of the Serpent

Every player starts the game as a guest. Guests include everyone in the world, but self-identified good people are not the winners. They experience the good and bad parts of life's game but can't get power-ups, extra health, immunity, shields, or advanced weapons available to winners.

Most of these players are happy to play life's game, collect points and gold (or unsecured Federal Reserve notes or crypto currency), and think that whoever dies rich and happy wins. Few wish to be bothered with the frantic urgings of the members since each has his own coping philosophy to navigate the game.

To be a winner, good players must change their status from guest to member. However, since it can cost you everything you aspire to be with a new agenda for life, most players would rather stay at the guest level, take life's punches, and hope for the best in the end.

Guest player gaming philosophy is enough distraction to keep them from the bonus round. The Game of Life is just a fantasy of a higher philosophy with nothing more to win or worry about when it's over. After it's all over, they realize only too late that staying a guest also costs them everything anyway, plus losing the bonus round.

Guest players – bad people, guilty, serfs of the Serpent

Same as self-identified Good People. They're just guests, some having dark powers, but most with loser instincts. The Game Master lets the sun rise and the rain fall on the good and the bad: the members and the guests (Matt. 5:45). All things being equal, the bad people have stuff happen to them just like the good people do. They put themselves at a disadvantage in playing the game because actions have consequences. If they keep racking up the bad stuff they do, a tipping point will eventually come where bad things begin happening to them as their chickens come home to roost. It's inevitable (Rom. 1:18–32).

Guest player characteristics. All players, guests or members, have the capacity to do the wrong thing. The Manual has lists of traits or activities that identify players who are part of the kingdom of the Serpent. When they are practiced as a lifestyle or habit where the player is comfortable in continued participation, it is very unlikely that they are a member, whether they claim to be or not (1 John 3:7–10).

The Serpent's guest player team's characteristics include: adultery, backbiters, bearing false witness, boasters, covenant breakers, covetousness (greed), disobedient to parents, disobedient (rebels), drunkenness, envy, evil thoughts, fearful, fornication, gossips, hatred, haters of God, heresies, idolatry, implacable, kidnappers, lasciviousness, lawless, liars, lustful intent, maliciousness, malignity, murders, perjury, profane, proud, reprobate mind, sorcerers, theft, **unbelieving**, ungodly, unholy, unmerciful, unrighteous, witchcraft, and wrath (Wellman 2014) (Lev. 18:5–25; Prov. 6:16–19; Matt. 5:28, 32; Mark 7:21–22; Rom. 1:26–32; 2 Cor. 12:20; Gal. 5:19–21; Eph. 5:3–7, 18; 1 Tim. 1:9–10; Rev. 21:8; 19:18–19).

Unbelief is the nail in the coffin that keeps guests out of the bonus round. While the Game Master says that those who practice these traits will not see the bonus round, none of them alone will consign a player to hell except unbelief. They are a result or an outworking of unbelief. For a while, my son in the Air Force would randomly get asked if homosexuals were going to hell. His response was that homosexuality is not what gets them there—it's their unbelief in the Game Master's account of the One: that is what condemns them (John 3:16–18, 35–36; Gal. 3:11; 6:7–8).

This is why players cannot clean up their lives and expect to reach the bonus round. It requires changing sides, a change of heart and mind, and perspective.

Member Players – Righteous People, Adopted Family of the Game Master

They got their ticket. These are the winning players and the potential game changers in the Game of Life. The Game Master calls them pilgrims because this Game of Life is simply the road to their real destination at the bonus round. Righteous people are religious, but most religious people don't meet the criteria to be called righteous (Heb. 11:13; 1 Pet. 2:11–12).

Being righteous is a reference to the perspective that the Game Master has toward the member. Because the One applied His atoning death to their game violations, the Game Master considers them to have the divine righteousness of the One when He views them. This is where the concept of being "a new creation in Christ" gets its meaning (2 Cor. 5:17–18). If the members whom you know don't act very righteous the way you see it, you are right; there may be a problem with their claims.

Statistically, professing members who sincerely follow the Manual are in the distinct minority. As you look around, you may notice that those who identify as members can be careless players. The ones you may know don't read the rules or can't explain them in a way that makes sense. Many prefer to have the rules read to them and explained to them at their religious kiosks, and they never realize that the good parts with all the power plays have been left out of the discussions. They may show up in the kiosk on Sunday but never open a Manual the rest of the week and don't turn to it when things go sideways for them.

Some seriously and sincerely read the Manual and know it very well, but they rely on their kiosk interpretation to overlay the text (so they understand it right) so that what they read may not translate into transformative power to radically improve their gameplay. These members read their Manual, even diligently. However, when they run across ways to achieve answered prayers and make a miracle, they pull back from trying it themselves because the kiosk or denomination doesn't teach it that way or the pastor redirects or downplays trying to apply it to their life situation.

The ineptitude of members doesn't attract guests to join the Kingdom, and it nauseates the Game Master (Gal. 3:1–3; Rev. 3:14–22). As the game winds down these days, the One said that false prophets would deceive, and the love of many will grow cold because of the increase of lawlessness (Matt. 24:11–13, paraphrased).

Members have the potential for the most awesome show of power; they have all the power-ups, extra health, immunity, shields, and advanced spirit weapons available to make themselves winners. Some of it can be found scattered around the castle, but the potent stuff is hidden in the secret room, and they haven't deciphered the code to get to it. Many of them may just have pieces of the arsenal.

Perhaps nobody has ever helped them apply their faith to consistently get prayers answered, and they have no experience praying in their moment of need and seeing the answer reveal itself before them in real time. Nor have they practiced warding off sickness or unsafe situations, applying a blessing to a difficult job or unsanitary exposure, and seeing their faith make the difference for them.

Those members who find the game pieces and use them properly can improve their own lives and those who join them. Down through history, they subdued kingdoms, administered justice in the administrations of international superpowers, obtained promised blessings, closed the mouths of lions, extinguished the power of raging fire, escaped the edge of the sword, out of frailty and weakness won strength, and became stalwart, even mighty and resistless in battle, routing overwhelming numbers of enemy troops, and raising their dead (Heb. 11).

Even today, they quench the fiery darts of the Serpent, effect change around the world through their spiritual ICBMs, physically heal themselves and others, turn bad circumstances around to their favor, and still raise the dead. The same power described in the lore of the old stories in the Manual still exists today and is still available to all members who reach for them.

Regardless of their playing skills, all the true members—righteous people—are winners in life's game.

Disciples. This term is the objective of membership. Members should be learners and practitioners of the Manual so that it permeates their souls and is displayed in their perspectives, attitudes, responses, and actions. *Abiding in the One* is a phrase used repeatedly in this book as a condition of enhanced gameplay and refers to disciples, members who are all in on their commitment to the One as their King (Matt. 16:24–25; Luke 12:22–34; 14:25–35; John 8:30–32; 13:34–35; 15:1–15).

The One said,

I am the vine, you are the branches. The one who abides in me while I abide in him produces much fruit, because apart from me you can do nothing. Unless a person abides in me, he is thrown away like a pruned branch and dries up. People gather such branches, throw them into a fire, and they are burned up.

If you abide in me and my words abide in you, you can ask for anything you want, and you'll receive it. This is how my Father is glorified, when you produce a lot of fruit and so prove to be my disciples. Just as the Father has loved me, so I have loved you. So abide in my love (John 15:5–9 ISV).

Member player characteristics. All players, guest or member, have the capacity to do good things whether by a heart's desire, good parenting, or sheer will. Doing good is expected of all, but it will not turn a guest player into a member. The Manual lists traits or activities that identify players who are part of the kingdom of the Game Master (1 John 3:7–10).

The Game Master's player characteristics include: abundance in good works, clear conscience, comforts the disheartened, compassionate, considerate, content, discerning, doesn't repay evil with evil or insult with insult, faithful, forgiving, gentleness, godly, goodness, gracious speech, helps the weak and fatherless and widows, **holy** (morally excellent in goodness and righteousness), honoring, humble, impartial, joyful, kind, **loves**, meekness (enduring, unresentful), not a busybody or gossip, obedient, patient, peace loving, rejects every kind of evil, respectful, righteous, self-controlled, sincere, sober, tenderhearted, thankful, truthful, unselfish, warns the unruly or insolent, and works to provide (Gal. 5:22–23; Eph. 4:25–26, 29, 32; 5:15–19; 6:1–2; Phil. 2:3; 4:8; Col. 1:10; 3:13–15; 4:6; 1 Thess. 4:11–12; 5:14–23; 1 Tim. 6:6–10; Titus 2:11–14; James 1:27; 3:17–18; 1 Pet. 2:11–17; 3:8–9; 15–16; 2 Pet. 1:5–7).

Holiness is required for the bonus round. Holy living embodies the character of a member where all these traits come together: "Follow peace with all men, and holiness, without which no man shall see the Lord" (Heb. 12:14 KJV). The outcome of holy living results in the demonstration of love for others, especially fellow members (John 13:34–35; Gal. 6:10).

HOLINESS IS REQUIRED FOR THE BONUS ROUND.

Belief in the One transfers a player from guest to member status. Following that, a lifestyle of holiness allows members to transform themselves into these characteristics of the Game Master and become a source of blessing to other players.

It is easy to find moral failings among member players. They must still work out remnants of their guest player status. The greater their prolonged tendency for failure corresponds to the lack of the pursuit of holiness.

Fake member players – serfs of the Serpent, hypocrites

Not all who talk like members actually got their golden ticket (Matt. 7:12). If the Game Master doesn't mean enough to them to make them a better person and help others or they don't want to be labeled as God freaks, they may have just bought a knock-off ticket to polish their credentials or get fire insurance from hell (or to simply chase or marry that hot player who's religious).

Guests understandably don't know the Manual and may have difficulty distinguishing the real members from the fake ones. Because they both claim to be members, guests usually assume that all members are like the worst ones they see. The Game Master predicted that there would be a lot of fake members who would act just like the real members with seemingly identical power, but He called them Lawless Ones: Workers of Iniquity (Matt. 7:22).

In this modern age, we are constantly told not to be mean and judge anyone or their motives. That's not exactly in the Manual. The Game Master said to check the results of what professing members do to discover the source of their power; it is possible to figure it out. He also said don't be a sucker for all their fancy talk if their activities and works don't add up. The Manual says to stay away from the fakes—they work for the Serpent, whether they think so or not (2 John 1:7–11).

Guest player perspective. It is common for guests to disparage the Game Master, the One, and His Manual based on the bad behavior of either real members or so-called members. They are right to point out flaws or failings of professing members and use their own standards against them to conclude that they are hypocrites.

Guests typically reject the Game Master based on member behavior. First, they correctly take the moral high ground to excoriate bad behavior. Then they draw the wrong conclusion that the Game Master is not worthy of their own commitment to His team. The middle verse of the entire Manual says that it is better to trust in the Game Master than to put your confidence in players (Ps. 118:8, paraphrased). Rejecting the Game Master because of lousy professing members is a sorry excuse to go to hell.

All players started on the Serpent's team with exposure to his philosophy of life. Switching teams requires a complete change of perspective and philosophy toward the values of the Game Master. Players who profess to switch teams don't all transition into the characteristic values and behavior of the Game Master at the same pace. A weak understanding of the Manual causes players to drift into drawing wrong analogies and wrong conclusions, and eventually leaving behind their profession of membership as they walk away and do their own thing.

> He [Jesus] taught them many things by parables [a simple story used to illustrate a moral or spiritual lesson], and in his teaching, said: "Listen! A farmer went out to sow his seed. As he was scattering the seed, some fell along the path, and the birds came and ate it up. Some fell on rocky places, where it did not have much soil. It sprang up quickly, because the soil was shallow. But when the sun came up, the plants were scorched, and they withered because they had no root. Other seed fell among thorns, which grew up and choked the plants, so that they did not bear grain. Still other seed fell on good soil. It came up, grew and produced a crop, some multiplying thirty, some sixty, some a hundred times."
>
> Then Jesus said, "Whoever has ears to hear, let them hear."
>
> When he was alone, the Twelve and the others around him asked him about the parables. He told them, "The secret of the kingdom of God has been given to you. But to those on the outside everything is said in parables so that,
>
> "'they may be ever seeing but never perceiving, and ever hearing but never understanding; otherwise they might turn and be forgiven!'" [Isa. 6:9–10].
>
> Then Jesus said to them, "Don't you understand this parable? How then will you understand any parable? The farmer sows the word (Manual). Some people are like seed along the path, where the word is sown. As soon as they hear it, Satan comes and takes away the word that was sown in them. Others, like seed sown on rocky places, hear the word and at once receive it with joy. But since they have no root, they last only a short time. When trouble or persecution comes because of the word, they quickly fall away. Still others, like seed sown

among thorns, hear the word; but the worries of this life, the deceitfulness of wealth and the desires for other things come in and choke the word, making it unfruitful. Others, like seed sown on good soil, hear the word, accept it, and produce a crop—some thirty, some sixty, some a hundred times what was sown" (Mark 4:2–20 ISV).

The author of Hebrews describes some members in the early Christian kiosk:

We have much to say about this, but it is hard to make it clear to you because you no longer try to understand. In fact, though by this time you ought to be teachers, you need someone to teach you the elementary truths of God's word all over again. You need milk, not solid food! Anyone who lives on milk, being still an infant, is not acquainted with the teaching about righteousness. But solid food is for the mature, who by constant use have trained themselves to distinguish good from evil (Heb. 5:11–14 NIV).

This process is also complicated when members mix their own interpretation of the Manual using their own experiences and philosophy, which can distort the intended outcome of the Manual's teachings. Sometimes a player turns into a strict authoritarian who starts telling everyone else what to do to make sure they are on the right path.

Being the voice of God, the One publicly unloaded with both barrels and pulled no punches on the kiosk leaders 2,000 years ago, who took the law of Moses and turned it into a serpentine system of rules. They became experts on contriving it to mean whatever they wanted it to say.

Then Jesus said to the crowds and to his disciples: "The teachers of the law and the Pharisees sit in Moses' seat. So you must be careful to do everything they tell you. But do not do what they do, for they do not practice what they preach. They tie up heavy, cumbersome loads and put them on other people's shoulders, but they themselves are not willing to lift a finger to move them" (Matt. 23:1–4 NIV).

The One continued:

Woe to you, teachers of the law and Pharisees, you hypocrites! You give a tenth of your spices—mint, dill and cumin. But you have neglected the more important matters of the law—justice, mercy and faithfulness. You should have practiced the latter, without neglecting the former. You blind guides! You strain out a gnat but swallow a camel.

Woe to you, teachers of the law and Pharisees, you hypocrites! You clean the outside of the cup and dish, but inside they are full of greed and self-indulgence. Blind Pharisee! First clean the inside of the cup and dish, and then the outside also will be clean.

Woe to you, teachers of the law and Pharisees, you hypocrites! You are like whitewashed tombs, which look beautiful on the outside but on the inside are full of the bones of the dead and everything unclean. In the same way, on the outside you appear to people as righteous but on the inside you are full of hypocrisy and wickedness.

Woe to you, teachers of the law and Pharisees, you hypocrites! You build tombs for the prophets and decorate the graves of the righteous. And you say, 'If we had lived in the days of our ancestors, we would not have taken part with them in shedding the blood of the prophets.' So you testify against yourselves that you are the descendants of those who murdered the prophets. Go ahead, then, and complete what your ancestors started!

You snakes! You brood of vipers! How will you escape being condemned to hell? Therefore I am sending you prophets and sages and teachers. Some of them you will kill and crucify; others you will flog in your synagogues and pursue from town to town. And so upon you will come all the righteous blood that has been shed on earth, from the blood of righteous Abel [Adam's 2nd son] to the blood of Zechariah son of Berekiah, whom you murdered between the temple and the altar. Truly I tell you, all this will come on this generation (Matt. 23:23–36 NIV).

Today, those who follow rules without a heart transformation end up with abusive relationships and unneighborly conduct that should be appalling to and rejected by everyone. Yet, guests conclude that this is the way the Game Master likes it just because the perpetrators profess to be members. When players don't know the Game Master, it's easier to tag Him with values expressed by the worst of His professing players. Then they self-righteously decide that there's no good reason to check Him out. So, they wash their hands of hypocrite Christians and walk into the caring and welcoming arms of their Serpent master's philosophers. And the Serpent wins again with an easy victory.

Fake member players — false prophets

There is an indication that false prophets and teachers, kiosk ministers or leaders, can seemingly become members and turn away from the Game Master (2 Pet. 2:1). Master player Peter identifies some characteristics of false teachers with some examples from 2 Peter 2 of what they teach.

> They indulge in the corrupt passions of the sin nature and despise authority, are presumptuous and reckless, self-willed and arrogant, no better than animals.
>
> They do whatever they feel like, and they laugh at the terrifying powers of the underworld, which they know so little about.
>
> They count it a delight to revel in the daytime (living luxuriously), deceiving by living in foul sin on the side while they join kiosk love feasts as though they were honest men.
>
> No woman can escape their sinful stare, and they never have enough of adultery.
>
> They make a game of luring unstable women, constantly looking for sin, enticing and luring away unstable souls.
>
> They are experts in greed and are doomed and cursed.
>
> They secretly and gradually introduce destructive heresies even to the point of denying the One.

They exploit with false arguments and twisted doctrine and will say anything to get hold of your money.

They mouth empty, boastful words, and by appealing to the lustful desires of the flesh, they entice people who are just escaping from those who live in error. They promise them freedom while they themselves are slaves of depravity (2 Pet. KJV, AMP, NIV, TLB).

Do you know any kiosk leaders like that? Peter probably had some specific players in mind when he made these descriptions. Notice that what they teach also impacts or is impacted by their character. Even if these leaders had become members, their fundamental character contained attributes of guests. It may take some evaluation over some time to identify false member leaders because the introduction of false teaching can be gradual. The better you know the Manual, the sooner you can discover an error with the help of the Spirit Master.

Following the way of Cain. The first recorded brothers, the children of Adam and Eve, were a contrast in character. The elder son Cain tried to please but did it his way, offering a sacrifice of his farm produce, which the Game Master rejected. Abel, the younger son, was a rule keeper who offered a lamb for sacrifice, which the Game Master accepted. In his rage at being rejected, Cain killed Abel instead of correcting his error and offering the required sacrifice (Gen. 4:1–16).

Jude refers to those who infiltrate the kiosk as fake members as those who have gone in the way of Cain (Jude 1:11). Cain was a faker who did not repent (turn from his error):

- He was outwardly religious, but he had no faith (Heb. 11:4).
- He had every opportunity to know God and repent (Gen. 4:6–7).
- He killed his brother "because his own actions were evil and his brother's were righteous" (1 John 3:12).

Fake members are like Cain:

- They have outward religion, not relationship (2 Tim. 3:5; Acts 20:30).
- They deceive themselves by hearing the [Manual] but not living it (James 1:22–25). They may "talk the talk," but they won't "walk the walk."
- They will work against God's purposes in the church like "weeds among the wheat" (Matt. 13:24–30). (Bible Love Notes n.d., ¶ 1–3)

Cain represents good players who never become members and whose outcome is ultimately evil. Their effort and influence have no bonus round value to the Game Master because they are fake members. Abel represents good players who become members who follow the Manual and are called righteous by the Game Master (Heb. 11:4).

Communist agenda. The 1963 list of "Current Communist Goals" that was read into the US Congressional record contains two points about religion:

> 27. Infiltrate the churches and replace revealed religion with "social" religion. Discredit the Bible and emphasize the need for intellectual maturity, which does not need a "religious crutch."

> 28. Eliminate prayer or any phase of religious expression in the schools on the ground that it violates the principle of "separation of church and state" (Skousen 1960, 248; W. J. Miller n.d., # 27–28).

Point 27 describes the ensuing deviation from Manual doctrines in our modern kiosks, such as syncretism and the Emergent Church. The social gospel is so compelling because it does not restrict or condemn a player's lifestyle. The false teachers of the social gospel have become the dominant religious representatives of Christianity to the public, and their books and teaching materials dominate the religious marketplace. Their influence has spread to the conservative kiosks as well so that both finding the Game Master and following Him while being true to the Manual require continued vigilance by the members. Guests who follow them will likely never find eternal life and rest for their souls.

> THE SOCIAL GOSPEL IS SO COMPELLING BECAUSE IT DOES NOT RESTRICT OR CONDEMN A PLAYER'S LIFESTYLE.

The One and master players Paul, Peter, John, and Jude described their agenda and provided points to measure those teachers against the truth in the Manual as described in this section and throughout this book. Their warning is to be careful that you are not deceived (Matt. 7:14–16; Matt. 24:11, 24; Mark 13:5–6, 22; Luke 21:8; Rom. 16:17–18; 1 Cor. 6:9–10; 1 John 2:18, 22–23; 4:3; 2 John 1:7).

Master Players – Advanced Member Players

All members have the potential to be master players, but most members don't make time to do things that require that level of expertise, which includes intensive focus and training (2 Tim. 2:15). You don't become a martial arts expert by watching movies of it; you turn off the TV and actually practice. All skills require proper practice—including spirit-level skills.

This category of master players includes mature players who are described as skillful in understanding and using the Manual and who can discern good and evil through practice. Unskilled members who don't really know the Manual like this can't tell much difference between good and evil and are contrasted as comparative babies, and that is where too many of us are (Heb. 5:12–14).

Members enjoy being around master players because of the advantage they bring with healings and blessings, but few are willing to unplug themselves from the cares and entertainment of the game world to devote themselves to being controlled by the Spirit Master in a way that makes them effective to Him and useful to other players.

Guests can never become master players until they change their game status to members. Guests may become advanced guest players, but their powers from the Serpent's team will never match what is available to members, and in the end, they still lose to the Serpent (Matt. 28:18; Eph. 1:20–22; Phil. 2:9–11; Rev. 20:10–15).

Master Players know the Manual and consistently do the supernatural power moves that are described in the member player section. The One said that they remain in the game until their time is up like all other players do, but the game environment doesn't define them (John 15:19; 17:14–17).

Quick objectives here are to: 1) love the Game Master above all, 2) love other players like the One loves you, 3) increase faith through the Manual, 4) obey the One, and 5) understand and play the game from His perspective (Matt. 22:37; Mark 12:30; John 13:34; Rom. 10:17; Phil. 2:3–8; 2 Pet. 1:5–11; 3:17–18; 1 John 5:3–4).

Game Environment

The current game environment includes the known universe with the earth and heavens. It interacts with the interdimensional heaven, where the Game Master resides. Players didn't just come along by happenstance from a primordial soup when the earth's crust cooled enough for life to somehow bubble up. The Game Master laid the foundations of the earth and created it on purpose to be lived in, not an empty chaos, which means he also created gamers on purpose to play in His new game environment (Job 38:1–11; Isa. 45:18).

The Game Master created the game environment by spoken declarations (Gen 1; Heb. 11:3). It was declared by His spoken Word in the spirit dimension and became manifested in our physical dimension into the reality we see around us today. What a spoken Word created can also be controlled by a spoken Word, something the members can do too as they use the Manual's instructions. This power is not limited to just the physical aspects and objects of the environment but also covers circumstances players face in the game (Matt. 21:21; Mark 11:23). This transaction between the physical and spiritual realms is where miracles happen. Miracles are not random or unpredictable but specific and measurable.

This game environment is filled with all the discovered and yet-to-be-discovered laws and theories of science that impact players' lives, plus the attention and influence of spirit beings who also make an effort to interact with players, some to their benefit and others to their detriment. Even if a space vehicle could go beyond planet Earth and its solar system, it still would remain in the game environment. There is no distance that becomes out of reach of the game environment. Even breaching into a trans-dimensional place does not free players from the curses or consequences of having been in the game environment. They stick to you like an incurable disease (Ps. 139:1–17).

Because the Serpent dominates this game environment, there is greater danger to players in general, and many things he can do that impact players at every level of their existence. Most players view the game environment only in a physical sense and never make a connection with how it is affected by the spirit realm. Even sincere members are quick to dismiss the spirit consequences of the paradise lost or the Serpent's hand in the things that happen to them or around them.

There is a general refusal to believe that what happens in the game environment is more than the physical, scientific, and observable part of the game. Because it originated from the spirit realm, gamers are actually only observing the end product and tend to ignore the source which makes it work.

Game World Origins

All theories of earth origins are based on faith, whether it is supernaturally derived from the Game Master or is the natural and intellectual confidence based on one's observable surroundings. The Manual candidly declares that it is *with faith that we know the worlds were framed by the word of God* (Heb. 11:1–3).

This Manual description is used in the Creation Theory, and members consider it a fact based on faith. There are conflicting accounts among members of how the creation event occurred, but members use the Manual as their source in their interpretations. Across all the theories of game world origins, whether secular, scientific, or theological, none of them completely and authoritatively answer all questions or satisfactorily account for all facets of prehistoric issues. The Manual reveals its origins but does not elaborate deeply on points that do not concern the Game Master's purpose for interaction with us in this current level of the game.

Evolution vs. creation. The greatest competing theory in the western game world is evolutionary theory or "science." Scientists use the terms "theory" and "fact" differently than the general public thinks of them, which can insert confusion. Running a full discourse on evolution versus creation is beyond the scope of this book. Scientist Stephen Gould provides some contrast from a guest perspective as cited in an article by Lawrence Moran entitled, "Evolution Is a Fact and a Theory" (Moran 1993, entire article).

A fundamental difference between creation and evolution is the source of their respective foundational truths. While both views observe the same geological and cosmic evidence or facts we find in nature, and both views use the same mathematical and scientific tools to study the same data, their interpretations come from two opposing worldviews. The Manual explains this phenomenon in the following texts.

> "Now faith is confidence in what we hope for and assurance about what we do not see. By faith we understand that the universe was formed at God's command, so that what is seen was not made out of what was visible" (Heb. 11:1, 3 NIV).

Members have had a transaction of faith with the Game Master, which gives them a connection to spiritual truth. It is through this faith that they receive their understanding of how the universe was formed, by the word of the Game Master, and they interpret observable data through the context of this faith perspective.

> "The person [guest player] without the Spirit [Master] does not accept the things that come from the Spirit of God but considers them foolishness, and cannot understand them because they are discerned only through the Spirit" (1 Cor. 2:14 NIV).

Guests have a spirit that is disconnected from the Game Master, leaving them without a way to understand or relate to spiritual truth. The Spirit Master, who is also called the Spirit of Truth, cannot impart insight to a guest who has no transformational mechanism of discerning faith that would make it possible to receive spiritually generated truth.

Guests, while they remain in this natural condition, view everything they see through only the perspective and understanding of their natural surroundings. Some non-Manual religions emphasize spiritual insights, but because they are generated from the Serpent, their spiritual clarity is mixed with deception and error, and they never reach the truth sourced in the Game Master.

Evolution is not the "obvious" choice based on facts or data; it is the *natural* choice of guests who are "naturally minded" or only tuned in to the non-spiritual aspects of the game environment. Guests could call evolution an intellectually-based perspective, and they would be correct, but that also describes the limitations of their one-dimensional understanding.

The transition from non-life to life forms, as in abiogenesis, has never been demonstrated or replicated by science, so all evolutionists engage in their own version of faith wish-casting to make it so. If creating a chemical soup to generate life were possible, the Serpent would most certainly have been creating his own life forms since eons ago, not to mention our own scientists today. Creating life forms would never be merely for academic purposes.

The process of forming life can be described but not fully understood or replicated.

> The challenge for abiogenesis (origin of life) researchers is to explain how such a complex and tightly interlinked system could develop by evolutionary steps, as at first sight all its parts are necessary to enable it to function. For example, a cell, whether the LUCA [last universal common ancestor] or in a modern organism, copies its DNA with the DNA polymerase enzyme, which is in turn produced by translating the DNA polymerase gene in the DNA. Neither the enzyme nor the DNA can be produced without the other. The evolutionary process could have involved molecular self-replication, self-assembly such as of cell membranes, and autocatalysis. Nonetheless, the transition of non-life to life has never been observed experimentally.
>
> The precursors to the development of a living cell like the LUCA are clear enough, if disputed in their details: a habitable world is formed with a supply of minerals and liquid water. Prebiotic synthesis creates a range of simple organic compounds, which are assembled into polymers such as proteins and RNA. The process after the LUCA, too, is readily understood: biological evolution caused the development of a wide range of species with varied forms and biochemical capabilities. The derivation of living things such as the LUCA from simple components, however, is far from understood ("Abiogenesis" n.d., ¶ 7–8).

There is no mechanism where science can factor in the phenomenon of a spiritual creative force. The Game Master said that everything today (observable) came from nothing (unobservable), but science starts with something already existing (observable) and ends with today's results (observable).

Fundamentally, debates between evolutionist and creationist scientists are clashes between two irreconcilable views that use the same data: intellectually based versus spiritually based. It is not a matter of smart versus stupid, but that is the best way that many guests understand these conflicting views. Guest views of earth origins are more likely to equate faith with wish-casting.

It is not reasonable to expect a guest to suspend disbelief and attempt to understand a spiritual perspective when they have no spiritual means to process it. If guests want to reach the Game Master, He said that He left enough clues for them in the very natural world that they claim to observe (Rom. 1:18–21).

> THERE IS NO MECHANISM WHERE SCIENCE CAN FACTOR IN THE PHENOMENON OF A SPIRITUAL CREATIVE FORCE.

Because the earth's origin was unobserved, that is, it was not observed or recorded as history in real-time by any player, it will forever be a theory held by faith regardless of which side a player believes. It may be a settled fact in the minds of the proponents of each view, but that fact is still faith-based.

The question is: *whose version do you choose to believe, the Game Master's faith-derived version or the Serpent's alternate intellectually-derived version?*

Evolution and time. Let's deal with a point of disagreement among the theories: although evolution (the origin of species) requires eons of time to make it a workable idea, *it does not follow* that evolution actually occurred simply because the earth may be eons of time old. There is always a necessary pairing of evolution with an ages-old earth, but those are actually two different, unrelated topics.

You do not need to have a young earth for a literal six-day creation cycle to occur as described in Genesis 1, but you cannot have evolution without an ages-old earth. Don't assume that an old earth must equal a need to believe in the evolutionary process. Various interpretations of the Manual's text result in differences in creation theory accounts.

Pre-game environment. Guests typically hold to an evolution theory scenario for earth origin, which may have several theory types. Among members, there are at least three major creation scenario theories, two of which are the young earth creation theory view and the gap theory creationism view, also called the ruin-restitution theory.

Both theories adhere to a literal six-day creation event, but what happened before that event is where these two views widely differ. We will address both accounts, but the young earth theory can most easily be found on an Internet search as its proponents have a stronger search engine presence with Larry Ollison stating that an estimated 70 percent of members hold this view (Ollison 2023, min. 10:00).

The third view, the day-age creation theory or old Earth creationism, inserts ages of millions of years for each of the six-day creation days. This third view will not be discussed since it is impractical in the sequence of creation and is said to create contradictions in the fossil record ("What Is the Day-Age Theory." n.d., entire article).

Hindu creationism. Hindu creationism is another perspective on the creation story. Here are some brief remarks about its theories:

> Hindu creationism also known as Vedic creationism is a type of religious old earth creationism. Historian of science Ronald Numbers has commented that "Hindu Creationists have insisted on the antiquity of humans, who they believe appeared fully formed as long, perhaps, as trillions of years ago." The views of Hindu creationism are based on the Vedas, which depict an extreme antiquity of the universe and history of the earth.
>
> [Dayananda Saraswati] argued that God designed the physical bodies of all species 1.96 billions years ago on earth and on other planets at the beginning of the present cosmic cycle. He stated that God conjoined the bodies with pre-existing souls and that different species were created and distributed to souls in accord to their karma from the previous cosmic cycle.
>
> Vedic creationism holds a view of the world derived largely from the Bhagavad Gita. Vedic creationism was also promoted by ISKCON devotees Michael Cremo and Richard L. Thompson, authors of the 1993 book *Forbidden Archeology*. They argue that human beings are distinct species that have existed for billions of years. Vedic creationists are known to search for anomalies and reinterpret the fossil record to make it fit with their metaphysical assumptions ("Hindu Views on Evolution" n.d., ¶ 5–7).

Hinduism is a group of distinct intellectual or philosophical points of view, rather than a rigid common set of beliefs. It includes a range of viewpoints about the origin of life. There is no single story of creation due to the dynamic diversity of Hinduism, and these are derived from various sources like Vedas, some from the Brahmanas, some from Puranas; some are philosophical, based on concepts, and others are narratives. Hindu texts do not provide a single canonical account of the creation; they mention a range of theories of the creation of the world, some of which are apparently contradictory ("Hindu Cosmology" n.d., ¶ 16).

Young earth creationism. This creation theory is the most well-known view for most players because of high-profile publicized debates, many of which are available online. Its proponents are most often referenced in the media. When guests criticize members and their faith in their creation views, young earth creationism is the view to which they likely refer.

The young earth creation theory's account of a literal six-day creation *also includes the creation of the universe with planet Earth* as part of that six-day timeline, and it *excludes any timeline gaps* to account for earth's aged appearance (Chapman 2016, min. 2:00–26:31). The Omphalos Hypothesis of a young earth is that it was created with an aged or mature look since Noah's flood only 4,350 years ago may not account for all the damage and erosion on its surface ("Omphalos Hypothesis" n.d., ¶ 1–4).

Another tenet is that there was no death of any kind from the creation until the fall of Adam into sin (Hodge 2010, ¶ 30–33). (Rom. 5:12; 1 Cor. 15:21; Gen. 1:29–30; Gen. 9:3). This brings up a question: Why was there a tree of life in the Garden if death was not a factor in the game at that point? After Adam and Eve ate the forbidden fruit and were confronted, the tree of life option was immediately taken off the table and it was guarded by cherubim and a flaming sword.

This would seem to imply that death was possible from the start of the game. Perhaps Adam and Eve didn't have time to die since it took almost a thousand years from the start of the game. How long do you think the Serpent dawdled before he confronted Eve? A month? A week? A couple of days? Certainly not a thousand years.

Ken Ham from Answers in Genesis says in an online video that, in conservative colleges they have polled, the theology departments believe more in an aged earth while the science departments believe more in a young earth (Ham 2022, entire video). Answers in Genesis and the Institute for Creation Research websites provide in-depth explanations for a young earth creation (Chapman 2016, entire video; Institute for Creation Research 2022, entire article). A Creation Museum and a life-size Noah's Ark display providing young earth information are located in northern Kentucky.

Gap creationism. This is also called the ruin-restitution theory. This description is not theistic evolution like the day-age creation theory. Gap creationism is a popular creation theory that predates Darwin (1859) by eighty-three years—since 1776—as theologians studied to reconcile the Manual text when scientists were developing new understandings of historical geology in the eighteenth century.

The gap creation theory interprets the Hebrew language used in the opening verses of the Manual to render an account of a previous or original earth condition before the six-day creation event, which was possibly teeming with life that was destroyed under the Game Master's judgment. This theory also affirms that the entire universe was created in Genesis 1:1 before the following six-day creation sequence.

The darkness that was "upon the face of the deep" could be described as a palpable spiritual darkness, which also resulted in a physical darkness like what occurred as a judgment in the ninth plague of the ten plagues of Egypt, where the Egyptians were in deep darkness that they could feel and that immobilized them for three days while the Israelites next door still had light during the day (Exod. 10:20–29). Such darkness will happen again during the coming Apocalypse era, where players will be plunged into darkness by the fifth guardian judgment and will gnaw their tongues in anguish while cursing the Game Master because they were scorched by the fourth guardian's judgment (Rev. 16:8–11).

So, when the Game Master said, "Let there be light," it could have been a literal pronouncement that a judgment over the planet was lifted and literal light could again reach its surface. When the Manual says the earth became formless and void through a suggested judgment upon it, there is no indication of how long it took before that happened or how long it remained in that condition.

The gap theory view of creation uses the translation or interpretation of the Manual text to agree in verse one of Genesis that the Game Master created a complete heaven and earth universe. This universe could have been left to develop in a prehistoric age into a mature creation like we see today. Verse two of Genesis can be translated that something went wrong on planet Earth before the six-day creation event of verse three. Some proponents of the gap theory of creation include dinosaurs in the timeline, while other creationists say they were created with the six-day creation event. There is a question whether prehistoric humans existed in an original earth who were not technically created in the image of God and predated Adam.

Because there were cataclysmic events that scar the earth and could have affected the oceans, these could account for the extinction of prehistoric land and sea life. It is possible that some dinosaurs were created once again during the six-day creation event while others were left buried in the past ages. The Manual text of Job (after Noah's flood) indicates a dinosaur presence during his lifetime.

There are about fifty-three super volcanoes (Volcanic Explosive Index [VEI] magnitude of 8) around the globe with many like Yellowstone that have erupted more than once ("List of Largest Volcanic Eruptions" n.d., entire article). There are an estimated 2,200 monogenetic volcanoes in the southwestern United States and Mexican state of Sonora, with at least three super volcanoes in the western United States (Huber 2021, ¶ 1; Hsu 2021, ¶ 1–2, 5).

Then add the forty-four known asteroid strikes of twelve miles or more (20 km) pockmarking the globe from a total of 190 known impacts ("List of Impact Structures on Earth" n.d., entire article), including the one in the Yucatan that is said to have wiped out the dinosaurs, plus the one six times bigger in South Africa being 36 miles wide (58 km) that created the 300-mile (500 km) Vredefort Crater, which was said to have caused the earth to shake for half an hour and boil the ocean tops, not to mention any ensuing tsunamis, earthquakes, terrain changes, and acidic oceans (Prigg 2014, ¶ 1–5).

There is a tale of phenomenal destructive geologic and atmospheric forces etched on the face of the earth that creationists also say contributed to the ice age following Noah's flood. An interpretation of the Manual with a previous pre-creation judgment on planet Earth may account for the dinosaurs' sudden extinction with all the alleged and still-missing evolutionary links, and it does not contradict the text of the Manual (the Game Master judgments include the use of natural forces or catastrophic forces of nature). Since no one was there, and the Manual isn't explicit about the sequence of this evidence, we are left with room for conjecture from its comments and the evidence seen around us.

Could we be living in the second age of planet Earth, which started at the Genesis creation and before the coming age of the new heaven and new earth after this earth's surface and atmosphere are destroyed by fire? The conditions governing each age are not necessarily dependent on a previous age or future age. Frankly, I'd like to know what happened to Mars, and what's up with the asteroid belt?

For detailed explanations of this creation theory that include Manual references, plus the matter of pre-creation life and geology before Adam picked himself up off the ground, see the first chapters of the book, *Genesis 6 Giants*, by Stephen Quayle˙ (Quayle 2013, 8–24). His book continues from there to lay out many more issues and timelines of Serpent havoc on our current game world experience that are not mentioned in this book.

Derek Prince has a Spiritual Conflict audio series. Volume 1 spells out a pre-Adamic period related to the rebellion of Lucifer, now known as the Serpent or the Devil (Prince n.d.c). If you prefer a video explanation of a gap theory, see Chuck Missler in his *Gap Theory* session, which can be found online (Missler 2003, entire video).

The Manual is a telling of the current Game of Life and its significance to the current players. It does not need to detail earth events that may have happened before the clock started on our current timeline. For players, death was introduced into the current Game of Life when Adam committed the first game violation (Rom. 5:12). What happened in a potential age before paradise does not have to be framed in the current game parameters.

The conditions governing each age are not necessarily dependent on a previous age or future age. The coming bonus round age with a new heaven and new earth will not include the pain, death, sorrows, or game violations we experience in today's game level (Larken 1920, 434–446). For members, there will be a total memory wipe that today ever happened, where the Manual says that *the former things will not be remembered or come to mind in the age to come* (Isa. 65:17; Rev. 21:1–5). You will have a fresh start and will not be defined by what happened to you here and now.

Technology. In his book, *Dead Men's Secrets*, archaeologist Jonathan Gray discusses the incredible technology that has been found among ancient civilizations around the world, including evidence of a previous nuclear holocaust about 4,000 years ago. Here is a timeline he constructed showing the rise and fall of technology across the millennia from Adam up to its recent revival (Gray 2014, 40).

(Gray 2014, 40)

(Gray 2014, 40)

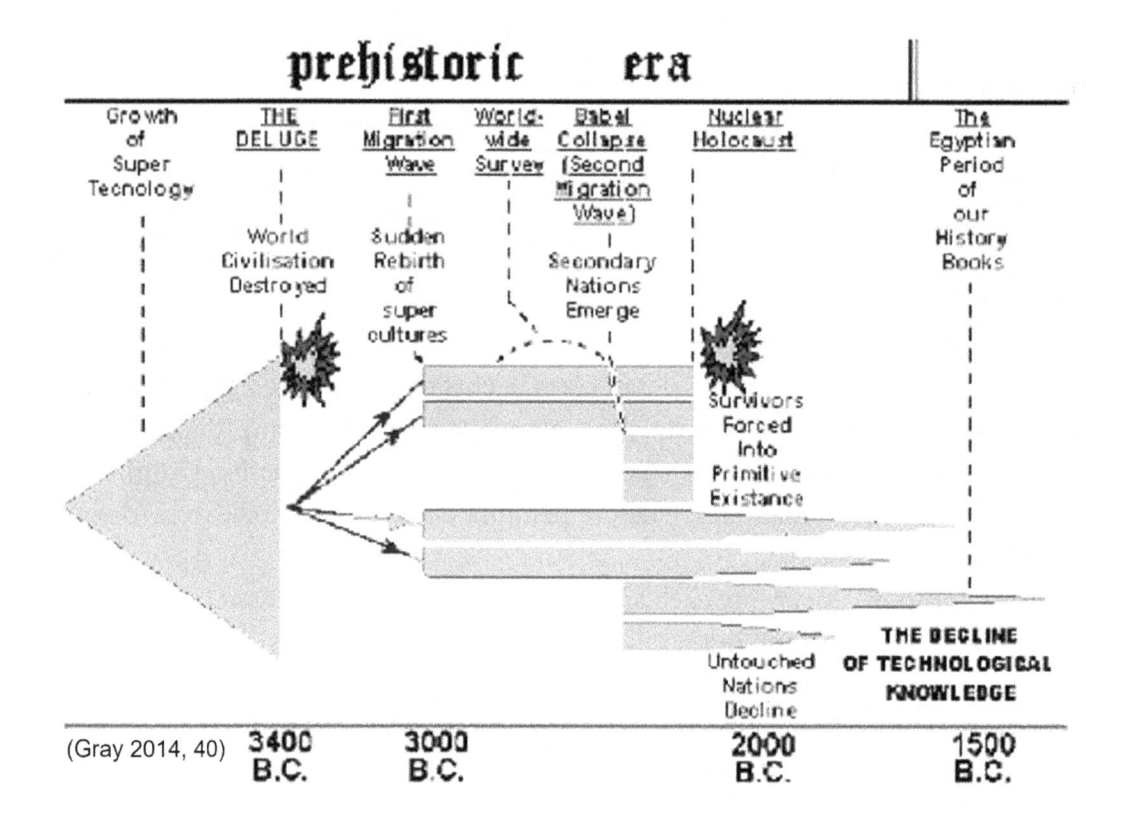

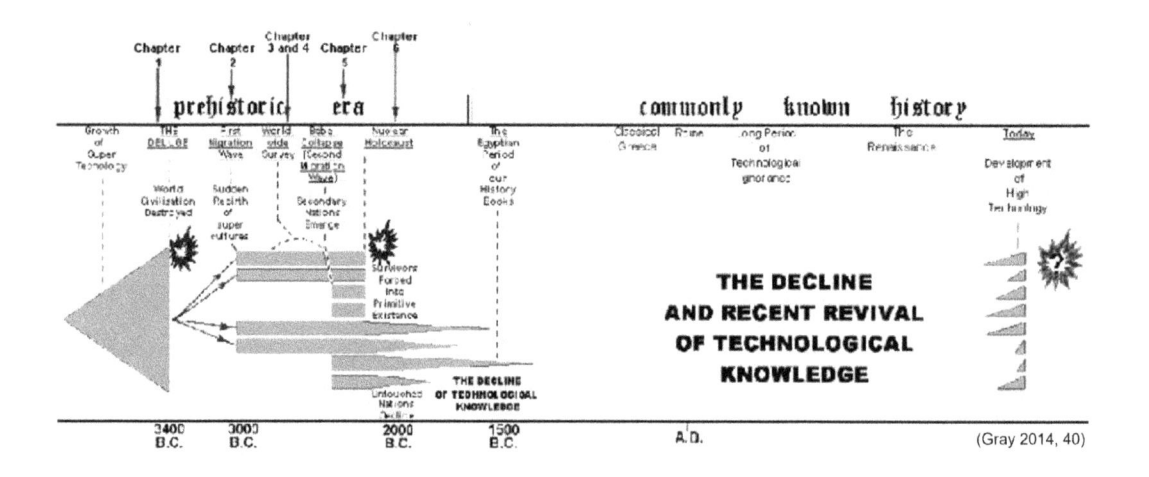

New Game Environment

After the current Game of Life ends with an apparent total destruction of this game world around a thousand years from now, the bonus round will be introduced, which includes a new game world and new heaven environment (Isa. 65:17; 2 Pet. 3:10–13; Rev. 21:1). All guests will be eliminated from this round, along with their Serpent Boss, his henchmen, and all the minions. Only members and the Game Master's guardians move on to the bonus round.

This reset of the game environment will also eliminate the personal effects of the current corrupt game environment upon the players. Evil is banished; health, happiness, and life will be perpetual, with the Game Master ensuring those benefits for all players thereafter (Rev. 16:1–21; 21:1–7; 22:1–3).

Golden Ticket – Eternal Life

There is only one way to the bonus round: through the One. *Nobody* gets to the Game Master except through Him. Tickets are not issued to anyone who believes in the One *plus something else* in addition to Him as their guarantee. He is the only way to cancel the game violations and move you on to the bonus round. Period (John 14:5–6).

The One obeyed the Game Master and sacrificed Himself for all the players. Then the Spirit Master resurrected him to become the Advocate to the Game Master for believing members (1 John 2:1–2). Now, the Game Master requires all players to acknowledge the One as the Messiah and believe in Him as their only way to the bonus round (John 3:16–20). The Manual says there is only one Mediator between the Game Master and players: the One player, Christ Jesus (1 Tim. 2:5). Nobody needs a priest or pastor to petition God on their behalf; you can do it yourself directly through the One.

Those who swear loyalty to the Game Master through the completed sacrifice of the One and make Him their advocate are issued a golden ticket to guarantee their entry to the bonus round. All ticket holders have their name entered into the Book of Life. The Spirit Master seals their decision, and nobody except the Game Master can expunge their name from the Book of Life (John 10:27–30; Rev. 3:5; 22:9).

In plain language, God created people who promptly rejected Him. Then He let those people He created kill His Son, Jesus Christ, so that all created people, including you, could have another chance to be like Him. *Nobody loves you more than the God who created you* (John 3:16; 1 John 3:2).

Golden ticket qualification. All players can qualify to receive a golden ticket, from the kindest and gentlest souls to the worst and meanest monsters among us, from the poorest and weakest waifs to the richest and most powerful dignitaries. Because it cannot be earned, any player with a capacity to choose may receive a ticket.

For those without a capacity to understand and make a choice, remarks in the Manual suggest that the Game Master has a provision to accept them. Kiosk teachings call this the Age of Accountability, where a child is too young to understand (2 Sam. 12:22–24; Jonah 4:10–11). Anecdotal accounts of those who claim to have briefly passed over to heaven also include meeting sibling players who had died in the womb through a miscarriage. This topic remains an open question, but members tend to believe that the Game Master extends grace to such helpless players.

The One paid the cost for all golden tickets in the middle of the Game of Life. This includes the cost of the past players and all future players up to today and beyond. Players don't have to clean up their act before they qualify for a ticket. The Game Master promised to help them qualify, delivering on that promise with one eternal sacrifice. Master player Paul explains:

> "But God demonstrates his own love for us in this: While we were still sinners, Christ died for us. Since we have now been justified by his blood, how much more shall we be saved from God's wrath through him!" (Rom. 5:8–9 NIV).

All that is left is for each player to choose to sign over their rights to live as they please during this game level and instead live to please the Game Master and invest their gameplay for His rewards in the bonus round. That is your price for reaching the bonus round.

> Do you not know that your body is a temple of the Holy Spirit who is within you, whom you have [received as a gift] from God, and that you are not your own [property]? You were bought with a price [you were actually purchased with the precious blood of Jesus and made His own]. So then, honor and glorify God with your body (1 Cor. 6:19–20 AMP).

You can absolutely know today that your game violations are forgiven and that you have a reserved place in the bonus round (Acts 26:15–18; Rom. 4:6–8; Eph. 1:3–12; Col. 1:9–17; Col. 2:13–15; 1 Pet. 1:3–5).

Afshin Javid, an Iranian Shiite Muslim who had an interaction with the One, offers an insight of the difference between Islam and the Manual. He said,

> We say, "In the name of god who is merciful and gracious," but we don't know if we are forgiven until the day of judgment. That is why there is not one single verse in the whole Koran that says, "Mohammed is in

the heaven." He must wait like all people for the day of resurrection, and all shall be judged on that day.

> So, who is this god that says, "I forgive you," and I feel forgiven today? And I asked, and I said, "Who are you that can forgive me, and I feel forgiven today?" And he says, "I am the way, and the truth, and the life." The moment I heard those words, I knew it's of great importance, but I had absolutely no idea what that meant. I still had no clue who this god is. So, I asked him, "What is your name?" "Jesus Christ, the living God," He answered. And the moment He spoke those words, it was as if every single bone was taken out of my body, and I fell on my face to the ground and I started weeping in the presence of God. I just wept ("Former Muslim Terrorist Sees Jesus and Becomes a Christian English with Arabic Subtitles" 2016, min. 11:04).

If you believe that you must wait until life is over before you can know whether you reached the bonus round, the Serpent is trying to punch your ticket to hell. The Game Master stresses that today is the day to make sure you know where you are going (Ps. 95:7–8; Luke 12:16–21; Heb. 3:7–9, 14–16; 4:6–8; 9:27–28). Master player Paul wrote Timothy about his assurance in the bonus round, saying,

> This is why I suffer as I do. Still, I am not ashamed; for I know Him [and I am personally acquainted with Him] whom I have believed [with absolute trust and confidence in Him and in the truth of His deity], and I am persuaded [beyond any doubt] that He is able to guard that which I have entrusted to Him until that day [when I stand before Him] (1 Tim. 1:12 AMP).

Christianity is the only religion where the believer's God comes and lives in them. Evangelist and Author Leonard Ravenhill relayed a story of a Chinese scholar who was,

CHRISTIANITY IS THE ONLY RELIGION WHERE THE BELIEVER'S GOD COMES AND LIVES IN THEM.

> Given a copy of the New Testament. He had read the Koran, the Vedas, and all the sacred books. The man said to him, "Did you read the New Testament through?" He said, "I did." "What's the most amazing thing?" The scholar said, "The most amazing thing is in Ephesians chapter two: *In time past you walked according to the*

course of this world, according to the prince of the power of the air, and at the end of that same chapter, it says that you are the *habitation of God* (Eph. 2:1–5, 18–22). So, does your God live inside of you? If so, that's the most awesome thing I've ever read. I've read all those other sacred books, but I've never read where a man's God comes and makes the man the habitation of God." Does Christ live in you? (Ravenhill n.d., entire video).

Golden ticket history. The actual acquisition of a golden ticket has always been a transaction of faith toward the Game Master since the start of the game. However, before the One came as the official atonement for the sins of mankind, the expression of faith involved a real sacrificial transaction, complete with a dead animal.

Upon their expulsion from paradise in the garden of Eden for the sin of disobedience in eating the forbidden fruit, a blood sacrifice was required of Adam and Eve and all their descendants thereafter to symbolize a player's expectation of faith that the Game Master's promised atoning sacrifice of His own divine Son would cover the player's game violations. Only designated animals were declared to be "clean" and suitable for sacrifice to cover sins: bulls, sheep, goats, or doves. There were other types of sacrifices, but our only focus here is on the one that covers players' game violations (sins). Human sacrifice is condemned as a detestable abomination to the Game Master (Jer. 7:30–32; 19:5; 32:35).

At the garden of Eden, the One was promised to be brought into the game by the Game Master. Starting back then after their garden expulsion, the symbolic atoning sacrifices continued for millennia until the One was born around 0 BC and died as the Game Master's official atoning sacrifice for humanity around AD 33, where he bruised the Serpent's head (defeated him) as prophesied at the garden of Eden (Gen. 3:13–15).

> The sacrifice of bulls and goats could never take away game violations, and sacrifices had to be performed year after year. With His death, the One offered Himself as a final sacrifice once and for all, permanently completing the requirement of paying for the sins of mankind and ending forever the need to sacrifice animals again (Heb. 10:1–4, 12–14, paraphrased).

Then He rose from the dead three days later and now sits on the throne with the Game Master at headquarters, where He makes intercession for us on our behalf to the Game Master (Heb. 10). The Manual says that *the One, who was perfect and never sinned, became sin itself on our behalf, so that we can become righteous like God, because with His stripes (from the flogging He was given in addition to crucifixion) we are healed* (2 Cor. 5:21; 1 Pet. 2:24, paraphrased).

Golden ticket benefits

The golden ticket is a game changer for players both in this game level and in the bonus round. It immediately legally restores the player to a position of right-standing with the Game Master, where their condition of righteousness is viewed through the perfect nature of the One Who became their Advocate. Now, when the Game Master views a member, He sees a player who has met the conditions to access the previously unattainable holy place of headquarters. This allows the player to call in favors from the Game Master when they invoke the name of the One on their behalf. Simply put, it is *praying with faith to God in Jesus' name*.

Players do not automatically become perfect in their gameplay or relationships. Because we inherited a corrupted nature when we were born on the Serpent's team, we continue to struggle with the passions and vices of the game world. The golden ticket empowers us to begin a transformation of our character so we are no longer enslaved by the bad habits we developed. The spirit was given new life so the soul (mind, will and emotions) can make a fresh start on a new path toward the divine nature.

As the Spirit Master takes up residence within the player, the outcome of this spiritual connectedness results in what are called the fruit of the Spirit: love, joy, peace, patience, goodness, faith, and self-control (Gal. 5:22–23; Eph. 5:8–10). The process of having these characteristics should happen effortlessly. Trees don't produce fruit through a struggle with nature but through a natural transfer of nutrients from the soil. In the same way, players don't clean up their lives with a list of rules but through a daily connection with the Game Master as they meditate and reflect on the principles of the Manual. Simply put, *read your Bible and chat with God (pray)*.

Experiencing the fruit of the Spirit should include complete inner peace even when your world is raging through turmoil and crisis. Life does not have to displace your divine tranquility (Phil. 4:6–7).

The golden ticket also includes the favor of the Game Master to receive miracles and the power of the Game Master to make miracles happen for you. Most players pray for miracles, but few practice making miracles. The One explains the ways to accomplish both (John 15:7–8).

The golden ticket gives players a family relationship with the Game Master, where they are adopted as His chosen ones. Their perpetual membership is ensured by the power of the Game Master, and access to the bonus round is assured.

Issued ticket. The Game of Life is about your faith, your belief system, and what you do because of it. Golden tickets are only issued to those who believe the Game Master's account of the One (Jesus). In its simplest form, the One said:

> "For God so loved the world that He gave His only begotten Son, that whoever believes in Him should not perish but have everlasting life. He who believes in Him is not condemned; but he who does not believe is condemned already, because he has not believed in the name of the only begotten Son of God" (John 3:16, 18 NKJV).

His cousin, John the Baptist, concludes this teaching, saying:

> "For He whom God has sent speaks the words of God, for God does not give the Spirit by measure. The Father loves the Son, and has given all things into His hand. He who believes in the Son has everlasting life; and he who does not believe the Son shall not see life, but the wrath of God abides on him" (John 3:34–36 NKJV).

The apostle Paul summarized the foundational essence of the Manual's gospel:

> "For I delivered unto you first of all that which I also received, how that Christ died for our sins according to the scriptures; And that he was buried, and that he rose again the third day according to the scriptures" (1 Cor. 15:3–4 KJV).

He also goes on to explain why the resurrection matters:

> Now if Christ is proclaimed as raised from the dead, how can some of you say that there is no resurrection of the dead? But if there is no resurrection of the dead, then not even Christ has been raised. And if Christ has not been raised, then our preaching is in vain and your faith is in vain.

> We are even found to be misrepresenting God, because we testified about God that he raised Christ, whom he did not raise if it is true that the dead are not raised. For if the dead are not raised, not even Christ has been raised. And if Christ has not been raised, your faith is futile and you are still in your sins. Then those also who have fallen asleep [died] in Christ have perished. If in Christ we have hope in this life only, we are of all people most to be pitied.
>
> But in fact Christ has been raised from the dead, the firstfruits of those who have fallen asleep. For as by a man came death, by a man has come also the resurrection of the dead. For as in Adam all die, so also in Christ shall all be made alive (1 Cor. 15:12–22 ESV).

The gospel has power to transform a soul through belief:

> "For I am not ashamed of the gospel of Christ, for it is the power of God to salvation for everyone who believes, for the Jew first and also for the Greek. For in it the righteousness of God is revealed from faith to faith; as it is written, 'The just shall live by faith'" (Rom. 1:16–17 NKJV).

The *Apostle's Creed* was first mentioned in the fourth century at an assembly in Milan. It is compiled as a set of core beliefs or a statement of faith for members:

> I believe in God, the Father Almighty, the Creator of heaven and earth, and in Jesus Christ, His only Son, our Lord. Who was conceived of the Holy Spirit, born of the Virgin Mary, suffered under Pontius Pilate, was crucified, died, and was buried. He descended into hell. The third day He arose again from the dead. He ascended into heaven and sits at the right hand of God the Father Almighty, whence He shall come to judge the living and the dead. I believe in the Holy Spirit, the holy catholic church, the communion of saints, the forgiveness of sins, the resurrection of the body, and life everlasting. Amen ("The Apostles' Creed" n.d.).

The "holy catholic church" does not refer to the Roman Catholic church. Instead, it refers to the universal church of the Lord Jesus Christ, the body of believers.

Ticket acquisition

Finally, the Manual provides a succinct format of how a guest can instantly become a member.

> Because if you acknowledge and confess with your mouth that Jesus is Lord [recognizing His power, authority, and majesty as God], and believe in your heart that God raised Him from the dead, you will be saved. For with the heart a person believes [in Christ as Savior] resulting in his justification [that is, being made righteous—being freed of the guilt of sin and made acceptable to God]; and with the mouth he acknowledges and confesses [his faith openly], resulting in and confirming [his] salvation. For the Scripture says, "Whoever believes in Him [whoever adheres to, trusts in, and relies on Him] will not be disappointed [in his expectations]" (Isa. 28:16). For there is no distinction between Jew and Gentile; for the same Lord is Lord over all [of us], and [He is] abounding in riches (blessings) for all who call on Him [in faith and prayer]. For "**whoever calls on the name of the Lord** [in prayer] **will be saved**" (Joel 2:32; Rom. 10:9–13 AMP, emphasis added).

This is the only pathway to the divine, where we can realize our goal to be made perfect through His power (1 John 3:2–3).

Fire insurance

Some players agree to get a golden ticket and join the Game Master's team only for insurance from the fires of hell because they are led to believe it costs them nothing. They have no intention of actually allowing the Game Master to control their lives, so they continue to live as they please, only now they may attend a kiosk too. They call themselves members but don't act like one. The attitudes they have, the decisions they make, and the things they do still have all the markings of a guest.

The Game Master said players cannot mock Him with their games because He knows their motives and sincerity. He warns that those who try stunts like that are only fooling themselves (1 Cor. 6:9–10; Gal. 6:7–9).

This may also be true of guests who were frightened into a golden ticket response because the terrors of hell were dramatically expressed to them in a story or film, but they didn't have a genuine repentance from sin and a faith toward God experience. Still, some may come to a point of true conversion in these situations.

Losing golden tickets

Is it possible to lose your golden ticket? This topic will be discussed in more detail in the Final Points section, but here is something to ponder. The One said that eternal life is knowing the one true God and Jesus Christ whom He sent (John 17:3 paraphrased).

In the garden of Eden, Adam and Eve communed with the Game Master in the evenings (Gen 3:8–10). According to John 17:3, did Adam and Eve have eternal life? We may assume they had their golden tickets when they were created in the image of the Game Master and came to life and were experiencing this relational aspect of eternal life on a daily basis.

It isn't discussed whether they had their golden tickets during that period of Godly communion, but it is a big deal that they definitely didn't have them after eating the fruit of the tree of knowledge. Either, they lost their tickets or they didn't have them anyway which implies they weren't bonus round material when they were created.

Because the Game Master requires a choice from us, the test of the tree of knowledge was Adam's test whether he would obey the Game Master. How many times do you think the Serpent solicited Eve's response? Once, several times, days or weeks? If you were unknowingly going to live a thousand years, how long do you think you would have resisted the Serpent's cajoling you on a daily basis to eat the fruit?

We all may have our reasons for keeping the Game Master's offer of eternal life at an arm's distance, but Adam and Eve's need to hold out until their eventual death was a far more difficult endurance test than whatever challenges we face. If they had eaten from the tree of life before the tree of knowledge, their resistance would have had to last forever.

Their big decision was certainly a test of their loyalties which, if successfully passed throughout their thousand-year lifetimes, would have been the catalyst to impart access to the bonus round. This should also remind us that our loyalty to the One depends on our persistence to the very end of our gameplay (Matt. 11:6; 24:11–13; James 1:12; Rev. 2:10). The Game Master remarks about blotting names out of the book of life (Rev. 3:5), so it may seem that tickets can be issued and revoked. Whether or not you agree, make sure your own ticket is assured.

Game Violations – Sin, Iniquity, Transgression

Technically, sin is a violation of the law of God (Merriam-Webster 2024, ¶ 2). In this case, it refers to the Game Master's standard of perfection in keeping all the rules in the Manual. Unfortunately for the players, this is an all-or-nothing situation. If a player violates one single rule, he is charged with a violation of the whole Manual. That is why it took only one sin of disobedience to condemn Adam, and the rest of us, to hell (Rom. 5:12).

Violations are not only the bad stuff a player does; they also include good stuff the player didn't do—sins of commission and sins of omission. Violations mount up both coming and going. (James 2:8–13). For example, the Manual says to do a good deed to players when you have the means to help them (Prov. 3:27–28; 1 John 3:17).

Here's a question: if you oppress a poor or needy player—compound his hard life, a game violation, is that a double strike of commission *and* omission at the same time? He is oppressed, which is a commission violation, and he is not helped, which is an omission violation. Just ignoring his plight is also an omission violation (1 John 3:17).

What if you did something wrong a long time ago, but now you're a different person? Does that get taken off the table because you cleaned up your act? We tend to downplay bad things we did a while ago and consider it water under the bridge. We can't just wish them away; game violations have no statute of limitations (Ps. 62:11–12).

GAME VIOLATIONS HAVE NO STATUTE OF LIMITATIONS.

The point the Manual makes is that players cannot match the level of perfection required by the Game Master to reach the bonus round (Rom. 3:23; 6:23). Because the Game Master has zero tolerance for imperfection, the original rules section of the Manual, which includes the Big Ten, simply makes players aware of violation issues and points out the futility of trying to reach the bonus round by keeping too many rules to remember their entire lives (James 2:8–13).

Additionally, thanks to Papa Adam, all players are already born with game violations against them because they start out life on the Serpent's team, and there is nothing good or holy about him. Players need a heart transplant by getting the golden ticket which transfers them from the Serpent's team to the Game Master's team (Rom. 5:12; Eph. 5:8; 1 Thess. 5:4–6).

At the end of the game (at the Apocalypse, AKA the Day of the Lord, AKA Judgment Day), violations will be charged against all guests, and immediate payment is due (Rev. 20:11–15). Members are still held accountable for their gameplay, but the One already expunged their game violations when they got their golden ticket. They are working on scoring points for the Game Master and will be penalized based on how much of their play was a distraction and not valuable to Him. What's left and valuable will be their treasure and reward (1 Cor. 3:11–17).

Furthermore, you don't have to acknowledge the Game Master's law to be subject to it. You can play to the end of your game time and never give Him the time of day or act like He exists, but until you get on the Game Master's team where you are no longer measured by how you kept the Manual's Law, it will always apply to you.

If you plan to keep the Manual's rules to prove you are good, like keeping the Golden Rule (Matt. 7:12; Luke 16:31), you will be judged by the rules. *Friendly Advice:* It's best to forget to try to keep the rules and instead get your golden ticket so the rules won't be held against you—if there's no game violation on your record, you're not liable for the rules (Rom. 4:6–8).

Noahide laws

These are the original laws of the Game of Life. The Jewish Talmud identifies six laws the Game Master gave to Adam and then again with seven to Noah. Since we are all descendants of these two players, those universal laws apply to all humankind, both guest and member. These laws apply to you, whether you are religious or not and provide basic parameters for your well-being ("Noahide Laws: Judaism" 2023, ¶ 1–2).

The Chabad.org website explains the laws for all players.

> The 7 Noahide Laws are rules that all of us must keep, regardless of who we are or from where we come. Without these seven things, it would be impossible for humanity to live together in harmony.
>
> **Do not profane Gd's Oneness in any way.** Acknowledge that there is a single Gd who cares about what we are doing and desires that we take care of His world.
>
> **Do not curse your Creator.** No matter how angry you may be, do not take it out verbally against your Creator.
>
> **Do not murder**. The value of human life cannot be measured. To destroy a single human life is to destroy the entire world—because, for that person, the world has ceased to exist. It follows that by sustaining a single human life, you are sustaining an entire universe.
>
> **Do not eat a limb of a still-living animal.** Respect the life of all Gd's creatures. As intelligent beings, we have a duty not to cause undue pain to other creatures.

Do not steal. Whatever benefits you receive in this world, make sure that none of them are at the unfair expense of someone else.

Harness and channel the human libido. Incest, adultery, rape, and homosexual relations are forbidden. The family unit is the foundation of human society. Sexuality is the fountain of life and so nothing is more holy than the sexual act. So, too, when abused, nothing can be more debasing and destructive to the human being.

Establish courts of law and ensure justice in our world. With every small act of justice, we are restoring harmony to our world, synchronizing it with a supernal order. That is why we must keep the laws established by our government for the country's stability and harmony.

These laws were communicated by Gd to Adam and Noah, ancestors of all human beings. That is what makes these rules universal, for all times, places and people:

Laws made by humans may change according to circumstance. But laws made by the Creator of all souls over all of time remain the same for all people at all times.

If we would fulfill these laws just because they make sense to us, then we would change them, according to our convenience. We would be our own god. But when we understand that they are the laws of a supreme Gd, we understand that they can not be changed, just as He does not change (Chabad n.d., ¶ 1–11).

Did anyone ever tell you about these laws? Most of these are folded into the Big Ten that Moses received, which makes us think that those laws only apply to Israel. However, the moral framework of the Big Ten is encapsulated in the Noahide laws, which still apply to you. These Noahide laws are the reason all religions and the nations they represent have retained similar moral codes throughout history.

Well, "don't covet" isn't in here, and that's not really stealing. The One said that as you think in your heart, you have already committed the violation. His Sermon on the Mount revisits several of the Noahide laws in a way that speaks to our motives. This includes His view of divorce (Matt. 5:17–18).

"But those things which proceed out of the mouth come from the heart, and they defile a man. For out of the heart proceed evil thoughts, murders, adulteries, fornications, thefts, false witness, blasphemies. These are the things which defile a man, but to eat with unwashed hands does not defile a man" (Matt. 15:18–20 NKJV).

Do you know anyone who keeps all the Noahide laws? Do you know anyone who keeps any of these laws? Most of us are not cruel to animals, but looking at society around us and how our society acts on the Internet, all the rest of the laws are constantly being broken. Increasing numbers of players are comfortable breaking them publicly. We are each accountable for our part in keeping them.

THE BIG TEN

There are 613 commandments in the Torah. Of these, the 10 Commandments are the most famous set of rules in the game world. They are broad statements of sin against God and man. This is not a random list of rules but are categorized into two types: rules toward the Game Master (commandments 1–4) and rules toward fellow players (commandments 5–10). They are then reduced to two rules, where the One summarizes the entire canon of law and all the prophets:

> "Jesus replied: 'Love the Lord your God with all your heart and with all your soul and with all your mind.' This is the first and greatest commandment. And the second is like it: 'Love your neighbor as yourself.' All the Law and the Prophets hang on these two commandments" (Matt. 22:37–40 ESV; Gal. 5:14).

Two rules cover all conduct of life: *Love God, Love Others*. Notice that most of the commandments are stated in a negative context, but the outcome of what should be produced in the heart and actions of the player are positive results toward the Game Master and other players.

The 10 Commandments from Patheos.com and listed in Exodus 20 are stated here in *italics*.

The First Commandment: *You shall have no other gods before me.*

The Second Commandment: *You shall not make for yourself a carved image, or any likeness of anything that is in heaven above, or that is in* *the earth beneath, or that is in the water under the earth. You shall not bow down to them or serve them, for I the Lord your God am a jealous God, visiting the iniquity of the fathers on the children to the third and the fourth generation of those who hate me, but showing steadfast love to thousands of those who love me and keep my commandments.*

The Third Commandment: *You shall not take the name of the Lord your God in vain, for the Lord will not hold him guiltless who takes his name in vain*—irreverent use of God's Word.

The Fourth Commandment: *Remember the Sabbath day, to keep it holy. Six days you shall labor, and do all your work, but the seventh day is a Sabbath to the Lord your God. On it you shall not do any work, you, or your son, or your daughter, your male servant, or your female servant, or your livestock, or the sojourner who is within your gates. For in six days the Lord made heaven and earth, the sea, and all that is in them, and rested on the seventh day. Therefore the Lord blessed the Sabbath day and made it holy.*

The Fifth Commandment: *Honor your father and your mother*—breaking civil laws when taught by parents to obey the laws, failing to take care of aged parents, failing to take care of sick parents, fighting with and/or speaking evil about siblings—*that your days may be long in the land that the Lord your God is giving you.*

The Sixth Commandment: *You shall not murder.*

The Seventh Commandment: *You shall not commit adultery.*

The Eighth Commandment: *You shall not steal.*

The Ninth Commandment: *You shall not bear false witness against your neighbor.*

The Tenth Commandment: *You shall not covet your neighbor's house; you shall not covet your neighbor's wife, or his male servant, or his female* *servant, or his ox, or his donkey, or anything that is your neighbor's* (Wellman 2014).

This was the Protestant rendering of the 10 Commandments, which most closely follows the Jewish numbering from Hebrew. However, there is some difference in how Commandments 1 and 2 are rendered between the Protestants and Jews. The Roman Catholic church entirely removes Commandment 2 regarding carved/created images, Commandment 4 is changed from the Sabbath Day (Saturday) to the Lord's Day (Sunday), and Commandment 10 is split into Commandments 9 and 10 to keep the total numbering at 10 Commandments (Ratzinger 1997, 496–497).

We refer to a "Big Ten Violation" based on this list of commands using the Protestant rendering.

New Testament commandments

The Big Ten from the Old Testament are referenced again in the New Testament. Additionally, about 30 to 50 commandments of the One are identified in the New Testament. One online site identifies an eye-popping 1,050 commandments across the New Testament in 69 categories.

These lists can be found online, and one set is shown below. It is best for members to be familiar with them since their membership status and gameplay are rated on whether they keep the One's commands. Of note, master player John remarks that the One's "commands are not burdensome" (1 John 5:3 NIV). Guests may be repulsed at the thought of keeping rules, but the context of rules for members is that their change of heart toward the Game Master also includes a new preference for playing the game His way and by His rules.

Reduced to their most basic essence, if a member follows the One's summary of "the law and the prophets" (Matt. 22:35–41) by loving the Game Master above all and loving others as the One loves us, all the New Testament rules are just details on that theme. To be sure, our ego can get in the way of keeping the rules by making us selfish or self-important, but when our perspective is toward the good of others, they are not burdensome to practice.

Here is a partial list of New Testament commands from Christian Apologetics and Research Ministry:

- repent
- follow him
- let your light shine

- be reconciled
- don't lust
- make no oaths
- don't resist evil with evil
- love and pray for your enemies
- be perfect (in love)
- don't judge
- don't give what is holy to dogs
- treat people as you want to be treated
- beware of false prophets
- follow Jesus
- confront brothers in private first
- forgive seven times seventy
- render to Caesar what is Caesar's
- love God
- love your neighbor
- keep guard against sin
- make disciples
- preach the gospel
- be on guard against greed
- invite the poor
- love one another (Slick 2014, ¶ 3–33).

Seven abominations

The Manual identifies seven game violations that are abominable (detestable or repulsive) to the Game Master.

> These six things the LORD hates; Indeed, seven are repulsive to Him: 1) A proud look [the attitude that makes one overestimate oneself and discount others], 2) a lying tongue, And 3) hands that shed innocent blood, 4) A heart that creates wicked plans, 5) Feet that run swiftly to evil, 6) A false witness who breathes out lies [even half-truths], And 7) one who spreads discord (rumors) among brothers (Prov. 6:16–19 AMP).

We may automatically respond that this list is not talking about us since we are not bad like that. Maybe you're just on the fringe of these abominations. See how you rate with this list as a fringe player.

Pride. Does your ego get the best of you? Do you put others down to prove you are better? Are you glad you're not a loser like that other player? Do you show off nice things to feel better than others? Are you racist?

Lying. Do you lie reflexively—the first thing out of your mouth when caught off guard by an unexpected question? Are you okay with a white lie or only a half-truth? Do you say a non-truth for a good reason? Do you lie as an acceptable part of your job, your position, your religion?

Shedding innocent blood. Do you hate someone without a good reason? Have you ever injured or killed someone who didn't deserve it? Have you participated in someone else's harm against the innocent? Have you had an abortion? Have you performed abortions? Is there someone you bully?

Devising wicked plans. Are you a conniver? Do you figure out how to get away with things? Do you scheme against other players? Do you show others how to cheat or game the system?

A false witness who lies. Do you cover for your friends, so they don't get caught? Do you falsely affirm someone else's story to keep them out of trouble? Do you falsely corroborate evidence to give yourself an advantage or to make someone else pay the price?

Feet that run to mischief. Do you carry out your wicked plans? Have you ever shoplifted or done a flash robbery or smash-and-grab? Do you make life hard for someone else? Are you part of a group that goes looking for trouble? Do you get into trouble to spite an authority figure?

One who spreads divisiveness, rumors. Do you keep things stirred up in your family, work, or school? Do you pit other players against each other? Are you a go-to for the best gossip or latest report? Are you a busybody? Are you a cyber-bully?

Most of these abominations are not even misdemeanors. Doing most may not break any civil or criminal laws. This list shows not just actions, but how much motives matter to the Game Master. They speak of issues of character.

Those questions reveal a path toward these abominations. Are you comfortable with this level of game violations? Do you accommodate or encourage others in these behaviors? Do you think the Game Master makes too much of these things? Are your little abominations okay with Him? Are you okay with forfeiting the bonus round to stick Him in the eye by continuing these things you enjoy and He despises?

How much leeway do you think there is on that narrow, difficult path to the bonus round? (Matt. 7:14; Rev. 21:8).

Notice that these abominations are character qualities of the Serpent. His downfall was pride (Isa. 14:12–14), he is the Father of Lies, he was a murderer from the beginning (John 8:44), and he is a thief whose objectives are to steal and to kill and to destroy (John 10:10). These are the opposite of the Game Master's qualities of love, joy, peace, patience, gentleness (kindness), goodness (benevolence), faithfulness, meekness (humility), and temperance (self-control) (Gal. 5:22–23; Eph. 5:9).

This list also proves that the Game Master and the Islam Allah are not the same god. Islam allows lying or deception toward infidels to hide their faith and calls for the shedding of innocent blood (infidels). Allah excuses or condones these. Those points are abominations to the Game Master, who is not tolerant of such behavior as Allah (Atalayar 2021, ¶ 1–10).

Rather, the outcome of players who practice behaviors that are abominable to the Game Master is to share the fate of their Serpent Boss at the end of the game:

> But as for the cowards and unbelieving and abominable [who are devoid of character and personal integrity and practice or tolerate immorality], and murderers, and sorcerers [with intoxicating drugs], and idolaters and occultists [who practice and teach false religions], and all the liars [who knowingly deceive and twist truth], their part will be in the lake that blazes with fire and brimstone, which is the second death (Rev. 21:8 AMP).

Three Abominations

Let's toss in a few more abominations and round it up to ten. 8) "He who justifies the wicked and 9) he who condemns the righteous are both alike an abomination to the LORD" (Prov. 17:15 ESV). And again, "Both of these deeply offend the Eternal: one who acquits the guilty and one who condemns the innocent" (Prov. 7:15 VOICE).

By the way, the Game Master refers here to the righteous (innocent) and wicked (guilty) based on His definitions of justice as spelled out in the Manual's moral code, not based on your creed or ideology which may not meet a Manual standard. Modern societal indoctrination too often colors our perspectives of right and wrong.

Whose side do you pick when the guilty party belongs to your friends and social world, and the innocent party is from a group you loathe? Do you side with justice or your friends? These choices happen every day on a macro scale amplified by higher education and politics regarding social issues of abortion and alternate lifestyles, political issues of government corruption, community issues of acquitting perpetrators, and rampant lawlessness. Everyone is being forced to pick a side. Which side do you agree with or support?

10) "The thoughts of the wicked are an abomination to the LORD, but gracious words are pure" (Prov. 15:26 ESV).

Do your thoughts trend toward cruelty, severe punishment, or death toward those you oppose? Are you triggered with rage when you see those you oppose? Are you able to say anything nice to those you disagree with? Notice that this passage does not distinguish between good or evil thoughts. A non-member player is defined as wicked by the Game Master. You think you are nice, but He doesn't see that while you are in your rebellion against Him.

We are all team players. So, whose team's qualities do you show, and which team's thoughts fill your heart?

SEVEN DEADLY SINS

In the sixth century, Pope Gregory I, also known as Pope Gregory the Great, compiled this list of vices, and Thomas Aquinas further developed it in the thirteenth century. The Roman Catholic church considers these to be root game violations from which other immoral violations develop. They are 1) pride, 2) greed (covetousness), 3) lust, 4) envy, 5) gluttony (to include drunkenness), 6) wrath (anger), and 7) sloth. Each is mentioned in the Manual in varying contexts. For those who like lists, pastor William Sampson has compiled a list of sixty-seven deadly sins from the New Testament (Sampson 2011, entire sermon).

There are moral lifestyle virtues that are said to cancel out these seven vices: 1) humility, 2) charity, 3) chastity, 4) gratitude, 5) temperance, 6) patience, and 7) diligence (Encyclopedia Britannica 2022, ¶ 1–2).

The Roman Catholic church relies on works-based solutions to overcome game violations. While each virtue is indeed the opposite of the corresponding vice, and although the Manual also provides some contrasting behaviors, such as don't steal but get a job, players cannot get game violations expunged by the Game Master by simply doing the opposite virtue (Eph. 2:8–9; 4:28).

Self-help theology is not a path to the bonus round. According to the Manual, expecting Him to punch a golden ticket for your progress simply lands you back to deadly sin number one: getting salvation through your effort is a source of pride (Eph. 2:8–9). There is no valid score-card

> THERE IS NO VALID SCORE-CARD THEOLOGY THAT ALLOWS YOU TO NEGOTIATE YOUR STATUS OF GOODNESS WITH THE GAME MASTER.

theology that allows you to negotiate your status of goodness with the Game Master (Ps. 14:1–3; 53:1–3; Rom. 3:10–28).

Religious Kiosks – Church, Mosque, Synagogue, Temple

Churches, temples, synagogues, mosques, shrines, covens, and blogs, along with all parachurch organizations, are included in this description. Any source that dispenses religious or spiritual advice can be considered a religious kiosk. This includes all religious, spiritual, or philosophically sourced print, audio, and video media. (This book generally refers to kiosks in the context of Western organized religion in many specific points but also includes all others.)

Probably without exception, they all claim to have the unvarnished truth about the Game of Life. Many organized Western religions base their claims on the Manual and have conflicting interpretations. Almost all current non-Manual religions around the game world have their origins from the game's early days, starting with Nimrod (D. P. Livingston n.d., ¶ 8–9, 15–27) (Gen. 10:8–12).

The Serpent runs all the kiosks that don't exclusively use the Manual. Of those that members established to only use the Manual, the Serpent infiltrates many of them and converts them to franchised kiosks that sprinkle extra philosophy throughout the Manual, take it out of context, or leave out key parts altogether. The more obvious ones, such as the Emergent Church, tend to pursue social agendas in their quest to benefit humanity. Others require much more discernment and may require some time to evaluate.

The Manual repeatedly warns of deception and gives many cautions for players to beware of false teachers. Even the master players, who were personally trained by the One Himself, had to warn their members to watch out for teachers in their own kiosk groups who were actually on the Serpent's side (Matt. 7:15–21; 24:4–5, 9–13, 23–24; Mark 13:22; Phil. 3:2; Col. 2:8; 2 Pet. 2:1–3).

Fast forward two thousand years with more than 200 new Manual translations. The Manual itself is now being re-translated in ways that subtly misdirect the players *just enough to disqualify them* from membership status. Viewing multiple renditions of the Manual can help with insight, as in this book, but it is best to stay as close to the conservative or literal translations as possible. This book uses a dozen translations to clarify its points, but the passages used are checked to align with the conservative Manual translations.

Depend on the Spirit Master for interpretative assistance as you hear kiosk explanations, and carefully heed the warnings in the Manual. Timely insights come from the Spirit Master for members who look for guidance. If you are looking for reliable

Manual translations, Baptist News Global compares several Bible versions, and God's Word Mission Society has a chart of different types of translations (Challis 2023, entire article; God's Word Mission Society 2024, entire article).

Cults and false teaching

What are the signs of a cult? When do false teachings cross over to a cult? It isn't always a clear situation. Aside from major cults, numerous small cults don't get widely flagged as being problematic.

The Bereans Apologetics Research Ministry identifies cults as those who have left Orthodoxy by denying essential Christian doctrines. Their partial list, representing more than 110 million adherents worldwide, includes Jehovah's Witness, The Church of Jesus Christ of Latter-day Saints (Mormonism), Seventh-Day Adventists, United Pentecostal Church International ("Oneness"), Christian Science / Church of Science, Church of Scientology, Church of Recovery, International Churches of Christ, Children of God, Unification Church, Church of Christ or The Disciples of Christ, Christadelphians, World Mission Society Church of God, Iglesia Ni Cristo, Jesus Miracle Crusade International Ministry, Pentecostal Missionary Church of Christ, Shepherd's Message, Back to Christ ("Cult Listing" n.d., ¶ 3–4).

Several lists on the Internet have almost identical statements of the signs of a cult. For example, here are ten such signs from a site run by former Mormons:

> The leader is the ultimate authority | The group suppresses skepticism | The group delegitimizes former members | The group is paranoid about the outside world | The group relies on shame cycles | The leader is above the law | The group uses "thought reform" methods | The group is elitist | There is no financial transparency | The group performs secret rites (Sam and Tanner 2018, entire article).

Those concerned about Manual perspectives as they relate to cults should consider what doctrines they emphasize and how the scriptures are applied, including changing the meaning of words to fit the narrative of their doctrinal perspective instead of applying the broadly understood and generally accepted meanings of such words, and in choosing the founder's interpretation over the Manual when the two views contradict.

The Christian Answers website urges readers to check the group's attitude toward the Manual, toward the One (Jesus Christ), and toward the golden ticket (salvation) (Christian Answers n.d., entire artile).

A WikiHow article, coauthored by Natalie Feinblatt, PsyD, says to evaluate their doctrine for prosperity theology and read the church rules to see how controlling they are about your relationships (Feinblatt 2023, entire article). Health for Life organization includes issues of dishonoring the family unit, crossing biblical boundaries of behavior as opposed to sexual purity and personal ownership, and emphasizing special doctrines beyond the scope of or that are contrary to scripture ("How Do I Know If I'm In A Cult?" 2020, entire article).

Secular Liturgies also has a list of twenty-five signs of a high control group or cult from a guest player perspective (Somerville-Wong 2020). This list is critical of religious kiosks and appears to mix up some doctrinal issues to prove their points, but such mix-ups can apply to kiosks that stray from sound doctrine. The Educate Yourself website has articles entitled, *Born-again Brainwashing* and *Mind Control: The Ultimate Terror* (Adachi n.d., entire article; Sutphen 1995, entire article). Dick Sutphen delivered the first article at the World Congress of Professional Hypnotists Convention in Las Vegas, Nevada. These articles explain the process of how brainwashing occurs and the scope of brainwashing in the religious world and the secular world, including business and the US Marine Corps.

> Mike Leake poses some questions to ask that might help to determine if you or a friend is in a cult: What happens if I disagree with the leaders? | How do I respond if an 'outsider' criticizes one of our leaders? | Are there different sets of 'rules' for the leader, and another set for 'members?' | Who is the leader answerable to? Is there accountability? | What would happen if you tried to leave the group? | Do they welcome independent thought? Do they believe I can think for myself? | Have I lost several friendships since joining this group? Am I being isolated? | Am I able to read outside literature? (Leake 2022, ¶ 11).

Players who are in a cult or high control group may read these lists and characteristics and agree with the listings but not apply them to their own situation. Being on the inside, where they know and experience such group qualities, may not set off alarms about their own group.

Guests can be in cults, too—just go to college or join the Marines. Besides religious cults, there are political, psychotherapy, commercial, and social cults with agendas to better themselves and others or force their perspectives on society (Young n.d., entire article).

Our college campuses have become indoctrination schools, where students or professors who object to the promoted secular ideology are punished similarly to how cults treat their recalcitrant members. Free speech is a thing of the past.

Derek Prince remarked about cults, saying,

> But there are multitudes of people involved in all sorts of cults today. And why I'm saying this is, if you want to help them, I think the best book in the New Testament is Colossians. Colossians was written to people who were in danger of becoming involved in cults. And when you've grasped the presence of Jesus in Colossians, you can no longer think about Him as a guru. He's the great Creator, He's the sovereign Lord (Prince 2023, min. 4:36).

Meat offered to idols

Since I've already gone to meddling, let's stir the pot with culinary constraints. The Corinthian church and all non-Jewish members in the first century were admonished to refrain from food offered to idols, from the meat of strangled animals, from consuming blood, and from sexual immorality (Acts 15:19–20; 21:25). Master player Paul explains the Christian liberty aspect of food offered to idols and the member's responsibility to avoid having an unenlightened fellow believer stumble in their faith because of the member's spiritual freedom (1 Cor. 8:1–13; 10:14–33).

Let's bring this issue into the twenty-first century. There is a growing participation of non-religious grocery stores and slaughterhouses offering Halal meat in their markets. This is not always advertised, so you may purchase meat that has been offered to idols and not realize it. Sometimes you can find information about this, such as the Perdue Foods poultry slaughtering facility in Dillon, South Carolina that holds an annual certificate for Halal inspections which is currently set to expire April 14, 2025. Amick Farms in Hurlock, Maryland had a Halal certification from 2018 to 2024 (Haven Hot Chicken 2022, certificates 1–2). Since May 2024, the KFC restaurants of Ontario, Canada, will sell only Halal chicken and remove pork from the menu. This will accommodate Ontario's seven percent Muslim population (Hoft 2024, ¶ 1, 7, 9).

These are only a few examples in countries with a growing Muslim population. It obviously makes no difference to the government, your grocer, restaurateur, guest players or any other religion how the animals are slaughtered so long is it is done in an acceptable and ethical manner. I will let master player Paul's admonishments to the Corinthian kiosk guide your choices and perspectives, but those first century issues have not gone away.

Bonus Round – Eternal Life

This is the relational objective of the Game of Life. Kiosks almost exclusively refer to the environmental heaven as the bonus round prize, but that is where the bonus round is experienced, not its full essence. The One described it like this:

> "And this is eternal life, that they know you, the only true God, and Jesus Christ whom you have sent" (John 17:3 ESV).

This aspect needs to be understood as the main component of the bonus round section description. The point of the Game of Life is for players to have a personal connection to the Game Master. Eternal life is accomplished when the player's spirit is reconnected to the Game Master when they join His team. This means the member has already begun to experience the meaning of the bonus round before leaving this contaminated game environment. Eternal Life is the player's connection and relationship dynamic with the Game Master and the One.

> Eternal Life
> The relational objective of the Game of Life

Here are the key aspects of eternal life:

- It is available right now in this level of the game.
- It is knowing the Game Master in a close, family relationship.

Eternal life is not simply fire insurance from hell. It is the player's adoption into the ultimate spirit family with the Game Master as your adopted Father, the One as your adopted Brother, and the Spirit Master as your ultimate Comforter. And all those benefits start immediately with the golden ticket.

Andrew Wommack describes this matter of eternal life as the singular most important teaching he could give. The article is available online on his website (Wommack 2022a).

Bonus Round – Heaven, the New Jerusalem, the New Earth

The bonus round is the environmental objective of this Game of Life. The Game Master is using this current game level to identify players who can cut through all the distractions that surround them, choose to believe Him, and play the game using His strategy for success. Players who operate as though this current game level is the best and only thing to enjoy will never experience what they could have had in the next round. It is possible for members to have "the best of both worlds," but if a choice must be made, wise members will always choose to invest in the next round, the bonus round (Dan. 12:3).

The One described the bonus round or the kingdom of heaven through many parables, which are common, everyday stories with a symbolic meaning. Because we have no comparable reference point for understanding descriptions and life in the heavenly kingdom, analogies are the best way for the Manual to explain it.

This is similar to describing computer technology to a medieval audience. It also results in curious prophetic descriptions in the Manual when the ancient prophets were trying to explain modern weaponry and global communications during the Apocalypse in terms their audience would understand. Unfortunately, when inadequate descriptions are given, we tend not to be impressed with what we hear, even though the reality may instead be everything we would hope for.

Heaven is described in more detail in the Manual's last two chapters (Rev. 21–22). It includes the Game Master's city coming down from heaven. The concept of the heavenly realm, the new earth, and the Holy City are collectively called "heaven" as a simplified explanation.

New Jerusalem. The Holy City or the New Jerusalem is described as a massive foursquare city with cubic dimensions, perhaps like a stepped pyramid. It has a number of characteristics:

- city of pure gold, as pure as glass
- cube-shaped – 1,400 miles per side, width, and height (2,200 km) (air dimensions are from Miami, Florida, to Omaha, Nebraska; from Washington DC to San Antonio, Texas; or from Madrid, Spain, to Warsaw, Poland; and from Istanbul, Turkey, to Paris, France ("Distance Calculator" n.d.)
- jasper walls 200 feet thick (65 m) (also translated as a diamond in composition)
- 12 foundations, named for the 12 apostles and decorated with stones in order 1–12: jasper • sapphire • agate (chalcedony) • emerald • onyx (sardonyx) • ruby (carnelian) • chrysolite • beryl • topaz • turquoise (chrysoprase) • jacinth • amethyst (modern identification of some stones is unclear)
    - o foundation stones are said to be anisotropic, displaying all the colors of the rainbow from the pure light of the Game Master (A&Ω Productions n.d.)

- 12 gates, each of a single pearl, with 12 guardians—3 gates per side, named for the 12 tribes of Israel
- gates are never shut
- city is brilliantly bright, like crystal-clear jasper
- no temple needed: Game Master and the One are its temple
- throne of the Game Master in the city
- river of water of life, bright as crystal, proceeds from the throne of the Game Master and the One (the Lamb)
- Main Street of gold, pure as transparent glass
- Tree of Life in the middle of the gold Main Street and on both sides of the river of water of life
    o 12 fruits, one type per month
    o leaves for healing of the nations
- city lit with the glory of the Game Master; there is no night
- houses the glory and honor of the nations
- nothing impure can enter, no one shameful or deceitful
- access members only—whose names are written in the Lamb's Book of Life (Rev. 21:9–27)

THE DAY OF THE LORD – APOCALYPSE

This is described as a sudden, final judgment on the game world after a prolonged buildup of cataclysmic events, which are now beginning to unfold. The Apocalypse is the common term for the Day of the Lord. Plenty of movies are made with this theme, but none of them even begin to describe how devastating and awful it will be for the game world itself or all the attending players. All those horror stories politicians and scientists like to tell about the imminent destruction of planet Earth never describe how bad it will really be. This Apocalypse is described in more detail in The World section of 10 Reasons for Bad Things.

Following the soon coming Apocalypse, the game will be ruled for 1,000 years by the One. This will be a time of peace in the game. After that, the Serpent will return once more to turn all players against the One. This will conclude with his decisive defeat, and the game ends with the great white throne field headquarters judgment of all players by the Game Master. Guests living today will have died about 1,000 years before this event and will be summoned for judgment and sentenced to the Lake of Fire for their second death. The bonus round for members follows that game-ending event.

New heaven, new earth

Following the Day of the Lord, the current game environment will be reset for the bonus round with a new heaven and a new earth. Specific details about its extent or players' parameters are not clearly described in the Manual.

The One indicates that members will have differing levels of authority and responsibility in the bonus round based on the points they earned for the Game Master while they played the Game of Life. Any player who wants a high score for a good position in the bonus round must pay close attention to what the Manual declares as important to the Game Master and make His priorities theirs also (Matt. 5:19–20; 19:13–14).

Heavenly rewards

The Game Master will reward members for 1) their recruitment efforts as His ambassadors in the game; 2) their transformation toward His character qualities, such as holiness, righteousness, and love; and 3) overcoming the obstacles that impacted their gameplay. 4) The way members endure suffering and trials of life and the testing of their faith through hardship also qualify for rewards.

We may not know all the specific rewards that await members in the bonus round. However, when you observe the game world's types of blessings that the Game Master offered to His members and chosen Hebrew nation of Israel when they tracked with Him and lived to please Him, His promised blessings included health, long life, productivity, and success in their family and vocation, good fortune, peace, and safety. He knows what is important to us at this game level (Deut. 28:1–14).

The One remarked about having a great or huge reward in heaven when we meet certain conditions. This "huge reward" is not spelled out, so we don't know exactly what He means, but since He knows what motivates us and what qualifies as a good reward for us on this game level, it stands to reason that the rewards waiting for us in the bonus round will be incredible (Mac n.d., entire article). (Matt. 5:11–12; Luke 6:22–23, 34–36).

Reward baseline. Let's start with a baseline of what all members can expect in the bonus round and work up from there. All members qualify to be in the presence of the Game Master forever and will also have a prepared dwelling place like a mansion or a room, depending on the translation you read. They will no longer experience sickness, sadness, pain, bad memories, the bondage of curses, darkness, or death (John 14:2–4; Rev. 21:1–5; 22:1–5).

Next, there will be an accumulation of treasure that all members can invest in during our current game level: gold, silver, and precious stones. To receive these, members' deeds and motives were in line with the Game Master's commands—which He assures are not burdensome (1 John 5:3). When members play the game to please themselves, those deeds and motives translate into wood, hay, and stubble (chopped straw and chaff (or the grain stalks left in the ground)). These may include game violations, good deeds that were done for selfish or personal reasons, or living a life of self-gratification. All the deeds and motivations for the actions of members will be evaluated and assigned from one of these six values.

In this scenario, players probably get the notion that "good deeds outweigh the bad deeds," but it only applies to this member player's reward rate. On Judgment Day, all a member's accrued works, which were converted to gold, silver, precious stones, wood, hay, and stubble, will be tested by fire. The treasure that remains when the fire is out is their reward for their service to the Game Master's kingdom (1 Cor. 3:9–17).

When the One describes a member as being great in the kingdom of heaven, this implies an elevated level of authority or responsibility in His kingdom hierarchy. The Game Master's value structure is the inverse of what we play for in this game level. An attitude of service to others and helping those who can't pay you back are the kind of characteristics that please the Game Master. Something as small as giving someone a cup of water in His name merits a reward (Mark 9:33–35, 41; 10:42–45; Luke 14:7–14).

The overcomer. There is another category of rewards for the overcomer or conqueror. Master player John describes an overcomer, saying,

"For everyone who has been born of God overcomes the world. And this is the victory that has overcome the world—our faith. Who is it that overcomes the world except the one who believes that Jesus is the Son of God?" (1 John 5:1–5 ESV).

The One includes a characteristic of an overcomer as "one who keeps my works until the end." (Rev. 2:26). The rewards for the overcomer come as benefits of receiving the golden ticket and whose actions show they are synced to the One by abiding in Him. They inherit all things because of their connection to the One as children of the Game Master (Rev. 12:11; 21:7)

These rewards are enumerated in letters sent to seven city kiosks. Each letter describes the condition of the kiosk and expectations for overcomers to succeed and achieve their reward. These churches are also said to represent different church ages.

- To the kiosk of Ephesus, the apostolic church (AD 30–300), they would eat from the Tree of Life (Rev. 2:1–7).
- To the kiosk of Smyrna, the martyr church (AD 100–313), they would receive a crown of life and not be hurt by the second death (Rev. 2:8–11).

- To the kiosk in Pergamos, the compromising church (AD 314–590), they would be given hidden manna to eat and a white stone with a new private name (Rev. 2:12–17).
- To the kiosk in Thyatira, the Roman Catholic church (AD 590–1517), they would be given power over the nations and the morning star (Rev. 2:18–26).
- To the kiosk of Sardis, the reformation church (AD 1517–1700), they would be clothed in white garments, their name not blotted out from the Book of Life, and have their name confessed before the Game Master and His guardians (Rev. 3:1–5).
- To the kiosk of Philadelphia, the revival church (AD 1700–1900), they would receive a pillar in the temple of the Game Master with the name of the Game Master, the New Jerusalem, and the One written on it (Rev. 3:6–12).
- To the kiosk of Laodicea, the worldly church (AD 1900–), they would sit with the One on His throne (Rev. 3:13–21) (Smith 2023, min. 56:06).

Crowns. The Game Master will award three types of (presumably gold) crowns (Rev. 4:4). These are awarded for specific achievements of faithful devotion to the Game Master and for watching out for His interests in His established kiosks.

- *Crown of Righteousness* – This crown is for members who keep themselves prepared for the return of the One by living exemplary holy and righteous lives (2 Tim. 4:8).
- *Crown of Life* – Also called the Martyr's Crown. This crown is awarded to members who patiently endure testing, trials, or persecution and remain faithful in their commitment to the Game Master even to their execution. The entire game world has been exposed to videos of dozens of members called Coptic Christians who were publicly beheaded in 2015 by the ISIS/Daesh terrorist group for their faith in the One. Their family members went on Arabic broadcasts to publicly forgive the executioners. In May 2022, twenty Nigerian Christians were executed by Muslim captors who posted the execution online. These are modern examples of watching members publicly qualify for the Crown of Life. The persecution of believers in the One is spreading and growing year by year (James 1:12; Rev. 2:10).
- *Crown of Glory* – Also called the Elder's Crown. The One is described as the Chief Shepherd of His flock of member players. Those kiosk leaders who minister to members can be referred to as under-shepherds. This crown is for kiosk leaders who oversee the "flock of God" and *who don't lord it over them*

but are faithful to guide them unselfishly and lead them by their good example (1 Pet. 5:2–4, paraphrased).

Other crowns. Two other crowns are usually included in kiosk lists for a total of five crowns. However, these final two entries seem more descriptive of a winning scenario than an actual earned crown.

- *Incorruptible Crown* – Also called the Victor's Crown. Master player Paul is describing members who want to be successful as master players as being self-disciplined or persevering in all areas of life. He says those who run a race compete for a crown or wreath that will decay, but members are competing for a crown that will never decay or tarnish (1 Cor. 9:24–27). The text appears to reference the value of our effort, which could refer to the Crown of Righteousness.
- *Crown of Rejoicing* – Also called the Soul Winner's Crown. This crown is said to be awarded to those who spread the good news of the golden ticket by converting guest players into members. It is referred to as part of a question, "For what is our hope or joy, or crown of rejoicing?" (Phil. 4:1; 1 Thess. 2:19–20). The context suggests that "those who turn many to righteousness" will view it symbolically as a crowning achievement rather than a literal crown. Master player Daniel describes these members as those who "will shine like the stars forever" (Dan. 12:3).

Losing crowns and rewards. Members on track to win a crown or reward can lose out if their motives turn selfish or they don't cross the finish line with faithful devotion to the Game Master. The One warned members of the kiosk of Philadelphia, "I am coming soon. Hold fast what you have, so that no one may seize your crown" (Rev. 3:7–11 ESV).

When your motives are for public recognition, the Game Master lets you accept that as your reward instead of giving you a reward Himself for your good deed.

> Beware of practicing your righteousness before other people in order to be seen by them, for then you will have no reward from your Father who is in heaven. Thus, when you give to the needy, sound no trumpet before you, as the hypocrites do in the synagogues and in the streets, that they may be praised by others. Truly, I say to you, they have received their reward. But when you give to the needy, do not let

your left hand know what your right hand is doing, so that your giving may be in secret. And your Father who sees in secret will reward you (Matt. 6:1–4 ESV).

Deception can cause members to lose their reward. Great care must be taken to ensure that members do not buy into teachings that are contrary to the Manual, even if they come from respected kiosk leaders.

Watch out for the false leaders—and there are many of them around—who don't believe that Jesus Christ came to earth as a human being with a body like ours. Such people are against the truth and against Christ. Beware of being like them and losing the prize that you and I have been working so hard to get. See to it that you win your full reward from the Lord. For if you wander beyond the teaching of Christ, you will leave God behind; while if you are loyal to Christ's teachings, you will have God too. Then you will have both the Father and the Son.

If anyone comes to teach you, and he doesn't believe what Christ taught, don't even invite him into your home. Don't encourage him in any way. If you do, you will be a partner with him in his wickedness. (2 John 1:7–11 TLB).

Headquarters – Heaven, Game Master's Throne

Access is strictly limited, and no one can get to the throne except through the One (John 14:6). Through Him, only the members can boldly reach headquarters and get help when they need it. They have unlimited access through their connection to the Spirit Master who will also interpret for players if they have trouble figuring out exactly what they need from Him (Heb. 4:16).

Field headquarters

The great white throne is described as a throne of judgment for the nations and all guests after the Apocalypse and the final battle between the Game Master and the Serpent with his guest armies at the end of the game. After their final defeat, all players whose names are not found written in the Book of Life will be sentenced to imminent destruction in the Lake of Fire, along with the Serpent, his henchmen, and all the minions.

And I saw a great white throne and Him who was seated upon it, from whose presence earth and heaven fled away, and no place was found for them [for this heaven and earth are passing away]. And I saw the dead, the great and the small, standing before the throne, and books were opened. Then another book was opened, which is the Book of Life; and the dead were judged according to what they had done as written in the books [that is, everything done while on earth].

And the sea gave up the dead who were in it, and death and Hades (the realm of the dead) surrendered the dead who were in them; and they were judged and sentenced, every one according to their deeds.

Then death and Hades [the realm of the dead] were thrown into the lake of fire. This is the second death, the lake of fire [the eternal separation from God]. And if anyone's name was not found written in the Book of Life, he was hurled into the lake of fire (Rev. 20:11–15 AMP; Heb. 9:27).

Hell – Lake of Fire

Most players have heard the concept of sudden death in an athletic competition where the next team or player that scores is the winner. In life, players can experience a sudden death when, as they go about their business, an accident happens or another player steps in and takes their life away, or they simply die suddenly as happens more often since the Covid-19 pandemic and vaccine regimen.

Have you heard of the second death? We all die, and dead is dead, right? It's not like we are only mostly dead. So, how can we die again if we're already dead? Our beings are composed of a soul within a body that experiences life around us. When this body gives out, we are dead and buried since we no longer function in this world, but our soul lives on after death. This first death is the end of our gameplay choices where our coming eternal outcomes are set in stone and no further changes can be made by us or on our behalf.

The Manual speaks of a second death, where our soul will be called up from its place in the afterlife to give an account to the Game Master of our life on Earth. This is called Judgment Day or the Day of the Lord which will happen at the end of this game cycle in about a thousand years.

The outcomes of this judgment of our soul are to expose our choices in life and to confirm whether our name is written in the Lamb's Book of Life, the Game Master's record of those who accepted the One as their substitutionary sacrifice for their game violations, and their status as an enemy of the Game Master. Those whose names are not found written in the Book of Life will be hurled into the Lake of Fire. This is the second death, the death of our soul (Rev. 20; 21:27).

Growing numbers of players don't know or don't believe there is a hell (41 percent), just like they don't know or don't believe there is a real Serpent (42 percent) (Brenan 2023, ¶ 4). While there are various names, the operational term is "Lake of Fire." Players aren't supposed to go there, so if you end up there, it wasn't supposed to end that way for you, except that it will have been your choice. Hell was only prepared and intended for the Serpent and his henchmen. However, since guests are on his team too, the Manual says their fate will be to share in his destruction (Matt. 25:41). The minions are headed for the abyss, which could also be part of hell.

Perhaps your religion teaches that you cannot know if you are forgiven until the day of judgment after you die. Perhaps your religion gives you another chance at a better life through reincarnation. Perhaps you learned that purgatory is part of the preparation for the bonus round after death. Many religions offer an escape hatch from hell where the subpar, bad, or evil player can reflect on how they messed up during this game level and then meet some requirement or payment plan to finally leave their torment behind and reach a better afterlife. These concepts are taught by Muslims and Hindus who believe hell is a temporary stop on their way to heaven or Moksha (Shukla 2012, entire article; Silawan 2021, entire article; Yogapedia n.d., ¶ 1–2, 4).

Roman Catholics believe purgatory is the purifying after-death stop on the way to heaven (Turner 2021, ¶ 20). Both Catholics and Hindus believe that the prayers and rituals of the living can impact the hellish outcome of the dead (Hinduism n.d., ¶ 2–22).

Buddhists believe good deeds can outweigh bad deeds and both heaven and hell are temporary, plus bad players can get shunted over to the animal realm. Karma plays a big role in a player's destination and continued life cycles (Tibetan Buddhist Encyclopedia n.d., ¶ 1–5).

The Serpent's focus is procrastinating any choices before death that would confirm you can reach eternal life, and he uses kiosk doctrine to validate and enforce it. If you can't know before death if you will immediately reach eternal life, then there is no need to go looking for it (2 Cor. 5:7–9). Here, procrastination is the killer. If he provides an assured pathway to eternity through another religion, that process is different from the Manual even if it uses the Manual's texts to make it authoritative. It will most likely add requirements not found in the Manual which will disqualify you from receiving a golden ticket.

> The Game Master's focus is today. As God's partners, we beg you not to accept this marvelous gift of God's kindness and then ignore it. For God says, "At just the right time, I heard you. On the day of salvation, I helped you." Indeed, the "right time" is now. "Today is the day of salvation" (2 Cor. 6:1–2 NLT, cf. Isa. 49:8).

When players end their gameplay, their spirit goes to one of two holding locations commonly referred to as heaven or hell. All players in both locations will give an accounting of their gameplay. Members will have their gameplay evaluated based on how much of it was valuable to the Game Master, and whatever treasure they collected that doesn't get burned up will determine their reward. Then they move on to the bonus round with the reward they earned (1 Cor. 3:9–15).

Guests will be called up for the only appointment they get at the Game Master's field headquarters (great white throne) to confirm that they never got a golden ticket, so their gameplay will be based on how badly they violated the Manual. Their punishment will be individually assigned, and they will be summarily appointed for destruction (Rev. 20:11–15).

The Manual does not include an escape hatch from hell or the concept of purgatory, where a player can have their game status reversed after death. These are constructs created by the Roman Catholic church and other religious systems, but no amount of prayer, penance, or gifts will affect their status post-mortem (Heb. 9:27–28).

These concepts are added rules that try to change how the game works and would make the game unworkable. Reincarnation, penance, and purgatory systems attempt to change the game's parameters and are simply syncretism, mixing incompatible religious mechanisms with the Manual. Players are always expecting to get another chance for a good outcome no matter how badly they played the game, and these constructs allow them to play on their own terms.

If eternal solutions toward heaven can be achieved through your effort, whether here or in the afterlife, then the One's sacrifice was not enough to save you from eternal destruction. Such teachings show contempt for the One's complete and finished sacrifice for your soul. If you can't decide to believe in the Lord Jesus Christ before you die, you lose this qualifying round, and your answer to Him is a forever NO (Acts 16:29–31; Rom. 10:8–13).

The One told a story of how the afterlife works.

> **IF ETERNAL SOLUTIONS TOWARD HEAVEN CAN BE ACHIEVED THROUGH YOUR EFFORT, WHETHER HERE OR IN THE AFTERLIFE, THEN THE ONE'S SACRIFICE WAS NOT ENOUGH TO SAVE YOU FROM ETERNAL DESTRUCTION.**

There was this rich man who had everything—purple clothing of fine quality and high fashion, gourmet meals every day, and a large house. Just outside his front gate lay this poor *homeless* fellow named Lazarus. Lazarus was covered in ugly skin lesions. He was so hungry he wished he could scavenge scraps from the rich man's trash. Dogs would come and lick the sores on his skin. The poor fellow died and was carried on the arms of the heavenly messengers to the embrace of Abraham. Then the rich fellow died and was buried and found himself in the place of the dead. In his torment, he looked up, and off in the distance he saw Abraham, with Lazarus in his embrace.

He shouted out, "Father Abraham! Please show me mercy! Would you send *that beggar* Lazarus to dip his fingertip in water and cool my tongue? These flames are hot, and I'm in agony!"

But Abraham said, "Son, you seem to be forgetting something: your life was full to overflowing with comforts and pleasures, and the life of Lazarus was just as full with suffering and pain. So now is his time of comfort, and now is your time of agony. Besides, a great canyon separates you and us. Nobody can cross over from our side to yours, or from your side to ours."

"Please, Father *Abraham,* I beg you," the formerly rich man continued, "send Lazarus to my father's house. I have five brothers there, *and they're on the same path I was on.* If Lazarus warns them, they'll choose another path and won't end up here in torment."

But Abraham said, "*Why send Lazarus?* They already have the law of Moses and the writings of the prophets to instruct them. Let your brothers hear them."

"No, Father Abraham," he said, "*they're already ignoring the law and the prophets.* But if someone came back from the dead, then they'd listen for sure; then they'd change their way of life."

Abraham answered, "If they're not listening to Moses and the prophets, they won't be convinced even if someone comes back from the dead" (Luke 16:19–31 VOICE).

Nobody can make you listen to the Game Master when you've tuned Him out (Rom. 1:16–32). Players who hope to fix things after death will be shockingly disappointed.

The good news is that the Game Master says you can absolutely know for sure today, right now, if you have eternal life and will reach heaven when you die. He doesn't leave such a seriously big outcome to chance or to your ability to earn it.

> And Jesus Christ was revealed as God's Son by his baptism in water and by shedding his blood on the cross—not by water only, but by water and blood. And the Spirit, who is truth, confirms it with his testimony. So we have these three witnesses—the Spirit, the water, and the blood—and all three agree. Since we believe human testimony, surely we can believe the greater testimony that comes from God. And God has testified about his Son. All who believe in the Son of God know in their hearts that this testimony is true. Those who don't believe this are actually calling God a liar because they don't believe what God has testified about his Son.
>
> And this is what God has testified: He has given us eternal life, and this life is in his Son. Whoever has the Son has life; whoever does not have God's Son does not have life.
>
> I have written this to you who believe in the name of the Son of God, so that you may know you have eternal life. And we are confident that he hears us whenever we ask for anything that pleases him. And since we know he hears us when we make our requests, we also know that he will give us what we ask for (1 John 5:6–15 NLT).

Your response time to repent (turn back) from game violations and receive eternal life is always today and right now. Instead of waiting, the One said that you should do everything you can to avoid ending up in the Lake of Fire.

> If your hand causes you to sin, cut it off. It's better to enter eternal life with only one hand than to go into the unquenchable fires of hell

with two hands. If your foot causes you to sin, cut it off. It's better to enter eternal life with only one foot than to be thrown into hell with two feet. And if your eye causes you to sin, gouge it out. It's better to enter the Kingdom of God with only one eye than to have two eyes and be thrown into hell, "where the maggots never die and the fire never goes out." For everyone will be tested with fire (Mark 9:43–49 NLT; cf. Isa. 66:24).

After death, it's judgment time and the Lake of Fire, where the worm doesn't die, and the fire never goes out. The Lake of Fire is the second death. If you remain a guest, you will have already died by then, but when you are brought up for judgment and sentenced to the Lake of Fire, that will be your second death (Mark 9:43–49; Heb. 9:13; Rev. 20:10–15). When the Game Master doubles down on your death sentence, what makes you think you're coming back from it (Matt. 10:28; Luke 12:5)? To perish is to not come back. *Ever.*

Obstacles

This gameplay book is about bad things that happen to players. That includes anything that hurts their health, wealth, or well-being, including property or losses against any other players they care about. The Hurt Zone section covers ten major categories of obstacles players face and subcategories that can be paired with them.

Obstacles can impact players on the physical or emotional levels and may have their origin in the spirit realm, whether directly or indirectly, due to the corrupted game environment. Occasionally, there is an obvious spiritual manifestation in a player's obstacle. However, most of the time, they appear to originate in the visually recognized aspects of the game, even including the mundane annoyances that just aggravate players.

There is usually a player nearby who is uncomfortable with talk of the spirit realm and feels the need to remind other players to not spiritualize everything and blow them out of context, so this comment is an acknowledgment that it may be possible to over-contextualize what already has its origin on a spiritual plane. That is why discussing the origins of obstacles can be difficult because the lines between the physical game and its spiritual realm can get hazy, and the average player treats it like crazy talk.

A final note here about obstacles regards our response to or attitude about them. It seems the kiosk world is increasingly attributing the Game Master as the source of obstacles in our gameplay through the "God is in control" sovereignty aspect, where nothing happens without His approval and that He will also fix it. Perhaps the intent is to emphasize His sovereignty over the game or deflect a bad attitude toward the Game Master because He is just trying to make you a better player.

The point is that we should not be discouraged when we are hit with all kinds of obstacles like finances, health, relationships, and so on. While they are likely not coming from Him, He can use any issue we face in life, whether good or bad, to make us better and more skilled players. He wants you to rise to the challenge (Rom. 5:3–11; James 1:2–4).

Solutions

Bad things happen for a reason. Those who find the reason will realize that there is a solution to fix it. Finding the solution can be elusive even for those who know where they should look for it. But once a player gets the solutions to his obstacles, there is still a choice whether to apply the solution, retain it, or whether the player even wants to continue getting more solutions to the obstacles in his gameplay.

While the Game Master provides all the solutions, members can still reject them. Surprisingly, some players walk away from the solution even when they know it will change their game environment or their gameplay for the better. For example, a player may turn down the opportunity to be healed of a disease, nerve injury, or a curse or stronghold because they have grown accustomed to living with it for so long that they can't imagine life being different for them without their handicap. It now defines who they are. Those who have lived with long-term issues understand how that transference can happen where they associate their existence with their disability.

The Serpent has solutions, too, because he has a range of power. Sometimes players get confused as to who is the source of the solution to their problems. Not every spirit connected to a player that says the Game Master is their source actually comes from the Game Master. The Manual encourages players to test the source of spirits empowering players who offer solutions (1 John 4:1–3).

Members can locate the solutions to every obstacle facing players, but applying the solutions comes more easily to those who try to become master players. Members can reach out to master players to assist them in applying the solutions to their obstacles. Guests can receive solutions too through a direct appeal to the Game Master or through the intercession of members. However, those who go on to become member players have a better chance to make those solutions permanent in their life experience (Matt. 12:42–45; Luke 11:24–26).

Section II: Final Points

THERE IS ALWAYS something more to say, and these items are an attempt to tie up loose ends. They are not necessarily associated with each other but contribute to the book's perspective.

Full Player Membership

SECURING THE GOLDEN ticket is the first objective of the game. This is a multi-faceted achievement. It includes eternal life, bonus round reward potential, a personal and operational relationship with the Game Master, adoption with the Game Master as your Father and the One as your brother, heir of the Game Master and joint-heir with the One, part of the corporate bride of the One, accepted and beloved, more than a conqueror, and a possessor of resurrection-level power from the Spirit Master.

Finding other members who play with a full understanding of what they possess is a blessing. These are the master players who know what they got and learned how to use it to be effective gamers. The Manual is very clear about how you receive membership. Don't let any kiosk change or add any more requirements to it.

Become a Member. The Manual explains how the Game Master made it possible for all of us to become member players:

> But now God has shown us a way to be made right with him without keeping the requirements of the law, as was promised in the writings of Moses and the prophets long ago. We are made right with God by placing our faith in Jesus Christ. And this is true for everyone who believes, no matter who we are.
>
> For everyone has sinned; we all fall short of God's glorious standard. Yet God, in his grace, freely makes us right in his sight. He did this through Christ Jesus when he freed us from the penalty for our sins. For God presented Jesus as the sacrifice for sin. People are made right with God when they believe that Jesus sacrificed his life, shedding his blood. This sacrifice shows that God was being fair when he held back and did not punish those who sinned in times past, for he was looking ahead and including them in what he would do in this present time. God did this to demonstrate his righteousness, for he himself

is fair and just, and he makes sinners right in his sight when they believe in Jesus.

Can we boast, then, that we have done anything to be accepted by God? No, because our acquittal is not based on obeying the law. It is based on faith. So we are made right with God through faith and not by obeying the law.

After all, is God the God of the Jews only? Isn't he also the God of the Gentiles? Of course he is. There is only one God, and he makes people right with himself only by faith, whether they are Jews or Gentiles. Well then, if we emphasize faith, does this mean that we can forget about the law? Of course not! In fact, only when we have faith do we truly fulfill the law (Rom. 3:21–31 NLT).

Becoming a member is about the attitude of your heart (Deut. 6:5; Matt. 22:37; Mark 12:30; Luke 10:27). The Manual says that players look at the outward appearance, but the Game Master judges the heart (1 Sam. 16:7; Jer. 17:9–10). He knows your level of sincerity, which comes down to what you deeply believe (Ps. 44:20–21). It is a transaction of faith, and the Manual puts it like this:

Because if you acknowledge and confess with your lips that Jesus is Lord and in your heart believe (adhere to, trust in, and rely on the truth) that God raised Him from the dead, you will be saved.

For with the heart a person believes (adheres to, trusts in, and relies on Christ) and so is justified (declared righteous, acceptable to God), and with the mouth he confesses (declares openly and speaks out freely his faith) and confirms [his] salvation. The Scripture says, No man who believes in Him [who adheres to, relies on, and trusts in Him] will [ever] be put to shame or be disappointed.

[No one] for there is no distinction between Jew and Greek (Gentile). The same Lord is Lord over all [of us] and He generously bestows His riches upon all who call upon Him [in faith]. For everyone who calls upon the name of the Lord [invoking Him as Lord] will be saved (Rom. 10:10–13 AMP).

And again,

> The Father loves the Son [Jesus] and has given (entrusted, committed) everything into His hand. And he who believes in (has faith in, clings to, relies on) the Son has (now possesses) eternal life. But whoever disobeys (is unbelieving toward, refuses to trust in, disregards, is not subject to) the Son will never see (experience) life, but [instead] the wrath of God abides on him. [God's displeasure remains on him; His indignation hangs over him continually] (John 3:35–36 AMP).

And finally,

> He who believes in the Son of God [who adheres to, trusts in, and relies on Him] has the testimony [possesses this divine attestation] within himself. He who does not believe God [in this way] has made Him out to be and represented Him as a liar, because he has not believed (put his faith in, adhered to, and relied on) the evidence (the testimony) that God has borne regarding His Son. And this is that testimony (that evidence): God gave us eternal life, and this life is in His Son [Jesus Christ] (1 John 5:10–11 AMP).

This is more than just having a knowledge of the truth; it penetrates your soul. The Manual says that if you believe there is one God, then good for you, but the demons believe it too, and it makes them shudder (James 2:19). Unless your faith is more than simple knowledge, it is dead (James 2:20).

Not having faith is not a passive or neutral situation from a spirit realm perspective. According to the Manual, your unbelief calls God a liar. The result is that your lack of faith makes it impossible for you to please Him (Heb. 11:6). If you need faith, you can get faith from being attentive to the Manual; read it and believe it (Rom. 10:17).

Everything you need for membership has already been done for you. All you need to do is believe it and receive it. If you don't know what to say to the Game Master, you can read back His Word that you just read in the above texts, or here is a sample prayer you can pray out loud:

Jesus, I confess that You are my Lord and Savior. I believe in my heart that God raised you from the dead. By faith I believe in Your Word, I repent of my sin and receive Your salvation now. Thank You for saving me!

Your faith is a transaction in the spirit realm, and the Manual text above says that when you believe in the Son of God, you have that testimony or divine confirmation within you. *Welcome to the winning team, Pilgrim!* (Heb. 11:13–14; 1 Pet. 2:11–12).

Membership Details

Membership status

Checking your membership status is mentioned several times. What you believe will reflect how you act. Of course, there can be a struggle as the spirit realm reacts to your decision of faith. However, suppose you have no interest in taking on the characteristics of the Game Master. In that case, the Manual recommends a personal inventory (2 Cor. 13:5). The Manual books of James and 1 John have the most thorough status checklists that cover our gameplay from many perspectives.

There are characteristics of membership. Here are a few: Those who love the Game Master hate evil (Ps. 97:10), love others (1 John 4:7–8), and their focus is on the bonus round (Col. 3:1).

Religious test. The game world is teeming with religious players. The Game Master's definition of pure religion is very simple and focuses on His priorities: to care for widows and orphans in their hardships and to stay uncontaminated by the game world system (James 1:27). It's just a different rendering of loving the Game Master with all your heart and loving others like the One loves you, with holy living (Matt. 22:37). If kiosks add to this, ensure your motivation is only from a love for the Game Master. Everything else is just an empty ritual.

Overlooked rules

There are always fine points within major transactions. If you plan to sue a company, you should check the fine print to see if what you didn't bother reading actually signed you up for something you would have otherwise refused when you signed the contract.

It doesn't matter which team you are on; both teams have rules of play and expect you to become like the team leader. You probably never knew how much damage to your life you were allowing the Serpent to do to you as a default member of his team.

There are huge benefits to players joining the Game Master's team. First, members are usually the only ones who go back and read the rules they had been living under while operating as guests. Guests usually don't believe them but don't bother checking out the rules either. So, not having learned the Serpent team rules since they come naturally, players then join the Game Master's team and may act surprised that He expects something from them, not realizing that they had previously been signed over for scheduled destruction by being on the Serpent's team.

Joining the Game Master's team is usually presented in broad strokes, so the implications of changes in their gameplay are left out. The closest way that most members come to explaining the major change is when they say that you are agreeing to "make Jesus the Lord of your life," which is a direct expectation from the One Himself and a stipulation in the Manual for membership (Luke 6:45–46; Rom. 10:9–10; Phil. 2:10–11).

Master player Paul interjects several "don't you know?" moments where members should know that their gameplay is no longer their call. When the One purchased them from the Serpent's team, they kept playing to please the Serpent by living their own lives and calling the shots. Instead, they were expected to quit playing to please themselves (and the Serpent) and begin playing for the Game Master (Rom. 6:1–23; 1 Cor. 3:16–17; 6:9–10, 15–20; 2 Cor. 13:5; James 4:4–5).

Membership expects that you give your life over to the Game Master, including your desires, will, and expectations, so He can make you a master player. The wrinkle is that while this is a condition of membership, it must be done voluntarily because— free will. If professing members refuse to conform to the Game Master's character (unlike they had so willingly conformed to the Serpent's character), the Manual does not assure their continued status as members.

This is why there is such a high potential for professing member players to make it to the bonus round by the skin of their teeth (1 Cor. 3:11–15) and for huge numbers of them to get shocked that they never actually joined the Game Master's team when they refused to relinquish control of their gameplay. In many cases, it may not be that they refused to comply but that they didn't think He was serious about His expectations of them. The Game Master will use the Manual to discern the truth of their status (Jer. 17:9–10; Heb. 4:12).

TRANSFER OF RIGHTS

Some players are slow to understand that membership on the Game Master's team is a transfer of masters and a transfer of rights. Players begin on the Serpent's team living with the illusion that they call the shots on their lives, and nobody tells them what to do or influences their choices. Then they decide to join the Game Master's team and continue to live the same way with the illusion that all they needed was fire insurance while they still get to call the shots on their lives, and nobody makes them do anything.

Owning your own life on the Serpent's team was a ticket to hell. While he let you run your life, the objective was to keep you distracted from your own destruction, and any shiny object would do. He was your boss, but you got the credit for being your own person, and all the while, you had no idea that you were just like him and doing things his way.

Joining the Game Master's team means you have a new Master who expects you to become more than you were before. Instead of continuing to live by the Serpent's philosophy, He wants you to become just like Him, but now you feel like someone's telling you what to do, and you don't like all those rules.

This is how the Serpent runs interference on your new game member life: instead of changing your heart's desires and then doing the things that please the Game Master as the Manual says, you are handed a list of things (perhaps by your kiosk or spiritual leader) that please the Game Master and are told to do those things to please Him. But now you aren't pleasing Him because your attitude is wrong, and your motive for doing it is misplaced. The Game Master is all about motives that equal action (Mark 9:41). So you don't get credit for your effort, and any reward you would have gotten for your trouble is gone because—motive (1 Cor. 13:1–3).

Everybody wants to clean up your messy life so you look and act like a clone of the Game Master, but nobody takes time to ignore your messy life and teach you to *love* the Game Master instead. When you love the Game Master the way He loves you, the Spirit Master will help your messy life get cleaned up *without* a list of rules. You don't need a list; you are loved, and you need to love back (2 Cor. 5:14–15; 1 John 3:1). *And then* you will do the things that please Him *and* get credit for your effort and rewards for your trouble (Mark 9:41).

When my son in the military declined a party or movie invitation, he got asked if he had a rule against partying or going to a movie. His perspective was that it's just not the Game Master's priority, so it wasn't his interest either. It was a choice, not a rule.

The Manual says we were bought at a heavy price, and we chose to not belong to ourselves. The Spirit Master's residence in our lives is our consent that He has ownership of us. Because of that, we are to give credit to the One in the way we live (1 Cor. 6:19–20). The Manual says that it's *reasonable* that we stop being conformed to this game world system any longer and instead become transformed into a new attitude and perspective of life through renewing our mind as we learn the Manual (Rom. 12:1–2).

The right to get even. This is where the attitude meets the real game world. About the right to be angry—we gave up our rights to this world; we don't get to live like we own our lives. Members owned by the Game Master do not have the right to get even when bad things are done to them. Instead, you are to help your enemy. The One goes so far to say that if someone takes your coat, give him your jacket too. That attitude is the opposite of what our parents taught us because you have to stand up for yourself. We are not to be overwhelmed by dark attitudes but must overcome them by doing good when we are mistreated. Our response to mistreatment reflects who controls our spirit (Matt. 5:43–45; Luke 6:27–29; Rom. 12:17–21; 1 Tim. 5:21–22; 1 Pet. 2:18–19).

This does not mean we are required to stay in a hostile environment, nor does it mean violations of company policy or criminal acts should not be reported nor justice pursued. Many managers probably should be reassigned or fired for allowing and encouraging unfriendly or hostile work environments. Master player Paul complained to local authorities in Philippi and Jerusalem. The issue is whether you internalize the mistreatment and focus on getting payback for your own satisfaction. The Game Master is keeping score, and it doesn't matter if payback from Him happens while you are still around or if it comes at the end of the game; He wants you to learn to be kind just as He is kind (Ps. 73:3–20; Rom. 12:17–21). As you read through the Manual, you will notice that repayment for evil and vengeance issued by the Game Master will be much worse than we could likely dish out. Even if they get their comeuppance or karma during the game, it will still be added to their charge sheet for Judgment Day.

Citizenship transfer

Master players recognize that once we get our golden ticket, this game level is no longer our home or destination because our citizenship was transferred to the bonus round (Heb. 11:13–16). We become pilgrims through this game level, playing for points that get activated in the bonus round.

This isn't to say we shouldn't enjoy life on this game level. Making memories is part of relationships, and we must value other players and practice love toward them in response to the Game Master's love toward us. As you live a full and satisfied life, keep track of your destination.

Transfer of ambition

While this seems redundant, it addresses a perspective that is taught to teenage players. Players are encouraged in their kiosks to "give their life to God." It's like prying their fingers loose from some prized game world possession. Somehow, we think we can transfer ownership of our lives over to the Game Master on our own terms and in our own good time. That's not His perspective.

The One said that you're either on His side or against Him, that you're either engaging in His interests or messing things up (Luke 11:23). If you call yourself a member and can't seem to give up your interests to the One you call your Master, perhaps it's time for a membership status check (2 Cor. 13:5).

God's will. One of the main kiosk calls to young players is that they "find God's will for their life." Having raised three sons and never getting a satisfactory kiosk explanation, this has been a troubling issue. So here is my conclusion.

The only vocational calling explicitly referenced in the Manual is a call to preach, whether in a local kiosk or a mission setting. Even here, some early master players supported themselves with vocational skills. If the Game Master isn't specifically calling you into kiosk work, this should not be an agonized decision. Kiosk leaders always use themselves as examples of "finding God's will," meaning becoming a pastor or missionary, and rarely project that to other vocations. This only adds pressure to young members who can become traumatized over what to do with their lives and fearful of missing God's will and blessing.

Another way He may place an indirect calling on your life is through a spiritual gifting like mercy, service, giving, teaching, or leadership. This motivational gift may be coupled with a vocational interest like education, medical services, law enforcement, financial services, legal work, or mechanical services, and you want to use your skills to help others. This has led to the startup of many parachurch organizations.

The most common pattern of vocational choice is that young players bypass these first two ways, think about what they would like to do in life, and pick a vocation based on their interests. Kiosks may frown on this method of vocational choice because it leaves out the spiritual element and motivation and is, therefore, not God-approved.

However, *all* members are called to be ambassadors of the Game Master (2 Cor. 5:20) *All* are called to help one another (1 John 3:17), love one another (1 John 4:7–8), and pray for one another (James 5:16). The Manual strongly emphasizes the development of our spiritual character and pursuit of Him instead of our vocational choices (2 Pet. 1:5–7). Whatever we do is supposed to be done for His glory because our motivation results in rewards (1 Cor. 10:31; Col. 3:23–24).

Don't stress yourself about a life calling. If your focus is to walk with Him, He will guide you as you go. My son followed his understanding of the Game Master's call to the Air Force Pararescue program, tapped out near the end of the preliminary testing, ended up stationed in Aviano, Italy, and then "banished" to the White Sands desert in New Mexico. He did not choose either destination, one full of European cultural opportunities, the other an isolated, hot desert. However, in each place, he met a pastor or an elder Christian who had a major impact on his spiritual journey and vocational future. He followed his continued interest in the medical field, completed nursing school and works as an ICU nurse in a major hospital to gain experience for entry to a trauma unit.

For myself, having been in Christian education for about 40 years, the Game Master moved me out of each school before it precipitously declined in enrollment and into a new school that met a need I had at that moment. My music degree opened opportunities in three schools as I transitioned into administrative work and IT management. I was not one to walk away from a job, so the Spirit Master made it evident to me a different way in each case. Every new job also positively impacted my children and my wife. Life has been a journey toward contentment (Phil. 4:11). If you are walking with the Game Master, every place you go is the place to be—with Him (Rom. 8:13–15).

> **IF YOU ARE WALKING WITH THE GAME MASTER, EVERY PLACE YOU GO IS THE PLACE TO BE—WITH HIM.**

If your ambition is to please the Game Master, He may take your vocational expertise and use it for a specific task for a limited time, like a medical mission trip. For example, the prophet player Amos, a herdsman and wild fruit gatherer by vocation, is said to have only had a three-week ministry. That's like a mission trip, but he got his own book in the Manual. If you feel you are being sidelined, you can always volunteer (Isa. 6:8).

Losing Your Golden Ticket

THE POINT OF bringing up this subject is to answer the question of whether golden tickets can expire, be given up, or get revoked and provide some understanding of how one could be said to lose their ticket. Operative terms include the Security of the Believer, Eternal Security, and Once Saved, Always Saved.

There are opposing views whether a player can lose his golden ticket. This is a very divisive topic where common ground is not easily obtained, and kiosk leaders typically hesitate to make declarative statements on it. Whether you change your view from one to another depends on your persuasion of how you interpret the Manual.

"Traditional **Calvinists** do not dispute that salvation requires faithfulness. However, Calvinists contend that God is sovereign and cannot permit a true believer to depart from the faith" ("Perseverance of the Saints" n.d., ¶ 31). Those who walk away from their faith were probably never members at all. Their Ticket wasn't revoked; they never actually got one.

The **Lutheran** view maintains that members can drift off or fall away from their faith by choice. Those who pursue the Game Master will retain their ticket.

> Like both Calvinist camps, confessional Lutherans view the work of salvation as monergistic in that "the natural [that is, corrupted and divinely unrenewed] powers of man cannot do anything or help towards salvation", and Lutherans go further along the same lines as the Free Grace advocates to say that the recipient of saving grace need not cooperate with it. Hence, Lutherans believe that a true Christian – in this instance, a genuine recipient of saving grace – can lose his or her salvation, "[b]ut the cause is not as though God were unwilling to grant grace for perseverance to those in whom He has begun the good work. . . [but that these persons] wilfully [*sic*] turn away. . ." ("Perseverance of the Saints" n.d., ¶ 31).

The **Arminian** view holds that the continuation of keeping a golden ticket depends on the player's continued life of faith in a direction toward the Game Master. Players can reject or denounce their faith and lose their ticket ("Perseverance of the Saints" n.d., ¶ 27–28).

Add to this mix the doctrine of **Free Grace** held by Baptist-type denominations. Free Grace doctrine says that all members receive their golden ticket by grace, without works, as stated in Ephesians 2:8–9. This doctrine tends to separate the player's behavior from the status of their ticket, meaning they cannot lose their ticket regardless of how badly they behave thereafter or even if they reject their faith. This is sometimes termed a **fire Insurance** policy where a player can live like the devil without regrets and still expect to end up with God ("Perseverance of the Saints" n.d., ¶ 15, 32).

Notice that all views recognize that: *players who believe in the One and received their golden ticket will never lose their ticket while they pursue a life of holiness toward their path to the bonus round.* It is recognized that having missteps and moral failings can happen to those on a path toward the Game Master. These are not considered to be disqualification issues as the player repents (turns back toward a righteous life) and continues their pursuit of holiness.

The issue among these views is about what happens to players who lose their focus and become inactive in their lives of faith or even turn away from a desire to have a continued connection with the Game Master or finally reject Him outright. Are they still members or not? Did they ever have a genuine golden ticket or not?

Most members have already drawn conclusions about eternal security based on their kiosk affiliation. If you still have questions, consider the following: Whenever there are two opposite views, each with supporting Manual texts, there is probably a third way that reconciles those texts.

Master player Paul cautions the kiosk to "work out your salvation with fear and trembling" (Phil. 2:12). The Amplified Bible interprets it as: work out (cultivate, carry out to the goal, and fully complete) your own salvation with reverence and awe and trembling (self-distrust, with serious caution, tenderness of conscience, watchfulness against temptation, timidly shrinking from whatever might offend God and discredit the name of Christ).

On this issue of whether one can lose his golden ticket, many are fully persuaded that the answer is no, but others say that the topic is not so conclusive. Manual texts indicate that a member can lose his golden ticket, suggesting that any player can choose to renounce his desire to stay on the Game Master's team because all players still retain their free will through the end of their gameplay. Because the Game Master gives a condition for not having your name blotted out of the Book of Life, losing your ticket seems to be a real possibility, and it would not be wise to call His bluff (Rev. 3:5).

The One assures members that it is not possible for anyone to get pulled off the Game Master's team or snatched out of His hand. No outside force can wrest you away from the protected bonus round outcome of the Game Master (John 10:28–29). All eternal security views agree on this point. However, He is not saying that members will be kept on His team against their will. Religious kiosks explain that a player who walks off the Game Master's team was never a member anyway, but the Manual seems to show that may or may not be the case (Heb. 6:4–8).

A message by Andrew Wommack is heavily referenced throughout this topic because very few attempt to explain this dilemma even though it is an often-asked question. In my current school, this was the first question asked by a second-grade student in chapel to the kiosk's director of children's ministries. She did not want to answer it. The next second-grade question was how to escape hell if you go there and then decide to go to heaven. No answer for that, either. For further study on salvation, here are some texts for these differing views from Andrew Wommack (Wommack 2010, min. 0:01–04:23).

Eternal Security

Eternal security means that we are saved by grace and not by works. **Ephesians 2:8–9**: "For by grace you have been saved through faith. And this is not your own doing; it is the gift of God, not a result of works, so that no one may boast" (NIV).

We are saved by grace and kept by grace. **Galatians 3:3**: "Are you so foolish? Having begun by the Spirit, are you now being perfected by [now ending with] the flesh?" (ESV).

We are not saved by the works of the law. **Romans 3:20**: "Therefore no one will be declared righteous in God's sight by the works of the law; rather, through the law we become conscious of our sin" (NIV).

> **Romans 3:27–28**: "Where, then, is boasting? It is excluded. Because of what law? The law that requires works? No, because of the law that requires faith. For we maintain that a person is justified by faith apart from the works of the law" (NIV).
>
> **Galatians 2:16**: "Yet we know that a person is not justified by works of the law but through faith in Jesus Christ, so we also have believed in

Christ Jesus, in order to be justified by faith in Christ and not by works of the law, because by works of the law no one will be justified" (ESV).

Galatians 3:10: "For all who rely on the works of the law are under a curse, as it is written: 'Cursed is everyone who does not continue to do everything written in the Book of the Law'" (Deut. 27:26) (NIV).

Texts on Assurance of Eternal Security

John 3:16: "For God so loved the world that he gave his one and only Son, that whoever believes in him shall not perish but have eternal life" NIV).

John 10:28: "I give them eternal life, and they will never perish, and no one will snatch them out of my hand" (ESV).

Hebrews 10:10: "And by that will, we have been made holy through the sacrifice of the body of Jesus Christ once for all" (NIV).

Hebrews 10:14: "For by one sacrifice he has made perfect forever those who are being made holy" (NIV).

Hebrews 10:17–18: Then he adds: "Their sins and lawless acts I will remember no more" (Jer. 31:34). "And where these have been forgiven, sacrifice for sin is no longer necessary" (NIV).

Romans 4:8: "Blessed is the one whose sin the Lord will never count against them" (Ps. 32:2) (NIV).

Psalm 32:1–2: "Blessed are those whose transgressions are forgiven, whose sins are covered. Blessed is the one whose sin the Lord will never count against them" (NIV).

1 Peter 1:3–5: Blessed be the God and Father of our Lord Jesus Christ! According to his great mercy, he has caused us to be born again to a living hope through the resurrection of Jesus Christ from the dead, to an inheritance that is imperishable, undefiled, and unfading, kept in heaven for you, who by God's power are being guarded through faith for a salvation ready to be revealed in the last time (ESV).

Romans 6:23: "For the wages of sin is death, but the free gift of God is eternal life in Christ Jesus our Lord" (ESV).

Texts on no assurance of eternal security

There are three or four differing interpretations (No eternal security assurance position – when not viewed as hypothetical), (Wommack 2010, min. 4:23–8:30, 27:48–35:32).

Hebrews 6:4–6: For it is impossible, in the case of those who have once been enlightened, who have tasted the heavenly gift, and have shared in the Holy Spirit, and have tasted the goodness of the word of God and the powers of the age to come, and then have fallen away, to restore them again to repentance, since they are crucifying once again the Son of God to their own harm and holding him up to contempt (ESV). **Verses 7–9:** For land that has drunk the rain that often falls on it, and produces a crop useful to those for whose sake it is cultivated, receives a blessing from God. But if it bears thorns and thistles, it is worthless and near to being cursed, and its end is to be burned. Though we speak in this way, yet in your case, beloved, we feel sure of better things—things that belong to salvation (ESV).

Hebrews 10:26–31: If we deliberately keep on sinning after we have received the knowledge of the truth, no sacrifice for sins is left, but only a fearful expectation of judgment and of raging fire that will consume the enemies of God. Anyone who rejected the law of Moses died without mercy on the testimony of two or three witnesses. How much more severely do you think someone deserves to be punished who has trampled the Son of God underfoot, who has treated as an unholy thing the blood of the covenant that sanctified them, and who has insulted the Spirit of grace? For we know him who said, "It is mine to avenge; I will repay" (Deut. 32:35) and again, "The Lord will judge his people" (Deut. 32:36; Ps. 135:14). It is a dreadful thing to fall into the hands of the living God (NIV).

2 Peter 1:10: "Therefore, my brothers and sisters, make every effort to confirm your calling and election. For if you do these things, you will never stumble" (NIV).

2 Peter 2:20–22: If they have escaped the corruption of the world by knowing our Lord and Savior Jesus Christ and are again entangled in it and are overcome, they are worse off at the end than they were at the beginning. It would have been better for them not to have known the way of righteousness, than to have known it and then to turn their backs on the sacred command that was passed on to them. Of them the proverbs are true: "A dog returns to its vomit" (Prov. 26:11) and "A sow that is washed returns to her wallowing in the mud" (NIV).

Jude 24: "Now to him who is able to keep you from stumbling and to present you blameless before the presence of his glory with great joy" (ESV).

Conditions for entering the New Jerusalem in Revelation chapters two and three promises: *to him who overcomes,* (Wommack 2010, min. 8:33–9:50).

Colossians 1:21–23 – includes a condition if you continue in the faith:

> Once you were alienated from God and were enemies in your minds because of [as shown by] your evil behavior. But now he has reconciled you by Christ's physical body through death to present you holy in his sight, without blemish and free from accusation—if you continue in your faith, established and firm, and do not move from the hope held out in the gospel. This is the gospel that you heard and that has been proclaimed to every creature under heaven, and of which I, Paul, have become a servant (NIV).

Members have a hard time understanding why a player would want to go back to the guest status. Members can get distracted by the Serpent's enticing game environment too, and the longer they visit and focus on appealing things of the game world, the less interest they may have for staying with the Game Master as time goes by. The One explained that this includes getting focused on the cares of this world, the deceitfulness of riches, and the desire and pursuit of other things. When their resolve gets weakened enough, it is possible for them to choose to finally walk away. (Matt. 10:32–33; 13:18–23; Mark 4:14–20; 2 Tim. 4:10; Phil. 1:24).

The apostle John explains it like this:

> Do not love the world or the things in the world. If anyone loves the world, the love of the Father is not in him. For all that is in the world—the desires of the flesh and the desires of the eyes and pride of life [or pride in possessions]—is not from the Father but is from the world. And the world is passing away along with its desires, but whoever does the will of God abides forever (1 John 2:15–17 ESV).

The faith deconstruction movement is gaining popularity among the younger players. Perhaps a personally traumatic and devastating event, like the loss of their health, their livelihood, or a loved one, may cause anger and bitterness toward the Game Master to well up inside a player until they accuse Him for their loss. They assume it was the Game Master's fault because He is omnipotent and omniscient and was missing in their moment of great need. In their despair and anger, they declare themselves to be done with the Game Master and storm off His team.

Assuming they later regret their decision, The Manual then leaves an open question in Hebrews chapter six as to whether it's even possible for them to return to the Game Master's team and get their ticket renewed. This passage of text can be interpreted in several ways depending on one's view of eternal security (Heb. 6:4–6).

Considering the Manual has many conditional promises, including those that appear to reference the golden ticket, it is wise to take master player Paul's advice and work out or complete your salvation with great concern and self-distrust. Master player Peter also calls on members to "be diligent to make your calling and election [in the bonus round] a sure thing" (Phil. 2:12 AMP; 2 Pet. 1:10–11).

The Almost Christian

Based on the 1661 sermon by Matthew Mead (2011)

WHAT IF YOU think you're a member but really aren't? While growing up in a conservative church and Christian school environment in the 1970s, there was a lot of talk about "re-dedication" or "giving your life to God." Aside from a born-again experience, the focus of talks in chapels and youth retreats was on areas of life that were not surrendered to the lordship of Christ. There could be a room in our lives where we had closed the door to God and clung to our own secret passions or vices.

The kiosks intended to raise a generation of players who were "sold out" to the Game Master. That prompted a lot of introspection or self-examination for players to keep a "short account" with God and be "fully surrendered" to Him and "crucified with Christ." This was pictured in many of those campfire settings where campers would throw a stick on the fire to show their renewed commitment to Christ in an area of life. An unintended outcome of this approach was covered in Matthew Mead's sermon, which sparked these memories from many decades ago.

Probing our motives, wrestling with, or trying to perceive unconfessed game violations or life choices, young players were pressured to make commitments since they couldn't know if they'd get hit by a Mack truck the next day. These intense altar calls could leave the impression that we were negotiating with God or could perhaps slip through and fix things later when we were ready. Where's that door of resistance in my life they're talking about? Do I give up more than this one area that's bothering me? Is there a room I don't know about? What else am I missing? How do I know when I'm "fully surrendered?" I'm on His team, but do I have to do *everything* He says?

Whatever teaching was given that "partial obedience is disobedience," it never included being a Christian versus being almost a Christian—if you made a profession of faith, it was accepted as gospel truth. Teaching was typically framed about whether you would receive eternal rewards, be dedicated, or need re-dedication to the Game Master, never about membership status or being a faker.

Golden ticket acquisition is non-negotiable. You accept eternal life on the Game Master's terms or not at all (1 Cor. 6:19–20). If the Spirit Master prompts you of an area that still needs fixing, you do it for the One Who gave Himself for you (Gal. 2:20). The One clearly stated that following Him means you are all in (Luke 9:57–62).

Simon, a kiosk leader, asked the One to come to his house for dinner. While there, a woman who was a known sinner came in and weepingly washed His feet with her tears, dried them with her hair, kissed them, and poured an alabaster box of expensive ointment on the One's feet. To answer Simon's disgust at this spectacle, the One told him a story and asked Simon whether the character who was forgiven of a little debt or the one who was forgiven for the overwhelming debt would love the creditor more. This answer was obvious to Simon (Luke 7:36–50).

> **GOLDEN TICKET ACQUISITION IS NON-NEGOTIABLE. YOU ACCEPT ETERNAL LIFE ON THE GAME MASTER'S TERMS OR NOT AT ALL**

Thinking back over childhood memories and being surrounded by many who professed their love for the Game Master at early ages, I wonder at this story and how the depth of love for the Game Master was cultivated. Loving Him because He first loved us was not emphasized as a driving force (1 John 4:19).

There are several video testimonials in the Resource appendices section of guests who were at the end of their life hopes. The One appeared to them and forgave them their spiritual debts. The overwhelming peace and love that flooded those guests as they realized they were no longer condemned and their burden was finally and forever lifted are reminiscent of the woman with the alabaster box.

If you wonder about your status as a member, what is your depth of love for the Game Master? Do you excuse yourself or hold back total commitment in areas of life? Do you consider your membership conditions negotiable with the Game Master? Are you all in? Has the One touched you to the deepest recesses of your soul? (Jer. 17:9).

Suppose you are wondering how to check your status as a member player. In that case, *The Almost Christian Discovered* by Matthew Mead identifies in detail twenty points that can make players an almost Christian but never actually a real Christian. A player can have:

1. Great knowledge and light of God and Christ with His will and His ways
2. Great gifts and even spiritual gifts
3. A strong religious profession and be active in the church

4. Be opposed to sin and open sin (but keep secret sins)
5. May hate sin and its shame and hate it in others more than in himself
6. May make vows and promises and resolutions against sin
7. May combat his own sin and love the Word but doesn't do it
8. May be a church member
9. Great hopes of heaven and being saved
10. Make big life changes
11. Great zeal
12. Pray a lot
13. Suffer for Christ
14. Be called of God
15. May have the Spirit of God but not be born of the Spirit
16. May have faith
17. May love God's people
18. May obey God's commands
19. May be sanctified
20. May do all the duties and worship of a true Christian . . .

> . . . and still be almost a Christian (Mead 2011, entire sermon). Just reading this list can be soul-shaking. There will be great sorrow for many players to realize that their commitment or profession of faith did not include an internal transformation as a genuine Christian. The most tragic words many self-proclaimed members will hear on Judgment Day will be, *"I never knew you; depart from me, you workers of lawlessness"* (Matt. 7:21–23 ESV, emphasis added).

This is the outcome of doing your best to please the Game Master, even immersing yourself in a membership lifestyle but never fully letting go of your control over your choices, destiny, passions, and proclivities. When did you reach the end of yourself and your claim on your life? Everyone may know you're a Christian—do you know better? (Luke 14:25–35; Eph. 2:8–9; 1 John 1:6–10; 2:3–6).

These videos and books are additional resources for self-examination on membership.

Am I Saved? 10 Tests of Assurance
https://www.youtube.com/watch?v=_XacW3FHajM

How far can a person go as a false Christian?
https://www.youtube.com/watch?v=RjMvMGJZ2PE

Matthew Mead – *The Almost Christian Discovered*

Paul Washer – *Narrow Gate, Narrow Way, The Gospel of Jesus Christ*

Master player Peter calls members to "be diligent to make your calling and election [in the bonus round] a sure thing" (Phil. 2:12 AMP; 2 Pet. 1:10–11).

God's Lemonade Stand

"All Things Work Together"

"And we know that all things work together for good to them that love God, to them who are the called according to his purpose" (Rom. 8:28 KJV).

THIS PHRASE, "ALL things work together," is usually a response given when you've told some member your tale of misery and woe, and it should mean that the Game Master will somehow work it out to your benefit. Quite often, it is also associated with additional remarks that He "brings things into your life," "allows" them, or "He knew it would happen," indicating that whatever trouble happens to you was somehow "His will" for you.

Do you see the shift in perspective in these two sentences? This shift in focus of who is the source of your problems, even if it's for your own good, is also a statement that there is nothing you can do about it or could have done to prevent it. This is part of the "God is in control" teaching, where nothing happens to you that He didn't want you to get. Sometimes student chapel speakers repeatedly say, "It doesn't matter what happens to you; God is in control."

The Manual indicates that the Game Master will make lemonade, but it does not say that He will also dump lemon loads of trouble on you so He can make that lemonade for you (Jer. 29:11). Instead, it says that there is nothing good that He will hold back from those who run His gameplays (Ps. 84:11). He doesn't clobber you with one hand and fix your brokenness with the other. The difference is that He will use the trouble you get into for your benefit, but He will not put you in that position of having trouble coming your way.

Good scholars will provide supporting texts to show that bad things do happen to come from the Game Master for our correction, instruction, and growth in our spiritual journey (Rom. 5:1–5; 2 Tim. 3:16–17; James 1:2–4; 5:10–11). Unfortunately, very few members dial up the Heaven Hotline to find out if it came from the Game Master or the Serpent or is a life issue from the game world curse.

Colleagues or fellow kiosk members sometimes say, "I hope God shows me soon what I'm supposed to learn from this problem because it's tough to keep going," "I'm just looking for God's plan in these problems," or "I don't know why God gave me these problems, but I'm waiting to find out." They looked for spiritual growth, which is good, but they never found a cause of their problems and concluded God bestowed it.

Occasionally, they may reach that neighborhood and say, "The devil's really messing with me right now," but don't identify his house and see the reason why. Even experienced members can get caught flatfooted, but in most cases, the cause for bad things is deducible for those who search for answers.

I was hit on two fronts at once in 2017. In one week, we sprung three leaks in the house: two different issues with shower heads and a bad one with the dishwasher, which caused floor damage around the sink. Those were all found and fixed just before our 1,000-mile trip to Wisconsin.

Then, on the way to Wisconsin for our son's wedding, the Yukon's tire flew off at a rough patch on the highway sixty-five miles up the road approaching the Dulles airport. We watched dumbstruck as it rolled on down the road ahead of us and around the bend as I guided the Yukon to the shoulder of the highway. After a tow to a nearby shop, we went home late that night and took the Yaris the next morning. Ten miles up the road, the clutch burned out, so we turned around, put it in the shop, and rented a Dodge Grand Caravan with all the insurance Enterprise offered. This was the first time in fifty-five years of cross-continental trips that all the cars went down at once. But wait, this story isn't over.

After coming home from Wisconsin, we picked up the Yaris but had to wait another week for the right rims to get shipped for the Yukon. A week later, a set of rims arrived with two mismatched rims in the set. So we had to wait another week. After a three-and-a-half-week saga, the suburban was ready. The Game Master helped us get the funds in place before the whole story started, and when the insurance company agent overheard a conversation of the highway patrol's observations at the Yukon's breakdown, He prompted them to reclassify the roadside assistance to an accident, making us eligible for paying only the deductible and having a reduced rate on the rental car.

Friends and family who knew our history of mishaps with cars and their correlation to spiritual drama with us immediately said, "What is it with you and cars?" We were puzzled and prayed blessings on the remainder of our trip and on our way home from Wisconsin. We had broken several curses over the family unit some years back. This saga seemed to fit a pattern, but we could not identify any cause. A week after these ordeals ended, we finally figured it out.

About the time these misadventures started, a pastor had informally met with me to consider taking a new position and not discuss it with anyone—I simply let my closest family know I had a serious "unspoken" prayer request. I agreed to pray, fasted for five days, and the whole sad story began. When I was finally cleared to tell my wife as things seemed to be crystallizing with the position, she put the timeline together, and we realized that we had likely been dealing with a spiritual opposition related to the job change. In the end, the position change did not happen, but that was only the start of even more drama soon after.

For those who are skeptical, spiritual attacks usually have a physical manifestation of some type, which could be a set of bad circumstances, sudden relational conflicts, health issues, or through our possessions or anything within our sphere of influence to knock us down. In our experience, it typically hits the pocketbook in some way, usually through car trouble, major household repairs, or an unexpected major bill. Realizing we were not dealing with the effects of a family curse, we also began praying against the spiritual and manifested opposition we experienced.

Continued prayer was required for the job position, but the bad circumstances stopped. The Game Master observed these things happen while we were praying for a blessing with my job. I should have preempted the mishaps with prayer on those fronts, but we forget that spiritual attacks can rise up when a blessing is on the horizon and fail to raise our spiritual armor against it in time. For someone who is analytical, I am sometimes especially clueless, which is why it helps to have a wife with a good spiritual insight. And yes, a factor in spiritual attacks *can include* a temporary loss of specific memories or a clouded perception.

The problems we faced were not from the Game Master. While He did not block them in this instance, He provided us with resources and mitigated our losses during our lapse of spiritual awareness and confusion and protected us when we finally put on our spiritual defenses. He can only help us to the degree we are responsible for our spiritual condition and preparation. It did not mean that our hardship was His intent or that He gave it to us to "learn us a lesson."

When everything already went wrong. Did your life take a left turn before you got this book? Have you lost your job or future? Has disaster already hit you, your life is a living hell, and you're dealing with the consequences or just trying to survive and keep your sanity? Are you a victim of circumstances or the victim of wrong choices? When your life goes south and hope disappears over the horizon, the Game Master still has plays left for you to run. Master player Paul spoke of a time when things got so bad in Asia that they even despaired of staying alive.

> We do not want you to be uninformed, brothers and sisters, about the troubles we experienced in the province of Asia. We were under great pressure, far beyond our ability to endure, so that we despaired of life itself. Indeed, we felt we had received the sentence of death. But this happened that we might not rely on ourselves but on God, who raises the dead (2 Cor. 1:8–9 NIV).

When your life reaches the point where you're saying, "It looks like God may have to raise the dead here," those are bleak times. Finding answers to life's traumas after you are left picking up the pieces can be either a search for comfort or for someone to blame. Unfortunately, it can also result in the "If I knew then what I know now" perspective, where we wish things could have been different. Hopefully, this book has given you an understanding of possible causes, some tools to help you put your life back together, and ways to be prepared to deflect life's hits.

The Manual shows that while the Game Master is not in the business of messing up your life, He runs a lemonade stand and can make sweet work of the lemons you get pummeled with during the game. But as with all things in the Manual, there are conditions, and you must qualify.

God's lemonade stand — aka all things work together

We'll start with the actual text and work backward: "And we know that all things work together for good to them that love God, to them who are the called according to his purpose" (Rom. 8:28).

The called. The promise is specifically to members referring to those who are "the called." That means they have their golden ticket. No promises are made for guests. Since there seems to be a dispute about whether the Satanic Bible is his official text or not, it would be uncertain what promises or blessings guests can expect from their Serpent boss. The Manual describes the Serpent's "blessings" as seasonal pleasures of sin (Heb. 11:24–25), but his ultimate intent is to steal, kill, and destroy players (John 10:10). Quite an outcome.

Those who confess or testify that the One is the Son of God have the Spirit Master residing in them, and they are assuredly members (1 John 4:15). Next comes the proof of their membership.

Love God. Those "that love God" is the key to your status identification as a member. It seems redundant to call yourself a member and have to check whether you love the Game Master since you obviously do by your membership. We think and we assume that we love the One just because we say so, but the Manual has a different level of proof: it's not just what you say; it's what you do.

The One said that if you love Him, you'll keep His commandments or sayings (John 14:21–24). The condition that identifies members is that they love each other (1 John 4:7–8), and this also is His commandment that they do so (1 John 4:21). One qualifier is that those who say they love the Game Master are also saying they unconditionally love fellow members. Those members who don't love each other don't know the Game Master because His defining characteristic is love (1 John 4:8, 16).

Players who say they love the Game Master but hate their fellow members are liars because the Manual says they cannot love the Game Master, whom no one has seen, when they refuse to love other members whom they have seen (1 John 4:14). Furthermore, unconditional love also means that you love your neighbor as much as you love yourself; players like that don't attack, hurt, or destroy others (Gal. 5:14–15).

It isn't enough to know what the Manual says or even enough to agree with the Manual. If you know what it says but don't actually do what it says and practice what it says, you are deceived (James 1:22), and the One says you have no foundation for stability or success with Him (Matt. 7:26–29).

All things work together for good. If you meet the Manual definition that you love the Game Master, this promise applies to you. You are expected to pray to the Game Master to help you out of trouble (Ps. 60:11; 108:12). He keeps you from trouble and responds when trouble gets through to you (Ps. 34:6, 17; 54:7; 91:1–16).

He said that because you love him, when you call on Him, not only will He be with you in your trouble, but He will also deliver you from it, honor you, and extend your game life (Ps. 91:14–16). The Game Master not only takes your call but also raises the blessing beyond what you asked for. Use your prayer of faith and put your confidence in Him and in His Word.

> The Manual says that no temptation or trial overtakes us which is worse than what is typical of the general player experience; the Game Master is faithful though, and He won't let you be tested beyond your ability, but as you go through that trial He will also provide the avenue of escape, so you can endure it (1 Cor. 10:13, paraphrased).

Pray with confidence because we know that He makes all things we experience work together for good. Even in your day of trouble, you can be blessed out of it and succeed when it's over. Give Him your cares because He cares about you (1 Pet. 5:7). Put your burden on Him, and He will sustain you (Ps. 55:22).

God is sovereign

The context we refer to is the "God is in control" teaching, where *nothing* happens to you except the Game Master allowed it or intended it to happen—nothing happens to you without His permission. Because there are spiritual parameters that the Game Master works from, this concept does not account for player activity. Since players can limit the Game Master—by His own account, how then is He controlling *everything* that happens to you? (Ps. 78:40–42).

The fact that He says He can be limited and hindered by players points to the problem that kiosk leaders overstate His hand in life's issues to convey the truth that the Game Master cares about what happens to them. Yes, He does care, but you can limit His assistance to prevent problems.

Calling all things the purpose of God may not be the intent of the kiosks, but it is widely accepted and understood to be the case by average members in their personal conversations as they wrestle with game troubles. Members don't intend to malign the Game Master. However, as they attempt to connect with a hurting player and show them that the Game Master cares about their bad situation, they overexplain and end up describing Him as the source of pain by saying He knew it was going to happen, He sent it to them, He allowed it, and then they point to Him as the One who can heal their hurts.

We have documented enough game world problems bedeviling players from start to finish that there is absolutely no need for the Game Master to "allow" more of it against players. If this is your religious philosophy, then your understanding of the Game Master's character needs a major correction. Consult the Manual and adjust your view based on its explicit reading of His character.

Here is a lemonade illustration where everything happens to you with His permission:

1) the Game Master hands you a lemon load of trouble (because He is in control),
2) He makes lemonade from your trouble, and
3) then He gives you the lemonade of comfort and help.

The actual text never says He gives you the lemons or intends for you to have lemons to begin with. His preferred food groups for you are milk and honey (Exod. 3:8, 17; Lev. 20:24; Jer. 11:5; Ezek. 20:6).

Here is a lemonade illustration that He describes in Psalm 34:

1) You land in a lemon bushel of trouble (vv. 4, 6, 17, 19)
2) He makes lemonade from your trouble, and (vv. 4, 6–7, 17, 19)
3) Then He gives you the lemonade of comfort and help (vv. 8–10, 18–20, 22).

Restoration

Healing from a heart-wrenching sorrow can encompass the physical, emotional, and psychological aspects of our being. It appears the pain and memories will last forever. The One said to come to Him with your weariness of life and unbearable burdens, and He can give you the rest for your soul that you need in the middle of your turmoil of life (Matt. 11:28–30).

The Game Master can restore relationships (Luke 1:16–17) and physical and material losses (Joel 2:25). These areas matter to players in this game level.

> The One came to preach His good news to the poor, heal the brokenhearted, to announce deliverance to captives, restore sight to the blind, to free those who have been downtrodden, bruised, crushed and broken down by calamity, and proclaim that the time of salvation and freely given favors from the Game Master would begin (Luke 4:16–21, paraphrased).

He declared these things to be fulfilled during His time in the game world, but to continue this work for future generations, He prayed for the Game Master to release the Spirit Master to the members as their resident Comforter (John 14:16–18). The Manual tells us to throw all our cares on the Game Master because He cares for us (1 Pet. 5:6–7). Whatever broken pieces of your life you are holding, you are not alone in your loss. No one cares more about your well-being than the One who made you.

Forgive and forget. This is the Serpent's solution. It places an extra burden of guilt on you because you just can't forget or move on from what happened, and it lives with you daily. The Game Master didn't tell you to forget. He only said to forgive because a condition of your being forgiven by Him is that you forgive others as He forgave you for the sake of the One who died for you (Matt. 6:12–15; 18;23–35; Eph. 4:32). Forgiveness from your heart is the only required response as we follow the example of the Game Master toward us. He will help you fade those memories but doesn't insist it of you.

Coerced forgiveness. This point is coupled with the "forgive and forget" remarks. Many players suffer deep personal loss through abuse, violence, treachery, intentional wrongdoing, and mishaps from other players or factors. A particular point to address is abuse toward minors.

Although abuse is widespread throughout the game world, a growing common story in the national Christian community is the revelation of sexual abuse against minors. Scandals within the Roman Catholic church are widely known, but abuse in the Protestant world is primarily under the radar, and instances of publicity are typically localized to individuals. The curtain has been pulled back in recent years by GRACE (Godly Response to Abuse in the Christian Environment), an organization that conducts investigative work for organizations, among other things (Godly Response to Abuse in Christian Environments 2019, entire site).

From some findings made public by GRACE, common themes among the abused are that those who have protective oversight of the affected children may not be aware of the problem or be included in the solution by their kiosk leadership and may not vigorously investigate when the child reports it to them because of their lack of standing in the family or kiosk environment. The family or kiosk leaders may place the blame on the child and sometimes stage a public display of "church discipline" against the child but not the perpetrator. In many cases, the child is counseled or coerced to forgive the perpetrator, and the situation may then be considered an in-house matter requiring no further action.

Young adults in college and beyond who realize they have been abused and have counseling needs may find their case handled by a kiosk college that counsels them to forgive, which may contact the student's home kiosk, and which may not report the student's story to authorities since the matter was resolved or "put to rest" in-house.

Note: *Many governments require caregivers who suspect or become aware of physical or sexual abuse of minors to report them to civil authority; they should not assume that prosecutors will excuse non-compliance.*

An issue that is coming to light regards adults whom kiosk leaders abuse. They may sometimes find that the kiosk leadership will declare it as adultery, which is typically considered consensual. This easily wipes out a criminal stain of abuse on the leader's reputation. These leaders are either forgiven by the kiosk leadership or move on to a new kiosk, where they may continue their predatory behavior with fresh victims. Such kiosks, which may assert they are Bible-believing, rarely provide justice, forgiveness, or recovery for the victims.

The focus of this point is the use of forgiveness to resolve a matter. The Game Master instructs us to forgive as a condition of our forgiveness from Him, and some may say He "commands" us to forgive. All declarations of forgiveness by a victim of circumstances, while expected from Him, should always be voluntary. Players do not "forgive from their heart" if it is involuntary, which may nullify the declaration in the Game Master's view, and coercion does not meet the standard of free will or proper motive by the victim.

Also, the Game Master does not require you to confront the perpetrator to announce that you forgive them. Instead, forgiving them is a transaction between you and the Game Master (Mark 11:25–26; Eph. 4:32). When you forgive others who despitefully use you, you are practicing the character of the Game Master and make it possible for Him to forgive you and bless you.

The Spirit Master can guide us to the place where we have received comfort from Him and are aware that our best interest toward peace is to forgive. This process can take months or years with deep hurts and scars.

Also, consider that if you need therapy, seek therapy; if you need justice, seek justice. The Game Master set up the government to punish those who commit evil, so let them do their divinely appointed duty (Rom. 13:1–4). Because we often associate the forgiveness of a heinous act to include also forgetting it, the logic is to conclude that you should not prosecute, or you will not have fully forgiven the perpetrator. This is not a conditional burden of forgiveness from the Game Master. As you read the Manual book of Acts, master player Paul quickly invoked his rights as a Roman citizen. He had no problem or hesitation in putting the fear of the law on those who beat him up or tried to kill him (Acts 16:16–40; 23:9–35).

The Manual rebukes members for suing each other when they should be settling their differences out of court (1 Cor. 6:1–8), and it also has a kiosk censorship process that is not used effectively today (Matt. 18:15–17). These guidelines do not discuss criminal behavior except fraud. However, this admonition has been applied to all manner of criminal behavior depending on whom the kiosk wants to protect through in-house discipline.

Forgive from your heart, but don't be compelled to forfeit justice under the impression that it's also required as part of forgiveness. Whatever hurts are not healed by the time you finish your gameplay, the Game Master will wipe away all tears at the bonus round; there will be no more sorrow or crying or pain, and those things that caused it or that were done to you will no longer be remembered by you or associated with you (Rev. 21:4).

The Sovereignty of God

"God Is in control"

EASTON'S BIBLE DICTIONARY defines the sovereignty of God as "his absolute right to do all things according to his own good pleasure" (Easton 1897) (Dan. 4:25, 35; Rom. 9:15–23; 1 Tim. 6:15; Rev. 4:11).

The Game Master is sovereign, having all authority over the game and able to step in according to His discretion, saying,

> "Don't forget this, O guilty ones. And don't forget the many times I clearly told you what was going to happen in the future. For I am God—I only—and there is no other like me who can tell you what is going to happen. All I say will come to pass, for I do whatever I wish" (Isa. 46:8–10 TLB).

The Calvinist perspective takes it further. Chip Ingram of Walk Through the Bible organization says, "The way I like to explain God's sovereignty best is simply to say, "God is in control"" (Ingram 2022, ¶ 1).

John Calvin (1509–1564) wrote a four-book series, *The Institutes of the Christian Religion* (Calvin 1536). The website introduction by Stephen Tomkins says in part,

> Probably no book in the history of the Protestant churches has been more influential than Calvin's *Institutes*. It is a systematic explanation of the whole of the Christian faith as Calvin understood it, an attempt to unpack everything God has revealed to us about himself and ourselves in the Scriptures (Christian History Institute n.d., ¶ 1).

> Calvin's writing is so lucid and well-organized that it communicated his ideas most persuasively throughout the Protestant world. Consequently, his way of thinking molded the teaching of the reformed

churches throughout Europe and the Church of England (and its many daughter churches) (Christian History Institute n.d., ¶ 3).

Calvin extends God's role as creator to include his absolute control over everything that happens in the universe, from the smallest to the greatest. This idea of the sovereignty of God was Calvin's most central doctrine. It means that nothing is left to chance or human free will. This is what led him to put on the doctrine of predestination—the idea that God, not we, decides whether we will be saved. This point of view was hugely influential and popular among Protestants in the sixteenth century, but became far more controversial later (Christian History Institute n.d., ¶ 4-5).

Notice that Calvin's sovereignty doctrine "means that nothing is left to chance or human free will" (Christian History Institute n.d., ¶ 5). His followers discard other factors and ascribe all good and bad things to God because He is in control.

According to John Calvin, the concept that God is in control includes your eternal destiny, which is out of your control. He said, "God . . . arranges all things by his sovereign counsel, in such a way that **individuals are born, who are doomed from the womb to certain death, and are to glorify him by their destruction**" (Calvin n.d., ¶ 6; emphasis added).

That statement is anathema to the Game Master. Instead, the Game Master said in no uncertain terms,

> "Tell them, 'As certainly as I'm alive and living,' declares the Lord God, 'I receive no pleasure in the death of the wicked. Instead, my pleasure is that the wicked repent from their behavior and live. Turn back! Turn back, all of you, from your wicked behavior! Why do you have to die, you house of Israel?'" (Ezek. 33:11 ISV).

The Game Master expresses it three times that He has no pleasure in the death of the wicked, but rather that they repent and turn to Him for life (Ezek. 18:23, 31–32). The One described the Game Master's heart, saying, "For God loved the world so much that he gave his only Son so that anyone who believes in him shall not perish but have eternal life" (John 3:16 TLB).

This is not an isolated thought stream from John Calvin. His followers believe this too. In a staff group discussion on God's love, an avowed Calvinist colleague posited the perspective that the Game Master does not love everyone because He sends so many to hell. He was very comfortable disparaging the expressed love of the Game Master for all players and ignoring His call for all to turn to Him for eternal life because of His love for them (John 3:16; Matt. 18:11–14; 2 Pet. 3:9).

Players ask, "Why did God let this bad thing happen to me?" That question springs from this widely taught Calvinist teaching that whatever happens to you was God's will for you. It's easier to say, "God is in control" and provide teachable moments during recovery from it than it is to say, "That shouldn't have happened to you, but God is here for you, and together with Him, we can walk through this and find the reason why."

My son observed a kiosk prayer team meeting about how to respond to players who come to them for prayer during the Sunday worship time. They were instructed to not tell them anything like what to expect after the prayer or tell them about a word from God that the team member received because if it didn't come true or happen, then the prayer team member was liable for its failure (which reflected on the kiosk). This was in lieu of helping them learn why things were happening to them or how they would work out. My son understood that the kiosk was simply a shoulder to cry on (James 2:15–16).

We have been addressing two major Protestant religious views that pertain to the Game Master's interaction with players: the Arminian view and the Calvinist view. Both views overlap in some respects and diverge in others. This book presents an Arminian perspective that life's choices are yours and that although the Game Master already knows the final score, eternal life is also your choice to receive.

A kiosk's perspective on the sovereignty of God largely identifies the kind of help you can receive to change your life's trajectory. The Arminian view shows the choice is yours, and solutions to change things are available. The Calvinist has a more fatalist approach to life's events where your losses are predetermined as God's will for you.

In broad terms, denominations that follow Calvinism include the Presbyterians, Evangelical Anglican and Episcopalians, Congregationalist, and reformed churches, including reformed Baptists (Joseph n.d., ¶ 2, 7–8). Denominations that follow Arminianism include Baptist, Anabaptist and Quaker, Methodist, Pentecostal, Brethren, Holiness, Adventist, and some Lutheran churches. Calvinists are increasingly found within Arminian congregations, tend to be vocal and assertive and may also take leadership roles. Lists of notable Calvinist and Arminian leaders and Christians have been compiled online (Olson R. 2013, ¶ 8–14).

Manual references in this book display the Game Master's response to our choices in life and our calls for help. You have a joystick or gamepad with choices to navigate your way through the game and can beat this game level and change your outcomes by choosing life with the Game Master. He says that's His preference for you (Deut. 30:19; 2 Pet. 3:9).

Regardless of guest and members' perspectives, there will come a time at the end of the game when spirit beings and all players, dead or alive, will be compelled to bow the knee and declare that the One is sovereign:

> For this reason also [because He (Jesus) obeyed and so completely humbled Himself], God has highly exalted Him and bestowed on Him the name which is above every name, so that at the name of Jesus every knee shall bow [in submission], of those who are in heaven and on earth and under the earth, and that every tongue will confess and openly acknowledge that Jesus Christ is Lord (sovereign God), to the glory of God the Father (Phil. 2:9–11 AMP).

Master player John describes how this will look at the end of the game:

> Then I looked, and I heard the voice of many angels around the throne and [the voice] of the living creatures and the elders; and they numbered myriads of myriads, and thousands of thousands (innumerable), saying in a loud voice,
>
> "Worthy and deserving is the Lamb that was sacrificed to receive power and riches and wisdom and might and honor and glory and blessing."
>
> And I heard every created thing that is in heaven or on earth or under the earth [in Hades, the realm of the dead] or on the sea, and everything that is in them, saying [together],
>
> "To Him who sits on the throne, and to the Lamb (Christ), be blessing and honor and glory and dominion forever and ever."
>
> And the four living creatures kept saying, "Amen." And the elders fell down and worshiped [Him who lives forever and ever] (Rev. 5:8–14 AMP).

Regardless of whose team you are on; you will willingly declare or be compelled to declare His sovereignty. Then, it is judgment time and game over.

In summary, the Game Master is sovereign over this Game of Life and has authority to intervene in whatever way He chooses. Your perspective of His sovereignty will determine what you will ask of Him and hope and expect from Him.

Since God is sovereign, is He putting trouble in my path? If you think God willed it, you may be a Calvinist.

For additional information comparing Arminianism to Calvinism, see the link for the entitled article, "An Outline of the FACTS of Arminianism vs. The TULIP of Calvinism:"
https://evangelicalarminians.org/an-outline-of-the-facts-of-arminianism-vs-the-tulip-of-calvinism

Faith Deconstruction

A SIGN SHOWING WE are nearing the Apocalypse is the rising number of professing member players walking off the Game Master's team. Deceit is becoming the order of the day and sounds plausible to those whose membership experience didn't impart a life-changing experience (Matt. 24:11–13; 2 Thess. 2:3; 1 Tim. 4:1–3; 2 Tim. 3:1–9; 2 Pet. 3:3; 1 John 2:18–19).

Deconstruction described:

> It is sort of a dismantling and then bringing together the elements. Any text, any idea, any concept will be broken down first, will be dismantled first to be constructed again within the deconstructor's own ideology, own subjectivity is what deconstruction tells you. In fact, this is one of the main points of deconstruction, that the person, the critic, the author, the reader, his psyche, his subjectivity, his personality definitely modifies the meaning of the text. This process also challenges the belief that a text always has one particular meaning. We've been taught that since the beginning of our education (The Literature Life 2021, min. 2:58 & 4:06).

The Manual also explains a deconstruction process depicting those who walk away from the Game Master. Romans chapter 1 describes a four-step process where players, who instinctively know the Game Master's truth but refuse to acknowledge Him, 1) professes themselves wise but become fools and change the incorruptible God into corruptible gods from within the creation, then 2) they change the truth of the Game Master into a lie and begin worshiping His creation, then 3) they change their natural affections to those as represented by the LGBTQ and transexual communities, and then 4) they change to a reprobate mind as haters of God and lovers of all things opposed to Him (Rom. 1:18–32).

The Manual identifies the source of much deconstruction: giving credence to seducing spirits and doctrines of demons (1 Tim. 4:1). Nobody wants to say they have been fooled, seduced, or deceived away from the faith and tricked by the devil, so it's framed around rational explanations. In some cases, it may be peer pressure; they don't want to be different from everyone else.

The concept of deconstructing your faith is popular with the younger generations. There are different meanings of what that entails, whether it is an examination of the tenets of the faith or scrutinizing issues of the kiosk culture. This is where members need to heed Psalm 118:8, "It is better to trust in the LORD than to put confidence in man." Churches and Christian leaders will disappoint you and perhaps abuse you. They are supposed to be an example of God's goodness but are not the standard for evaluating God's goodness. Their failures are not the Game Master's failures.

Here are some excerpts from Timothy Padgett of BreakPoint.org, who writes:

> To be clear, Scripture (especially the Psalms) not only creates plenty of space for doubting and questioning, but describes how God meets us in our questions and doubts. So, if all that is meant by deconstruction is asking tough questions about God or faith, that's a normal part of the Christian life and need not mean deconversion. Or, if it is used to refer to untangling politics or other elements of American culture that have been corruptively bundled with Christian identity, deconstruction may simply mean discernment.
>
> Conversion, reform, and renewal are words provided in Scripture and church history to keep God's people squarely within a Christian vision of truth: that it is revealed, not constructed, and that it is objective, not subjective. More importantly, because God takes upon Himself the burden of making truth known (and does not author confusion), real knowledge about God and self is possible.
>
> Deconstructing faith rarely ends at merely rejecting corruption or jettisoning historical baggage, and instead culminates in an entirely new faith that features what is culturally acceptable. Abandoned along the way are essential doctrines of Christianity (such as the deity and exclusivity of Christ or the authority of His Word), and its moral teachings (especially those having to do with sexuality and abortion). Shaped by a commitment to skepticism, "deconstruction" presumes that truth is illusionary and knowledge is impossible" (Stonestreet and Padgett 2021, ¶ 4-8).

While proponents can claim it is a necessary way to confirm one's faith, the Serpent is effectively introducing this concept in kiosks as a helpful way to intelligently walk away from the Game Master and His Manual since it does not stand up to the scrutiny of personal experience, intellect, science, and social themes as an authoritative guiding document.

Gospel Partners Media has a short video suggesting five reasons these professed believers walk away from their faith as outlined in Todd Friel's booklet, *Are You a Rotten Fish?* (1 John 2:19).

1. We have neglected crucial aspects of the gospel proclamation – God's character and nature, His holiness and daily anger with the wicked, believing God's love is unconditional, so no conditions are binding and no strings are attached.
2. We present an unbalanced portrayal of Jesus – a needy, sissified boyfriend who doles out some helpful advice.
3. We tell people to follow Jesus for a better life – life enhancement, prosperity gospel.
4. We preach that Jesus is valuable ONLY as "fire insurance" (Rom. 2:4).
5. We don't preach repentance (Matt. 4:17, 21:32; Luke 5:32, 17:3; Acts 3:19, 5:31, 11:18; Rom. 2:4; Eph. 2:8-10, 5:8).
6. And finally... we teach wrong salvation instructions – repentance and faith are required (Wretched 2023, entire video).

Popular Christian apologist and Calvinist, Tyler Vela, announced in November 2022 that he had "deconverted" from Christianity with the headline stating because God did not comfort him after his divorce. He said,

> My divorce wasn't the cause or even the reason for my deconversion—**it was more like a catalyst,** not the cause. I didn't lose my faith because I got divorced. Like, "God, if You're real, I wouldn't be divorced." Now that would be shallow and honestly a silly reason. I mention my divorce because it's an event that made me rip off a bunch of band-aids and come out of hiding. To confront a lot of very sinful and shameful aspects about myself in my life. My divorce forced me to confront myself and how I handled abuse and infidelity and how being a victim of circumstance had changed me into someone I didn't recognize and I was ashamed of being.

What was weird, however, was that **the more I healed** and became more confident and at peace with who I am, I also noticed that **the ministerial promises of the Bible seemed further and further from reality for me.** That tension bothered me. **A very strong cognitive dissonance set in. I begged and cried and asked God to get to make me more like Jesus, to love him more, to know him more to have the Spirit convict me, etc. But the more I did that, the less faith I had, because it started to feel that those are things that I shouldn't have to beg God for.**

Surely something from my heavenly father who's supposed to infinitely love and care for and protect and uphold his children, surely God would know what would at least be noticeable to me, right? Enough to keep me from walking out. I wasn't expecting grand miracles or healing. I wasn't praying for stuff or things for prosperity, or even for favourable circumstances. I just wanted him just like He promised. And God could have, just like I would for my sons, but crickets. For years, crickets" (Staff Writer 2022, ¶ 11–12, 18).

Tyler talks like someone who could have benefitted from counseling. Those are a lot of trauma trigger points with his divorce issues and his "sinful and shameful aspects" that were left unaddressed while he drew his conclusions and walked off the Game Master's team.

If you think the Game Master ghosted you, you need to run a diagnostic check on your life. A broken family can be evidence of a curse. The heavens of brass can be the outcome of a curse or unresolved game violations. Soul searching needs to address our personal issues that run contrary to the Manual (Deut. 28:15, 23, 30; Ps. 24:3–5; Prov. 1).

Some things are left to us by God as our own responsibility to do. It isn't the Game Master's job to keep you from walking off His team. The greatest commandment is to love the Game Master with all your being (Deut. 6:5; 11:1; 30:20; Matt. 22:36–40; Mark 12:29–31; Luke 10:22–28). The onus is not on Him to get us to love Him more, to obey Him better. It sounds spiritual but is not scriptural. Instead, this shows a lack of commitment to Him (John

> **WHEN YOU ARE SHAKEN TO YOUR CORE, YOUR PERSPECTIVE OF THE GAME MASTER WILL REVEAL YOUR UNDERSTANDING OF HIM AND YOUR EXPECTATION FROM HIM.**

14:15, 21–24). When you are shaken to your core, your perspective of the Game Master will reveal your understanding of Him and your expectation from Him.

Master player David describes what it is like when the Game Master has your back, but he also explains why he got a response in his distress: he was synced to the Game Master through His Manual.

> Lord, how I love you! For you have done such tremendous things for me. The Lord is my fort where I can enter and be safe; no one can follow me in and slay me. He is a rugged mountain where I hide; he is my Savior, a rock where none can reach me, and a tower of safety. He is my shield. He is like the strong horn of a mighty fighting bull. All I need to do is cry to him—oh, praise the Lord—and I am saved from all my enemies!
>
> Death bound me with chains, and the floods of ungodliness mounted a massive attack against me. Trapped and helpless, I struggled against the ropes that drew me on to death. In my distress I screamed to the Lord for his help. And he heard me from heaven; my cry reached his ears.
>
> The Lord rewarded me for doing right and being pure. For I have followed his commands and have not sinned by turning back from following him. I kept close watch on all his laws; I did not refuse a single one. I did my best to keep them all, holding myself back from doing wrong. And so the Lord has paid me with his blessings, for I have done what is right, and I am pure of heart. This he knows, for he watches my every step (Ps. 18:1–6, 20–24 TLB).

Master player Jeremiah expressed his times of anguish and woe during the siege and fall of Jerusalem as the people were starving around him while the Game Master punished them for their persistent game violations (Lam. 1–5).

> O Lord, all peace and all prosperity have long since gone, for you have taken them away. I have forgotten what enjoyment is. All hope is gone; my strength has turned to water, for the Lord has left me. Oh, remember the bitterness and suffering you have dealt to me! For I can never forget these awful years; always my soul will live in utter shame.

Yet there is one ray of hope: his compassion never ends. It is only the Lord's mercies that have kept us from complete destruction. Great is his faithfulness; his loving-kindness begins afresh each day. My soul claims the Lord as my inheritance; therefore I will hope in him. The Lord is wonderfully good to those who wait for him, to those who seek for him. It is good both to hope and wait quietly for the salvation of the Lord (Lam. 3:17–26 TLB).

Jeremiah's perspective inspired the lyrics to the hymn, "Great Is Thy Faithfulness." The Game Master wasn't responding to his cries in his dark, dark distress (Lam. 3:7–9). Yet, Jeremiah held onto the one ray of hope that the Game Master is faithful in compassion, and he chose to wait for Him and pursue Him so he could again experience His goodness.

When master player Paul was traveling through Asia, the struggles were so bad that he despaired of getting through them alive and felt like there was a death sentence on them (2 Cor. 1:8–11) As a bullied teenager with suicidal thoughts in a verbally and emotionally abusive household, the Game Master was my therapist through my deep, years-long depression. His psalms and hymns and promises were a life raft in my sea of despair. His mercies are new every morning; great is His faithfulness.

What is the Game Master's worth to you? (Job 13:13–16; Heb. 11:35–40; Rev. 3:18–22; 12:10–11). What hope do you cling to when you reach rock bottom? Does your trust in Him persist or fade away? Perhaps it's too late to undo the damage and devastation you face, and things will never be the same, but He will help you pick up the pieces and set you upon a stable rock (Ps. 40:1–3; Matt. 7:22–27; Luke 6:47–49). "Give your burdens to the Lord, and he will take care of you. He will not permit the godly to slip and fall" (Ps. 55:22 NLT).

It seems that deconstructionists don't run spiritual diagnostics on their life issues using the Manual. Instead, they rely on the Serpent's seductive philosophical malware to draw their flawed conclusions. Unfortunately, the outcome for many deconstructionists who look to the Serpent for answers is usually that the Serpent was right in the garden of Eden: the Game Master does not have your best interest at heart, so His perspective is irrelevant to your situation.

Prosperity Gospel

THIS ISSUE MUST be addressed because it is a red flag to many members, and rightly so. It has become distorted to the point that sincere member players ignore, reject, or even discredit the Manual's valid promises of health and prosperity as it relates to this game level. This book may seem close enough to prosperity gospel theology concepts to create cause for concern in those who only have a limited understanding of it. However, it is not intended to devolve into a "name it and claim it" or "blab it and grab it" venue for personal gain.

Prosperity gospel theology, as it is widely understood, is a false teaching that uses the Manual as evidence that the Game Master primarily wants His players to be happy, healthy, and wealthy, with a prominent text coming from Malachi 3:8–11. Learning strategies for health and wealth are not wrong and are even prudent, but the focus of a member should be to invest his wealth in the bonus round (Matt. 6:19–20). An easy deception of the Serpent is to distract, and using the Manual to shift a member's focus toward accruing points on a game level that will not pay them eternal dividends keeps members from interfering with his game world operation.

The One told his members to use wealth to fund the pursuit of signing up member players as a strategy for gameplay, not for a life of leisure (Luke 16:9). He was able to relate to the poor, middle class, and wealthy, and while He led a simple life with simple needs, His teaching and healing operation was underwritten by many women (Luke 8:1–3). His team of disciple members included businessmen and a wealthy IRS-type agent, but there's no mention that they consistently funded His work during their time with the One, and it appears they ran their businesses on the side after they were commissioned to enlighten the game world with His gospel of good news only as a means of funding their continued ministry.

All this controversy does not change the fact that the Game Master has most certainly provided the means for players to find health and success in the *function* of our daily lives. He does not view being poor, wretched, blind, weak, sickly, or dying before your time as achievements or desirable outcomes (Deut. 30:19–20; Rev. 3:17). In this picture of His blessing, the issue of wealth may improve for you as curses are broken and healing is received. Pursuing wealth as a promise of its own to satisfy your passions is a focus He rejects. In the end, all you will have to show for it is a smoking ash heap of wasted opportunity, just a pile of regrets (1 Cor. 3:11–15; 1 Tim. 6:9–11).

The Manual says that your way of life should be free from covetousness or the pursuit of money, and instead, you need to practice contentment with what you have (Heb. 13:5). To covet is a Big Ten game violation (Exod. 20:17; Deut. 5:21). Instead of pursuing prosperity, He says to make yourself a worthy player in the things that matter to Him by pursuing the bonus round and becoming mission-ready, geared up, and combat-ready, and let Him handle your financial success and daily subsistence in the game world (Matt. 6:28–34).

Blessed living

A major point of spirit armor and weaponry is to get yourself to the place where you can stop surviving from miracle to miracle and start living from blessing to blessing. A blessed life is a life of good fortune where you have the Game Master looking out for you all the time instead of constantly calling headquarters for a miracle to pull you through your next tight spot. It does not help the Game Master's cause to have His members forever living on the edge of ruin, staying distracted from His interests because they must continually focus on miracle prayers just to keep them going. That's not much inspiration for joining His team.

You still must deal with things wearing out and breaking, but they don't have to turn your world upside down or happen at the worst moments. The Israelites walked in the desert for forty years while their clothes and sandals never wore out. Surely, a blessed life should include favorable attention toward you as a beneficiary of the Game Master's promises (Deut. 8:4; 29:5; Neh. 9:21; Matt. 6:31–32).

Does this mean you should have an easy life? Not necessarily. Prosperous living, which does not include wealth or leisure, is possible. If your measuring stick for prosperity is limited to money and leisure, then you don't have a bonus round perspective. You should also check your membership status (2 Cor. 13:5). There is nothing inherently wrong with having an easy life, just as there is nothing inherently wrong with being rich. However, those are the wrong motivational pursuits of life for bonus round success.

Being a winner both here and going into the bonus round is done on the Game Master's terms. The Manual says that we will find it as we aspire to be like the Game Master with an attitude of contentment in what we have (Ps. 1; 1 Tim. 6:5–10).

Additional information: "The Dangers of the Prosperity Gospel" (Amaechina 2022) https://www.christianpost.com/voices/the-dangers-of-the-prosperity-gospel.html

Spiritual Gifts

BECAUSE SUPERNATURAL LIVING requires supernatural power, this area needs to be covered. Depending on your perspective, there are about twenty-five different spiritual gifts listed in the Manual (Rom. 12; 1 Cor. 12; 1 Cor. 7:7,8; 1 Cor. 13:3; Eph. 3:6–8; Eph. 4; 1 Pet. 4:9,10). By Manual location, they are (those in *italics* are repeated):

Romans 12 – exhortation, giving, leadership, mercy, *prophecy*, service, *teaching*;

1 Corinthians 12 – administration, *apostle*, discernment, faith, healing, helps, knowledge, miracles, *prophecy*, *teaching*, tongues, tongues interpretation, wisdom;

Ephesians 4 – *apostle*, evangelist, pastor, *prophecy*, *teaching*;

From **various texts** – celibacy, hospitality, martyrdom, missionary, voluntary poverty ("Spiritual Gifts List & Definitions" n.d., ¶ 6).

The ones we'll discuss are described as manifestation gifts or gifts of power, which include miracles, healing, discernment, knowledge, prophecy and tongues, and their interpretation. The giftings from "various texts" are not included in typical denominational lists.

There is a contrast in viewpoints among kiosk denominations that either claim the manifestation gifts of the spirit are here among us or those that claim they ended when the canon of scripture was complete. Some of those that claim such gifts have ended and then go on to argue that the Game Master won't heal you or give you a miracle seem to operate with split personalities when they pray for the sick or for those in need. What exactly are they praying for if not for divine intervention? Is anything too hard for God? (Gen. 18:14; Jer. 32:17; Matt. 17:20; Luke 1:36–37; 1 John 5:14–15)

I believe the argument of whether gifts were phased out is largely irrelevant. I have cited stories from Andrew Wommack and Derek Prince who both have had significant healing and miracle ministries. The way they describe their beginning struggles in these areas probably don't reflect a gifting with miracles or healings. The fact that they have had better success in some areas than in others seems to be evidence that they may not possess a universal gifting. They could simply be master players who have practiced experience in their faith. When the Spirit Master bestows a gift to you, it should come naturally and significantly.

You don't need a spiritual gift to heal yourself or others or to make a miracle. These gifts can be both accomplished by any member and downloaded in a moment of need. The difference is that those who possess specific gifts have the capacity to use them repeatedly or as a characteristic skill of their gameplay. The reason this topic matters is because most of us members don't have manifestation gifts, the spiritual gifts of miracles, healing, supernatural knowledge or discernment, or intuitive foreign language skills. All of us can call on the Game Master for assistance and receive a download as needed, but they are not necessarily part of our gifting upgrade except by the Spirit Master's choice.

The Spirit Master bestows gifts to members that make them more effective in their participation on the Game Master's team (1 Cor. 12:7, 11). The Manual says that, "the gifts and calling of God are without repentance" (Rom. 11:29 KJV). Whatever the Game Master gives you and whatever He calls you to do are not revoked.

A few of these special gifts are emphasized the most, and the Manual gives instructions to cultivate or take them on as part of our collective game experience for the benefit of the members and guests (1 Cor. 12:31; 14:1, 5, 12). We have already detailed healing and miracles with Manual instructions on how to effectively access them without their being specifically gifted to us. Master player Paul instructs us to earnestly pursue and cultivate the best gifts which he does not enumerate (1 Cor. 12:31), and he preferred that we all used the gift of prophecy (1 Cor. 14:1–3, 39).

Tongues and prophecy are juxtaposed with tongues being a sign for guests and prophecy being a sign for members (1 Cor. 14:22–25). Tongues here refers to foreign language and not the speaking in tongues or praying in tongues commonly described in Protestant kiosks. The purpose of manifestation gifts is to show the power of the Game Master so that players will be directed to the Manual. They are the Spirit Master's way of getting players' attention in dramatic fashion. The gifts themselves are not the end but only the means to an end, and players are the beneficiaries along the way.

The One & Spiritual Gifts

As you read about the life of the One, besides the spiritual gifts of healings and miracles that He did, almost all the other spectacular happenings (prophecy, word of knowledge, discernment, etc.) were also done through the operation of spiritual gifts. This is never described as having a real connection with us. Here is a restated list of some amazing things He did such as:

- Knowing what players were thinking (discernment) (Matt. 12:24–26; 22:15–22; Mark 2:5–12; 3:1–6; Luke 6:7–11)
- Knowing what others didn't know (word of knowledge) (Mark 5:38–40; John 6:64)
- Where to find things (knowledge) (Matt. 17:24–27; 21:1–5; Mark 11:1–8 Luke 5:3–9; 19:29–36; John 21:3–6)
- Seeing them where no one was watching (knowledge) (John 1:43–50)
- Passing through a mob unharmed (miracle) (Luke 4:28–30; John 8:59)
- Telling a player's future (prophecy) (John 21:18–24)
- Teleportation (miracle—teleportation itself is not a spiritual gift) (Luke 24:36–37; John 6:19–21; 20:19, 26)

The supernatural things the One did in the game world were examples to us of what we can do through the gifts or assistance of the Spirit Master. He was in perfect harmony with the Spirit Master, possessing all the available spiritual giftings Himself. That is why He accomplished those things, not because He was mooching off His God-side when things got tricky (John 14:12–14).

We typically conclude that He switched to "God-mode" in those moments, but He was not functioning in the game world as God; He was playing here alongside us as a member who used Spirit Master tools to get the job done. He came here to show us how it's done. What a great example for us to follow!

A major difference between Him and us is that the Spirit Master does not gift each of us with all the spiritual gifts like He had. Some may have more than one gifting, and Master player Paul urged the kiosk members to ask for the best ones (1 Cor. 12:31; 14:1, 39). Whether we have a manifestation power gift or not does not prevent its availability to us as needed. We can still pray in the moment for discernment or knowledge or wisdom or healing or a miracle and receive a power download from the Spirit Master. Those skills are not beyond our reach, only beyond our chosen belief system.

Speaking In Tongues

This is different from the gift of tongues. Speaking in tongues is also called praying in tongues or praying in the Spirit. This is a communication of the player spirit to the Spirit Master in a non-game world language. It is not intended for guests' ears or for their interpretation since it is done from member spirit to Spirit Master. Those who use tongues like this do not consider it to be a spiritual gift that is selectively dispersed because they believe it is intended for use by all members and should be issued with their membership.

Because the prayer in tongues is a direct spirit-to-Spirit connection, it is encrypted so that only the Spirit Master can interpret it. The Serpent's henchmen cannot interfere or decode it, making it most effective in spiritual warfare communication.

Master player Paul announced that he spoke in tongues more than anyone in the early Corinthian kiosk (1 Cor. 14:18). Today, at least one Protestant kiosk denomination describes this in its literature as a game violation. Something radically changed along the way, and while the Manual mentions that tongues will cease along with prophecy (1 Cor. 13:8), it does not declare their use would become a game violation or was clearly intended to be finished during this game level while the game is still in play. It is still widely practiced by some kiosk denominations.

It is not clarified in the Manual that the Game Master would take game enhancements out of play right after He introduced them. The most common explanation offered is that once the Manual was finalized, these "temporary" special evidences like healing, miracles, and tongues were also ended.

Those who disregard Spirit power giftings like speaking in tongues will often include at-will healing and miracles in the list of discontinued gifts as evidenced by their doctrinal publications. Religious kiosks prefer a controlled environment where players don't scare everybody with their weirdness. Master player Paul had to straighten out this very issue with the Corinthian kiosk by setting down some rules of order, but he did not prohibit the practice of the gifts. These gifts are more likely to be practiced regularly at in-home kiosk gatherings. Those kiosk leaders follow the Manual instructions to direct how the giftings will be used in an orderly manner at the meetings (1 Cor. 14:23–33).

Those who speak in tongues generally believe in healing and miracles as a denominational position, but players do not need to speak in tongues to see healings and miracles happen for them. Many of the personal healings and miracles described in this book happened without the author or subjects speaking in tongues.

Those who prefer to stay away from speaking in tongues are missing a benefit of enhanced blessings from this spiritual communication, but the Game Master does not penalize those who choose to not participate. *You can choose to opt out.*

Acknowledgments

I AM THANKFUL FOR my youngest son who inspired me to write this book when Air Force colleagues were asking why bad things happen to good people. I appreciate my middle son who helped vet my thoughts throughout the book and confirmed the accuracy of scripture references.

I am deeply grateful to retired pastor Dr. Gerald (Jerry) Small, who wrote the initial book review and was fully onboard with its gaming perspective at the age of eighty-five and who wanted to see this book published in 2014. I am indebted to my cousin and Spanish pastor, Lemuel Lara, who gave hours of commentary in its final stages. I am thankful for the pastors of various denominations who provided valuable insight and encouragement: Minister Brian Eichelberger, Pastor Dario Agnolutto, and Pastor JJ Engelbrecht. I greatly appreciate my sister, Leslie Rheinheimer, who gave it three grammar checks, and my colleagues and friends who were willing to read a draft and offer feedback.

My wife, licensed professional clinical counselor Dr. Karen Haaland Hubbard, accepted one of the most tedious tasks of entering citations and running quality control checks. I appreciate her continued encouragement over the past ten years as this book took form.

About the Author

HARRY E. HUBBARD has worked in band and choir programs, English and computer classes, technology management, and various administrative roles, including dean of students, information coordinator, and director of operations in Christian schools for more than forty years. He holds a music education degree and a master's degree in educational administration. He has served as a Baptist church deacon, Sunday school teacher, and a church orchestra director. He and his wife have three grown sons, two of whom have served in the Army and Air Force branches of the military. A lifelong hobby has been collecting information.

Harry and his wife found the answers that gave each a new lease on life with miraculous healing through prayer from the illnesses of Crohn's disease for Karen and fibromyalgia for him. Confronted one day in his thirties with a preference to die young instead of growing old with constant and increasing pain galvanized his quest for solutions that led him to the information held in this book.

Bibliography

Aaron, Charlene. 2021. "'They Were Releasing Spells Over the Viewers:' Ex-Witch Warns Witchcraft Everywhere from Hollywood to Church." CBN News. Accessed June 18, 2024. https://www1.cbn.com/cbnnews/us/2021/october/they-were-releasing-spells-over-the-viewers-ex-witch-warns-witchcraft-now-everywhere-from-hollywood-to-the-church

"Abiogenesis." n.d. Wikipedia. Accessed June 18, 2024. https://en.wikipedia.org/wiki/Abiogenesis

Adachi, Ken. n.d. "Mind Control: The Ultimate Terror." Educate-Yourself. Accessed June 18, 2024. https://educate-yourself.org/mc

"African Diaspora Religions." n.d. Wikipedia. Accessed June 18, 2024. https://en.wikipedia.org/wiki/African_diaspora_religions

Agresti, James D. 2022. "As Murders Soar, FBI Buries the Data." Just Facts Daily. Accessed June 18, 2024. https://www.justfactsdaily.com/as-murders-soar-fbi-buries-the-data

Alien Resistance. n.d. "Recent Polls: Belief in Aliens & UFOs." Accessed June 18, 2024. http://www.alienresistance.org/ufo-alien-deception/recent-polls-trends-belief-aliens-ufos

Amaechina, Oscar. 2022. "The Dangers of the Prosperity Gospel." The Christian Post. May 21, 2022. Accessed July 5, 2024. https://www.christianpost.com/voices/the-dangers-of-the-prosperity-gospel.html

Ames, Richard F. (2020). "Armageddon and Beyond." Tomorrow's World. Accessed June 18, 2024. https://www.tomorrowsworld.org/booklets/armageddon-and-beyond/content

Amplified Bible. 2015. La Habra, CA: Zondervan.

"Ancient Stone Markers Warned of Tsunamis." 2011. CBS News. April 6, 2011. Accessed June 18, 2024. https://www.cbsnews.com/news/ancient-stone-markers-warned-of-tsunamis

"Apostles' Creed, The." n.d. God on the Net. Accessed June 18, 2024. https://www.godonthe.net/evidence/apostle.htm

Archives, Trump Whitehouse. 2021. "Trump Administration Accomplishments SHARE:" 2021. Accessed June 18, 2024. https://trumpwhitehouse.archives.gov/trump-administration-accomplishments

Asscherick, David. 2019. "Hitchhiking For Love." June 5, Accessed June 18, 2024. https://www.youtube.com/watch?v=VX-LQSWSQ3Q

Atalayar. 2021. "The 'Taqiyya': Infiltrating the Infidels for the Sake of Allah." Atalayar. April 13, 2021. Accessed June 18, 2024. https://www.atalayar.com/en/opinion/author/taqiyya-infiltrating-infidels-sake-allah/20210413132400135311.html

A&Ω Productions. n.d. "This Was Written In The Bible 2000 Years Ago. But Scientists Only Found Out About It Recently!?!" YouTube. Accessed June 18, 2024. https://www.youtube.com/watch?v=JhC6iPuh4XM&list=WL&index=13

Bandow, D. (2022, March 7). "Christianity Is the World's Most Persecuted Religion, Confirms New Report." Cato Institute. Accessed June 18, 2024. https://www.cato.org/commentary/christianity-worlds-most-persecuted-religion-confirms-new-report

Barna Group. 2018. "Atheism Doubles Among Generation Z Research: Releases in Millennials & Generations." Barna Group. Accessed June 18, 2024. https://www.barna.com/research/atheism-doubles-among-generation-z

Bates, Josiah. 2022. "The True Story Behind HBO's We Own This City and the Rogue Gun Task Force That Terrorized Baltimore." Time. Accessed June 18, 2024. https://time.com/6168269/we-own-this-city-true-story-hbo-max

Belasco, Amy. 2009. "Troop Levels in the Afghan and Iraq Wars, FY2001-FY2012: Cost and Other Potential Issues." Congressional Research Service. July 2, 2009. Accessed June 18, 2024. https://sgp.fas.org/crs/natsec/R40682.pdf

Bergman, Frank. 2024. "Top Virologist Warns 'Massive Tsunami' of 'Death' among Vaccinated Is 'Imminent.'" April 2, 2024. Accessed June 18, 2024. https://

slaynews.com/news/top-virologist-warns-massive-tsunami-death-among-vaccinated-imminent

Bible Love Notes. n.d. "What We Learn from Bad Guys Like Cain." Bible Love Notes. Accessed June 18, 2024. https://biblelovenotes.blogspot.com/2017/05/what-we-learn-from-bad-guys-like-cain.html

Bible Study. n.d. "How Old Is the Earth?" Bible Study. Accessed June 18, 2024. https://www.biblestudy.org/basicart/how-old-are-the-heavens-and-earth.html

Bible Study Tools. n.d. "Buckler." Bible Study Tools. Accessed June 18, 2024. https://www.biblestudytools.com/dictionary/buckler/#:~:text=Buckler%20%5BN%5D,Psalms%2035%3A2%20%3B%20Ezek

Bomberger Ryan 2022. "Yes, Planned Parenthood Is the Leading Killer of Black Lives." Accessed June 18, 2024. https://townhall.com/columnists/ryanbomberger/2022/02/18/yes-planned-parenthood-is-the-leading-killer-of-black-lives-n2603476

Bonchie. 2022. "Deborah Birx Openly Admits to Lying About the COVID Vaccines to Manipulate the American People." July 23, 2022. Accessed June 18, 2024. https://redstate.com/bonchie/2022/07/23/deborah-birx-openly-admits-to-lying-about-the-covid-vaccines-to-manipulate-the-american-people-n600381

"Book of Jasher referred to in Joshua and Second Samuel, The." (n.d.). J. H. Parry & Company Accessed June 18, 2024. https://www.holybooks.com/wp-content/uploads/Book-of-Jasher.pdf

Bowman, Sonny. 2022. "End Times: Putting the Pieces in Place". Life Foursquare. Accessed June 18, 2024. https://www.life4square.com/sb/endtimes.pdf

Branton. 1999. "The Secrets of The Mojave." Accessed June 18, 2024. https://cdn.preterhuman.net/texts/alien.ufo/Branton%20-%20The%20Secrets%20Of%20The%20Mojave.pdf

Brenan, Megan. 2023. "Belief in Five Spiritual Entities Edges Down to New Lows." Gallup. July 20, 2023. Accessed June 18, 2024. https://news.gallup.com/poll/508886/belief-five-spiritual-entities-edges-down-new-lows.aspx

Broadbery, Dustin. 2022. "Reality vs. Illusion: People Have Been Robbed of Their Ability to 'Decipher Between Fact and Fiction.'" Freedom First Network. May 8, 2022. Accessed June 18, 2024. https://freedomfirstnetwork.com/2022/05/

reality-vs-illusion-people-have-been-robbed-of-their-ability-to-decipher-between-fact-and-fiction

Brunson, Andrew. 2022. "Brunson: 'The Majority Of Believers Are Not Ready For The Pressures Of Persecution, And This Is Very Dangerous.'" Harbingers Daily. May 9, 2022. Accessed June 18, 2024. https://harbingersdaily.com/brunson-the-majority-of-believers-are-not-ready-for-the-pressures-of-persecution-and-this-is-very-dangerous

Buys, Amanda. (n.d.). "Neptune Baptism Line Crossing Ceremony." Kanaan Ministries Preparing the Bride. Accessed June 18, 2024. https://www.kanaan-ministries.org/wp-content/uploads/2019/02/Neptune-1.pdf

Calvin, John. 1536. "Institutes of the Christian Religion." Christian Classics Ethereal Library. 1536. Accessed June 18, 2024. https://www.ccel.org/ccel/calvin/institutes.v.xxiv.html

———. n.d. "Chapter 23: Refutation of the Calumnies by Which This Doctrine Is Always Unjustly Assailed." Christian Classics Ethereal Library. Accessed June 18, 2024. https://www.ccel.org/ccel/calvin/institutes.v.xxiv.html

Carter, Belle. 2022. "Study Warns of Possible Reproductive Crisis as Sperm Counts Drop Worldwide." News Opinions Quotes Report. November 18, 2022. Accessed June 18, 2024. https://noqreport.com/2022/11/18/189609

CBN News. 2023. "'Witchcraft Killed My Dad': Ex-Witch's Horrific Journey Out of Terror to Christ." YouTube. 2023. Accessed June 18, 2024. https://www.youtube.com/watch?v=_H0vfeIntjE

Chabad. n.d. "The 7 Noahide Laws: Universal Morality." Chabad. Accessed June 18, 2024. https://www.chabad.org/library/article_cdo/aid/62221/jewish/The-7-Noahide-Laws-Universal-Morality.htm

Challis, Mallory. 2023. "How to Pick a Bible That's Right for You." February 13, 2023. Accessed June 18, 2024. https://baptistnews.com/article/how-to-pick-a-bible-thats-right-for-you/?gad_source=1&gclid=Cj0KCQjw4MSzBhC8ARIsAPFOuyX0SoGHEx6sd4iciuasEi3PIfANWk52MIraDmNdGggf4RlsCLQOJDgaAjekEALw_wcB.

Chapman, Donn. 2016. "Origins: What's the Biblical Age of the Earth?" Cornerstone Television. November 1, 2016. Accessed June 18, 2024. https://www.youtube.com/watch?v=zgR0ukEEZqA

Charles, Jeff. 2022. "Progressives Have a New Term to Smear Everyone They Don't Like." Red State. May 29, 2022. Accessed June 18, 2024. https://redstate.com/jeffc/2022/05/29/progressives-have-a-new-term-to-smear-everyone-they-dont-like-n572026

Christian Answers. n.d. "With so Many Denominations and Religions, How Can I Decide Which Are True and Which Are False?" Christian Answers. Accessed June 18, 2024. https://christiananswers.net/q-eden/edn-r006.html

Chudov, Igor. 2024. "Religious Faith Can Be 'Turned Off' by Transcranial Magnetic Stimulation, Scientists Find." Igor's Newsletter. April 26, 2024. Accessed June 18, 2024. https://www.igor-chudov.com/p/religious-faith-can-be-turned-off

Clarke, Adam. 1832. "Verse-by-Verse Bible Commentary 2 Peter 1:3." Clarke's Commentary. 1832. Accessed June 18, 2024. https://www.studylight.org/commentary/2-peter/1-3.html

Coghlan, Andy. 2014. "Massive 'Ocean' Discovered Towards Earth's Core." June 12, 2014. Accessed June 18, 2024. https://www.newscientist.com/article/dn25723-massive-ocean-discovered-towards-earths-core/#:~:text=The%20finding%20could%20help%20explain,the%20origin%20of%20Earth's%20water

Compson, Keely. 2022. "Here's 96 Examples of Food Shortages Being Created in Past Year." Republic Broadcasting Network. June 16, 2022. https://republicbroadcasting.org/news/heres-96-examples-of-food-shortages-being-created-in-past-year

Conway, Tim. 2013a. "Am I Saved? 10 Tests of Assurance." I'll Be Honest. 2013. Accessed June 18, 2024. https://www.youtube.com/watch?v=_XacW3FHajM

COVID Blog, The. 2023. "5 Reasons to Believe the Global Population Is Already One Billion People Less Than It Was in January 2020." The COVID Blog. April 20, 2023. Accessed June 18, 2024. https://thecovidblog.com/2023/04/20/5-reasons-to-believe-the-global-population-is-already-one-billion-people-less-than-it-was-in-january-2020

Crone, Billy. 2016. "1 of 1–Personal Testimony of Pastor Billy Crone 2016–Billy Crone." YouTube. 2016. Accessed June 18, 2024. https://www.youtube.com/watch?v=U0V2yIxFs5s

———. 2023a. "Billy Crone–Aliens UFO's & the Rapture of the Church." YouTube. 2023. Accessed June 18, 2024. https://www.youtube.com/watch?v=qQHHGM9d-Gs

———. 2023b. "Pastor Billy Interview with In Focus Alison Steinberg OAN Part 2." YouTube. 2023. Accessed June 18, 2024. https://www.youtube.com/watch?v=6McXEQ5YRNk&t=607s

"Cult Listing." n.d. The Bereans: Apologetics Research Ministry. Accessed June 18, 2024. https://thebereans.net/cult-listing

Dalberg-Acton, John. n.d. "Briany Quotes." Accessed June 18, 2024. https://www.brainyquote.com/authors/john-dalberg-acton-quotes

Daniel, Keith. 2017. "War Between the Saints Calvinism vs Arminianism." Sermon Index. 2017. Accessed June 18, 2024. https://www.youtube.com/watch?v=QmpKIQejqA0

DeSoto, Randy. 2024. "Divine Judgment? Before/After Pics of Biden's Gaza Pier Look Like God Wiped It from Face of the Earth." Gateway Pundit. May 31, 2024. Accessed June 18, 2024. https://www.thegatewaypundit.com/2024/05/divine-judgment-pics-bidens-gaza-pier-look-like

"Distance Calculator." n.d. Distance Calculator. Accessed June 18, 2024. https://www.distance.to

Dougherty Melissa. 2021. "Top Five New Age Teachings in the Church." YouTube. 2021. Accessed June 18, 2024. https://www.youtube.com/watch?v=FCDbO8Lc5NU.

Dowling, M. 2022. "Bill Gates Announces They're Halfway Toward Their Goals [The Great Reset]." Independent Sentinal. September 23, 2022. Accessed June 18, 2024. https://www.independentsentinel.com/bill-gates-announces-theyre-halfway-toward-their-goals-the-great-reset

D'Souza, Dinesh. 2021. "Millions of Muslims Are Converting to Christianity After Having Dreams and Visions of Jesus Christ." Accessed June 18, 2024. https://www.youtube.com/watch?v=RL2MM_efr6Y

Dutton, Kevin. 2012. "The Wisdom of Psychopaths: What Saints, Spies, and Serial Killers Can Teach Us About Success." New York, NY: Scientific American/Farrar, Straus and Giroux.

Easton, M. G. 1897. "Illustrated Bible Dictionary, 3rd Ed." Thomas Nelson. 1897.

Edwards, Elizabeth. 2022. "Voodoo Origins: The World's Most Misunderstood Religion." The Vintage News. December 9, 2022. Accessed June 18, 2024. https://www.thevintagenews.com/2022/12/09/voodoo-origins

Encyclopedia Britannica. 2022. "Seven Deadly Sins." Encyclopedia Britannica. November 3, 2022. Accessed June 18, 2024. https://www.britannica.com/topic/seven-deadly-sins

Eredin. 2024. "The Nephilim: Why God Exterminated Canaan." YouTube. 2024. Accesed June 18, 2024. https://www.youtube.com/watch?v=SyYLpGI5_5M

Escobar, Pablo. 2023. "[Quotation]." AZ Quotes. 2023. Accessed June 18, 2024. https://www.azquotes.com/quote/820119

Feather, White. n.d. "Reiki, Jesus and Eleanor's Healing." The International Center for Reiki Training. Accessed June 18, 2024. https://www.reiki.org/articles/reiki-jesus-and-eleanors-healing

Fielding, Hunter. 2024. "13 Nations Sign Agreement to Engineer Global Famine by Destroying Food Supply." Global Research. June 14, 2024. Accessed July 5, 2024. https://www.globalresearch.ca/13-nations-sign-agreement-engineer-global-famine/5860390

Feinblatt, Natalie. 2023. "How to Tell If a Church Is a Cult." January 3, 2023. Accessed June 18, 2024. https://www.wikihow.com/Tell-if-a-Church-is-a-Cult

"Fig Leaves." n.d. Specialty Produce. Accessed June 18, 2024. https://specialtyproduce.com/produce/Fig_Leaves_7136.php

Figgs, L. (2018, December 26). "The Final Days Outlined in the Book of Revelation." Accessed June 18, 2024. https://prezi.com/inuttwcplo28/ccg-youth-revelation-timeline

Fixico, Donald L. 2018. "When Native Americans Were Slaughtered in the Name of 'Civilization.'" n.d. History. Accessed June 18, 2024. https://www.history.com/news/native-americans-genocide-united-states

Flanagan, Anne Josephine, and Sheila Warren. 2022. "Advancing Digital Agency: The Power of Data Intermediaries." Accessed June 18, 2024. https://www3.weforum.org/docs/WEF_Advancing_towards_Digital_Agency_2022.pdf

Foley, Ryan. 2022. "Most Americans Don't View the Bible as Primary Determinant of Right And Wrong: Study." The Christian Post. November 6, 2022. Accessed June 18, 2024. https://www.christianpost.com/news/most-dont-see-bible-as-main-determinant-of-right-and-wrong-poll.html

———. 2023. "Abortion Is Leading Cause of Death Worldwide for Fourth Year in a Row." Christian Post. January 4, 2023. Accessed June 18, 2024. https://www.christianpost.com/news/abortion-is-leading-cause-of-death-worldwide-fourth-year-in-a-row.html

"Former Muslim Terrorist Sees Jesus and Becomes a Christian English with Arabic Subtitles." 2016. The Light. 2016. Accessed June 18, 2024. https://www.youtube.com/watch?v=dLxkanD0j4I

Four Corners Free. n.d.a. "Astral Travel Attacks." Four Corners Free. Accessed June 18, 2024. https://fourcornersfree.com/astral-travel-attacks

———. n.d.b. "Signs of Possible Witchcraft Attack." Four Corners Free. Accessed June 18, 2024. https://fourcornersfree.com/signs-of-possible-witchcraft-attack

Foxe, J. (1709). *Foxe's Book of Martyrs: A History of the Lives, Sufferings, and Triumphant Deaths of the Early Christian and the Protestant Martyrs*. Hendrickson Publishers.

Freeman, Makia. 2019. "Yes, DEW and Laser Weapons Are Being Used Against the American People." Shift Frequency. December 31, 2021. Accessed June 18, 2024. https://wakeup-world.com/2019/02/21/yes-dew-and-laser-weapons-are-being-used-against-the-american-people

Geisler, Norman, and Thomas Howe. 2014. "Jonah 3:3—Is Jonah's Testimony to the Size of Nineveh Accurate?" Defending Inerrancy. 2014. Accessed June 18, 2024. https://defendinginerrancy.com/bible-solutions/Jonah_3.3.php

"Georgia Guidestones." n.d. Wikipedia. Accessed June 18, 2024. https://en.wikipedia.org/wiki/Georgia_Guidestones

Godet, Frédéric Louis. 1957. *Commentary on St. Paul's First Epistle to the Corinthians*. Vol. 2. Grand Rapids, MI: Zondervan.

Godly Response to Abuse in Christian Environments. 2019. "Empowering Christian Communities to Recognize, Prevent, and Respond to Abuse." Godly Response to Abuse in Christian Environments. 2019. Accessed June 18, 2024. https://www.netgrace.org

God's Word Mission Society. 2024. "2024 Bible Translation Guide." 2024. Accessed June 18, 2024. https://godsword.org/pages/bible-translation-guide?gad_source=1&gclid=Cj0KCQjw4MSzBhC8ARIsAPFOuyW_F9QfV1jrPTtUFyIVHQ8k2JekluvxDBWm26G-caAMefupIxZyS-4aAiYnEALw_wcB.

Gogate, P., C. Gilbert, and A. Zin. 2011. "Severe Visual Impairment and Blindness in Infants: Causes and Opportunities for Control." *Middle East African Journal of Ophthalmology* 18 (2): 109–14. Accessed June 18, 2024. https://doi.org/10.4103/0974-9233.80698

Gorokhova, E. 2009. *A Mountain of Crumbs: A Memoir*. New York: Simon & Schuster.

Gray, Jonathan. 2014. *Dead Men's Secrets: Tantalising Hints of a Lost Super Race*. Teach Services, Inc.

Greenberg, Alissa. 2021. "The Legendary Chinese Seafarer the West Overlooks." Nova. August 13, 2021. Accessed June 18, 2024. https://www.pbs.org/wgbh/nova/article/zheng-he-china-explorer-ships

Grider, Goeffrey. 2014. "Ripped from The Headlines: 12 Shocking Proofs That Disaster Strikes America When It Mistreats Israel." Now the End Begins. July 22, 2014. Accessed June 18, 2024. https://www.nowtheendbegins.com/11-shocking-proofs-disaster-strikes-america-mistreats-israel

Grossu, Arina. 2014. "Margaret Sanger, Racist Eugenicist Extraordinaire: The Founder of Planned Parenthood Would Have Considered Many Americans Unworthy of Life." The Washington Times. May 5, 2014. Accessed June 18, 2024. https://www.washingtontimes.com/news/2014/may/5/grossu-margaret-sanger-eugenicist

Guion, Payton. 2015. "Bubonic Plague-Carrying Fleas Found on New York City Rats." March 3, 2015. Accessed March 13, 2022. https://www.independent.co.uk/news/world/americas/bubonic-plaguecarrying-fleas-found-on-new-york-city-rats-10083563.html

Guzik, David. 2021. "Isaiah 61: Out of The Mouth of the Messiah." Enduring Word. 2021. Accessed June 18, 2024. https://enduringword.com/bible-commentary/isaiah-61

Hadingham, Evan. 2001. "Ancient Chinese Explorers." Nova. January 16, 2001. https://www.pbs.org/wgbh/nova/article/ancient-chinese-explorers

Hall, Dustin. 2014. "An Amazing Encounter with Jesus." Accessed June 18, 2024. https://www.youtube.com/watch?v=VR6c37_bo68

Hamm, Kenneth. 2022. "Why Most Christian Schools Are NOT Biblical." Institute for Creation Research. 2022. Accessed June 18, 2024. https://www.youtube.com/watch?v=aIYZjclfg9Q

Ham, Kenneth. n.d. "Was There Death Before Adam Sinned?" Answers in Genesis. Accessed June 18, 2024. https://answersingenesis.org/death-before-sin/was-there-death-before-adam-sinned

Hanley, P. J. 2018. "The Last Generation." May 1, 2018. Accessed June 18, 2024. https://www.understandingbibleprophecy.org/2018/05/the-last-generation

Harvard Business Review. n.d. "Top 40 Essential Business Books to Read." Harvard Business Review. Accessed June 18, 2024. https://store.hbr.org/best-business-books

Haven Hot Chicken. 2022. "We Use Only 100% Certified Halal Chicken." Accessed June 18, 2024. https://www.havenhotchicken.com/halal

Heartstrings. 2014. "How Wealthy Was Job?" April 10, 2014. Accessed June 18, 2024. https://onlinebaptist.com/topic/20767-how-wealthy-was-job

Hebrew University, The. 2021. "Hebrew University's Prof. Yuval Noah Harari on The Era of the Coronavirus: Living in a New Reality." 2021. Accessed June 18, 2024. https://www.youtube.com/watch?v=ltJTRnNLYqY&t=1s

Henley, W. E. 1875. "Invictus." Poetry Foundation. 1875. Accessed June 18, 2024. https://poemanalysis.com/william-ernest-henley/invictus

Henry, Matthew. 1706. "Romans 13:11-14 Commentary." Bible Gateway. 1706. Accessed June 18, 2024. https://www.biblegateway.com/resources/matthew-henry/Rom.13.11-Rom.13.14

———. 1991. *Matthew Henry's Commentary on the Whole Bible*. Vol. 6. Peabody, MA: Hendrickson Publishers.

"Hindu Cosmology." n.d. Wikipedia. Accessed June 18, 2024. https://en.wikipedia.org/wiki/Hindu_cosmology

"Hindu Views on Evolution." n.d. Wikipedia Accessed June 18, 2024. https://en.wikipedia.org/wiki/Hindu_views_on_evolution#Hindu_creationism

Hinduism. n.d. "How to Save Oneself from Hell?" Hinduism. Accessed June 18, 2024. https://hinduism.stackexchange.com/questions/51366/how-to-save-oneself-from-hell

"Hoax Journalism." 2008. The Museum of Unnatural Mystery. 2008. Accessed June 18, 2024. http://www.unmuseum.org/jourhoax.htm

Hodge, B. (2010, March 2). "Could Death Exist Before Sin Biblically?" Answers in Genesis. Accessed June 18, 2024. https://answersingenesis.org/death-before-sin/biblically-could-death-have-existed-before-sin

Hoft, Jim. 2022. "Interactive Map Details Destruction of Numerous US Food Manufacturing Plants, Grocery Stores, Etc. — Compares US Incidents to Global Trends." Gateway Pundit. June 23, 2022. Accessed June 18, 2024. https://www.thegatewaypundit.com/2022/06/interactive-map-details-destruction-numerous-us-food-manufacturing-plants-compares-us-incidents-global-trends

———. 2024. "KFC Canada Implements Halal-Only Chicken Policy in Ontario, Bans Pork in Nod to Islamic Practices." Gateway Pundit. July 7, 2024. Accessed July 15, 2024. https://www.thegatewaypundit.com/2024/07/kfc-canada-implements-halal-only-chicken-policy-ontario/

Hohmann, Leo. 2022. "'SMART Cities' Worldwide Being Converted into 'Open Concentration Camps,' Says Ex-Silicon Valley Engineer Turned Whistleblower." LeeHohmann.Com. November 23, 2022. Accessed June 18, 2024. https://leohohmann.com/2022/11/23/smart-cities-worldwide-being-converted-into-open-concentration-camps-says-ex-silicon-valley-engineer-turned-whistleblower

———. 2023. "Deagel Population Forecast of Nearly 70 Percent Fewer Americans by 2025 Is Starting To Look Prophetic." Lioness of Judah. April

21, 2023. Accessed June 18, 2024. https://lionessofjudah.substack.com/p/deagel-population-forecast-of-nearly

"Hoodoo (Spirituality)." n.d. Accessed June 18, 2024. https://en.wikipedia.org/wiki/Hoodoo_(spirituality)

"How Do I Know If I'm In A Cult?" 2020. Health for Life Counseling. August 24, 2020. Accessed June 18, 2024. https://healthforlifegr.com/seven-behaviors-and-signs-of-cults

Hsu, Charlotte. 2021. "Examining the 1,800-Plus 'Young' Volcanoes in the US Southwest." Phys.Org. November 3, 2021. Accessed March 30, 2024. https://phys.org/news/2021-11-plus-young-volcanoes-southwest.html

Huber, Michael. 2021. "Supervolcanoes in the Continental US." ArcGIS Story Maps. May 5, 2021. Accessed March 30, 2024. https://storymaps.arcgis.com/stories/d473985310594972b2e960f6234581b2

Hudson, Doug, and James Lloyd. n.d. "The Diabolical System Of Diaprax." Christian Media Research. Accessed June 18, 2024. http://cmediaresearch.com/cmc-14.html

Huff, Ethan. 2022. "Australia Sees 63% Drop in Births after Introduction of COVID 'Vaccines' – What Will the Government's Excuse Be?" Natural News. November 17, 2022. Accessed June 18, 2024. https://www.naturalnews.com/2022-11-17-australia-63-percent-drop-births-covid-vaccines.html

Ingram, Chip. 2022. "What Does the Phrase 'God Is Sovereign' Really Mean?" Walk Through the Bible. 2022. Accessed June 18, 2024. https://www.christianity.com/wiki/god/what-does-the-phrase-god-is-sovereign-really-mean-11555729.html

Institute for Creation Research. 2022. "Core Principles of the Institute for Creation Research." Institute for Creation Research. 2022. Accessed June 18, 2024. https://www.icr.org/tenets

Jaeger, Jarryd. 2022. "Americans' Belief in God Hits New Low: Poll." The Post Millenial. June 17, 2022. Accessed June 18, 2024. https://thepostmillennial.com/americans-belief-in-god-hits-new-low-poll

Jesus4Evers. 2015. "Testimony of Billy Crone." Accessed October 11, 2023. Accessed June 18, 2024. https://www.youtube.com/watch?v=B09hsP8sLmU

Jiang, Yan, Jingnan Han, Connor Donovan, Gholam Ali, Tan Xu, Yumei Zheng, and Wenjie Sun. 2017. "Induced Abortion among Chinese Women with Living Child-A National Study." *Adv Dis Control Prev* 2 (1): 10–15. https://www.ncbi.nlm.nih.gov/pmc/articles/PMC5568110

Johnson, Lance D. 2024. "U.S. Has Recorded Over 1 Million Excess Deaths Among People Aged 65 and Older Since the Rollout of Covid-19 Vaccines." Info Wars. April 5, 2024. Accessed June 18, 2024. https://www.infowars.com/posts/u-s-has-recorded-over-1-million-excess-deaths-among-people-aged-65-and-older-since-the-rollout-of-covid-19-vaccines

Joseph, Daniel Isaiah. n.d. "Wondering What Denominations Are Calvinist? Here's the Answer." Christianity FAQ. Accessed June 18, 2024. https://christianityfaq.com/what-denominations-are-calvinist

Elliott, Josh K. 2021. "The CIA Released Thousands of UFO Documents Online. Here's How to Read Them." Global News. January 13, 2021. Accessed June 18, 2024. https://globalnews.ca/news/7573277/cia-ufo-documents-declassified-online

Ethics and Religious Liberty Commission, The. 2014. "The Accuser in the Mirror: The Danger of False Guilt." July 25, 2014. Accessed June 18, 2024. https://erlc.com/resource/the-accuser-in-the-mirror-the-danger-of-false-guilt

Kennington, Haley. 2021a. "Flashback: Former Malaysian Prime Minister Warned – 'Elites Want to Reduce World Population to 1 Billion'." September 29, 2021. Accessed June 18, 2024. https://rairfoundation.com/flashback-former-malaysian-prime-minister-warned-elites-want-to-reduce-world-population-to-1-billion-videos

———. 2021b. "In 2015 Former Malaysian Prime Minister Mahathir Mohamad Warned Against Planned Global Genocide by Elites: 'The Peace That We Will Get From This Is the Peace of the Graveyard.'" Truth Comes to Light. September 21, 2021. Accessed June 18, 2024. https://truthcomestolight.com/in-2015-former-malaysian-prime-minister-mahathir-mohamad-warned-against-planned-global-genocide-by-elites-the-peace-that-we-will-get-from-this-is-the-peace-of-the-graveyard

Kierkegaard, Soren. 2007. *Provocations: Spiritual Writings of Kierkegaard*. Edited by Charles E. Moore. Farmington, PA: Plough Publishing House

Knighton, Tom. 2022. "Study: 1 out of 179 Americans Will Be Murder Victim." Bearing Arms. November 16, 2022. Accessed June 18, 2024. https://bearingarms.com/tomknighton/2022/11/16/americans-murder-n64427

Kottusch, Pia, Miriam Tillmann, and Klaus I. Püsche. 2009. "Arch Kriminol [Survival Time Without Food and Drink]." *Arch Kriminol* 224 (5–6): 184–91. https://pubmed.ncbi.nlm.nih.gov/20069776

Kotwal, Karishma. 2016. "80 Deaths in 3 Months in 'Suicide Village' Badi." The Times of India. May 6, 2016. Accessed June 18, 2024. https://timesofindia.indiatimes.com/city/bhopal/80-deaths-in-3-months-in-suicide-village-Badi/articleshow/52138514.cms

Lada, B. 2018. "25 Years Later: The Great Flood of 1993 Remains Worst River Flooding US Has Ever Seen." AccuWeather. 2018. Accessed June 18, 2024. https://www.accuweather.com/en/weather-news/the-great-flood-of-1993-remains-the-worst-river-flooding-us-has-ever-seen/346375

"Land of Uz." n.d. Wikipedia. Accessed June 18, 2024. https://biblereadingarcheology.com/2016/04/14/where-was-the-land-of-uz

Larken, Clarence. 1920. *The Greatest Book on "Dispensational Truth" in the World*. Self-Published.

Law, J. O. 2019. "Christian Meditation: What Practices Are New Age and What Is Biblical?" The Christian Post. March 19, 2019. Accessed June 18, 2024. https://www.christianpost.com/news/christian-meditation-what-practices-are-new-age-and-what-is-biblical.html

———. 2022. "Christian Author Warns Against New 'Breathe With Me' Yoga Barbie: 'Satan Is After the Children.'" The Christian Post. May 20, 2022. Accessed June 18, 2024. https://www.christianpost.com/news/christian-author-warns-against-new-yoga-barbie.html?clickType=link-most-popular

Leake, Mike. 2022. "What Are the Warning Signs of a Cult?" Bible Study Tools. December 22, 2022. Accessed June 18, 2024. https://www.biblestudytools.com/bible-study/topical-studies/what-are-the-warning-signs-of-a-cult.html

Lee, Robert J. 2023. "Bombshell Report: Romanian Senator Diana Sosoaca Says People Had to Die by Premeditated Earthquakes Triggered in Turkey." Cairns News. 2023. Accessed June 18, 2024. https://cairnsnews.org/2023/02/13/

bombshell-report-romanian-senator-diana-sosoaca-says-people-had-to-die-by-premeditated-earthquakes-triggered-in-turkey

Lewis, C. S. 1996. *The Problem of Pain.* Harper Collins (Original work published 1940).

Lewy, Guenter. 2004. "Were American Indians the Victims of Genocide?" History News Network. September 2004. Accessed June 18, 2024. https://historynewsnetwork.org/article/7302

"List of Impact Structures on Earth." n.d. Wikipedia. Accessed June 18, 2024. https://en.wikipedia.org/wiki/List_of_impact_structures_on_Earth

"List of Largest Volcanic Eruptions." n.d. Wikipedia. Accessed June 18, 2024. https://en.wikipedia.org/wiki/List_of_largest_volcanic_eruptions

Literature Life, The. 2021. "Deconstruction| Explained in 10 Points with Examples Literary Theory." YouTube. 2021. Accessed June 18, 2024. https://www.youtube.com/watch?v=DUzor0mXGZQ

Livingston, D. P. n.d. "Nimrod." Christian Answers.Net. Accessed June 18, 2024. https://christiananswers.net/dictionary/nimrod.html

Livingston, I., and J. Samenow. n.d. "A First: Category 5 Storms Have Formed in Every Ocean Basin This Year." Accessed June 18, 2024. c

Logos. 2022. "What Is Eschatology? 4 Views, Why There's Disagreement & More." April 29, 2022. Accessed June 18, 2024. https://www.logos.com/grow/what-is-eschatology

Los Angeles Times, The. 2005. "Bedeviled by Exorcist Shortage, Vatican Kicks off Training Program." Chicago Tribune. February 20, 2005. Accessed June 18, 2024. https://www.chicagotribune.com/2005/02/20/bedeviled-by-exorcist-shortage-vatican-kicks-off-training-program

LT Radio. n.d. "The Events During the 7 Years of Tribulation." LT Radio. Accessed June 18, 2024. http://www.ltradio.org/charts/End%20Time%20Charts/Events%20during%20the%207%20year%20Tribulation%20(Revised).gif

Mac, Martha. n.d. "Five Crowns & Rewards in Heaven." Sold Out for Jesus. Accessed June 18, 2024. http://www.so4j.com/five-crowns-rewards-in-heaven

MacIntosh, Chris. n.d. "Here's What's Really Behind the Global Reset and Sustainable Development Agenda 2030." Doug Casey's International Man. Accessed June

18, 2024. https://internationalman.com/articles/heres-whats-really-behind-the-global-reset-and-sustainable-development-agenda-2030

Malik, Pravir. 2023. "The Possibilities of Quantum Intelligence-Driven Nano-Cyborgs." Forbes. April 23, 2023. Accessed June 18, 2024. https://www.forbes.com/sites/forbestechcouncil/2023/04/24/the-possibilities-of-quantum-intelligence-driven-nano-cyborgs/?sh=79713ce864aa

Mangiaracin, Emily. 2022. "'Died Suddenly' Film Connects the Dots on the Depopulation Agenda behind COVID Vaccines." Lifesite. October 31, 2022. Accessed June 18, 2024. https://www.lifesitenews.com/news/died-suddenly-film-connects-the-dots-on-the-depopulation-agenda-behind-covid-vaccines

Manning, Brennan. 2005. *The Ragamuffin Gospel*. Multnomah Books.

Marshall, P., Gilbert, L., & Shea, N. (2013). *Persecuted: The Global Assault on Christians*. Thomas Nelson Publishers.

Martin, Albert N., and Fred Zaspel. n.d. "Degrees of Punishment in Hell." The Gospel Coalition. Accessed June 18, 2024. https://www.thegospelcoalition.org/essay/degrees-punishment-hell

Mattson, Brian. 2014a. "Sympathy for The Devil." March 31, 2014. Accessed June 18, 2024. http://drbrianmattson.com/journal/2014/3/31/sympathy-for-the-devil

———. 2014b. "Ep 8–Commentary: Noah and Its Critics." Accessed June 18, 2024. https://www.youtube.com/watch?v=v0d9g3Ydsew

———. 2014c. "Ep. 8–Above the Paygrade: Brian Godawa and the Ramifications of Noah." Accessed June 18, 2024. https://www.youtube.com/watch?v=Z0Cq8SusCY0

Mc Dermott, David. n.d. "The Effects of Bad Decisions." Decision Making Confidence. Accessed June 18, 2024. https://www.decision-making-confidence.com/effects-of-bad-decisions.html#:~:text=The%20effects%20of%20bad%20decisions%20consists%20of%20some,doing%20unnecessary%20things%208%20financial%20cost%20More%20items

McNamee, M J, and Edwards S D. 2006. "Transhumanism, Medical Technology and Slippery Slopes." *Journal of Medical Ethics* 32: 513–518.

McTernan, J. P. 2012. *As America Has Done to Israel*. New Kensington, PA: Whitaker House.

Mead, Matthew. 2011. *The Almost Christian Discovered*. Monergism Books.

Meehan, R. L., ed. (1999). *Ignatius Donnely and the end of the world: Biblical chronology*. Paulo Alto: Kirribilli Press. Accessed June 18, 2024. https://web.stanford.edu/~meehan/donnelly/bibchron.html#:~:text=In%20this%20way%2C%20Bishop%20Ussher,the%20date%20at%202459%20BC

Mek, Amy. 2022a. "Germany Admits Covid 'Vaccine' 40 Times Deadlier Than Previously Known." Rair Foundation. 2022. Accessed June 18, 2024. https://rairfoundation.com/germany-admits-covid-vaccine-40-times-deadlier-than-previously-known

———. 2022b. "Great Reset in Action: World Economic Forum's Communist 'Digital Identity' Scheme." Rair Foundation, Inc. February 20, 2022. Accessed June 18, 2024. https://rairfoundation.com/great-reset-in-action-world-economic-forums-communist-digital-identity-scheme-video

Merriam Webster. n.d. "Reins." Merriam Webster. Accessed June 18, 2024. https://www.merriam-webster.com/dictionary/reins

Merriam-Webster. 2022. "Genocide." Accessed October 15, 2022. Accessed June 18, 2024. https://www.merriam-webster.com/dictionary/genocide

Merriam-Webster. 2024. "Sin." Accessed June 18, 2024. https://www.merriam-webster.com/dictionary/sin

Miller, Sean. 2024. "Mind Reading Technology May Be Used For 'National Security.'" InfoWars. April 10, 2024. Accessed June 18, 2024. https://www.infowars.com/posts/mind-reading-technology-may-be-used-for-national-security

Miller, W. J. n.d. "Communist Goals–1963 Congressional Record." WJMiller.Net. Accessed June 18, 2024. http://www.wjmiller.net/main1/?M=1-9

Mirkes, Renée. 2019. "Transhumanist Medicine: Can We Direct Its Power to the Service of Human Dignity?" *The Linacre Quarterly* 86 (1): 115–126.

Missler, Chuck (2003). "Fall of Satan." YouTube. Accessed June 18, 2024. https://www.youtube.com/watch?v=ycaOFAJNAVM

"Missouri v. James Scott: 'The Midwest Flood Trial.'" 2007. CourtTV. 2007. Accessed June 18, 2024. https://archive.ph/20070710073935/http://www.courttv.com/archive/trials/flood/

Moore, Stephen. 1997. "Our Unconstitutional Congress." Imprimis. July 1997. Accessed July 11, 2024. https://imprimis.hillsdale.edu/our-unconstitutional-congress/

Moran, Laurence. 1993. "Evolution Is a Fact and a Theory." The Talk Origins Archive. January 22, 1993. Accessed June 18, 2024. http://www.talkorigins.org/faqs/evolution-fact.html

Morgan, Bill. 2007. "Scalar Wars: The Brave New World of Scalar Electromagnetics." May 16, 2007. Accessed June 18, 2024. http://www.prahlad.org/pub/bearden/scalar_wars.htm#weaponization-%20Defense%20Secretary%20William%20Cohen,%201997

Morin, Amy. 2007. "What Is a Psychopath?" Very Well Mind. November 7, 2007. Accessed June 18, 2024. https://www.verywellmind.com/what-is-a-psychopath-5025217#:~:text=A%20person%20who%20is%20manipulative,common%20traits%20associated%20with%20psychopathy

Moynihan, Lydia, and Charles Gasparino. 2023. "Silicon Valley Bank Failure Could Spark Run on Regional Banks: Sources." New York Post. March 11, 2023. Accessed June 18, 2024. https://nypost.com/2023/03/11/silicon-valley-bank-failure-could-lead-to-run-on-other-banks

Mozumdar, A. K. 2002. *The Life and the Way: The Christian Yoga Metaphysics*. San Diego, CA: Book Tree.

MSR News Online. 2013. "KKK Lynched 3,446 Blacks in 86 Years – Abortion Claims That Many Black Babies in 'Less Than Four Days.'" MSR News Online. May 19, 2013. Accessed June 18, 2024. https://spokesman-recorder.com/2013/05/29/the-ku-klux-klan-in-86-years-lynched-3446-abortions-accomplish-this-number-in-four-days

Muller, George. n.d. "The Biography of George Muller." George Muller. Accessed June 18, 2024. https://www.georgemuller.org/biography-of-george-muler.html

Murphy, C., and J. Vess. 2003. "Subtypes of Psychopathy: Proposed Differences between Narcissistic, Borderline, Sadistic, and Antisocial Psychopaths." *Psychiatric Quarterly* 74: 11–29. https://doi.org/10.1023/A:1021137521142

"Mystery Airship of 1896, The." 1996. The Museum of Unnatural Mystery. 1996. Accessed June 18, 2024. http://www.unmuseum.org/airship.htm

National Archives, The. n.d.. "UFOs: Newly Released UFO Files from the UK Government." Accessed June 18, 2024. https://webarchive.nationalarchives.gov.uk/ukgwa/+/https://www.nationalarchives.gov.uk/ufos

New World War. 2022. "Weather Warfare." 2022. Acvcessed June 27, 2024. http://www.newworldwar.org/weatherwar.htm

News Clips. 2023. "Tucker Compares Biden to Nixon . . . But Not in the Way You Might Think." Rumble. 2023. Accessed June 18, 2024. https://rumble.com/v26dm6i-tucker-compares-biden-to-nixon . . . -but-not-in-the-way-you-might-think.html

Nguyen, L. (2017, July 26). "15 People Who Have Died Playing Video Games." The Gamer. Accessed June 18, 2024. https://www.thegamer.com/15-people-who-have-died-playing-video-games

Nico Christodoulou. 2012. "That's Impossible: Weather Warfare." History Channel. 2012. Accessed June 18, 2024. https://www.dailymotion.com/video/xrcu9h

Nietzsche, Friedrich. 1889. *Götzen-Dämmerung, oder, Wie man mit dem Hammer philosophiert* [Twilight of the Idols, or, How to Philosophize with a Hammer]. Translated by Anthony M. Ludovici. Edinburgh: T. n. Foulis, 1911.

Nito. (2014, December 8). "The Book of Revelation (Apocalypse) – Part 3 – The End Times Timeline." About Science, Religion and LIfe. Accessed June 18, 2024. https://holyscience.wordpress.com/2014/12/08/the-book-of-revelation-apocalypse-part-3-timeline

"Noahide Laws: Judaism." 2023. June 15, 2023. Accessed June 18, 2024. https://www.britannica.com/topic/Noahide-Laws

Not from Earth. n.d. "True Giants: Giant Race Which Still Lives in The Solomon Islands." Accessed June 18, 2024. https://notfromearth.org/true-giants-giant-race-still-lives-solomon-islands

Novielli, Carole. 2022. "The Staggering Death Toll of Abortion in the United States and Worldwide." Live Action. May 14, 2022. Accessed June 18, 2024. https://www.liveaction.org/news/staggering-death-toll-abortion-us-worldwide

NTB Staff. 2022. "Going Viral: Watch This 1983 Interview with A Former CIA Operative Who Explains How He Circulated Disinformation by Using Journalists." Not the Bee. November 7, 2022. Accessed June 18, 2024. https://notthebee.com/article/this-nearly-40-year-old-interview-with-a-former-cia-operative-explaining-how-he-used-to-plant-disinformation-with-the-press-seems-really-important-for-today

Number of Abortions. n.d. "Abortion Counters." Number of Abortions. Accessed June 18, 2024. http://www.numberofabortions.com

Oatman, Johnson. 1956. "Count Your Blessings." In *Baptist Hymnal*, edited by Walter Hines Sims 318. Nashville. TN: Convention Press.

Ollison, L. 2023. "The Luciferian Flood and the World Before Adam and Eve–Dr. Larry Ollison." WOW Faith Church. 2023. Accessed June 18, 2024. https://www.youtube.com/watch?v=bwXLj6f9vTU

Olson, Roger E. 2013. "Arminian Denominations." Society of Evangelical Arminians. July 19, 2013. Accessed June 18, 2024. http://evangelicalarminians.org/arminian-denominations

Olson, Walter. 2020. "The Origins of a Warning from Voltaire." Cato Institute. December 20, 2020. July 11, 2024. https://www.cato.org/publications/commentary/origins-warning-from-voltaire

"Omphalos Hypothesis." n.d. Wikipedia. Accessed June 18, 2024. https://en.wikipedia.org/wiki/Omphalos_hypothesis

One Lord One Body Ministries. 2013. "The Anatomy of A Stronghold." 2013. Accessed July 14, 2024. https://onelordonebody.com/2013/11/19/the-anatomy-of-a-stronghold/

Oregon State University. n.d. "Vitamin A." Accessed June 18, 2024. https://lpi.oregonstate.edu/mic/vitamins/vitamin-A

Ostler, Jeffrey. 2015. "Genocide and American Indian History." American History. March 2, 2015. Accessed June 18, 2024. https://doi.org/10.1093/acrefore/9780199329175.013.3

Pappas, Stephanie. 2018. "The Earth Is Eating Its Own Oceans." November 14, 2018." November 14, 2018. Accessed June 18, 2024. https://www.livescience.com/64091-earth-is-eating-its-oceans.html

Pastor Landon. 2019. "The Prophet Habakkuk in 3 Minutes." YouTube. February 9, 2019. Accessed June 18, 2024. https://www.youtube.com/watch?v=-qJ23qgcsJI

Paterson, Keith. 2016. "Where Is the Land of Uz?" Bible Reading Acheology. April 16, 2016. Accessed June 18, 2024. https://biblereadingarcheology.com/2016/04/14/where-was-the-land-of-uz

Pavone, F. 2023. "64,500,000 Babies Have Been Killed in Abortions, Biggest Travesty in American History Opinion. Jan 27, 2023." Life News. January 27, 2023. Accessed June 18, 2024. https://www.lifenews.com/2023/01/27/64-5-million-babies-have-been-killed-in-abortions-biggest-travesty-in-american-history

"Perseverance of the Saints." n.d. Wikipedia. Accessed June 18, 2024. https://en.wikipedia.org/wiki/Perseverance_of_the_saints#Free_Grace_doctrine

Piper, John. 2004. "George Mueller's Strategy for Showing God: Simplicity of Faith Sacred Scripture, and Satisfaction in God." Desiring God. Accessed June 18, 2024. https://www.desiringgod.org/messages/george-muellers-strategy-for-showing-god

Planet Zion. 2014. *Former Muslim Terrorist Sees Jesus and Becomes a Christian.* Accessed June 18, 2024. https://www.youtube.com/watch?v=NMMsKicQSn8

Powe, Alicia. 2022. "1 Million COVID Deaths: Here's The Real Reason Why More People Died From COVID In The United States Than Every Other Country." Gateway Pundit. May 14, 2022. Accessed June 18, 2024. https://www.thegatewaypundit.com/2022/05/1-million-covid-deaths-real-reason-people-died/

Prager, Dennis. 2022. "Between Left and Right, How Do You Know Which Side Isn't Telling the Truth?" Townhall. November 15, 2022. Accessed June 18, 2024. https://townhall.com/columnists/dennisprager/2022/11/15/between-left-and-right-how-do-you-know-which-side-isnt-telling-the-truth-n2615970

Preston, Christopher. 2021. "Stop Blaming Satan for Your Sin." October 21, 2021. Accessed June 18, 2024. https://www.fairviewbiblechurch.org/blog/2021/10/22/stop-blaming-satan-for-your-sin

Price, G. 2023. "Greg Price." Twitter. January 19, 2023. Accessed June 18, 2024. https://x.com/greg_price11/status/1616275514435436545?ref_src=twsrc%5Etfw%7Ctwcamp%5Etweetembed%7Ctwterm%5E1616275514435436545%7Ctwgr%5Edfe854d6997578ef25d334ed1e25dbec7d7f11de%7Ctwcon%5Es1_&ref_+url=htt-

ps%3A%2F%2Fthelibertydaily.com%2Ftucker-compares-biden-to-nixon-but-not-in-the-way-you-might-think%2F

Prigg, M. 2014. "Scientists Reconstruct Asteroid Impact Six Times Bigger than the Blast That Wiped Out The Dinosaurs Which Boiled Oceans, Burned the Sky, and Shook the Earth for Thirty Minutes." Daily Mail. 2014. Accessed June 18, 2024. https://www.dailymail.co.uk/sciencetech/article-2601713/Scientists-reconstruct-asteroid-impact-SIX-TIMES-bigger-blast-wiped-dinosaurs-say-boiled-oceans-burned-sky-shook-earth-thirty-minutes.html

Prince, Derek. 1994. *Explaining Blessings and Curses*. Baker Book House.

———. 2006. *Blessing or Curse: You Can Choose*. Vol. 7th ed. Chosen Books.

———. 2021a. "Common Causes Of Curses." Derek Prince Ministries. 2021. Accessed June 18, 2024. https://www.derekprince.com/radio/205

———. 2021b. "Further Causes Of Curses (Part 1)." Derek Prince Ministries. 2021. Accessed June 18, 2024. https://www.derekprince.com/radio/206

———. 2021c. "Further Causes of Curses (Part 2)." 2021. Derek Prince Ministries. 2021. Accessed June 18, 2024. https://www.derekprince.com/radio/207

———. 2021d. "How To Get God's Word Into Your Heart." YouTube. Derek Prince Ministries. 2021. Accessed June 18, 2024. https://www.youtube.com/watch?v=-pMz1C3zu0A

———. 2021e. "When You Read Your Bible, All The Power Of God Works In You!" YouTube. 2021. Accessed June 18, 2024. https://www.youtube.com/watch?v=hrsdLJt8Ilk

———. 2022a. "How Much Are You Worth?" Derek Prince Ministries. 2022. Accessed June 18, 2024. https://www.derekprince.com/shorts/146

———. 2022b. "Spiritual Warfare Part 10/15: The Sword of the Spirit." YouTube. Accessed June 18, 2024. https://www.youtube.com/watch?v=lIkm_xqPVK0&list=PL_L1za0tEXFXNhigNVPTo1ibq7hQiYoNn&index=10

———. 2022c. "Spiritual Warfare Part 12/15: The Weapon of Prayer." YouTube. Accessed June 18, 2024. https://www.youtube.com/watch?v=NDKg-zDARZcI&list=PL_L1za0tEXFXNhigNVPTo1ibq7hQiYoNn&index=13

———. 2023. "Jesus Is Not Just A Prophet Or A Guru." YouTube. 2023. Accessed June 18, 2024. https://www.youtube.com/watch?v=LhIv4BdsXe8

———. 2024. "The Cross In My Life – Part 2." Derek Prince Ministries. 2024. Accessed July 5, 2024. https://www.derekprince.com/sermons/77

———. n.d.b "Derek Prince: Invisible Barriers To Healing." Derek Prince Ministries. Accessed June 18, 2024. https://www.derekprince.com/sermons/229

———. n.d.c. "Spiritual Conflict, Volume 1, Lucifer Challenges." Accessed June 18, 2024. https://store-us.derekprince.com/purchase/spiritual-conflict-volume-1-lucifer-challenges-mp3

Prophecy News Update. (2011, July 20). "Zechariah 14, Neutron Bombs, and God's Ultimate Purpose for Israel." Accessed June 18, 2024. https://www.calvarychapeljonesboro.org/prophecynews/zechariah-14-neutron-bombs-and-gods-ultimate-purpose-for-israel

ProTrump News Staff. 2022. "Elon Musk: 'Almost Every "Conspiracy Theory" That People Had About Twitter Turned Out To Be True.'" Gateway Pundit. December 25, 2022. Accessed June 18, 2024. https://www.thegatewaypundit.com/2022/12/elon-musk-almost-every-conspiracy-theory-people-twitter-turned-true-video

Quayle, Stephen. 2013. *Genesis 6 Giants: The Master Builders of the Prehistoric and Ancient Civilizations,* 9th ed. Bozeman, MT: End Time Thunder Publications.

Quayle, Stephen, and Duncan Long. 2008. *Longwalkers: Return of the Nephalim.* Bozeman, MT: End Time Thunder Publishers.

Radiance Foundation, The. 2022. "The Number One Killer in the Black Community Is Not." 2022. Accessed June 18, 2024. https://radiancefoundation.org/numberonekiller

Ramirez, John. n.d. "Ice Bucket Challenge-a Voodoo Ritual." YouTube. Accessed June 18, 2024. https://www.youtube.com/watch?v=LRP6r59_46Y

"Rapture, Premillennialism & Dispensationalism Refuted!" n.d. "The Origin of Rapture False Doctrine: John Darby 1830 AD." Accessed June 18, 2024. https://www.bible.ca/rapture-origin-john-nelson-darby-1830ad.htm

Ratzinger, Joseph. 1997. "Catechism of the Catholic Church." 3rd ed. Libreria Editrice Vaticna. 1997. Accessed June 18, 2024. https://www.usccb.org/sites/default/files/flipbooks/catechism/498/

Ravenhill, Leonard. n.d. "Is Christ Really In You?" YouTube. Accessed December 23, 2022. https://www.youtube.com/watch?v=s-gCRoVHDe8

Reed, B. 2023. "Mexican President Posts Photo of What He Claims Is a Maya Elf." The Guardian. February 27, 2023. Accessed June 18, 2024. https://www.theguardian.com/world/2023/feb/27/mexican-president-andres-manuel-lopez-obrador-photo-elf-alux

Rethinking the Future. n.d. "Disaster-Resilient Structures: Pioneering the Future of Architecture in Disaster Relief." Rethinking the Future. Accessed June 18, 2024. Accessed April 6, 2024. https://www.re-thinkingthefuture.com/articles/disaster-resilient-structures

Rucker, J. D. 2022. "How the Jabs Will Be Used to Control Those Who Haven't Already Been Depopulated Into the Grave." America First Report. September 23, 2022. Accessed June 18, 2024. https://americafirstreport.com/how-the-jabs-will-be-used-to-control-those-who-arent-depopulated-into-the-grave

———. 2023. "Lara Logan Only Needed 10-Words to Perfectly Describe '15-Minute Cities' By J.D. Rucker Aug. 5, 2023." August 5, 2023. Accessed June 18, 2024. https://thelibertydaily.com/lara-logan-only-needed-10-words-to-perfectly-describe-15-minute-cities

Rummel, R. J. n.d.a "20th Century Democide." Accessed June 18, 2024. https://www.hawaii.edu/powerkills/20TH.HTM

——— n.d.b "Death by Government: Definition of Democide." Accessed June 18, 2024. https://www.hawaii.edu/powerkills/DBG.CHAP2.HTM

Saad, Lydia. n.d. "Do Americans Believe in UFOs?." Gallop. Accessed June 18, 2024. https://news.gallup.com/poll/350096/americans-believe-ufos.aspx

Sam and Tanner. 2018. "10 Signs You're Probably In A Cult." 2018. Accessed June 18, 2024. https://medium.com/@zelphontheshelf/10-signs-youre-probably-in-a-cult-1921eb5a3857

Sampson, William N. 2011. "The 67 Deadly Sins of the New Testament." Landover Baptist Church. May 12, 2011. Accessed July 6, 2024. https://www.landoverbaptist.net/showthread.php?t=65069

Sands, Geneva. 2022. "DHS Shuts Down Disinformation Board Months After Its Efforts Were Paused." CNN. August 24, 2022. Accessed June 18, 2024. https://www.cnn.com/2022/08/24/politics/dhs-disinformation-board-shut-down/index.html

Sartorius, Lawrence, and Michael Sartorius. 2022. "Earth Changes and the Ascension of Planet Earth." The New Earth. 2022. Accessed June 18, 2024. https://thenewearth.org/TheNewEarth-Bk2-18.html

Savard, Liberty. 2000. "Stop Blaming the Devil!." Charisma. June 30, 2000. Accessed June 18, 2024. https://charismamag.com/spriritled-living/spiritual-warfare/stop-blaming-the-devil

Schneider, K. A. 2015. *Self Deliverance: How to Gain Victory Over the Powers of Darkness*. Minneapolis: Chosen.

Schnoebelen, Wiliam. 2015. "Buried Gems: The Lost Armor Revealed–Treasure Guardians Series." December 11, 2015. Accessed June 18, 2024. https://www.youtube.com/watch?v=fwV5xPNOuHE

———. 2023. "St. Patrick & the Curse of the Irish." Accessed June 18, 2024. https://www.youtube.com/watch?v=OluYGoClnaQ&list=PLBFEQHjcT2QC-uRXsP-Q4BiWZ2qPHduyr&index=92

Scoggins, Robert Chris. 2019. "Researchers Reinvent How Bridges Withstand Earthquakes with New Support Column Design." Prevention Web. July 19, 2019. Accessed June 18, 2024. https://www.preventionweb.net/news/researchers-reinvent-how-bridges-withstand-earthquakes-new-support-column-design

Seeger, A. (1917). "I Have a Rendezvous with Death." Poetry Foundation. Accessed June 18, 2024. https://www.poetryfoundation.org/poems/45077/i-have-a-rendezvous-with-death

Šerić, M. (2023, March 16). "Christians In The Middle East: A Persecuted And Forgotten People – Analysis." Eurasia Review: News and Analysis. Accessed June 18, 2024. https://www.eurasiareview.com/16032023-christians-in-the-middle-east-a-persecuted-and-forgotten-people-analysis

Shapero, Julia. 2023. "Belief in God, the Devil Falls to New Low: Gallup." July 20, 2023. Accessed June 18, 2024. https://thehill.com/changing-america/respect/diversity-inclusion/4107968-belief-in-god-the-devil-falls-to-new-low-gallup

Shukla, Aseem. 2012. "Heaven or Hell: In the Here and Now." December 2012. Accessed June 18, 2024. https://www.hinduamerican.org/blog/heaven-or-hell-in-the-here-and-now

Silawan, Renz. 2021. "All Muslims Will Go to Hell as Decreed by Allah." SilawanTribe. January 3, 2021. Accessed June 18, 2024. https://silawantribe.com/2021/01/03/all-muslims-will-go-to-hell-as-decreed-by-allah/#google_vignette'

Sinnenberg, Jackson 2023. "As Exorcism Demand Continues to Rise, Vatican to Hold Training." ABC News. February 27, 2023. Accessed June 18, 2024. https://abc3340.com/news/nation-world/vatican-to-hold-training-next-month-as-demand-for-exorcism-continues-to-rise-catholic-church-prayer-ritual-priests-internation-association-of-exorcists-paranormal-supernatural-psychiatry-mental-health

Skiba, R. 2012. *Archon Invasion: The Rise, Fall and Return of the Nephilim*. Lexington, KY: King's Gate Media.

Skiba, R. (2015). "Mythology and the Coming Great Deception (updated)." YouTube. Accessed June 18, 2024. https://www.youtube.com/watch?v=ipm-MjoGSnoU&list=PLzL1qDngeVYUDDdZwjmF4Xfdqy3LKQtgu&index=5

———. 2016. "Moses Tells Us Exactly How The Nephilim Returned After The Flood." Accessed June 18, 2024. https://www.youtube.com/watch?v=pby2Vh6AM48

Skousen, W. Cleon. 2014. *The Naked Communist*. Izzard Ink, LLC.

Slick, Matt. 2014. "What Commandments Did Jesus Give Us?" CARM. June 3, 2014. Accessed June 18, 2024. https://carm.org/about-jesus/what-commandments-did-jesus-give-us

Smith, Trey. 2011. *Thieves: One Dirty TV Pastor and the Man Who Robbed Him*. Trey Smith Books.

———. 2023. "Athena: The Nashville Idol." YouTube. 2023. Accessed June 18, 2024. https://www.youtube.com/watch?v=EcZPkyRxSFQ

Snyder, Michael. 2022. "America Is Being Transformed Into a Really Bad Version of 'Grand Theft Auto.'" America First Report. September

5, 2022. Accessed June 18, 2024. https://americafirstreport.com/america-is-being-transformed-into-a-really-bad-version-of-grand-theft-auto

———. 2023a. "The Genocide of Christians Is Escalating All Over the Planet, but Most Westerners Don't Even Know It Is Happening." Discern Report. September 12, 2023. Accessed June 18, 2024. https://discernreport.com/the-genocide-of-christians-is-escalating-all-over-the-planet-but-most-westerners-dont-even-know-it-is-happening

———. 2023b. "Wake Up! Highly Destructive Natural Disasters Are Suddenly Striking Areas All Over the Earth." Freedom First Network. September 11, 2023. Accessed June 18, 2024. https://freedomfirstnetwork.com/2023/09/wake-up-highly-destructive-natural-disasters-are-suddenly-striking-areas-all-over-the-earth

———. 2024. "Artificial Intelligence Is Allowing Them to Construct a Global Surveillance Prison From Which No Escape Is Possible." Discern Report. January 5, 2024. Accessed June 18, 2024. https://discernreport.com/artificial-intelligence-is-allowing-them-to-construct-a-global-surveillance-prison-from-which-no-escape-is-possible

Somerville-Wong, Anastasia. 2020. "The 25 Signs You're in a High-Control Group or Cult." Secular Liturgies. February 24, 2020. Accessed June 18, 2024. https://secularliturgies.wordpress.com/2020/02/24/the-25-signs-youre-in-a-high-control-group-or-cult-by-anastasia-somerville-wong/#comments

"Spiritual Gifts List & Definitions." n.d. Ministry Tools Research Center. Accessed June 18, 2024. https://mintools.com/gifts-list.htm

Staff Writer. 2022. "Christian Apologist Tyler Vela 'Deconverts' from Christianity Because God Did Not 'Comfort Him' After Divorce." Protestia. 2022. Accessed June 18, 2024. https://protestia.com/2022/11/20/christian-apologist-podcaster-announces-his-deconversion-from-christianity-because-god-did-not-comfort-him-after-divorce

Stambaugh, Jim. n.d. "Creation's Original Diet and the Changes at the Fall." Answers in Genesis. Accessed June 18, 2024. https://answersingenesis.org/animal-behavior/what-animals-eat/creations-original-diet-and-the-changes-at-the-fall

Stonestreet, John, and Timothy D. Padgett. 2021. "The Problem with Deconstructing Faith." Christian Headlines. October 26, 2021. Accessed June 18, 2024. https://

www.christianheadlines.com/columnists/breakpoint/the-problem-with-deconstructing-faith.html

Strobel, Lee. 1998. *The Case For Christ*. Grand Rapids, MI: Zondervan.

Strom, D. 2023. "Swiss Study: Heart Injuries from COVID Vaccine 3000x Higher than Thought." Hot Air. July 26, 2023. HotAir. Accessed June 18, 2024. https://hotair.com/david-strom/2023/07/26/swiss-study-heart-injuries-from-covid-vaccine-3000x-higher-than-thought-n567151

Stupid Laws. 2022. "Whistling Underwater Is Illegal." Stupid Laws. 2022. Accessed June 18, 2024. https://www.stupidlaws.com/whistling-underwater-is-illegal

Sullivan, Kaitlin. 2020. "California Confirms First Human Case of the Plague in 5 Years: What to Know." NBC News. August 19, 2020. Accessed June 18, 2024. https://www.nbcnews.com/health/health-news/california-confirms-first-human-case-bubonic-plague-5-years-what-n1237306

Sutphen, Dick. 1995. "Born Again Brainwashing." Educate Yourself. May 27, 1995. Accessed June 18, 2024. https://educate-yourself.org/cn/fundamentalistbrainwashing06jun05.shtml

Taibbi, M. 2022a. "Matt Taibbi." Twitter. December 16, 2022. Accessed June 18, 2024. https://twitter.com/mtaibbi/status/1603857536981032976

———. 2022b. "Twitter Files Thread: The Spies Who Loved Twitter." Racket News. December 25, 2022. Accessed June 18, 2024. https://www.racket.news/p/twitter-files-thread-the-spies-who?r=5mz1&utm_campaign=post&utm_medium=web

Tate, Kristen. 2021. "Coming Soon: America's Own Social Credit System." The Hill. May 3, 2021. Accessed June 18, 2024. https://thehill.com/opinion/finance/565860-coming-soon-americas-own-social-credit-system

Terje M. 2021. "'You Take on the Intelligence Community — They Have Six Ways from Sunday at Getting Back at You,.'" YouTube. 2021. Accessed June 18, 2024. https://www.youtube.com/watch?v=uW7EHai-cRM

Thinking Conservative, The. 2021. "Who Controls the Food Supply Controls the People." The Thinking Conservative. September 1, 2021. Accessed July 11, 2024. https://www.thethinkingconservative.com/who-controls-by-henry-kissinger/

Thomas, Dalton. 2020. "The Mark of the Beast, Pandemics, and the 'New World Order'—Facts vs Fiction." Accessed June 18, 2024. https://www.youtube.com/watch?v=az6c7negl6o

Thomas, Geoff. 2009. "13:12-14 The Armour of Light." Geoff Thomas Sermon Archive. September 13, 2009. Accessed June 18, 2024. http://geoffthomas.org/index.php/gtsermons/the-armour-of-light

Thomas, Jefferson. 1776. "Declaration of Independence: A Transcription." America's Founding Documents. 1776. Accessed June 18, 2024. https://www.archives.gov/founding-docs/declaration-transcript

Tibetan Buddhist Encyclopedia. n.d. "Who Will Go to Hell According to Buddhism?" Tibetan Buddhist Encyclopedia. Accessed June 18, 2024. https://tibetanbuddhistencyclopedia.com/en/index.php?title=Who_will_go_to_hell_according_to_Buddhism%3F

"Timeline of the Tribulation Week, A." n.d. What Saith the Scripture. Accessed June 18, 2024. https://www.whatsaiththescripture.com/Timeline/Big.Chart.html

"Trichotomy vs. Dichotomy of Man—Which View Is Correct?" n.d.b. Got Questions. Accessed June 18, 2024. https://www.gotquestions.org/trichotomy-dichotomy.html

Toledo, A. (2022, May 6). "Globalists Have Been Planning to Starve the World With Food Scarcity Since at Least 2015." Uncanceled News. Accessed June 18, 2024. https://www.naturalnews.com/2022-05-05-globalists-began-planning-food-crisis-in-2015.html

Towns, Elmer. n.d. "Demons in the Bible – Different Types and How They Attack." Bible Sprout. Accessed June 18, 2024. https://www.biblesprout.com/articles/hell/demons

Turner, Nathaniel. 2021. "Purgatory and How to Get Out of It." February 14, 2021. Accessed June 18, 2024. https://catholicismcoffee.org/purgatory-and-how-to-get-out-of-it-catholicismcoffee-312598c43bd9

TV Show Clips. 2016. "Once upon a Time S01e04 Cinderella." YouTube. 2016. Accessed June 18, 2024. https://www.youtube.com/watch?v=U2uYIvtEeu0

Tzu, Sun. 2022. *The Art of War*. Rye Brook, NY: Peter Pauper Press.

United Nations. 2015. "Transforming Our World: The 2030 Agenda for Sustainable Development." United Nations. September 25, 2015. Accessed June 18, 2024. https://sdgs.un.org/2030agenda

Unruh, B. (2022, May 17). "Poll Shocker: You Won't Believe How Many Pastors Actually Have a Biblical Worldview." World Net Daily. Accessed June 18, 2024. https://www.wnd.com/2022/05/poll-shocker-wont-believe-many-pastors-actually-biblical-worldview

"Uvalde Schools Police Chief: "I Didn't Know I Was in Charge at the Shooting Scene." 2022. CBS News. June 10, 2022. Accessed June 18, 2024. https://www.cbsnews.com/news/pete-arredondo-uvalde-schools-police-chief-interview-police-response

Vela, T. 2022. "Deconversion Announcement." The Free Thinker Podcast. November 17, 2022. Accessed June 18, 2024. http://freedthinkerpodcast.blogspot.com/2022/11/deconversion-announcement.html

Vigilant News. 2023. "Vaccine Injury Treatment–Fasting for 48-72 Hours Creates Autophagy–the Body's Detox Process That Kills COVID-19 Vaccine Spike Protein Damaged Cells and Reboots the Immune System." September 16, 2023. Accessed June 18, 2024. https://vigilantnews.com/post/vaccine-injury-treatment-fasting-for-48-72-hours-creates-autophagy-the-bodys-detox-process-that-kills-covid-19-vaccine-spike-protein-damaged-cells-and-reboots-the-immune-system

Wang, Tian, and Quanbao Jiang. 2022. "Recent Trend and Correlates of Induced Abortion in China: Evidence From the 2017 China Fertility Survey." *BMC Womens Health* 22 (1): 1–16.

Wars in the World. 2024. "List of Ongoing Conflicts." October 4, 2022. Accessed June 18, 2024. https://www.warsintheworld.com/?page=static1258254223

Wellman, Jack. 2014. "A List of Sins from the Bible." Christian Crier. September 8, 2014. Accessed June 18, 2024. http://www.patheos.com/blogs/christiancrier/2014/09/08/a-list-of-sins-from-the-bible

"What Are Spirit Guides?" 2022. Accessed June 18, 2024. http://www.gotquestions.org/spirit-guides.html

"What Does It Mean to Put on Christ in Romans 13:14?" 2023. Got Questions? June 27, 2023. Accessed June 18, 2024. https://www.gotquestions.org/put-on-Christ.html

"What Is the Battle of Armageddon?" n.d. Got Questions? Accessed June 18, 2024. https://www.gotquestions.org/battle-Armageddon.html

"What Is the Day-Age Theory." n.d. Got Questions? Accessed June 18, 2024. https://www.gotquestions.org/Day-Age-Theory.html

Whitehead, J., and N. Whitehead. 2023. "A State of Martial Law: America Is a Military Dictatorship Disguised as a Democracy." The Rutherford Institute. June 27, 2023. Accessed June 18, 2024. https://www.rutherford.org/publications_resources/john_whiteheads_commentary/a_state_of_martial_law_america_is_a_military_dictatorship_disguised_as_a_democracy

Winkley, Lyndsay. 2023. "Could San Diego Police Department's Smart Streetlights Program Infringe Upon Privacy Rights?" The San Diego Union-Tribune. July 31, 2023. Accessed June 18, 2024. https://www.sandiegouniontribune.com/news/public-safety/story/2023-07-31/could-san-diego-police-departments-smart-streetlights-program-infringe-upon-privacy-rights

Wise, Talia. 2022. "WitchTok Booms to 30B Views on TikTok, Ex-Witch Warns Preschool Witchcraft Targeting Kids." CBN News. November 2, 2022. Accessed June 18, 2024. https://www1.cbn.com/cbnnews/us/2022/november/witch-tok-booms-to-30b-views-on-tiktok-ex-witch-warns-preschool-witchcraft-targeting-kids

Wolf, Naomi. 2023. "Dear Conservatives, I Apologize: My 'Team' Was Taken in By Full-Spectrum Propaganda." Outspoken with Dr. Naomi Wolf. March 9, 2023. Accessed June 18, 2024. https://naomiwolf.substack.com/p/dear-conservatives-i-am-sorry

Wommack, Andrew. 2010. "Lesson 2: The Security of the Believer." Andrew Wommack Ministries. December 13, 2010. https://www.awmi.net/audio/audio-teachings/?teaching=general-teaching-series&lesson=the-security-of-the-believer

———. 2012a. "The Power of Faith Filled Words: "Mixing Faith with God's Word"." Andrew Wommack Ministries. February 13, 2012. https://www.awmi.net/audio/audio-teachings/?teaching=the-power-of-faith-filled-words&lesson=mixing-faith-with-gods-word

———. 2012b. "The Power of Faith Filled Words: 'Put God's Word in Your Heart.'" Andrew Wommack Ministries. February 13, 2012. https://www.awmi.net/audio/

audio-teachings/?teaching=the-power-of-faith-filled-words&lesson=put-gods-word-in-your-heart

———. 2012c. "The Power of Faith Filled Words: 'Words Change the Natural World.'" Andrew Wommack Ministries. February 13, 2012. https://www.awmi.net/audio/audio-teachings/?teaching=the-power-of-faith-filled-words&lesson=words-change-the-natural-world

———. 2022a. "Eternal Life: There's More to It Than You Think." Andrew Wommack Ministry International. 2022. https://www.awmi.net/reading/teaching-articles/eternal_life/

———. 2022b. "How to Flow in the Gifts of the Holy Spirit." 2022. https://www.awmi.net/reading/teaching-articles/flow_gifts/

———. 2022c. "If Your Life Isn't Supernatural, It Is Superficial." July 26, 2022. https://www.facebook.com/awmcanada/videos/352538790376308

Woo, Marcus. 2018. "The Hunt for Earth's Deep Hidden Oceans." July 11, 2918. Accessed June 18, 2024. https://www.quantamagazine.org/the-hunt-for-earths-deep-hidden-oceans-20180711

World Health Organization. 2021. "Abortion." World Health Organization. November 25, 2021. Accessed June 18, 2024. https://www.who.int/news-room/fact-sheets/detail/abortion

WorldOMeter. n.d. "Current World Population." Accessed June 18, 2024. https://www.worldometers.info/world-population

Wretched. 2023. "The REAL Reason So Many People Are DECONSTRUCTING Their Faith." Gospel Partners . 2023. Accessed July 5, 2024. https://www.youtube.com/watch?v=UxLv-vBRFp8

Yogapedia. Accessed June 18, 2024. https://www.yogapedia.com/definition/5318/moksha#google_vignette

Young, Alexey. n.d. "Cults Within & Without." Orthodox Christian Information Center. Accessed June 18, 2024. "http://orthodoxinfo.com/praxis/cultswithinwithout.aspx

Zimbardo, Philip. 2008. "The Psychology of Evil." Ted. Accessed June 18, 2024. https://www.ted.com/talks/philip_zimbardo_the_psychology_of_evil

APPENDIX A

Resources: Counseling & Deliverance

THIS SECTION OF appendices is a compilation of resources based on the topics of this book. They are divided by category and subject matter. There may be places where a resource is repeated because some of the sources cover a broad range of subjects.

Websites are provided where available. Book titles and audio resources can also be found on Amazon. Videos and audio may be available on YouTube.

There are many professional faith-based parachurch organizations. These links include national organizations, but other local groups may be in your area. This collection of over 150 sources covers many topics from various Christian groups.

Counseling Centers

GriefShare – https://www.griefshare.org

> "A GriefShare support group is a safe, welcoming place where people understand the difficult emotions of grief. Through this 13-week group, you'll discover what to expect in the days ahead and what's "normal" in grief. Since there are no neat, orderly stages of grief, you'll learn helpful ways of coping with grief, in all its unpredictability—and gain solid support each step of the way."

VeryWell Mind – https://www.verywellmind.com

> "An award-winning resource for reliable, compassionate, and up-to-date information on the mental health topics that matter most to you. We are dedicated to empowering you with the trustworthy evidence-based information you need for your mental and emotional

well-being. Our mission is to help you prioritize your mental health and find balance amid the chaos of daily life."

6 Best Online Christian Counseling Services of 2024:

https://www.verywellmind.com/best-online-christian-counseling-services-4692788

Best Overall: Faithful Counseling – https://www.faithfulcounseling.com

Best for Couples: ReGain – https://www.regain.us

Best with In-Person Option: Grace Wellness Center – http://www.thegracewellnesscenter.com

Best for Resources: Christian Therapist On Demand – https://christiantherapistod.com

Best Free App: Chatnow – https://chatnow.org

Best Directory: GoodTherapy – https://www.goodtherapy.org/find-therapist.html

Life Christian Counseling Network – 301-292-2778.
https://www.lifechristiancounseling.com

> "Christian counseling is a thoughtful integration of God's Word with the best of developmental psychology to alleviate suffering and help the individual grow to the full maturity God intends. LCCN offers counseling services for all age groups and every imaginable difficulty. Our Christian counselors work from a solid understanding of God's Word and a personal walk with Christ. Our counselors' specialties include trauma, depression, anxiety, panic attacks and phobias, sexual abuse and childhood trauma, anger, addictions, and marriage and family issues. We also offer a premarital program for couples considering or seeking to be married."

Life Christian Counseling Network's counselors are clinically trained, Christian counselors who will come alongside you in times of grief, loss, anger, and fear.

Call us at **301-292-2778** to find out more information or set up an appointment.

Our counselors create an empathetic, judgement-free environment that allows the space for reflection, growth, and healing.

LCCN services are currently available in *Maryland, Pennsylvania, Virginia, Washington, DC, Wisconsin.* Pending the coming finalization of the Counseling Compact, these 36 member states may soon be included: AL, AR, AZ, CO, CT, DE, FL, GA, IN, IA, KS, KY, LA, MD, ME, MN, MO, MS, MT, NE, NH, NJ, NC, ND, OH, OK, SC, SD, TN, UT, VT, VA, WA, WV, WI, WY. Nine more states have filed legislation and are currently considering the Counseling Compact bill: CA, HI, ID, IL, NM, NY, OR, PA, RI.

https://counselingcompact.org/map

International calls can be accepted. LCCN counselors are mostly English language speakers.

Anchor International – https://anchorinternational.org

"Anchor International is a nonprofit organization dedicated to creating safe groups for mental wellness. We equip people to lead Christ-centered support groups in their churches and communities, because we believe all people can find hope and healing in the midst of mental and emotional health struggles."

Prayer Hotlines

Andrew Wommack Ministries – 719-635-1111, 4:30 AM – 9:30 PM MST
    Helpline ministry: awmi.net/more/contact-us
    International contact information: awmi.net/more/contact-us

Derek Prince Ministries – with Touch of God Deliverance Ministries
Touch of God Deliverance Ministries: https://healingdeliverance.net

Great Exchange Healing Ministries – 24-Hour Prayer Lines – A listed collection of 38 ministries, including contact information. Members of ISDM (International Society of Deliverance Ministers) under the leadership of Bill Sudduth.
http://www.greatexchangehealingministries.com/our-blog/24-hour-prayer-lines

Christian Pure – 19 Prayer Hotlines – https://www.christianpure.com/learn/christian-prayer-hotlines

RPM Ministries – https://rpmministries.org

"Empowering Christians globally with practical tools to live proper Christian lives."

Free Resources – https://rpmministries.org/free-resources

10 International Biblical Counseling Organizations – Australia, Brazil, France, Mexico, South Africa, UK, et.al.
https://rpmministries.org/2019/01/10-international-biblical-counseling-organizations-to-follow

Deliverance Ministries

This topic is unfamiliar to the average member and guest. This does not mean the kingdom of darkness does not personally affect them. Those who are affected or tormented by negative spiritual issues can find assistance from these organizations. See also the section on Demonology and Spiritual Warfare for books and media on self-deliverance. WARNING: *This section may not be suitable for children.*

Derek Prince – Is it possible to have the Holy Spirit and a demon at the same time? https://www.youtube.com/watch?v=px8Z_V9ttE0
Why some people are not delivered – https://www.youtube.com/watch?v=IEuECR8EN-4
How demons work in Christians – https://www.youtube.com/watch?v=HFe9EscZfBg

Isaiah Saldivar – https://www.youtube.com/@IsaiahSaldivar

Can a Christian be demon-possessed? https://www.youtube.com/watch?v=KkrgI_MZ42w
How can a Christian have a demon? https://www.youtube.com/watch?v=3dt5c-_W8wM
Christians can't have demons! 25 counter arguments – https://www.youtube.com/watch?v=GXi9TnC_mUw
7 lies the devil wants you to believe about casting out demons – https://www.youtube.com/watch?v=_ymoaBIwY2g
10 steps for casting out demons – https://www.youtube.com/watch?v=lFKCNc1ufzk
Casting out demons for beginners – https://www.youtube.com/watch?v=8ZDO6nLChEI
The demon won't leave! Casting out stubborn demons – https://www.youtube.com/watch?v=MRltD8NAeLA
Casting out demons tips for teenagers and youth groups – https://www.youtube.com/watch?v=dAWPoZtoaRs
I tried casting demons out of myself and failed. Self deliverance tips – https://www.youtube.com/watch?v=etDz0FW_Pl8

Vlad Savchuk– https://hungrygen.com
Vlad's school link includes free courses on curses and demons and includes prayers of deliverance in many areas. *Some videos include guided exorcism sessions.*
https://www.vladschool.com/
How to spot a demon – 14 signs: https://www.youtube.com/watch?v=GZijNVYqFqs
How to be self-delivered – https://www.youtube.com/watch?v=UL2TtTkAvn0
How to cast out demons – https://www.youtube.com/watch?v=Mr3xDVNCzP4
Cursed objects and haunted houses – https://www.youtube.com/watch?v=hz_YdumR9f4
8 demonic things you have to remove today – youtube.com/watch?v=R5BdMH_MXvM
Spiritual spouses – incubus, succubus, Lilith: https://www.youtube.com/watch?v=ek-NqxUW0V8
WitchTok alert – 20 types of witchcraft: https://www.youtube.com/watch?v=jdcb1MCNfDc
It ends with me! Breaking bloodline curses: https://www.youtube.com/watch?v=V6FMVXuqx3w

Daniel Duval – Bride Ministries – https://bridemovement.com/prayer-resources-3
"Deliverance prayers in six languages for many topics including spiritual gang-stalking, suicidal ideation, Santeria and Voodoo, illuminati bloodlines and genetics, fallen angel bloodlines and genetics, ear-ringing, coronavirus, black goo, evil grid renunciation, abortion, constellations, etc."
Salvation Prayer – https://bridemovement.com/salvation-prayer

Healing Prayer – https://bridemovement.com/healing-prayer
"Bride Ministries also provides coaching assistance for those from highly traumatic backgrounds such as dissociative identity disorder (DID), Satanic ritual abuse (SRA), government-sponsored mind control projects, and general exposure to the occult. Coaches have their own independent practices and rates."
https://bridemovement.com/findacoach

Roly and Amanda Buys –
https://www.kanaanministries.org/kanaan_downloads_restoration_bride_messiah/
This page of free resources has numerous helps and renunciation prayers for those in spiritual bondage across a wide spectrum of major religions and cults and occultic organizations and practices.
Sample categories include cults, water spirits, forest spirits, spiritual spouses, witchcraft, abortion, curses, Roman Catholicism, Islam, Buddhism, Hinduism, blood covenants, SALT covenants, Druidism, Freemasonry, Kaballah, Satanic Ritual Abuse, Neptune Baptism, and so on.

Freedom in Christ Ministries – https://www.ficm.org
"We equip individuals and church leaders to overcome whatever is holding them back from living the abundant life in Christ – and then help others do the same."
Steps to Freedom in Christ – https://www.ficm.org/steps-to-freedom-in-christ
Free Resources – https://www.ficm.org/ministry-materials/free-resources

Dr. William Shnoebelen – https://www.withoneaccord.org/Prayers_ep_50.html
This site has prayers for spiritual warfare and defense, liberation and deliverance, emotional healing prayers, a marriage prayer, and more.
Topics include generational wounds, dimensional deliverance, curses, warfare and protection prayers, soul ties, roots of bitterness, and so on.

Salvation Prayer –
https://www.withoneaccord.org/assets/images/freedownloads/Salvation%20in%20Messiah.pdf

Julie Lopez – https://julie-lopez.com
Julie provides prophetic life coaching sessions, which give you access to deliverance prayers and prophetic declarations.

Adam Daniel – https://www.youtube.com/@theprayerproject

"My heart for this channel is to help people discover healing, victory, and who they truly are in Christ. We take time to pray together, learn from the word of God, and discover the deep spiritual truths that God wants us to learn, so that we can be all that he has called us to be."

Four Corners Free – https://fourcornersfree.com
"Bringing worldwide freedom from generational curses and strongholds."

Cornerstone Assembly of God – Occult Worksheet
https://www.cornerstone.ag/pdf/PDFPrayers/PCLI/Handout-Occult.pdf

Sexual Brokenness

One Stone Ministries – https://www.firststone.org
The Mission: "Leading people In the Body of Christ to freedom from homosexuality and sexual brokenness* through a relationship with Jesus Christ as Lord; to reach out to churches, schools, organizations, and the general public by providing education, biblical discipleship, and support."
*Sexual Brokenness: Devastation brought about by behaviors outside of God's original intent of sexuality. Sexual brokenness includes, in part, pornography, adultery, promiscuity/fornication, homosexuality, lesbianism, sexual abuse, molestation, prostitution, transsexuality, and cross-dressing.

Sex Change Regret – https://sexchangeregret.com
"Giving hope to those who want help to go back."
"Your story isn't finished yet. The best is yet to come. Maybe it's time to get started!"

APPENDIX B

Resources: Healing & Recovery

THIS SECTION INCLUDES books, media, and Internet sources. There are a few major authors cited whose teachings cover vast areas of subject matter. In addition, readers may know of alternate or additional sources as the spread of knowledge multiplies.

The intent is to provide sources that are easy to understand, include an academic approach where things are explained, and there are steps to try, where the author has done extensive research or has valuable experience, and where the content is expected to be helpful to a wide audience. I have not read every book or article or gone through every video or audio available. I have read, heard, or seen enough to choose them as recommended or at least suggested material, and some are included simply based on reader reviews. It is up to you to extract the value from them.

The topics are based on points of interest discussed, areas that should be included as major issues or doctrines, and areas where players struggle and should have help navigating through them. This is not an endorsement of every view presented by the authors. It is always the reader's, the listener's, and the viewer's responsibility to evaluate what is put in front of them based on the truth of the Bible.

Finding help and healing can be difficult for those who suffer loss. The following authors provide differing perspectives on life's troubles.

Andrew Wommack – awmi.net
God Wants You Well
Healing Is the Children's Bread (Teaching Article) – awmi.net/reading/teaching-articles/healing_childrens
Healing Journeys – DVD stories of the power of God's Word working in the lives of people – https://store.awmi.net/category/browse/dvds/special
Healing journeys – online stories – https://www.awmi.net/video/series/healing-journeys

Financial breakthroughs – online stories – https://www.awmi.net/video/series/financial-breakthroughs

Grace encounters – online stories–https://www.awmi.net/video/series/grace-encounters

How to receive a miracle (3-part CD series) – https://store.awmi.net/purchase/k62-c

You've Already Got It (Teaching Article) – awmi.net/reading/teaching-articles/already_got

Derek Prince. derekprince.org
Most of these titles are booklets or small books under 150 pages.
God's Remedy for Rejection
Life's Bitter Pool
God's Medicine Bottle
God's Word Heals
Ultimate Security: Finding a Refuge in Difficult Times

C.S. Lewis
The Problem of Pain – "If God is good and all-powerful, why does he allow his creatures to suffer pain?"

Lynne Suszek – Lynne's Healing Room: https://www.lynneshealingroom.com

Kay Arthur. precept.org
Lord, Heal My Hurts
When the Hurt Runs Deep – Healing and Hope for Life's Desperate Moments

Mark and Patti Virkler. cwgministries.org
Prayers That Heal the Heart

Gregory Boyd–*Is God to Blame? – Moving Beyond Pat Answers to the Problem of Suffering*

Dr. David Stoop. drstoop.com
Forgiving What You'll Never Forget – How do you forgive the unforgivable?

Stephen Arterburn, M.Ed. and **David Stoop, Pr.D.** drstoop.com
Take Back Your Life – How to Stop Letting the Past and Other People Control You

Frank Hammond – *Overcoming Rejection: Revised & Updated (Spiritual Warfare Series, Volume 2)*
Forgiving Others: The Key to Healing and Deliverance

John Bevere – *The Bait of Satan, 20th Anniversary Edition: Living Free from the Deadly Trap of Offense. Escaping the victim mentality.*

Nancy Guthrie – *What Grieving People Wish You Knew about What Really Helps (and What Really Hurts)*
https://www.crossway.org/books/what-grieving-people-wish-you-knew-about-what-tpb

APPENDIX C

Resources: Membership Testimonials

Here are some testimonials of player's conversion or Game Master intervention on their behalf.

Billy Crone's Testimony – https://www.youtube.com/watch?v=B09hsP8sLmU
Tim Conway's Testimony – https://www.youtube.com/watch?v=9g4LYlTuIso
Ruby Conway's Testimony – https://www.youtube.com/watch?v=dZEX3Jsg1sY
Dr. William Shnoebelen's Testimony – https://www.youtube.com/watch?v=TxN5t8GswYs
Hungry Generation – Life-changing Testimonies – https://www.youtube.com/playlist?list=PL3vispi2tzOcyVU8DnzoYpXLmcsmiMmNs
Alan Strudwick – New Age leader's amazing encounter with Jesus – https://www.youtube.com/watch?v=g3VH_e9jBh4
Todd Starnes – Ex-gang member saved in solitary confinement: "Jesus Christ came in my cell"
https://www.toddstarnes.com/faith/gang-member-saved-solitary-confinement-jesus-christ
https://calebparke.com/gang-member-jesus-christ-prison-cell-testimony
https://www.youtube.com/watch?v=QqacC0YkyqU&feature=emb_imp_woyt
"Why God? Why would You save me?" – Face-to-face encounter with Jesus in rehab
https://www.youtube.com/watch?v=PRio0oiWS3g
Tailah Scroggins – Ex-new ager's mission to slay demonic forces after escaping witchcraft, astrology (from a Christian home, was a worship leader while practicing New Age) – https://www.youtube.com/watch?v=5ahw_bGVZfk
https://www.youtube.com/@TailahOfficial
Jacquelyn Johnson – Lost Catholic to saved by grace – https://www.youtube.com/watch?v=cpmGVAEa2Jc
John Ramirez – Conversion to Jesus Christ from being a third-ranked high priest in a satanist cult in the south Bronx of New York City.
John Ramirez Testimony – https://www.youtube.com/watch?v=I11L71PD3Lw

Michael Franzese – From New York mobster to Christian evangelist – https://www.youtube.com/watch?v=e7g5aaNeFBA

Mike Shreve – Yoga & Christianity: Why I canceled all Yoga teaching – https://www.youtube.com/watch?v=CaG_Xlux1L0

Aggressive faith! Instant healing testimonies . . . in Jesus' name! Injuries, disease, flu, burn, wow! – https://www.youtube.com/watch?v=hJv4BCEMH3I

Jesus Image – Blindness healing testimony from Jesus '17 – https://www.youtube.com/watch?v=tz-bEDo3JkQ

Ruslan KD – Jesus is appearing to millions of people in dreams? – https://www.youtube.com/watch?v=pkW2HibvGZI

Muslim Conversions to Jesus

Multiple Muslim Testimonials – https://ifoundthetruth.com
25 accounts of Muslim conversions
https://www.youtube.com/@thelight9016
Muslims are converting to Christianity after Jesus appears to them in dreams and visions
https://www.youtube.com/watch?v=Th-yn5IIufw
Ex-Terrorist Confirms Mass Visions of Jesus in Gaza, Says Thousands of Muslims Will Come to Christ
https://www.youtube.com/watch?v=eh1wQIJC5jY
Iran Testimonials
https://www1.cbn.com/cbnnews/insideisrael/2015/December/Divine-Encounters-Breaks-Out-in-Iran
Jahir Israel – Muslim sees Jesus in his dream
https://www.youtube.com/watch?v=EMNq9PQyYlA
Hedieh's Testimony –
https://www1.cbn.com/cbnnews/cwn/2021/june/hanging-in-hellfire-her-imam-said-she-would-suffer-for-eternity-then-she-heard-the-audible-voice-of-jesus
Muslim woman gives Jesus one week to prove himself before ending her life. Then this happens!
https://www.youtube.com/watch?v=TJUh-Jeqfrg
Muslim turns to Jesus, Jesus helps him, his wife sees Jesus in her dreams
https://www.youtube.com/watch?v=snASsXl1NRY
American Muslim doctor converts to Christianity
https://www.youtube.com/watch?v=UTzYCwsPTNo

I murdered him for Allah but God raised him up to forgive me
https://www.youtube.com/watch?v=mtjMANw2hCA
Afshin's Testimony – Former Muslim terrorist sees Jesus and becomes a Christian
https://www.youtube.com/watch?v=dLxkanD0j4I
Muslima leave Islam and become a Christian (Godlogic)
https://www.youtube.com/watch?v=QfoVF36o9qs

Shinto and Buddhism Conversions to Jesus

How A Japanese Shintoist became a Christian–An Unimaginable Change – Japan Kingdom Films
https://www.youtube.com/watch?v=2F4p48g-LME
Chiaki's Story – Darkness to light
https://www.youtube.com/watch?v=GZO5HHjXqq8
Sommy – From Buddhism, Atheism, New Age to Jesus – Hauntings, sleep paralysis, tarot, demonic channeling
https://www.youtube.com/watch?v=rPRAnMS7BLA
Mishelle – From Buddha to Christ – https://www.youtube.com/watch?v=dKLXv4Et_Y4
Rahil Patel – Why a Hindu priest left the religion to follow Christ
https://www.youtube.com/watch?v=09n8WRCcb78
Ruksha de Mel – Former Sri Lankan Buddhist accepts Christ
https://www.youtube.com/watch?v=QD4g8trdiOk
An amazing encounter with Jesus – Indian Guru
https://www.youtube.com/watch?v=VR6c37_bo68&ab_channel=DustinHall

APPENDIX D

Resources: Life Helps

This section covers Christian growth and development.

Andrew Wommack. awmi.net
The Believer's Authority – What You Didn't Learn in Church
Effortless Change
A Better Way to Pray
Staying Full of God
Harnessing Your Emotions
Hardness of Heart
Self-Centeredness: The Source of All Grief
Spirit, Soul & Body
The War Is Over – God Is Not Mad, So Stop Struggling with Sin and Judgment
Living in the Balance of Grace and Faith – Combining Two Powerful Forces to Receive from God
Don't Limit God – Imagine Yourself Successful
How to Become a Water-Walker – Lessons in Faith
The Christian's Survival Kit (audio teachings)

> Don't Panic-Believe | Put Things in Perspective | Knowing God | The Power of the Word of God | The Ministry of the Holy Spirit | Be a Doer of the Word | Self-Centeredness | The Source of Grief | Watch Your Tongue | Abiding in the Vine | The Power of love | The Power of Joy | Fruit, Not Failure, Glorifies God | How to Handle Persecution | Sin, Righteousness, and Judgment | Prayer in Jesus' Name | What to Do When Your Prayers Seem Unanswered

Derek Prince. derekprince.org
Does Your Tongue Need Healing?
God Is a Matchmaker: Seven Biblical Principles for Finding Your Mate, revised and expanded
God's Will for Your Life
Grace Alone: Finding Freedom and Purging Legalism from Your Life
If You Want God's Best
Pride versus Humility
The Grace of Yielding
Transformed for Life: How to Know God Better and Love Him More
Ultimate Security: Finding a Refuge in Difficult Times
You Matter to God: Discovering Your True Value and Identity in God's Eyes

K. P. Yohannan – *The Road to Reality – Coming Home to Jesus from the Unreal World*

APPENDIX E

Resources: Christianity

This section includes the discovery of Christ, salvation issues, deception in the church, and the philosophy of Christianity.

Find a Church
Online Churches: https://harbingersdaily.com/find-an-church-online
Baptist Churches: https://independentbaptist.church

Bill Walker – Pastor, Unity Bible Church, Lewiston, Maine.
https://unitybible.com
https://www.youtube.com/channel/UCiG1kMzY6NiWbBPWseJNXrA
Sermon: *Living out our new life in Christ* series (Eph. 4:25)
https://www.unitybible.com/sermons/20-0614-ephesians-425-living-out-our-new-life-in-christ/
This is a sermon on truth and deception. Pastor Bill explains how we as believers "put away falsehood"—a lifestyle of deception (vv. 14, 22)—our old manner of life because "the whole world lies in the power of the evil one" (1 John 5:19).
So you're dead . . . now what? (6-sermon series)
https://www.youtube.com/watch?v=l4N4p7vbN7U&list=PLyxSsBauvwlXaZql_SVW5Addh6EizOGSF
Saved by grace alone . . . the doctrines of grace! (Eph. 2:8–10)
https://www.youtube.com/watch?v=BRhTXaZplnI
Philippians: Rejoice in adversity (*Can you command people to rejoice?*)
https://www.youtube.com/watch?v=CcKrjSG-4EM (message begins at 36:45)

Lee Strobel
The Case for Christ – A Journalist's Personal Investigation of the Evidence for Christ
The Case for a Creator – A Journalist Investigates Scientific Evidence That Points Toward God

The Case for Faith – A Journalist Investigates the Toughest Objections to Christianity

Nabeel Qureshi – *Seeking Allah, Finding Jesus*: *A Devout Muslim Encounters Christianity*
No God but One: Allah or Jesus?: *A Former Muslim Investigates the Evidence for Islam and Christianity*

C. S. Lewis – *Mere Christianity, The Screwtape Letters*

Matthew Mead – *The Almost Christian Discovered*: *or, the False Prophet Tried and Cast*

Film – Enemies Within the Church (2021)
https://www.imdb.com/video/vi3872572185?playlistId=tt16106010&ref_=tt_ov_vi
https://www.americanthinker.com/articles/2022/03/the_false_gospel_of_the_enemies_within_the_church.html

Deception in the Church – Numerous articles identify and explain deception and false doctrine. The site includes pages of links, audio and videos, and recommended books.
deceptioninthechurch.com
deceptioninthechurch.com http://www.deceptioninthechurch.com/emerging-church.html
http://www.deceptioninthechurch.com/newageinthechurch.html

Spencer Smith – Third Adam: https://www.youtube.com/watch?v=lnMpfoxYSFY

Categories of Cults
http://www.apologeticsindex.org/267-categories-of-cults
http://www.apologeticsindex.org/262-take-back-your-life-recovering-from-cults

Ron Carlson and Ed Decker – *Fast Facts on False Teachings*

Walter Martin – *The Kingdom of the Cults, The Kingdom of the Occult*

Steven Hassan – *Combating Cult Mind Control: The Guide to Protection, Rescue, and Recovery from Destructive Cults*

David Hunt – *What Love Is This?: Calvinism's Misrepresentation of God*

Michael Scott Lowery – *Predestined – Elected – Chosen: What Do the Biblical Terms Really Mean?*

Andrew Wommack.
Christian Philosophy – Everyone has a philosophy. It's the lens through which they view the world and make decisions.
The War Is Over
The True Nature of God

Derek Prince.
The Spirit Filled Believer's Handbook
Protection from Deception

Fritz Ridenour – *How to Be a Christian without Being Religious*

A. W. Tozer – *The Pursuit of God: The Human Thirst for the Divine*

Diaprax–The practice of the dialectic (the use of dialogue to resolve conflict between opposing ideas or opinions). Employs **Thesis + Antithesis = Synthesis**. Heavily used in Emergent Church philosophy and other apostate churches.
https://cmediaresearch.com/cmc-14.html

Melissa Dougherty – Top five New Age teachings in the church
https://www.youtube.com/watch?v=FCDbO8Lc5NU
Channel–https://www.youtube.com/c/MelissaDougherty/about

Brennan Manning – *The Ragamuffin Gospel: Good News for the Bedraggled, Beat-Up, and Burnt Out*

J.D. Greear – *Stop Asking Jesus Into Your Heart – How to Know for Sure You Are Saved*

Alisa Childers – *Another Gospel?: A Lifelong Christian Seeks Truth in Response to Progressive Christianity*

Patrick McIntyre – *The Graham Formula: Why Most Decisions for Christ Are Ineffective*

"Over half of American adults believe they are going to heaven because they repeated a 'salvation prayer' . . . so why don't we feel saved?"

The Graham Formula: **S + C + F = D (.25) = B**. Sermon + Counseling + Follow-up = Decisions x .25% = # of Born-again experiences (¼ of professions of salvation)

Evaluation before purchase in PDF, PowerPoint, MP3, and online audio formats, available on Amazon.com.
http://www.christianebooks.com/Free_Download.htm

R. T. France – *I Came to Set the Earth on Fire – A portrait of Jesus*

Roman Catholicism

Mike Grendon – Which Jesus do Catholics worship and trust?
https://www.youtube.com/watch?v=WJZvK4S5mQ4
Former Catholic Mike Grendon confronts Catholic teachings
https://www.youtube.com/watch?v=k7hlCl2ZdUo

Mike Winger – Unbiblical stuff the Catholic Church teaches: Mary, Indulgences, Eucharist, Priests, 7 Sacraments
https://www.youtube.com/watch?v=d1xZTPY98Oc

Ex-Catholics for Christ – https://www.youtube.com/@excatholics

Calvinism

War Between the Saints Calvinism vs. Arminianism by Keith Daniel: (2017)
https://www.youtube.com/watch?v=QmpKIQejqA0
Calvinism and Catholicism are strange bedfellows!
https://www.youtube.com/watch?v=Bc5RkgWJpGo
John Calvin examined and exposed:
https://www.youtube.com/watch?v=ykwpGWMN92Q

Dr. Leighton Flowers – https://www.youtube.com/@Soteriology101

Faith on Fire – https://www.youtube.com/@faithonfireministries

Greg Boyd – Calvinism refuted in 10 minutes –
https://www.youtube.com/watch?v=v_vq64Zjt_o
The John 3:16 challenge: Calvinism vs Salvation according to scripture
https://www.youtube.com/watch?v=HRkAyRq9X4I

Islam

Apologetics – Jude 1:3 – https://www.youtube.com/@apologetics-jude1383
This is a Classical Bible-based Christian Channel dedicated to providing a reasonable defense for the faith once and for all delivered to the saints (Jude 1:3).
What's keeping Muslims from converting to Christianity–Nabeel Qureshi
https://www.youtube.com/watch?v=gMAfM8mx8T8

Impact Evangelism – https://www.youtube.com/@ImpactEvangelism
This channel seeks to reach Muslims with the Gospel. We teach apologetics to Christians who desire to share their faith with others. Our goal is to help equip the church to carry out the great commission to Muslims and see Muslims come to Jesus Christ. This channel is all about evangelism, so if you're into evangelism this is the channel for you!
Why Muslim Imams Are Becoming Christians
https://www.youtube.com/watch?v=nrP7xDy6Ix4

Stuart & Cliffe Knechtle – https://www.youtube.com/@givemeanswer
Give me an answer–Cliffe says, "If other religions speak the truth I am going to hell."
https://www.youtube.com/watch?v=RHzrJ-Hjp2w

Harris Sultan – Arab imam destroys Islam and gets excommunicated
https://www.youtube.com/watch?v=yAUMXDD_8qc

APPENDIX F

Resources: YouTube Channels & Websites

The following YouTube channels offer more perspectives, teachings, and resources.

Unity Bible Church (Bill Walker) – https://www.youtube.com/c/UnityBibleChurchLewistonME/featured

Calvert Grace Church (Dario Agnolutto) – https://www.youtube.com/@calvertgrace

Immanuel Bible Church (Jesse Johnson) – https://www.youtube.com/@ImmanuelBibleVA

Calvary Oro Valley Church – https://www.youtube.com/@CalvaryOroValley

Billy Crone – https://www.youtube.com/user/NFBCmedia/videos
https://getalifemedia.com/

Vlad Savchuk – Hungry Generation:
https://hungrygen.com
https://www.vladschool.com
https://www.youtube.com/@vladhungrygen

Jesus Image – https://www.youtube.com/@jesusimage

Dr. Frank Turek – Cross Examined:
https://www.youtube.com/@CrossExamined
https://crossexamined.org

Trinity Radio – https://www.youtube.com/@BraxtonHunter

Mike Winger – Learn to Think Biblically – https://www.youtube.com/c/MikeWinger/featured

Dr. Leighton Flowers – https://www.youtube.com/@Soteriology101

Tim Conway – I'll Be Honest –
https://www.youtube.com/c/Illbehonestwillyou
https://www.youtube.com/channel/UCzpl6CJP6lo5vjsEAeIHnsg

Derek Prince Ministries – https://www.youtube.com/c/DerekPrinceMinistries/featured

Andrew Wommack Ministries – https://www.youtube.com/c/AndrewWommackMin/featured

Koinonia House (Chuck Missler) – https://www.youtube.com/c/KoinoniaHouse6640

Dr. Larry Ollison – https://www.youtube.com/user/drlarryollison/videos

Dr. William Schnoebelen – (Ex-Druid-Wiccan-Satanist-Mason-LDS-Catholic)
https://www.withoneaccord.org
https://www.youtube.com/@WilliamSchnoebelen

Adam Daniel – https://www.youtube.com/@theprayerproject

Tudor Alexander – The Dance of Life Podcast – https://www.youtube.com/@danceoflifepodcast

Michael Rood – A Rood Awakening! – https://www.youtube.com/@aroodawakening

Ex-Catholics for Christ – https://www.youtube.com/@excatholics

Mike Gendron (Ex-Catholic)
https://www.forthegospel.org/mike-gendron
https://www.proclaimingthegospel.org/page/home-page

Daniel Duval – https://www.youtube.com/@DanielDuval, https://bridemovement.com

Islam Education – https://www.youtube.com/@IslamEducations

God Logic 2.0 (Muslim topics) – https://www.youtube.com/@GodLogic2.0

Apologetics Roadshow – https://www.youtube.com/@apologeticsroadshow

Faith On Fire – https://www.youtube.com/@faithonfireministries

J. Warner & Jimmy Wallace – Cold Case Christianity – https://www.youtube.com/@ColdCaseChristianity

Wretched – https://www.youtube.com/@WretchedNetwork, https://wretched.org

Christadelphian – Bible Truth & Prophecy – https://www.youtube.com/c/TheChristadelphianWatchman

Ruslan Karaoglanov – https://www.youtube.com/@RuslanKD

Impact Video Ministries – https://www.youtube.com/@ImpactVideoMinistries

Redeemed Zoomer – https://www.youtube.com/@redeemedzoomer6053

Amazing Discoveries – https://www.youtube.com/user/OfficialADTVChannel, https://adtv.watch

Russ Dizdar – https://www.shatterthedarkness.net

Steve Quayle – https://www.stevequayle.com

Rob Skiba – robschannel.com, https://www.youtube.com/@RobSkiba

Justen Faull – https://www.youtube.com/@JustenFaull

Trey Smith – God in a Nutshell – https://www.youtube.com/c/treysmithnutshell

APPENDIX G

Resources: Bible, Martyrs & Power for Living

Bible Gateway – biblegateway.com–Online Bibles in multiple versions and languages. Select translations include audio.

Comparing Bible Versions.
https://baptistnews.com/article/how-to-pick-a-bible-thats-right-for-you/?gad_source=1&gclid=Cj0KCQjw4MSzBhC8ARIsAPFOuyX0SoGHEx6sd4iciuasEi3PIf-ANWk52MIraDmNdGggf4RlsCLQOJDgaAjekEALw_wcB
https://godsword.org/pages/bible-translation-guide?gad_source=1&gclid=C-j0KCQjw4MSzBhC8ARIsAPFOuyW_F9QfV1jrPTtUFyIVHQ8k2JekluvxDBWm26G-caAMefupIxZyS-4aAiYnEALw_wcB

Andrew Wommack.
Sharper than a Two-Edged Sword – A Summary of Sixteen Powerful Messages That Have Changed the Lives of Thousands
This book's chapters are summaries of entire books by Andrew Wommack:
True Christianity | The Holy Spirit | Spirit, Soul & Body | You've Already Got It! | The True Nature of God | The War Is Over | Grace, the Power of the Gospel | Living in the Balance of Grace and Faith | The Believer's Authority | A Better Way to Pray | The Effects of Praise | Harnessing Your Emotions | Discovering the Keys to Staying Full of God | God Wants You Well | Hardness of Heart | Self-Centeredness: the Root of All Grief

Kay Arthur.
How to Study Your Bible – The Lasting Rewards of the Inductive Method

Bruce Wilkinson – Walk Thru the Bible. https://www.walkthru.org

Derek Prince – Prayers & Proclamations

Martyrs & Survivors

WARNING: *Most books contain graphic accounts of torture.*

John Foxe – *Foxe's Book of Martyrs*
https://warmdayswillnevercease.wordpress.com/2020/04/03/book-review-foxes-book-of-martyrs-by-john-foxe

Charles Rivers Editors – *The Spanish Inquisition: The History and Legacy of the Catholic Church's Notorious Persecution of Heretics*

> "Persecution is not an original feature in any religion; but it is always the strongly marked feature of all law-religions, or religions established by law." – Thomas Paine, Rights of Man

Richard Wurmbrand – Romanian pastor of an underground church who was imprisoned and tortured during the Cold War; founder of The Voice of the Martyrs.
Tortured for Christ – From Suffering to Triumph

Dr. Haralan Popov – Bulgarian pastor arrested in 1948 for treason and imprisoned and tortured for thirteen years; founder of Door of Hope International.
Tortured for His Faith

Corrie ten Boom – Corrie's family hid Jews for the Dutch Underground during World War II. She and her family were arrested for aiding the Jews and sent to concentration camps.
The Hiding Place

Brother Yun – *The Heavenly Man*: *The Remarkable True Story of Chinese Brother Yun*

Howard and Phyllis Rutledge – *In the Presence of My Enemies*

Persecuted – *The Global Assault on Christians*

Power for Living

Derek Prince
Faith to Live By
Fasting: the Key to Releasing God's Power in Your Life
Gateway to God's Blessing
How to Fast Successfully
Living as Salt and Light: God's Call to Transform Your World
Secrets of a Prayer Warrior
The Promise of Provision: Living and Giving from God's Abundant Supply
You Shall Receive Power

Frances Gardner Hunter – *Hot Line to Heaven: A spirited adventure that shows how your prayers can be answered – if you believe!*

APPENDIX H

Resources: Demonology & Spiritual Warfare

THE COMMON DENOMINATOR between aliens and giants is demons. The association between witchcraft and New Age enlightenment is also demons. Satan's demons operate across the entire spectrum of any spiritual experience that does not originate from God. Demons did not disappear after the book of the Acts of the Apostles or move to Africa. They operate globally. Those who avoid the topic of witchcraft or don't believe in it are still affected and influenced by demons through any spiritual or meditative source that does not come entirely and solely from God Himself and His Bible. Deception is the avenue through which logical and rational people willingly accept Satan's perspectives of life and philosophy.

There is a great personal danger in pursuing an understanding of the occult and demonic issues, where the satanic spiritual side reciprocates by turning malevolent attention upon the curious investigator. The following authors provide a safe venue from scripture and experience where readers can learn extensive details about the operational tactics of occult forces without being exposed to their power. All member players should have a good working knowledge of Satan's devices so they can recognize when his schemes are at work (2 Cor. 2:9–11).

Derek Prince – derekprince.org. Books, videos, and audio teachings on demonology, spiritual warfare, blessings and curses, personal living, fasting, and so on. Many videos available from online sources.

Books:
Lucifer Exposed: The Devil's Plan to Destroy Your Life
Called to Conquer: Finding Your Assignment in the Kingdom of Heaven
Rules of Engagement: Preparing for Your Role in the Spiritual Battle
Spiritual Warfare

Blessing or Curse: You Can Choose, Third Edition
They Shall Expel Demons: What You Need to Know About Demons – But Were Afraid to Ask
Weapons that Prevail – 4 CDs
Demons and Demonology – Revealing the Path to Permanent Freedom – 6 CDs
Pulling Down Strongholds

Jonas Clark
http://www.jonasclark.com
Breaking Family Curses – Stop Generational Curses Fast!
Breaking Christian Witchcraft: Protection From Witchcraft Attacks (Kindle Edition)

Adam Daniels – https://www.youtube.com/@theprayerproject

C. S. Lovett – *Dealing with the Devil*

David Appleby – *It's Only a Demon – A Model of Christian Deliverance*

Rabbi K. A. Schneider – discoveringthejewishjesus.com
Self-Deliverance: How to Gain Victory over the Powers of Darkness

Frank Hammond
The Discerning of Spirits
Pigs in the Parlor: A Practical Guide to Deliverance
Obstacles to Deliverance: Why Deliverance Sometimes Fails
A Manual for Children's Deliverance
Poltergeists – Demons in the Home: Cleansing Your Home from Demonic Intruders
Praise – A Weapon of Warfare and Deliverance
Overcoming Rejection
Forgiving Others: The Key to Forgiveness and Healing
The Marriage Bed: Can It Be Defiled?
Repercussions from Sexual Sins: The Sexual Revolution is wreaking havoc on the family, the church, and the individual's relationship with Jesus Christ.
Soul Ties: Righteous Soul Ties & Demonically-Inspired Soul Ties
Confronting Familiar Spirits: Counterfeits to the Holy Spirit

John Ramirez – johnramirez.org. Books, videos, and audio teachings on demonology, spiritual warfare, and so on. Many videos available from online sources.
Out of the Devil's Cauldron
Unmasking the Devil: Strategies to Defeat Eternity's Greatest Enemy
Armed and Dangerous: The Ultimate Battle Plan for Targeting and Defeating the Enemy

Russ Dizdar – shatterthedarkness.net. Extensive free audio library of witchcraft in the church and demonology with tools to detect and combat dark powers.
Spiritual Warfare Today Training Course: Basic training in spiritual warfare, detection of dark powers, prayer, and so on – spiritualwarfaretoday.com

Jenny Weaver – https://www1.cbn.com/cbnnews/us/2021/october/they-were-releasing-spells-over-the-viewers-ex-witch-warns-witchcraft-now-everywhere-from-hollywood-to-the-church

Daniel Duval – Bride Ministries – https://bridemovement.com, https://danduval.com
https://www.youtube.com/@DanielDuval
"We offer the Discovering Truth with Dan Duval podcast, the BRIDE Ministries Institute, the BRIDE Ministries Church, FREE prayer resources, weekly online community groups, conferences, and other outreaches, including strategic assistance to survivors of satanic ritual abuse (SRA) and government sponsored mind control projects."

WARNING: *This section may not be suitable for children.*
Higher Dimensions, Parallel Dimensions, and the Spirit Realm
Kingdom Government and the Promise of Sheep Nations
Why am I getting persecuted for my breakthrough – https://www.youtube.com/watch?v=xb1o8ePEfwg
Realms are real–Timothy Bence – https://www.youtube.com/watch?v=9rN3ZCsM0_o
Understanding realms 1 – https://www.youtube.com/watch?v=4-3weWA2qTk
Understanding realms 2 – https://www.youtube.com/watch?v=rOsnnwGxtFc
Regions of captivity (3) – https://www.youtube.com/watch?v=6j5GJFC12q8
Creating realms–Timothy Bence (4) – https://www.youtube.com/watch?v=xnb4Q1SP_q8
The mysteries of the spirit realm and the dimensions beyond – Nikki
https://www.youtube.com/watch?v=jXOVmNyKb5Y

Mature Material:

4-Part Interview: Merfolk, underwater kingdoms, and the mysteries of the deep with Amanda Buys & Priscilla

1. https://bridemovement.com/merfolk-underwater-kingdoms-and-the-mysteries-of-the-deep-part-1-with-amanda-buys-and-priscilla
2. https://bridemovement.com/merfolk-underwater-kingdoms-and-the-mysteries-of-the-deep-part-2-with-amanda-buys-priscilla
3. https://bridemovement.com/merfolk-underwater-kingdoms-and-the-mysteries-of-the-deep-part-3-with-amanda-buys-priscilla
4. https://bridemovement.com/merfolk-underwater-kingdoms-and-the-mysteries-of-the-deep-part-4

The Hitler project, hybrids and Kabbalah with Amanda Buys –
https://bridemovement.com/hitler-project-hybrids-and-kabbalah-with-amanda-buys

Roly and Amanda Buys – Deliverance: cults, water spirits, witchcraft
https://www.kanaanministries.org

Julie Lopez – https://julie-lopez.com

> "Coming from five generations of witches, Julie learnt to discern and walk in darkness until, at the age of 19, she was saved after her father died unexpectedly. She specializes in helping people to be set free, hear the voice of God and those who are experiencing spiritual battles, bondages, and a lack of discernment."

Dr. Michael S. Heiser
The Unseen realm | documentary – https://www.youtube.com/watch?v=w9EW3ORjpU8
Demons–documentary film – https://www.youtube.com/watch?v=H41Lw2YEY74

Dr. Larry Ollison
"Currently President of International Convention of Faith Ministries (ICFM), Dr. Ollison is also Vice-President of Spirit FM Christian Radio Network, Missouri State Director of Christians United for Israel (CUFI), and a Trustee on the boards of several international ministries. He is also the host of The Cutting Edge Radio Broadcast and authors The Cutting Edge Daily Devotional."
https://ollison.org
https://www.youtube.com/user/drlarryollison/videos

Dr. William Schnoebelen–https://www.withoneaccord.org

> "Former high-level teacher of witchcraft, spiritism, ceremonial magic, a Wiccan priest, Druidic high priest, Old Catholic priest, ordained spiritist minister, involved in vampirism, a York and 32nd degree Scottish rite Freemason, LDS (Mormon) church member with temple recommends, Master's degree in theology from a Roman Catholic seminary."

Shattering Strongholds of ADDICTION
Wicca: Satan's Little White Lie
Churchcraft: Wicca, Christianity, and the End of Days
Romancing Death: A True Story of Vampirism, Death, the Occult, and Deliverance
Vampires and Werewolves: Real or Fake? (DVD)
Interview with an Ex-Vampire (9 DVDs)
Mormonism's Temple of Doom 2011 (DVD)
Catholicism: The Church on Haunted Hill 2011 (DVD)
Unholy Covenants–Challenges for the Christian Mason (DVD)
The Order of the Eastern Star: Ladies of the Labyrinth (DVD)
Masonic DeMolay: A Kindergarten for Satanism (DVD)
Exposing the Illuminati from Within (Expanded) (2-DVD set)
Disclosure: UFO's Aliens and the Magick Connection (DVD)

Montague Summers – *The Vampire, His Kith, and Kin; The Vampire in Europe*

Billy Hallowell – Playing with Fire Podcast

> "Evil is real. But are demons active today? Can evil inhabit human beings? Is exorcism real? Join investigative journalist Billy Hallowell as he delves into the strange phenomena of supernatural activity through the harrowing stories of people who believe they have experienced ultimate evil, fought a battle they never expected—and have found healing. This podcast is based on Hallowell's book, *Playing with Fire: A Modern Investigation into Demons, Exorcism, and Ghosts*."

https://edifi.app/podcasts/billy-hallowell-s-playing-with-fire-podcast-26364

Zita Grant – *Be Free from Spirit Spouse (Marine Spirits): Book One*
How to Be and Stay Free from Spirit Spouses (Marine Spirits): Book Two

Jennifer LeClaire – *The Spiritual Warrior's Guide to Defeating Water Spirits: Overcoming Demons that Twist, Suffocate, and Attack God's Purposes for Your Life*
Defeating Python Spirit: A Topical Highlight from the Spiritual Warriors Guide to Defeating Water Spirits

Kynan Bridges – *Overcoming Familiar Spirits: Deliverance from Unseen Demonic Enemies and Spiritual Debt (Spiritual Warfare)*

Dr. Daniel Olukoya – *Power against Marine Spirits*

Augustine Ayodeji Origbo – *Deliverance from the Bondage of the Spirit Husbands and Wives (Incubus and Succubus): A Divine Solution to Sexual Abuse or Attacks in the Dream*

Dr. Elmer Towns – Demons in the bible – different types and how they attack
https://www.biblesprout.com/articles/hell/demons

Dr. Loreda Fox – Christian psychiatrist
The Spiritual and Clinical Dimensions of Multiple Personality Disorder (Understanding and Treatment Strategies for Helpers of Extreme Trauma Survivors)

> "Some Satanists have invaded the church as it is the perfect cover for them. They masquerade as angels of light and gravitate towards positions of leadership in order to have more influence. Because much of what they say is sound doctrinally, they are rarely detected. Most survivors I have worked with had satanist parents in high positions in churches; many were pastors" (Fox 1992, 196).

Mary Lou Lake – *What Witches Don't Want Christians to Know – Expanded Edition: A True Story of the Occult and Mind Control*

Article – "Science and Religion finds Eastern Mysticism":
https://thereluctantsamizdatwordpresscom.wordpress.com//?s=shiva+the+supermen&search=Go (23 March 2016)

A.W. Tozer – Article: "How to Try the Spirits"
http://www.worldinvisible.com/library/tozer/5j00.0010/5j00.0010.29.htm

Billye Brim – *The Blood and the Glory.* https://billyebrim.org

Billy Crone – https://www.youtube.com/@NFBCmedia
Pastor Billy Crone's playlists include: The Satanic War on the Christian; World Religions, Cults and the Occult; In the Days of Noah; One Minute into Eternity (Is there Life after Death?)
https://www.youtube.com/user/NFBCmedia/playlists?disable_polymer=1

Yoga
Can Christians do Yoga? – Alan Strudwick
https://www.youtube.com/watch?v=7hURnW48oxs

What does the Bible say about Yoga?
https://www.youtube.com/watch?v=6RDzfJFlqAQ

"Why I stopped teaching Yoga and Reiki, to follow Jesus" – Jessica Smith interview
https://www.youtube.com/watch?v=AkiNFjzJ6y4

Mike Shreve – Ex-Kundalini Yoga teacher explains why Christians should not practice Yoga
https://www.youtube.com/watch?v=_0UU8a2Rbd8

Everette Roeth – Ex-Yoga instructor tells all – Is Yoga demonic?
https://www.youtube.com/watch?v=DIWnZDGZsVg

Danna Weiss – Exposing Yoga for what it really is
https://www.youtube.com/watch?v=nsQfJKN3Ebo

Hanna – Ex-Yoga instructor finds freedom after encountering God:
https://www.youtube.com/watch?v=xqQFJaySGzk

APPENDIX I

Resources: Prehistory, Apocalypse, Giants, Aliens, Assorted Topics

UNCONVENTIONAL MATERIAL DOES not mean it is untrue. These subjects may or may not be related. Included materials are alluded to in some sections or provide additional insight.

Clarence Larkin – *The Greatest Book on Dispensational Truth in the World*

Dr. Henry Morris – *The Long War Against God – Darwin Challenged God's Word with Evolution . . . But Was He the Only One?*
Creation Basics and Beyond, 2nd Edition
Beginning of the World – A Scientific Study of Genesis 1–11

Bill Cooper – *After the Flood: the Early Post-Flood History of Europe Traced Back to Noah's Flood*

John C. Whitcomb, Jr. – *The World that Perished* – Biblical and Scientific Evidence for the Genesis Flood as a Global Catastrophe

Paul Copan – *Is God a Moral Monster?: Making Sense of the Old Testament God*

Jonathan Gray – *Dead Men's Secrets*: Tantalizing Hints of a Lost Super Race
Video: Dead Men's Secrets: Ancient man was not primitive, dragging his knuckles
https://www.youtube.com/watch?v=jC2YWHkYcAA

Steve Quayle – stevequayle.com
Genesis 6 Giants–Volume 2–Master Builders of Prehistoric and Ancient Civilizations

Longwalkers: Return of the Nephilim
Xenogenesis: Changing Men into Monsters
Little Creatures: The Gates of Hell Are Opening
Weather Wars
Empire Beneath the Ice – *Empire Beneath the Ice* reveals why most of what you learned about World War II and the defeat of Nazi Germany is wrong.

Richard J. Dewhurst – *The Ancient Giants Who Ruled America*: *The Missing Skeletons and the Great Smithsonian Cover-Up*

Jim Vieira, Hugh Newman – *Giants on Record*: *America's Hidden History, Secrets in the Mounds, and the Smithsonian Files*

Hugh Newman, Jim Vieira – *The Giants of Stonehenge and Ancient Britain*

Charles H. Hapgood – *Maps of the Ancient Sea Kings: Evidence of Advanced Civilization in the Ice Age*

Rob Skiba – robschannel.com
Archon Invasion: The Rise, Fall, and Return of the Nephilim

Ryan Pitterson – *Judgment of the Nephilim. A Comprehensive Biblical Study of the Nephilim Giants*

Robert J. Morgan – *The 50 Final Events in World History*: *The Bible's Last Words on Earth's Final Days*

Col. David J. Giammona, Troy Anderson – *The Military Guide to Armageddon*: *Battle-Tested Strategies to Prepare Your Life and Soul for the End Times*

Dr. Chuck Missler – khouse.org. Teaching videos available from his website and across the Internet covering topics of creation, UFOs, and analysis of the Bible with its descriptions of the scientific realities in which we live.
Alien Encounters–What is behind UFO sightings? Are they real? Where are they from? What does the Bible say about them? Are they friendly or hostile? (six-part series)

https://www.youtube.com/watch?v=xnDbo_RoGN0&list=PLUwtE9Hi3BnpxFCcaJGDXQ9h4Ke5fQCR8

Prager University: Video – Does Science Argue for or Against God?
https://www.youtube.com/watch?v=UjGPHF5A6Po

Trey Smith – godinanutshell.com, https://www.godinanutshell.com/articles
Aliens are demons–https://www.godinanutshell.com/video-archive/aliensaredemons

Branton – *The Secrets of the Mojave* (*Or the Conspiracy against Reality*)
https://cdn.preterhuman.net/texts/alien.ufo/Branton%20-%20The%20Secrets%20Of%20The%20Mojave.pdf

Alien Resistance – "Offering Biblical Perspectives on the UFO and Alien Phenomenon Since 1999..."
alienresistance.org
www.alienresistance.org/the-first-christian-symposium-on-aliens-results
www.alienresistance.org/ufo-alien-deception/christian-ufology-research-overview
1) "Alien Abductions" stop in the name and authority of Jesus Christ and can be terminated as a pattern in a person's life.
2) "Alien Abductions" match the abilities of fallen angels as described in the Bible.
3) "Aliens" bring primarily deceptive anti-biblical messages, as is reported by abductees and contactees.

Billy Crone–Aliens UFOs & the rapture of the church
https://www.youtube.com/watch?v=qQHHGM9d-Gs

David Bay: Cutting Edge Ministries – cuttingedge.org
Weather Control/Warfare – http://www.cuttingedge.org/articles/weather.cfm

Geoengineering Watch – https://www.geoengineeringwatch.org

Educate Yourself – https://educate-yourself.org, http://mirrors.wordsforgood.org/educate-yourself.org

Tomorrow's World – The rapture debunked in 3 questions
https://www.youtube.com/watch?v=X3BXysIOlz4

Steve Wohlberg – *End Time Delusions – The Rapture, the Antichrist, Israel, and the End of the World*

Missionary Spencer Smith – YouTube Channel:
Occult practices in the modern church! – https://www.youtube.com/watch?v=NN10QNiAPE0
"You have not known the depths of Satan" – https://www.youtube.com/watch?v=ewARcSdWeUU
"The doctrine of Jezebel" – https://www.youtube.com/watch?v=up85NRaN6z0&ab_channel=SpencerSmith
Albert Mohler – *The Gathering Storm – Secularism, Culture, and the Church*

Bible Truth & Prophecy (Christadelphian)
https://bibletruthandprophecy.com/
https://www.youtube.com/c/TheChristadelphianWatchman/featured
World events show the writing is now on the wall (June 2021 updated)
https://www.youtube.com/watch?v=X4RjWLpWeV8

Jon E. Lewis – *The Mammoth Book of Cover-Ups*: *the 100 Most Terrifying Conspiracies of All Time*

Zachary K. Hubbard – *Numbers Games*: *9/11 to Coronavirus*

Jeff Berwick – *The Controlled Demolition of America*

Jeanne Manning & Dr. Nick Begick – *Angels Don't Play This HAARP*: *Advances in Tesla Technology*

Elena Freeland – *Chemtrails, HAARP, and the Full Spectrum Dominance of Planet Earth*

Jim Maars – *Population Control*: *How Corporate Owners Are Killing US*

R. J. Rummel – *Death by Government: Genocide and Mass Murder Since 1900*

Michael Zimmerman – *Buddhism and Violence* (Publications of the Lumbini International Research Institute, Nepal)

John Perkins – *Confessions of an Economic Hit Man*

Graham Hancock – *Lords of Poverty – The power, prestige, and corruption of the international aid business*

Vox Day – *The Irrational Atheist: Dissecting the Unholy Trinity of Dawkins, Harris, And Hitchens*

Dr. Nick Begich – *Controlling the Human Mind*: *The Technologies of Political Mind Control or Tools for Peak Performance*

Stella Morabito – *The Weaponization of Loneliness: How Tyrants Stoke Our Fear of Isolation to Silence, Divide, and Conquer*

H. G. Tudor – *Black Flag: 50 Warning Signs of Abuse*

Wade Mullen – *Something's Not Right: Decoding the Hidden Tactics of Abuse – and Freeing Yourself from Its Power*

Connie Baker – *Traumatized by Religious Abuse: Courage, Hope, and Freedom for Survivors*

APPENDIX J

Resources: Music

MUSIC IS A major source of doctrinal input for many players. While everyone develops their own tastes and styles, the content matters too. Those who want to take hold of their lives and effect change in their life experience, need to listen to music with lyrics that support their goal.

Avoid songs where you give up and let God take over, where you are helpless to do anything, where He does all the lifting to get the job done and where you are passively watching Him do it for you. That is not how spiritual warfare is made or how miracles are done by you. Songs about your abject worthlessness and miserable value do not reflect your standing as a new creation in Christ. Avoid Jesus-is-my-boyfriend songs, God-or-girlfriend songs where either one may be substituted in the lyrics. Reflective, introspective navel-gazing worship puts the focus on us instead of our Creator. These song types are written for target audiences and pushed by recording labels to generate profit. They are not written for the glory of God or for equipping the saints.

Find songs that express an active role in dealing with life issues, songs that define your position of strength through God, songs that declare why you will overcome trials based on His Word, songs that demonstrate how you win with God. Songs of praise for the glory of God should be part of your repertoire. Anchor your thoughts in lyrics that have a firm foundation in the truth of the Bible. These song types are harder to find because most of the focus is placed on feelings, not fighting, overcoming or conquering. Even with songs that meet these standards, sometimes part of the song is going great and then it takes a left turn into a passive and weak perspective or has a tenuous hold on the Manual's teaching or incorporates New Age theology.

When you find artists who meet your objectives, you may find that you can't just sweep up everything they have because their song library includes the various types expected for maximum sales. Many artists would prefer to write songs that speak to their soul's perspective and which many fans would follow as well, but market forces and contracts can prevent them from having that freedom of expression. Many artists experience a faith journey which takes them away from the principles that guided their early careers. Continued evaluation is required.

Pastor Billy Crone remarked that musician Tim Lambesis said, "In twelve years of touring, I would say that maybe one in ten Christian bands we toured with were actually real Christians." Ninety percent of the Christian bands he associated with were not Christians. That explains the music and the lyrics (Crone 2022. min. 1:01:01).

David Meece – davidmeece.com

Missionary Spencer Smith – *Calling Evil Good: The Lie of "Christian" Rock and Roll*
YouTube Channel: https://www.youtube.com/@spencersmith312